Britain's Empire

Britain's Empire

RESISTANCE, REPRESSION AND REVOLT

Richard Gott

VERSO
London • New York

First published by Verso 2011

3 5 7 9 10 8 6 4 2

Verso
UK: 6 Meard Street, London W1F 0EG
US: 20 Jay Street, Suite 1010, Brooklyn, NY 11201
www.versobooks.com

Verso is the imprint of New Left Books

ISBN-13: 978-1-84467-738-2

British Library Cataloguing in Publication Data
A catalogue record for this book is available from the British Library

Library of Congress Cataloging-in-Publication Data
A catalog record for this book is available from the Library of Congress

Typeset in Minion Pro by Hewer UK Ltd, Edinburgh
Printed in Sweden by ScandBook AB

Contents

Introduction

Just over a century ago, in 1908, Henrietta Elizabeth Marshall published a large illustrated book for children called *Our Empire Story*.[1] Within its covers were tales of 'India and the greater colonies', then defined as Canada, Australia, New Zealand and South Africa, and the book included evocative colour illustrations by J. R. Skelton. For the children of Empire, for much of the twentieth century, this work provided all that they were ever to know about the history of the world they lived in. Sound, if partial, history, and easy to read, it had a profoundly influential impact.

Henrietta Marshall told the story from an imperial perspective. For the most part, she took no notice of the existence of the various native populations that the empire-builders encountered, though her thumbnail sketches of the inhabitants of southern Africa were clearly designed to summon up a tiny frisson in the mind of her young readers. They were, she wrote, 'very wild and ignorant . . . They hated each other and were constantly at war, and some of them, it was said, were cannibals.'

A distinguished popular historian and a woman of her time, Henrietta Marshall was proud of the British Empire. Yet she was also aware of a downside to her tale. 'The stories are not always bright', she wrote. 'How could they be? We have made mistakes, we have been checked here, we have stumbled there. We may own it without shame, perhaps almost without sorrow, and still love our Empire and its builders.'

Such uncritical expressions of affection, seen from the perspective of a century later, are difficult to justify. Descendants of the empire-builders and of their formerly subject peoples now share the small island whose inhabitants once sailed away to change the face of the world. A history of empire today must take account of two imperial traditions, that of the conquerors and that of the conquered. Traditionally, that second tradition has been conspicuous by its absence. One purpose of this book is to provide a balance to the version of events published in older histories of Empire.

The creation of the British Empire caused large portions of the global map to be tinted a rich vermilion. Although not meant that way, the colour turned out to be peculiarly appropriate, for Britain's Empire was established, and maintained for more than two centuries, through bloodshed, violence, brutality, conquest and war. Not a year went by without the inhabitants of Empire being obliged to suffer for their involuntary participation in the colonial experience. Slavery, famine, prison, battle, murder, extermination – these were their various fates.

Wherever the British sought to plant their flag, they met with opposition. In almost every colony they had to fight their way ashore. While they could sometimes count on a handful of friends and allies, they never arrived as welcome guests, for the expansion of empire was invariably conducted as a military operation. The initial opposition continued off and on, and in varying forms, in almost every colonial territory until independence. To retain control, the British were obliged to establish systems of oppression on a global scale, both brutal and sophisticated. These in turn were to create new outbreaks of revolt.

Yet the subject peoples of Empire did not go quietly into history's good night. Underneath the veneer of the official record exists another, rather different, story. Year in, year out, there was resistance to conquest, and rebellion against occupation, often followed by mutiny and revolt – by individuals, groups, armies and entire peoples. At one time or another, the British seizure of distant lands was hindered, halted, and even derailed by the vehemence of local opposition.

A high price was paid by the British involved. Settlers, soldiers, convicts – those people who freshly populated the Empire – were often recruited to the imperial cause as a result of the failures of government in the British Isles. These involuntary participants bore the brunt of conquest in faraway continents – death by drowning in ships that never arrived, death by the hands of indigenous peoples who refused to submit, death in foreign battles for which they bore no responsibility, death by cholera and yellow fever (the two great plagues of Empire).

Many of the early settlers and colonists had been forced out of Scotland by the Highland Clearances, in which avaricious landlords replaced peasants with sheep. Many were driven from Ireland in a similar manner, escaping from centuries of continuing oppression and periodic famine. Convicts and political prisoners were sent to far-off gulags for minor infringements of draconian laws. Soldiers and sailors were press-ganged from the ranks of the unemployed.

Then, tragically, and almost overnight, many of the formerly oppressed became themselves, in the colonies, the imperial oppressors. White settlers – in the Americas, Australia, New Zealand, South Africa, Canada, Rhodesia and Kenya – simply took over land that was not theirs, often slaughtering, and even purposefully exterminating, the local indigenous population as if they were vermin.

The British Empire was not established, as some of the old histories liked to suggest, in virgin territory. Far from it. In some places that the British seized to create their empire, they encountered resistance from local people who had lived there for centuries or, in some cases, since time began. In other regions, notably at the end of the eighteenth century, lands were wrenched out of the hands of other competing colonial powers that had already begun their self-imposed task of settlement. The British, as a result, were often involved in a three-sided contest. Battles for imperial survival had to be fought *both* with the native inhabitants *and* with already existing settlers – usually of French or Dutch origin. This was particularly true in the West Indies in the 1790s, where freed slaves and slaves in revolt, Maroons and Caribs, linked up with French Republicans in attempts to curb the overweening ambition of the British to put the clock back.

None of this has been, during the sixty-year post-colonial period since 1947, the generally accepted view of the Empire in Britain. The British understandably try to forget that their Empire was the fruit of military conquest and of brutal wars involving physical and cultural extermination. Although the Empire itself, at the start of the twenty-first century, has almost ceased to exist, there remains an ineradicable tendency to view the imperial experience through the rose-tinted spectacles of heritage culture.

A self-satisfied and largely hegemonic belief survives in Britain that the Empire was an imaginative, civilising enterprise, reluctantly undertaken, that brought the benefits of modern society to backward peoples. Indeed it is often suggested that the British Empire was something of a model experience, unlike that of the French, the Dutch, the Germans, the Spaniards, the Portuguese – or, of course, the Americans. There is a widespread opinion that the British Empire was obtained and maintained with a minimum degree of force and with maximum cooperation from a grateful indigenous population.

This benign, biscuit-tin view of the past is not an understanding of their history that young people in the territories that once made up the Empire would now recognise. A myriad of revisionist historians have been at work in each individual country producing fresh evidence to suggest that the colonial experience – for those who actually 'experienced' it – was just as horrific as the opponents of Empire had always maintained that it was, perhaps more so. New generations have been recovering tales of rebellion, repression and resistance that make nonsense of the accepted imperial version of what went on. Focusing on resistance has been a way of challenging not just the traditional, self-indulgent view of empire, but also the customary depiction of the colonised as *victims*, lacking in agency or political will.

Many of the rebellions discussed in this book fall into four basic categories. First, as in America, Australia, Canada, New Zealand, and parts of Africa, there are the revolts of the indigenous peoples against the British imposition of white settlement and extermination.

Second, there are the revolts of people reluctantly dragooned into the imperial sphere, notably in areas such as India or West Africa, where there was no substantial white settlement and no policy of overt extermination. Here the rebellions often took the straightforward form of resistance to foreign rule.

Third, as in the example of the American colonies, there are the revolts against British rule by the white settlers themselves. These occurred on every continent and were often complicated by a history of previous allegiances – to the French (in Canada and the islands of the Indian Ocean), or to the Dutch (in South Africa though not in Indonesia, where the planned British settlement never materialised).

Fourth, as in the case of the innumerable slave rebellions in the Caribbean and elsewhere, there are the revolts of the workforce in the colonies, slaves in the first instance. Then, when slavery was abolished, cheap labour was provided by indentured labourers brought from overseas, who also resisted. By the twentieth century, many workers had begun to organise themselves with embryonic trade unions, capable of withdrawing their labour and going on strike.

The theme of repression has often been underplayed in traditional accounts, although a few particular instances are customarily highlighted – the slaughter after the Indian Mutiny in 1857, the massacre at Amritsar in 1919, the crushing of the Jamaican rebellion in 1867. These have been unavoidable tales. Yet the sheer scale and continuity of imperial repression over the years has never been properly laid out and documented.

No colony in their Empire gave the British more trouble than the island of Ireland. No subject people proved more rebellious than the Irish. From misty start to unending finish, Irish revolt against colonial rule has been the leitmotif that runs through the entire history of Empire, causing problems in Ireland, in England itself, and in the most distant corners of the British globe.

Endless rebellion in colonial Ireland, followed by fierce repression, famine and economic disaster helped to create an immense Irish diaspora spread over the world, where little Irelands arose to endlessly tease and irritate the British. The British affected to ignore or forget the Irish dimension to their Empire, yet the Irish were always present within it, and wherever they landed and established themselves, they never forgot where they had come from. The memory of past oppression, and the barely suppressed rage at the treatment of previous generations, grew with compound interest over the years.

The British often perceived the Irish as 'savages', and they used Ireland as an experimental laboratory for the other parts of their overseas empire, as a place to ship settlers to and from, as well as a crucible for the development of techniques of repression and control. Entire armies were recruited in Ireland, and officers learned their trade in its peat bogs and among its burning cottages. Some of the great names of British military history – from Wellington and Wolseley to Kitchener and Montgomery – were indelibly associated with Ireland. The particular tradition of armed policing, first patented in Ireland in the 1820s, was to become the established pattern for the rest of the Empire.

Irish soldiers – the 'wild geese' of legend – fought over the years in almost every European army except the British, serving in France and Spain, in Naples and Austria. Irish Catholics were not permitted officially to serve in the British forces until 1760, when 1,200 men were recruited for service in the marines, although some had infiltrated other regiments before that date. The rules were relaxed during the French and Indian War, and Catholics were more readily recruited.

Protestant landlords remained hostile to this development, arguing that arming such men, who might one day turn against them, was dangerous. They were right to be worried, for a fresh outbreak of violent rebellion occurred in 1761, led by the Whiteboys.

This book highlights the rebellions and resistance of the subject peoples. Implicit in its argument is the belief that Britain's imperial experience ranks more closely with the exploits of Genghiz Khan or Attila the Hun than with those of Alexander the Great, although these particular historic leaders have themselves been subjected to considerable historical revisionism in recent years. It is suggested here that the rulers of the British Empire will one day be perceived to rank with the dictators of the twentieth century as the authors of crimes against humanity on an infamous scale.

The drive towards the annihilation of dissidents and peoples in twentieth-century Europe certainly had precedents in the nineteenth-century imperial operations in the colonial world, where the elimination of 'inferior' peoples was seen by some to be historically inevitable, and where the experience helped in the construction of the racist ideologies that arose subsequently in Europe.[2] Later technologies merely enlarged the scale of what had gone before.

Throughout the period of the British Empire, the British were for the most part loathed and despised by those they colonised. While a thin crust of colonial society in the Empire – princes, bureaucrats, settlers, mercenary soldiers – often gave open support to the British, the majority of the people always held the colonial occupiers in contempt, and they made their views plain whenever the opportunity arose. Resistance, revolt and rebellion were permanent facts of empire, and the imperial power, endlessly challenged, was tireless in its repression. The sullen passivity, for most of the time, of the mass of the population gave a true indication of popular feeling. Individual murder, killings and assassination were sometimes the simplest responses that poor people could summon up to express their resentment of their alien conquerors, yet the long story of Empire is littered with large-scale outbreaks of rage and fury, suppressed with great brutality.

For much of its history, the British Empire was run as a military dictatorship. Colonial governors in the early years were military men who imposed martial law whenever trouble threatened. 'Special' courts and courts martial were set up to deal with dissidents, and handed out rough and speedy injustice. Normal judicial procedures were replaced by rule through terror; resistance was crushed, rebellion suffocated.

While many indigenous peoples joined rebellions, others took the imperial shilling. In most of their colonies, the British encountered resistance, but they often had local allies who, for reasons of class or money, or simply with an eye to the main chance, supported the conquering legions. Without these fifth columns the imperial project would never have been possible.

The use of indigenous peoples to fight imperial wars was a significant development in these early years, and became a central element in the future strategy of Europe's empires. This was as true of India as of the Caribbean and the Americas. Without Indian mercenary soldiers, known as sepoys, Britain could never have conquered and controlled the Indian subcontinent. Clive's victorious army at Plassey in 1757 was relatively small: 1,000 European troops and 2,000 Indian soldiers. Soon it became necessary to recruit a much larger army of local soldiers to provide protection for the British merchants, traders, and tax collectors moving into the inland markets of Bengal. These mercenaries were subsequently deployed in the 1760s in battles against the Bengali Nawab Mir Kassim.

Indian sepoys played a crucial role in the unfolding history of the Empire, fighting not just in India, but in predatory expeditions sent to Ceylon, to Indonesia, to Burma, to Africa, and eventually to Europe during the great European inter-imperial wars of the twentieth century. They established a pattern for the other mercenary armies of the Empire: the black, originally slave, regiments raised in the West Indies and sent to fight in Africa in the nineteenth century, and to Europe in the twentieth; and the African troops that would fight both in Africa itself, and as far afield as Burma. Without these locally recruited mercenary armies, the expansion and survival of the British Empire would not have been possible.

Yet not every Indian of military age served in the British army. The sepoys who served the British did so because they were paid to do so, and because they were too terrified to withdraw their labour. Britain controlled her mercenary armies with cash and with terror. Much of the early fighting in India in the eighteenth century was devised to secure booty with which to pay the troops. Yet many early campaigns were characterised by sepoy disaffection. Britain's harsh treatment of sepoy mutineers at Manjee in 1764, with the order that they should be 'shot from guns', was a terrible warning to others not to step out of line.

Mutiny, as the British discovered a century later, was a formidable weapon of resistance at the disposal of the soldiers they had trained. Crushing it through 'cannonading' – standing the condemned prisoner with his shoulders placed against the muzzle of a cannon – was essential to the maintenance of imperial control. This simple threat kept the sepoys in line throughout most of imperial history.

To defend its empire, to construct its rudimentary systems of communication and transport, and to man its plantation economies, the British used forced labour on a gigantic scale. For the first eighty years of the period covered by this book, from the mid-eighteenth century until 1834, the use of non-indigenous black slave labour originally shipped from Africa was the rule. Indigenous manpower in many imperial states was also subjected to slave conditions, dragooned into the imperial armies, or forcibly recruited into road gangs building the primitive communication networks that facilitated the speedy repression of rebellion. When black slavery was abolished in the 1830s, the imperial landowners' thirst for labour brought a new type of slavery into existence, in which workers from India and China were dragged from their homelands to be employed in distant parts of the world – a phenomenon that soon brought its own contradictions and conflicts.

As with other great imperial constructs, the British Empire involved vast movements of peoples. Armies were redeployed from one part of the world to another; settlers changed continents and hemispheres; prisoners were relocated from country to country; indigenous inhabitants were corralled, driven away into oblivion, or exterminated with smallpox infection (as in North America) or arsenic poisoning (Australia).

There was nothing historically unique about the British Empire. Virtually all European countries with sea coasts and navies had embarked on programmes of expansion in the sixteenth century, trading, fighting and settling in distant parts of the globe. Sometimes, having made some corner of the world their own, they would exchange it for another piece 'owned' by another power, and often these exchanges occurred as the byproduct of dynastic marriages. The Spanish, the Portuguese and the Dutch had empires; so too did the French, the Italians, the Germans and the Belgians. World empire, in the sense of a far-flung operation far from home, was a European development that changed the world over four centuries.

While the origins of the British Empire can be traced back to those early years, this book concentrates on the period since the defeats and victories of the 1750s. The Empire had earlier roots, but what is sometimes called 'the second British Empire' was basically a creation of the second half of the eighteenth century. The formation of British Canada, the white settlement of Australia, the move into central India, the early experimental incursions into Africa: these were all made possible in the period after Britain and the British colonies in America had gone their separate ways in the wake of the settler war of independence.

At that time, the British Empire was but a few small dots on the map. The colonies established on the Atlantic shores of North America had already been lost, and the tiny English settlements in Canada clung desperately to the eastern seaboard, together with a handful of riverine towns captured from the French. In India, a few coastal cities and their hinterland – Calcutta, Madras, Bombay – were Britain's only footholds, while the British slave islands in the Caribbean were under constant threat of rebellion. The capture and subjection of Australia, Ceylon, Burma, New Zealand, Tasmania and South Africa lay in the future. So too did the seizure of strategic outposts like Penang and Hong Kong, Singapore and Aden.

The mood in Britain after the loss of the American colonies had hardly been expansionist. William Pitt's India Act of 1784 famously declared that wars of aggression, and augmentation of territory, were contrary to the interests and injurious to the honour of the British nation. Yet well-meaning phrases formulated in London had no impact on the fresh patterns of domination soon to be established on the ground.

The story of British colonial settlement in America ended for the British in 1781, after two great rebellions, one by the Native Americans, the other by the white settlers. Events in the British Empire in subsequent centuries continued that tradition. Over the next 200 years, not a year went by without major instances of resistance and rebellion occurring somewhere in the Empire. In some years, the rebellions are almost uncountable, reaching a crescendo of resistance that the imperial cohorts were hard-pressed to crush.

While the stories of some individual revolts have often been told, the tale of resistance over two centuries has never before been considered over the wide sweep of Empire. We know about, and are still taught about, the generals and the proconsuls. Shelves groan under their innumerable biographies. In recent decades, we have also been told of the contribution to Empire of the 'subalterns' and the British working class. Much less familiar are the stories and the biographies of those who resisted, rebelled, and struggled against the Empire's great military machine.

Over two centuries, this resistance took many forms and had many leaders. Sometimes kings and nobles led the revolts, sometimes priests or slaves. Some have famous names and biographies; others have disappeared almost without trace. Many died violent deaths. Few even have a walk-on part in traditional accounts of Empire. Here, in this book, many of these forgotten peoples are resurrected and given the attention they deserve. For they lie at the heart of Our Empire Story.

Part I

THE CHALLENGE TO IMPERIAL POWER: NATIVE AMERICANS, CARIBBEAN SLAVES, INDIAN PRINCES AND IRISH PEASANTS, 1755–1772

The middle of the eighteenth century marks a significant watershed in the history of the British Empire. It was a time when the indigenous inhabitants of the United States fought their last battles against the British, and when the princes of India began the unequal struggle that would eventually lead to their subjugation. The resistance to Empire ignited in this period took place against the background of a global struggle between Britain and France, the first 'world war' of modern times, spreading out from the battlefields of Europe to embrace the colonial territories of India, North America and the Caribbean.

The conflict in the years between 1756 and 1763 is familiar to European historians as 'The Seven Years War', a European war in which the Prussian army and the British navy triumphed over France and Austria (the Holy Roman Empire). Spain, the ruler of much of Latin America and the Caribbean, joined the war in support of France and Austria in 1761, provoking the British to seize Spain's Cuban colony in 1762, while Russia and Sweden were also to be found fighting on the French side.

A yet wider war, known to American historians as 'The French and Indian War', overlapped with the European conflict and took place over a slightly longer period, the nine years from 1754 to 1763. Fighting between Britain and France began on the Ohio River in 1754, the result of long and unresolved disputes about the interior territories of North America, and Britain formally declared war on France in May 1756. Three years later, in September 1759, a British army advanced into New France, or French Canada, and captured Quebec. France held on briefly in Louisiana, but was no longer to play an important role in the north of North America. Both Quebec and Louisiana were lost by France at the Paris peace conference of 1763.

This inter-imperial conflict led to the largest and longest Native American resistance war in American history. The Ohio valley became the epicentre of a Native American battleground that spread north to the Great Lakes and the St Lawrence River on the Canadian border, and south to the Carolinas and Georgia. This cataclysmic conflict has often been overshadowed in conventional American accounts by the settler war of independence in the 1770s, and it is almost entirely forgotten in the standard histories of Britain and its overseas possessions.

Another arena of the great British war with France was India, where rival trading stations – the British at Calcutta, the French at Chandernagore – had long been established on the Hughli River, and where British and French armies had already clashed in the 1740s. A successful British attack on the French fort at Chandernagore in 1757 was followed by the defeat of France's uncertain ally, Siraj-ud-Daula, the rebellious Muslim ruler of Bengal, at the battle of Plassey. The marginalisation of French influence and the British conquest of India had begun.

The global struggle of the 1750s and the eventual British defeat of the French, formalised by the Treaty of Paris in 1763, led to the creation of what is often called the 'Second British Empire'. With British armies deployed in different parts of the world, the struggle enabled this embryonic 'Second Empire' to increase in size by leaps and bounds. It also provided the Empire's subject peoples with the opportunity to participate in acts of resistance that might have been difficult to sustain in years of general peace. Many opponents of colonial rule perceived that this was a good moment to rebel. In North America and India, and in the slave islands of the Caribbean, a fleeting chance was offered to peasants and princes, as well as to slaves and indigenous peoples, to challenge British power.

Four distinct groupings sought to stem the imperial tide at the start of this era: first were the Native Americans in the North American hinterland to the west of the thirteen coastal colonies, peoples already caught up in the tide of white settlement; second were the inhabitants of the coastal states of India, threatened for the first time by Britain's military advance; third were the slaves in Britain's West Indian islands, notably Jamaica, who sought to escape from their enforced servitude; and fourth were the peasants in Ireland, mobilised against their settler landlords by the rural insurgents known as the Whiteboys.

Rebels everywhere did as best they could with the weapons they had to hand, and two successful uprisings occurred at the start of this period. One took place in the Americas in 1755, when Shingas roused the other Delaware chiefs to join the French in defeating the British on the Ohio River, killing the British commander-in-chief as he advanced into the Ohio valley. Another uprising was the one staged in Bengal the following year, in 1756, when Siraj-ud-Daula expelled the British from their military base at Calcutta, after holding prisoners in the famous Black Hole prison.

Other acts of colonial insubordination followed. In America, the Abenaki went on to slaughter British soldiers on Lake George in 1757, and, with the Micmacs, maintained a hostile posture along the Canadian frontier. A few years later, the Delaware ordered the British to leave Pittsburgh, and, inspired by Neolin and led by Pontiac, their nation rose up along the banks of the Ohio in 1763. Finally, the Cherokee engaged in fresh hostilities in the Carolinas in the 1760s.

Elsewhere in that decade, with Caribbean islands changing hands during the war, and with a consequent loosening in imperial systems of control, African slaves seized their chance to rebel. A plantation revolt in Jamaica in 1760 was to smoulder on for several years.

Fresh leaders in India – Mir Jafar and Haidar Ali – took up the anti-imperial cause in Bengal and Mysore. These varied resistance struggles in different parts of the world paved the way to a sustained period of imperial rejection throughout the newly expanded empire. Though ultimately unsuccessful, they nourished a tradition of resistance that was to be incubated by succeeding generations.

CHAPTER 1

Native American Resistance during the French and Indian War

On 9 July 1755, in a ravine of the Monongahela River, a few miles from Pittsburgh, a troop of 600 Native American guerrilla fighters ambushed a British army advancing into their territory along the Ohio valley. A thousand British soldiers were casualties of the ensuing battle, and the commander-in-chief of British forces in America, the sixty-year-old General Edward Braddock, was killed. The Native Americans, chiefly Delaware and Shawnee, together with 250 French soldiers with whom they were allied, could savour for a moment a significant victory against an imperial army, and rejoice as its defeated remnants retreated to the Atlantic coast.

The indigenous inhabitants of North America were always aware of the different colonial strategies of the British and the French, and they thought they were better off under the French. An Iroquois at a French mission outpost run by the Jesuits in Canada described their rival merits:

> Go see the forts our [French] Father has erected, and you will see that the land beneath his walls is still hunting ground, having fixed himself in those places we frequent only to supply our wants; whilst the British, on the contrary, no sooner get possession of a country than the game is forced to leave it; the trees fall down before them, the earth becomes bare, and we find among them hardly the wherewithal to shelter us when the night falls.[1]

Several Native American nations accepted the implicit advice in the Iroquois letter, and when war broke out between the European rivals in 1754 they made temporary alliances with the French, whose rule appeared less threatening to their interests than the impositions of the British settlers.

In the Ohio valley, the Delaware took time to decide which way to jump. They had only recently moved into the upper reaches of the valley, driven there by British settlers from Pennsylvania and other coastal colonies, and were soon made aware that this too was territory into which settlers were planning to expand. Fur traders were to be found travelling along the rivers, as well as groups of armed settlers from Virginia. Two of these pioneering expeditions in the early 1750s were led by Major George Washington, a young, slave-owning Virginian landowner with a part-time military position who was to take a speculative interest in these western territories for the rest of his life. The Virginian pioneers were soon followed by settlers from the rival colony of Pennsylvania.

These Virginian probes into the Ohio valley coincided with a revival of French interest in the future of these lands situated between their existing colonies: Canadian 'New France' to the north, and Louisiana on the Gulf of Mexico to the south. France's strategic aim was to establish French 'protectorates' in the vast Native American territory stretching from the Gulf to the St Lawrence River, to be controlled from a string of military outposts. The first to be constructed was Fort Duquesne, later to become Pittsburgh.

In the early stages of this war, the British had hopes of recruiting the Native American nations to their side, but the French experience of making tactical alliances with local people had proved more effective. The Delaware supported the French move against the British in 1755, and the British commander was their first victim.

Braddock had been sent out to North America in January 1755. Sailing with two Irish regiments from Cork to Virginia, he advanced westward from Maryland. His soldiers built a rough road across the Allegheny mountains and into the territory of the Delaware. Their task was to seize Fort Duquesne from the French.

Benjamin Franklin, one of the white settler leaders in Pennsylvania, warned the British general of the uncertain loyalties of the Delaware, but Braddock took no notice. 'These savages may, indeed, be a formidable enemy to your raw American militia, but upon the King's regular and disciplined troops, sir, it is impossible that they should make an impression.'[2]

Shingas, one of the Delaware resistance leaders in the Ohio valley, had long been known as 'a terror' to the British frontier settlements.[3] Yet in recent years he had seemed more friendly. He was invited with other chiefs to a meeting with Braddock, and came under pressure to join the British against the French. He sought to bargain, and a settler recalled what he had requested:

> Shingas asked General Braddock whether the Indians that were friends to the British might not be permitted to live and trade among the British, and have hunting grounds sufficient to support themselves and their families, as they had nowhere to flee to but into the hands of the French and *their* Indians, who were their enemies.[4]

This was a straightforward request, but Braddock had no experience in dealing with Native Americans and no mandate to give Shingas what he asked for. The hunting grounds of the Delaware were already destined to be handed over to the settlers of Virginia, represented in Braddock's army by Major Washington.

Shingas received a one-sentence reply from Braddock that echoes through the chronicles of Empire: 'No savage should inherit the land.'[5] Tactical alliances might be made with indigenous peoples, for short-term opportunistic reasons, but such people could never be granted *rights* in exchange for their cooperation, least of all rights to land scheduled for white settlement.

Shingas and the Delaware chiefs gave a blunt response. 'If they might not have liberty to live on the land', they told Braddock, they would not join the British in fighting for it. They withdrew from the talks; the general told them dismissively that 'he did not need their help'.[6] He lived long enough to regret his decision, for their assistance would have been useful. They alone were familiar with the terrain through which his army was about to march.

Shingas and his men, 'very much enraged' by Braddock's remarks, went off to join the forces of France. Travelling back to Fort Duquesne, they met the French officer in charge, Captain Daniel de Beaujeu, who was more appreciative of their needs. When Captain Beaujeu 'began the Warsong', it was said, 'all the Indian Nations immediately joined him'.[7] Soon a powerful fighting force of Native Americans came out in support of the French – the army with French officers that defeated the British at Monongahela in July 1755.[8] Washington was one of the few survivors.

The victory of the Native Americans, albeit with French help, could be chalked up as a major success in their long resistance war. For a short while, they had cause to congratulate themselves on a notable victory, and, according to settler legend, they avenged their own losses by burning several prisoners alive. Their success was widely noted, and raised the spirits of other victims of settler oppression. The huge population of black slaves in the Thirteen Colonies were much encouraged by the result of the battle.

The military governor of Virginia, where 120,000 slaves worked on the plantations, noted with alarm that the blacks had become 'very audacious on the defeat on the Ohio . . . These poor creatures imagine the French will give them their freedom.' The white settlers of Virginia, numbering 170,000, were nearly outnumbered by their slave workforce, and had good cause to be worried. The threat of black rebellion was deemed so alarming that the governor placed 'a proper number of soldiers in each county to protect it from the combinations of the negro slaves'.[9]

Resistance by the indigenous inhabitants of the coastal colonies of North America was not new; it had occurred at intervals since the arrival of white settlers at the end of the sixteenth century. The first 'Indian War' took place in Virginia on the shores of Chesapeake Bay between 1609 and 1614. A second rebellion in the same area in 1622 almost destroyed the nascent colony, leaving nearly 400 settlers dead. A further rebellion in Virginia in 1644 was considered the bloodiest day for the British in the history of seventeenth-century America.[10]

Further north, the river towns of Connecticut were attacked by the Pequots in 1637, while the Algonquin warriors of Metacom, known to the English as 'King Philip', besieged half the settler towns of New England, destroying twelve of them in 1675. What became known as 'King Philip's war' was the deadliest conflict, in terms of the proportion of casualties to the population, in the history of the Americas. By the time it was over, hundreds had died on both sides.[11] To the south, in the Carolinas, the Creeks and the Yamasees were also no strangers to rebellion, joining forces early in the eighteenth century to kill several hundred settlers.

Native American resistance was met by the settler strategy of extermination. In the brutal conflict of the Chesapeake war, the English, with their banner of 'King Jesus', destroyed entire villages, slaughtering their inhabitants.[12] During the subsequent rebellion in Virginia in 1622, settlers murdered 200 Indians with poisoned wine.[13] Fifty fell in an ambush the following year, and 800 were killed in July 1624.

The Pequot rebellion in Connecticut in 1637 also evoked a savage English response, culminating in the massacre of several hundred Pequots. Male survivors were rounded up by British soldiers and executed, while the women and children were sold into slavery.[14] The Creek rebellion in South Carolina in 1715 was also harshly repressed: the settlers armed their African slaves, burned Native American villages, and killed an estimated thousand men, women and children.[15] Huge areas of Native American land were then cleared and prepared for settler occupation.

The folk memory of these ferocious killings caused a lull in the resistance wars, but in the 1750s and 1760s, during what were to be the final decades of British rule, the Native Americans renewed their struggle against the tide of white settlement with a determination born of desperation.

After the Delaware victory at Monongahela in July 1755, the Native Americans retained their supremacy in the Ohio valley over the next two years. Destroying the farms established by settlers from Virginia and Pennsylvania,[16] they forced these unwelcome predators back over the mountains to the east. More than 2,500 settlers were killed, and their rough cabins burned brightly along the frontier. The British commander at Fort Cumberland, in Maryland, described how 'the smoke of the burning plantations darkens the day, and hides the neighbouring mountains from our sight'.[17]

Yet the Native Americans soon found the tide of war turning against them. The British sent a fresh army across the Atlantic to fight them and their French allies; they were no longer faced by simple settler militias. Several Delaware chiefs in the Ohio valley, once led by Shingas, took note of the winds of change: they swapped sides. Accepting the overlordship of the Iroquois, who had re-established close relations with the British, they facilitated a British advance through Pennsylvania in 1758. The British army moved quickly over the Allegheny mountains and headed for Fort Duquesne. It was accompanied once again by Colonel Washington, now the commander of the Virginia militia.

Lacking reliable Native American allies, and short of supplies as a result of defeats further north, the French abandoned Fort Duquesne in December 1758 and burned it down. When the British arrived, Custaloga, one of the new Delaware chiefs, emerged from its still-smoking ruins and gathered with others to discuss a new treaty. They were content to see the French depart, but were loth to welcome the British. They knew that if British soldiers remained in the Ohio valley the Pennsylvania settlers would soon move in, avid to regain their old farms and to seize fresh Indian lands.

Custaloga told the British curtly that he had just one request: they should leave at once, both from the ruined fort and from the Ohio valley.

> We have great reason to believe you intend to drive us away and settle the country, or else why do you come to fight in the land that God has given us? . . . Why don't you and the French fight in the old country, and on the sea? Why do you come to fight on our land? This makes everybody believe you want to take the land from us, by force, and settle it.

Custaloga's argument was powerful, but the British ignored it. The Delaware were clearly hostile to the British, although in negotiations they seemed prepared to accept the presence of 200 soldiers stationed at Pittsburgh 'to support and defend the traders'. Yet the prospect of a permanent British settlement was a matter of continuing concern. A Quaker trader reported from the Ohio six months later that the Indians disliked 'the British coming here with an army; they seem jealous of their lands being settled'.[18]

The Delaware were right to be worried, for the solidarity that had once existed among the Native American nations was being rapidly eroded. The Iroquois had joined up permanently with the British, beguiled by the promises of Sir William Johnson, an officer appointed to be the 'superintendent' of the Indians. In 1759 they marched north with him towards French Canada to assist in the capture of Fort Niagara, thus helping to pave the way for the British seizure of Canada, and for the eventual white settlement of all Native American lands to the west.

The Delaware in the Ohio valley soon felt the adverse impact of the British conquest of French Canada. They were now without allies, isolated and alone. Yet three years later, in a last desperate effort, an inspired figure arose among them to preach rebellion against the white man. Neolin the prophet, for a brief moment, was to revive their faith in themselves.[19]

Other Native Americans were to suffer from having bound their future too closely to the French cause, notably the Micmacs in the British Canadian territory of Acadia, known to the British since 1713 as Nova Scotia.[20] This territory, originally French, had been moved into the British orbit under the terms of the 1713 Treaty of Utrecht. It was an unsatisfactory settlement both for the Micmacs and for the French settlers, and both groups showed signs of resistance during the first half-century of British control. The British solution was to introduce more settlers into the territory: some 4,000 arrived in 1749, mostly Protestants from New England, and a fort was constructed at Halifax to protect them.

The Micmacs, advised by a French missionary, Abbé Jean-Louis de Loutre, joined the French in efforts to force out the new settlers. The Micmac chief reminded the British with a rhetorical flourish that they were not the owners of the land: 'The place where you are, where you are building dwellings, where you are now building a fort, where you want as it were to enthrone yourself, this land of which you want to make yourself the absolute master: this land belongs to me.'[21]

Yet conventional forms of resistance proved ineffective against the tide of British settlement. Major Charles Lawrence, the governor, soon had the upper hand. The rebellious French inhabitants of Acadia were required to swear an oath of allegiance to the British monarch, a symbolic instrument of imperial control used throughout the Empire. A worse fate was reserved for the Micmacs: the governor offered a reward for their scalps.

These methods of coercion were only partially successful. Many French settlers refused to change their loyalties, while the Micmacs embarked on a guerrilla war. Major Lawrence then announced a yet more radical policy: the entire territory of Acadia would be emptied of its non-British inhabitants, both Micmac and French. Both groups – in the circumstances of the world war – were deemed a threat to British rule. In the autumn of 1755, orders were given for both the French settlers and the Micmacs to be deported. To be driven from their lands was an already familiar phenomenon to the Native Americans, but less so to European settlers. Given a taste of the imperial medicine usually handed out to indigenous peoples, the French were forced from their farms and expelled from the territory.

Opposition to Empire often arose among settlers who resented distant imperial rule; it came notably from European settlers from other empires who had found themselves in lands under British control. In later years, rebellions in Canada were organised by French settlers unhappy about their role within an Empire to which they had no ties of faith or nation. Dutch settlers in South Africa behaved in the same way.

A handful of the Acadians escaped into the hills, to continue the guerrilla war. Some 10,000 fled to the mainland, while 6,000 were forced from their homes and herded onto ships. Some of the French population eventually resettled in Louisiana, taking with them their Cajun culture and music. Others returned to France, where they re-established themselves with pensions granted by the French king. After the Paris Treaty of 1763, their lands were repopulated with 5,000 fresh settlers brought from New England.[22]

Native American resistance further west took a new turn in July 1757, when an army of 6,000 Native Americans moved across Lake George and seized the British outpost of Fort William Henry, a military base with a garrison of 2,000 men. Lake George was a stretch of water that lay in Native American territory north of Albany, on the track running north from the British colonies in North America to the French colony of Quebec; the fort had been constructed two years earlier on the lake's southern shore.

Prominent in this Native American force were members of the Abenaki nation, a people driven out of New England in the seventeenth century who had subsequently established themselves in settlements along the St Lawrence River. They had joined together with other nations, including the Micmacs of Acadia, to oppose the British, but all had then been forcibly pushed west by the settlers on the coast. Abenaki warriors were frequently involved in anti-British campaigns; now, defending their own lands, they were allied with a comparable number of French soldiers.[23] At Fort William Henry, they took their revenge on an army whose traditional task was to defend the land seizures of the settlers.[24]

After several days' bombardment by French guns, the British surrendered. Louis-Joseph, Marquis de Montcalm, the French commander in Canada, and Colonel George Munro, the fort's British commander, agreed that the soldiers of the fort's garrison should be disarmed and sent north as prisoners to Montreal.

The large force of Abenaki warriors, working to a separate agenda, had other plans. The following morning, they attacked and killed the British prisoners: one account suggests that some 200 prisoners were killed or carried away. The Abenaki did not keep to European rules of war when defending their own country. News of the slaughter of the prisoners created an hysterical atmosphere in the surviving white settlements along the frontier. Native Americans were now victorious from the St Lawrence to the Ohio. Any triumphalism, though, would have been premature.

Two years later, in September 1759, the Native Americans were on the receiving end of British revenge. Many of the Abenaki were based at the old Jesuit settlement at Odanak, between Montreal and Quebec.[25] There, the Abenaki had constantly tried to resist the advancing settlers on the frontier. Atecouando, their chief, had challenged a group of land surveyors sent in to measure up their territory a few years earlier, in 1752. 'We forbid you very expressly to kill a single beaver or to take a single stick of wood on the lands we live on', he warned. 'If you want wood, we will sell it to you, but you shall not have it without our permission.'

Surveyors were the advance guard of imperial expansion – in the Americas, in the Caribbean, and in Australia and South Africa. Usually protected by a small military force, they moved into indigenous or aboriginal territory to map the lands for future white settlement. At Odanak, they ignored the warnings of Atecouando and continued their work. The Abenaki killed them.

In September 1759, the Abenaki were attacked by a troop led by Major Robert Rogers. 'Take your revenge', Rogers was told by General Jeffrey Amherst, his commander-in-chief. The British massacre of the Abenaki was justified, Rogers argued subsequently, on account of their past misdeeds:

> This nation of Indians was notoriously attached to the French, and had for near a century past harassed the frontiers of New England, killing people of all ages and sexes in a most barbarous manner, at a time when they did not in the least expect them; and to my knowledge, in six years time, carried into captivity, and killed on the afore-mentioned frontiers, four hundred persons. We found in the town, hanging on poles over the doors, etc., about six hundred scalps, mostly British.[26]

The Abenaki settlement was surrounded before dawn, and Rogers recorded a version of events in his journal:

> I surprised the town when they were all fast asleep . . . which was done with so much alacrity by both the officers and men that the enemy had not time to recover themselves or take arms for their defence, till they were chiefly destroyed, except some few of them that took to the water.
>
> About forty of my people pursued them, who destroyed such as attempted to make their escape that way, and sunk both them and their boats. A little after sunrise, I set fire to all their houses, except three in which there was corn that I reserved for the use of the party.
>
> The fire consumed many of the Indians who had concealed themselves in the cellars and lofts of their houses. About seven o'clock in the morning, the affair was completely over, in which time we had killed at least two hundred Indians, and taken twenty of the women and children prisoner . . .

The Odanak massacre destroyed the Abenaki as a significant nation, and was one of several similar events that led to their eventual decimation. Today, some 250 years later, they barely survive. Their language is all but extinct in Canada, 'and few traits distinguish their reserves from surrounding French-speaking villages'.[27]

The slaughter coincided with a further event in September 1759 – one that would change the history of the continent. Before the ice closed over the St Lawrence River that year, the French-Canadian city of Quebec was captured for the British by General James Wolfe following a three-month siege. For the French settlers in the town, and for the Native Americans beyond, this was a defeat of more than symbolic importance. It led to the end of the French Empire in Canada, the start of a new British-influenced era for the Native Americans in the north of North America, and the beginning of the end of British ownership of the white settler colonies further south, where the settlers would stage a successful rebellion in the years after 1776.

The British capture of Quebec was followed by the fall of Montreal in 1769. The lands of Canada belonging to the Native Americans, formerly held by the French, were ceded to Britain by the Paris Treaty of February 1763. The French territory of New France was brought within the frontiers of the British Empire – with its forests, its French settler population of 70,000, and its immense but uncounted indigenous population. The lands of British 'Canada' were initially defined not just as the former French territory along the St Lawrence River, but as the entire central hinterland of America to the west of the Allegheny mountains and the Ohio River. The seeds of future conflict were sown in these remote areas. The existing Thirteen Colonies, perched along the Atlantic seaboard for more than a century, were bulging at the seams, over-full with settlers bent on territorial expansion into Native American lands. At stake were the vast American spaces to the west of the Appalachians.

CHAPTER 2

The Last Great Native American Rebellions

At the end of the French and Indian War, Native American resistance continued in the borderlands of the British colonies, seemingly unaffected by the departure of their sometime French allies from Canada. The Cherokee, a mountain people living in and around the Appalachians, were the largest Native American nation on the frontiers of British America, and in January 1760 they erupted in a great rebellion in South Carolina, after a fresh influx of settlers had threatened to seize yet more of their land.

The Cherokee had been engaged in relatively peaceful commerce with European traders for more than a century, although fighting and hostage-taking, punctuated by impermanent peace treaties, had characterised life on the unstable and eroding frontier. When caught between the French and the British in the war of the 1750s, they had allowed the British to construct a handful of forts on their land. The settlers took advantage of this military protection to expand their landholdings further, tentatively establishing themselves along the Savannah River, inland from Charleston. The Cherokee disliked both the soldiers and the settlers, complaining of several incidents of soldiers raping Cherokee women. Matters came to a head late in 1759, when twenty Cherokee were kidnapped and detained at a newly established British camp at Fort Prince George, where they were held as hostages by Lieutenant Coytmore, the British commander.

Seroweh, a Cherokee chief based at the neighbouring town of Estatoe, summoned several hundred warriors to blockade the fort in February 1760. His immediate purpose was to secure the release of the hostages, but his strategic aim was to halt further white settlement in the Carolinas and to eliminate the existing forts. When he came out for talks, Coytmore was killed, and the hostages were promptly shot by soldiers within the fort. Their deaths added fuel to Seroweh's incipient rebellion. Some Cherokee headed off to threaten the settlements in North Carolina and Virginia, while others advanced on Georgia.

Settlers further south, on the Long Canes River, received warning of a Cherokee attack and took evasive action. Fifty families fled towards the British camp at Fort More, but the Cherokee overtook them and attacked while they were stranded with their wagons beside a stream. The male settlers escaped, but women and children were scalped or taken prisoner.[1]

Cherokee attacks against the settlements continued throughout February and March. Scores of settlers were killed or taken prisoner; hundreds of buildings and thousands of cattle were destroyed. The entire region around the forts, with garrisons of 300 men each, was cleared of its settler population, and the forts were left isolated in a sea of Cherokee hostility. Further west, in Tennessee, the Cherokee surrounded the camp at Fort Loudoun.

Yet the rebels' triumph could not last long. Seroweh's forces were overextended, short of weapons and ammunition. They lacked allies from neighbouring Native American nations, some of whom had remained neutral or openly sided with the settlers. No support came from the French forts to the west.

Seroweh sought to make a tactical peace agreement with the British in May, and he came with eight other chiefs to the gates of Fort Prince George. Offering to negotiate, they were invited in for a meal by Ensign Milne, Coytmore's successor as local commander. The tables were turned. Milne appeared friendly enough, but the lunch invitation was a deception. Seroweh and the other chiefs were bundled inside the fort and held hostage.

News of Seroweh's rebellion had reached New York in February, and General Amherst, the British commander, ordered Colonel Archibald Montgomerie to prepare an expedition to crush it. An army of 1,200 Scottish Highlanders was assembled in New York, together with 1,000 local militiamen drawn from the settler community of South Carolina. The colony's assembly raised money for the expedition, offering £25 for each Native American scalp collected. North Carolina's assembly made a similar offer, but suggested that Cherokee prisoners might usefully be employed as slaves.

With Seroweh himself still detained at Fort Prince George, Seroweh's town of Estatoe was attacked by Montgomerie's regiment in June. All Cherokee found there were killed, though many had already escaped. 'A pretty town of 200 houses, it was well supplied with corn, ammunition, bearskins, and plunder from the British settlements. The troops looted and burned every house and killed a dozen persons who had lingered.'[2]

Montgomerie believed that 'after one or two of their towns had been burnt', the Indians would 'be very desirous to come to terms'. His soldiers hurried on to give other villages the same treatment. Major James Grant, one of the officers, described 'the disconsolate Cherokees on the hills watching flames destroy their villages and the looting soldiers running from house to house'. He wrote to headquarters explaining that 'the correction you'll allow has been pretty severe. I dare say the whole nation will readily come to terms . . .'[3]

With the hope that the Cherokee were now 'ready' to negotiate, Montgomerie released Seroweh from detention. If the Cherokee wanted peace, he told him, they had only to display a white flag. Outraged by the earlier treachery of Ensign Milne and by the subsequent humiliations he had suffered, Seroweh rejected these overtures, and returned to his smouldering village. He told his assembled warriors of his fear that 'the British overture was a feint to draw the headmen together in order to put them to death'. He urged them to prepare for a longer war, and his rebellion resumed.

A year later, in June 1761, the Cherokee were faced by a fresh battalion, led by Major Grant. Once again the Cherokee towns were burned and their fields destroyed, and many were killed. Grant had fought the rebels to a standstill, having 'burned fifteen Cherokee towns, ruined fifteen hundred acres of corn, and destroyed the Cherokee appetite for war'. Yet the battles took their toll on the British as well as the Cherokee. Grant returned to Fort Prince George after a punishing month-long expedition, with his army in a wretched condition.

It was the end of the road for the Cherokee. This time they were forced to make a permanent peace, with disastrous results for the future of their nation. Within twenty years their lands in Georgia and Kentucky had been seized and parcelled out among a fresh influx of settlers – Scotch-Irish immigrants from Ulster, and another group from Germany. Later, during the settler war of independence in the 1770s, a tactical alliance with the British against the rebel settlers was to lead to further tragedy for the Cherokee. In succeeding decades, the survivors were force-marched ever further to the west, a handful ending up in Oklahoma in the nineteenth century. Their displacement was the result of policies pursued by the new settler government of the United States, but responsibility for their earlier decimation lay at the door of the British.

The Cherokee had been defeated in 1761, but other Native Americans in the strategic frontier territory of the upper Ohio began the following year to listen to the revolutionary appeals of Neolin, a religious leader among the Delaware known as 'the Delaware Prophet'. Neolin argued for a fresh union of Native American nations that would join together to expel the white settlers from the Americas. The Native Americans had lost their French allies in 1760, and had greeted the British conquerors of Canada with 'sullen hostility'. Now they could rely only on themselves. That was the gist of Neolin's sermons.

Neolin preached rebellion among the peoples west of Pittsburgh, along the banks of the Muskingum River, a tributary of the Ohio. He sought to inspire fresh forms of resistance against the tide of settlement, urging his audience to return to the way of life that had existed before the arrival of the settlers. 'I warn you,' he said with the wisdom of experience, 'that if you allow the British among you, you are dead. Maladies, smallpox, and their poison, will destroy you totally.'[4]

Neolin was an authoritarian preacher, obliged by the drama of the times to insist on absolute obedience. 'You must pray to me,' he told them, 'and only do my will.' Much that is known of him comes from the evidence of a French prisoner who was captured and held by the Delaware, and subsequently escaped. The Frenchman wrote of having seen 'strange hieroglyphics' painted on deerskin that contained the prophet's message. Neolin had constructed a pictorial chart that showed the path from earth to heaven along which 'their forefathers used to ascend to happiness'; the path was clearly blocked by a symbol that represented 'the White people'. The French prisoner gave a detailed account of the philosophy of Neolin and his acolytes:

> The first doctrine they taught them was to purify themselves from sin, which they taught they could do by the use of emetics and abstinence from carnal knowledge of the different sexes; to quit the use of fire-arms, and to live entirely in their original state that they were in before the white people found out their country; nay, they taught that the fire was not pure that was made by steel and flint, but that they should make it by rubbing two sticks together.[5]

Neolin's message, with its emphasis on the age-old traditions of the Native American nations, soon spread throughout the upper Ohio, exploding the following year in the great rebellion known by the name of Pontiac, chief of the Ottawa.[6]

Pontiac's rebellion was the last and most geographically widespread revolt staged by the Native Americans against British rule in the Americas. A charismatic leader of the Ottawa, Pontiac took advantage of the religious fervour engendered by Neolin to plot the destruction of the British forts at Pittsburgh, Detroit, and Niagara. Born around 1720, he was noted by contemporaries for his powers of organisation. 'He is in a manner adored by all the nations hereabout', wrote Alexander Fraser, a British lieutenant, 'and he is more remarkable for his integrity and humanity than either Frenchman or Indian.'[7] By origin an Ottawa, Pontiac was the head of a loose Native American confederacy that included the Potawatomi and the Ojibwa. He had witnessed (and possibly participated in) the British victory over the French in Canada in 1759, but had subsequently become suspicious of British intentions. He well understood that plans for increased white settlement in the backlands of America, in territory where the French had been content simply to trade, would seriously damage the interests of the Native Americans.

Pontiac's rebellion began in May 1763 when a troop of Chippewas led by Chief Minavavana attacked the fort of Michilimackinac (now Mackinaw), a British base on the straits between Lake Huron and Lake Michigan. 'I heard an Indian war cry and a noise of general confusion', wrote Alexander Henry, a British fur trader living at the fort who was captured, and who later gave an account of the attack. The Chippewas had entered the fort, Henry recorded, after suggesting a friendly game of lacrosse. 'Going instantly to my window', he recorded, 'I saw a crowd of Indians within the fort furiously cutting down and scalping every Englishman they found.'[8]

Chief Pontiac of Ottawa led a federation of Native American nations against the British in 1763. Portrait painted by John Mix Stanley, circa 1850.

Henry described a meeting of Indians where a triumphant announcement had been made; those present were told that 'Pontiac had taken Detroit, that the King of France had awoke and repossessed himself of Quebec and Montreal, and that the British were meeting destruction, not only at Michilimackinac but in every other part of the world'.

In the summer of 1763 Pontiac's warriors advanced on the forward forts of the British, capturing and destroying outlying settlements in Michigan, Ohio, Indiana and Pennsylvania. Hundreds of settlers and traders were killed, and several military units sent out from Fort Niagara by General Amherst were ambushed and destroyed.

The Native Americans showed conclusively that, when united, they could occupy and hold large spaces in the interior of the continent against all comers. Yet Pontiac's armies, in the end, were unable to prevail against the base at Detroit, under siege from May to October, or at Fort Duquesne (now renamed Fort Pitt). There, on 5 August, a few miles from Pittsburgh, the scene of the Delaware victory over General Braddock in 1755, an army of Delawares, Shawnees, Mingoes and Hurons from Sandusky fell on a British contingent led by Colonel Henry Bouquet.[9]

After two days' fighting, Pontiac's warriors withdrew and the British retained their control of the fort. 'The action', records Fortescue, 'was one of the fiercest ever fought with Indians.' Fierce arguments broke out among the Native American allies in the wake of the defeat, and Pontiac's rebellion slowly foundered. Gaining the upper hand, the settlers took their revenge. In December, at a workhouse in Lancaster, Pennsylvania, an entire community of Susquehannock Indians were slaughtered by a posse known as the 'Paxton Boys', led by a Presbyterian elder.[10]

Terrified by their narrow escape at Bushy Run, the British turned again to thoughts of extermination. General Amherst advocated a return to the tried and tested way of curbing the power of the Native Americans, and when two Delaware chiefs came for peace talks at Fort Pitt, a British officer, William Trent, noted in his journal what was done. 'We gave them two blankets and a handkerchief out of the Smallpox hospital', he wrote, adding that he hoped it would have 'the desired effect'. It certainly did.[11]

Amherst hoped to make the experiment at Fort Pitt more systematic. 'Could it not be contrived to send the smallpox among those disaffected tribes of Indians?' he wrote to Colonel Bouquet, smallpox now being rife within the fort at Pittsburgh. 'I will try to inoculate [them] with some blankets that may fall into my hands', Bouquet replied, 'and take care not to get the disease myself.'[12] (He was to die three years later, of yellow fever.) Neolin's prophecy that contact with the British would mean that 'their poison will destroy you totally' was no idle warning.

In 1764 some 2,000 Native American delegates came to a peace conference at Fort Niagara, and agreed to return the prisoners they had captured. Pontiac was not present, but he signed a separate agreement the following year, in which he re-emphasised that the French surrender of their forts in 1760 gave no right to the British to seize Indian land. He lived on until April 1769, when he was murdered near St Louis by a Native American bribed by a trader.

Pontiac's experience illustrated a problem that recurs throughout the subsequent episodes of indigenous resistance elsewhere. A successful rebellion needs a united people as well as assistance from the enemy of the occupying power. Had Pontiac been able to rely on the unity of the disparate Native American nations that had initially been forged, and had he secured the French assistance he had been hoping for, the subsequent history of the British Empire – and of the United States – might have taken a different course.

Pontiac's revolt was paralleled by a growing sentiment of rebelliousness against British rule among the white settlers. Ever since Washington's probes along the Ohio in the early 1750s, the settlers had envisaged that the Native American land west of the Alleghenies would soon be theirs. Now, as the result of decisions taken in Europe, notably in the wording of Britain's 'Royal Proclamation' of 1763, their ambitions were thwarted. What loomed in the

1760s and 1770s was not just a Native American struggle against the white settlers, but a settler conflict with the British Empire that would change the history of the world.

Pontiac's great rebellion marked the end of the Delaware struggle to keep the Ohio valley free from white settlement. In subsequent years, individual settlers from Virginia, Pennsylvania and the Carolinas, as well as several speculative land companies, pressed on into Native American territory, ignoring demands from London to stop. George Washington was among those who took a continuing interest in the colonising ventures of the Ohio Company and the Mississippi Company.

Old divisions re-emerged between the Native American nations. Terrorised by the armed actions of the settlers and the land companies, the Iroquois saw little future in resistance, and renewed their alliance with the British. They put their faith in the 'superintendents' with whom some had worked during the 1750s. In November 1768, 3,000 Iroquois gathered at Fort Stanwix (now the town of Rome in New York state) to sign a treaty with British officials. The agreement was to benefit them at the expense of the Delaware and the Shawnees, for in exchange for guarantees to their existing homelands, they surrendered the title to a vast swathe of land in the interior held by those nations.[13] A number of Delaware and Shawnees were present at the gathering, but they did not sign the treaty; the Iroquois claimed to negotiate on their behalf.

The Cherokee on the frontiers of Virginia had also signed a treaty. Fatally weakened by their rebellion of 1760–61, they too suffered from a fresh influx of settlers. They had signed an agreement in September 1768, and agreed to new boundaries favourable to the settlers. Under the terms of this agreement, the Treaty of Hard Labour, immense new areas of Cherokee land were thrown open to white settlement, never to be recovered.

CHAPTER 3

Slave Rebellions in the Caribbean

The slave islands of the Caribbean were also affected by the course of the French and Indian War. Slave revolts in Jamaica in 1760 and 1765 posed fresh challenges to British rule. Slave workers from Africa had long contributed to the wealth of Empire, and the Empire itself seemed inconceivable at that time without the continued supply of the cheap labour they provided. Seized from the Spanish Empire a century earlier, Jamaica was England's largest, richest and most important possession in the Caribbean. Its riches came from sugar, grown on plantations worked by a huge slave population kept under fierce discipline.

During the Easter celebrations in 1760, slaves working on the Jamaica plantations exploded in a well-organised rebellion. Four hundred took part in the initial outbreak of slaves from a dozen plantations on the north coast. They were soon joined by thousands all over the island. According to the near-contemporary account of Edward Long, an established British planter, it was the most formidable uprising ever known in the West Indies to date.[1] Most of the slaves were 'Coromantins', imported from the Gold Coast (now known as Ghana), the area of Africa where the Ashanti would provide continued resistance against British rule throughout the nineteenth century.

The 'generalissimo' of the rebellion was Tacky – or 'chief' in the slave patois – 'a young man of good stature, and well made', according to Long's description. Other leaders were Fortune and Kingston, named after the plantations where they worked. Long had a poor opinion of Tacky, who 'did not appear to be a man of any extraordinary genius',[2] yet he led the rebellion for more than a year.

Much of the island was freed from imperial control. Large tracts were farmed by Maroons, the descendants of indigenous peoples and escaped slaves, whose free territory in the mountains had long provided a safe haven for fresh generations of runaways. Many slaves perceived it as an attractive model for an alternative society that might be created after they had secured their freedom. The rebel slaves of 1760, Long noted, were impressed by 'the happy circumstance of the Maroons'. They were perceived to have acquired 'very comfortable settlements, and a life of freedom and ease'.[3]

The Maroons had long sustained an independent existence and were quite capable, when provoked, of descending from the hills to cause havoc on the plantations. When the British had sought to eliminate them in the 1730s, the Maroons had fought the British forces to a standstill. A peace treaty signed in 1738 gave the Maroons rights to substantial territory, as well as guarantees of freedom, independence and self-government. The Maroons agreed, in return, to surrender all runaway slaves in future, and to allow two white 'residents' to live among them, to regulate disputes that might arise between white and black. This typical colonial device – the positioning in conquered territory of a 'resident', an 'agent', or a 'district commissioner' – was much used throughout the Empire. The Maroons pledged themselves to assist the British monarch against his enemies, and they were called out to help crush the rebellion of 1760, although it proved necessary to summon troops from other islands.

The planning of Tacky's rebellion was meticulous, 'conducted with such profound secrecy that almost all the Coromantin slaves throughout the island were privy to it, arousing no suspicion among the Whites'. The rebel aim, wrote Long, was to divide 'the island into small principalities in the African mode, to be distributed among their leaders and head men'.

Sure of victory, slaves in Kingston had already chosen their future queen: 'The Coromantins of that town had raised one Cubah, a female slave belonging to a Jewess, to the rank of royalty, and dubbed her queen of Kingston; at their meetings she had sat in state under a canopy, with a sort of robe on her shoulders and a crown upon her head.' General Tacky, for his part, wrote Long, 'had flattered himself with the hope of obtaining (among other fruits of victory) the lieutenant-governor's lady for his concubine'.

Many slaves had dreams of independence along the lines pioneered by the Maroons. One slave, subsequently captured, outlined his ideas to his guard, a Jewish militiaman. Jews on the island were unpopular with the other white settlers, since most had refused to join the militia. Aware of this prejudice, the slave explained his plan to his guard:

> You Jews, said he, and our nation (meaning the Coromantins), ought to consider ourselves as one people. You differ from the rest of the Whites, and they hate you. Surely then it is better for us to join in one common interest, drive them out of the country, and hold possession of it to ourselves. We will have . . . a fair division of estates, and we will make sugar and rum, and bring them to market.
>
> As for the sailors, you see they do not oppose us, they care not who is in possession of the country, Black or White, it makes no difference to them; so that after we are masters of it, you need not fear that they will come cap in hand to us (as they now do to the Whites) to trade with us. They'll bring us things from t'other side the sea, and be glad to take our goods in payment.

The Jewish militiaman listened to this story with interest, according to Long's account, but declined to join the rebellion.[4]

Many slaves were recently arrived from Africa, and their familiar customs were much in evidence. Long recounts the capture and execution of a famous 'obeiah man', or priest, 'tricked up with all his feathers, teeth, and other implements of magic':

> He was an old Coromantin, who, with others of his profession, had been a chief in counselling and instigating the credulous herd, to whom these priests administered a powder, which, being rubbed on their bodies was to make them invulnerable; they persuaded them into a belief that Tacky, their generalissimo in the woods, could not possibly be hurt by the white men, for he caught all the bullets fired at him in his hand, and hurled them back with destruction to his foes.

The firm though mistaken belief that it was possible to resist and survive the modern weapons of the white man, a view often held by slaves and indigenous peoples, is a permanent thread that runs through the empire story.

Tacky's rebellion spread through the island and lasted for several months. It was crushed by superior force, but a guerrilla war continued for a year. Tacky was eventually captured by the Maroons and shot. His severed head was taken to Spanish Town and stuck on a pole. His fellow rebels, Fortune and Kingston, were 'hung up alive in irons on a gibbet' in the centre of Kingston. Fortune lived for seven days; Kingston for nine. Some 400 rebels were shot; others were burned to death over a slow fire; many committed suicide. Long concluded that 'such exercises in frightfulness proved of doubtful value'.

A further 500 had their death sentences commuted, and were shipped to Britain's prison island of Roatán, one of the Bay Islands off the northern coast of Honduras.[5] Among those sentenced to exile was Queen Cubah, but she persuaded the ship's captain to leave her behind in Jamaica. She was eventually recaptured and executed.

Tacky's rebellion lasted for so long that it received newspaper coverage in Boston. It was also talked about in London, and sparked off the publication there of a pamphlet called 'Two Dialogues on the Man-Trade'. Its author, J. Philmore, an otherwise unknown eighteenth-century pamphleteer, supported the slaves' rebellion – in order that they might 'deliver themselves out of the miserable slavery they are in'. In an outspoken statement, revolutionary for the times, Philmore declared, 'all the black men now in our plantations, who are by unjust force deprived of their liberty and held in slavery . . . may lawfully repel that force with force and . . . destroy their oppressors'.[6]

Philmore went further, claiming that it was 'the duty of others, white as well as black, to assist those miserable creatures . . . in their attempts to deliver themselves out of slavery, and to rescue them out of the hands of their cruel tyrants'. Tacky's rebellion, and this subsequent appeal to whites for revolutionary solidarity with the slaves, was to feed into the anti-slavery movement of the eighteenth century that eventually secured an end to the slave trade within the British Empire in 1807.

A further rebellion of the Coromantin slaves took place in Jamaica in November 1765, organised by Blackwall, a survivor of the 1760 revolt. Put on trial at that time, he was acquitted for lack of evidence. On this later occasion, the slaves 'hoped to find the white people off their guard', wrote Edward Long in his history, 'and they had full confidence that, by their precautions and their secrecy, they should carry all before them and make amends for their former disappointment'.[7]

Following a plan similar to that of 1760, Blackwall organised a group of Coromantin slaves on the Whitehall estate, freshly arrived from the Gold Coast. That Christmas, they planned to stage revolts at seventeen estates. The aim, as Long described it, was 'to slaughter, or force the white inhabitants to take refuge on board the ships'. The slaves then planned 'to divide the conquered country with the Maroons, who, they alleged, had made choice of the woody uncultivated parts, as being most convenient for their hog-hunting'. The ambition of the slaves was to 'enjoy all the remainder, with the cattle and the sheep, and live like gentlemen'.

Unfortunately for the rebels, bonfires at the Whitehall estate were lit prematurely. Quamin, one of their number, was impetuous and 'would not wait the appointed time'. The plantation was seized for a while, but the slaves were checked at a neighbouring estate by the planters' militia. Some thirteen rebels were executed, and thirty-three were transported to Roatán island.

A further rebellion broke out the following year. Thirty-three Coromantins 'suddenly rose and, in the space of an hour, murdered and wounded no less than 19 white persons'. The slaves were soon defeated; some were killed on the spot, and others executed later or sent to Roatán. Yet they kept up the pressure, both in Jamaica and elsewhere in the Caribbean, as a new phase of slave resistance began.[8]

A rebellion on the British island of St Vincent some years later, in March 1772, was so serious that two British battalions had to be sent there from the North American colonies. A long-smouldering resistance movement by Black Caribs, who had organised themselves to oppose white settlement on the island, was led by Joseph Chatoyer.

The Black Caribs, like the Maroons elsewhere, were descendants of the indigenous inhabitants of the island who had intermarried with runaway and shipwrecked slaves. Their situation paralleled that of other British islands in the Caribbean, notably Jamaica and Dominica, which had significant Maroon populations who were neither white settlers from Europe nor black slaves from

Africa. The Caribs of St Vincent saw themselves as the indigenous owners of the island: they had never accepted the sovereignty of the French, nor, later, of the British.[9]

The British had acquired St Vincent from the French at the Paris peace conference of 1763. The acquisition had proved a mixed blessing: the Atlantic side of the island was occupied by 10,000 Black Caribs, while the Caribbean side was in the hands of 5,000 French settlers, originally from Martinique, who ran sugar plantations with slave labour. The British brought in fresh settlers from Britain, and planned to extend new plantations into Black Carib territory, the most fertile part of the island.

The large tracts occupied by the Black Caribs, effectively a free territory in the hills, were an irritant to the plantation owners and a significant attraction for the slaves, providing a safe haven for runaways and an attractive model for an alternative society. The British had begun building a road into the Carib half of the island in 1771, and surveyors, guarded by forty soldiers, were sent up into the hills. The plan was to survey and sell the Carib land and to place the Caribs in 'reserves'.

Armed Carib bands organised by Joseph Chatoyer were initially successful in halting the surveyors' work, and early in 1772 Chatoyer came with forty Carib chiefs to a meeting called by Sir William Young, the British Commissioner. Negotiations took place, but Young found the Caribs to be 'in a fixed resolution not to consent to our settling any part of the country claimed by them'.[10] Faced with a negotiating deadlock, the plantation owners demanded that more extreme measures should be taken against the Caribs. They should be expelled by force and sent to 'any unoccupied tract of 10,000 acres' in Africa, 'or to some desert island adjacent thereto'.[11]

Young and the plantation owners needed reinforcements to crush the Black Caribs, and two battalions arrived from North America in March. Chatoyer's followers held out for some months, but, facing defeat and a choice between extermination or exile, they abandoned their resistance war a year later, in February 1773.

Concern in Britain over events in the Caribbean had grown since the days of Tacky's Jamaican slave rebellion, and Chatoyer's Caribs now secured vocal support in the parliament in London. They were 'fighting for liberty', declared Colonel Isaac Barre MP in December 1772, 'and every English heart must applaud them'. Granville Sharpe, the philanthropic radical, wrote to the Earl of Dartmouth, the colonial secretary, pointing out that 'even a victory in so bad a cause will load the British government with indelible shame and dishonour'.

Fresh negotiations took place, and Chatoyer signed a treaty that allowed the Caribs to remain in occupation of the northern third of the island. Yet he remained distrustful, well aware that the plantation owners would never settle for less than the eventual destruction of the Caribs. After a brief period between 1779 and 1784, when the island again fell under French control, Chatoyer reignited his resistance against the returning British in 1785, and again in 1791; but the settlers eventually achieved their aim. The Black Caribs were defeated after Chatoyer's death, and the survivors were expelled to Roatán island, where a handful of their descendants remain to this day.

Two decades passed before the future of slavery began to interest political opinion in Britain, where most people shared the opinion of Adam Smith, delivered in a lecture in 1763, that 'slavery . . . has hardly any possibility of being abolished'. Smith explained that slavery 'has been universall in the beginnings of society, and the love of dominion and authority over others will probably make it perpetuall'.[12] Famed for his economic perspicacity, Smith was less far-sighted on this occasion.

CHAPTER 4

Treaties and Proclamation Mark the End of the French and Indian War

On 10 February 1763, Britain, France and Spain signed a treaty in Paris designed to mark a formal end to the French and Indian War. Spain recovered Havana from the British, but was obliged to exchange it for Florida. France surrendered all its territories on the North American mainland, with the exception of New Orleans and its Louisiana hinterland; it also gave up the Caribbean islands of Dominica, Grenada, St Vincent and Tobago.

The British returned Guadeloupe, Martinique and St Lucia to the French, while in India France regained Pondicherry. No mention was made of the indigenous inhabitants in the treaties that detailed the exchange of colonial acquisitions. Neither counted nor consulted, they were treated as though they were not there. It was an attitude that continued to characterise international treaties into the twentieth century.

Britain now had the beginnings of a large Empire to defend, to police, to administer, and to exploit. The dangers were clear: their West Indian islands were faced with the possibility of endless slave rebellions while North America lay exposed to permanent attack from Native Americans.[1] To protect their possessions, the British had barely 15,000 soldiers. More troops would need more money.

To recoup the costs of imperial defence, the British made plans to exploit the new colonial territories. For the West Indies, 'a Commissioner for the Sale of Land in the Ceded Islands' was appointed and sent out to the Caribbean to establish new plantations on the lands of the indigenous inhabitants and the Maroons.

For the American mainland, and for Native American territory, a more complicated procedure was devised. Alarmed by the implications of Pontiac's rebellion, the British drafted a Royal Proclamation in London on 7 October 1763. This outlined what were perceived to be the rights of the Native Americans in the newly enlarged territory of British America. The Proclamation dealt with a subject that the Treaty of Paris had ignored. For the first time in the history of the Americas, the British recognised the land titles of Native Americans, declaring that no land claimed by them could be alienated in future unless the title had been extinguished through purchase or treaty.

Patronising and sanctimonious as its language must now seem, the Proclamation made two other essential points. In the increasingly white-settled lands of the eastern colonies along the Atlantic seaboard, only the hunting grounds of the Native Americans were to be regarded as protected territories. In the largely unknown territories to the west – in the great unexplored areas of the American West and Pacific Canada – the Native Americans were to be left with a free hand:

> It is just and reasonable, and essential to our interest, and the security of our colonies, that the several nations or tribes of Indians with whom we are connected, and who live under our protection, should not be molested or disturbed in the possession of such parts of our dominions and territories as, not having been ceded to or purchased by us, are reserved to them, or any of them, as their hunting grounds . . .
>
> And we do further declare it to be our royal will and pleasure, for the present . . . to reserve under our sovereignty, protection and dominion, for the use of the said Indians, all the lands and territories not included within the limits of our . . . new governments, or within the territory granted to the Hudson's Bay Company, as also the land and territories lying to the westward of the sources of the rivers which fall into the sea from the west and the north-west.

The British, in other words, claimed sovereignty over the entire vast territory of America and Canada that they had not yet themselves explored, but they were happy to recognise Native American land ownership. Since the Native Americans were actually present on the ground, the British hoped that they would keep out other potential marauders – the Spanish, the French, or the Russians. The territory set aside for the Native Americans was to be denied to the land-hungry white settlers of the Thirteen Colonies. White settlement was now expressly forbidden in the newly designated Native American territory, and all existing settlers were told to withdraw.

Yet the Royal Proclamation was only a form of words, issued in London, and there was little obligation on anyone to obey its instructions. Nor did they do so. 'Few colonists were willing to acquiesce in royal attempts to keep them from western lands', writes Colin Calloway. 'Scotch-Irish settlers who had emigrated to escape British domination paid little heed to a British proclamation in the new world. Veterans of the "French and Indian wars" were not about to be deprived of the fruits of their hard-won victory.'[2] The leaders of the white settler colonies understood immediately that the Royal Proclamation was a direct threat to their right to expand into Native American lands.

The new territory, beyond the unmarked western borders of the existing white settlements, was now to be a responsibility of the British government, and control and defence of it were handed over to the British military. In future, it would be the job of the British soldier to keep the peace between settler and Native American along the ill-defined frontier.

This was a significant commitment, and funds would have to be found to pay for this additional military burden. When the white settlers discovered that they would be called upon themselves to bear the cost of policing the new territories – against their own incursions – they were soon in rebellious mood. Within twenty years their revolt prospered, and the British were thrown out of both their new middle American lands and their old coastal colonies.

The Royal Proclamation also made important concessions to the French settlers of Canada. By enticing the settlers to their side, the British retained their new Canadian territories without difficulty (although problems were stored up for the future). Here, as elsewhere in the Empire, military rule became the norm. The Native Americans in the frontier regions of Canada were effectively governed under martial law for seventy years, until 1830. The indigenous peoples were perceived as valuable military allies, and military policy was designed to ensure that they remained loyal and happy. Yet they were to lose their land. Over the years the British made treaties with them, and extinguished their land claims. Worthless 'presents' were handed out in exchange.

CHAPTER 5

Muslim Resistance in Bengal and Mysore

In June 1756, in the year after the British defeat on the Ohio and the expulsion of the Acadians, a large Bengali army destroyed an important British military and commercial base on the other side of the world. Siraj-ud-Daula, the twenty-seven-year-old Muslim Nawab of Bengal, forced the Europeans living and trading at Fort William, on the outskirts of Calcutta, to retreat in humiliating confusion to their ships. With a single blow, he removed one of Britain's strategic toe-holds on the coast of India, leaving the British southern base at Madras vulnerable to attack, both by local Muslims and by the French.

India was another significant zone of conflict during the war between England and France in the 1750s. A tradition of resistance to the British presence had built up ever since the East India Company had first established itself as a trading enterprise on the coast a century and a half earlier. The British company had been established in 1600; it survived in India by making tactical alliances with local rulers, securing privileges not always available to native merchants. In the course of the seventeenth century it had entrenched itself in the port cities of Surat on the west coast (in 1608), in Masulipatnam on the east coast (in 1611), and later at Madras (in 1639), at Bombay (in 1662), and at Calcutta (in 1690). For many decades, these were mere trading enclaves on the great Indian subcontinent, similar to those held by the Portuguese in earlier centuries. The Indian hinterland remained virtually unknown to the British, and advance into the interior was neither sought nor permitted. After 1756 this was all to change.

Siraj-ud-Daula had become the Nawab of Bengal, the richest province in the Mughal Empire, only three months before he seized Fort William. He had taken over on the death of his great-uncle, the Nawab Alivardi Khan, ruler since 1740. He expressed his contempt for all things British, and particularly disliked the far-reaching ambitions of the East India Company.[1] He sought to bring it under control by curbing the power of its commercial allies and partners, the Hindu bankers of Calcutta. Then, in May 1756, he sent an ultimatum to the British trading authorities in Calcutta, accusing them of constructing an illegal military fortification at Fort William. He told them that he would expel them 'totally out of the country' if the fort was not immediately dismantled. Receiving no reply, he advanced from his home town of Murshidabad in June with an army of 50,000 men.

Fort William was attacked and partially destroyed, and the Europeans were left to escape to their ships. Most sailed away to safety down the Hughli River, but sixty individuals, including the acting British governor, John Holwell, were rounded up by the Nawab's soldiers and crowded into the small 'Black Hole' prison within the British barracks. By the next morning, barely twenty had survived the heat and overcrowding to tell the tale.

'The Black Hole of Calcutta' became one of the more infamous events in British imperial memory, though similar atrocities perpetrated by the British remained less familiar. Holwell himself did not hold the Nawab responsible for this British humiliation, blaming the deaths on the callous brutality of the guards. He survived the experience to publicise and inflate the incident in a book entitled *Black Hole*.[2]

The Nawab's victory, and perhaps even the fate of the prisoners in the Black Hole prison, had an immediate and powerful impact on Indian morale. The Bengalis called the British 'cowards', seeing how swiftly they had fled to their ships, and for six months Calcutta was entirely free from British control. The Muslim Nawab now moved against the privileged Hindu bankers who had provided the British traders with financial support.[3]

Siraj-ud-Daula's triumph at Calcutta was short-lived. The British were still untroubled at their southern naval base at Madras, and they planned a revenge attack. The Nawab's predecessor, Alivardi Khan, had once compared the British to 'a hive of bees, of whose honey you may reap the benefit, but if you disturb their hive they will sting you to death'.[4] The bees soon arrived, and Siraj-ud-Daula was faced with a British naval force, commanded by Admiral Charles Watson, which sailed north from Madras later in the year with orders to recapture Calcutta. The fatal sting came from a small troop commanded by Robert Clive, a thirty-two-year-old colonel.

The armies of Siraj-ud-Daula were defeated at Plassey, outside Calcutta, by Clive's soldiers on 23 June 1757. The Bengali Nawab suffered the defection of his military commander, Mir Jafar, who believed that his own political ambitions would be furthered in alliance with the British. A tradition of Indian resistance had been established in earlier years, but so too had a parallel practice of corrupt and venal rulers giving in to British pressure, a pattern that continued well into the next century.

An Arab by birth, the sixty-six-year-old Mir Jafar had moved into the Bengali ruling elite by marrying the sister of the previous Nawab. Thwarted in his hopes of power, and unhappy with the radicalism of Siraj-ud-Daula, Mir Jafar plotted with the British to overthrow the regime. He abandoned the Nawab's army at the start of the battle and was handsomely rewarded. Colonel Clive appointed him the new Nawab of Bengal.

Siraj-ud-Daula retreated north to Murshidabad, his efforts at anti-imperial resistance betrayed by his own officers and family. Pursued there by the soldiers of Mir Jafar, he was captured after attempting to escape in disguise. Soon recognised and detained, he was promptly executed and his body was paraded on an elephant through the city. Yet the tradition of Bengali resistance that he had awakened survived and was endlessly replenished. A century later, during the Indian Mutiny of 1857, a new rebel leader, Nana Sahib, unleashed a fierce attack on the British Residency at Cawnpore, on a day – 23 June 1857 – chosen to mark the centenary of the Bengali defeat at Plassey.

In Mir Jafar, the British had a pliable Indian ally, and the revenues of Bengal were soon diverted into the coffers of the developing British Empire. Mir Jafar paid out £500,000 to the East India Company, and £250,000,000 to the European traders of Calcutta, to recompense them for their losses the previous year. Large sums were also made available to the British military and naval authorities. Much of the money was spent on an immense new base at Fort William, modelled on the designs of the French military engineer Marshal Vauban, and capable of housing an army of 15,000 men.[5]

Mir Jafar was ambitious but, old and incompetent, he did not serve British purposes for long, and was deposed four years later. He was replaced in 1761 by Mir Kassim, his efficient son-in-law, whom British officials described as 'a very enterprising man of great abilities'. He faithfully discharged the Bengali debts due to the East India Company, and historians have praised his achievements, arguing that 'he retrenched expenditure, repressed disorders, and did what he could for the general welfare of the people'.[6] Yet, like Siraj-ud-Daula, he criticised the trading privileges of the British, and sought to tax the Company. Soon, he posed a fresh threat to the tenuous British position in India, and some officials sought to restore the more amenable Mir Jafar.

Having lost the confidence of the British, Mir Kassim moved his capital north from Murshidabad to Monghyr, on the Ganges. There he planned resistance, constructed powerful fortifications, and recruited experienced European officers to train his army. A foundry was established for the manufacture of military cannon, producing weapons 'as good as those from Woolwich'. Soon he had assembled a well-trained army, with 25,000 foot soldiers and a regiment of gunners.

Mir Kassim controlled the important strategic town of Patna further up the Ganges, some 300 miles north-west of Calcutta, and was well prepared for a British counter-attack. The British seized Patna in a pre-emptive strike in June 1763, but Mir Kassim's armies quickly recaptured it and pursued the retreating British. West of Patna on 1 July, at a battle near Manjee, his forces destroyed one quarter of the British army of Bengal and killed its commander.

Mohammed Taki Khan, the Nawab's senior general, prepared his troops for a British revenge attack, and on 19 July at Agurdeep, near Plassey, a larger British force deployed from Calcutta confronted them. The Bengali general, eager to avenge the defeat at Plassey six years earlier, told his troops that a victory would bring an end to foreign rule in Bengal. But as he charged towards the British battalions on horseback, he was shot and killed.

Dismayed by the loss of their commander, the Bengali army fled. The way through to Mir Kassim's headquarters now lay open to the British, and he was quickly detained. He escaped, but his throne was lost; the aged Mir Jafar was again named as the Nawab.

In the succeeding weeks, the armies of Mir Kassim recovered their morale and continued their resistance, but defeat could not be long postponed. Mir Kassim sent a message to the British commander threatening to kill the officers held hostage at Patna unless military operations were suspended, but his offer was not accepted (neither was his threat carried out). The British seized Monghyr in October, and Patna was recaptured in November. Mir Kassim retreated across the Ganges to the relative safety of Oudh, where he was welcomed by its Nawab, Shuja-ud-Daula. There, the two Nawabs made fresh plans to resist and subvert the advancing armies of the British.

In March 1764, the armies of three Indian states joined forces to confront the British. One army was that of Mir Kassim; the second was that of Shuja-ud-Daula, the Muslim Nawab of Oudh; and the third was that of Shuja Alam, India's ageing Mughal emperor. This alliance of the three most powerful Muslim rulers on the continent was the first and last attempt by the Mughal Empire to halt the British conquest of India.

Joining forces at Benares, the armies crossed the Ganges and advanced to attack the British garrison at Patna. The timing was good. A series of minor mutinies had undermined the structure of British military power in the region. It seemed an opportune moment to launch a joint campaign to expel the foreigners.[7]

The Mughal attack on Patna was a failure; both sides now prepared for further engagement. The Muslim leaders were optimistic that they might yet defeat the British, yet when battle was joined in October, at Buxar, near Bihar, south-east of Patna, the Indians and their Afghan allies proved no match for the British troops commanded by Major Hector Munro.

The defeat at Buxar was a disaster for the Indian cause. The British now held undisputed mastery over the whole of Bengal, extending south into Bihar and Orissa. The Indian princes had not performed well. Shah Alam, the Mughal emperor in Delhi, had already abandoned the allied cause before the battle. Mir Kassim escaped with him to Delhi, and died there years later. Much of the territory of Oudh, home of Shuja-ud-Daula, was laid waste by a British detachment in the aftermath of the battle, and the Nawab eventually surrendered and made peace with the British.

The British hoped to use Oudh as a buffer state capable of defending Bengal against the Marathas to the south, and the Nawab requested an attack on a Rohilla chieftain, Hafiz Rahmat Khan, who operated on the borders of Rohilkhand, a territory centred on Bareilly, north-west of Oudh. The Rohillas were customarily denigrated by the British as adventurers from Afghanistan, and the task of subduing them was carried out in April 1774 by Colonel Champion of the British army in Bengal.

The war was short. The Rohilla army of 40,000 men fought well, but could offer no effective resistance to the superior fire of Colonel Champion's artillery. Hafiz Rahmat and 2,000 of his soldiers were killed. A century later, his grandson Khan Bahadur Khan would join the great rebellion of 1857, and would hold the territory around Bareilly for nearly a year.

Shuja-ud-Daula remained at Lucknow until his death in 1775, when he was succeeded as Nawab of Oudh by his son Asaf-ud-Daula, who ruled under British advice for a further twenty years. With Oudh and Bengal under their tight control, the British foothold in India was now vastly enlarged and unchallenged. The East India Company happily collected taxes, and soon began looking avariciously at other parts of the continent into which to expand.

But although the British were well established at their base at Manjee, in August 1764 their 'native battalions' mutinied. The 'sepoys' marched onto the parade ground without orders, seized their European officers, and put them behind bars, declaring that they would no longer serve the British.

Sepoy was the name given to an Indian private soldier in the service of a European country in Asia, be it Portugal (*sipaio*), France (*cipayo*), or England. The British enforced their control over the Indian sepoys in two ways – through money and through terror. The sepoys were usually paid well, both in wages and in prize money, but when their pay failed to arrive, or if they were forced to adopt practices that conflicted with their own customs or religions, they would often mutiny. The late arrival of the sepoys' pay was largely to blame for the Manjee mutiny, and the local British commanders had been reluctant to take punitive measures.

A series of sepoy mutinies had already taken place earlier in the year, undermining the structure of British military power in the region. Soon, however, the mutineers at Manjee were faced with Major Hector Munro, sent out from Patna to crush their rebellion. The mutinous sepoys would be treated in a dramatically brutal fashion, to teach them an unforgettable lesson. They were to be shot from guns.

The British liked to claim that they had inherited the practice of 'cannonading' from the Mughal emperors. It was a tradition they continued throughout the nineteenth century. During the Indian Mutiny in June 1857, a young officer, Lieutenant George Cracklow, was witness to a 'cannonading', and he wrote a detailed description in a letter to his mother:

> The prisoners were marched up to the guns, their irons knocked off, and [they were] lashed to the muzzles with drag ropes, the muzzles pointing just between their shoulders . . . I shut my eyes for half a second and the guns exploded with one report. I could hardly see for the smoke for about 2 seconds when down came something with a thud about 5 yards from me. This was the head and neck of one of the men. You can't imagine such a horrible sight. On each side of the guns, about 10 yards, lay the arms torn out at the shoulders. Under the muzzle and between the wheels lay the remainder of the bodies with the entrails scattered about. The heads had flown up in the air and fallen in rear of the guns. I would never have imagined bodies would go to pieces so easily.[8]

Lieutenant Cracklow soon hardened himself to the experience, like other officers in India. Writing again to his mother a month later, he described himself as 'an executioner-general': 'I . . . think no more of stringing up or blowing away half a dozen mutineers before breakfast than I do of eating the same meal.'[9]

Indian soldiers, both Hindu and Muslim, were particularly fearful of this very special form of violent death. 'What the sepoys object to', wrote William Butler, a missionary at the time of the Mutiny, 'was the dishonour done to the body, its integrity being destroyed, so that the 'Shraad' could not be performed for them.' This was a funeral ceremony that Hindus believed to be 'essential to their having a happy transmigration'. The dismantling of the remains of a man executed by cannonading 'would necessarily . . . expose the disembodied ghost . . . to a wandering, indefinite condition in the other world, which they regard as dreadful'. To avoid this happening, the sepoys, when condemned to die, 'would plead, as a mercy, to be hung or shot with a musket – any mode – but not to be blown away'.[10]

The sepoy revolt of 1764 was crushed on the parade ground at Patna, where twenty-four of the ringleaders from Manjee were sentenced to be blown from guns.[11] The tradition of dismemberment, part and parcel of the British experience in India, is usually discussed solely in the context of the Mutiny of 1857. Yet it began a century earlier, providing the glue of terror that enabled the British to maintain their mercenary armies over such an extended period. British rule in India, so many ruled by so few, was maintained by the memory of the terror meted out to the Manjee mutineers at Patna in 1764.

* * *

Blowing from Guns in British India by Vasily Verestchagin, circa 1882–83. Verestchagin travelled in India in 1874–76 and 1882–83, and this painting may depict the execution of fifty Sikh Kukas in the Punjab in 1872.

The threat of sepoy mutinies had been reduced by the terror tactics of Major Munro, but in May 1766 it was the turn of European officers to show signs of disaffection. More than forty of them, across three brigades of the army of Bengal, complained about the loss of their 'allowances', and resigned their commissions simultaneously – a gesture perceived as mutiny.

In India, as in America, the expense of imperial warfare had become a serious problem for the Empire. British military power in India was based on a large army of sepoys with a handful of British officers. Both groups had to be well and regularly paid. Successful battle and conquest secured plunder, but in the lean years of peace, money had to be found from revenue. Without pay, the troops would rebel. While the sepoy mutiny in 1764 had been brutally crushed, a mutiny by British officers required a more delicate approach.

Robert Clive, now a general and the military governor of Bengal, summoned reinforcements from Madras. Advancing to the camps of the British mutineers, at Monghyr, Patna and Allahabad, he was relieved to find that the loyalties of the sepoys had not wavered – memories of the 'cannonading' at Patna still lingered. European troops, however, were in sympathy with their rebellious officers, and were on the verge of mutiny themselves.

Summoned by Clive to the parade ground, the mutinous officers refused to report for duty. Two sepoy battalions were promptly deployed to a point overlooking the ground. With muskets loaded, the Indian soldiers forced the European officers to return to their barracks, and were later rewarded by Clive with two months' pay. The mutinous officers were marched off to Calcutta, guarded by a sepoy battalion, to be court-martialled and sent back to England. The British had relied on their Indian mercenaries to enforce control over their army's European commanders. Fearing that the army was now dangerously depleted of officers, most of the mutineers eventually returned to duty.

The pressing need for revenues to pay for the armies of occupation soon had an adverse impact on Bengal's economy: the lack of food and money, arising out of the high taxation that the East India Company enforced in Bengal – thereby siphoning off the country's wealth to Britain – coincided with a disastrous drought.[12] In 1770, a devastating famine killed a third of the population of Bengal, perhaps 10 million people. 'The suffering of the hapless victims was aggravated by the monopolies of rice and other commodities enforced by the Company's senior officers and their Indian associates.'[13]

An account published a century later gives a flavour of the extent of the tragedy:

> All through the stifling summer of 1770 the people went on dying. The husbandmen sold their cattle; they sold their implements of agriculture; they devoured their seed-grain; they sold their sons and daughters, till at length no buyer of children could be found; they ate the leaves of trees and the grass of the field; and in June, 1770, the Resident at the Durbar affirmed that the living were feeding on the dead. Day and night a torrent of famished and disease-stricken wretches poured into the great cities. At an early period of the year pestilence had broken out. In March we find small-pox at Moorshedabad, where it glided through the vice-regal mutes, and cut off the Prince Syfut in his palace. The streets were blocked up with promiscuous heaps of the dying and dead. Interment could not do its work quick enough; even the dogs and jackals, the public scavengers of the East, became unable to accomplish their revolting work, and the multitude of mangled and festering corpses at length threatened the existence of the citizens . . .[14]

Imperial disruption and taxation, coupled with drought and famine, marked the start of the British Empire in India; it was a pattern to be sustained over the next 200 years.

The defeat of the three Muslim rulers at Buxar in 1764 was a disaster for the Indian cause. The British were now freshly confident of their power in the continent and had secured the support of several local princes. Yet they had

Haidar Ali, the Muslim ruler of Mysore and a formidable opponent of British rule, in his younger years.

over-reached themselves, and their sepoy forces often proved unreliable. Other rulers emerged to take up the British challenge. Haidar Ali, the Muslim ruler of the great, formerly Hindu kingdom of Mysore, was soon to become the most formidable opponent of British rule.

Haidar Ali was an illiterate Punjabi who rose from the ranks of the Mysore army to become its commander, and master of the kingdom, basing himself in the central Indian city of Bangalore. Considered by the British to be 'unscrupulous and a master of intrigue', he was also perceived as a brave and capable soldier, and a dangerous and resourceful opponent. An admirer of all things French, he had first made contact with the alternative European power in the 1750s at its coastal enclave of Pondicherry, south of Madras. Later, with French assistance, he had reorganised the Mysore army on European lines, creating a disciplined force that was a match for the British.

Early in 1767, Haidar Ali faced an army led by Colonel Joseph Smith, the British commander at Madras. Historians of empire call this the First Anglo-Mysore War, a conflict that went well for Haidar and badly for the British. At their first encounter, Haidar's troops outnumbered those of Colonel Smith and forced him to retreat to the coast. Haidar pursued him to the outskirts of Madras.

Haidar's army raided the suburbs of Madras later in the year, seizing the country houses of the East India Company officials. It was led by Haidar's seventeen-year-old son and successor, Tipu Sultan, the next Indian leader to oppose the Empire: he would do so vigorously for more than three decades.

Haidar Ali's forces returned to Madras two years later, in March 1769. Once again they battled against the army of Colonel Joseph Smith, which had been dispatched to Mysore to attack Bangalore. Smith's advance had met with some success, and Haidar had put forward peace proposals in September. Rejecting his offer, Smith renewed his offensive; but Haidar seized the initiative, recovering much lost ground. When his soldiers threatened Madras, the British abandoned the fight, and the war ended with a treaty in April 1769. Both sides agreed to hand back the territory they had seized and the prisoners they had captured.

Haidar hoped that the British would be his ally against other Indian principalities, and the treaty stipulated that they would come to his assistance if he were attacked. Yet when Haidar was attacked by an army of the Marathas from western India the following year, the British failed to help him. For this, he never forgave them.

The directors of the East India Company were unhappy with the outcome of the war against Haidar. They complained that it had been 'very improperly conducted and most disadvantageously concluded'. Haidar's success left them with grave doubts about their future:

> The Company's interest and influence in India have suffered such diminution and discredit that the most consummate abilities, persevering assiduity, unshaken fidelity and intrepid courage in our future servants, may perhaps be insufficient in many years to restore the British East India Company to a proper degree of credit and dignity in the eyes of the nations and inhabitants of Indostan.

A bleak indictment of Company rule.

In fact, the British had reason to be thankful for the treaty made with the Mysore ruler. The peace lasted for a decade, the 1770s, in which the forces of the Empire were to be fully occupied in the expensive, and ultimately unsuccessful, defence of their colonial possessions on the other side of the world, in North America.

Haidar's triumph was considerable. He had fought successive British armies to a standstill, and secured a breathing space of his own. A pattern of Mysore resistance to British rule had been established. It would continue under father and son until the end of the century, with Tipu's final defeat and death at Seringapatam in 1799.

CHAPTER 6

Peasant Resistance in Ireland

Rather closer to the seat of empire in London, a new resistance movement appeared among Catholic peasants in the colony of Ireland in December 1761. It was first noted by John Wesley, an itinerant preacher and the founder of Methodism, who noted that the Irish rebels called themselves 'the Whiteboys', and that they named their leader 'Queen Sive'.

'A few men met by night near Nenagh, in the county of Limerick', wrote Wesley,

> and threw down the fences of some commons which had been lately inclosed. Near the same time, others met in the counties of Tipperary, Waterford, and Cork. As no one offered to suppress or hinder them, they increased in numbers continually, calling themselves Whiteboys, wearing white cockades and white linen frocks.[1]

Queen Sive and 'her fairies', described as 'all the able young fellows from Clonmel to Mitchelstown', waged war against a variety of enemies – cloth-weavers and tithe-collectors as well as landlords. Their purpose was to recover properties seized by settler landlords for non-payment of rent, and to force weavers to lower their prices. They also gave notice of their aim 'to do justice to the poor by restoring the ancient commons and redressing other grievances.'[2]

Rebellious elements within Ireland's peasantry, hostile to the British programme of settlement and colonisation, had a well-established tradition of protest on which to draw. England's closest neighbour and its oldest colony, established in the twelfth century, Ireland remained endlessly rebellious. The white settler population had first taken root under Queen Elizabeth and Oliver Cromwell, when impoverished Protestants were sent from England and Scotland to establish themselves in a predominantly Irish (and Catholic) society. War in 1690, when the Catholic King James Stuart was defeated at the Battle of the Boyne by his son-in-law, the Protestant Prince William of Orange, served to solidify the settler occupation.

A British programme of settlement remained in progress throughout the eighteenth century, as though the island were virgin territory which could be settled indefinitely by outsiders. A model for the wider Empire in the nineteenth century, the Protestant settlers continued to arrive from Britain; they then drove out, and if necessary destroyed, the indigenous population. Yet in spite of the steady inroads made by settlers, three-quarters of Ireland's population in the eighteenth century were Irish peasants who remained obstinately Catholic. Resistance to settlement, followed by fierce repression, remained the rule.

The Whiteboys of the 1760s were the latest in a long line of paramilitary resistance movements in Ireland, secret anti-settler societies entrenched among the Catholic population in rural areas. Yet they were more than a simple peasant self-help organisation; in one of their oaths, recorded at the end of the eighteenth century, they revealed their wider, political ambitions: 'I sware, I will to the best of my power, Cut Down Kings, Queens, and Princes, Earls, Lords, and all such with Land Jobbin and Herrisy.'[3]

According to Wesley's account, a diary note of June 1762, the Whiteboys' insurrectionary forces would assemble after dark. There would be

> five or six parties of them, 200 to 300 men in each, who moved up and down chiefly in the night . . . levelled a few fences, dug up some grounds, and hamstrung some cattle, perhaps fifty or sixty in all. One body of them came into Clogheen, of about 500 foot, and 200 horse. They moved as exactly as regular troops, and appeared to be thoroughly disciplined.[4]

The Whiteboys that Wesley had heard news of were dispersed at Easter 1762 by a troop of light horse. 'Many were apprehended and committed to gaol; the rest of them disappeared.'[5] But resistance continued, and over subsequent decades the rebellion threatened the established order in the colony, forcing the government to pass draconian legislation and to send out additional troops. Over time, the repression was successful, but the Whiteboys were to emerge in different disguises in Ireland in later years, creating the longest rebellious tradition in the history of empire.

Queen Sive was just one of the names given to the hydra-headed leadership of the Whiteboys. In later generations, the resistance leaders received names like Captain Rock and Captain Right, or Captain Moonlight. The Whiteboys changed over time into the Whitefeet, the Blackfeet, and the Defenders. Their organisation, wrote the historian William Lecky a century later, took deep root in Ireland and spread rapidly and silently. 'The names of those who constructed it will never be known, but they were evidently men of some education and of no small organising ability.'[6]

The Whiteboys would often send menacing letters to Protestant landlords to try to prevent them from seizing common land, and, when the enclosures went ahead, would tear them down. The fences would be 'levelled' and the cattle of the settlers killed; the Whiteboys, indeed, were sometimes referred to as the 'Levellers'.

To curb their power and influence, the colonial authorities drafted fresh laws. The 'Whiteboys Act' of 1775 made all secret agrarian societies illegal, and described the menace they were perceived to pose:

> It is frequently of late years, in different parts of this kingdom, that several persons calling themselves Whiteboys, and others, as well by night and in daytime, have in a riotous, disorderly, and tumultuous manner, assembled together, and have abused and injured the persons, habitations, and properties of many of his Majesty's loyal subjects, and have taken away and carried away their horses and arms, and have compelled them to surrender up, quit, and leave their habitations, farms, and places of abode . . .[7]

To prevent their ranks being infiltrated by government informers – a problem that would dog all Irish rebellious activity from that day to this – the peasant supporters of the Whiteboys were required to swear an oath of allegiance to 'Queen Sive', and threatened with punishment if they refused to obey her commands.

The tradition of swearing oaths of allegiance, both to their cause and to each other, became a pattern throughout the Empire. Instead of an oath being sworn to the British monarch, a procedure normally required of all colonial subjects in positions of authority, one would be sworn to the rebel organisation. Perceiving the dangers in a religious society of allowing people to swear subversive oaths, the Irish parliament passed a further Whiteboys Act in 1787. Those found participating in illegal oath-taking would be transported for life to other colonies. An additional clause declared that anyone advertising an event likely to end in a riot would be executed.

The Whiteboys represented and defended the peasants, but they were not exclusively Catholic. Indeed, part of their programme was to undermine the hold of the Catholic clergy on the peasant population. Their actions, wrote Lecky, were seriously to diminish the influence of the priests, and 'in some cases the chapel doors were actually nailed up against them by their congregations'. Tithes, the regular payments made to the priests by their congregations, began to dry up, and several priests abandoned their parishes. Others, however, fought back, and the Whiteboys were constantly excommunicated. The anti-Catholic emphasis of the Whiteboys had a practical element as well. In Munster, a notion was spread abroad 'that if the Whiteboys for a time abandoned their own worship, and attended the Protestant churches, they would acquire, like the Protestants, the right of keeping arms in their possession . . .'.[8]

As the century progressed, the repression became more violent, yet the Whiteboys sustained their resistance. A manifesto issued in Munster in 1786 emphasised their continuing determination to 'oppose our oppressors by the most justifiable means in our power, either until they are glutted with our blood, or until humanity raises her angry voice in the councils of the nation to protect the toiling peasant and lighten his burden'.[9]

The sheer weight of repressive legislation, coupled with the deployment of military reinforcements, eventually took its toll. The convict ships to Australia, established as a prison colony in 1788, always carried a solid cargo of Irish resistance fighters. After thirty years' activity in the late eighteenth century, the Whiteboys slowly faded away, yet they were to be continuously replaced over time by organisations with similar ambitions.

Protestants as well as Catholics were involved in the resistance movements of Ireland. In 1770, in the northern province, an incipient rural insurrection had been bubbling away over several months. Absentee landlords had expropriated the farms of their tenants, and the farmers had begun to fight back in the only way they knew how. In December 1770 the rural uprising came to Belfast. A large number of Protestant 'Steelboys', accompanied by their peasant supporters, marched into the town and stormed the military barracks.

The Steelboys, or the 'Hearts of Steel', had their origin in County Antrim, on the estate of the Earl of Donegal. They were tenant farmers and labourers, the descendants of Protestant and Presbyterian planters. The cause that led them to rebel – the loss of their land – was similar to that which had led to the formation of the Whiteboys in the 1760s, and their rebellion took similar forms: the destruction of cattle and administering of oaths of loyalty to cement their purpose.

Viscount Townsend, the lord lieutenant of Ireland, gave a report on their activities. 'Since the month of July 1770,' he wrote,

> many wicked and dangerous insurgents have, in a most daring and illegal manner, assembled themselves with arms in large bodies in the counties of Antrim, Down, Armagh, [the] city and county of Derry and county of Tyrone, and have committed divers treasonable and other capital and enormous offences subversive of public order and tranquillity, and ruinous to the morals and industry of the people . . .[10]

A paragraph in a Ballynure newspaper expressed the outrage of the landlords at the peasant protests: 'Several outrages of a very wicked and pernicious nature have been lately committed in many parts of this county – such as houghing and killing cattle, robbing, firing into, and burning houses, stacks of hay and corn, and writing and dropping incendiary letters, full of horrid oaths and imprecations.'

The Steelboys' protest of December 1770 against the colonial authorities in Belfast was caused by the arrest of David Douglas, an Ulster farmer from Templepatrick, who had been held prisoner on charges of 'houghing', or maiming, the cattle of Thomas Gregg, a Belfast merchant. Gathering reinforcements on the way, the Steelboys were formed into regular order by an old soldier called

Nathaniel Mathews as they marched towards the city. They were led by a man on horseback who carried iron crowbars rolled in hay ropes to break open doors and gates.

Arriving in Belfast some three years later, John Wesley wrote clear-sightedly about 'the real cause' of the insurrection:

> Lord Donegal, the proprietor of almost the whole county, came hither to give his tenants new leases. But when they came they found two merchants of the town had taken their farms over their heads; so that multitudes of them, with their wives and children, were turned out to the wide world. It is no wonder that, as their lives were now bitter to them, they should fly out as they did. It is rather a wonder that they did not go much further.[11]

After an exchange of fire at the Belfast barracks, in which two men were killed, the Steelboys secured Douglas's release and he was carried back in triumph to Templepatrick. Yet the farmers' victory was short-lived, for the military were ordered out to the disturbed districts. Several Steelboys were put on trial in Carrickfergus, and when local juries refused to convict, their cases were transferred to Dublin.

The insurrection continued for some while but had died down by 1773. Its collapse was caused partly by the ferocity of the military repression, and partly by an increase in Protestant emigration from Ulster. Thousands of peasants and smallholders fled from Ulster to America – among them David Douglas, the farmer from Templepatrick, who sold his farm that year with the intention of leaving for America 'as soon as possible'. Some of the tenants thrown out by Lord Donegal were soon active again elsewhere, recruited into the rebel armies in America that fought to sever the link with England.

Part II

WHITE SETTLER REVOLT IN AMERICA, AND FRESH RESISTANCE IN CANADA, INDIA AND THE CARIBBEAN, 1770–89

A fresh and lasting phenomenon in the history of imperial resistance emerged between 1770 and 1785: revolts by white settlers. While most rebellions came from indigenous peoples and slaves, a stronger and often more successful strand arose within the ranks of migrants who had made the Empire their home. The first of these settler rebellions occurred in the colonies of British North America. The Declaration of Independence, devised by the American settler leadership in 1776, was to become a model, admired and repeated at different moments in different parts of the world. Yet while this American rebellion appeared to be inspired by idealistic and revolutionary rhetoric, it arose from a far from selfless motive: the desire to seize other people's land.

The white settlers in North America were a minority, sharing what they thought of as *their* continent with millions of Native Americans and hundreds of thousands of black slaves. The settlers wanted independence not for the high-minded reasons with which they are often credited, but because the British colonial power was thwarting their ambition to occupy native territory. The pattern of all future white settler rebellions, driven by the thirst for land, was etched in the 1770s, and recurred constantly until the end of the twentieth century. To achieve their goal, the settlers organised rebellions, resistance and revolutionary war. They were often successful.

The American rebellion of 1776 involved the outbreak of another world war, a repeat of the French and Indian War of the 1750s. France and Spain came out in support of the settlers and against Britain, their historic enemy. Rebellion and war created opportunities for others, and both in India and the Caribbean various groups sought to break loose from the imperial embrace.

The crisis in relations between Britain and its American colonies arose largely as a result of the expense involved in crushing Pontiac's great Native American rebellion in 1763. The colonial expenditure of the London government had more than doubled during the hostilities of the 1750s, and Pontiac's rebellion was the final straw, creating political trouble in England. Heavily taxed to pay for colonial wars, British landowners and legislators now sought, understandably, to extend taxation to the colonies. It was a burden the settlers were unwilling to shoulder.

Worse was to come, for the extension of taxation was accompanied by a more serious threat to the settlers' future. The British effectively dashed their hopes of territorial expansion. The October 1763 Royal Proclamation on the

Native Americans had outlined the future of the newly enlarged territory of British America, but the details were not well received in the Thirteen Colonies. The great hinterland of the continent, west of a line from Quebec to New Orleans, had once been notionally in the sphere of the French, but it had also long been in the sights of ambitious and expansionist settlers from Britain. To their surprise and irritation, the Proclamation decreed that the land rights in these territories of the Native Americans, many of whom had already been pushed westwards by the settlers on the Atlantic seaboard, were to be recognised and respected. White settlement was to be expressly forbidden in these Native American lands, and all existing settlers were ordered to withdraw.

To control this new territory, and to police it against settler incursions, was the task of the British army – but now, the British government argued, the funds for these military operations were to be met by the white settlers. In order to raise revenues in the colonies for this purpose, in March 1765 George Grenville, the British first lord of the treasury, secured a parliamentary measure. The Stamp Act decreed that newspapers and pamphlets in the American colonies, as well as commercial and legal publications, were to be taxed. Grenville hoped this tax would meet the added cost of military defence, including the control of the new Native American territory in the west.

Grenville gave due warning of his scheme, but the white settlers were enraged. 'No taxation without representation' was their cry – although they had no intention of allowing 'representation' to their black slaves or to the Native American population. They soon embarked on a campaign of resistance to the proposed measure, encouraged by their about-to-be-taxed newspapers. Though relatively peaceful at first, their passive resistance soon exploded into full-scale war.

The settlers in the early stages had allies in the British parliament, which voted in 1766 to repeal the Stamp Act, albeit reiterating its right to tax the colonies. Yet money to pay for military operations in America had still to be found. One bright idea was to persuade the settlers to pay in kind for the British soldiers policing the settlers' frontiers. An amendment to the Mutiny Act in 1766 allowed military commanders to secure lodging and food for their troops in the homes of the local inhabitants. This measure aroused almost as much resistance from the settlers as the stamp duty, notably in the town of Boston, Massachusetts.

An additional cause of settler unrest was Britain's developing relationship with Canada. The Royal Proclamation gave fresh rights to Canada's Native Americans, and had also made concessions to the large population of French settlers. Most of the white settlers in the former French province of Quebec were French-speaking Catholics – 100,000 lived there, and only 400 Protestants, according to General Guy Carleton, British governor of Canada. (Figures for the Native American population were not recorded.) If the French Canadians were not to prove rebellious like the British settlers further south, their wishes would have to be taken into account. General Carleton made a tactical alliance with the French landowners and the Catholic church, who became the power-brokers of the new colony, and his proposals were given legislative form in the Quebec Act of May 1774.

One effect of this Act, which repealed the Royal Proclamation of 1763, was to extend the frontiers of British Canada into the Native American territory to the south, as far as the junction between the Ohio and the Mississippi. The present-day American states of Ohio, Indiana and Illinois were effectively included within Canada. At the same time, the Act removed the guarantee of the Native Americans' land rights that had been awarded to them in the Royal Proclamation ten years earlier. Although the Native Americans were still seen as valuable military allies, and the British wanted them to remain content and loyal, their land claims were extinguished in exchange for 'presents'. In most of Canada, as elsewhere in the Empire, military rule became the norm. Native Americans in the frontier regions were placed under martial law, and remained so until 1830.

This solution to Canada's constitutional problems was to compound the anger and distrust of the white settlers in the American colonies. The largely Protestant settlers were shocked by the details of the Quebec Act: not only were Canada's frontiers being extended into the uncharted territory that they believed they had a right to occupy, but Quebec itself was handed over to the Catholic Church. The fact that the British now planned to depend on the formerly French settlers of Canada as their only reliable ally on the continent raised fears among settlers in the Thirteen Colonies that the British would soon have adequate military force at hand to limit their ambition to move west into Native American territory.

While the writing had been on the wall for the settlers ever since the Royal Proclamation of 1763, the Quebec Act appeared to extinguish for all time the settlers' long-imagined right both to seize land beyond their existing frontiers and to exterminate the Native Americans when necessary. When the settlers' rebellion finally broke out, in 1776, the slaughter of the Native Americans, many of whom sided in desperation with the British, was high on their agenda. American patriots might call their rebellion a war for liberty, but the indigenous people understood it as a struggle for land.[1]

While the British government and the American settlers squared up for battle on the mainland, the native peoples of the Caribbean also faced new threats to their lands, and embarked on their final acts of resistance. The Caribs and the Maroons, sometimes in tandem with the slaves and sometimes against them, fought their last battles against the Empire before being slaughtered or expelled. Black Caribs in St Vincent in 1772, and Maroons in Dominica in 1785, were drawn into revolt. Slaves too, notably in Jamaica, again seized the chance to try to break free.

The British also met with steady resistance in India in these years, in spite of the peace agreement achieved in 1769 with Haidar Ali and the kingdom of Mysore. Trouble now came from the Marathas, first in 1779 and again the following year – this time from Haidar Ali and his son Tipu Sultan, with renewed French backing. The Marathas of Nana Farnavis were successful in inflicting a humiliating defeat on the British at Wargaon in 1779, paving the way for further Maratha resistance in the early years of the nineteenth century, while Tipu Sultan's memorable victory over Colonel William Baillie in 1780 was to remain in the annals of Empire as a signal defeat for the imperial forces.

CHAPTER 7

Episodes of Resistance during the American War of Independence

On 5 March 1770, a protest demonstration by settlers in the Massachusetts city of Boston soon developed into an attack on British soldiers billeted in the town. Settlers armed with sticks and snowballs threatened a British sentry outside the customs house, and soldiers fired on them, killing three and wounding several others. One of those killed in what came to be called the 'Boston massacre' was Crispus Attucks, a labourer of mixed ancestry, both Native American and black.

The Boston riot was caused by settler resentment at the imperial taxation deemed necessary to pay for imperial troops, and hostility was inevitably directed at the soldiers themselves. As a result of the initial settler unrest, given a focus by the Stamp Act of 1765, the British had removed their regiments from the Native American frontier regions in the west (where they were supposed to be safeguarding the interests of the Native Americans against the inroads of the settlers). They were deployed back east, to keep order in the fractious coastal settlements. Settlers in Boston and other towns, under the terms of the Mutiny Act of 1766, were expected to pay for the board and lodging of the soldiers, who increasingly acquired the appearance of an occupying force.

British troops had first been quartered in Boston in 1768, and reinforcements had arrived the following year. The dubiously loyal settlers of Massachusetts – who were already supporting schemes for the boycott of British goods – regarded the soldiers as troops of occupation, and openly showed their hostility. The episode outside the customs house encouraged some of them to argue for a more violent response, but the majority felt that matters should not be allowed to get out of hand. Three years later, in 1773, in the wake of the famous Boston 'tea party', the settler rebellion acquired a new head of steam.

In the wake of the 'Boston massacre' of 1770, the settlers began to fall out among themselves. Some in the coastal cities refused to countenance a break with Britain. Others, close to the Native American frontier and squeezed between the fierce hostility of the Native Americans and the coercive pressure of Britain's colonial government, thought they had little to lose.

On 16 May 1771, an army of 2,000 impoverished settlers on the western frontiers of North Carolina faced a colonial militia half its size on the banks of the Alamance River. The settlers called themselves 'the Regulators', a movement formed in 1768 in opposition to the local colonial government, which was perceived as overbearing and corrupt. The Regulators refused to pay taxes or to recognise the corrupt colonial courts, and they carried out physical attacks on state officials. Now they were in open rebellion against the authorities. ' "The Regulation" was not a revolution', wrote a nineteenth-century historian, 'it was rather a peasants' uprising, a popular upheaval.'[1]

The militia was led by Colonel William Tryon, Britain's governor in North Carolina since 1764, when the London parliament was asserting its right to tax its American colonies to pay for the frontier armies. The Stamp Act of 1765 had aroused opposition throughout North Carolina, and when a British warship arrived with the government's stamped paper, the settlers refused to allow it to be brought ashore. They obliged the stamp distributor to take an oath that he would not do his job. It was a scene replicated throughout the coastal settlements. Matters could only get worse. Governor Tryon 'sought to conciliate the colonists by an ostentatious parade of hospitality. He caused an ox to be roasted whole, and several barrels of beer to be provided as a feast for the common people. They attended on his invitation but it was to throw the untasted meal into the river, and empty the beer on the ground.'[2]

Inland, on the frontier, a more serious settler rebellion was brewing. The settlers, many of them poor whites who included emigrants from the land war in Ulster, were in the front line against the Cherokee Indians. They were the people most affected by the British decision to draw a frontier line beyond which further settlement would be forbidden.

Deciding to take the temperature on the western frontier, Colonel Tryon arrived there to patrol the line between the settlements and the hunting grounds of the Indians. Delighted by the physical presence of the governor, whose task was to protect them against the inroads of the settlers, the Cherokee gave him the title of 'Great Wolf'. After Tryon returned to the coast, the Regulators grew ever more restive. Apart from the problem of the blocked-off frontier, denied to future settlement, their grievances included 'excessive taxes, dishonest sheriffs, and extortionate fees'. Among the Regulators' leaders was Hermon Husband, a radical Quaker described as an 'agitator', while another, James Hunter, was spoken of as their 'general'.

When they emerged in open rebellion, Colonel Tryon moved to suppress it. Battle was joined on the banks of the Alamance River on 16 May 1771, and the Regulators were defeated by the governor's militia. Of the fifteen that were captured, six were charged with treason and hanged. Yet Colonel Tryon was so alarmed by the extent of the insurrection that he obliged every male inhabitant in the area of Piedmont to swear an oath of allegiance to the British king.

Hundreds of the surviving Regulators subsequently moved out of North Carolina westwards into Tennessee. The Alamance is not usually regarded as the first battle in the War of Independence, but the Regulators were undoubtedly an influence on what happened next. According to John Bassett, the battle 'set people to thinking of armed resistance. Failure as it was, the Alamance showed how weak the British army would be in a hostile country.'[3] In Tennessee, still alienated from the local settler government but abiding by the terms of the oath to the King that they had been obliged to swear, the Regulators sided with the British in the years after 1776.

The settler rebellion in the Americas was soon to take a new turn. In Boston, Massachusetts, on 16 December 1773, a group of forty settlers, dressed in blankets and Mohawk headdresses, boarded three British ships tied up at the wharf. Once on deck, they threw 342 chests of tea imported from India into the waters of the harbour.

This bizarre event, known to history as the 'Boston Tea Party', was sparked by Britain's attempt to solve a new problem in one part of the Empire, in the process exacerbating an old one in another. In serious financial trouble caused by the military costs of its imperial expansion in the wars against Mir Kassim and Haidar Ali, the East India Company had been granted a monopoly on all tea sold to British colonies (under the terms of the Tea Act of 1773).[4] The Empire's nascent needs in India were thus given precedence over those in its more established American zone – with unforeseen results.

The dramatic gesture of Boston's radicalised settlers was made in the belief that the arrival of cheap tea from the Empire in India would undermine their own boycott of British goods, which had been running for several years as a political protest against their colonial rulers. The British authorities refused to countenance such a challenge, and a blockade of Boston was ordered until the tea chests had been paid for. The following year, in 1774, General Thomas Gage, the new governor of Massachusetts and commander-in-chief in North America, added insult to injury by giving orders for the British army to be billeted on the citizens of Boston. The embers of a fresh rebellion were soon to be coaxed into flame.

During 1774, a fresh Native American resistance war arose in the Americas, the first since Pontiac's rebellion in the previous decade. The conflict preceded and then ran in tandem with the white settler rebellion that erupted in 1775. Shawnee warriors faced an attack in west Virginia on the banks of the Ohio River by 1,200 members of the Virginia militia. Cornstalk, the Shawnee chief, was a veteran opponent of the British; he had taken part in Pontiac's rebellion and had subsequently been held as a hostage in Pittsburgh by Colonel Bouquet. He was supported by White Eyes, chief of the Delaware, and by Kayashuta, chief of the Mingo Iroquois.

The conflict occurred against the background of the continuing movement into the Native American lands of the upper Ohio of hunters, squatters, traders and surveyors. The settlers had been urged to press on westward into Kentucky by John Murray, Lord Dunsmore, Virginia's governor since 1771. Land surveyors, the familiar precursors of imperial expansion, had been sent out by Major George Washington in 1773, with orders to survey 200,000 acres of Native American territory.[5] Although the Royal Proclamation of 1763 had attempted to prevent the settlers moving into the upper Ohio, no legislation could impede their pressure to seek more land.

The settlers were soon quarrelling among themselves, and a dispute broke out at the new settlement of Pittsburgh between rival groups from Virginia and Pennsylvania. Lord Dunsmore ruled the town to be part of Virginia, and sent a representative to enforce his decree. The Pennsylvanian settlers thought the town should be theirs, and a judge ordered the detention of Dunsmore's official.

Alarmed by the rising tide of white immigration rolling down from the Alleghenies, Native American leaders took advantage of the settler conflict to begin a campaign of harassment against the surveyors. The lands of the Shawnee were among those under threat. Although they secured support from individuals from other Native American nations, many of the Delaware, the Wyandots, the Miamis and the Ottawas were reluctant to join in, recalling the defeat of Pontiac. A prominent Mingo Iroquois, James Logan, feared that the 'Long Knife' (the white man) would prove invincible. With acquired pessimism, he warned the Native American council that 'by a war they could but harass and distress the frontier settlements for a short time, that the Long Knife would come like the trees in the woods, and that ultimately, they would be drove from their good land that they now possessed'.[6]

Logan favoured peace, but events changed his mind. His Shawnee wife and family were killed in April 1774 by traders on the Ohio River – an event recalled as the Yellow Creek Massacre.[7] Many versions of the massacre were published, but the clearest comes from the reminiscences of Judge Henry Jolley, who described what happened to a party of Indians camped on the creek, on the opposite side to the sheds of an English trader called Daniel Greathouse:[8]

> The Indians came over to the white party – I think five men, one woman, and an infant babe. The whites gave them rum, which three of them drank, and in a short time became very drunk. The other two men and the woman refused.
>
> The sober Indians were challenged to shoot at a mark, to which they agreed, and, as soon as they emptied their guns, the whites shot them down. The woman attempted to escape by flight, but was also shot down. She lived long enough however to beg mercy for her babe, telling them that it was kin to themselves.

> They had a man in the cabin prepared with a tomahawk for the purpose of killing the three drunk Indians, which was immediately done.

Logan moved into open opposition, helping Cornstalk and other chiefs to organise raids on the surveyors and the settlers.

The Shawnees and the Mingos were soon faced by the Virginian militia mobilised by Lord Dunsmore, and were defeated in October at a battle at Point Pleasant. The fighting was evenly balanced. Colonel William Christian described the tenacity of the Shawnee and the competence of their leaders: 'I cannot describe the bravery of the enemy in battle. It exceeded every man's expectations. They had men planted on each river to kill our men as they would swim over, making no doubt I think of gaining complete victory.' Even when reinforcements arrived, the Shawnee retreated slowly 'and killed and wounded our men at every advance'.[9]

After the battle, most of the Shawnees sued for peace. Bravery was to no avail. They were forced to surrender all their lands south of the Ohio River, and to hand over Cornstalk's son, Elenipsico, as a hostage. Logan and the Mingo Iroquois refused to take part in the peace negotiations and fought on. Like several other chiefs, Logan was to join forces with the British during the coming War of Independence, to continue his own personal war against the settlers. Dunsmore, who had had a conflictive relationship with the settlers, also supported the British side. Three years later, in 1777, Cornstalk was detained by the settlers and held hostage with Elenipsico at Fort Randolph. Both men were murdered there by vigilantes. The Shawnee resistance had come to a brutal conclusion.

The long-brewing settler rebellion in the American colonies finally broke to the surface in April 1775. A revolt by the settlers' militia outside Boston, at Concord, led to the first armed clash at Lexington. The local militia, known as the 'Minutemen', fought against British soldiers loyal to the crown. Armed rebellion was now on the agenda, and Lexington was followed by a further battle in the south in June, at Bunker's Hill, near Charlestown.

Formerly of the Virginia militia, and the castigator of the Native Americans on the Ohio in the 1760s, Colonel George Washington was chosen as the commander-in-chief of the rebel forces, who initially numbered some 20,000 men, most of them farmers. The American colonies were now formally at war with Britain, and soon the rebels were facing a reinforced British army numbering some 42,000 troops, assisted by 30,000 German mercenaries.

The initial rebel strategy was to advance towards Canada, the perceived source of all their troubles. Under the Quebec Act of 1774, British Canada had acquired Ohio, Indiana and Illinois – three of the Native American territories within which the rebel settlers had hoped to establish new colonies for their surplus populations. An attack on Canada would deprive the British of their secure northern base. A rebel army commanded by General Richard Montgomery captured Montreal in the autumn of 1775, but the French settlers remained loyal to Britain. A further American attack was beaten off, and Montgomery was killed. A British fleet was sent over to America the following year, with orders to pardon the rebel settlers should they wish to surrender, but the settlers were in no mood for compromise. On 4 July 1776, on the balcony of the town hall of Boston, a settler spokesman declared the American colonies to be independent of British rule.

The Declaration of Independence, drafted by Thomas Jefferson, inaugurated what was to become the first successful white settler rebellion in British imperial history. It marked the symbolic start of an important new historical era: for England, for the Americas, and for the population of the embryonic British Empire.

The Declaration took place against a background of simmering unrest among the Native American nations. Although the British had helped to crush Pontiac's rebellion in 1763, the settlers were well aware that their imperial rulers had envisaged a long-term policy of peaceful coexistence with the Native Americans. The aim of the settlers themselves – implicit in their actions and given voice by frontier soldiers like General Amherst and Colonel Bouquet – was to allow the Native Americans to be inexorably rubbed out, something that had already happened to the Shawnee of Kentucky and to the Cherokee in the Carolinas. This was to be the policy pursued by white settlers in many territories of the Empire in the following century. Colonel George Morgan, Britain's Indian agent at Pittsburgh, knew what was at stake. The rebel settlers, he said, had 'an ardent desire for an Indian war, on account of the fine lands these poor people possess'.

Not surprisingly, the Creek and Cherokee on the western frontier volunteered to fight for the British. They sensed that the settlers would soon launch another war of extermination against them, and they believed that association with Britain was now their best hope of survival.

The settler rebellion was sustained over the following five years, but with considerable difficulty. Both the settlers and the British made tentative efforts to attract the Native American nations to their side; both also sought the support of the black slave population. Slaves were an important minority in the territories of Britain's American colonies, with nearly a million of them among a settler population of barely two and a half million.

Lord Dunsmore, who remained loyal to Britain, promised the slaves freedom if they would fight on the British side. When drafting his Declaration of Independence, Jefferson had denounced Dunsmore's move as a cynical

British manoeuvre, yet the offer was well received by the slaves, bringing an initial thousand men into the British ranks. Dunsmore called his black recruits 'Lord Dunsmore's Ethiopian Regiment', and the legend 'Liberty to Slaves' was emblazoned across their uniforms. Dunmore and his black regiment were defeated in December 1775, and many of his former slaves fell victim to smallpox. Dunmore's gesture was premature: slavery was to continue in the southern states of independent America for nearly a century, until 1863, while it survived in Britain's Caribbean islands for another sixty years, until the 1830s.

In July 1776, just as the settlers of North America were gearing up for war with Britain, slaves in Jamaica were again discovered by their white masters to be planning a rebellion, as they had done in 1760 and 1765. 'Though happily discovered in good time, and easily crushed in the bud', wrote the author of the Annual Register, the consequences of the rebellion did much 'to increase the general calamities both at home and in the islands.'

The rich sugar islands of the Caribbean were constantly changing hands in the second half of the eighteenth century, chiefly between the British and the French. This frequent change of ownership, consequent upon European imperial dissension, was the chief cause of the increased unrest in the region, long before the French Revolution helped to spark a major slave explosion in Santo Domingo in 1791.

In several islands the initial reaction among the small class of white plantation owners was to support the settler rebellion in America, both in the islands where a substantial proportion of the planters were of French origin, and in the more British islands. In Bermuda the whites openly sided with the American settlers, and British authority was only restored there in 1779. The Bahamas, too, were openly defiant of the British, as was the plantation assembly at St Kitts. Just as problematic for the British were the native Caribs and Maroons, as well as the black slave populations. So restless were the populations of the former French islands of St Vincent, Grenada and Dominica that additional British troops were garrisoned there permanently throughout the American war.

The French took advantage of the uncertain loyalties of these peoples, occupying several formerly British islands and arming the native population. The French re-captured Dominica in September 1778, and seized St Vincent in June 1779, enlisting the support of Chatoyer's Black Caribs.

The need to send reinforcements to America placed heavy demands on Britain's small military force on Jamaica. When a great fleet of merchantmen was about to set sail in July 1776, guarded by ships from the Jamaica station, the plantation owners feared that their island would be left entirely defenceless.

This, indeed, was the moment fixed upon by the slaves 'for carrying their design into execution'.

The threat of slave rebellion was so serious that the English fleet, with supplies for the American war, was obliged to postpone sailing for a month. As a direct result of the delay, the Register's chronicler noted, 'many ships of that rich fleet fell into the hands of the enemy'. Although the Jamaican rebellion was swiftly crushed, groups of slaves on other West Indian islands took advantage of the confused situation in the Americas to take up arms against their oppressors, obliging the British to keep troops behind in the Caribbean that might otherwise have been deployed on the mainland.

In October 1777, at Saratoga, New York, a rebel settler army led by General Horatio Gates surrounded a British force of 5,000 men, commanded by General John Burgoyne, Canada's commander-in-chief. Burgoyne had moved south from Canada with a force of 8,000 men, capturing Fort Ticonderoga in July 1777. Gates was a former British officer who had fought in America during the French and Indian War during the 1750s, and who had subsequently settled in west Virginia. Burgoyne was outnumbered and, lacking adequate supplies, he surrendered. His troops were released on condition that they did not serve in America again.

The battle at Saratoga was the settlers' first major victory. The previous year they had been forced back on the defensive, and General Washington had already been defeated twice at New York. He had failed to prevent the British from capturing Philadelphia in September 1776, but had dealt them a couple of severe blows during the winter.

Few events in the history of Britain's Empire were to prove so momentous as Burgoyne's surrender. Although the British fought on for another five years, Saratoga was the writing on the wall for British control of its North American colonies. It was read as such at the time by the rulers of France and Spain, who joined the settlers' war against England. Soon the British were no longer trying to crush a simple rebellion in a distant colony; the action of the rebel settlers had provoked another world war.

In June 1778, a large force of Iroquois and 1,000 soldiers loyal to Britain, led by Colonel John Butler, marched into the valley of the Wyoming in Pennsylvania. There, some 5,000 white settlers had recently established their farms on land seized from the Iroquois; now, Native Americans, in alliance with the British, were gearing up to retaliate.

In the early months of 1778, the settler war was stalled. The British were pinned down in New York, and the intervention of the French had yet to take effect. For the British, therefore, the Iroquois attack in Pennsylvania was a useful diversion.

Alarmed by the Iroquois-British advance, women and children from the new settlements took refuge within Forty Fort on the Susquehanna River; the men and boys went out to confront the hostile force. The Iroquois brushed them aside and destroyed the fort: some 350 settlers were killed, many of them women and children; others escaped into the forest, to die of starvation. The Iroquois and Colonel Butler then moved north to attack the frontier settlements of New York. There they came under attack the following year from a scorched-earth expedition sent out by George Washington, and commanded by General John Sullivan. Forty Iroquois villages were destroyed, and thousands starved to death in the harsh winter conditions. In the process, the Iroquois were effectively destroyed as a significant independent nation.

The final significant conflict in the American settler war took place at Yorktown, near the mouth of the Chesapeake River, in the southern colony of Virginia. In October 1781, Washington's settler rebels drove a British army, commanded by General Charles Cornwallis, to humiliating surrender. Washington had besieged the town for several weeks and many British soldiers were out of action, through wounds or illness, and with their guns unable to fire. A fleet sent to their rescue arrived five days too late: by then, nearly 7,000 soldiers had surrendered. Cornwallis and other senior officers returned to Britain, and the experience of this generation of imperial soldiers, tempered by defeat, was soon to be made available for other duties elsewhere in the Empire – in India, Ireland and the Caribbean.

Yorktown had effectively put an end to the war, and early in 1782 the British parliament in London voted to abandon the struggle. The success of the settlers' rebellion would remain a salutary warning to imperial politicians and colonial governors throughout the next 200 years of empire.

In March 1782, six months after Yorktown but a year before the final peace treaty that would separate Britain from America, nearly a hundred unarmed Native Americans – men, women and children – were slaughtered on the upper Ohio. This was an area that had seen much conflict over the previous thirty years, and the massacre, by a settler group led by David Williamson, was a foretaste of the fate to which the British were soon to abandon the Native Americans.

Two massacres took place, at the Moravian missionary towns of Gnãdenhütten and Salem, not far from Pittsburgh. Some of the victims at Gnãdenhütten were Shawnee, some were Unamis, and most were Munsees. This was not a spontaneous outbreak of frontier frenzy, but a calculated act of repression through terror. Williamson's vigilantes were no strangers to this type of action: they had already caused the death of Cornstalk, the Shawnee leader, held hostage in 1777.

A graphic account of the event at Gnādenhütten was recorded by Frederick Leinbach, a Moravian who had heard the details from two neighbours: 'Some time in February, 160 men living upon the Monongahela set off on horseback to the Muskingum, in order to destroy three Indian settlements, of which they seemed to be sure of being the towns of some enemy Indians.' On arrival at Gnādenhütten, this vengeful posse killed the son of the Moravian minister and captured ninety-five Indians. These captives, true to their religious training, joined together in prayer: 'The women met together and sang hymns and psalms all night, and so likewise did the men, and kept on singing as long as there were three alive.'

On the next day, they were clubbed to death. 'In the morning the militia chose two houses, which they called the slaughter houses, where they knocked them down; then they set these two houses on fire; as likewise all the other houses.' The lawyer of the Moravian missionaries also described what occurred, concluding that 'the tragic scenes of erecting two butcher houses, or sheds, and killing in cold blood 95 brown or tawny sheep of Jesus Christ, one by one, is certainly taken note of by the Shepherd, their Creator and Redeemer.'

Reprisals against the white killers involved in the Gnādenhütten massacre were subsequently taken by the Native Americans whenever an opportunity arose. 'As soon as it is known that any prisoner had part in that affair', noted David Zeisberger, another missionary, 'he is forthwith bound, tortured, and burnt.'[10] Reprisals and counter-reprisals came thick and fast, and later in 1782 Williamson and Colonel William Crawford led a fresh militia force into the Native American lands of the old North-West to destroy their settlement at Sandusky, north-west of Pittsburgh. They made no secret of their genocidal mission, 'not only by words but even by exposing effigies which they left hanging by the heels in every camp'.

Crawford had been involved in the war against Cornstalk in 1774, and in June 1782 his posse came under attack from a Native American troop. His men were captured, tortured, and put to death. Native Americans seized one of the whites 'and having stripped him naked, black'd him with coal and water: this was a sign of being burnt: the man seem'd to surmise it, and shed tears'. The Native Americans had secured their revenge for the events at Gnādenhütten.

In September 1783, the victorious settler regime in the Americas signed a definitive peace treaty with Britain in Paris (a preliminary document had been agreed the previous November). The independence of the new state was formally recognised by Britain, and the western boundaries of the United States were extended as far as the Mississippi River. The British were allowed to retain navigation rights on the river, but were told to move out from their forts in Native American territory 'with all convenient speed'. In practice, they held on to them for a further decade.

Many of the 'Empire Loyalists' who had fought for the British against the settlers, both white and black, were given special attention and granted asylum in Canada, but no rights were secured for the Native Americans who had fought on the British side. Their fate was now sealed.

The settlers proclaimed their triumph. 'We are now Masters of this island', declared rebel General Philip Schuyler, 'and can dispose of the Lands as we think proper or most convenient to ourselves.' Many soldiers returned from expeditions into Native American territory with stories of the rich lands that awaited them once independence had been secured. These were now to be the spoils of war. With peace came a new era of land speculation.[11]

The peace terms made no mention of the Native American peoples who had fought and died, and who actually inhabited the territory that was to be transferred. As details of the peace filtered out, 'Indian speakers in council after council expressed their anger and disbelief that their British allies had betrayed them, and handed their lands over to their American and Spanish enemies.' The Native Americans learned the hard lesson of empire: whenever a metropolitan power abandons its colonies, and delivers it into the hands of a white settler elite, the days of the indigenous people are numbered.

The Paris treaty formally concluded Britain's war with France and Spain, and allowed Britain to recover the Caribbean islands of Grenada and Dominica, while St Lucia was returned to France. The islands' change of ownership would prove a contributory cause of future rebellions.

One further item in the treaty would have a future consequence of signal importance. The British agreed that convicted criminals would no longer be transported from Britain to the United States, nor to any part of the North American continent. Soon the River Thames was to be clogged with prison ships, until eventually, at the end of the decade, a solution was found to this problem – on the other side of the world, in Australia.

CHAPTER 8

Native American Resistance to Fur Traders in Western Canada

Native Americans had been adversely affected by the outcome of the settler independence war, and in the western lands of Canada beyond Lake Winnipeg (in what today is Saskatchewan) they had encountered serious trouble from white traders pressing into their traditional lands. In 1780 they attacked a party of fur traders at the Eagle Hill Creek, on the North Saskatchewan River. Several traders were killed and the survivors fled, abandoning the goods they had hoped to exchange.

The traders had spent the winter at a settlement on the creek, initially unmolested by the Native Americans, but a few days before they planned to move on, a large band had been 'engaged in drinking about their houses'. One of the traders, 'to ease himself of the troublesome importunities of an Indian, gave him a dose of laudanum in a glass of grog'. This effectively prevented him 'from giving further trouble to anyone by setting him asleep forever'. Almost at once, according to a correspondent of the *Winnipeg Free Press* who recalled the story to his readers a century later, in 1885, the traders reaped their due reward.

While many Native Americans were prepared to trade with the whites, they could not allow a member of their community to be murdered with impunity. 'This was the signal for a war of extermination of the whites', wrote the Winnipeg correspondent, and the rage of the Native Americans was 'only arrested by the greatest calamity that could have affected' them. Here again, as at the time of Pontiac's rebellion in 1763, the whites protected themselves by unleashing smallpox. 'It spread with destructive and desolating power as the fire consumes the dry grass of the field. The fatal infection spread around with a baneful rapidity which no fighter could escape, and with a fatal effect that nothing could resist.'

The notion that early contacts between traders and Native Americans were friendly and mutually convenient is contradicted by this report. For what took place at Eagle Hill Creek was symptomatic of what was to go on in Canada, and elsewhere in the Empire, wherever white settlers made contact with indigenous peoples. With laudanum for the individual and smallpox for larger Native American groups, the white man had the upper hand. Poisoning and the spreading of disease among indigenous peoples were two essential weapons of Empire. First practised in America, they were soon adopted elsewhere.

Conflicts to the west of Lake Winnipeg continued through the years after the attacks at Eagle Hill Creek. These skirmishes often developed out of inter-tribal fighting among the Native Americans themselves – quarrels exacerbated by the presence of the fur traders. In the summer of 1793, a group of Native Americans from the A'ani tribe arrived on horseback in the same neighbourhood, on the shore of the North Saskatchewan River. They planned to sell skins of wolf and fox at the trading post on Pine Island established by the North-West Company, a fur-trading enterprise based in Montreal. They also hoped to seize weapons from the traders' store.

Living in the territory between Saskatoon and Edmonton, the A'ani were known to the French traders as Gros Ventres ('Big Bellies') and referred to by the British as (Water)Fall Indians. In theory, the various European trading posts along the river welcomed all Native American groups and happily purchased the skins that they offered for sale, exchanging them for weapons and other goods. In practice, the Cree were more favoured than the Gros Ventres since they brought the valuable beaver, while the Gros Ventres only sold the cheaper wolf and fox. As a result, the Cree were usually better armed than their rivals. Yet fighting between these rivals was not welcomed by the traders, since in the eyes of the Gros Ventres they were perceived as the allies of the Cree.[1]

The decision of the Gros Ventres to target the Pine Island fort arose from their need to revenge themselves on the Cree. Once inside the fort they made their intentions clear. James Finlay, the trader in charge, sought to placate them with presents, but James Hughes, his young clerk, called out '*Aux armes!* To arms, men!' The result was a typical frontier skirmish. Caught within the fort, the Indians turned and fled, though not before seizing the traders' equipment and driving off their horses. The traders survived, but the North-West Company abandoned the fort. The Gros Ventres made a further attack later that year on Manchester House, another of the North-West Company's trading stations. Stripping the traders of their clothes, they took the goods in the storehouse. The traders fled.

Encouraged by this success, the Gros Ventres made a further attack in 1794 on two forts on the South Saskatchewan River, north of Saskatoon. One belonged to the North-West Company while the other, the South Branch fort, had been established by the rival Hudson's Bay Company. A cavalcade of 150 Indians descended on the South Branch fort where a trader, Hugh Brough, stood outside with his horses. His Indian interpreter warned Brough that the Indians were on the warpath, and quickly fled. Brough was shot and scalped, as was another trader, Magnus Annal. Two other traders, Van Driel and William Fea, were within the fort with a handful of Indian families. Feeling secure, they had made no preparations to defend themselves. Fea hid in a cellar, but was discovered and killed. Van Driel escaped downriver in a canoe to the fort at Nipawin to tell his story.

The North-West Company's fort was on the far side of the river, manned that day by a skeleton summer team, commanded by Louis Chatelain. Here the traders had had the foresight to stay at home, and to reinforce the palisades. When an A'ani chief advanced towards them, he was shot, and the Indian force withdrew. Traders had received a fright, and Chatelain abandoned the post.

These and other attacks were successful in driving out the traders in the short term, and the spirit of resistance spread to other Indian groups. The North-West Company gave up its fort on Pine Island and their settlement on the South Saskatchewan River. A traveller through the area some ten years later found the Native Americans still in control. Arriving in April 1805 at the fort of Montagne à la Basse, on the Qu'Appelle River, to the south, Daniel Harmon found the gates firmly shut. About 'eighty lodges of Crees and Assiniboins' were encamped outside, threatening 'to massacre all the white people' within the gates.[2]

Considerable and continuing animosity towards the traders characterised the Saskatchewan frontier region. The Native Americans in this part of Canada were often well armed and capable of devising strategies of resistance. They had no intention of being exterminated without a fight.

CHAPTER 9

The Resistance in Southern India

Following the American settler rebellion, war between Britain and France would have immediate repercussions in India during the 1770s. During the two decades since Plassey, in 1757, the rulers of the eastern states had observed the British consolidating their power: in Bengal from their base at Calcutta, and in the Carnatic from their garrison at Madras. On India's western shores, the British had a foothold at Bombay, the gateway to the extensive territory of the Maratha Confederacy, a loose and often warring alliance of related Hindu chieftains that stretched across the whole of central India. These lands were the legacy of the seventeenth-century conquests of Shivaji, a Maratha chief who had seized them from the Mughal empire. The Marathas at Poona had played little part in the early drama of imperial consolidation, and throughout the resistance wars of Haidar Ali of Mysore they had negotiated with the British and remained neutral.

Now they perceived that it might be to their advantage to ally themselves with the French, a tempting prospect that soon led to internal quarrels among the Maratha chiefs. Nana Farnavis, who was friendly to the French, was one; Ragunath Rao (or Ragoba), who secured an alliance with the British, was another.

In December 1778, outside Poona, some 50,000 Maratha soldiers commanded by Nana Farnavis, armed with rockets, cannon and muskets, harassed a British column as it climbed up from Bombay. The British had sent a two-pronged expedition to Poona in an ill-planned venture to defend the claims of their ally Ragoba against those of Nana Farnavis. One army had been despatched from Calcutta to march across the entire width of India; a smaller force of 4,000 men had advanced inland over the hills from Bombay, slowed down by its baggage trains drawn by 19,000 bullocks.

It was this second force that Nana Farnavis's army confronted in January 1779, outside Poona. Aware that they were greatly outnumbered, the British had planned to slip away in the night, jettisoning their heavy guns and burning their stores; but the Marathas attacked before dawn, and the British suffered large casualties. The survivors straggled away to the village of Wargaon, where they surrendered. The Marathas were to fight with the British over a period of forty years, and in this, their first encounter, they had been victorious.

The Marathas obliged the British to sign a humiliating document, the Convention of Wargaon. The British were forced to send back the army advancing from Bengal, to give up the territories and revenues they had acquired from Ragoba, and to surrender two hostages as a guarantee.

Two years later, in October 1781, the same month as the British defeat at Yorktown, the Marathas obliged the British to sign a second humiliating peace agreement, after a further successful attack, in April 1971, on another British army as it fell back from Poona to Bombay, with the loss of 500 men.

In the Carnatic, after a truce that had lasted for more than a decade, the forces of Tipu Sultan posed a fresh threat to the British. Tipu, the 'Tiger of Mysore', was the son of Haidar Ali, the Mysore ruler who had driven the British back to the gates of Madras in an earlier decade. In September 1780, Tipu secured a notable victory over a British army, at Conjeveram, near Madras (sometimes called the battle of Pollilur), in what was the most serious defeat of the time suffered by the British at the hands of an Indian army; Tipu would later decorate his palace at Seringapatam with murals of his victory at Conjeveram.

This was the start of a four-year struggle for supremacy in south India. The Mysore army destroyed a British force of 4,000 men led by Colonel William Baillie; seventy British officers were killed or wounded. Two hundred Europeans were captured and held in the prisons of Mysore for many years, where several, including Baillie, died.

Tipu was the most formidable opponent encountered by the British in their long march to conquer India. The state of Mysore stood alone in the 1780s as a bulwark against the British advance into central India – and Britain's eventual supremacy. Tipu resisted the encroachments of the Christian British on India's Islamic realm for nearly two decades. In his prime, he was the most feared enemy of the Empire, but the nineteenth-century historian of India James Mill left a fair description of him: 'Rather above the middle size, and about five feet eight inches high, Tipu had a short neck and square shoulders, and . . . bordered on corpulency; but his limbs were slender, and his feet and hands remarkably small. His complexion was brown, his eyes large and full, his eyebrows small and arched, his nose aquiline; and in the expression of his countenance there was a dignity, which even the English, in spite of their antipathy and prejudices, felt and confessed.'[1]

Tipu survives in the imperial memory as a famous villain, a monster of cruelty, and a bloodstained tyrant. He was all of these things; but by the standards of his time, he was a Napoleon in his pursuit of efficiency and progress. He was popular with both his Hindu and Muslim subjects, and to later generations of nationalists he was a hero. Only at the end of the twentieth century did his role begin to be reconsidered, as Hindu fundamentalists criticised his policy of Islamisation, perceiving him as a fanatical Muslim persecutor of Hindus.

Tipu was a competent general and, like his father, was one of a generation of rulers who had learned their military strategy, European-style, from the French. The British complained about the perceived harshness of native rulers, but their real objection to Tipu was his alliance with France. In the years after the French Revolution he picked up the rhetoric of the time, and liked to be called 'Citizen' Tipu.

As Tipu's army celebrated their victory at Conjeveram, the British reflected on the disaster that had befallen them. The man held most responsible was not Colonel Baillie but General Hector Munro, the victor at Buxar in 1764 and enthusiast for 'cannonading' mutinous sepoys from guns. Munro had fled in panic to Madras, throwing away his stores and ditching his heavy guns.[2] Worse than defeat for the British was the perceived humiliation of the captives held in prison in Seringapatam. Penderel Moon records how

> a number of English prisoners belonging to the ranks, many of whom were mere boys in their teens, were persuaded or forced to be circumcised into Islam, and then, with slave rings in their ears, were trained as janissaries or turned into palace servants or even dancing boys. Tipu . . . retained a number of prisoners of this class, thereby exciting intense resentment among the English.[3]

Years later, when the Mysore state again came under British attack in 1792, several of these English dancers were killed.

Two years after Conjeveram, in February 1782, Tipu Sultan caused the British to suffer a further disaster, to the south of Pondicherry. With French reinforcements, he attacked a British force led by Colonel Brathwaite, encamped with 1,600 sepoys and nearly 100 Europeans to the south of the Coleroon River. After a desperate fight, the colonel surrendered, with nearly all his officers killed or wounded. Brathwaite and a few survivors joined Baillie in prison in Seringapatam.

Later that year Tipu faced a new threat from the west, as General Matthews, the British commander at Bombay, sailed down the Malabar coast with plans to seize Tipu's fort at Bednore, believed to be stuffed with treasure. Tipu's commanders made a tactical retreat from the fort, leaving it to be captured by Matthews' soldiers in January 1783. The British subsequently seized Bednore, Anantpoor and the port at Mangalore.

Tipu launched a counter-attack from Seringapatam, recapturing Bednore in May. British officers were marched off in chains. Mangalore was recovered by Tipu in January 1784 after a long siege.

On 11 March 1784, Tipu's resistance war was brought to a temporary close. With Britain and France at peace after the conflict in America, the Indians lacked an inter-imperial conflict from which they might benefit. Tipu signed a treaty with the British at Mangalore, and, as in previous such peace deals, the two sides swapped the territory they had seized and released their prisoners. 'So ended at length this weary and desolating war', commented Colonel Fortescue, 'which so nearly cost us the possession of India.'[4] Within a decade, it would start up all over again.

Part III

THE LOSS OF AMERICA CREATES A NEED FOR NEW PRISONS ABROAD AND A PLACE TO SETTLE BLACK 'EMPIRE LOYALISTS', 1786–1802

The loss of their North American colonies in 1783 caused considerable heartache to the British, yet a solution to one of the irritating by-products of that loss proved a spur to imperial expansion in other parts of the world. Britain was short of prisons. Successive British governments over the previous two centuries had sent the bulk of the country's convicted prisoners into distant exile. By tradition and custom, the 'convicts' would be shipped off – 'transported' – to the colonies across the Atlantic, chiefly to the North American mainland and the Caribbean. There they would be put to work on plantations.

This somewhat irregular form of punishment, permitted since the time of Queen Elizabeth I, was given fresh impetus during the English Civil War of the mid seventeenth century. Oliver Cromwell ordered a number of Royalists captured after the battle of Worcester to be transported to North America. Later he sent prisoners captured in Ireland to the sugar plantations of Barbados and to the recently acquired island of Jamaica. James II sent the survivors of Monmouth's Rebellion of 1685 to Virginia, where they worked alongside the existing black slave population. Early in the eighteenth century, this practice received additional legal authority: a law of 1718 permitted convicted thieves and vagabonds to be transported to North America, noting that their labour in the colonies 'would benefit the nation'.

Now, sixty years later, this outlet for convicted criminals was suddenly unavailable. The 1783 Treaty of Paris declared that British convicts could no longer be sent to North America. Unless somewhere else could be found quickly, prisoners would have to be kept at home. Britain's prisons – many of them privately owned; some of them ancient wooden hulks kept moored in the Thames and other southern rivers – were soon brimming with prisoners who would previously have been sent abroad.

The British began a search for fresh sites to establish their forced-labour gulags. Somewhere far away was needed to which Britain's 'criminalised' population could be packed off and set to work. The first place considered as a convict dumping ground was the coast of uncolonised West Africa. Dr Henry Smeathman, a Swedish botanist, was the chief source of the government's information on the region at the time. He was familiar with the Sierra Leone River, in a region that housed one of the historic ports of the Atlantic slave trade, and he was asked in 1785 to comment on its suitability as a penal colony.

Smeathman's initial reply was forthright: the climate was not good, and 'not one in a hundred would be left alive in six months'; local African hostility would make settlement difficult. This bleak view did not stop the British from considering the territory suitable for black settlement. Sierra Leone was soon to be the destination for black settlers from Britain, for black 'Empire Loyalists' from Canada, and for Maroons forcibly exiled from Jamaica.

Yet to establish a permanent gulag for its white prisoners, the British government would have to look elsewhere, and it soon decided on a more distant location. Botany Bay in Australia had been warmly recommended to the government as a potential site for settlement by Sir Joseph Banks, who had visited the Australian coast in 1770 with Captain Cook. This idea was given urgent priority, and a dozen convict ships were prepared in 1787. They sailed to Australia from Portsmouth, via Rio de Janeiro and Cape Town, with 700 convicted prisoners on board. They arrived on 26 January 1788 at Sydney Cove, an aboriginal territory that the British were to call New South Wales.

Apart from the pressing need to do something about convicted prisoners in Britain itself, as well as in Ireland, a demand for extra prison facilities soon arose in the embryonic Empire in India. As Indian resistance to conquest grew, the authorities searched for sites to establish convict settlements for both political and civil prisoners. Two officers were sent out from Calcutta in 1788 to survey the 200 islands in the Andaman archipelago in the Bay of Bengal, and to report on their suitability as a prison. Their advice led to the construction in September 1789 of a small prison settlement on the south-east side of Great Andaman, subsequently called Port Blair. It was ill-chosen, for the climate was unsatisfactory. The mortality rate was so high that the settlement was closed in 1796, and the Bengal government had to search for a new gulag. The 700 prisoners held on Great Andaman were transferred to Penang, an island colony off the Malayan coast that Britain had acquired in 1786.[1]

Later, in 1810, the British seized the Seychelles from France. These islands had been used by the French to incarcerate political prisoners, and the British were to follow in their footsteps. Later still, in the 1830s, Singapore became a prison for Indian and Chinese convicts.

CHAPTER 10

The British Search for Distant Gulags

In August 1786 Sultan Abdullah – the Muslim ruler of Kedah, a region on the west coast of what is now Malaysia – agreed to allow the British to acquire the island of Penang. Ten years later, in 1796, a convict settlement was established there, and the island continued as an imperial prison for many years, remaining in British hands until it was captured by Japan in 1942.

Initially, Penang served as Britain's principal military base in the East, and from it British power was eventually extended to Indonesia, to Singapore and to Hong Kong. Britain became an important player in the region, and small states in the vicinity perceived that developing a relationship with it might be to their advantage. Kedah was one of them.

Sultan Abdullah's reason for associating himself with the British was the arrival in 1782 of a dynamic military ruler in neighbouring Thailand, General Chao Phraya Chakri, Rama I. Kedah had traditionally been a vassal state of Thailand, but the new Thai ruler threatened its relative independence. Abdullah hoped that a deal with Britain over Penang might provide protection against the Thais, but he was soon disillusioned.

The British offered little in return for their acquisition of Penang, and several dissident chiefs in Kedah called for them to leave. In March 1791 these chiefs appealed to the native population of Penang, in the name of 'Our Lord Mohammed, the Guardian of the Moslems, and the last of all the Prophets', to rise up and throw the British out.[1] With the assistance of the Illanun, a powerful group of pirates or sea-faring 'gypsies', the chiefs attacked the British base. Their attack was repulsed, for the British were well-entrenched and well-prepared. Retaliating the following year, the British destroyed the Kedah forts. They were to occupy this mainland territory in 1800, renaming it Province Wellesley in honour of the governor of India.

Some years before Britain lost its American empire, a British explorer laid claim to a territory on the other side of the globe, whose future as a prison colony would be a direct result of that loss. On Sunday 29 April 1770, two of Australia's aboriginal inhabitants stood their ground on a beach as the ship of Captain James Cook nosed into a small bay on the eastern shore of their continent. It was just six weeks after the 'massacre' on the Boston seafront that marked the first settler stirrings that would lead to the American rebellion.

Australia, like America, was already inhabited when the British arrived, and, on the first day of the British 'discovery' of what was to become New South Wales, the Aborigines registered their hostility towards the newcomers. The two men on shore 'seemed resolved to oppose our landing', noted Captain Cook in his diary, for 'as soon as we put the boat in, they again came to oppose us'.[2] The British explorer took immediate offensive action, provoking a further hostile response: 'I fired a musket between the two which had no other effect than to make them retire back where bundles of their darts lay, and one of them took up a stone and threw [it] at us, which caused my firing a second musket, load[ed] with small shot . . .'[3]

Although initially aggressive, the Aborigines were found by Captain Cook to be personally pleasing, and his appreciative description of them, written a few months later, is quite unlike anything written by subsequent British settlers, who despised and exterminated them.[4] Cook thought the society developed by the Aborigines was unusually attractive. To some people they might seem wretched, he wrote – in what seems like an eighteenth-century condemnation of the consumer society – but in reality they are far happier than Europeans:

> Being wholly unacquainted not only with the superfluous but the necessary conveniences so much sought after in Europe, they are happy in not knowing the use of them. They live in a tranquillity which is not disturb'd by the inequality of condition: the earth and sea of their own accord furnishes them with all things necessary for life; they covet not magnificent houses, household stuff etc., they live in a warm and fine climate, and enjoy a very wholesome air, so that they have very little need of clothing, and this they seem to be fully sensible of, for many to whom we gave cloth etc., left it carelessly on the sea beach and in the woods, as a thing they had no manner of use for.

If their state of self-sufficiency was indeed as desirable as Captain Cook suggested, the initial opposition of the Aborigines to his sailors was fully justified. A boatload of white men had arrived in their bay that April day in 1770 and fired their muskets with the bleak intention, as revealed in Cook's diary, of taking them captive. The Aborigines fought back:

> Immediately after this we landed, which we had no sooner done than they throwed two darts at us. This obliged me to fire a third shot, soon after which they made off, but not in such haste but what we might have taken one, but Mr [Joseph] Banks, being of the opinion that the darts were poisoned, made me cautious how I advanced into the woods.

On the following day, when a group of Cook's sailors came ashore to replenish their water-barrels, a group of sixteen aborigines 'came boldly up' to register their displeasure. An officer 'did all in his power to entice them to him by offering presents, etc., but it was to no purpose. All they seemed to want was for us to be gone.'

The Aborigines were clearly content with their lot, and, to the obvious surprise of Cook, they had no desire to participate in international trade – a revelation that surprised the mercantile British captain. 'They seem'd to set no value upon anything we gave them', wrote Cook, 'nor would they ever part with anything of their own for any one article we could offer them. This in my opinion argues that they think themselves provided with all the necessaries of life, and that they have no superfluities.'

Captain Cook left the Aborigines in their desirable state of nature and sailed on. He was killed on the Sandwich Islands some years later, in 1779. Two further decades passed before the Aborigines were greeted by the first colonising expedition bearing British settlers and convicts, which arrived on their shores in 1788. The disdainful message from the Aborigines on that occasion was the same as the one that had greeted Captain Cook – 'Go away!' – and those who survived the extermination campaigns were to repeat it over the next two centuries.

In January 1788, some 1,500 Aborigines were living in the immediate vicinity of the Australian beach at Botany Bay, near Sydney, where the first British ships bearing convicts made their landing. Port Jackson was to be the first tiny British settlement in Australia, and it was one expressly established for the purpose of receiving these prisoners.[5] An Aboriginal group from the Gamaraigal people observed that Captain Arthur Phillip, the man appointed to be the British 'governor' of the territory, was setting off to explore the coast in two small boats. They came down to the water and, in the words of an eyewitness, 'greeted them in the same words, and in the same tone of vociferation, shouting everywhere, "Warra, Warra, Warra" – words which, by the gestures that accompanied them, could not be interpreted as invitations to land, or expressions of welcome.'[6] Far from it. By shouting 'Warra, warra, warra!', the Aborigines were giving eloquent expression to their demands, crying out clearly in their own language: 'Go away, go away, go away!'

European ships had called in at Botany Bay from time to time, but their custom had been to sail away again. An occasional sailor might remain behind, but never before had there been a systematic plan of settlement. Now the Aborigines discovered that this particular batch of Europeans intended to stay. This intention, as much as acts of overt hostility from the settlers, provoked the Aborigines into open opposition.

Life was tough for the British convicts as well, of course, and not just when they reached Australia. The journey out was often harrowing. During the first eight years of the Sydney settlement, at least one in ten of the prisoners died on the voyage. In 1790, according to a report by Captain Phillip, the losses were numerous: 'Of the 939 males sent out by the last ships, 261 died on board, and 50 have died since landing. The number of sick this day is 450, and many who are not reckoned as sick have barely strength to attend to themselves.'[7]

The British should have been expert at moving large numbers of people across the globe, for British ships were still transporting thousands of slaves from Africa to the Americas. Yet British expertise with sailing ships carrying cargo had never run to the provision of adequate travelling conditions for passengers, whether slave, convict or free.[8] Convicts in the early years were sometimes attacked and killed by the ships' crew, who, for their part, were afraid that the prisoners might mutiny. Other hazards arose on the voyage out, especially for women prisoners. 'The captain and each officer enjoy the right of selection', wrote a Captain Bertram in 1806. 'Thus they continue the habit of concubinage until the convicts arrive at Sydney town. Each sailor or soldier is permitted to attach himself to one of the females.'[9]

Some were ordinary criminals, but many were political prisoners, writers of seditious tracts, or dissenters who had spoken out of turn. Others had committed minor economic crimes. As resistance grew in Ireland, many of the early prisoners were Irish rebels; later, Australia would receive convicts from other parts of the Empire, including South Africa and the West Indies.

Although these were prisoners, not slaves, they were transported with no guarantee of eventual freedom. A commonplace sentence was to be 'transported' for a specified number of years – seven, fourteen, or twenty-one, and sometimes for life. Some received their 'emancipation' earlier, but many remained convicts until they died. The colonial authorities often received no record of the crimes committed or of the sentences passed. Many of the political prisoners from Ireland were sentenced to transportation without trial. Their status would remain endlessly unresolved because they had no papers – a typical gulag situation.

The convicts were the first victims of the Aborigines, who showed their displeasure from the start. In May 1788, four months after landfall, two convicts had gone out to cut rushes in a distant cove. One returned 'very dangerously wounded', for a barbed spear had entered 'about the depth of three inches into his back between the shoulders'. The other had seemingly run away, but a day or two later his clothes were recovered, 'torn, bloody, and pierced with spears'. There was every reason 'to suppose that the poor wretch had fallen a sacrifice to his own folly and the barbarity of the natives'.

Nor was this an isolated incident. A week later, the bodies of two more convicts were brought back from a cove further up the harbour, 'pierced through in many places with spears, and the head of one beaten to jelly'. The two men had stolen an Aborigine canoe, and suffered the consequences. Theft by the convicts was an irritant to the indigenous inhabitants, but the main problem lay elsewhere: the Aborigines were not prepared to tolerate the white settlers remaining on their land. Their resistance was absolute.

An early record of these encounters was made by Colonel David Collins, commander of the Royal Marine detachment that travelled with the first ships. As secretary to Captain Phillip, he was well placed to write revealing memoirs, and he took some pride in his role as the territory's first participant-observer. Only perhaps once in a century, he wrote, were colonies 'established in the most remote part of the habitable globe', and it was seldom that men were found 'existing perfectly in a state of nature'.[10] Nor is it usual, he might have added, for such men to tell the colonial newcomers to go away – on the very first day.

'Warra, warra, warra!' was hardly the message that the British party expected to hear. They planned to occupy the Aborigines' land, certainly; but they also wished rather desperately to be friends. On a hostile and unfamiliar shore, they needed assistance and information. Their most pressing problem was lack of food. In the early months of settlement, with no help from the Aborigines, they faced starvation; seven soldiers were hanged in January 1789 for stealing food from the public store.

Colonel Collins was only faintly aware of the contradiction in the British position. 'It was natural to suppose', he recorded after a few weeks, 'that the curiosity of these people would be attracted by observing that, instead of quitting, we were occupied in works that indicated an intention of remaining in the country'. This intention provoked hostility rather than curiosity.

Six months after landing, in August 1788, Colonel Collins was still recording the endless saga of rejection: 'The natives continued to molest our people whenever they chanced to meet any of them straggling and unarmed'; in December he noted how they were becoming 'every day more troublesome and hostile'. The Aborigines caused great disappointment to the new colony's leaders. It was one thing to set up a gulag at the bottom of the world, with shiploads of recalcitrant prisoners, but quite another to do so against a backdrop of native resistance that was to prove both dangerous and relentless.

In December 1790, in the hinterland of Sydney Cove, 'a native named Pemulwy' speared a convict called John McEntire. The first Aborigine to have a name recorded by British settlers has received little historical recognition over the years, although he is a hero revered by many Aborigines today. As a leader in an ancient civilisation that did not have leaders, Pemulwy went on to harass the infant British prison settlement for a further decade.

Pimbloy (or Pemulwy) a native of New Holland (Australia), 1804. This engraving, by Samuel John Neele, is the only known image of Pemulwy, the first Aborigine encountered by the settlers. 'The resemblance is thought to be striking by those who have seen him', wrote Captain James Grant of the Lady Nelson.

Governor Phillip blamed the crew of the French expedition of Jean-François La Pérouse for the initial trouble with the Aborigines at Sydney Cove. Two French ships had sailed into the bay on a round-the-world cruise in January 1788, in the week of the British arrival. French sailors had fired on the natives 'in consequence of which, with the bad behaviour of some of the transport boats, and some convicts, the natives have lately avoided us'.

McEntire had arrived in the first convict ship in 1788 and was regarded as a 'trusted' convict, often being employed by Governor Phillip to shoot animals and game – and, so some of the settlers believed, Aborigines as well. He died of the wound that Pemulwy had inflicted. He was not the first Briton to fall to an Aborigine's spear, but the first to have a named killer.

Phillip had hopes of finding an Aborigine to be trained as an interpreter, but there were no volunteers. If he was to make contact, he would have to seize an individual Aborigine by force.[11] The first captured Aborigine died when the settlement was swept by smallpox. A second attempt at capture was made in November 1789, and two men were seized. One escaped, still attached to his iron fetter, while the other, called Bennilong, became the desired interpreter, and was eventually brought into colonial service. Like many other colonial inhabitants prepared to work with the British conquerors, he was rewarded with a scholarship to London, and he sailed there with Governor Phillip in 1792.

The death of McEntire in December 1790 provided the British with an excuse to respond in a new and harsher way. Captain Phillip ordered a punitive expedition to be sent out against Pemulwy's Bidjigal tribe. The soldiers were told to capture six Aborigines and, failing that, to kill six of them and bring back their heads. The governor wanted to make a 'severe example'. Yet two expeditions proved fruitless, for Pemulwy and his companions melted into the bush.

A month later, in January 1791, a further clash occurred between settlers and Aborigines in which the governor's guards shot and killed an Aborigine. 'It was much to be regretted that any necessity existed for adopting these sanguinary punishments', noted the governor, but he had additional cause for regret. They had failed, he wrote, 'to reconcile the natives to the deprivation of those parts of the harbour which we occupied'. As was to be the case in Sierra Leone, the colonial occupation of a traditional harbour would become the cause of fierce resentment among the local population. The Aborigines were soon to lose rather more than their harbour.

Colonel Collins reflected on the permanent problem that lay ahead. 'While they entertain the idea of our having dispossessed them of their residences, they must always consider us as enemies; and upon this principle they made a point of attacking the white people whenever opportunity and safety concurred.' These Aborigine attacks provoked inevitable reprisals, and James Bonwick – a sensitive historian writing a century later, in the 1880s – described how 'a wholesale slaughter' became the usual mode of revenge adopted by the Christian strangers. 'The convicts slew and ill-treated native children, seized upon young women to subject them to their brutal passions, and wounded or slew complaining husbands and fathers.'[12]

The age-old colonial curse of imported European disease soon struck Australia. 'Shortly after the English landed, a fearful pestilence set in' among the Aborigines, 'and very many bodies were left unburied in the bush.' The disease was described as a kind of smallpox. Memories of the decimation of the Indians of South America, as a result of the Spanish conquest, were uneasily evoked by British officers.[13]

With unequal combat between spear and musket, Pemulwy's resistance could not last forever. With his son Tedbury, he crops up from time to time in the records of the 1790s, until finally, in March 1797, 'a strong party of natives' with Pemulwy at their head was surrounded by soldiers. Pemulwy was shot seven times in the encounter, thereafter disappearing into legend.[14] He was captured and taken to hospital, according to one version, escaping with an iron manacle still fixed to his leg. Later, in 1801, he was reportedly joined by two escaped convicts, and together they launched attacks on farms along the Georges River.

Finally cornered in June 1802, Pemulwy was shot dead, and his severed head was sent to Britain to be held in the collection of Sir Joseph Banks. A new governor, Captain Philip King, wrote to Banks saying that he understood 'that the possession of a New Hollander's head is among the desiderata, I have put it in spirits and forwarded it by the Speedy'.[15] He said that, although he regarded Pemulwy as 'a terrible pest to the colony, he was a brave and independent character'. [16] Pemulwy's was just one among the many severed heads that the British sent home from distant parts of the Empire as souvenirs. His skull has disappeared without trace.[17]

CHAPTER 11

The Black Settlers of Sierra Leone

When Britain had first been looking around for an African territory in which to dump its convict population in 1785, it had been warned by Henry Smeathman of the unsuitability of Sierra Leone: the climate was unhealthy and the natives hostile. The government shelved the convict project, but came up with another idea. If it was not possible to transport white convicts to West Africa, might not poor blacks usefully be shipped out? Perhaps they might not mind the climate.

Many impoverished blacks lived in London at the time, some of them former slaves or veterans of the war in North America. The British government felt little responsibility for them, and existing Poor Law legislation decreed only that paupers were the responsibility of their 'parish of origin'. Former slaves could hardly be returned to their 'parish' in America, so what better idea than to ship them off to Africa? Smeathman suggested that the local Temne population 'would not be inconvenienced by the newcomers'.[1]

Granville Sharp was the leader of a group of wealthy English radicals who sought ways of mitigating the plight of British blacks. He was the financial supporter of a proposed new settlement on the Sierra Leone River, but he believed that it should be established with 'the consent (and association, if possible) of the native inhabitants'. This did not happen. Conflict between the black settlers and the indigenous population was inevitable from the start, for the message of Islam, brought from across the Sahara, had long ago reached the western coastal region. Some of the inland Mandingos could speak and write in Arabic.[2] European ships sailing down the coast of Africa had stopped there over the centuries to load up with food and fresh water. Others, filled with slaves, still left regularly for the Americas. The Africans were all too aware of a wider world beyond their river, and it was not unusual to find an African speaking a European language: English or French, Dutch or Portuguese. Sharp was an evangelical Christian and thought that 'Pagans, Papists, Mahometans, Infidels, etc.' should not be allowed in the new colony.[3]

A British warship, HMS *Nautilus*, arrived at the Sierra Leone River in May 1787 accompanied by three transport vessels. On board were 400 free blacks from Britain, with sixty white prostitutes brought along at the last moment. All had been told they could have a new life as settlers in Sierra Leone. A Temne chief, 'King' Tom, who controlled the lands bordering the river, made a commercial deal with Captain Thomas Thompson of the *Nautilus*. The chief was a small-time supplier of slaves to European purchasers, and he lived with his followers in Romarong, a village of fifty huts built under the hills on the south side of the harbour. The Temne chiefs had grown accustomed over the years to securing a substantial income from the slave traders.

Tom agreed to provide the settlers with a tract of land, twenty miles square, on the edge of the harbour. In exchange for £59 worth of goods, he signed away his rights to the land 'for ever'. The settlers measured out plots and built simple huts, calling their settlement Granville Town, in honour of their philanthropic benefactor.

A rival Temne chief, 'King' Jimmy, was not a party to the agreement, and was hostile to the black settlers from the start. It transpired that the territory that Tom had given away 'for ever' included the watering place of Jimmy's people, a harbour from which his predecessors had received rent from ocean-going ships. Several Temne villagers claimed that the area was holy ground and was being profaned by the presence of the settlers.

The following year, 1788, Jimmy seized power from Tom and sought to remove the unwelcome intruders. First he demanded tribute from them, and when this was not forthcoming he took some of them captive, selling them to slave traders to compensate for his loss of earnings. By the end of the first year, some 300 of the original black settlers had melted away; those who remained felt isolated and nervous.

In November 1789 a passing British warship, HMS *Pomona*, commanded by Captain Henry Savage, sent a party ashore to Romarong to protect the survivors, burning a Temne hut as a punishment. Jimmy's villagers put up a fierce resistance, forcing the British to withdraw. Captain Savage poured a heavy bombardment into the village before sailing away. Then, with the British safely over the horizon, Jimmy took his revenge, attacking the surviving settlers and burning down their huts at Granville Town.

The victory of 'King' Jimmy and the Temne did not last long. The colony's supporters in London argued that a larger group of settlers might fare better, and in faraway Canada they knew of a problem to which Sierra Leone might provide an answer. In 1783, at the end of the American war, the British had felt obliged to look after the settlers, known as 'Empire Loyalists', who had fought with them against the rebels. These were shipped up to Canada and given settlement grants, some 30,000 being established in Halifax, Nova Scotia, the former lands of the Acadians expelled in 1755.[4] Among them were 3,000 former black slaves, granted their freedom in exchange for fighting on the British side.

Although free men, and pensioners of the British state, these 'Black Loyalists' found Nova Scotia unattractive. The climate was bleak, and the existing white settlers were unwelcoming and racist. The blacks learned of the African schemes of Granville Sharp and his band of evangelicals in London, and discussed among themselves their possible transfer from Canada to West Africa. Many greeted the idea with enthusiasm, and in 1792 – after a group of London evangelicals had taken over Sharpe's colonisation project, renaming it as the 'Sierra Leone Company' – the project to transfer some of the 'Black Loyalists' went ahead. They sailed in fifteen ships for the new settlement in Sierra Leone, now called Freetown.

The arrival in Africa of 1,000 American-Canadian former slaves introduced a new era in the history of empire, one characterised by the inter-imperial transfer of populations. William Dawes, the new colony's governor, was already an expert at such transcontinental migration, having been a junior officer accompanying the first shipload of convicts to New South Wales in 1788. He was replaced by Zachary Macaulay, father of the British historian, who had also had imperial experience working on a plantation in Jamaica, following which he had become an opponent of the slave trade.

Freetown lay 'a musket's shot distant' from 'King' Jimmy's village of Romarong, and the Temne looked on in amazement at the arrival of the large group from Canada, fearing that they would take over their land. The black settlers quickly asked for guns. 'King' Naimbanna, a more senior chief than Jimmy, was located and befriended by the officials of the Sierra Leone Company. His son was sent on a scholarship to England – always a popular bribe with the native elites of Empire.[5] Naimbanna accepted a deal which provided the settlers with rather less land than the earlier group had had, and gave the Temne guaranteed access to their ancient watering place.

The local Africans remained hostile and unfriendly, yet the first significant threat to Macaulay's colony came not from the Temne but from the settlers' opposition to the governor's autocratic rule, and from their tactical alliance with a French naval squadron during an attack in September 1794. The squadron, operating without challenge off the West African coast, had bombarded the town, and the black settlers had joined forces with the French sailors to loot the offices of the Sierra Leone Company. Macaulay protested to the French that his was a humanitarian colony. 'That's as may be, *citoyen*', replied the Republican French captain, 'but you're still English.' Many black settlers claimed that they were American, which in a sense they were.[6] The immediate problem was solved when the French sailed away, and the colony's internal disputes subsided after the pugnacious Macaulay returned to London in 1795.

As with Sharp's earlier project, the Sierra Leone Company had an evangelical Christian enthusiasm, and hoped to use Freetown as a base from which to Christianise the African continent. Yet the Mandingos, inland from Freetown, had already embraced another religion. As converts to Islam, they stood ready with an indigenous challenge to this imperial ambition.

* * *

Some years later, in 1802, the Temne living along the Sierra Leone River laid siege to the fort at Freetown in an attempt to recapture it from the settlers. They were led by Nathaniel Wansey, a settler from Canada banished into the interior two years earlier. 'Supported by a number of marksmen who kept up a very destructive fire on those who advanced to repel them', Wansey attacked and captured the fort, and, according to a report sent back to London, Lieutenant Laidlaw, Sergeant Blackwood and a private from the Africa Corps were killed. Several others were wounded, including William Dawes, the former governor.[7]

The fighting lasted for more than two weeks, and a fresh group of black settlers – 500 Maroons from Jamaica who had sailed into Freetown harbour in October 1800 – were called in to crush it. The Maroons had been forcibly exiled to Nova Scotia after a rebellion in 1795, and had found Canada no more welcoming than had the 'Black Loyalists' from America.[8] The Canadians had jumped at the chance to shunt them on to Sierra Leone. On their arrival at Freetown, the Jamaican Maroons found that the existing population of 'Black Loyalists' were engaged in a rebellion against the colonial authorities. Their first task was to help crush it.

Robert Dallas, a contemporary chronicler, explains how useful they were to the British authorities: 'Had the Maroons been the disciples of revolutionary emissaries, or the abettors of anarchy and equality, they would in all probability have joined the people of their own complexion to extirpate the white tyrant; on the contrary, they joined with alacrity in quelling the insurrection.'[9] Some of the rebels were killed; others were captured and tried. A few were executed, and some, like Wansey, were banished into the interior. Not until 1807 did the Temne finally agree to sign a peace treaty.

Part IV

BRITAIN EXPANDS ITS COUNTER-REVOLUTIONARY EMPIRE DURING THE WAR AGAINST REVOLUTIONARY FRANCE, 1793–1802

The Fall of the Bastille on 14 July 1789 was the formal start of a great revolutionary process that brought an era of French history to a dramatic close. Yet the overthrow of the old order in Paris was also to influence the future of Europe and, via the colonial connections of the European powers, to have significant implications for the rest of the world. It marked a decisive moment in the development of the British Empire.

Revolutionary France declared war on Britain and Holland on 31 January 1793, having sent the French King Louis XVI to the guillotine ten days earlier. This new war between Royalist England and Republican France was to last on and off for more than twenty years, until 1815. Its impact reverberated throughout the world, from Canada to India and the Indian Ocean, from South Africa to the islands of the West Indies. The conflict had a profound effect on the new British Empire, which in the process acquired great tracts of territory once held by France and Holland.

While the Europeans fought each other, peoples elsewhere, in the extra-European world threatened by colonial expansion, used this fratricidal strife to pursue their own projects of liberation or emancipation. Indian princes tried to keep their states free from the British embrace; black slaves in the West Indies, as well as Maroons and Caribs, rose up to demand their freedom or their traditional lands; Dutch farmers in South Africa imagined a Republican and Jacobin future, and so too did the Defenders in Ireland and the United Irishmen of Dublin and Belfast. These revolutionary enthusiasms were crushed by the British wherever they were on display.

Once at war with revolutionary France, Britain's ruling elite often seemed less worried by the fighting on the European continent than by the threat to British interests in distant parts of the globe, where the French message of freedom and Republicanism fell on fertile soil. Only at the end of the decade, in 1798, when a French-supported rebellion in Ireland required the attention of every senior general in the British army, were the British forced to pay serious attention to events nearer home.

Britain's real interest lay beyond Europe's shores. With eyes fixed on distant horizons, Britain's rulers glimpsed a golden opportunity to expand their empire in the world beyond, and they seized the chance. In the West Indies, British armies took over the sugar- and slave-rich islands of Tobago, Guadeloupe and St Lucia from the French; they seized Guyana from the Dutch, and Trinidad from Spain. They even tried to drag the French island of Saint-Domingue – known later as Haiti – into their empire.[1]

Elsewhere, in opposition to the alliance between the revolutionary Republicans of France and Holland, the Royalist British seized Ceylon, Malacca and Cape Town from the Dutch. All such enclaves became significant pieces in the jigsaw of empire. The British also used the threat posed by revolutionary France to entrench themselves ever deeper into India, crushing princely states on the grounds that they were potential allies of Jacobin France. On the route to India, they challenged France's occupation of Egypt in 1798 by briefly seizing it themselves in 1801. None of these were peaceful acquisitions. They were the work of a conquering army, murdering and looting as it went. The human cost to the British themselves was also considerable: frequent military disasters marked this period of empire-building. So too did medical breakdown: no rank or class was spared the ravages of yellow fever, that great disease of imperialism that decimated European armies in the Caribbean.

In fighting against the country that had written the Declaration of the Rights of Man, the British began the construction of an empire that would keep those rights off the agenda. Conceived in a decade of revolution, this expanded British Empire was counter-revolutionary from the start. Anything that smacked of Jacobinism – the French creed of revolution – was rooted out. The democratic greeting of 'citizen', from the French *citoyen*, was often taken up in colonial territories and used as a defiant anti-imperial expression. Its public use in British possessions as far apart as Ireland, South Africa, the West Indies and India was seen as a challenge to British hegemony.

Tipu Sultan, the 'Tiger of Mysore', was the first to call himself *citoyen* in honour of his French allies. Yet even before the French declaration of war in 1793, he had been faced with fresh British moves towards the high plateau of Mysore. Ever since 1767, when his father Haidar Ali had forced the British to retreat from Bangalore, the Mysore rulers had resisted the encroachments of the Christian British on their Muslim realm. Years of war were followed by a peace agreement signed in 1784, but by the 1790s the British were again on the warpath. Tipu was initially successful, defeating a British regiment at the Gajalhatti pass in 1790. With the arrival of a new British commander sent south from Calcutta, however, Tipu found the scales moving against him.

The new officer in charge, the overseer of further imperial expansion in India, was Charles Cornwallis, the general defeated at Yorktown in 1781. He was to have better fortune in India. Tipu faced attacks from two sides in February 1791, with Cornwallis advancing from Madras and the opportunistic Marathas pressing in from the north. Tipu lost the strategic town of Bangalore, a serious blow, but was providentially rescued by the weather. Torrential storms and faulty planning left Cornwallis's army without adequate supplies, and the British abandoned their campaign for the rest of the year.

Tipu Sultan's sons are handed over as hostages to General Lord Cornwallis at Seringapatam, 1792. Painting by Robert Home

In February 1792, Tipu's inland fortress at Seringapatam was besieged by Cornwallis's army, made up of 6,000 European soldiers, 16,000 Indian sepoys and some 12,000 Marathas.[2] Tipu's soldiers fought outside the gates for a week before calling a truce. Tipu faced a demand from the British for large sums of money and half his kingdom, including the western coastal region of Malabar.[3] He also had to hand over two sons as hostages. The British did not often take hostages, fearing that it would put them on the same level as the 'barbarians' with whom they were dealing. They soothed their consciences by putting Tipu's boys into a comfortable house in Madras, from which they were taken occasionally to concerts to listen to the music of Handel. They were sent back home to Seringapatam two years later. Cornwallis returned to England in 1793 to join the war cabinet, taking with him a 'hawking ring' seized from Tipu.[4] Six years later, in 1799, Tipu Sultan was overthrown and killed.

Other parts of the colonial world were soon affected by the spreading ripples of the French Revolution and its message of liberty and freedom. In February 1795 a group of Dutch settlers in the Dutch colony at Cape Town, in the South African hinterland, threw off the yoke of the Dutch East India Company and proclaimed a Republic. They had heard news of the revolution in Holland that January, which had overthrown William of Orange and established the Batavian Republic – a country now in solidarity with the revolutionaries in France. Soon too they were calling each other 'citizen'.

This European extension of the French Revolution soon had global repercussions. Would the Dutch possessions abroad declare themselves for Republican Holland and Republican France, or would they ally themselves with the exiled Prince of Orange and his counter-revolutionary friends in England? What would happen in Dutch Ceylon and Dutch Java? What would happen at Dutch Cape Town?

These Dutch Republicans were hardly revolutionaries. Their desire for freedom was the old white settler desire, when surrounded and threatened by alien and hostile forces, for freedom to do exactly what they liked, untrammelled by the laws of any central or colonial government. Just as the American settler 'revolutionaries' of the 1770s had wanted 'freedom' to seize the land of the Native Americans, so the Afrikaner settlers wanted a free hand to steal the land of the Xhosa. Yet in keeping with the times, the rhetoric of the Dutch Republicans owed much to the ideas unleashed in Europe in 1789, and they decked themselves out in the red, white and blue of the French revolutionary tricolour. A British fleet was sent out in 1795 to crush them.

In the same year, another fleet began dismantling the Dutch Empire in Asia. Ships from Madras anchored off Ceylon's northern port of Trincomalee that August with more than 1,000 European troops and two battalions of sepoys on board. Dutch troops and their Malay soldiers put up considerable resistance to the British landings, and the British lost more than seventy soldiers. The local population, the Sinhalese, were barely involved, but the Dutch and their Malay auxiliaries fought all the way down the island, forcing the British to summon reinforcements from Madras and Bombay. Not until February 1796, with 2,000 Europeans and some 4,000 Indians, were the British able to capture Colombo. After the Dutch surrender, the British held the coastal areas but the central mountainous heartland, the independent kingdom of Kandy, remained untouched. They did not feel strong enough to take on the Kandyans while already engaged in dealing with a Sinhalese rebellion on the coast led by Sinno Appu.

In all their imperial territories, old and new, conquest was met with resistance. The British did not just walk ashore. The slave islands of the Caribbean, in particular, saw rebellions on an unprecedented scale in the 1790s. British armies were often greeted by black guerrilla forces. In the British islands of Jamaica, Dominica, Grenada and St Vincent, and in the French islands that the British sought to occupy (Haiti, Guadeloupe and St Lucia), slaves, Maroons and mulattoes (usually free men of colour) fought vigorously, alone or with French assistance, against armadas sent out from Britain.

War in the Caribbean began with the 1791 slave rebellion in Haiti and the flight of the island's French planters. The message of the French Revolution had created serious divisions within the island's white elite, and the slaves were alert to their chance. Exploding at Cap Français on the north coast, their rebellion spread rapidly over the northern plains, involving tens of thousands of slaves. The initial casualty figures were large, with 10,000 slaves killed, and 2,000 whites.

Many French planters fled the island, some moving to Spanish Cuba, others to British Jamaica. There they asked Colonel Adam Williamson, the military governor, for troops and weapons to recover their island. Williamson could only provide a handful of men, as he needed all his troops to guard against a possible slave revolt in Jamaica itself. 'Many slaves here are very inquisitive and intelligent', he told London, 'and are immediately informed of every kind of news that arrives . . . They have composed songs of the negroes having made a rebellion at Hispaniola [Haiti] . . . and there are numbers who are ripe for any mischief.' Martial law was declared at Christmas 1791, after news of an imminent rebellion on a plantation at Trelawny. Williamson requested troops from Britain, but they were slow in coming.

The fugitive French planters from Haiti were not an isolated phenomenon. When slave rebellions quickly followed on the French islands of Martinique, Guadeloupe and St Lucia, other planters were forced to flee. Some landed on the British island of Dominica, itself affected by the rebellion of Jean-Louis Polinaire and the Maroons of Pharcelle. The panic among the whites was understandable. On six French islands[5] there were 55,000 whites and the same number of mulattoes, overshadowed by nearly 600,000 black slaves. Barely 50,000 whites lived on the British islands, and most of them were concentrated in Jamaica (23,000) and Barbados (16,000). They lived in close proximity to nearly half a million (465,000) black slaves, and 10,000 'free coloureds'. The revolutionary rhetoric flowing from Paris threatened the stability of the entire region.

The British had long hoped to expand their empire by including the rich French colonies of the West Indies, and now the dispossessed French planters pressed them to take up the challenge, and to sponsor an invasion of Haiti.[6] War with France gave the British a chance, and invasion plans were prepared for all the French islands. The simple proposal was to invade, to crush the slave rebellions, and to return the plantations to their white owners under British rule. In April 1793 an expedition sailed from the British military base at Barbados and captured tiny Tobago. In June, at Martinique, the British were less successful, for the slaves, who had combined with the free coloureds, made such a show of resistance that the French planters accompanying the British forces grew nervous. The British withdrew in September, and instead established a bridgehead on Haiti.

They lacked soldiers, and their commanders made urgent appeals to London for reinforcements. The government eventually responded, and an armada with nineteen battalions on board – nearly a quarter of the entire British army – was sent out late in 1793. It was the start of a flurry of naval activity. A second armada was despatched to the Caribbean two years later, at the same time as another fleet was sent to the south Atlantic to seize Dutch South Africa, and a third sailed from Madras to capture Dutch Ceylon.

The first fleet destined for the Caribbean, commanded by Admiral Sir John Jervis and General Sir Charles Grey, sailed in from Gibraltar, from Nova Scotia and Canada, and from Ireland – itself in a state of incipient rebellion. It arrived at Barbados in December 1793 with orders to seize Guadeloupe, Martinique and St Lucia, and to consolidate the Empire's foothold in Haiti. Soon they faced slave rebellions in every island, aided and supported by French Republicans.

The drama in the West Indies, sparked off by the slave rebellion in Saint-Domingue in 1791, unfolded against a background of continuing debate in Europe and the Americas about slavery and the slave trade. Rebellions by slaves and Caribs had long aroused interest and concern in London. Tacky's revolt in Jamaica in 1760 had brought calls for white solidarity and support, while Chatoyer's Carib resistance in St Vincent had been discussed in parliament in 1773, the year after slavery in Britain had been formally outlawed. The American states of Delaware and New Jersey had followed suit in the 1780s, and Republican France voted to abolish slavery throughout its empire in 1794.

The slave trade was a tougher nut to crack. The Danes voted to end the trade to their Caribbean colonies in March 1792, and the British made a guarded promise the following month, declaring that 'the slave trade ought to be gradually abolished'. The weasel word 'gradually' was introduced by an influential politician from Scotland, Henry Dundas, who successfully postponed the trade's abolition for fifteen years, until 1807. This long delay allowed the evil practices of the Atlantic passage to continue, as well as enabling the British to purchase blacks in slave markets to serve in their imperial wars.

During their occupation of Haiti between 1793 and 1798, the British learned painfully that territory in the West Indies could only be held with the assistance of local black soldiers. General Sir John Vaughan, commander of British forces in Guadeloupe, advised London in December 1794 that a regiment of black troops should be assembled, either by recruiting slaves on the islands or by importing them directly from Africa. Soon a substantial portion of the British army in the West Indies in these years was bought at the slave market. Black battalions were formed in several Caribbean islands after 1795, and 13,000 slave soldiers were purchased locally to help in the suppression of rebellion. The slave soldiers were promised their freedom when hostilities ended, but the promise was usually forgotten. The slave rebellions were often followed by slave soldier mutinies, both leading to a litany of floggings and executions. Elsewhere, blacks were imported from the slave market in Goa, and from Mozambique, to fight in the British war of conquest in Ceylon. While Republican France and Holland gave slaves their freedom, the British purchased fresh ones to defend their expanding Empire.

The French Revolution had sparked off trouble for the British in the Caribbean; it also created new inspiration and opportunities for rebellion nearer home. A revolt in Ireland in 1798 was part of the great tidal wave of revolutionary resistance that had started in Paris nine years before. General Charles Cornwallis, who had defeated Tipu Sultan in 1792, was sent out to Ireland, and he rightly perceived the revolt there as a 'deep-laid conspiracy to revolutionise Ireland on French principles'. A nervous British government believed itself to be faced with insurrectionary agitation that would make its colony ungovernable. In the typical reflex action of imperial rule, an Insurrection Act was drafted to suspend habeas corpus and trial by jury, and to impose a nightly curfew. The penalty for disobedience was seven years' transportation to the new prison colony of Australia.

Ireland was a colonial classic, exquisite in its simplicity: an impoverished indigenous people, Irish Catholics, faced a tiny and arrogant white settler class of British Protestants. Feeble imperial representatives, biased towards the Protestant settlers, tried to keep the territory under control, often through terror. This was the model of Empire that Britain presented to the world in the eighteenth century, and maintained for nearly two centuries.

CHAPTER 12

Resistance to Empire in the Caribbean in the Wake of the French Revolution

On the evening of 20 January 1791, at Grand Bay in the parish of St Patrick, the Maroons of Dominica joined forces with plantation slaves and 'free coloureds' to threaten British control of the island. Their leader was Pharcelle. A participant in an earlier rebellion of 1785, Pharcelle was not a Maroon himself but a slave shipped in from the Guinea coast. His revolt in Dominica anticipated the great slave rebellion that was to explode a few months later, in August 1791, in Saint-Domingue (Haiti), and its course was influenced by events there and in the other French-speaking islands of the Caribbean.

A small but mountainous island lying between Guadeloupe to the north and Martinique to the south, Dominica had been under British control for only eight years.[1] The British had had nothing but trouble from this acquisition. With a largely French-speaking population, disagreements and conflicts within the white population – between French and English settlers and plantation owners – were inevitable. These quarrels had an impact on the slaves, which in turn affected the 'free coloureds' and the *Nègres Marrons* – the large population of former slaves who lived in the central mountains. The strength of these 'Maroons' lay in their ability to recruit slaves and in their inaccessible retreat in the hills, which the British lacked sufficient military strength to recover.

Typical in this regard were the slaves from the formerly Jesuit-owned plantations in the south-east of the island. The French Jesuits had left after the first British takeover in 1763, and their slaves had removed themselves swiftly into the woods with their families. 'They were joined from time to time here by others from different estates', wrote Thomas Atwood in his history of the island, published in 1791. 'There they secreted themselves for a number of years, formed companies under different chiefs, built good houses and planted gardens in the woods, where they raised poultry, hogs, and other small stock.' Compared with the conditions of slavery, this was an attractive, almost idyllic existence: 'With what the sea, rivers, and woods afforded, and what they got from the negroes they had intercourse with on the plantations, they lived very comfortably, and were seldom disturbed in their haunts.'

The Maroons were hostile to the British occupation of the island, as were the 'free coloureds', many of them mulatto landowners and tradesmen of French origin who lived in Dominica but moved easily between the various French islands. Their loyalty to the British Empire was weak. With a pragmatic outlook, they used their dual nationality to their advantage whenever possible.

The existence of the Maroons was a permanent enticement to the slaves to slip away, and an ever-present threat to the plantation owners. By establishing self-sufficient communities that could be used to attack the slave plantations, the Maroons called the entire plantation system into question. They were 'an internal enemy of the most alarming kind', wrote Captain John Orde, the military governor, which threatened 'to destroy every English estate in the island'.

Pharcelle was among those who had escaped a life sentence on the plantations to join the free Maroons in the hills, and to fight for independence. The governor described him as 'formidable', yet as with so many imperial rebels, he flits through the archives leaving an enigmatic trace. His rebellion in 1785 had lasted for several months, and was only suppressed when additional troops arrived from St Vincent and Grenada. Pharcelle himself survived, holed up in the hills for several years, his presence a permanent reproach to the plantation owners. He was known as a gun-runner, and, from an impregnable base above the town of Colihaut, he remained in contact with other islands in the Caribbean still in French hands.

After the Revolution in Paris in 1789, French Royalists and Republicans took part in serious political debate throughout the Caribbean. Much of the French-speaking population in British-controlled Dominica was sympathetic to the new revolutionary Republic, and many sought to make common cause with Maroons and slaves against the British authorities. Among the prominent supporters of the French Republic was Jean-Louis Polinaire, a 'free coloured' originally from Martinique who published revolutionary pamphlets – much to the anger of the island's white assembly, which complained that his pamphlets gave encouragement to their already discontented slaves. Only a small spark was needed to set off a slave explosion on the plantations.

Polinaire lit the fuse. Plantation slaves, according to law, had a right to two days in the week to work for themselves, and Polinaire had been urging them to demand this right throughout 1790. The request was common enough, but most plantation owners refused to consider it. Their slaves grew increasingly resentful. 'Some individuals had absconded and others would not go to work', noted Captain Orde, just before the rebellion broke out.

The revolt of January 1791 had an unusual degree of support: from the 'free coloureds', from the Maroons, and from slaves on virtually every plantation. Pharcelle provided 500 muskets that he had squirrelled away in the hills after the earlier rebellion. Yet the authorities were well prepared. The principal rebel positions were seized by British military detachments within a week. 'Great numbers of negroes' surrendered, Orde recorded, and only Pharcelle escaped to fight another day.

Orde had offered a substantial reward to anyone who captured an escaped slave, and Polinaire, the pamphleteer, was betrayed by a treacherous Carib who informed a British plantation owner of his hiding place, and claimed the reward. Polinaire was tried at Roseau before a jury of French and English residents, found guilty of rebellion, and hanged.

This was fierce justice, yet the message of freedom and rebellion was not entirely rubbed away. Orde wrote to London to deplore the fact that things would never be the same. 'Notions and opinions have certainly got root in the minds of slaves in general, which I much apprehend will militate against their ever again being such faithful, obedient and contented servants as they were formerly.' Orde was right to be pessimistic, and he himself soon lost the confidence of the plantation owners. The authorities ordered him back to Britain.

Maroon resistance continued over the next twenty years, for Pharcelle was a great survivor. He was able to stay in contact with French Republicans in Guadeloupe, who promised French assistance in 1794 if he would help to fight the British. Plans were made for a fresh rebellion to coincide with a French invasion. Pharcelle was captured before he could go into action and the British sought to negotiate a deal, for they were alarmed by the extent of his plans.[2] Pharcelle made the deal to save his life, but his promise did not last long. When the French invasion took place in May 1795, he guided the French force through the mountains.

Pharcelle was to be found over the next few years working for both the French and the British, sometimes rounding up runaway slaves, sometimes guiding black troops through the mountains. Something eventually went wrong with his balancing act. In 1800 he was detained and accused of 'insolent and highly suspicious conduct'. The white assembly ordered him to be sent into exile. From the records of Dominica, he disappears without further trace.

Throughout 1793, large black armies of former slaves were operating on the French island of Saint-Domingue (later known as Haiti), fighting to maintain their freedom after an historic and successful rebellion in August 1791. Then, in September 1793, the rebel slaves were confronted at Jérémie, on the south-western tip of the island, by 600 red-coated British soldiers who had landed there after crossing from Jamaica. Two days later, the rebels noted the arrival of British ships at the important strategic base at Mole St Nicolas, considered the 'Gibraltar of the Caribbean', after sailing across the bight of Léogane. The British troops, under the command of Colonel Adam Williamson, the governor of Jamaica, included French Royalist landowners seeking to recover their sugar plantations. The former slaves put up substantial resistance to this British attempt to include Haiti into the Empire, forcing them to withdraw five years later.[3]

In the weeks before the British landing, rebel forces had been swollen as the result of the end to slavery on the island declared by Léger Félicité Sonthonax, a Revolutionary 'commissioner' sent out by the Republican government in Paris. Sonthonax promised freedom to all slaves who joined the resistance forces of the Republic, thus anticipating the formal end to slavery throughout the French dominions announced in Paris in February 1794. (The slaves in Haiti had already taken matters into their own hands in 1791.)

Five months after the initial British landings, the rebel army was under siege at the principal city of Port-au-Prince, fighting off a British naval squadron as well as a troop advancing by land from Tiburón, a town seized by the British. Called upon to surrender by the British naval commander in February 1794, Sonthonax refused: 'Were we ever forced to leave this place, nothing would be left of your ships but smoke, since the rest of them would be at the bottom of the sea.' Acknowledging the truth of his words, the British retreated.

Spurred on by their success, the rebel army attacked isolated British garrisons in the west, causing 2,000 white refugees to escape into the British zone, and in April General André Rigaud, one of the mulatto leaders of the revolution, advanced on British-held Tiburón. Commander of the most formidable black army in the south of the island, Rigaud bore the brunt of the early resistance against the British, although another leader, Toussaint L'Ouverture, would receive much of the credit.[4] The climate was on the side of the black revolutionaries, for British troops found the tropical conditions intolerable. Their numbers began to dwindle as yellow fever made its devastating impact.

Control of Haiti would require thousands of soldiers as a permanent garrison, and the British sent out an armada to the Caribbean, commanded by Admiral Jervis and General Grey, that arrived at Barbados in December 1793. Before reinforcements could be sent to Haiti, the British commanders had preliminary tasks in Martinique, St Lucia and Guadeloupe,[5] and not until May 1794 were troops available to assist the British enclaves on Haiti.[6]

The rebel army and Commissioner Sonthonax were driven out of Port-au-Prince by the British with the help of a unit of French Royalists, but the rebels ensured that no further advance was possible. Yellow fever took its toll of the new troops, as it had done of the old. Ships arrived with half their complement dying – or already cast overboard. Some 700 soldiers had died by the end of August. They 'dropt like the leaves in autumn', noted one long-established planter.[7]

The British position in Haiti was bleak, and to survive at all they recruited local blacks.[8] They sought to preserve the old Royalist slave regime while offering freedom to individual slaves if they joined the British army. Black soldiers were fighting on both sides by the autumn of 1794. But the British offer came too late, and Rigaud's revolutionary army gradually got the upper hand, finally recapturing Tiburón in December. The local British commander committed suicide in despair.

The rebel armies were not strong enough to force out the British until another four years had passed, but in 1798 their continuing resistance caused Britain to accept that their toe-hold in Haiti was too expensive to maintain.

In May 1798, the leader of Haiti's victorious black forces, Toussaint L'Ouverture, accepted the surrender of British forces at Port-au-Prince, forcing them to abandon the island. Among the terms of surrender, L'Ouverture stated that the thousands of black slaves recruited into the British army were to remain in free Haiti – they were not to be shipped away for resale elsewhere. General Thomas Maitland, the British commander, and later the commander in Ceylon, agreed immediately. He knew that the white planters on the sugar estates of the other Caribbean islands would have little desire to employ the black soldiers of Haiti.

On the final day of the British retreat, Toussaint entered Mole St Nicolas with an escort of officers – black, mulatto and white. Church bells rang, heavy guns were fired, and the British fleet greeted his arrival with salvoes and salutes. A special Te Deum was sung in the church, and General Maitland walked with Toussaint after the service to the Place des Armes, where a tent had been decorated with red velvet. A thousand British soldiers took part in a formal military display, and after a ceremonial banquet the senior British admiral presented the silver tableware to Toussaint in the name of King George III.

'Toussaint's triumph could not have been greater', notes the Haitian writer Stephen Alexis. 'The proudest nation on earth was honouring in him a whole race which had till recently dwelt in shameful degradation.'[9] The phenomenon of a senior British officer surrendering to a black general was not much mentioned at the time, nor has it been dwelt on much since.

CHAPTER 13

Slaves and 'Free Coloureds' in the French Islands of the Caribbean Resist Absorption in the Empire

Resistance to British attack or occupation took place in several islands in the Caribbean in the mid-1790s, with French-backed slave rebellions breaking out in Guadeloupe in 1794, in Grenada and St Vincent in March 1795, and in St Lucia in June. A fresh Maroon revolt began in Jamaica in July 1795. Under the pressures and demands of global war, social and military controls on the islands fell apart, providing an unprecedented opportunity for slaves, as well as Maroons and Caribs, to make a bid for freedom.

In April 1794, slaves and free coloureds gathered at the Fleur d'Épée fort on the French island of Guadeloupe to resist an attack by a British armada recently arrived in the Caribbean. Led by French officers, the slaves made up the bulk of the French Republican forces, now exhausted by the extended civil war between Royalists and Republicans that had taken place on the island since 1790. Successive slave rebellions had led many French settlers to abandon their plantations and seek shelter on British islands.

The British were no strangers to Guadeloupe. They had occupied it from 1759 to 1763, returning it to France at the Paris peace conference that year as a makeweight in the negotiations over the future of French Canada. In the 1790s the island had a population of some 115,000, of which nearly 90,000 were slaves and 3,000 were mulattoes (or freed men of colour). Only 14,000 inhabitants were white. Most of the white population were terrified by the Jacobins in their midst, fearful of their former slaves, and appreciative of a British occupation.

Guadeloupe is formed from two adjacent islands, Grand Terre and Basseterre. The black Republicans tried to defend the Fleur d'Épée fort at Pointe-à-Pitre on Grand Terre, but were overwhelmed by a British force that landed near the town in April 1794. The British commander, General Thomas Dundas – a veteran of the Yorktown defeat in 1781 – secured a swift victory and took no prisoners. Prolonged repression of the inhabitants followed this initial British massacre. The blacks resisted for ten days, but the British soon controlled most of both islands, though not for long.

Guadeloupe was the third French possession seized that year: Martinique had been captured in February, and St Lucia in April. These islands fell under nominal British control, although largely occupied by slaves, free mulattoes and

French Republicans who refused to accept this alien rule. As in Haiti, the British had insufficient soldiers to control the islands, and they looked for black allies. A 'Black Ranger' battalion of 250 slaves was recruited in 1794.[1]

French help for the resistance on Guadeloupe was soon at hand. A small Republican fleet was sent out that year – seven ships with 1,500 men – to recover the West Indian colonies. The troops were led by two fresh 'Commissioners', Pierre Chrétien and Victor Hugues, a wealthy mulatto who had once lived in Haiti. They brought the news that the Revolutionary Convention in Paris had declared an end to slavery in February: 'Today the English are dead', Danton had cried. The recipe for slave rebellion that had proved so effective in Haiti was to be extended throughout the French Caribbean.

The French fleet arrived off Grand Terre on 2 June, and the British occupation of Guadeloupe began to unravel. The ferocious General Dundas had died at his base on Basseterre, leaving his invasion force rudderless. Victor Hugues made an unopposed landing and ordered the new anti-slavery message to be announced publicly throughout the island. He offered equality, decreeing that blacks would be given the same privileges as whites. Many slaves flocked to join his revolutionary army, and on 6 June these makeshift troops recaptured the Fleur d'Épée fort, and took Point-à-Pitre the following day.

One fort, however, was not the whole island, and British reinforcements soon arrived at Basseterre from other islands. The black forces were heavily outnumbered, and Pierre Chrétien and two French generals were killed. Over the next three months the black slave army occupied Grand Terre to the north, while the British remained in control of Basseterre, restoring slavery and French Royalist institutions. The population was required to swear an oath of loyalty to George III, king of England. On Grand Terre, the Republican revolution proceeded apace – with the aid of a portable guillotine, a new gadget that Victor Hugues had thoughtfully brought from Paris.

Receiving French reinforcements in October, the black slave army moved across the straits to Basseterre, to lay siege to the British camp at Berville, commanded by Brigadier Colin Graham. Cut off from all outside assistance, the brigadier surrendered, but with one condition: he requested that his troops might be allowed to march out with the honours of war before being shipped home to Britain.[2] This was permitted, but Graham failed to secure pardons for the 700 French Royalists under his command; he was forced to watch while 300 of them were fed to the guillotine.

That December, the black army forced the British to withdraw from Basseterre and retreat to Martinique. Guadeloupe's inclusion within the Empire had lasted for barely eight months. Its loss proved to be the least of the troubles facing British officers in the Caribbean.[3] British troops suffered as well. The soldiers that had surrendered lingered as prisoners on Guadeloupe for a further year, though many died in the weeks after their surrender.[4] The real killer that year was yellow fever, though this was not a new experience for the British.[5] Napoleon's troops captured Guadeloupe in 1802,[6] and the British recovered it in 1810. They held it for another six years before finally returning it to France in 1816.

Rebellion erupted on Grenada in March 1795, led by Julien Fédon, a mulatto landowner from the French-speaking Catholic community. The island had been acquired by Britain from France in 1763, was seized back by France in 1779, and became British again four years later. Freeing the ninety-five slaves on his own plantation at Belleville, Fédon offered liberty to all slaves who would join his rebellion. His rebel army soon attracted thousands of supporters from neighbouring plantations. Seizing the towns of Goujave and Grenville, his soldiers spread through the central mountains and forests. They captured the anti-French governor, Ninian Home, a Protestant Scots planter, while he was out on a day's sailing with a group of forty friends. Fédon's men held them all as hostages, threatening their execution if British troops were to advance on their mountain hideouts.

With a fresh Anglo-French war in 1793, and with Home's appointment as governor, the situation of the French minority on the island had already begun to deteriorate. Catholics were excluded from government, church property was confiscated, and use of the French language was discouraged. Groups of French 'free coloureds' gathered at Fédon's plantation in 1794 to plan a rebellion. Many were well-off mulattoes, non-British and non-white, who had come to the island during the period of French ownership between 1779 and 1783. Their rebellion, as elsewhere in the Caribbean, was both a slave revolt and a French insurrection against British rule, assisted by Victor Hugues in Guadeloupe. Black slaves and the French inhabitants of the island of all classes and colours threw in their lot with the resistance. Like other rebels that year, Fédon raised the flag of the French Republic, fighting against the British with the slogan 'Liberté, Egalité, ou la Mort' – Liberty, Equality, or Death.[7]

A fighting force of 7,000 slaves armed with cutlasses assembled at Fédon's camp on Mount St Catherine, the island's highest peak; they were joined by 600 whites and coloureds with muskets. In April they were attacked by British troops brought from Barbados, but they repelled the attack with musket fire and took their revenge on their hostages. They cut the throat of Governor Home and of those captured with him.

More slaves joined in as the British retreated, and Fédon's army swelled to 10,000 men. The British position was desperate, for only 500 regular troops and 380 militiamen were based on the island. They had just lost Guadeloupe, their forces were over-extended in Haiti, and now Grenada appeared lost. They retained control of St George's, but the rest of the island was in rebel hands.

Fédon had promised slaves their freedom, and the British commander now did the same, offering an amnesty to rebel slaves in May and recruiting a corps of 'Black Rangers'. This new slave corps was deployed in the mountainous areas in Fédon's heartland, unfamiliar to white troops, and reinforcements were brought in from Martinique and Barbados, and from Spanish Trinidad. Fédon's army received French help from Guadeloupe and kept the British forces corralled in St George's, where they were soon being decimated by yellow fever. The rebels held most of the island for the rest of the year – a black republic under arms.

The tide began to turn against Fédon in 1796. Alarmed by endless reverses, the British dispatched a second armada to the West Indies, commanded by General Sir Ralph Abercromby. With 100 ships and 30,000 men, this was one of the largest expeditions ever sent across the Atlantic. Some 5,000 fresh troops came ashore on Grenada, landing near St Andrew's Bay in March 1796, bringing succour to the enfeebled British garrison at St George's.

Fédon's forces came under sustained attack, and two French ships bringing reinforcements from Guadeloupe were not sufficient to prevent defeat. Fédon's army was driven into the hills, from where he organised a war of guerrilla resistance south of the Grand Etang. No quarter was given, no prisoners taken, and when his hideout was eventually surrounded, Fédon ordered twenty white prisoners to be shot.

The British took their revenge. Lieutenant Thomas Hislop was the famously brutal new commander,[8] and when eighty whites who had fought with Fédon surrendered, fourteen were hanged. Fédon's surviving followers were hunted down, and Fédon himself was discovered in July in a hut on the brink of a precipice. He disappeared over the cliff and was heard of no more. Some said he was killed; others believed he escaped to Trinidad to fight another day. The year-long Grenada rebellion had been crushed.

In March 1795, in the month that Julien Fédon raised the Republican flag of rebellion in Grenada, Joseph Chatoyer, veteran leader of the Black Caribs of St Vincent, summoned his followers to join him in a fresh rebellion against British occupation. He called himself King Chatoyer, and he too received support from the French Republican forces of Victor Hugues in Guadeloupe, to whom he was known as 'Chateaugai'. The director of the botanic gardens in St Vincent described him as 'brave, desperate, and accustomed to warfare and bloodshed'.[9]

Chatoyer had fought a resistance war against the British twenty years earlier that ended with a treaty in 1773. Occupied subsequently by the French in 1779, St Vincent acquired a sizeable French population of small farmers. Chatoyer continued to be wary of the British when they recovered the island in 1783, conscious that the returning landowners would still nurse an ambition to seize Carib lands.

Grignion sculpt
CHATOYER the CHIEF of the BLACK CHARAIBES in St. VINCENT with his five WIVES.
Drawn from the life by Agostino Brunyas 1773. From an original painting in the possession of Sir Wm. Young Bart. F.R.S.

Chatoyer, the Chief of the Black Charaibes in St Vincent with his five wives. Drawn from the life by Augustino Brunyas in 1773.

From his camp on Dorsetshire Hill, above Kingstown, the island's capital, Chatoyer called on the French population to unite with the Black Caribs in the cause of liberty. Were they to refuse to do so, he added fiercely, they would be destroyed. His words were recorded in a British propaganda sheet: 'We do swear that both fire and sword shall be employed against them, that we are going to have their estates, and that we will murder their wives and children, in order to annihilate their race.' Since the lands of many small French farmers had been seized to create large British sugar plantations, the French needed little encouragement to join Chatoyer.

The Carib rebellion, according to the lurid account of Bryan Edwards, the Jamaican planter, was long and bloody: 'The windward plantations were set in flames, the unarmed slaves and defenceless women and children were slaughtered, and . . . several English prisoners . . . were massacred in cold blood, upon Dorsetshire Hill, four days subsequent to their capture. Had the insurgents been joined by the negroes, all would, doubtless, have been lost.'[10]

The weakness of the Carib rebellion was its failure to make common cause with slaves on the sugar plantations. Slaves were reluctant to support them, for a history of dislike and betrayal characterised their relationship. The Caribs failed to echo the French appeal for an end to slavery, and the British quickly turned to the slaves for help. Here as elsewhere, a slave battalion of 'Black Rangers' was recruited to fight the Caribs.

Carib hopes of victory were thwarted by British reinforcements from outside. A small British force was landed from HMS *Zebra* in April, and moved swiftly towards the Carib encampment on Dorsetshire Hill. Chatoyer himself was bayoneted by a Major Leith, and twenty of his immediate followers were killed. Yet their deaths were not immediately decisive, for Duvalle, a new Carib leader, emerged to continue the rebellion, launching an attack on the British base at Calliaqua. Forced back into their jungle retreats in May, after the British had burned their farms in the plains, the Caribs received French assistance from St Lucia and repelled a British attack in July.

Much of the island remained in the hands of the Caribs for another year, with the British marooned in their base at Fort Charlotte. When Carib forces seized a food convoy destined for British troops, it was the turn of the British to be starved out. 'There is talk of capitulation', a Colonel Myers wrote despondently to his commanding officer, 'the people being tired of the war and of lending their negroes for defence.' Myers noted 'a degree of apathy and indifference' that 'seems to have overtaken not only the troops but all the people in the island.'[11]

Carib resistance could only be broken with fresh troops, and in June 1796 some 4,000 British soldiers were landed at Kingstown. Carib positions at Vigie came under attack, and they fought back with considerable energy and skill, killing seventeen British officers. Among their new leaders was Marin Padre, a free black landowner described as 'a brave and daring man of great military parts', who had come with the French reinforcements from St Lucia. Perceiving eventually that his forces were outnumbered, Marin Padre negotiated an armistice. The 600 men under his direct command agreed to surrender and were granted all the honours of war, but hundreds of others rejected the surrender terms. Led by Maunpedos, Marin's brother-in-law, they escaped to the forest to stage a final show of resistance.

The surviving Caribs finally surrendered in November, and this time the surrender terms were harsh. The British insisted – as had been foreshadowed in 1772 and as Chatoyer had always feared – that the Black Caribs should be expelled from the island, prefiguring the eventual fate of the Maroons of Jamaica. More than 5,000 Caribs were transferred to the small offshore island of Balliceaux, a place with 'no springs or rivulets'. They took a serious illness with them, and nearly half of them died. Alexander Anderson, the director of the botanical gardens on St Vincent, surmised that many succumbed to diseases contracted 'during their miserable situation in the woods without shelter', but he feared there was 'another powerful cause – the agonising reflection that they were to be forever transported from their native country to another they never saw'.[12]

With no water at Balliceaux, the colonial authorities gave orders in April 1797 for the 2,700 survivors to be sent off to their final destination, the island of Roatán, Britain's prison colony off Honduras. Anderson reflected on their fate: 'Who can avoid melancholy sensations on a whole race of mankind transported forever from their native land, inhabited by them for many generations, and not conceive there has been something radically wrong in the principles of that government necessitated to that act?'

The Maroons of Jamaica were well aware of the embattled position of the British in the Caribbean in the 1790s, and in July 1795 they embarked on their own revolt, though they may well have been provoked. The island's plantation owners believed the situation to be too dangerous to permit the continued existence of free men whose loyalties to Britain were in doubt, and the new British military governor, General Alexander Lindsay, Earl of Balcarres, welcomed the opportunity to crush them.

Sixty years earlier, the Maroons had fought the British to a standstill, and a peace treaty in 1738 had given them rights over a substantial territory, with guarantees of freedom, independence and self-government. In return, the Maroons agreed to capture and surrender runaway slaves, to assist the British king against his enemies, and to allow two white officials to regulate disputes between white and black. Under the terms of this treaty they had been called out to help crush Tacky's slave revolt in 1760.

Ever since the slave rebellion in Haiti in August 1791, the authorities in Jamaica had perceived themselves to be in the frontline. A correspondent in Kingston that November had noted a change in the attitude of the slaves: 'I am convinced the ideas of liberty have sunk so deep in the minds of all Negroes that, whenever the greatest precautions are not taken, they will rise.' A slave revolt was indeed planned at Christmas, but was frustrated by the imposition of martial law and the mobilisation of the militia. Brutus, the slave leader on an estate in Trelawny, was captured before the rebellion could get underway, and five years later the slaves were still quiescent. The chief threat to British rule now came from the Maroons.

The rebellion of July 1795 was sparked off by an incident in Montego Bay.[13] Two Maroons accused of stealing pigs were flogged, at a time when the white official charged with resolving their disputes was absent and in the process of being replaced. A Maroon delegation that came down to the town to negotiate was detained and imprisoned on a ship in the harbour.

General Lindsay declared martial law, and the settler militia was again summoned to active service. Troops destined for Haiti were retained on the island, and the mountain passes leading to the Maroon settlements were closed. The Maroons retreated further into the hills, challenging the government to follow them.

Over the next eight months, more than 300 Maroons and 200 runaway slaves held out against an army of 1,500 British soldiers and several thousand militia. Maroon resistance was reinforced by the excesses of the militia, who burned the homes and gardens of Maroon villagers who had actually remained friendly to the whites.[14] General Lindsay tried to cordon off the Maroon lands, but after a month of war not a single Maroon had been wounded, while the British had lost more than seventy killed. Five officers were killed in an ambush in August, while the senior British officer in the field, Colonel Fitch, was killed in September, throwing 'a gloom over the entire island'.

British morale was low. Colonel George Walpole, the new commander, found the troops at the army's base camp 'very much dispirited by the recent misfortunes, jaded and fatigued to the greatest degree, badly hutted and ill-accommodated'. A plantation owner, Simon Taylor, wrote pessimistically to a cousin in London in September:

> This cursed Maroon war still continues, and I see little prospect of its ending . . . It is true the Maroons have had their town taken and burnt, the greatest part of their provisions destroyed, and have been forced to fly into almost inaccessible mountains and caves, but still they at times make sallies, destroy small settlements, pick off some of our people, but the article that is much dreaded is this: that of our slaves joining them, and I find some few have lately done so.

As in Dominica, the Maroons found it difficult to secure slave support. In October a Maroon leader tried to recruit the slaves on the Amity Hall estate, explaining that 'he did not mean to force them, but he was fighting to make all the Negroes free'.[15] His small group of Maroons burned down the plantation house and killed the bookkeeper, but they failed to persuade the slaves to join their resistance war. A generation later, during the great slave rebellion of 1831, the positions were reversed. The slaves asked the Maroons for help and were met with blank indifference.

The Maroons soon faced a new strategy devised by Colonel Walpole. Working in pairs, Walpole's soldiers moved slowly towards the Maroon stronghold, firing howitzer shells into their camps. This had some limited success, but the Maroons still held out. William Quarrell, a colonel in the militia, suggested a fresh tactic. He had once met a Spaniard from Cuba who told him of the success they had had in using dogs to crush a rebellion by Native Americans at Bluefields, on the Mosquito coast of Nicaragua. Thirty-six dogs and twelve Cuban handlers had expelled the Miskito Indians from the coastal zone.

The Jamaican planters were enchanted with this story, and Colonel Quarrell was ordered to Cuba to recruit some 'chasseurs' or dog-handlers. He returned in December with one hundred dogs, accompanied by forty-three Spanish-speaking black handlers. 'The savages have the utmost dread of a large dog', noted the governor, 'the Negroes the same.'[16] The arrival of the Cuban dogs was a turning point in the war. The plantation slaves fled as the dogs came by, and soon the Maroons in the mountains heard news of what was planned.

After two months of constant prodding by Walpole, together with the threat of unleashing the dogs, the Maroons came down from their secret refuge. Driven back by fear of the dogs and by Walpole's howitzers, their leaders gave in. In January 1796, they submitted to Walpole's humiliating surrender terms, which included three conditions: to go on their knees to beg the king's pardon for their rebellion; to settle wherever the governor might deem appropriate; and to surrender any runaway slaves in their midst.

The Maroons insisted on a fourth and secret condition to which Walpole promised to agree: they would not be banished from the island. But General Lindsay, the governor, was less generous than Walpole. His surrender terms were harsher. Runaway slaves and free blacks who had joined the Maroons were put on trial, and many were executed. Walpole's promise to the Maroons was ignored. The white settlers who owned the plantations were determined to free the island of the Maroon threat forever. They insisted on deportation, and got their way. So eager were they to rid Jamaica of the Maroons that they paid for their passage to Halifax, Nova Scotia.

In June 1796, some 600 Maroons and their families sailed away in three transport ships, accompanied by Colonel Quarrell. Several died on the six-week journey to Canada.[17] The original plan was for them to join the Canadian community of 'Black Loyalists' – the slaves who had supported the British during the American war and been given land in British Canada. Yet these former slaves, as has been recorded earlier, had not prospered in Canada, and many had sailed for Sierra Leone in 1792. The Jamaican Maroons, in cold and gloomy exile in Canada for four years, fared no better.[18]

Eventually, in 1800, 500 Maroons from Jamaica were shipped off from Canada across the Atlantic, to join the Black Loyalists on the Sierra Leone River. They were given land and settled down, but they retained a burning desire to return home. 'The Maroons universally harbour a desire of going back, at some period of their lives, to Jamaica', reported a House of Commons committee in 1802.

Colonel Walpole was embittered by Lindsay's refusal to support the surrender terms he had negotiated in 1796, and refused the sword of honour granted to him by the Jamaican assembly. He resigned from the army and returned to Britain. He was elected a member of parliament in the Whig interest, and spoke out against the slave trade. Years later, in 1827, some surviving Jamaican Maroons in Sierra Leone wrote to him to complain of their endless suffering 'in a most horrid condition'. The main problem, they wrote, was unemployment caused by European prejudice: 'in fact we all live begging'. They asked for Walpole's assistance to return to Jamaica, but Walpole could do nothing to help. He died in 1835.

In 1838, 200 exiled Maroons in Sierra Leone petitioned Queen Victoria with the same request, blaming their 'insurmountable hardships' on 'the great number of liberated Africans annually thrown upon this colony', the involuntary victims of Britain's campaign against the slave trade. Their jobs, their farms and their trade had all been overrun by these newcomers, and they begged to be allowed to return to Jamaica. In 1841 their prayers were answered. The emancipation of the slaves in the West Indies in the 1830s caused a great demand for labour, and Jamaican planters sent out recruiting agents all over the world. Some came to Freetown, and, after more than forty years, 200 Maroons were finally able to return to their Jamaican home.

In April 1796, rebel slaves and French settlers on St Lucia, led by a French Republican officer, Captain Lacroix, prepared to resist an assault on the island by British forces. They had controlled the island since June 1795, after defeating the British occupation force deployed by General Grey's armada, sent out in 1794. Now they were faced by fresh troops from the second armada, commanded by General Abercromby.

St Lucia was an island of considerable strategic significance – the first to be captured in war, and the first to be negotiated away at subsequent conferences of peace. Populated by black slaves and French settlers, it had been occupied by the British from time to time in the eighteenth century, the frequent change of ownership causing unrest in the slave population. The French had recovered St Lucia in 1784, under the terms of the Treaty of Paris, and two Republican agents had arrived in 1791 to expel the Royalist governor and to raise the tricolour flag. In December 1792, Captain Lacroix arrived in the Caribbean to spread the new revolutionary doctrines. Receiving little enthusiasm in Martinique and Dominica, he was greeted with sympathy and support in St Lucia, and became the island's Republican governor. St Lucia was renamed La Fidèle, and its new status was celebrated with much singing of the Marseillaise, the planting of trees of liberty, and the wearing of red caps and bonnets.

A landlord historian of the island, writing some fifty years later, recalled his impact:

> The incendiary pamphlets and proclamations which this crazy adventurer caused to be circulated throughout the island, contributed not a little to foster that unfortunate partiality for the doctrines of the new school, which had already but too strongly manifested itself. The work of the estates was discontinued, the plantations were deserted, and nothing prevailed but anarchy and terror, in the midst of which the Negroes under arms were discussing the 'rights of man'.[19]

In April 1794, the island was captured by British troops from General Grey's armada. The former slave population soon organised resistance to the new owners, retreating tactically to the inland labyrinth of wooded mountains that the British were unable to penetrate. Victor Hugues provided continuing French support from Guadeloupe, despatching troops with Commissioner Goyrand. The slaves controlled several small ports where they could land arms and supplies, threatening the British-held towns of Morne Fortuné and Castries.

The slave resistance prospered throughout 1794, but in April 1795 the British brought in more troops. A large force landed near Vieuxfort. With them came a corps of 400 'Black Rangers' recruited from the slave population of Barbados and trained by Captain Malcolm. The St Lucia resistance forces retreated to the woods, but secured a victory on the road to Soufrière, where the British lost nine officers in a week. Sickness made half the invasion force unfit for service, and desertion further thinned the ranks. The British withdrew in June, leaving the resistance forces in control.

In April 1796 the resistance was faced by General Abercromby's great armada, which arrived off St Lucia with 12,000 fresh troops. With such a weight of numbers on the British side, the resistance army of 2,000 black soldiers and a few hundred whites was doomed. They held out for a month at Morne Fortuné, inflicting casualties on the invading force, but in May they surrendered. The British lost thirty-nine officers and 520 men, killed, wounded or missing.

General Abercromby thought it was a barren conquest. 'The island except as a military post had ceased to be of any value; and there was every reason to suppose that the brigands still hiding in the jungle would give much trouble.' John Moore, a British brigadier, was left behind with 4,000 soldiers, and, as Abercromby had suspected, the resistance did not collapse. 'The blacks are to a man our enemy', one officer noted.

Regular military operations ceased on the surrender of Morne Fortuné, but the rest of the island remained unsubdued. Captain Lacroix reappeared as the commander of what became known as the 'French Army in the Woods', and his guerrilla forces attacked whenever Brigadier Moore tried to advance into the interior. One British regiment, once 915 men strong, lost 841 soldiers and twenty-two officers in a year's operations – through war and disease. Moore noted later that it had been his wish 'to have governed the colony with mildness, but I have been forced to adopt the most violent measures from the perverseness and bad composition of those I have had to deal with'. More than 300 rebels were slaughtered or hanged.[20]

Lacroix and his 'French Army in the Woods' eventually agreed to lay down their arms at the end of 1797. Having been free men for so long, his soldiers requested that they should not be returned to slavery. Colonel James Drummond, the new British commander, was happy to agree to almost anything, for his men were exhausted by the struggle and defeated by the climate.[21] Many of Lacroix's soldiers were later integrated into a black battalion, and, like the Maroons from Jamaica, were sent off to serve the British in the new African colony of Sierra Leone.

CHAPTER 14

Europe's Revolutionary Conflict Spreads to South Africa

Amid all their troubles elsewhere, the British were obliged to turn their attention in 1795 to a revolt in the distant Dutch enclave in southern Africa, following the rebellion in Holland in January that had overthrown William of Orange. The embryonic settler revolutionaries only controlled the inland districts of Graaff-Reinet and Swellendam, but their aim was to take over the entire colony and establish an independent Republic. Their leader, Adriaan van Jaarsveld, was the military commander of the eastern frontier region, a settler prominent in an earlier war in 1779 against the Xhosa, the frontier inhabitants referred to contemptuously by the settlers as Kaffirs.

This Dutch colony had been in the hands of the Dutch East India Company for more than a century, since 1652. A tiny band of settlers had established themselves in the hinterland of Cape Town and imported a large slave population to work for them. Many of these were Malay Muslims from the Dutch territories in Indonesia. The various African tribes that lived in the territory soon came under attack: the San, the indigenous African population on the northern border, known familiarly as Bushmen, and the Xhosa, or Kaffirs, to the east. The San began serious resistance, and more than 500 were killed by a Dutch force in 1774. The Xhosa faced similar punitive expeditions. A third tribal group in the territory – the Khoi-Khoi, or Hottentots – were used by the Dutch as cheap labour, as slaves and as mercenary soldiers. A 'Hottentot Regiment' raised in March 1795 was subsequently taken over by the British.

Van Jaarsveld and his friends at Graaff-Reinet had been inspired by the revolutionary events in Europe, and had a fleet from Republican France appeared off the coast, the settlers would have welcomed it. Yet it was a British fleet that arrived at Cape Town in June, just four months after their republic had been established. The British intention was to occupy the Dutch colonial enclave and to ensure, belatedly, that it did not fall into the hands of republican revolutionaries. Most of the local population, General James Craig, the British commander, observed with distaste, were 'infested with the rankest poison of Jacobinism'.

When his ships anchored off Cape Town, they found no sign of a French fleet. They had got there first. Craig had brought a letter from William of Orange, exiled in England, urging the Dutch governor at the Cape to treat the British as allies. Yet no one welcomed him ashore, for the settlers were politically divided. Those involved in administration were conservative and supported the British, while the settlers up-country were firmly on the side of the French and Dutch revolutions, interpreting them in their own special way. Many of them had joined a militia to resist foreign intervention.

After weeks of negotiation with the Dutch governor, Craig was allowed to land his force of 1,600 men. The soldiers came ashore at Simonstown in July, and camped on the track to Cape Town; the Dutch militia and the Hottentot Regiment fired on their camp from the surrounding hills. The British force was only able to move forward after sepoy reinforcements arrived in September from India – some 3,000 soldiers transported by a fleet of fourteen ships, in the first deployment of Britain's imperial army in India on the African continent. Faced with this overwhelming force, the Dutch governor formally surrendered.

Much of the European population of the colony remained suspicious and hostile; the Africans were indifferent. The only onshore allies of the British were a few traders and merchants. The Dutch settlers inclined to republicanism had been using the word 'citizen' as a comradely term of address, and they found it hard to take an oath of allegiance to King George III. Soon they received the traditional punishment inflicted by a British occupying force for such disrespect towards the British monarch: dragoons were billeted in their homes, and they were obliged to provide them with food.[1] This had happened in America in the 1760s and would often occur subsequently in Ireland.

The settler militia that had travelled down to Cape Town to challenge the British returned to their farms, declaring that they would not be bound by the surrender terms. Realising that here, as in the Caribbean, he would have a serious policing problem, the new British governor arranged for the sepoys to remain behind in the new colony to keep order.[2]

The Graaff-Reinet territory had survived as an independent Jacobin republic since February. Another year passed before, in February 1796, an official in the service of the new British government of the colony journeyed across country to their 'free' territory. He brought a British flag with him, and had it hauled up the flagpole of the courthouse. The republican settlers tore it down, still hoping that French or Dutch republicans would come to their aid. Yet no assistance ever got through to their isolated inland republic, and they were soon obliged to submit. The arrival of fresh forces from Britain and India, and the defeat in August of a Dutch armada sent to recover the colony, spelled an end to their ambitions for independence. Yet resistance continued in Graaff-Reinet; the settler submission was only temporary. They proclaimed their freedom from British rule again in 1798, sparking off an even more dangerous rebellion by the Xhosa and the Khoi-Khoi.

* * *

A triple rebellion faced the British in Cape Colony in January 1799 as the republican farmers at Graaff-Reinet embarked on a second revolt, a repeat of the Jacobin unrest of 1795 and a prelude to a period of chaos and fighting in the region. In May, a large party of Xhosa in the coastal area of the Zuurveld attacked a British patrol, killing sixteen soldiers with assegais. At the same time, the Khoi-Khoi who provided slave labour to the Dutch farmers, joined forces with the Xhosa to demand their independence.

This was 'Britain's first war against black men in Africa', according to Noël Mostert, the historian of the Xhosa nation, underlining the significance of the encounter.[3] It was the first of many campaigns the British would have to fight. This initial Xhosa resistance continued sporadically until after the Treaty of Amiens in 1802, when the British were obliged to return the colony to the Dutch.

The rebels had chosen a good moment, for the colonial authorities were ill-prepared. The global scares affecting the British Empire at the time – the Irish rebellion, a landing by Napoleon in Egypt, and the continuing resistance in Mysore of Tipu Sultan – had reduced the British garrison in South Africa to the bone. Three regiments had had to be sent urgently across the Indian Ocean to Madras, and supplies in Cape Town were decimated by a warehouse fire. Lord Macartney, the gout-ridden governor appointed in 1796, had recently retired to England.

The British had not been able to judge whether the Dutch settlers were friends or enemies. The farmers were needed to produce food for the garrison at the Cape; they were also needed as 'commandos' on the frontier, to fight off the marauding Xhosa. Yet they were always regarded with suspicion, perceived as not much different from the other 'savages' with which the colony was peopled. Henry Dundas, the British war minister, thought of the Dutch settlers as 'distant tribes' who might one day perhaps be civilised: 'Considering the extent of the country over which the latter are dispersed, the rude and uncultivated state in which they have hitherto lived, and the wild notions of independence that prevail among them, I am afraid that any attempt to introduce civilisation, and a strict administration of justice, will be slow.'

The Dutch rebellion was sparked off by the arrest of Adriaan Van Jaarsveld, still the settlers' leader at Graaff-Reinet. His rebels were soon faced by a force sent out from Cape Town led by Colonel Thomas Vandeleur, yet neither the British nor the Dutch imagined that this apparently minor squabble would spark off a far more serious African rebellion. But the Xhosa in the frontier zone now took advantage of the prevailing disorder to join with the Khoi-Khoi in attacking and looting the white farms. The principal Xhosa tribe living in the Zuurveld were the Gqunukhwebe, a people of mixed origin (having both Xhosa and Khoi-Khoi as ancestors). Occupying the land between the Fish and the Sunday rivers, they had been led since 1794 by Chief Chungwa, a man with 'a tall muscular figure' and a 'prepossessing countenance'.

The colony being short of British troops, Colonel Vandeleur had included a corps of Khoi-Khoi soldiers in the force he took to Graaff-Reinet. His decision ignited a wider fire, since other groups of Khoi-Khoi formed the principal workforce on the Dutch farms, where they worked in near-slave conditions. Many of them had left their employers to form irregular bands that lived off the cattle and produce of the settlers – a similar phenomenon to that of the Maroons in the Caribbean. 'The planters pursue them with great avidity', wrote Major Robert Percival, a traveller through the area at this time, 'and never spare any, except for slaves. At certain places are posts for the farmers to assemble with dogs, in order to hunt these unfortunate people; and whenever they are surprised by the Dutch, cruel massacre never fails to take place.'[4]

When the Khoi-Khoi farmworkers saw Khoi-Khoi soldiers in the company of British troops, they imagined that the British had come as their allies in the struggle they were having with the Dutch farmers. Klaas Stuurman, the local Khoi-Khoi leader, held a meeting with Colonel Vandeleur to tell him that his people were ready to rebel. They could no longer tolerate the 'calamities and sufferings' they had experienced 'under the yoke of the Boers', who had deprived them of their country. He requested British assistance in securing independence and freedom for the Khoi-Khoi.

Cut off from their sources of labour and their supplies of ammunition, the Dutch Republicans surrendered in April, and nineteen of their leaders were held in the castle dungeons at Cape Town with eighty other political prisoners. They were put on trial in August 1800, and Van Jaarsveld and Willem Prinsloo were condemned to death. Eight others were condemned to be struck over the head with the flat blade of a sword and banished for life. Particular attention was paid to Cornelis Edeman who, as a teacher, was condemned to be publicly flogged on the scaffold, and then banished. It was intolerable to the British authorities that a simple schoolmaster should be a republican, presumably inciting his pupils to rebellion. After the flogging, Edeman was shipped out to the Australian gulag in New South Wales. Van Jaarsveld and Prinsloo survived their death sentences, and were released from prison when Holland recovered the colony in 1803.

When Vandeleur defeated the Dutch settlers and deprived them of their ammunition supplies, Stuurman's Khoi-Khoi joined forces with Chungwa's Xhosa to organise a rebellion of their own. In May they attacked a British patrol led by Lieutenant John Champney. The attack arose out of an incident provoked by Vandeleur, who had warned Chungwa to withdraw from the Zuurveld, underlining his message with 'two or three rounds of grape'.

For the Xhosa, the moment was too good to miss. The large number of warriors that they could field, coupled with Khoi-Khoi familiarity with European weapons and settler properties, led to widespread devastation. Vandeleur wisely concluded that it would be a mistake 'to wage an unequal contest with savages in the midst of impenetrable thickets', and he pulled his troops back from the frontier to Algoa Bay, returning from there to Cape Town by sea.

John Shipp, a fourteen-year-old private soldier, recorded his impressions of the Xhosa resistance:

> The Caffres are most certainly a formidable enemy. They are . . . such expert marksmen with their darts that they can be certain of their aim at sixty, or seventy, paces distance . . . They live in the woods and, when pressed, retire to hidden and almost inaccessible places, so that offensive warfare against them is inconceivably difficult.[5]

Dutch farms were burned and stock destroyed far to the west of the established frontier. Some of the white families, forced to abandon their farms, found themselves living permanently in their wagons. Shipp described the impact of the rebellion on the settler lands through which the retreating British passed: 'Beautiful homesteads, still smoking from the fire that had destroyed them, lay deserted by their owners, who were either killed or fled to safety . . .'.

In August, General Francis Dundas, governor at the Cape, decided that a fresh effort should be made to recover the frontier zone from the Africans. He was reminded, he wrote as he set out to the east with 800 soldiers, of 'the unfortunate events at Santo Domingo'. The previous September in Haiti, Toussaint L'Ouverture had escorted General Maitland to his ship. Was this also to be the fate of the British in South Africa – to be defeated at the hands of a black ruler, and driven into the sea?

On arriving at the Zuurveld, Dundas realised that the Africans could not be defeated in a war; it would expose 'the whole country to ruin'. The pursuit of peace was the only possible strategy. Vandeleur was not pleased, arguing that 'every advance on our part towards reconciliation will be construed into timidity, and nothing but a sound drubbing will bring these savages to any reason'.

Dundas won the argument, and Honoratus Maynier, an old frontier hand, was sent out to secure peace terms from both Stuurman of the Khoi-Khoi and Chungwa of the Xhosa.[6] The British government agreed to protect the Khoi-Khoi 'against the ill-treatment of the Boers', and to ensure that those who returned to work for them would be 'well paid and well treated'. Klaas Stuurman and his immediate followers, whose 'individual safety would be endangered' by going back to work, were granted land on which they might settle.

Chungwa did rather better out of the negotiations, securing the right for his people to remain in the Zuurveld. Dundas announced in October that hostilities were now at an end, although there was little peace on the frontier until the British withdrew from South Africa in 1803. Peace with the Khoi-Khoi did not come until after the return of a Dutch government that year, when Stuurman again agreed that his supporters would stop fighting in exchange for a portion of territory they could call their own. They were given land on the Gamtoos River, close to Algoa Bay, but Stuurman did not live to appreciate it. He was killed in a hunting accident, and leadership of the embryonic Khoi-Khoi colony devolved to his brother David.

The British returned to the Cape in 1806, and in 1809 they schemed to crush David Stuurman's Khoi-Khoi settlement on the Gamtoos River and to send his people back to work for the settlers. Stuurman was lured to a friendly house, arrested and taken to Cape Town. Given a life sentence, he was sent to the prison on Robben Island, to work there in chains. He escaped, but after his recapture in 1816 he was kept in solitary confinement until 1823, when he was despatched to the Australian gulag. He died there in 1830.

The treatment of Chungwa was yet more harsh. In January 1812, when ill and dying, he was killed by a British force while sleeping, shot down in cold blood during a renewed British effort to exterminate the African inhabitants of the Zuurveld.

CHAPTER 15

The Dutch Empire in Ceylon

The Sinhalese peasants of Ceylon organised a formidable revolt in June 1797, during the first full year of British rule. The rebellion led by Sinno Appu took place in the coastal area close to Colombo, but it also received support from Kandy, in the highlands. It was caused by the deployment of eager tax-gatherers from India, sent out to extract payment from the peasants for the costs of the conquest. The colonial authorities indicated their true purpose too crudely: to raise money from subject peoples to pay for the troops that kept them in subjection.

Sinno Appu established himself at Sitavaka, inland from Colombo, but when the British attacked he took refuge in the jungle. His rebel forces adopted guerrilla tactics, as they had done during the period of Dutch rule. The character of the country, with large areas of dense jungle broken only by scattered villages and rough paths, placed regular troops at a disadvantage. Refusing to be drawn into pitched battles, his guerrillas made unexpected attacks on the forces sent out against them.

Captain Robert Percival, a British officer who travelled to Kandy in 1800, took the measure of one of the rebel forts at Cudavilli, east of Colombo: 'This entrenchment, if held by an enemy possessed of any degree of military skill, could not be forced without considerable difficulty . . . We had several sepoys killed and wounded here at different times before the rebellious Sinhalese could be subdued.'[1] An isolated British fort in rebel territory, at Gurrawaddi, was occupied for months by sepoys from Madras, who 'lost many of their men from the fire of the rebels who concealed themselves in the neighbouring thickets'.

Percival and General Welbore Doyle, the British commander-in-chief, were well aware that tax collection lay at the heart of the revolt. 'Revenue can only be collected at the point of a bayonet,' wrote Doyle, and the 'rapacious dispositions' of the tax-gatherers 'are perpetually urged forward by the precariousness of their tenure.'[2] Percival reported further resistance to the collection of taxes at the garrison of Manaar: 'This cannot always be done without compulsion, and the exaction has even sometimes been resisted. In June 1800, a body of natives . . . assembled before the fort in a tumultuous manner, and seemed determined not to submit to the exaction.'

Sinno Appu withdrew to Kandy in 1798 and disappeared from the scene, but the coastal revolt spluttered on for several years before the British were engulfed in a wider catastrophe. Seeking to enlarge their control of the island in 1803 by invading Kandy, they were to be dramatically rebuffed.

In February 1803, Wickrama Sinha, youthful ruler of Ceylon's mountainous inland kingdom of Kandy, staged a successful resistance to a British attack, destroying one quarter of the island's British garrison. The ambition of the new governor, Frederick North, had been to capture the unconquered centre of the island, and to turn Kandy into a protectorate, on the model of 'protected' states established in India.[3] Some 3,000 soldiers were sent out in two columns to advance into the hills, from Colombo in the west and from Trincomalee in the east.

Wickrama Sinha planned a subtle form of resistance, for he knew that British unfamiliarity with the terrain, combined with inclement weather conditions later in the year, would take its toll on unseasoned troops. He could afford to play a waiting game, since supplies for the occupying army would run short once the rainy season had started. He withdrew from Kandy to the town of Hanguranketa.

Arriving in the royal capital, the British behaved in the arrogant fashion to which they had become accustomed in India, choosing a member from the Kandyan nobility, Muttusamy, to be the new ruler. Required to do what was expected of him, Muttusamy agreed to pay the costs of the British garrison, surrendered the kingdom's cinnamon monopoly, and signed away the coastal province of the Seven Korales.

British triumphalism did not last long. A detachment sent out to Hanguranketa to capture Wickrama was ambushed. It sustained heavy casualties, and the survivors retreated to the coast. Wickrama's men now laid siege to Kandy, and what remained of the British garrison – made up of 300 European soldiers, 700 Malays and a handful of Indian gunners. Kandyan guerrillas ambushed convoys bringing supplies from the coast, and the physical condition of the garrison deteriorated, with many soldiers affected by hunger and fever. Most Europeans were unfit for duty, and the commanding officer died in May.[4]

Wickrama attacked in June, and the British surrendered. They were promised safe passage down to the coast at Trincomalee, and allowed to take their pretender, Muttusamy, with them. Wickrama's forces kept the retreating band under constant surveillance, and at one stage, when the British sought to cross a wide river, the Kandyans said they would only supply ferry boats if Muttusamy was surrendered. When Major Davie, the British commander, handed him over, he was promptly beheaded. Davie was spared, but he remained a prisoner in Kandy for nine years, regularly sending out bleak messages appealing for rescue until his death in 1812.

Wickrama and the Kandyans followed up their successful rout of the British in the mountains by pushing down into the maritime provinces, advancing to within twenty miles of Colombo. Governor North requested reinforcements from India, and only the arrival of 800 sepoys from Madras was sufficient to turn back the Kandyan tide. The Kandyans fought a border war along the frontiers of the British-controlled provinces over the next two years, confronting small detachments that North had authorised to make terror raids into Kandyan territory. People were forced from their homes and their crops destroyed, actions that further united the Kandyans against the British occupation.[5]

North blamed his defeat on the poor performance of his Malay and sepoy regiments, and he told London that he could reconquer Kandy with better troops. He asked for 4,000 soldiers to be sent from the black regiments operating in the Caribbean. The request was considered, but they could not easily be made available because of fresh commitments in the Caribbean as a result of the renewed conflict with Napoleon. Several units had already been disbanded under pressure from white landowners.

North requested permission to purchase African slaves for his army from the slave market in the Portuguese territory of Goa. This he was allowed to do, and the British ambassador in Goa sent a preliminary batch of 170 slave soldiers down to Colombo in November.[6] Further supplies dried up after Catholic priests in Goa protested at their flock being sold to Protestants. North began buying slaves directly from Mozambique, and these arrived in regular batches over the next few years.[7] The British had one entirely black regiment in 1810.[8] When Wickrama Sinha confronted a second invasion, in 1815, the British forces were larger and better prepared.

CHAPTER 16

The Great Irish Rebellion of 1798

The revolutionary French bacillus of 1789 had spread rapidly to Ireland. In July 1791, citizens of Belfast had celebrated the anniversary of the fall of the Bastille with a triumphal procession, and the execution of the French king in January 1793 caused many urban Irishmen to embrace the republican cause, cutting their hair short in the manner of the Jacobins and receiving the name of 'croppies'. The new revolutionary mood gave birth to a new independence movement, the Society of United Irishmen, established in Belfast in October 1791 and inspired by the ideals of the French Revolution and the ambitions of the rebellious settlers in North America. Wolfe Tone, a Protestant from Dublin, was the principal leader of a disparate coalition of Catholic priests and Ulster Dissenters that linked Catholic peasants to sections of the Protestant middle class.

The Society began by advocating parliamentary reform and ended up demanding independence from Britain. Wolfe Tone made an historic appeal to the Irish 'to break the connection with England . . . the never-failing source of all our political evils'. Recruiting both Catholics and Protestants, in town and country, small groups began to arm themselves to 'break the connection', and to overthrow British rule.[1] The aim of the rebels was independence, to be achieved through an insurrection that would receive military assistance from revolutionary France. The pattern established in the islands of the Caribbean was to be tried out in Britain's island next door.

The United Irishmen were not alone. The Catholic peasantry were already organised within the framework of their existing secret societies. The most powerful of these by the 1790s were the 'Defenders', an armed Catholic defence organisation formed in the 1780s that drew on the experience and the membership of the Whiteboys, the earlier resistance movement that had emerged in 1761. They were to coalesce imperceptibly after 1794 with the radicalised United Irishmen.

William Lecky, the nineteenth-century historian, was among the first to perceive the crucial importance of the Defenders. 'It appears to have been mainly through this channel that the great mass of the poorer Roman Catholics passed into the ranks of disaffection. It was ultimately connected with, and absorbed in, the United Irish movement, and it formed one of the chief Catholic elements in the rebellion of 1798.'[2] Roy Foster, a more recent historian, has described the steady growth of the Defenders along the Cavan–Monaghan border in the years since 1792. The burden of taxation and the exaction of tithes were among their chief concerns.[3]

> The disturbances spread out to east and west, and it became evident that this rural movement was based on a more coherent and threatening ideology than earlier agitations. It involved some claims for land redistribution as well as historical memories of the Stuart cause; archaic and conservative elements were mingled with a new subversiveness. The ideas and oaths of the Defenders were transmitted by the highly mobile rural workforce, and some rural schoolmasters were involved in the mid-1790s.

The Defenders were more than a simple movement of peasants. Created as a counterweight to a new Protestant militia, the 'Peep O'Day Boys', they soon controlled a large expanse of South Armagh and could assemble on signals given by whistle 'almost in an instant'. As 'Defenderism' developed, it became overtly anti-Protestant and anti-British, organising acts of spectacular violence.[4] Strong in towns and other centres of rural industry, the Defenders were sufficiently well organised to send arms-buying delegations to London.

An incident late in 1789 attracted considerable attention, and also marked them out for repression. The Defenders had been summoned by a group of Catholic squatters on an estate at Forkhill, near Dundalk, to prevent British Protestant settlers from making further inroads into what they perceived as their land. The conflict had arisen as the result of a large bequest from a wealthy Protestant landlord of settler origin called Richard Jackson. Owner of the Forkhill estate, Jackson had died in 1787, bequeathing his fortune to be spent on the education, at 'Jackson's School', of the Protestant children of the locality. They were to be trained as weavers, provided with looms, and then, at the age of twenty-five, settled on smallholdings on the estate. None of the existing Catholic tenants, it was claimed, would be displaced by this development, for only parkland and wasteland would be colonised by the industrious Protestants.

In practice, of course, this was not so. Much of Jackson's estate was already occupied by Catholic squatters, and the fulfilment of his legacy would certainly have involved their displacement. The Protestant rector of Forkhill, the Reverend Edward Hudson, was a trustee of Jackson's charitable bequest, and he wrote to an Irish politician, Lord Charlemont, in December 1789 to explain the background to what had occurred:

> This estate was for 35 years possessed by the most indolent man on earth. He kept more than half of it waste during that time, on which they [the squatters] in fact subsisted. The idea of its being let, set them mad. A report has been industriously spread, that several of the old tenants had been dispossessed.

According to the Reverend Hudson, no one had actually been deprived of any land, and this may indeed have been the case; but the Catholic peasants were simply not prepared to believe it, and they 'assembled the Defenders from all parts of the country' and drove out the Protestant settlers by force.

In recounting this tale of the Defender revolt, the nineteenth-century historian, William Lecky, himself a descendant of a Scots family that had settled in Ireland in the seventeenth century, was not immune from the bigotry of his own time. He described the Dundalk Irish of the late eighteenth century in words usually used by the British of his own time to refer to the inhabitants of Africa. The object of the Protestants, he wrote, 'was to plant a nucleus of industry and order in the midst of a savage, bigoted, idle, and entirely lawless population, who seem to have been allowed for many years to live and to multiply, without any kind of interference, guidance, or control'.[5]

The Reverend Hudson had gone further, explaining to Lord Charlemont how he wished to force the natives to be free. His sole concern, he wrote, was to introduce some small-scale economic activity into the district. 'I hope', he went on, 'to make our savages happy against their will, by establishing trade and industry among them', adding, with considerable distaste, that 'many traces of savage life' could still be detected in the population.[6] Hudson especially deplored their tendency towards inbreeding. 'The same laziness and improvidence, the same unrelenting ferocity in their combats, the same love of intoxication, the same hereditary animosities, [are] handed down from generation to generation. Add to this . . . that there are not at this moment ten families in the parish which are not related to every other in it . . .'

According to Hudson, the fierce conflict between the two groups 'struck such horror that none of those Protestants but half a dozen ever appeared here afterwards'.[7]

After this event, a detachment of British soldiers was sent to keep the peace on the Forkhill estate, and the Reverend Hudson arranged for some primary education to be provided for Catholic children. This soon became a further cause of controversy. A schoolteacher employed to teach Catholic prayers in the Irish language was soon dismissed and replaced by a new one – a prominent member of the Protestant colony, who refused to teach 'anything but Protestant prayers'. A group of Defenders broke into his house in January 1791, and cut out his tongue and that of his wife. Only one of those involved was captured and tried, and he refused to give evidence against his fellow Defenders. He went to the gallows attended by a priest, maintaining 'all the demeanour of a martyr'.

The colonial authorities now sought to crush the Defenders, as they had earlier destroyed the Whiteboys. Those under suspicion of being Defenders were sent off to join the navy during the imperial wars of the 1790s. General Henry Luttrell was charged with the 'pacification' of Connaught in 1795, and the magistrates under his direction, according to Lecky's account, 'took a great number of those whom they suspected of being Defenders, and without sentence, without trial, without even a colour of legality, they sent them to serve in the King's fleet – a tender sailing along the coast to receive them'. More than a thousand peasants were deported in this way.[8]

Alarmed by the possibility of joint action by Catholics and Protestants, the British authorities encouraged and exploited their divisions. Out of a particular local conflict in September 1795 in County Armagh, in which the Catholic Defenders were defeated by the Protestant Peep O'Day Boys, the Protestants formed an organisation calling itself the Orange Order: an armed group designed to preserve the privileges of the Protestant settler community, and to expel peasants from land purchased by Protestants. The creation of the Orange Order made a successful Protestant–Catholic uprising against British rule increasingly difficult.

The United Irishmen envisaged that their rebellion would be supported by an invasion from France, at war with Britain since 1793. French assistance was thought essential for victory. When Wolfe Tone sought to bolster his arguments to the French in February 1796, in seeking their military intervention, he claimed that the Defenders 'embraced the whole peasantry', or three-quarters of the nation. The French were impressed with his arguments, and in December 1796 a French army of 14,000 men arrived off the Irish coast, with Wolfe Tone on board. The weather was against them, and the French armada was scattered in the Channel mists. The revolution had to be postponed.

Alarmed by the threat of an invasion only narrowly averted, the British sent reinforcements to the north of Ireland early in 1797, where the United Irishmen were thought to be at their most powerful. General Gerard Lake, the new commander, was ordered to 'disarm' Ulster, and his task was to secure the surrender of the guns and pikes the peasants had stored away. 'Nothing but terror will keep them in order', Lake wrote.

Lake's name became a byword for repression, not just in Ireland but also in India (where he became commander-in-chief in 1800). In April he appealed to the civilian authorities in Ireland to make his task easier by introducing martial law:

> I think if they once knew military law was proclaimed, and that one or two of their large towns were threatened to be burnt unless arms of every kind were produced, it would have a very great effect; and if they did not bring in their arms, it would be advisable for the houses of some of the most disaffected to be set on fire. You may think me too violent, but I am convinced it will be mercy in the end.[9]

General Lake had few troops of his own, and left much of the work to a local yeomanry of Protestant settlers. Already fearful of the Defenders, they unleashed their hatred on the Catholics. Grim and cruel deeds were done in Ulster during the watch of General Lake.[10] Later that year, in November, General Francis Hastings, an Irish politician, noted that if the outrageous practice of house-burning was not quickly stopped, 'all hope would be lost of seeing Ireland connected five years longer with the British Empire'.[11]

In July 1797 the French had a second invasion fleet ready, with Wolfe Tone again on board. This time it was an armada of Dutch ships, but the result was the same. The winds were contrary, and the ships stayed in harbour. After waiting for six weeks, the invasion was again called off.

Still concerned by the Irish threat, the British arrested the leaders of the United Irishmen in March 1798. Martial law and a night-time curfew were proclaimed throughout the island, and soldiers and the yeomanry were ordered out to disarm the population. The cruelties of the Ulster disarmament, decreed by Lake in 1797, were repeated in the south, with floggings, house-burnings and indiscriminate shootings.

The scale of the repression led to a small-scale political victory for the rebels. In November 1797, General Sir Ralph Abercromby took up his appointment as commander-in-chief after returning from the West Indies, and he objected to the methods being used to cow the population. He published a famous order in February 1798 that referred to 'the very disgraceful frequency of courts-martial, and the many complaints of irregularities in the conduct of the troops of this kingdom'. These had 'unfortunately proved the army to be in a state of licentiousness which must render it formidable to everyone but the enemy'.

Abercromby's humanitarian concerns were rejected by the colonial authorities in Dublin, and he was forced to resign. It was a measure of the seriousness of the situation that General Charles Cornwallis – an elderly and experienced soldier-statesman, victor over Tipu Sultan in India in 1792 – was sent out to replace him.[12] Abercromby's resignation could hardly be construed as a victory for the rebels, for his departure led to a tightening of the existing screw of military violence. While Ireland awaited the arrival of Cornwallis, the acting commander was General Lake. The racist nature of the repression, arising from the great distance perceived between the ferocious indigenous 'savage' and the apparently benign advocates of trade and industry, would become the pattern for the Empire as it established itself on more solid foundations.

On 23 May 1798, unwilling to wait for assistance from France or Holland, those leaders of the United Irishmen not in prison gave orders for a general insurrection, spearheaded from Dublin. Swelled by the insurrectionary movement of the Defenders, the United Irishmen rebelled in several counties, and attacks were made on military garrisons in Kildare and Meath.[13] General Lake claimed he had 'full powers to put down the rebellion, and to punish rebels in the most summary manner, according to martial law', and his repression was effective. In most parts of the country, the rebellion fizzled out. William Lecky claims there were essentially two rebellions in 1798, at first distinct:

> One was purely political, and was directed by educated men, influenced by political theories and aiming at political ends. The other was a popular movement which speedily became agrarian, and was to a great extent directed against the owners of property. These two movements at last combined, and the result was the most bloody rebellion in modern Irish history.[14]

The fates were against the rebels from the start. Their principal urban leaders, infiltrated by British spies, were arrested before the rebellion began. Wolfe Tone was absent in France, still trying to secure French support. Resistance in the countryside was rapidly crushed in most regions, and the rebellion in Dublin was snuffed out almost at once. Only in County Wexford and County Wicklow, and briefly in County Down, were the rebels able to survive for more than a few days.

In Wexford, an important centre of the Defenders, hostility to the settlement of Protestant colonists was still strong.[15] One prominent Wexford leader, Father John Murphy, who had studied in Seville, captured the town of Enniscorthy on 28 May with a small group of men. They established themselves on Vinegar Hill outside the town, some eighty miles south of Dublin, and erected a Liberty Tree and drank toasts to the establishment of the Republic. Some 20,000 peasants joined the rebels, defending the hill for three weeks and dealing out summary justice against their opponents.[16]

The rebel success was short-lived. British troops were poured in from England, and yeomanry were rushed down from Ulster. The rebels abandoned the hill to Lake's troops on 21 June, and savage repression followed.[17] Reporting laconically on his inability to control his army, Lake wrote that 'the troops behave excessively well in action, but their determination to destroy everyone they think a rebel is beyond description, and wants much correction'.

The great Irish rebellion was effectively at an end.[18] Not until August did the awaited French invasion finally arrive, landing in County Mayo. The invading soldiers were quickly rounded up and sent home. A second French fleet, with Wolfe Tone on board, was intercepted by the British before it reached the coast, and Tone was captured and taken to prison in Dublin. In November, he cut his throat.

During three months of rebellion in Ireland, more than 30,000 people were killed. The government admitted to no more than eighty-one executions during the period of martial law. A further 418 were transported to Australia by sentence of court martial, and 'great numbers' as a result of sentence by the assize courts. General Cornwallis wrote from Dublin in July that 'the conversation even at my table . . . always turns on hanging, shooting, burning, etc., etc., and if a priest has been put to death, the greatest joy is expressed by the whole company'.

George Cruikshank
Rebels destroying a house and furniture.

'Rebels Destroying a House and Furniture during the Irish Rebellion of 1798', by George Cruikshank, 1845.

After Leinster had been subdued, one rebel leader, Joseph Holt, continued the struggle in the hills of Wicklow.[19] He is remembered by Lecky as a skilled and courageous leader, 'perhaps the most skilful who appeared in Ireland during the rebellion'. Uninterested in the politics of the rebellion, Holt claimed that, as a Protestant, he would have preferred to have been on the other side. He was a rebel because his house had been burned down and he was obliged to take to the hills. Once there he was found to have martial talents of a high order.

He surrendered at the end of the year and was transported to Australia, where he was a witness of the 'Battle of Colonial Vinegar Hill', outside Sydney in 1804. Travelling by coach in January 1799 from Dublin to Cork, on the first leg of his journey to New South Wales, Holt recorded a conversation with two troopers who travelled with him as guards. Their remarks point to the existence, always latent in colonial history but rarely brought out into the open, of a belief that action in one country might lead to the implosion of the whole system at its heart. The troopers 'spoke of the Insurrection, and declared themselves to favour it, which I was not disposed to doubt, having had so many desertions from the army of both English and Irish soldiers'.[20] They said that if they had 'been aware of what they would have had to do in Ireland, damn them, but they would have deserted sooner than have come over'. They complained that 'the leaders of the Insurrection were too precipitate, and commenced their operations before they had things ready', and believed that the Irish 'should have waited for assistance from England and Scotland, where people were really ready to support them, by making a disturbance in those countries, thus taking away the attention of the Government from Ireland'.

A postscript to the rebellion took place five years later, on 23 July 1803, when Robert Emmett organised a revolt in Dublin. He was hanged and beheaded, uttering his famous last words on the scaffold: 'When my country takes her place among the nations of the earth, then, and not till then, let my epitaph be written.'[21]

CHAPTER 17

Tipu Sultan and the Final Resistance of Indian Forces in Mysore

The chief obstacle in the way of British imperial expansion in India was Tipu Sultan, the combative ruler who occupied the southern gateway to the heart of the continent. He had been humbled by General Cornwallis in 1792, and now a new and more imperious governor-general had arrived, determined to destroy a ruler perceived to be too friendly to French interests and to the ideals of the French Revolution. 'Citizen' Tipu had to be overthrown.

Richard Wellesley, Lord Mornington, had become the new ruler of British India in 1797. He was also a man schooled in Ireland, and a civilian politician determined to end the years of pacific manipulation which had sometimes characterised British policy in India. Years later, in 1821, he was to return to Ireland as lord-lieutenant, with a mission to crush the rural resistance that continued after the suppression of the rebellion of 1798. With Wellesley was his younger brother, Colonel Arthur Wellesley, later famous as the Duke of Wellington.

Richard Wellesley ordered his officers in 1798 to prepare their armies to destroy Tipu, and secured support for this task from the Nizam of Hyderabad and his substantial army. Seringapatam came under attack in February 1799 from an army of 4,000 European soldiers and 16,000 sepoys, led by General George Harris, the British commander-in-chief. Yet another veteran of the American wars, Harris had fought in the campaigns against Tipu earlier in the decade. After a preliminary bombardment, a truce was ordered to discuss peace terms.

The terms laid before Tipu by General Harris were infinitely more onerous than those dictated by Cornwallis in 1792, and were clearly intended to be rejected. Tipu was required to give up half of his remaining kingdom, pay an immense fine, and send four of his sons and four of his generals to be kept as hostages by the British. Tipu refused to accept.

Battle was renewed, and the final bombardment of the fortress began on 4 May. Tipu himself died in the battle. In the scrum, as the British troops poured into the city, an attendant saved himself by creeping beneath Tipu's palanquin. He crawled out, faint and wounded, 'to show where his dead master lay. Corpse after corpse was lifted and passed out for examination under the ghastly torchlight until at last the body was found of a man . . . which the attendants recognised to be that of Tipu Sultan.'

Tipu was buried beside his father, Haidar Ali Khan, with ceremonial salutes and an escort of the British Grenadiers. A thunderstorm of unusual violence burst over Seringapatam that day, killing two officers of the Bombay army. The dynasty of Haidar Ali had come to an end, and the troops broke loose that night to pillage and plunder.[1]

Command of the city was secured the following morning by Colonel Arthur Wellesley. 'By the greatest exertion', he wrote in a letter to his mother, 'by hanging, flogging, etc, I restored order among the troops.' Tipu's possessions were sold at an improvised auction and the army eventually received a million pounds in treasure and jewels as prize money; the gilded tiger's head from the Sultan's throne was sent to the British monarch at Windsor Castle. One bizarre item, discovered in Tipu's 'music room', was a 'musical tyger'. This was, a London paper recorded,

> A most curious piece of mechanism, as large as life, representing a royal tyger in the act of devouring a prostrate European officer . . . There are some barrels in imitation of an organ within the body of the tyger, and a row of keys of natural notes. The sounds produced by the organ are intended to resemble the cries of a person in distress, intermixed with the horrid roar of the tyger. The machinery is so contrived that while the organ is playing, the hand of the European is often lifted up to express the agony of his helpless and deplorable condition.[2]

The British claimed that the mechanical tiger attacking the officer was proof of Tipu's 'deep hate and extreme loathing' towards them.[3] Certainly Tipu had good reason for such a view, shared by many of those who disliked the British presence in India. It was said that he had commissioned the piece and designed it himself, and gazed at it every afternoon.[4] The tiger was taken to London and displayed in the East India Company's museum. Eventually, later in the century, it found sanctuary in the Victoria and Albert Museum.

The British capture of the tiger symbolised the crushing of Tipu's Muslim dynasty in Mysore. This meant more than the mere division of his territory; it was a first step towards the establishment of British authority in southern India. Mysore was soon to be used by the British as a springboard for moving into the territories of the Marathas to the north.

In June 1800, Doondia Wao, known as 'King of the Two Worlds', watched as British soldiers advanced on his fortress at Bednore, in the north of Mysore. Doondia Wao appears in the annals of the British conquerors as a 'brigand', and is little more than a footnote in the career of Britain's Duke of Wellington, then still Colonel Wellesley. The campaign against him was to forge Wellington's formidable reputation as a soldier, but the greatest British soldier of his age did not have everything his own way. Doondia Wao outwitted him for several months.

Formerly a soldier in the Mysore army of Haidar Ali, Doondia had become an independent rebel leader. 'His extraordinary resourcefulness, boldness, and address', noted one contemporary, had been found 'highly useful by those he served.' Deserting from Tipu's service in the early 1790s, during Cornwallis's campaigns in Mysore, Doondia created his own rebel band, operating from a base in the district of Darwar. He was recaptured by Tipu's soldiers and detained at Seringapatam. There, as was the custom with Tipu's captives, he was converted to Islam. Escaping from prison during the great storm on the day of Tipu's funeral, he was joined by other veterans of Tipu's army, and established himself as the ruler of Bednore. As such, he was a clear threat to the hegemony of the new British rulers.

Great confusion and disorder in Mysore followed in the wake of Tipu's death. No Indian ruler had illusions about what lay ahead. The British were in an expansionist mood. Indian princes had to decide whether to accept the bribes the British offered to join their camp, or to resist. Many rulers paused before making a final decision, leaving small armies of leaderless men to roam through the territories of southern India that the British had nominally acquired. If a suitable leader emerged, either British or Indian, such men could be formed into a formidable resistance force. It was a time when 'any man possessed of a bold heart and a discerning brain might hope to carve out a kingdom for himself', wrote Colonel John Biddulph a century later.[5] Britain's Wellington was just such a man, yet so was Doondia. Aged about sixty in 1800, Doondia was a competent and popular guerrilla commander. A chief promising plunder could command a following that might eventually grow into an army. This was the strategy of the Indian resistance as well as that of the British.

With the destruction of Seringapatam, the British were anxious both to explore new territory and to mop up the resistance. Doondia was attacked in July 1799, and his district was occupied after much slaughter. Doondia himself escaped, to return in strength the following year. His army was said to number 40,000 men, and increased as it marched, wrote Wellington, like a snowball.

Doondia, wrote a later historian, 'was well served by the local population, imparting him correct [and] timely information of the plans and movements of his pursuers'.[6] This further challenge to British rule could not be allowed to go unchecked. Wellington was ordered by the governor-general to hunt him down, and to hang him from the nearest tree. A vast army was assembled at Chitteldroog.

Doondia retreated into the neighbouring territory of the Marathas, for Wellington's army had greater discipline and firepower. He was pursued to Bednore, where the fort was stormed. Some 500 of his men were slaughtered.

Doondia escaped, as he had done so often before; but eventually, in September, he was cornered and killed at Bhanu, near Bellary. Doondia had survived as an independent challenger to the British for more than a year, and his name was to live on. During the Maratha resistance in the Deccan over the next twenty years, other rebels, basking in reflected glory, sometimes gave themselves the name of Doondia Wao.

Part V

RESISTANCE TO IMPERIAL EXPANSION DURING THE WARS AGAINST NAPOLEON, 1803–15

New territories were incorporated into the Empire in the early years of the nineteenth century as a byproduct of Britain's counter-revolutionary war against France, resumed in 1803 after a breathing space registered by the Treaty of Amiens in 1802. The Treaty, signed by the British, the French, the Spanish and the Dutch, declared that 'peace, friendship, and good understanding' would henceforward exist between the signatories. Prisoners and hostages were exchanged,[1] and the British were obliged to abandon all their Caribbean conquests, with the exception of Trinidad and Tobago. They also returned Cape Colony in southern Africa to the Dutch, and withdrew their troops from Egypt; they were allowed to keep the new colony established at Ceylon.

The Amiens Treaty broke down in 1803, and a new war between Britain and France continued for a further twelve years, until the final defeat of Napoleon at Waterloo in June 1815. Napoleon, ruler of France since 1799, proclaimed himself Emperor in 1804, and France sought again to challenge the British in the Caribbean, as it had done with such success in the 1790s, with the support of its freed slaves. This time the French project was thwarted by the slave forces of Jean-Jacques Dessalines in Haiti and by the sea battle in October 1805 at Trafalgar, from which the British emerged victorious. Having lost Tipu, his ally in India, and having failed to build on his occupation of Egypt, Napoleon was obliged thereafter to concentrate his attention on Europe.

With the French engaged in military campaigns in Europe, the British continued the expansion of their empire elsewhere. White settlers first arrived in Tasmania in 1803; Cape Colony was again seized from the Dutch in 1806; Buenos Aires was briefly captured from Spain in the same year, and lost a few months later; Ra's al-Khaymah (today one of the United Arab Emirates) was seized in 1809; and Mauritius and the Seychelles were taken over in 1810. Indonesia was incorporated into the Empire in 1811 (though lost in 1816), Kandy (in central Ceylon) was taken in 1815, and Nepal in 1816.

In most of these territories, seized from the French or the Dutch, the change of imperial overlord was greeted with resistance from the local inhabitants, often more widespread than expected. Revolts and mutinies were frequent, notably in India in 1806 and 1809, while continuing rebellions in the Caribbean came from slaves and slave-soldiers, as well as from Maroons.

The resistance of princes continued in India in the early years of the nineteenth century, with a number of notable, though impermanent, military victories by the Maratha rulers, Daulat Rao Sindhia and Jeswant Rao Holkar. In Kandy, Wickrama Sinha outmanoeuvred a British army in 1803, and secured a postponement of the conquest of his kingdom until 1815. Resistance to the occupation of Indonesia in 1811 was also a protracted affair – the attempt to add this Asian jewel to the British crown being thwarted both by indigenous resistance and by the requirements of politics in Europe.

The local inhabitants also defeated the British when they attempted to move into Egypt and Latin America. The Egyptians destroyed a British army in 1807, leaving the great Mohamed Ali in supreme charge, while the Mayan Indians of British Honduras refused to accept incursions into their territory by loggers. Local resistance to British expeditions sent to seize Spanish-held territories along the River Plate in 1806 and 1807 was also successful. This period saw a revival of the tradition of white settler rebellion begun in North America in the 1770s. In Australia in 1808, and in South Africa in 1815, white settlers quarrelled among themselves, with some of them seeking to escape from the imperial embrace.

Meanwhile the native populations of conquered territories were treated according to the pattern of Britain's earlier experience in the Americas, establishing guidelines for the future conduct of Empire. The slaughter of the Aboriginal inhabitants on the island of Tasmania started almost on the first day of settlement, in 1803, while the fierce repression of convicts held in the colony of New South Wales, mostly prisoners from the Irish revolt of 1798, provoked rebellion in 1802 and 1804. The attacks on 'pirates' in the Persian Gulf in 1809, and off the coast of Java in 1812 and 1813, were a pointer to the future, as was the campaign to seize land from the Xhosa on the frontiers of Cape Colony in 1811 – the first of many wars of extermination.

The scale of the repression in the colonies of the Caribbean did not go unnoticed in London, and several overly violent governors were brought back prematurely to London, notably Colonel Cochrane and Colonel Ainslie in Dominica, and Colonel Picton in Trinidad. As a result of the growing campaign against the slave trade, the British authorities had become better informed about conditions in the colonies.

None of Britain's new imperial acquisitions were immune to the global desire to remove the shackles of slavery, and all were made more alert by the British parliamentary vote in 1807 to end the slave trade, believed by many to presage an end to slavery itself. The British had abolished slavery in Britain itself in 1772, but had continued to support the slave system within the Empire – an established institution that provided a welcome supply of cheap labour.

In March 1807, after long debate, the British parliament finally voted to end the slave trade.[2] The trade had been a central feature of Britain's foreign commerce for more than two centuries – endorsed, supported and profitably enjoyed by the royal family, as well as by the families of sundry courtiers, financiers, landowners and merchants. The personal and public wealth of Britain created by slave labour was a crucial element in the accumulation of capital that made possible both the Industrial Revolution and the expansion of the Empire.

The trade was brought to an end partly by the useful political work of Quakers and other Christian dissidents, and partly through the efforts of parliamentary radicals. Yet it was also the work of slaves in the Caribbean who engaged in propaganda of the deed. Driving the anti–slave trade agitation was the accelerating rate of slave rebellion in the late eighteenth century, notably Tacky's Jamaican rebellion in 1760, and Chatoyer's resistance in St Vincent. Then came the slave revolutionaries of Haiti, who rebelled in August 1791. They had seized power, abolished slavery, and established the first black Republic in the Americas. Other islands saw serious uprisings by slaves and Maroons, who, with French help, seized control of large parts of Dominica, Guadeloupe, Grenada, St Vincent, Jamaica, St Lucia and Trinidad.

These rebellions (with assistance from the French and from the twin weapons of malaria and yellow fever) had defeated the two British armadas sent to destroy them, and killed thousands of seamen and soldiers. They also deprived the British of income from their sugar plantations. Since those in the forefront of the struggle were slaves recently arrived from Africa, the stark danger to British commercial interests of the continuing trade could not have been more graphically revealed.[3]

The vote of 1807 did not put an end to the international trade by other nations, nor did it terminate slavery. Several countries continued the trade, with half a million slaves arriving in the Americas in the 1820s – more than 60,000 a year. Each year 3,000 slaves were still being landed in Brazil in the 1850s. Slavery itself was not abolished in the British Empire until 1838, in the French Empire until 1848, and in the United States until 1863. Slavery persisted in Spanish Cuba until 1886, and in Brazil until 1888. The vote of 1807 was not always respected. The British in Asia continued to take advantage of the continuing trade. The governor in Mauritius, which had been conquered from the French in 1810, sought to befriend the existing French settlers by allowing them to continue importing slaves – some 30,000 of them between 1811 and 1821.

One tragic and unforeseen result of the decision to end the trade was its arousal of the false expectation among slaves that their servitude might soon be abolished. Slave rebellions occurred in Trinidad (1805), in Jamaica (1808 and 1809) and in Dominica (1813). Even the slave state of Cape Colony witnessed a revolt in 1808. More than thirty years passed after 1807 before the British finally abandoned slavery in their Empire – years that saw major slave rebellions in Jamaica, Dominica, Barbados, Honduras and Guyana. All were savagely repressed. Some among their participants claimed that the trumpeted news of an end to the trade had led them to believe that slavery itself was over.

CHAPTER 18

Rebellions, Revolts and Mutinies in the Caribbean

While military triumphs in India after the overthrow of Tipu Sultan created fresh opportunities for the promoters of the developing empire, British authorities in the Caribbean were faced by the difficult aftermath of military defeat. Shortage of troops through illness, and the perceived failure of the two great naval expeditions sent out in 1793 and 1795, had left the slave population alert and rebellious. The settlers and the landowners, for their part, were nervous and fearful. Britain and France had been at war for eight years; both sides were exhausted.

Fresh slave revolts and mutinies marked the start of a long period of unrest in Britain's slave colonies, partly provoked by the continuing upheavals in Haiti, and partly by the more immediate belief that the parliamentary moves to end the slave trade was but a prelude to an end to slavery. Slavery itself, of course, remained legal in the colonies, but an end to slavery itself was now the firm goal of its victims, to the alarm of their owners.

The British-held island of Tobago, off the coast of Venezuela, perceived as a likely candidate to be returned to French rule,[1] was the first to reach the edge of the precipice, in December 1801. The slaves planned to take their chance at Christmas, and prepared a rebellion on sixteen plantations. Each plantation had a leader with the rank of colonel. Roger, a driver on the Belvedere estate, was to be the island's new governor; Thomas, a cooper, was to be the commander-in-chief; and a slave called Sandy was to be a major. More than 1,000 slaves were involved in the plot, against a militia force of barely 200.

Roger is described in the records as 'a remarkable, active and intelligent Creole'. Well aware of the winds of change blowing through the Caribbean, he had a print on his wall of the execution of Louis XVI. Several organisers of the rebellion were drivers or tradesmen – men with a wider knowledge of the world than most plantation slaves. Many were relatively well off, 'not only in possession of the comforts, but even the luxuries of life'. Two of them were former members of the Black Rangers, the unit of slave soldiers recruited in 1795. Disbanded in 1800 under pressure from the plantation owners, these free soldiers had been sold back into slavery.

Setting the sugar cane alight outside each overseer's house was the signal for the start of the revolt. 'It was hoped that the appearance of the flames would induce the whites to hasten to the spot', wrote the planter Bryan Edwards, a near-contemporary of these events, 'and that they might then be murdered with little difficulty'.[2] But the whites had heard rumours of the threatened rebellion, and Brigadier Hugh Carmichael, the garrison commander at Scarborough, ordered a special militia patrol to be mounted over the holiday. Martial law was declared and thirty plotters were arrested.

A macabre charade was enacted. Carmichael ordered that a single rebel should be hanged on the signal flagpole at dawn. After execution, his body was lowered and raised up again thirty times, with a gun fired on each occasion. 'The insurgents, who at a distance witnessed the execution, were thus led to believe that one of their chiefs perished at each fresh raising of the body; and the salutary effect of this belief was that, supposing themselves to be left without a leader, they surrendered or dispersed.'[3]

The rebellion was snuffed out; several hundred slaves and a number of free coloureds were arrested. Two were executed, including a coloured militiaman convicted of conspiring with the slaves. Martial law was lifted after reinforcements had arrived from Barbados in January – three infantry companies – and a further five men were hanged. Carmichael justified his action by claiming that the rebel leaders 'had sworn to the total extermination of the white and coloured people by a regular and systematic attack'.

This lurid picture, which most whites in the Caribbean had lodged in their imagination since the slave triumph in Haiti, was not to be realised in Tobago. The repression of Roger's rebellion knocked the spirit out of the slaves for a generation, and they did not finally secure their freedom until August 1834.

A fresh revolt broke out a few months later on the island of Dominica. On 9 April 1802, 500 black soldiers mutinied at Fort Shirley, near Cabrits, on the northern point of the island. 'Black Man' was their password, and among their number only the name of Private Hypolite has been recorded. The mutineers had justifiable grievances. Obliged to work without pay on the governor's private estate, they imagined that their military unit was about to be disbanded and that they would be returned to slavery, as had happened to the Black Rangers of Tobago.

The Black Regiment of Dominica had been formed in 1795, and in 1798, to swell their numbers, the governor had purchased 200 slaves from a market on a neighbouring island. Fighting for the British, they had been promised their eventual freedom. Fearing that this promise would not be kept, the black soldiers seized their barracks and killed three of the black non-commissioned officers and all the whites.

Colonel Andrew Cochrane, the island's governor, declared martial law and marched from Roseau to Fort Shirley with two regiments. The black soldiers held their ground, but the governor's force prevailed. Sixty of the mutineers were killed and 370 taken prisoner.[4] A court martial sentenced thirty-four to be hanged. Some escaped over the ramparts of Fort Shirley and made for the hills. Private Hypolite was among their number, and joined a surviving group of black Maroons.

A decade later, in 1813, a war of extermination was launched in Dominica against the Maroons. Pharcelle, the Maroon leader in the 1780s and 1790s, was long gone, but Quashee, the most recent chief, had kept alive the flames of resistance through the first decade of the nineteenth century – a struggle characterised by sporadic guerrilla activity and a 'very considerable desertion of negroes from the estates'. Hypolite was still active, and so too was a Maroon called Jacko, who had been fighting in the hills for forty years or more.

The continued existence of a Maroon 'free territory' in the mountains was an attraction for the plantation slaves. In July 1812 a group of seventy-five at the Castle Bruce plantation had slipped away to join them. With more than a thousand Maroons providing a safe refuge for runaways, the authorities felt obliged to act. Colonel George Ainslie, a governor freshly arrived, made some effort to negotiate. Maroons who surrendered would be offered a free pardon; those who refused would be treated 'with the utmost rigour of military execution, their provision grounds laid waste, and the punishment of death inflicted on those who are found in arms'.[5] Chief Quashee had no plans to surrender, and rejected the governor's terms. The Maroon courier who had brought the governor's message was accused of treason and shot.

Unwilling to use the army to put down what was perceived as an internal disturbance, Colonel Ainslie turned to a familiar Caribbean practice – recruiting slaves and forming them into a Black Ranger battalion. Soon the Maroons were faced by black troops as knowledgeable about the forests as they were, and under orders to exterminate them. Colonel Ainslie proclaimed that 'the Rangers have orders to take no prisoners, but to put to death men, women, and children, without exception'. Rewards were offered for the heads of Quashee and other individual Maroons. Quashee, not to be outdone, offered $2,000 for the head of the governor.

The Maroons held out against the Rangers for a year, but their resistance eventually crumbled. Their farms were burned down, and Colonel Ainslie boasted that they faced the choice of 'starving in the woods or surrendering'. Jacko's small band of 500 was finally surrounded in July 1814, and Jacko was shot. Eleven leaders were hanged; their heads were cut off and displayed on poles at prominent places around the island. Some of those who surrendered were escaped slaves: one hundred men, forty-eight women and eight children. Found guilty of 'loitering off plantations to which they belong without passes', they were imprisoned.

The Maroons of Dominica had long maintained a close alliance with the plantation slaves – not always the case in other islands – and it was this relationship that allowed them to survive for so long.[6] Yet their alliance caused panic among the white slave-owners, who had demanded action from the colonial authorities with such success. After the war in Jamaica in 1795, the Jamaicans Maroons had been banished from the islands for ever. In St-Dominica, twenty years later, they were effectively eliminated. The slave-owners triumphed.[7]

In December 1805, in the Caribbean island of Trinidad, two French planters with sugar estates in Diego Martin valley sounded the alarm when they heard their African slaves singing a subversive song. Its words referred to the rebellion in Saint-Domingue (Haiti) in 1791:

> The bread is the flesh of the white man, San Domingo!
> The wine is the blood of the white man, San Domingo!
> We will drink the white man's blood, San Domingo!
> The bread we eat is the white man's flesh
> The wine we drink is the white man's blood.

Under cover of organising their Christmas celebrations, the slaves were preparing a rebellion and rehearsing these evocative songs.[8] 'King' Samson, the rebellion's leader, appeared in the day to be a harmless old Ibo slave from Nigeria, but at clandestine meetings at night, he emerged as a powerful *obeah-man* in charge of the rebellion's organising committee. This was what the whites were led to believe.

The British had acquired Trinidad from the Spanish in 1797, and were ever-fearful of the continuing influence of French Republicans.[9] A slave revolt had broken out on neighbouring Tobago in 1801, and the authorities had heard rumours of a black underground and a network of secret societies. The whites knew that they were outnumbered. Trinidad had 20,000 slaves in 1803, and barely 2,000 whites. There were also 5,000 Maroons, some of whom had come from the other islands.

Many of these French-speaking Maroons, republican in their political enthusiasms, had taken to the hills in 1797 after raiding the armoury left behind by the Spaniards. Their existence posed a permanent threat to the white plantation owners. The *cabildo*, or assembly, of the whites called them 'the scum of the Revolution', who had found in Trinidad a 'Refugium Peccatorum' – a refuge from their sins. It would be 'an act of moral madness', the *cabildo* recorded in 1803, 'to relax the police when we still have 5,000 of these people, and daily increasing'; 'every precaution' had to be taken.[10]

The Maroons were perceived by Colonel Thomas Picton, the first British governor, as 'irredeemably Republican', and soon he was challenging them with a small but well-armed militia. The Maroon-controlled hinterland was successfully invaded by this force, and the captured Maroons were executed. Picton also suppressed a mutiny of coloured troops on the way. His methods were criticised in London in 1802 and, accused of the excessive use of torture, he was forced to resign.

With the power of the Maroons diminished, the chief threat to the white planters came from their African slaves. Brigadier Thomas Hislop, Picton's replacement as governor, heard rumours of an impending rebellion in December 1805; he imposed martial law and mobilised the militia. Informers had provided the names of slaves named as the future kings and queens, and the members of a future black government, and they were all arrested. Under torture, they confessed that a rising had indeed been planned for Christmas Day; two prominent planters, much hated by the slaves, were to have been the first to be killed.

Brought before a court martial, the three slaves held to be most responsible were found guilty and hanged. Six men were flogged, as were the women involved.[11] Among them was King Samson's queen, who was sentenced to wear chains for life, with a ten-pound iron ring fastened to her leg.

In the excitable imagination of Trinidad's tiny white population, the details of the Christmas plot of 1805 loomed ever larger as the years went by. The old French planters remained haunted by their fears of riot and massacre. They came to believe that the rebels had planned to kill every white man by grinding them up in Mr Shand's mill, and they recalled how 'lots were to be cast for the white ladies'. They were convinced that only the severest punishment would terrorise the Maroons and slaves into submission.[12]

Yet many free blacks believed that the Christmas plot was an invention of the terrified whites. They argued that the slaves had created an imaginary existence for themselves away from the world of the sugar plantation, and that when the slaves had talked of emperors and kings, they were simply planning their costumes for the Christmas carnival – and maybe they were.

Whether real or imaginary, the Christmas rebellion was brutally suppressed, and the white settlers remained on their guard. When a Methodist preacher arrived on the island in 1811 and preached sermons that favoured the slaves, he was drummed off the island. 'It is of no consequence of what colour ye are', the Reverend Thomas Talboys had preached to his slave flock, 'for the white man will be burning in hell, while all of you, who have faith in the gospel, will be enjoying bliss in heaven'.[13] This was not what the white *cabildo* liked to hear, and Talboys was charged with 'preaching doctrines tending to excite insubordination in the minds of the free people of colour, and slaves'.

Summoned before Brigadier Hislop, he was ordered into exile. 'Go instantly and shut up your Chapel', he was told, 'desist from preaching, and join a military corps.' The subversive priest was sent to Guyana, while the brigadier left for India, to become a significant player in the extermination of the Pindaris in 1817.

Even when slavery was abolished throughout the British empire, in August 1834, and replaced with a system of apprenticeship, the slaves in Trinidad 'shewed much resistance, but this, in most cases, was of a passive nature. The use of the cat-o'-nine tails convinced some of the most refractory that they were in the wrong, and the rest returned to their duty.' With the extensive use of flogging, the former slaves found it difficult to tell the difference between the old system and the new, and remained in the mood of intransigence to which they had been reduced by years of repression.

In Jamaica in May 1808, fifty slaves at the military base at Fort Augusta organised a mutiny and killed their two white officers. Recently arrived from Africa, they had been purchased by the governor to serve in the 2nd West Indian Regiment. These were the last batch of a total of 13,000 slaves enrolled by the British army in the Caribbean since 1795. A graphic account of the mutiny at Fort Augusta by an historian later in the nineteenth century suggests that the slave soldiers were 'influenced by some wild idea that, if they killed the officers, they would then be able to return to their own country'.[14] The contemporary planter historian Bryan Edwards also thought that they 'were desirous of returning to their native country', but claimed too that they were 'too often drilled'.[15]

The mutiny was confined to the new recruits, and was swiftly crushed when older soldiers not only refused to take part but actively joined in suppressing it. 'Ammunition being supplied, nearly half the mutineers were shot, and the rest made prisoners.'[16] Sixteen prisoners were tried by court martial, and condemned to death; nine were shot.

The mutiny's brutal suppression helped fuel a subsequent slave revolt planned in 1809. Setting fire to a plantation outside Kingston was to be the signal for the start of the rebellion – a sign for others to join in. They had hoped to do so, according to Edwards, by 'the firing of the towns and the murdering of the white inhabitants'.[17] Their aim was to establish a republican government on the model of Haiti.

'Duke' Watkins was appointed the slaves' commander-in-chief, with a title designed to echo that of the Duke of Manchester, the island's military governor, while his second-in-command, 'Sambo' John, was addressed as 'Captain'. The whites were saved almost by chance, for in spite of the recent mutiny the colonial authorities were poorly prepared.[18]

The plans were discovered when one of the survivors of the mutiny of 1808 was captured in March 1809. Burgess, a slave in the 2nd West Indian Regiment, had escaped after the mutiny, and became one of the plotters of the planned rebellion. Originally sentencing him to death for desertion, the authorities now prepared for his delayed execution. 'Just before the sentence was to be executed', according to Edwards's account, 'most probably with the hope of saving his life, he revealed the important secret which his friends had confided to him.'[19]

His allegations were investigated, and the authorities concluded that a slave rebellion was indeed imminent. Watkins and Sambo John and several others were arrested, while others escaped. Having provided such useful information, Burgess was pardoned, while Watkins and John were tried and executed. 'Thus ended the project of a negro republic in Jamaica', noted Edwards.

CHAPTER 19

The Resistance of the Marathas to the British Invasion of Central India

The lands of the Maharashtra in the north-central region of India had stood open to a British advance ever since the defeat and death of Tipu Sultan in 1799. North of Mysore and inland from Bombay, the immense plateau of the Deccan was the homeland of great Maratha armies, the legacy of the famous seventeenth-century leader Shivaji. North of the Deccan lay Rajasthan and Delhi, and the great fortress at Aligarh.

The long defensive struggle of the Marathas against the British had begun with the victories of Nana Farnavis in 1779, and it was now renewed on different fronts over the following two decades, producing numerous defeats as well as notable victories. Indeed, the cost in lives and in revenue of the Maratha wars was to lead to the eventual recall of Richard Wellesley, the governor, for his particular war had not been authorised in London. The Maratha resistance provoked his political downfall, even though his generals prevailed on the battlefield.

Daulat Rao Sindhia was the principal Maratha leader, forming part of the 'Maratha Confederacy', an informal grouping of the most powerful Maratha rulers in the vast inland territory of central India. These included the one-eyed Jeswant Rao Holkar, based at Indore, and Baji Rao II, known as 'the Peshwa', based at Poona. Sindhia, perceived as the heir to Shivaji, was also the protector of Shah Alam, the surviving Mughal emperor in Delhi, now old and blind.[1] In August 1803 he was faced with British armies advancing into the Deccan.

Sindhia and Holkar were both powerful chiefs, but they had a great capacity to fight among themselves – a considerable source of strength to the British.[2] Both were aware of the British threat, and understood Wellesley's need to enlarge his territory, for the governor was short of money to fund his armies; he needed the extra revenue that a conquest of the Maratha lands would provide. Baji Rao had taken the line of least resistance with the British, accepting their help in May 1803 to recover Poona from Holkar.

Sindhia was the first Maratha ruler in the way of the British advance, but he had to fight on two fronts. In the Deccan, he was threatened by the forces of General Arthur Wellesley, the governor's brother and later the Duke of Wellington, remembered as the victor at Seringapatam in 1799. Further north, in Rajasthan, Sindhia's French-trained armies confronted an invasion led by

General Gerard Lake, recently arrived from Ireland, considered a skilful tactician and a good organiser.[3]

The war began in August with Lake's army bombarding Sindhia's headquarters at Aligarh, south of Delhi. Sindhia was obliged to surrender after the loss of 2,000 men, and his southern fortress at Ahmadnagar in the Deccan, north of Poona, also had to be abandoned, after a similar heavy bombardment by Wellington's army. A final confrontation came in September, when his forces met those of Wellington at the battle of Assaye, further north – possibly the fiercest battle against the British invaders ever seen in India. Sindhia's soldiers acquitted themselves well, and British casualties were heavy, but the British were judged to have won when Sindhia's surviving forces retired from the field.[4]

Another fierce battle took place on the outskirts of Delhi, and General Lake's forces seized the city. Shah Alam, the old Mughal emperor, sat under a tattered canopy to receive the British general – and he did so, according to a contemporary report, 'with every external appearance of the misery of his condition'. He was now obliged to obey the orders of a 'British Resident' established in Delhi, and he died soon after, in 1806. His son, Akbar Shah, became the new emperor, but only in name. The British now ruled supreme in Delhi.

Sindhia watched helplessly while Lake rolled up parts of the Maratha map of India that had once been his. The capture of Delhi and the fortress at Agra yielded immense sums in prize money, distributed among British soldiers. The end came in October, at the village of Laswari, west of Agra. Sindhia's military commander, Abaji, fought a final battle against Lake, and here again the Marathas acquitted themselves well. Lake was to claim that he had been much impressed by the Marathas at Laswari, just as Wellington had been surprised by the strength of the resistance at Assaye. Yet Laswari was a serious Maratha defeat. They lost 7,000 men as well as their guns and ammunition. British losses were also substantial, with over 800 killed or wounded.[5]

Sindhia's principal army was now destroyed, and he signed a peace treaty seriously disadvantageous to his cause. He gave up a substantial slice of territory, formally handing over the Maratha lands north of the Jumna River, including Delhi and Agra, but he secured a fresh deal that allowed him to survive as a Maratha ruler with some of his powers intact. The Peshwa Baji Rao was less fortunate. A 'British Resident' was installed at Poona, assuming the powers and status that he had once held. The peace treaty was humiliating for the Maratha rulers, yet within two years the British political position had deteriorated.

The following year, in July 1804, Jeswant Rao Holkar, the only undefeated member of the Maratha triumvirate defending central India, launched a surprise attack on a British force at Sonara, south of Agra. This was the worst military reverse suffered by the British since Haidar Ali had defeated Colonel Baillie's army outside Madras in 1780, nearly a quarter of a century earlier. Five sepoy companies deserted during the retreat to Agra.

After the military defeats of Sindhia's forces at Assaye and Laswari in 1803, and the defection of the Peshwa Baji Rao, Holkar was the last member of the old Maratha Confederacy to remain at large. Safely ensconced in his fortress at Indore, he still had hopes of reviving the alliance with Sindhia and Baji Rao to fight against 'the infidel Christians'. He was a resolute opponent of the British, aware of their ambition to take over the continent, but Sindhia and Baji Rao distrusted him and were not prepared to join an anti-British alliance.[6]

Although weakened by Sindhia's defeat, Holkar was in a relatively strong position for the British were seriously over-extended. Holkar was a well-educated and intelligent ruler, with 'a mind more quick of conception and fertile in resources than any of the other Mahratta chiefs', according to Major William Thorn, who had fought against him.[7] He spoke Persian as well as Marathi, and although he lacked an eye, he was an excellent guerrilla leader.

'We are obliged to remain in the field at enormous cost,' Lake noted gloomily to Governor Wellesley in April. Wellington's army in the Deccan was also in poor shape, bogged down with few provisions. When Wellesley ordered Lake to prepare an attack on Holkar's armies in April 1804, the Marathas had considerable initial success. They shadowed Lake's forces in the neighbourhood of Tonk, south-west of Agra, and obliged them to withdraw to Agra when overcome by the summer's heat. Colonel William Monson was left behind to monitor the Marathas' movements, and he moved south across the Chambal River to Sonara, with reinforcements from the Rajah of Kotah. It was here that Holkar launched his devastating attack in July that forced Monson to retreat to Agra.[8] His victory was a severe blow to the British. Lake's biographer wrote how 'for a time the safety of Upper India was gravely imperilled . . . Permanent injury to British prestige was the result of so serious and complete a reverse. The natives of India had discovered that British armies were not invincible'.[9]

Throughout early autumn, everything went Holkar's way. Lake was retreated from Agra to Cawnpore, to await reinforcements from Calcutta, while one of Holkar's armies was sent to recapture Delhi. The city was surrounded for several weeks, and the siege was only abandoned when Lake's reinforced army arrived later in the year. Holkar's troops moved north, and the tide turned in Lake's favour.[10]

The war concluded in November when Holkar was ambushed by Lake's forces at Farrukhabad. Holkar escaped, but his soldiers were caught unready, sleeping beside their horses. Hundreds were cut down, and perhaps as many as 3,000 were killed or died of their wounds. Many of those who escaped simply abandoned Holkar's cause, and returned home. Holkar faced defeat, with little left except his immense fortress at Bharatpur. There he held out, and even when

Lake tried to capture it in January 1805, Holkar forced him to withdraw, after sustaining more than 3,000 casualties. The fortress was to stand alone, unconquered, for another twenty years.

The resistance war by Holkar and Sindhia, although ultimately unsuccessful, was not without effect. The Maratha rulers suffered serious military setbacks, but the British were wounded politically. Governor Wellesley had squandered money on waging wars that were designed to bring in extra revenue, not to spend it, and in 1805 he was reprimanded by his employers, the East India Company, and ordered home. He was not well received there either.[11]

His successor was the elderly and reliable General Charles Cornwallis, now aged sixty-six. He was an old India hand who had done battle with Tipu Sultan in 1792; he was a veteran of the American wars of the 1770s; and he had been the commander in Ireland in 1798. But the Maratha resistance had obliged him to return to India with a commitment to cut back on expenditure and to abandon the wilder schemes for the enlargement of empire. On his first day back, in August 1805, he wrote to Lake to tell of his 'earnest desire . . . to put an end to this most unprofitable and ruinous warfare'.

Sindhia, the loser in 1803, was courted by Cornwallis, who ignored Holkar and embarked on a peace deal. Sindhia found that everything under dispute with him was to be given back: Gohad and Gwalior were to be returned; Delhi was to be abandoned. He was allowed to restore Maratha influence in Hindustan; the British frontier was drawn back from the Chambal to the Jumna; and British protection was withdrawn from the native princes whose land lay between the rivers.

Sindhia's resistance had apparently been worthwhile. At least one Maratha ruler had triumphed, if only temporarily. The British were left with their empire in India facing an uncertain future. Cornwallis's policy exemplified the decline in the British position, and his own personal circumstances were not good. The exertions of his return to India had been severe. Shortly after the settlement with Sindhia, in October 1805, he collapsed and died.

Holkar remained out in the cold, accusing Sindhia of falling 'a prey to temporary selfish gain'. He remained hopeful of finding allies with whom to continue the anti-British struggle, and he retreated across the Sutlej River in November 1805. He camped in the Punjabi plain between Amritsar and Lahore, in the hope that he might secure the support of Ranjit Singh and other Sikh leaders.[12] These were vain hopes, and a further forty years were to pass before the heirs to Ranjit Singh were ready to battle the British.

Holkar agreed finally to make peace with the British, recognising that he had run out of friends. He signed a treaty with Lake at Amritsar, and pledged to abstain from all further incursions into the territories of the East India Company. The British, for their part, agreed to allow Holkar to remain sovereign in his own land.

Not everyone was content. This was a treaty through which Holkar 'was reinstated in dominions to which he never had any right', complained Major Thorn, who had battled alongside General Lake throughout the campaign, 'and which, even if he had, he deserved to have forfeited'.[13] Lake was so annoyed by the Cornwallis policy of abandoning in peace talks what had been gained in battle that he resigned and returned to England. He died in London three years later, still an angry man.

The Maratha rulers had been forced to allow Wellesley and Lake to greatly enlarge the British Empire in India. They had lost Mysore and Travancore, the Maratha principalities of Baroda and Poona, the territories of the Nizam of Hyderabad, and, to the north-west, the province of Oudh.

The British conquerors were well rewarded: Wellesley was knighted, Lake made a peer. Yet the Marathas had also done well. Two powerful rulers remained beyond British control – Sindhia at Gwalior and Holkar at Indore – and their fiefdoms were to remain independent for a further decade. With admirable strategic vision, Holkar devoted the rest of his short life to the construction of a gun factory. He died in 1811 at the age of thirty.[14] Sindhia died years later, in 1827. Yet the Maratha resistance of 1803–05 only postponed the evil hour. In the following decade, in 1817–18, the Marathas were to find that the British, freed from their European distractions, had time, energy, and money to encompass their destruction.

CHAPTER 20

Mutiny and Revolt by Muslim Sepoys and European Officers

Muslim sepoys staged a mutinous insurrection in July 1806 at the British-held fortress of Vellore, in the western region inland from Madras that had seen the resistance of Tipu Sultan in the 1790s. Ever since Tipu's death in 1799, the two sons of the old Mysore ruler had been kept under house arrest in Vellore, and the fortress had become a centre of incipient resistance.

Mutinies had been common in the slave states of the Caribbean, but in India, where British power and influence depended on huge native armies, mutiny among the sepoys had been largely prevented by the use of terror. The tradition of 'cannonading' – blowing away mutineers from the barrel of a large gun – ensured that sepoy rebellions were few and far between. Yet both sepoys and their white officers could be driven to extreme action when threatened by inconsiderate attacks on their culture or their pay. The troubled years after the Maratha armies had failed to stem the British advance into northern India saw unparalleled outbreaks of unrest among both groups.

The sepoy rebels at Vellore assembled on parade at 3 a.m., and fired on the European troops in their barracks. More than a hundred were killed, and a dozen British officers were shot as they came from their houses to see what was going on. The triumphant sepoys brought out one of the imprisoned sons of Tipu and proclaimed him the new Sultan. The flag of Mysore was hoisted from the ramparts.

The tinder that sparked off the insurrection was a new set of regulations for the sepoys, issued early in 1806 by General Sir John Cradock, the commander in Madras, an officer previously involved in the repression of the Irish rebellion of 1798. Cradock had ordered the sepoys to 'smarten up': they were told to stop wearing earrings, to shave their beards, and to sport a new pattern of turban 'very much ressembling a hat'.

The sepoys perceived the new turban as the thin end of the wedge. If they adopted the European custom of wearing a hat, worse might follow. Might they not soon be forcibly converted from Islam to Christianity? 'Next we shall be condemned to eat and drink with the outcast and infidel English, to give them our daughters in marriage, to become one people, and follow one faith.'[1] In May, the sepoys at Vellore announced firmly that they would not wear the new turban, and nineteen were arrested and sent for trial to Madras. Found guilty of disorderly conduct, two of them received 900 lashes. The remaining seventeen were to receive 500 lashes, but their sentences were commuted after they had expressed sentiments of contrition. Some 1,500 sepoys were stationed at Vellore, watched over by only 370 European soldiers. They nursed their anger and planned to avenge their humiliation.

Their mutiny in July was crushed almost by chance. Speedy intervention by a newcomer saved the day for the British. Colonel Robert Rollo Gillespie, a veteran of the imperial campaigns in the West Indies in the 1790s, had recently arrived as the new governor of Arcot, a town some fourteen miles away from Vellore.[2] Out riding before breakfast, Gillespie was told of the mutiny and galloped at once to the fortress, accompanied by soldiers from the 69th Light Dragoons.

The sepoys had surrounded the surviving Europeans in the fortress, but they were now faced by the reinforcements brought by Gillespie. He had himself quickly roped up into the fort, and he was soon in a position to rally the survivors from the ramparts. Large guns were dragged up from Arcot, and the gates of the fort were blown open. Several hundred sepoys were killed on the spot; others were taken prisoner; and some, who had escaped by jumping down from the walls, were rounded up later. A few survivors were tried and executed by 'cannonading'. The Indian princes, the sons of Tipu, were removed to Madras, and Gillespie made a tour of other British military outposts where mutinous symptoms had been detected.

The British had received warnings of an impending rebellion at Vellore, but had taken no notice. The attack took them completely by surprise. Both General Cradock and the governor at Madras, Lord William Bentinck, were recalled to London in disgrace, though they survived this setback to their careers.[3]

A yet more serious mutiny occurred in the Madras army in 1809, at three strategic forts spread over a wide area – at Seringapatam, Hyderabad and Masulipatam. The mutiny involved European officers, two dozen of whom seized the fort at Masulipatam and arrested the commanding officer. A similar mutiny took place at Seringapatam, and the officers at Hyderabad threatened to march south to Madras. Their complaints concerned the loss of financial perks and privileges imposed in a recent economy campaign, and were echoed throughout the army. One officer at Masulipatam wrote that 'there was not a [East India] Company corps from Cape Comorin to Ganjam that was not implicated in the general guilt, that is not pledged to rise up against government unless what they call their grievances are redressed'.[4]

A European mutiny threatened the entire British position in India, and this one lasted for four months, from May until September. Yet the government stood firm, and when the European mutineers failed to receive support from the Indian sepoys, their mutiny collapsed. After it was over, Gilbert Elliot, Earl of Minto, the governor-general, registered his official disgust, recorded in the Calcutta Gazette: 'The conduct of these officers in urging the innocent men under their command, who had the most powerful claims on their humanity and care, into the guilt and danger of rebellion, constitutes an aggravation of their offence, that cannot be contemplated without feelings of the deepest indignation and sorrow.' Minto further recorded his hope that 'the example of their crimes and their fate will . . . efface the deep stain which has been cast on the honour of the Madras army'.[5]

The punishment given to the mutineers was less of a lesson to others than Minto would have liked. The ringleader was drowned on his way back to Britain, but those brought before a court martial were simply dismissed from the service. Yet the lessons of the mutiny were not lost on the sepoys, who began to voice hopes of a British withdrawal: 'Before long, all white face gone. This Governor very fine Governor; he tell black men that they better than white men, and that sepoy never mind again what they say.'

The message of those who hoped for a British withdrawal may well have reached Travancore, a state in Kerala under British 'protection', whose Diwan, or ruler, Velu Tampi, disliked the financial obligations that British rule involved. Velu Tampi had previously owed allegiance to Tipu Sultan, but now, as a vassal of the British, he was required to pay for the upkeep of four sepoy battalions. Finding these demands excessively onerous, he had fallen behind in his payments. Eventually, with the assistance of the Rajah of Cochin, he organised a rebellion against his British overlords at the end of 1809. His plan was to assassinate Colonel Collin Macaulay, the British Resident, and to recover his state's independence. He persuaded his supporters that the British were seeking to impose Christianity upon them.

Velu Tampi had considerable popular support, and the war that followed was not small, with 140 casualties on a single day. The British were reduced to appealing to the government in Ceylon for additional military assistance, a reversal of the situation in 1803. Four British regiments and twelve sepoy battalions were needed to crush the rebellion. One nineteenth-century historian described British actions as 'among the least justifiable of the many questionable transactions by which British power in India had been acquired or preserved'.[6]

Macaulay managed to escape without injury, but the reprisals against Velu Tampi's supporters were harsh. His brother was hanged without a trial, while the Diwan himself committed suicide. Macaulay ordered that his body should be exposed on a gibbet – an action subsequently criticised by Minto, the governor-general, who considered the action to be 'repugnant to the feelings of common humanity and the principles of a civilised government'.

CHAPTER 21

Rebellion in Australia and the Slaughter of Aborigines

Many convicts arriving in Australia in the 1790s were Irish Republicans, some of them Defenders. Their numbers had increased dramatically after 1798, and the colonial authorities feared a repeat of the Irish rebellion.[1] Lieutenant Philip King, the governor of New South Wales, was familiar with Irish prisoners, having previously run Australia's own offshore gulag at Norfolk Island.[2] He described the 135 convicts who had arrived there from Cork in 1801 as 'the most desperate and diabolical characters that could be selected throughout that kingdom'. He thought they were just awaiting 'an opportunity to put their diabolical plans into execution' in New South Wales. Fifteen escaped from the prison farm in 1802; two were recaptured and hanged.

On the evening of 4 March 1804, several hundred convicts on the mainland justified the governor's fears. Held at Castle Hill, a prison farm north of Sydney, they overpowered the officers and seized muskets from the armoury. Their plan was to capture Parramatta, a settlement five miles away, and then to move to Sydney, fifteen miles to the south. From there they hoped to escape by ship. Philip Cunningham from Kerry was one of the leaders; another was William Johnstone. Their slogan was 'Death or Liberty'. Both were Irishmen deported from Cork.

Their rebellion was recalled as 'the Battle of Colonial Vinegar Hill', in memory of the Irish battle in 1798. Joseph Holt, the guerrilla leader in County Wicklow deported after 1798, left an account of the Australian revolt in his memoirs. While he did not participate in the Castle Hill insurrection, he was aware of what was going on and recorded his belief that the enterprise was doomed from the start:

> The lower people, convicts and others, both English and Irish, seeing their torment increasing in this most ill-managed colony, conceived an opinion that they could overpower the army, possess themselves of the settlement, and eventually make their escape from it. Where they were to go did not enter into the contemplation of these poor fellows, who fancied, at all events, they could not be worse off than they were already.[3]

The rebellion at Castle Hill was not quite as incompetently planned as Holt claimed. The rebels were sufficiently well organised to send teams from house to house to urge their fellow convicts to join their bid for freedom. The password was 'Saint Peter', and their initial plan was to move to the outlying farm settlements to secure muskets to add to their armoury of pitchforks and reaping hooks.

Martial law was proclaimed by the governor, who set out from Sydney with an armed unit from the New South Wales Corps, commanded by Major George Johnston. The rebels were stopped at dawn on 5 March, halfway between Parramatta and Hawkesbury, and ordered to surrender. Philip Cunningham stepped forward and, with his hat in one hand and a sword in the other, called out 'Death or Liberty!'[4]

Johnston pulled out his pistol and put it to Cunningham's head, and the soldiers opened fire. Cunningham and nine rebels were killed, and others captured. The remainder made a rapid retreat.[5] King later praised the 'active perseverance and zeal' of the soldiers, but Johnston thought that they were 'too fond of blood', and wrote of how he had tried to stop them killing their prisoners.[6]

Martial law was repealed, and 300 survivors of the revolt were distributed around the colony in separate labour gangs. Although most of the rebels were Irish, Holt claimed 'the English were as much involved in the business as the Irish'. With the rebellion crushed, Governor King moved rapidly against those members of the Irish community who might have been involved. Holt was among those charged with aiding the rebels, and he was sent to the Norfolk Island prison for two years. In 1805 he was transferred to Tasmania, an island that the British planned to develop as an additional prison colony, both for convicts and for yet more political prisoners from Ireland. Major Johnston re-enters the story in 1808, for he was to be the leader of a white settler rebellion.

Tasmania at this time was an island occupied by 7,000 Aborigines; the first British contingent of white settlers, soldiers and convicts had arrived just a year earlier. Their ship had sailed out from Britain with 400 people on board.[7] The Aborigines observed the settlers establishing a camp on their island, and conflicts with the settlers over food broke out almost at once. 'Famine in the camps of the British multiplied the misfortunes of the natives', wrote a historian years later, in 1884. 'Bands of lawless convicts were let loose over the country to gain subsistence as best they could. Without any check upon the indulgence of their evil passions, it can easily be conceived how the natives were molested on their hunting grounds.'[8] Herds of kangaroo, on which the Aborigines relied for subsistence, were killed for the use of the British settlement.

According to the later account, 'black women were lured away, and their husbands were shot. Babes were murdered and maidens violated. Cruelties such as these led to resentment still more savage. The inhumanity of the white man bore its bitter fruit. Cattle and sheep were wounded; men and women were speared if they ventured from home.'[9]

This was the background to the attack sustained by the Aborigines in May 1804. Some 300 Aborigines from the Moomairremener people had been driving herds of kangaroo across the hills above Risdon, on the far side of the river Derwent from what eventually became the Tasmanian settlement of Hobart. Accompanied by women and children, the men were armed solely with waddies – a short, thick club used when hunting. Suddenly, without warning, the Aborigines were fired on by British soldiers, and fifty were killed.

The attack was witnessed by Edward White, a settler who had been hoeing outside his hut. He gave an account of what he saw and did: 'They looked at me with all their eyes. I went down to the creek, and reported them to some soldiers, and then went back to my work. The natives did not threaten me; I was not afraid of them. They did not attack the soldiers.'

The soldiers alerted by White had few scruples. Under the command of Lieutenant William Moore, they moved up swiftly and opened fire. White recorded that many were slaughtered or wounded: 'I don't know how many . . . This was three or four months after we landed. They never came so close again afterwards. They had no spears with them – only waddies.' An official report in 1830 recorded that the death toll, including men, women and children, was as high as fifty.

Several decades of resistance were sparked off by the initial massacre, but the final outcome of settlement was the annihilation of the island's Aboriginal population. 'The spirit of animosity and revenge which this unmerited and atrocious act of barbarity engendered', W. C. Wentworth noted years later, in 1823, 'has been fostered and aggravated to the highest pitch by the incessant encounters that have subsequently taken place between them and the whites.'[10] Already in the first decade of the nineteenth century, the pattern of development, in Tasmania and in the Australian mainland, had been etched in blood.

In January 1808, the embryonic armed forces of the colony of New South Wales staged a mutiny in Sydney and detained the governor, Captain William Bligh, formerly the commander of the mutinous HMS *Bounty*.[11] This was a *coup d'état*, the first white settler rebellion in Australia and the first in the Empire since the South African rebellion of 1795. With the detention of the representative of the British Crown, the colony fell into the hands of a rebel white settler government, and remained under rebel rule for two years. The leader of the mutineers was Major George Johnston – the man who had slaughtered the Irish convicts at Colonial Vinegar Hill four years earlier.

New South Wales in 1808 was hardly America in 1776, or even South Africa in 1795; the prospect of maintaining an independent regime for any length of time was slim. The white settlers and Major Johnston's small corps shared a tiny strip of coastline with hundreds of convicts and a large population of Aborigines. They depended for their survival on their trading lifeline to other parts of the Empire.

The military had played an important role in the initial construction of colonial rule in New South Wales, as in Britain's other colonies. Two hundred Marines had stood guard over the first group of convicts transported to Australia in 1788, although the military had never been envisaged as a permanent solution to convict control. The demands of the counter-revolutionary war against the French in the 1790s meant that the Marines were needed elsewhere. To fill the gap, a unit was recruited specifically for service in Australia in 1792, and the New South Wales Corps, as it was called, was formed of 200 soldiers with criminal records, who could not get employment elsewhere. The governor complained to London in 1796 that 'characters who have been considered as disgraceful to every other regiment in His Majesty's Service have been thought fit and proper recruits for the New South Wales Corps'.

This was the origin of the group that seized power in Sydney in 1808. Many of its members had secured land grants in Aborigine territory, and officers financed their life-style through their monopoly control over the lucrative rum trade. The officer class was no stranger to power in the new colony, for as early as 1792, when Governor Arthur Phillip returned to London, the officers had run the colony for three years while waiting for a new governor to arrive. Now their successors planned to do the same again.

In 1807, Governor Bligh had accused the military of corruption and incompetence, and in January 1808 he ordered the arrest of John Macarthur, a former Corps officer who had become a powerful figure in the colony. The choleric Macarthur had come to the colony in one of the earliest ships, established himself as a sheep farmer at Parramatta, and been in constant disagreement with successive governors over land taxes, harbour dues and commodity prices. The immediate cause of his arrest was his illegal import of stills for the production of alcohol – a crime that gave the name 'Rum Rebellion' to the subsequent mutiny of the Corps.[12] By detaining Macarthur, Bligh was throwing down a gauntlet to the military and the embryonic settler leadership in Sydney, and challenging them to defy him. For Major Johnston, an ally of Macarthur, the detention was a call to arms, and he arrested the governor. Bligh was imprisoned on a ship on the Derwent River, and kept there for a year.

A new governor, General Lachlan MacQuarrie, a veteran of the American wars of the 1770s, was sent out from London. He arrived in December 1808 to impose imperial order, and the settler rebellion swiftly collapsed. The mutinous officers were found guilty of conspiracy. Major Johnston was sent to London for trial, found guilty and cashiered, returning to Australia in 1813. Macarthur was exiled to London, and came back to his farm in 1817. Captain Bligh was promoted to admiral. The New South Wales Corps was disbanded and its soldiers brought back to England.

In April 1816, a fresh resistance campaign was organised by Aborigines living along the Hawkesbury River, inland from Sydney. The Dharuk people had been in the forefront of the first anti-settler campaigns of the 1790s, but fierce repression had curbed their opposition. Now, as new settlements were established on their land, with an influx of post-war colonists, their hostility revived. Some of the new settlers were forced to abandon their farms and retreat to the town.

Soon the Aborigines were faced by three military units, sent out to curb their opposition by General Macquarrie. Noting grimly that the area surrounding the Hawkesbury River was 'infested' with Aborigines, Macquarrie ordered his soldiers to drive the Dharuk off the land. He told them to take few prisoners and to 'inflict exemplary and severe punishments', defined as shooting those who tried to escape. Soon Aborigine corpses were hung from trees in conspicuous places.

Macquarrie's units spent three weeks working along the riverbanks to the west of Sydney. One group, led by Captain Wallis, acting on the instructions laid down, found an Aborigine camp at Appin and killed fourteen. Some were shot and others, disposed of more cheaply, were forced over a precipice. In one infamous episode an Aborigine woman had the top of her head sliced off and was left with it dangling across her forehead, while her infant child was thrown into a fire and burned alive.

Soon the Hawkesbury River was made safe again for white settlement. Given carte blanche by the governor to exterminate the Aborigines, the returning settlers were not slow to take the law into their own hands.

CHAPTER 22

Resistance in South Africa, South America and Egypt

In January 1806, a British fleet commanded by Admiral Sir Home Popham anchored off the coast of South Africa, between Robben Island and the Blueberg. The ships had arrived to recover Cape Colony, the Dutch territory the British had first captured in 1795, and handed back to Holland in 1803 under the terms of the Amiens Treaty. Neither the large indigenous population of the colony – including the Khoi-Khoi, the Xhosa and the San – nor the Dutch white settlers expressed much interest in this change of imperial ownership, though it would soon have a dramatic effect on the fortunes of them all. Desultory resistance by Dutch colonial forces, under the command of General Jan Willem Janssens, did not hinder the British army of 6,000 men, led by Colonel Sir David Baird, from coming ashore and occupying Cape Town. The Dutch colony was once again in British hands.

Admiral Popham now sailed off across the South Atlantic on his own account, seeking to capture the Spanish Viceroyalty of Rio de la Plata – the River Plate – and its capital, Buenos Aires. His piratical fleet stopped on the way at the Atlantic island of St Helena to pick up reinforcements.

Spanish settlers had been living in South America rather longer than the Dutch in South Africa, and they too had been affected by the European upheavals in the wake of the French Revolution. Like the Dutch, they lived in a slave society where the majority population – native Indians and imported black slaves – remained a permanent threat to the white settlers, and where any threat of change of political ownership imposed from outside was bound to be unsettling.

Settlers and slaves were taken by surprise when they found some 1,500 British soldiers disembarking on the southern shore of the River Plate, near Buenos Aires, on 17 June, and they offered only sporadic resistance to the troops commanded by Colonel William Beresford. The city surrendered within ten days, and fifty-eight members of the city's ruling elite were happy to swear an oath of allegiance to King George of England, while the Marquis Rafael de Sobremonte, the Spanish viceroy, fled inland to Córdoba.[1]

Buenos Aires was wrong-footed for a few leaderless weeks, after which its citizens began to respond in a more adequate fashion. The population of the city itself was nearly 50,000, of whom only 10,000 were white.[2] Some 6,000 were black slaves, while most of the people were Indians and mixed-race mestizos, described variously as *pardos*, *morenos* and *chinos*. Several thousand men from this heterogeneous population – Indians, creoles and Spaniards – were organised by the Spanish settlers into a three-pronged militia force capable of confronting the British garrison established in the centre of the town.[3]

These motley troops laid siege to the British, and Beresford surrendered on 12 August – an event known to subsequent generations of Argentinians as 'La Reconquista'. The militia seized the colonel and a thousand of his soldiers, sending them under guard to various inland towns. Admiral Popham escaped to his flagship offshore, and retreated with his fleet downriver to the Atlantic. Reinforcements sent from South Africa arrived in the River Plate shortly after Beresford's defeat, and 2,000 men landed on the northern, Uruguayan side of the river, but they could do nothing to recover Buenos Aires.

The news of Beresford's initial success arrived in London in July, before the government heard of his defeat. 'Buenos Aires at the moment forms part of the British Empire', announced the *Times* on 13 September, hardly disguising its excitement in an editorial two days later: 'There can be hardly a doubt that the whole colony of La Plata will share the same fate as Buenos Aires; and from the flattering hopes held out to the inhabitants in the proclamations of General Beresford, they will see that it is their true interest to become a colony of the British empire.'

The British now planned to build on this Latin American triumph, and several fresh expeditions were organised. One fleet, commanded by General Sir Samuel Auchmuty, a veteran of the wars in America in the 1770s and the Indian wars against Tipu Sultan in the 1790s, was directed to Buenos Aires, and arrived in the River Plate in January 1807. A second fleet, led by Colonel Robert Craufurd, was ordered to make for the Chilean port of Valparaíso.[4] Craufurd was another veteran of the Indian wars, as well as of the Irish rebellion of 1798. Now in command of 4,000 men, he had orders to capture the Spanish province of Chile and to 'establish an uninterrupted communication with General Beresford, by a chain of posts or any other means'. The British planned to link up their (proposed) twin conquests, 750 miles apart, across the mountain chain of the Andes, just as they had once hoped to conquer Nicaragua in 1780.[5]

Craufurd's expeditionary force to Chile was soon obliged to divert to the River Plate, to help repair the damage done by Beresford's defeat. Auchmuty's armada, joining up with the troop reinforcements from South Africa camped on the north side of the river, captured the town of Montevideo in February 1807.[6] Honour demanded that the British recapture Buenos Aires, and fresh reinforcements were sent out from Britain that year – a third fleet, commanded by General Sir John Whitelocke.

* * *

Grandly named as the governor-general of South America, with orders to recover Buenos Aires, General Whitelocke sailed into the River Plate in May 1807 with a force of 8,000 men.[7] He assumed command of the two British expeditionary forces encamped north of the river at Montevideo. When Whitelock and Colonel Craufurd attacked early in July, the local militias in Buenos Aires were well prepared, and they secured a resounding victory.

Commanded by Spanish settlers, but largely composed of *gauchos*, blacks and Indians, the militias were more effective than those available a year earlier. Citizens had had a year to prepare for this second attack, and the *cabildo*, or town council, received support from the country's large Indian population. One group of Indian caciques offered to provide '20,000 of our subjects, all men of war, with five horses each', to attack the *colorados*, the red-faced Englishmen. Men from the Lonko, the Mapuches and the Indians of the pampas were mobilised against the British invaders.[8]

This was 'a victory for the city', wrote the Argentine historian Tulio Halperín Donghi, 'for its regiments – both Creole and Spanish – and for all its inhabitants'. Even the town's slaves were provided with weapons of steel, displaying a degree of loyalty that surprised those who had been reluctant to arm them.[9]

After the victory, Whitelock's troops were dragged through the streets of the city.[10] Their humiliating defeat at the hands of Indians and blacks was recorded in the diary of a British officer, Colonel Lancelot Holland: 'Nothing could be more mortifying than our passage through the streets amidst the rabble who had conquered us. They were very dark-skinned people, short and ill-made, covered with rags, armed with long muskets and some a sword. There was neither order nor uniformity among them.'

With such an unfortunate defeat, the imperial ambitions of the British in South America were at an end. Their surviving forces were swiftly withdrawn from Buenos Aires and Montevideo, and the depleted fleet sailed for home.[11] The military disasters led to another court martial, with Whitelocke proving less fortunate than Admiral Popham. He was thrown out of the army and 'declared totally unfit and unworthy to serve His Majesty in any military capacity whatsoever'.[12]

The mixed-race militias of Buenos Aires were soon rejoicing again, for they organised a revolution of their own in May 1810, against their Spanish rulers. A junta was established, whose most influential political figure, Mariano Moreno, was a 'Jacobin' supporter of the country's Indian population who unveiled a revolutionary programme. Equality between Indians and Spaniards was proclaimed, and copies of Rousseau's *Social Contract* were distributed throughout the country. This promising start to Argentina's independence was too radical for the times, and Moreno was detained and sent into exile. Banished to Europe, he died during the sea voyage.

* * *

The indigenous Indian inhabitants of a British territory further north, descendants of the Mayas, were also in the forefront of resistance in 1807, attacking the loggers in the mahogany forests of British Honduras that fringe the Atlantic coast of Guatemala. The archives of the colony record an urgent request that year for 'arms and ammunition for gangs working up the [Belize] river at Hogstyle Bank, who have been attacked by Indians.'[13]

These were continuing requests for help. A few years earlier, in 1802, Indians had been 'committing depredations upon the mahogany works', and British troops were called out. Later, in 1817, the archives refer to 'the exposed and unprotected state of the settlers' and to 'the vast hordes of Indians who are all in the constant habit of breaking in upon their works'.

Britain had formally wrested this coastal strip of territory from Spain in 1798, defeating a Spanish fleet sent to drive out the British loggers settled there. Logwood and lately mahogany had been cut along the coast since the seventeenth century, and while the whites gave the orders, the work of logging was done by slaves, known later as 'Belize Creoles', brought over from the islands of the Caribbean. European demand for luxury furniture in the eighteenth century had led a pioneering group of white settlers to penetrate ever further inland, in search of untouched stands of mahogany. Soon the loggers came up against the forest homes of the Mayan Indians – heirs to a great civilisation, and still unconquered at that time by the Spanish in the Yucatán, the neighbouring province of Mexico.

The British policed the slaves in the colony with black troops from the 5th West Indian Regiment, but the soldiers had little success in controlling the Mayan regions of the interior. Captain George Henderson, an officer stationed in Belize in 1809, noted how difficult it was to do so: 'Numerous tribes of hostile Indians often left their recesses in the woods for the purposes of plunder. This they often accomplished; and if resistance were offered, not infrequently committed the most sanguinary murders.'[14]

Familiar with the forest, the Mayans kept their hiding-places secret from the military. Captain Henderson recalled that, while it had been 'found expedient frequently to dispatch' soldiers in pursuit of fugitive Indians, 'the habitations of these people have never been traced'. Yet the Mayans were certainly affected by the British punitive expeditions, and Henderson noted proudly that although the Indians were 'peculiarly ferocious . . . the dread of the military . . . has latterly operated as a very effectual check'. Secure in their forest base, however, the Mayans sustained a continuing resistance struggle throughout the nineteenth century.

In March 1807, Mohamed Ali, the emerging nationalist ruler of Egypt, and its dominant figure in the early nineteenth century, received news that a British fleet had landed troops at Alexandria. The subsequent British invasion of Egypt lasted for six months, and ended in disaster for the British. It set the pattern for an uneasy relationship between Britain and Egypt that would last for 150 years, concluding with a comparable British humiliation at Suez in 1956.

British military expeditions had been in Egypt before, in 1801, when they had sought to prevent Napoleon from establishing a pro-French regime in the country and blocking the route to India. Sir Ralph Abercromby, the general who had fought in the Caribbean in the 1790s, had been killed there in 1801 on the eve of the French withdrawal. After the Amiens peace treaty in 1802, the British occupation forces also withdrew, leaving a Turkish governor in charge. The British returned to London with an Egyptian political figure, Mohamed Bey al-Alfi, who they hoped might be of future use in controlling Egypt in their own interest.[15]

Al-Alfi returned to Egypt in February 1804 with a view to establishing a government favourable to Britain, but the formidable Mohamed Ali had the support of the population of Cairo, and was confirmed as governor in 1805. Al-Alfi's position became increasingly marginal, and although a British fleet arrived off Alexandria in March 1807 to support his cause, officers were informed that he had died two months earlier.

The fleet, commanded by Admiral Sir John Duckworth and with an army on board led by General Alexander Mackenzie Fraser, continued with its original plan and made an unopposed landing close to Rosetta (Rashid). British troops advanced through the narrow streets of the town, but soon came under attack from the Egyptian garrison which 'opened a deadly fire on them from the latticed windows and the roofs of the houses'.[16] The Egyptians obliged General Fraser to retreat along the coast to Aboukir and Alexandria, and the British lost many soldiers along the way: 185 were killed and 281 wounded. The Egyptians displayed the heads of the dead soldiers on stakes in Cairo, on either side of the Ezbekia road, while the survivors, according to one account, were 'sold as slaves'.[17]

The Egyptians foiled a second British attempt to capture Rosetta the following month, when two British officers commanding 2,500 men oversaw the bombardment of the city over a period of two weeks. Egyptian reinforcements again obliged the British soldiers to retreat, and their advance guard was cut off and captured. Half the men straggled back to Alexandria, but many were killed or wounded. Others were again taken as prisoners to Cairo, and several hundred more British heads were fixed on stakes in the city. The surviving prisoners were marched between 'these mutilated remains of their countrymen'. Mohamed Ali forced Fraser to make a humiliating withdrawal from Alexandria in September.

Effectively establishing himself as a ruler largely independent of Turkey, Mohamed Ali went on to carve out an autonomous empire that extended southwards into the Sudan. He revolutionised the country's land ownership and embarked on its industrial development. His successors carried on his ambitious programmes, but were checked by another (more successful) British invasion in 1882. Ali's family lived on, and his great-great-grandson, King Farouk, was not finally removed from the throne until 1952.

CHAPTER 23

Slave Rebellion, Xhosa Resistance, and White Settler Revolt in Cape Colony

When the British recovered Cape Colony from the Dutch in 1806, they still had sharp memories of Chungwa's Xhosa rebellion of 1799 in the Zuurveld. Fearing further resistance from the Xhosa, a young officer, Colonel Richard Collins, was sent out in 1808 to explore the Xhosa land to the north and the east of Cape Colony's frontiers. He spent several months engaged on this task.

Chungwa was now old and ill, but Collins made contact with Ndlambe and other Xhosa chiefs, notably Ngqika and Hintsa. Ndlambe was a man in his seventies, a Xhosa ruler since 1782, described by a contemporary as a 'perfect specimen of a powerful chief of the olden times, before intercourse with the colonists'. He had long challenged his rival Chungwa for supremacy in the Zuurveld, and had fought and negotiated on the frontier with Dutch settlers long before the British arrived. He was to live on until 1828.

Collins reported back to the governor in August 1809, and his recommendations were forthright: the Xhosa in the Zuurveld, a territory later renamed the district of Albany, should be forcibly expelled, and plots of their land should be offered to European settlers. The Xhosa could be pushed across the Great Fish River, and allowed to live further east. When his report was first delivered, the British Empire was short of troops: some had been diverted to seize the River Plate; others were occupied in holding down India and in planning for campaigns in the Indian Ocean; still others were fighting against Napoleon in Spain. With the start of the Peninsula campaign in 1808, imperial resources were stretched to breaking-point. There were no soldiers to spare for frontier service in South Africa. The 'forcible expulsion' favoured by Collins would have to wait its turn.

Like many territories in the Empire, Cape Colony relied on slave labour for its workforce. When the British regained control of the colony in 1806, they found a country with 30,000 black slaves and perhaps 50,000 Khoi-Khoi, or Hottentots. There were thousands of Xhosa on the frontier, and only about 26,000 white settlers. All these groups were to rebel against the British at one time or another over the next hundred years, but the first to seek their freedom were the slaves.

The slaves at the Cape came from different parts of the world. Those known as 'Malay slaves' were Muslims, shipped in from all over the Indian Ocean – a legacy of Dutch rule. Indeed many of their forebears had arrived at the Cape as political prisoners from elsewhere in the Dutch Empire. Slaves from Africa had been brought to the Cape by the British during their earlier occupation, between 1795 and 1802. Of the fifty or so slaves brought to court after the rebellion in 1808, eighteen came from the Cape itself, seventeen from Mozambique, three from Madagascar, and one each from Mauritius, Ceylon, Malabar, Bengal, Timor, Batavia, Java and Bali.

The British parliament had voted to abolish the slave trade in March 1807, and in July the youthful British governor of the Cape, Du Pré Alexander, Earl of Caledon, proposed to free the 250 slaves who worked for the government. His proposal was a clear indication that the situation of the wider slave population might soon change, and slaves began to wake up and take notice – although the message must have been confusing, since a fresh shipment of slaves arrived at Cape Town in December.

Two slaves and two Irishmen combined together in October 1808 to organise a slave rebellion. A Muslim slave from Mauritius called Louis, described later in court as 'the chief and ringleader of the insurgents', was joined by James Hooper, an Irish labourer recently arrived in the colony. Hooper rented a room in Louis's house in Cape Town, and claimed that since there were no slaves in Ireland, the same situation should prevail at the Cape. The two of them went on to team up with Abraham, a slave born locally.

The three men formed a secret group to organise a slave revolt, designed to spark an end to slavery. They were joined later by Michael Kelly, a sailor and a countryman of Hooper's. Their plan, according to the subsequent court account, 'was to incite as much as possible the slaves in the interior to insurrection and rebellion'. Then, 'having assembled and armed them with such arms as were to be procured in the country', they were to march to Cape Town to seize the first military post. They planned to send a letter to the governor to demand freedom for the slaves, and if this was not forthcoming they would 'make themselves masters of the Magazines, to storm and force the Prison, release the prisoners, and fight for the liberty of the slaves'.[1]

Louis from Mauritius was a slave who worked independently around the town. He paid a rent to his owner, and was sufficiently light-skinned to pass as white. His wife was a free woman. With Hooper and Abraham, he sought out potential recruits for their conspiracy, and they soon heard that slaves at a Dutch farm in the Swartland, north of Cape Town, were likely candidates. Hooper and Abraham visited the farm in early October, and found the slaves willing to join their proposed rebellion. Returning to Cape Town, they encountered Kelly, and persuaded him to take part in their plot.

Later that month, the four organisers returned to the Swartland farm to unleash their rebellion. Louis was to be the 'Governor or Chief of the Blacks', while Hooper was 'to obtain a high position under him'. The operation began well enough. They arrived in a hired wagon, with Louis wearing full-dress military uniform, with gold epaulets and a sword. The Dutch farmer was away from home, and Kelly, who spoke some Dutch, explained to his wife that Louis was a Spanish captain. The woman was sufficiently impressed to invite the four men in for dinner, and pressed them to stay the night.

On the following morning, they persuaded ten of the slaves working on the farm to join them, and they moved on to other settlements in the neighbourhood, travelling in their own hired wagon and in a second one commandeered from the farm. They gave out a simple message (according to the court account): the British governor had ordered all slaves to proceed to Cape Town to be set free, and had declared that all white men should be made prisoner. Many slaves joined in with alacrity, and spread the news. Farms were occupied, wagons and carts were seized, guns and ammunition were taken, and wine was freely distributed. Several white farmers were seized and humiliated, and one farmer's wife was raped.

Although much drink was taken, several hundred slaves marched off to Cape Town in separate groups. The plan was bold and imaginative, if ill-prepared. Long before the slaves reached town, the authorities were alerted and the cavalry sent out. Three days after the slaves set off, they were surrounded and seized. More than 300 were arrested, and fifty brought to trial in Cape Town in December.

The court's judgment was typically harsh, with some sixteen rebel slaves sentenced to be hanged and quartered, 'the said quarters to be exposed upon stakes at the gibbets outside the town'. A further twenty-two were to be flogged, 'to be tied to a stake and severally scourged with rods on their bare backs'. The others were to be sent to the prison on Robben Island.

Yet the British governor was uncertain of the reaction within the slave community, and he recommended leniency. Only five rebels were hanged eventually, but fifty were flogged and sent to Robben Island. Louis, Hooper and Abraham, as the principal organisers, were among those hanged, but Kelly was reprieved. The remaining rebels were ordered to watch the executions before being returned to their masters' farms.

Another two decades were to pass before the slaves' dream of freedom was realised – an event that triggered off the Great Trek and a fresh twist to the history of South Africa. For many of the settlers of Dutch origin, the British decision to abolish slavery in 1833 was the final straw, and between 1835 and 1837 perhaps as many as 5,000 of them moved out of Cape Colony across the Orange River, to set up an independent state of their own – the Orange Free State. Within twenty years, a further 20,000 had followed them, taking their slaves with them.

* * *

A new and more severe military governor arrived at the Cape in 1811. General Sir John Cradock, last heard of creating the conditions for the sepoy rebellion at Vellore in 1806, had extensive imperial experience, for he had served in senior positions in the West Indies and Ireland, as well as in India and the Iberian Peninsula. In Spain, where his talents were considered inadequate, he was replaced by Wellington. Cradock studied Colonel Collins's report of the situation in the Zuurveld, and swiftly requested that it should be implemented forthwith. The Xhosa were to be rounded up and driven out of the Zuurveld. Martial law was proclaimed along the frontier.

Lack of troops was no longer an argument for inaction. The British could deploy the Khoi-Khoi regiment of Hottentot soldiers inherited from the Dutch, sometimes known as the Cape Corps, and their commander at Cape Town, Colonel John Graham, was put in charge of a small extermination force. His campaign began on Christmas Day. He marched out to the east with his Khoi-Khoi contingent, a handful of British soldiers and a few commando units formed by Dutch settlers. His principal weapons were fire and famine. He had chosen 'the season of the corn being on the ground', he explained later, 'in order that if the Kaffirs would not keep their promise of going away, we might the more severely punish them for their many crimes by destroying it'.[2]

Ndlambe, the oldest surviving Xhosa chief in the Zuurveld, encountered Graham's troops at the end of December. Shaking his spear, he shouted out his defiance in famous words: 'This country is mine; I won it in war, and shall maintain it.' Now he faced a British force intent on expelling his people from the frontier zone. He reiterated his claim to the land and disappeared into the bush, leaving his men to maintain a steady resistance. Several white settlers were killed, and for a moment the two forces seemed evenly matched.

A week later the tide turned against the Xhosa. Ndlambe had retreated, while Chungwa lay ill and dying, and was killed in cold blood while sleeping. Under the rules of martial law, Colonel Graham's orders were explicit: any male Xhosa seen out in the open was to be shot, and women were also killed.[3]

By the middle of January, Ndlambe's people had been forced out of the Zuurveld and across the Great Fish River. Colonel Graham's scorched-earth policy now began in earnest. 'Two parties of one hundred men each were sent to destroy the gardens, and burn the villages', wrote Lieutenant Hart on 17 January, reflecting on the prosperity of the area the soldiers had been called upon to obliterate. 'The gardens here are very large and numerous, and here also are the best garden pumpkins and the largest Indian corn I have ever seen . . . some of the pumpkins are five and a half feet round, and the corn ten feet high.' On the following day, Hart recorded, 300 men 'went early to destroy gardens and huts, taking with them 600 oxen to trample down the corn and vegetables'.

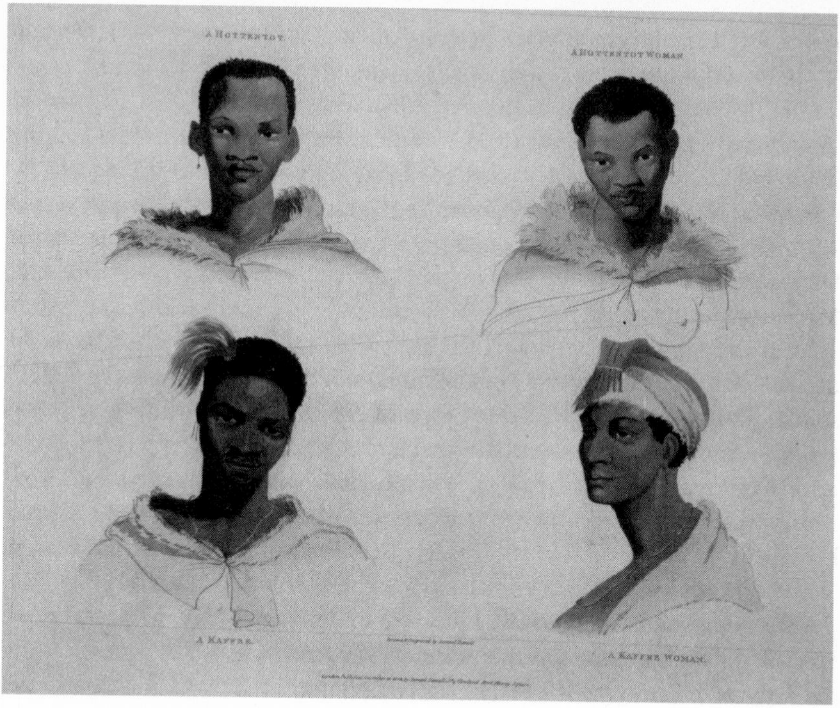

A Hottentot (Khoi-Khoi), a Hottentot Woman; a Kaffre (Xhosa), a Kaffre Woman. Four head-and-shoulder vignettes engraved by Samuel Daniell, 1804.

Many weeks were spent in this way, the soldiers ensuring that the Xhosa would never return to the land they had once made so prosperous. The British commander was entirely frank about his purpose. 'The only way of getting rid of them', Colonel Graham told a correspondent,

> is by depriving them of the means of subsistence and continually harassing them, for which purpose the whole force is constantly employed in destroying prodigious quantities of Indian corn and millet which they have planted . . . taking from them the few cattle which they conceal in the woods with great address, and shooting every man who can be found.

'This is detestable work', he added thoughtfully; 'we are forced to hunt them like wild beasts'. Graham's task was finished in March 1812. He had completed the first great 'removal' in the history of the British occupation of South Africa, driving some 20,000 Xhosa across the Fish River. Hundreds were killed in the process, and thousands of cattle seized.

Although Chungwa had been killed, Ndlambe escaped across the river to fight another day.

Ndlambe's nephew Ngqika (sometimes Gaika) was left behind to make peace with the British. A younger man, then barely thirty, he was to become their stooge Xhosa chief, working with them as he had once briefly worked with the Dutch in 1803. The Dutch, like the British, had nothing but praise for their African collaborators, describing Ngqika as 'one of the handsomest men that can be seen, even among the Caffres uncommonly tall, with strong limbs and very fine features'; 'there is in his whole appearance something that at once speaks the king, although there was nothing in his dress to distinguish him, except some rows of white beads which he wore round his neck . . . His countenance is expressive of the utmost benevolence and self-confidence.' [4]

Ngqika had thrown in his lot with the British, and was obliged to work under their command. Yet his role was never easy. Orders were given that any Xhosa remaining in the Zuurveld without a document bearing his signature would be shot on sight.

The Zuurveld was lost to the Xhosa for all time. Its idyllic landscape was described by John Campbell from the London Missionary Society, who travelled through it a year after Graham's extermination campaign had ended. The countryside is 'beautiful in the extreme', he wrote, 'much resembling a nobleman's park in England'. Yet he detected the harsh reality behind the surface appeal, for its slopes were still covered with the abandoned gardens of the Xhosa. 'The skeletons of many of their houses remained, and some tobacco was still growing, but all their cornfields were destroyed . . . not a living soul, but stillness reigns.'

Xhosa bitterness at being driven from their land was never wholly assuaged in later years. One of the old Dutch settlers, Andries Stockenstrom, recorded in his autobiography the views of those who had survived. After the war of 1811–12, he wrote, no honest man would deny that the Xhosa, if sure of success, would rise to a man 'and cut the throat of every white male and female whom they could overtake – as a measure partly of policy and partly of revenge'.[5] To celebrate Colonel Graham's success, the British named a new settlement in the Zuurveld in his honour. Grahamstown survives to this day.

A group of Dutch settlers in Cape Colony, unhappy with British rule, organised a rebellion in 1815. One of the causes of the rebellion, a pale replay of the Dutch resistance to British rule in 1795 and 1799, was the British use of the Khoi-Khoi to police the frontiers of the colony – an imperial strategy that gave offence to many old Dutch settlers. Their rebellion was crushed at what became known as 'the battle at Slachter's Nek', in which Khoi-Khoi soldiers participated.

Recognising that they would have to ally themselves with the Xhosa if they were to achieve their aim of throwing out the British, some of the rebels paid a visit to Ngqika's kraal to ask for his support. They offered him the old Xhosa territory of the Zuurveld, seized by the British in 1811, if he would agree to collaborate. The British were threatened with a white settler revolt, organised in league with the Africans, but fortunately for them, Ngqika remained loyal.

The rebellion was sparked off by the death of Frederick Bezuidenhout, a Dutch farmer charged with maltreating his Khoi-Khoi workers, who was killed by a British military unit while resisting arrest. Johannes, his brother, vowed to avenge Frederick's death, declaring that he would drive the British out of South Africa. He secured the support of Hendrik Prinsloo, the farmer son of Martinus Prinsloo, a prime mover of the settler rebellion of 1799. Hendrik had considerable influence in the province, and the chief participants in the rebellion were either close neighbours or members of his extended family, including his brother-in-law Theunis de Klerk.

A British officer at Grahamstown, made aware of the settlers' plans and of their contacts with Ngqika, took swift action. He sent soldiers to arrest Prinsloo and detain him at his farm. The rebels secured some settler support, but their overtures to Ngqika had an adverse effect on other Dutch settlers in the region. Many chose to support the British authorities rather than accept an alliance with the Xhosa.

Eventually a group of sixty rebels, led by Johannes Bezuidenhout in Prinsloo's enforced absence, assembled at Slachter's Nek, on a ridge overlooking the Little Fish River. Their immediate plan was to release Prinsloo from detention, though some had wider ambitions. One of the settlers, probably Bezuidenhout, made a formal oath: 'I swear by God Almighty never to rest till I have driven the oppressors of my nation from this land.'

No battle occurred at Slachter's Nek, for most of the rebels surrendered when faced by a superior British force led by Colonel Jacob Cuyler, by origin an 'Empire Loyalist' born in Albany in America. A handful of them escaped and fled to the territory of the Xhosa, but Bezuidenhout was killed. In December, Colonel Cuyler presided over a Special Court at Uitenhage, where forty-seven rebels were put on trial. Six of them, including Prinsloo, were found guilty of rebellion and sentenced to death. Five death sentences were upheld by the governor, General Lord Charles Somerset, as a warning to the settlers against further rebellion. Other rebels were exiled, but required to attend the executions before they left.

Colonel Cuyler presided over the execution of the five men, but the operation was so grossly bungled that Slachter's Nek and its gruesome aftermath entered into the folklore of the white settlers in Africa. The scaffold collapsed at the first attempt, and had to be rebuilt before the executions could finally take place.[6] The memory of this frightful event was to be resurrected on many subsequent occasions in the later history of South Africa, notably during the Boer War nearly one hundred years later.

CHAPTER 24

British Penetration into the Persian Gulf

On the morning of 13 November 1809, the Qawasim defenders of the walled town of Ra's al-Khaymah, in the Persian Gulf, prepared to resist a British invasion force disembarking from a fleet that had sailed from Bombay, via Muscat. Ra's al-Khaymah, the 'tented point', is today one of the states of the United Arab Emirates; it was then an important Muslim town in the Gulf, ruled since the previous year by Hassan ben Rahma, a sheikh of the Qawasim, an influential Arab nation on the Gulf coast traditionally at odds with the Omanis of Muscat.

The town's defences were subjected to heavy bombardment, but the Qawasim put up stiff, if eventually ineffective, resistance. 'The Arabs ran towards the point of debarkation with tumultuous shouts', wrote Captain John Wainwright, the British commander, 'but the grapeshot from the gunboats shook them a good deal, and the troops, landing in great style, soon overpowered them.' Soon the Qawasim were driven from the town, 'a great part of which, with the whole of the dhows and naval stores, was burnt by four o'clock. Thus, in a few hours, was this enterprising and powerful people reduced to poverty and weakness.'[1]

This was the first serious opposition the British had encountered at the start of their long campaign to bring the territories of the Persian Gulf under imperial control. Their ally was Sayyid Said, the new Sultan of Muscat and Oman, a Gulf territory further to the south. British support for his Sultanate was the result of their defeat of Tipu Sultan in 1799, for the Mysore ruler had long kept a political and commercial agent at Muscat, a relationship that the British inherited. Informal arrangements made with the Muscat Sultan were to last for the next two centuries.

The strategically placed port of Muscat, at the entrance to the Gulf, and on the trade routes to Europe and Africa, had attracted outside interest since the days of the Portuguese. Alfonso de Albuquerque had seized it in 1508. The Omanis threw out the Portuguese in the seventeenth century, forcing them to abandon most of their possessions along the coast of East Africa (including Zanzibar but not Mozambique). In the early nineteenth century it was the turn of the British, and Captain John Malcolm sailed into the Gulf in 1800, after the death of Tipu, and signed a treaty with Sultan ibn Ahmed, then the ruler of Muscat and Oman.[2]

Once allied with a friendly local ruler, the British now wished to control the region's trade. To do so effectively, they would need to set up a military base comparable to the one they had established at Penang in 1786.[3] Initially, they had their eyes on the strategic island of Qish, just off the Persian coast on the eastern side of the Gulf, controlled by the Qawasim of Ra's al-Khaymah. But they were not alone in taking an interest in the Gulf. In April 1803, the Wahhabis of Arabia, led by Saud ben Abdul Aziz, had swept across the desert and captured the city of Mecca, and then begun expanding eastwards towards the Gulf, threatening the traditional hegemony over its waters held by the Omani Sultanate.

The Qawasim were the first to perceive changes ahead. Sultan ibn Saqr, ruler at Ra's al-Khaymah, sought to make peace both with the Saudi Wahhabis, clearly seen as the emerging Arab force in the area, and with the British, the predominant European power. A balancing act was required that could not be long sustained. Sultan ben Saqr was perceived as too pro-British, and the Wahhabis detained him in 1808, replacing him with his nephew, Hassan ben Rahma, who favoured the Saudis.

The outlook was not promising for the Omanis, especially when their Sultan ibn Ahmed died, in 1804. His death was followed by a succession struggle, and a new imam, Sayyid Said, was not chosen until 1806. The British at Bombay perceived that the imam would fall into the hands of the Wahhabis, as the Qawasim had done, unless he was provided with military support. To weaken the Wahhabis, they decided to crush their new ally, the Qawasim.

The Qawasim found themselves denounced as 'pirates', a customary term of abuse during the early years of the nineteenth century given to any small nation that had ships of its own to challenge British control of the seas.[4] They heard news in October 1809 that the British had fitted out a naval taskforce at Bombay with a plan to attack R'as al-Khaymah. The force consisted of ten ships, 700 European soldiers, 500 sepoys, and 200 'camp followers'.

The Qawasim fortress was well defended, and Hassan ben Rahma had some 20,000 Bedouin Arabs he could summon to his assistance. Sayyid Said, the Oman imam, advised the British that the proposed attack was 'rash in the extreme'; but despite his pessimism, he promised to provide the expedition with pilots, provisions, and water. In practice, as Captain Wainwright noted later, very little was forthcoming.[5]

R'as Al-Khaymah was attacked on 11 November, with the British fleet anchored below its great walls. 'The town was cannonaded by the small cruisers and gun boats with visible effect', Wainwright recorded. 'So destitute of personal apprehension were the Arabs, that the moment a shot fell, numbers came to pick it up.' The Qawasim saw a hundred of their men killed and fifty of their dhows destroyed. When the troops went ashore the next day, they fell at once to plunder, 'securing considerable sums of money'. Hassan ben Rahma was not present at the destruction of the town, for he had crossed the Gulf earlier to the town of Luft. He was pursued there by the British, who destroyed both Luft and Linga. Hassan survived to fight another day.

Ra's al Khaymah, fortress of the Qawasim, under attack by British forces, 13 November 1809. 'The grapeshot from the gunboats shook them a good deal, and the troops, landing in great style, soon overpowered them.' Engraved by I. Clark after an aquatint by R. Temple.

Returning to the port of Muscat in December, the British found that Sultan Sayyid Said had a fresh task for them. The Omani town of Shinas had been occupied by the Wahhabi, and the Sultan urged the British force to remove them. In January 1810, the town was attacked by a joint British–Omani force, and its great curtain walls were breached. The Wahhabi put up an 'obstinate resistance', according to Captain Lionel Smith, a British officer present at the siege:[6]

> His defences were nearly battered to ruins, and the greatest part of his garrison lay around in mangled heaps. Still in this hopeless condition, after the body of his fort was occupied by the British and the Omanis, did he persevere, at the least cessation of our musketry, to fire upon us from two of his towers . . .

The Wahhabi occupying the fort at Shinas eventually surrendered, and the British fleet returned to Bombay in February. The Arab loss of life was put at 400, but it was a Pyrrhic victory for the British and the Omanis. Captain Smith noted drily that 'the fort was so demolished by our fire' that the Sultan of Oman and Muscat 'did not think it prudent to keep possession of it'.

Ten years later, in November 1819, Sheikh Hassan ben Rahma, the Muslim ruler of the Qawasim and the controller of the trading port at Ra's al-Khaymah, prepared his town's population of 6,000 fighters for yet another bombardment by the British. The Sheikh was aware of British complaints that the Qawasim were 'pirates' who interfered with free trade in the Gulf. Yet he also knew that the real reason for this fresh invasion, as before, was the British ambition to secure military control of the strategic waterway of the Gulf, in tandem with their ally, the Sultan of Oman. Sheikh Hassan's Qawasim were still at odds with Oman, and the British were again intervening on the side of its Sultan.

'Handsome in person, mild in demeanour', Sheikh Hassan was said by an imperial observer to have 'a look of sullen tiger-like ferocity lurking in his restless eye.' He remained at his post at Ra's al-Khaymah while it was subjected to a heavy attack from the sea. British troops came ashore on 3 December, and much of the town, its fortifications and its warehouses, rebuilt after the attack of 1809, were now again destroyed. This new punitive expedition was led by General Sir William Grant-Keir, formerly the commander of the Gujerat Field Force, responsible for exterminating the Pindaris in 1817. He had sailed from Bombay with an army of European soldiers and sepoys, the largest force ever sent to the Gulf. A second army moved overland from Muscat. Captain Perronet Thompson was his interpreter.

With his town destroyed, Sheikh Hassan withdrew inland to the hill fortress at Zaya,[7] and initially his defences there were sufficient to keep the British expeditionary force at bay. Grant-Keir ordered two large twenty-four-pound guns to be brought ashore and dragged inland to destroy the fortress. On 21 December, with Zaya filled with women and children as well as with fighting men, the fort was shelled. The sheikh gave in after a two-hour bombardment and was taken back to Ra's al-Khaymah in chains. Advancing into the ruins of the fort, the British found 400 women and children among the 400 male defenders.

The sheikh was obliged to sign a treaty with the British, drafted by Captain Perronet, which declared that 'there shall be a cessation of plunder and piracy by land and sea on the part of the Arabs, who are parties to this contract, forever'.[8]

With the humiliation of Sheikh Hassan and the destruction of his port city, no further obstacles remained to British military control of the Gulf, which survived as an integral part of Britain's informal empire for 150 years. The Qawasim watched helplessly as British ships sailed along the coast throughout January 1820, burning more than 200 of their boats and destroying their harbours and fortifications at Jazira al-Hamra, Ajman, Umm al-Qaiwain and Sharjah. When the ships eventually sailed back to Bombay in February 1820, a small garrison was established at the ruins of Ra's al-Khaymah, and Sheikh Hassan was replaced by his more pliable uncle, Sheikh Sultan ibn Saqr.

The British were now committed to the support of their only firm ally in the region, the imam of Oman and Muscat, Said bin Sultan. When the imam appealed, in November 1820, for help against the forces of one of his tribal chieftains – Sheikh Mohammed ben Ali, ruler of the Bani Bou Ali – a British force of sepoys commanded by Captain Perronet Thompson was sent out to deal with the problem. It met with disaster.

The sheikh's soldiers attacked, and the British captain ordered the sepoys to charge with their bayonets. 'Not a man moved forward', he wrote in a letter to his wife.

> I then ordered them to fire. They began a straggling and ineffectual fire, aided by the artillery; the Arabs all the while advancing, brandishing their swords.
>
> The sepoys stood still till the Arabs were within fifteen yards, when they turned and ran. I immediately galloped to the point where the sepoys were least confused, and endeavoured to make them stand; but they fired their musquets in the air and went off.[9]

Captain Thompson had been captured during the assault on Buenos Aires in 1807, and was accustomed to catastrophe.

> As the morning wore on, the full extent of the disaster became apparent. Only a handful of the wounded men had left the camp. Six European combatant officers, one medical officer, and no less than 317 others – out of a total of just over 400 – had been killed, including 17 of the artillerymen . . .[10]

The Omani sultan put his own losses at about 400.

The survivors of the British force abandoned the scene in ignominious retreat, spiking their guns and throwing their powder barrels down a well. Policing the Gulf over the years remained a costly business.

CHAPTER 25

The British Seizure of Mauritius, the Seychelles and Indonesia

The British had long coveted the extensive complex of French islands in the Indian Ocean. Mauritius was a significant prize, as were the islands associated with it – Réunion, the Seychelles and Diego Garcia (a coral atoll in the Chagos archipelago 1,000 miles to the north, still notionally a British colonial territory at the start of the twenty-first century). Yet British imperial planners had given little thought to the immense population of slaves on these islands, nor to the tiny group of French settlers who, in revolutionary times, had grown accustomed to ruling themselves.

Mauritius was a slave island producing sugar, with a tiny slave-owning settler class reminiscent of the French plantation owners of Haiti. These settlers, like the Dutch settlers in South Africa, had initially welcomed the French Revolution in 1789, perceiving that they could use it to their own ends. They formed a republican colonial assembly. Yet when two Revolutionary commissioners, Étienne-Laurent-Pierre Burnel and René-Gaston Baco de la Chapelle, arrived from Paris in June 1796 with 2,000 soldiers to enforce the abolition of slavery decreed in 1794, the white settlers quickly changed their tune. The French soldiers were locked up in their barracks, and Burnel and Baco were deported to the Philippines. For several years, out of touch with the metropolis, the islands came under the direct rule of the white settlers. They returned to French control in 1803, after Napoleon had supported the revival of slavery.

In 1810 a British fleet sailed from India, with 10,000 sepoys on board, to capture the French-ruled islands of Mauritius and the Seychelles, as well as Réunion. Using the sepoy army in India for imperial wars further afield was now an established custom, for sepoys had already travelled to South Africa in 1795, to Egypt in 1801, and to Ceylon in 1803. On this occasion the fleet sailed south from Calcutta, under the command of General Sir John Abercromby (the son of Ralph Abercromby, who had been killed in Egypt in 1807). They took additional soldiers on board at Madras, some of whom had sailed down from Bombay. This Indian fleet was soon joined by a second fleet that sailed up from Britain's recent acquisition at Cape Town, and in July the joint fleet captured Réunion, before sailing on to Mauritius.[1] It met with disaster in August when it encountered a French fleet off the south-east coast of Mauritius. At the 'Battle of

Grand Port', chalked up as a British defeat, three British ships ran aground and more than 2,000 sailors were captured.[2]

Three months later, in November 1810, the British were finally successful. The sepoys landed at Grand Bay, about twelve miles from Port Louis, and while the tiny French garrison of 1,000 men fought back for a while, the result was not in doubt. The 60,000 slaves working on the French-owned sugar plantations watched without lifting a finger as they came under the control of a new imperial overlord.

The sailors captured three months earlier were released, and the French garrison was sent home to France at British expense. The new ruler, Colonel Sir Robert Farquhar, a former governor of Penang, was known for his opposition to slavery. He was initially committed to uphold the decision in 1807 to abolish the slave trade throughout the British Empire. But abolition was very far from the minds of the slave-owners of Mauritius, and Colonel Farquhar was soon made to understand that he could not rule without their cooperation. He decreed that the French Code Noir, drawn up in 1685 in the reign of Louis XIV,[3] would remain in place, and that the legal position of the settlers concerning slavery would remain unchanged. The settlers were tacitly permitted to import the slaves they needed, and some 30,000 arrived between 1811 and 1821.[4]

Eleven years later, in December 1821, slaves imported from Madagascar took part in a rebellion organised with the assistance of Prince Ratsitatane, a member of Madagascar's ruling family. The tiny surviving French community of 7,000 white settlers on Mauritius lived in a state of barely suppressed terror, similar to that of the whites of British Honduras and the islands of the West Indies. They shared the island with 100,000 unfriendly workers – some 80,000 slaves, brought in from all over the Indian Ocean but especially from Madagascar and East Africa,[5] and 20,000 non-white Maroons who were nominally 'free'. For many years the white settlers had operated what was effectively a police state. A small militia of armed settlers, commanded by Captain Orieux, was organised to police the plantations, to fight against Maroons, to assist with the illegal trade, and to capture runaway slaves.

The British authorities had agreed to allow the French settlers to live according to their inherited traditions. Plantation owners were tacitly permitted to continue importing slave labour in spite of the formal end of the slave trade in 1807. Some 30,000 slaves were imported during the first decade of British rule, and most came from Madagascar – an independent kingdom ruled by King Radama.[6] In an attempt to curb the illegal trade, Robert Farquhar, the governor, had persuaded King Radama to close the slave market in Madagascar in 1817. From his base in Mauritius, Farquhar had ambitions to take over Madagascar on the familiar Indian pattern, enticing the royal family into a treaty relationship with Britain. He arranged for Radama's two younger brothers to be educated in Mauritius, and they later returned home with their Irish tutor, Sergeant James Hastie.

Other members of Madagascar's ruling family, including Prince Ratsitatane, were opposed to Radama's friendship with Farquhar. Recognising the British intention of taking over their island by the devious method of educating the scions around the throne, Ratsitatane planned the assassination of the Irish tutor. When his schemes were discovered, he was arrested and exiled to a prison in Mauritius.

Once there, Ratsitatane discovered that plans for a rebellion among the slaves from Madagascar were far advanced. Escaping from prison, he joined the rebels in the hills. The rebellion continued for several weeks, but the slaves were soon faced by Captain Orieux's militia force, deploying 1,000 armed settlers and Maroons. Informers sent reports of rebel movements to the militia, and Ratsitatane was eventually betrayed by a black named Laizafy. Captured and imprisoned for a second time, he was executed with three of the rebel leaders at Plaine Verte in April 1822; their severed heads were put on public display.

In December 1810, the British fleet had moved on from Mauritius, and the slaves on the cotton plantations of the Seychelles witnessed a similar British takeover.[7] The French settlers there were also allowed to continue importing slaves for many years to come. When slavery was officially abolished in the 1830s, they were obliged to abandon their cotton plantations to concentrate on less labour-intensive crops. British naval cruisers landed here throughout the nineteenth century, bringing slaves captured from slaving ships from East Africa to be set free.

The Seychelles were eventually to have more significance as a British gulag – the most privileged prison colony in the British Empire. The practice had been originally established by the French, but under the British the islands became one of the principal dustbins of empire, the place where imperial governors could cast away the kings and rulers they had overthrown or deposed – but were unable to execute.[8]

Prison islands were a significant part of the imperial experience. Caribbean rebels were sent to Roatán island, off Honduras; recalcitrant Indians were imprisoned on Penang and on the Andaman islands; Napoleon on Elba and St Helena became part of folk memory; and the export of political prisoners from Ireland to Australia had already begun before the Irish rebellion of 1798.

The story of the imperial gulag in the Indian Ocean is less familiar, although the Seychellois themselves have not been so forgetful. A history of the Seychelles published in 1940 noted that 'the colony is now recognised as the ideal health resort for deposed potentates, political prisoners and all persons of like ilk'. The

British sent important imperial prisoners there in the late nineteenth century – from Buganda, Somaliland, Zanzibar, Egypt, Ashanti (Ghana) and Perak.[9]

Whenever the British thought of using an out-of-the-way concentration camp, the Seychelles always came to mind.[10] In 1900 a proposal was made to incarcerate up to 2,000 Boer prisoners of war on the islands, as well as some Boer convicts. After some discussion, the authorities perceived that the resources of the colony were not up to such a large invasion, and it was reserved in the future, as in the past, for important individual prisoners and their retinues. Archbishop Makarios of Cyprus was sent there in 1956, and released a year later.[11]

In August 1811, the Muslim rulers of the island of Java, long part of the Dutch Empire, readied themselves for a British invasion. The period of shifting ownership occasioned by the Napoleonic wars had allowed Java's local rulers to establish a measure of freedom from European control before the British fleet arrived. For the Dutch themselves, in the heady atmosphere of revolution and liberty unleashed on the world since 1789, had begun to have fresh ideas about their colonial empire. Marshal Herman Willem Daendels, their governor-general at Jakarta from January 1808 to May 1811, had outlined plans to abolish the feudal system prevalent across the islands. He hoped to open the way to radical new forms of colonial government, including the sharing of power with those further down the social scale.

Such intriguing schemes were abandoned after Napoleon's annexation of Holland in June 1810. Daendels was replaced at Jakarta in May 1811 by General Jan Willem Janssens, a Dutch officer who received strict orders from the French emperor to keep the archipelago out of British hands. Britain had captured the French islands of Réunion, Mauritius and the Seychelles in 1810, and now clearly planned to drive the French and the Dutch from Java.

The British attempt to seize this fresh portion of the inhabited globe is an often-neglected episode in the imperial story. Of all the schemes to enlarge the Empire – after the failure to incorporate Nicaragua, Haiti and part of South America – the invasion and conquest of the archipelago of Indonesia, then notionally under the imperial rule of the Dutch and the French, was the most ambitious.

The visionary aim of Stamford Raffles, the thirty-year-old entrepreneur behind the scheme and a veteran of the colonial settlement at Penang, was to make Java 'the centre of an Eastern insular empire' to be peopled with white settlers from Britain.[12] He envisaged the country as a 'Second Raj' – a vast new territory that would rival the possessions of Britain in India. His view was shared by Major William Thorn, a quarter-master with the British forces, who thought that the country was 'particularly advantageous for new settlers'.[13] Making an early visit to Karang Sambong, one hundred miles east of Jakarta (Batavia),

Thorn was enchanted by its potential. 'If these districts were divided into farms of about fifty to one hundred acres, and superintended by European farmers', he wrote, with the prospect of white settlement in mind, 'the benefits would be incalculable.'

The population of Java did not share these ambitions for the region, although Raffles secured the support of a handful of local sultans. His wide-ranging dreams of imperial expansion were abandoned five years later. The islands of Indonesia proved difficult to capture and costly to control. Seized by the British in 1811, they were returned to Dutch rule in 1816.[14]

To seize and secure this potential new imperial territory in the Dutch islands, the governor-general of India, the Earl of Minto, ordered a large expeditionary force to be assembled at Penang in June 1811.[15] The following August, after heavy fighting, General Janssens, the Dutch officer commanding the island, was obliged to surrender to the British, as he had had to do in Cape Town in 1806. Minto sailed back to India in October, leaving Stamford Raffles in charge as the new governor-general of Java.[16] 'I am here alone', the new governor wrote in October 1812, 'without any advice, in a new country with a large native population of not less than six or seven millions of people, a great proportion of foreign Europeans, and a standing army of not less than seven thousand men'.

Several Muslim sultans had imagined that they might themselves become the beneficiaries of an end to Dutch imperial rule, and soon they organised resistance to the British. First to do so was Bagus-Rankin, a Muslim leader who had rebelled against the Dutch six years earlier. He operated from a secure mountain base in the hilly tracts of Indramayu, on the northern coast east of Jakarta. His rebel movement enjoyed considerable popular support, and had been reinforced by deserters and fugitives from the defeated French army. 'Such indeed was the fanaticism of the people', according to Major Thorn's account, 'that all the temptations arising from the rewards which were offered for his apprehension could not prevail on any of his adherents to seize or betray him.'

Bagus-Rankin controlled several villages and then, 'flushed with success', he laid siege to the fort at Indramayu. But the British felt threatened by his rebellion, perceiving it as 'a torrent which had already become formidable', and Bagus-Rankin soon faced a small British force sent out from Jakarta in November 1811.[17] He escaped into the hills, but was captured six months later. 'The check which his troops had received was decisive', wrote Major Thorn. 'The notion of the invincibility of their chief no longer swayed the misguided minds of his followers, [and] they abandoned his standard in great numbers.'

More serious resistance to the British presence in the archipelago came from Sultan Badru'din of Palembang, along the eastern shores of the neighbouring island of Sumatra. Hearing news of the British victory over the Dutch, the sultan thought that this would be a good moment to throw out the existing European settlers and traders and to establish his own rule free from colonial fetters. 'I am not like other native princes', he declared. 'I dread nobody, whoever it might be.' Assembling the colony of Dutch settlers and merchants at Palembang, he arranged for them to be taken out in boats and killed at sea.

The sultan soon faced a small force sent out from Jakarta and led by Colonel Rollo Gillespie. The sultan's palace at Palembang was captured in April 1812, and although he escaped into the hills with the contents of the royal treasury, his brother, Ahmad Najimu'd-din, was selected by Gillespie as his replacement.[18]

Java was made up of various seemingly independent kingdoms, some of whose rulers had formerly signed treaties with the Dutch. Two of the most significant states, created from the old Javanese kingdom of Mataram, were based at Surakarta and Jogjakarta. Raffles's first task as governor had been to make deals with their princes. The chiefs at Surakarta were soon brought into line. Pakhubuwana IV, the Susuhunan of Solo, was content to sign up with the British, recognising the arrival of a new imperial power. A second Surakarta chief, Mangkunegara II, known as the Prangwedana, took time to consider which way to jump, but by the middle of 1812 he too fell into line.

Of all the Java princes, Hameng Kubuwana II, sultan of Mataram, based at Jogjakarta, was the most formidable. Captain Thomas Travers, a British officer, described him as 'the most violent and intriguing of the native princes of Java', a man who 'entertained a rooted animosity against all the Europeans settled in the island'. The sultan had met Raffles in December 1811, arriving at the British camp 'accompanied by several thousands of armed followers'. His men, according to a British account, had 'expressed in their behaviour an infuriated spirit of insolence . . . and several of his own suite actually unsheathed their *krises*, to indicate plainly that they only waited for the signal to perpetrate the work of destruction'.

The sultan had asked Raffles to leave, and receiving no reply had marched smartly out of the camp, determined that the British should be expelled from the island. Raffles, for his part, decided that the city of Jogjakarta was too important to be left outside the British sphere of control. He hoped to depose the sultan and replace him with a more amenable prince.

Sumadiningrat, the sultan's army commander, was warned in July 1812 of an impending British assault on the city, and soldiers were sent out to ambush the advancing troops, led by Colonel Gillespie.[19] This army, formed from British soldiers, Indian sepoys, and pikemen supplied by the Prangwedana, moved south from Samarang and advanced towards the *kraton*, the great citadel at Jogjakarta. The sultan sent out small parties of pikemen, musketeers and cavalry to harass them on the road, and on 18 June a troop of twenty-five British dragoons fell into an ambush. Five were killed, 'mangled most shockingly', and thirteen badly wounded. 'It seems the enemy attacked them with great boldness', wrote one British officer, 'and dismounted them with spears of great length, while others fired from the jungle.' The ambush was the first and last success of the Javanese resistance that year, although the harassment of the invading force continued. Colonel Gillespie described how the inhabitants of the *kampungs* around Jogjakarta came out to throw stones at his advancing army.[20]

The fall of the great *kraton* was one of the few colonial attacks of the early nineteenth century to be witnessed and described in writing by someone from the defending side. Pangeran Arya Panular, a member of the royal family, wrote a splendid diary in verse about the British occupation of Java (now translated by Peter Carey), detailing the scenes of tragedy and treachery that accompanied the destruction and occupation of the *kraton*.[21]

From the moment of the first bombardment, on 20 June, the battle did not go well for the defenders. Sumadiningrat was the last of the *kraton*'s defenders to hold out. His residence in the inner *kraton* was bombarded by cannon, and then surrounded by the Prangwedana's pikemen and by sepoys led by John Deans, the secretary to the British Resident. According to Arya Panular's poem, Sumadiningrat had already been deserted by most of his followers, who took fright on first hearing the British cannon. He retreated to a nearby mosque, but was soon discovered there by John Deans and the sepoys, and the mosque was 'subjected to repeated volleys of gunfire and stormed by waves of pikemen'.[22] Further resistance was useless, for the attackers were too numerous:

> Sumadiningrat is killed and his close retainers are scattered. Not content with this, John Deans hacks at the neck of the dead Yogya commander with his sword, but does not sever it . . . Prangwedana now enters the mosque and gazes long and hard at Sumadiningrat's (bloody) corpse and bewhiskered (face), observing that stiff-necked people should not puff themselves up if they are not like Prangwedana.

With the death of Sumadiningrat, serious looting began, and his residence was set on fire. Before returning to report to Raffles, Deans and the Prangwedana allowed their troops to plunder at will in the Chinese settlements to the south of the *kraton*. Other disgraceful incidents were recorded by the Javanese verse diarist, including looting, rape, and the loss of control by British officers. Colonel Gillespie, after being lightly wounded in the left arm during a skirmish at another mosque within the *kraton*, lost his temper. He 'angrily order[ed] his men to fire repeated rifle volleys which kill[ed] many of the defendants'.

Sultan Hameng Kubuwana was taken prisoner in the course of the fighting. His personal belongings were looted, as was the *kraton* treasury and library, with its 150 manuscripts.[23] On the day after the battle, Raffles installed the crown prince as Sultan Hameng Kubuwana III – although he did not survive for long, dying in November 1814.

Pangeran Arya Panular recalled the extraordinary scenes as Raffles and other British officers took their seats at the victory parade, describing them as 'glowing blood-red like giants who have just devoured human beings'. With them was John Crawfurd, appointed as the British Resident in Jogjakarta.[24] British arrogance astonished even the chronicler. When Crawfurd saw a court official, Pangeran Kusumayuda, give a simple salaam to the new British-imposed sultan (who happened to be Kusumayuda's nephew), he immediately ordered him to get down on the floor and kiss the sultan's knees. The Pangeran had been slightly injured, with a cut over the eye, purposefully delivered by a British soldier after he had been captured. Now he was expected to bow down before the new rulers: 'Kusumayadu is startled at the unexpected nature of this order, and he becomes even more confused when Crawfurd forces his neck down and (demands) that he perform the same abeisance to Raffles, this being the first time that such homage has ever been paid to a Governor.'

In firm control of Jogjakarta, the British now ruled the entire island. 'European power is for the first time paramount in Java', Raffles wrote to Lord Minto at the end of the month. Colonel Gillespie, the conqueror of the *kraton*, was one of the first officers to be withdrawn, after quarrelling with Raffles and being accused of raping young girls. He was killed during the invasion of Nepal in 1814.

No further resistance to British rule came from the Javanese, but they faced other threats, in some ways more serious. A conspiracy broke out among the sepoys in Britain's army in October 1815. Together with Pakubuwana, one of the Surakarta princes, they planned to overthrow the British and the Jogjakarta puppet regime and to seize the territory for themselves. Their mutiny was crushed, and nearly seventy of the ringleaders were court-martialled. Seventeen were shot, and the rest were sent back to India in chains.

Britain's occupation of Java was over almost before it had begun. Raffles was not defeated by the local resistance but by diplomats in Europe. At the Convention of London in August 1814, the British and the Dutch agreed in principle that all Dutch colonies captured since the treaty of Amiens in 1803 should be returned (with the exception of Cape Colony and Demerara [Guyana]). The London government argued that Britain needed the friendship of Holland as a bulwark against a potentially resurgent France. The agreement was firmed up in the Treaty of Vienna in May 1815, and the British made plans to abandon their occupation of Java. Their withdrawal was delayed by the escape of Napoleon from Elba, news of whose final defeat at Waterloo in June 1815 did not reach Java until early in 1816. Stamford Raffles sailed away in March that year, and on 19 August 1816 the Dutch flag flew again over Batavia. The indigenous resistance to empire flared up again a decade later, but by then the British were merely spectators.

One form of resistance to British rule in the Indonesian archipelago was 'piracy' – a phenomenon that had long been a way of life in the islands of the eastern seas. 'Pirate' resistance to British encroachments in the area had started in the eighteenth century. A trading fort owned by the East India Company on the island of Balambangan, off the north coast of Borneo, had been destroyed by Solo 'pirates' in 1755. Later, in 1786, when the British first seized Penang, 'pirates' made tax demands on their shipping in the Straits of Malacca. Hardly a year went by without a British ship being stopped and taxed, and the British were powerless to react.

The capture of Java put the question of 'piracy' in these waters close to the top of the imperial agenda. Raffles himself had a clear idea of what was involved in 'piracy', explaining in a letter to Minto the hold it had on a sea-faring population: 'At present, piracy is considered an honourable profession, especially for young nobles and needy great men. The numerous uninhabited islands and tracts of desert coast on all the Eastern Seas render it very difficult to put a sudden and complete check to the practice.'[25]

'Pirates' operating off Java were attacked twice by expeditions sent out by Raffles, in 1812 and 1813, but John Hunt, an officer on Raffles' staff, hinted at the inherent difficulty of dealing with them:[26]

> The idea of extirpating whole hordes of piratical states, were it possible, must, from its cruelty, be incompatible with the liberal principles and humane policy of a British government. The simple burning down of a Malay town can prove no serious impediment to future piratical enterprises; constructed as they are of bamboos, mats, and atap leaves, a town is almost rebuilt in the same period of time as it takes to destroy it.

The 'pirates' of Indonesia resisted British attempts to clear them from these seas over the next fifty years. Yet with the decision of Raffles to occupy Singapore island in 1819, the extermination of 'pirates' in the Straits of Malacca become a top imperial priority, extending in ever wider circles to the shores of Sarawak and Borneo in the 1840s.[27]

CHAPTER 26

Bulbhadar Singh and the Gurkha Resistance in Nepal

The Gurkhas, a mountain nation, had established themselves in Kathmandu and the valley of Nepal in the eighteenth century, but with the extension of British conquests in the nineteenth century their territories came under threat from the British in Bengal. The British found time and energy in 1814 to embark on a new war of aggression on the northern frontier of their Indian empire, a signal that marked a fresh wave of imperial expansion. Over the next thirty-five years they were to absorb two-thirds of the subcontinent, as eager generals gobbled up the territories of the Marathas, the Burmese, the Rajputs, the Sindhis and the Sikhs. Nepal was the first new territory in their sights, and the Gurkhas were ready for them. In October 1814, at the great Nepalese fort at Kalanga – a few miles north of Dehra Dun, close to the border with India – the Gurkhas and their commander, Bulbhadar Singh, secured a spectacular victory over a British invading force.

General Sir Rollo Gillespie, recently returned to India after the conquest of Java, had advanced into Nepal with an army of 3,500 men, ostensibly to define the frontier between Bengal and Nepal. Negotiations were held to determine the exact nature of the frontier, and the Gurkhas made a point of defending what they regarded as theirs. The British officers did not have everything their own way.

Dissatisfied with the progress of the talks, the British moved to settle their northern frontier by force. This was an ambitious undertaking. The Gurkhas had only a small force of some 12,000 soldiers, but they were defending a difficult terrain with which they were uniquely familiar. In the mountains of Nepal, the British found it difficult even to locate the people they were supposed to be fighting, and their troops and transport animals suffered from the cold.

With victory at the Kalanga fort, the war began well for the Gurkhas. It was an unpleasant reverse for the British. Bulbhadar Singh had placed cannon beside the fort's main gate, and the British attack was beaten off with a chilling fire. When Gillespie tried to rally his men for a second charge, he himself was shot dead. Most of the casualties were British soldiers, and their two fruitless attacks resulted in 740 casualties. Charles Metcalfe, the British resident at Delhi, noted his disquiet in a letter of January 1815:[1]

> We have met with an enemy who shows decidedly greater bravery and greater steadiness than our troops possess; and it is impossible to say what may be the end of such a reverse of the order of things. In some instances our troops, European and native, have been repulsed by inferior numbers with sticks and stones. In others, our troops have been charged by the enemy, sword in hand, and driven for miles like a flock of sheep.

Yet the Gurkha defenders of Kalanga had also suffered severely, and Bulbhadar slipped away with only seventy men. When the British eventually entered the fortress, they found it 'in a shocking state, full of the mangled remains of men and women killed . . . by our batteries . . . The stench was intolerable. Upwards of ninety bodies were collected and burnt.'

The Gurkha victory at Kalanga was followed in November by the successful defence of a fort at Jaithak, north of the town of Nahan. The Gurkhas built a stockade to block the approach of British troops, and the British proved reluctant to advance. The Gurkhas fell on them with their kukris at the moment when the British were finally persuaded to storm the fort. The British soldiers took to their heels at once, as did their sepoys when they saw what was happening.

After these two Gurkha victories, with a third of Gillespie's army destroyed and the commander killed, the British abandoned further offensive operations against the Gurkhas for the rest of the year. 'Our power in India rests upon our military superiority', Charles Metcalfe noted perceptively in 1815. 'It has no foundations in the affections of our subjects. It cannot derive support from the good will or good faith of our neighbours.'[2] When the British failed to demonstrate their military superiority, the political repercussions were considerable.

The struggle of the Gurkhas resumed the following year, but their territory was not finally subjugated until March 1816. The Gurkha resistance caused the British an important political defeat. Others – notably the rulers of what was left of the old Maratha Confederacy in central India – were encouraged to believe that the British could still be defeated. A fresh resistance struggle began in 1817.

CHAPTER 27

The British Conquest of Kandy

In another mountainous territory, the rulers of Kandy in the island of Ceylon prepared for a fresh British invasion in January 1815, just as they had done twelve years earlier. Wickrama Sinha, defiant and independent as ever, was still the principal ruler, though beset with growing political problems exacerbated by the continuing presence of the British in the island's coastal provinces. Gradually increasing his domination over the court, he had disposed of several powerful rivals and turned for support, in populist fashion, to the people.

Pilama Talawuwe, long his adigar, or chief minister, had played an ambivalent role in the events of 1803. Arrested and accused of further plotting, he was executed in 1811. Ehelapola, Talawuwe's nephew, briefly took his place, but he too soon fell from favour. Seeking British help to overthrow Wickrama, Ehelapola had travelled secretly to Colombo, but on his return to Kandy he was accused of treachery. He escaped back to the British sanctuary of Colombo, leaving his wife and family behind.

Ehelapola was dealing with a new British governor in Colombo, who had arrived in 1811. General Sir Robert Brownrigg, who was born in Ireland and had fought in America and the West Indies, was aware of the humiliations the Kandyans had inflicted on his predecessor in 1803, and was initially reluctant to support Ehelapola's planned rebellion against Wickrama Sinha, or to move beyond the coastal enclaves that the British controlled. Yet the existence of Wickrama Sinha's independent kingdom remained a permanent challenge, and the possibility that Wickrama could be replaced by a British puppet ruler was an obvious temptation.

Stories of Wickrama's repressive regime in Kandy were legion, for the British have always enjoyed hearing and reading about the crimes of people they plan to overthrow. John Davy, a doctor with the British forces, recorded many of these tales. It was said, for example, that the young children of Ehelapola, abandoned in Kandy, were beheaded on Wickrama's orders, and that their mother witnessed their execution – and later pounded their severed heads with a pestle, before herself being drowned in a pond.[1]

Under pressure from those who listened to such stories, Brownrigg re-examined the possibility of occupying the entire island, including Kandy, but he needed a pretext. His chance came in 1814, when ten merchants trading in Kandy were accused of spying for Britain. They were mutilated as a punishment: the nose, right ear and right arm of each man was cut off. They were sent back to Colombo with their severed limbs tied around their necks. Only one man survived the journey. The British saw this 'wanton, arbitrary, and barbarous piece of cruelty' as an excuse for war against Kandy, and in January 1815 Wickrama Sinha was faced with a fresh invasion. Brownrigg himself took command of the British force, with Ehelapola in attendance.

Little fighting took place, for Wickrama Sinha simply withdrew into the surrounding countryside, as he had done in 1803. The British army of 4,000 men, reinforced by the black slave regiment purchased by Governor North, marched into Kandy in February, and the territory was formally annexed to the Empire. Ehelapola sent out a search party to locate Wickrama Sinha, who was eventually discovered. Brownrigg declared that Wickrama and his family were to be 'for ever excluded from the throne'. Wickrama himself, with ninety-four of his Tamil relations and followers, was banished to Colombo, and later sent to India and detained at Vellore. The temples of Kandy were looted, and Wickrama's regalia, his crown and sceptre, and a splendid golden throne studded with precious stones were packed up and sent off to join the British monarch's collection at Windsor Castle.[2]

In seizing Kandy, the British made several concessions to local custom. They were obliged to recognise the religion of Buddha, to leave the Buddhist priests with considerable political power, and to reinstate friendly nobles as provincial chiefs. Brownrigg had no illusions about the welcome he had received, and he ordered a large garrison to be maintained at Kandy. He wrote of the Kandyan dislike of their foreign conquerors, noting that 'they made no complaint of oppression or misrule, contenting themselves with expressing a wish that we should leave the country'. Three years later, many of them joined a great rebellion in which thousands were to die.

In March 1818, Kandy exploded in open rebellion against British rule. The Kandyan elite chose this most suitable moment, when imperial forces were over-stretched elsewhere, to launch a bold attempt to regain their independence and to throw out the British. The British authorities in Madras, in the midst of a campaign to exterminate the Pindaris and to curb the Marathas, were suddenly in receipt of urgent requests from Colombo to send sepoy reinforcements to Ceylon. The requests could not have come at a more inopportune time.

Kapitipola, the Dissawa of the province of Uva, was the effective leader of the insurrection.[3] He was the First adigar of Wilbawa, a prince who claimed to be the legitimate heir of Wickrama Sinha. Kapitipola was also the nephew of Ehelapola, the prince who had once asked the British to assist in Wickrama's overthrow. Kapitipola and Wilbawa had established themselves in the jungles of the province of Velassy towards the end of 1817. They had a plan to liberate Kandy from British control, and enjoyed considerable popular support.

'The outbreak of revolt in Velassy', wrote Henry Marshall, the medical officer in Kandy, 'was to act like a match thrown into a barrel of gunpowder upon the dissatisfied and disaffected population of the whole country'.[4]

In October, General Brownrigg ordered Wilson, the Resident in Badulla, to investigate the rumours of rebellion. Wilson advanced into Wilbawa's territory, but his small force of Malay soldiers was ambushed, and Wilson himself was killed. More troops were thrown into the region in December, but the rebels, following their customary practice, disappeared into the jungle.

In the early months of 1818, the revolt appeared to be consolidating, and in May a priest carried the sacred tooth of Buddha from its shrine in Kandy to the rebel camp, bringing comfort and divine assistance to the cause. Kapitipola's rebels refused to engage in pitched battles, preferring to organise ambushes into which small detachments of British troops and their supply convoys might fall. British forces were decimated by exhaustion and disease, and soon more than 1,000 soldiers, approximately one-fifth of the British force in Ceylon, were ill and out of action.[5]

The rebels forced General Brownrigg to abandon his more forward military positions, and if reinforcements had not arrived from India he might have been obliged to evacuate Kandy. Several sepoy battalions from the Madras Native Infantry reached Colombo in March, and a British battalion came later from Calcutta.

Desperate, but with renewed energy when the reinforcements arrived, the British general began to show his true colours. Martial law was declared, and the revolt was crushed with violence and terror. Brownrigg's soldiers laid waste to the countryside, and military posts were constructed in the rebellious districts. An official report sent to London described how 'the dwellings of the resisting inhabitants were burnt; their fruit trees were often cut down'. Ten thousand Kandyans died during the rebellion, from starvation or disease, or in battle. The British, too, suffered considerable loss.

Kapitipola's guerrilla forces slowly lost civilian support, and dissent began to emerge within his ranks. Madugala, one of his lieutenants, emerged to claim that Wilbawa was a former Buddhist priest and not really the legitimate monarch. A rival claimant was placed on the throne of Kandy, and Wilbawa and Kapitipola were both briefly detained by Kandy's quarrelling elite. As if to mark the change in fortune, the British claimed to have recovered Buddha's tooth, and when several rebel leaders surrendered, the rebellion was effectively at an end.

Kapitipola was eventually captured by British forces, and executed.[6] His severed head was packed up by the authorities and sent to Britain, being formally presented to the Phrenological Society of Edinburgh. Madugala was also executed, but twenty rebel leaders were banished to the imperial gulag on Mauritius.[7] Wilbawa, priest and would-be king of Kandy, escaped from British clutches and held out in the hills for more than a decade. Finally captured in 1830, he was tried for high treason and sentenced to life imprisonment – and then granted a pardon.

The entire island of Ceylon was now under British military control, and soon it became necessary to solidify the British presence with white settlers. These began to arrive in the 1820s, to grow coffee – and later tea. Colonel Fortescue wrote a hundred years later of the British habit of forgetfulness:

> Millions of Englishmen have drunk tea and coffee at their breakfasts, and cured their catarrhs with cinchona, all grown in Ceylon; but not one in a million thinks of the hundreds of British soldiers who died in 1803 and 1818 in order that Ceylon might become a peaceful tropical garden for the British nation.[8]

British recollection of the thousands of Kandyans who died in the same cause has been equally unforthcoming.

Part VI

SLAVE REVOLTS, WHITE SETTLEMENT, INDIGENOUS EXTERMINATION, AND THE ADVANCE INTO BURMA AND ASSAM, 1816–30

In the decade after 1815, the subject peoples of empire faced a fresh challenge from a new generation of imperial rulers in a mood of military euphoria. With the defeat of Napoleon at Waterloo, and thus the destruction of Britain's chief European rival, British soldiers began to take a renewed interest in their expanded empire. Many officers, notably those who had fought with Wellington during the war in Spain, received jobs as colonial governors – an excellent way of acquiring a personal pension.

These former soldiers ruled in the manner with which they were familiar, often placing their fiefdoms under martial law. This legal device allowed them to detain and torture, with no questions asked, and to annihilate those rash enough to dissent. As governors, they were overseers of the continuing and accelerated extermination of native peoples. The indigenous inhabitants of the new empire, now perceived as 'the enemy', were rooted out with the same energy as the armies of France had once been destroyed. In India and South Africa, in New South Wales and Tasmania, and in the seas off Singapore and the Arabian mainland, military governors helped create the climate in which British trade and investment – and the slave labour that continued to underpin the imperial project – could flourish, without the inconvenient presence of those unwilling to recognise its alleged advantages.

The military were also on hand to help crush revolts by black slave labourers, notably in Barbados, Guyana and Jamaica. The formal end of Britain's slave trade in 1807, and the various pieces of legislation that sought to improve the conditions of the slaves, led many of them to jump the gun in this period, believing mistakenly that their freedom was imminent. The growth and spread of dissenting churches contributed to this mood of anticipation, since slaves were allowed to meet formally and informally outside the plantation on church premises, and often listened to evangelical sermons that proclaimed the ideologies of freedom.

During the long period of warfare with France, little surplus manpower was available for peopling the Empire's allegedly open spaces. Now, as a result of economic mismanagement at home in the post-war era, thousands of new settlers were encouraged to abandon Britain to find a new life elsewhere. In 1816, the War Office discussed a plan to send war veterans to Canada, while others were packed off to Australia and South America. In 1820, the government funded the despatch of 5,000 settlers to South Africa, partly to create a barrier against the Xhosa on the contested eastern frontier, and partly to offset the influence of the long-established Dutch population, with its uncertain political allegiance. Many of the native inhabitants were already under threat in the areas taken over by these new settlers. Some were in the process of being destroyed.

In Australia, the Aborigines were cleared from the Hawkesbury River territory outside Sydney in 1816, and those around Bathurst were slaughtered by death squad in 1826. Aborigines in the Swan River territory, in south-west Australia, were attacked in 1829 and their land made ready for new settlers.

Some colonial settlements were government-funded, but most settlers arrived in the colonies as the result of private enterprise, in the form of the hare-brained schemes of individual entrepreneurs. One such development in Canada, the Red River settlement in Manitoba, destroyed by the Indian-French Métis in 1816 (see Chapter 29), was the pet project of Lord Selkirk.

The new military rulers sought to further increase the territory of empire through force of arms – in Kandy, Ceylon; in Ashanti, Ghana; and in the Burmese Empire. Yet resistance was stiff. There were slave rebellions in the Caribbean, the Aborigines in Australia did not go quietly into their long good night, and the embers of the Irish rebellion of 1798 were often coaxed into flame. In central India, the Marathas continued their efforts to throw out their British overlords, and in Ceylon, Ghana and Burma the imperial conquerors met with startling mutinies and military defeats. They were soon faced with rebellion in the newly acquired territory of Assam, on India's North-East Frontier, gobbled up in the wake of the war against Burma. Mass movements of protest, and the resistance of individuals, ensured that this was not an easy time for ambitious imperialists. The twin themes of empire – repression and revolt – continued long into the post-Napoleon twilight.

CHAPTER 28

Slave Rebellions in the Caribbean

On Easter Sunday, 14 April 1816 – a quarter of a century after the great slave revolt of 1791 in Haiti – slaves on the island of Barbados launched a substantial rebellion. Their leader was Bussa, a slave born in Africa who worked as the head ranger on Bailey's sugar plantation in the eastern parish of St Philip. The slaves torched the sugar cane at his plantation that Sunday, and their revolt spread rapidly through the southern and central parts of the island, home to 80,000 slaves. The planters were caught unawares, for they had had 'no apprehension of such a convulsion' – or so General Sir James Leith, the island's military governor, subsequently informed the authorities in London. Slaves questioned after the rebellion told their interrogators firmly that 'the island belonged to them, and not to white men, whom they proposed to destroy'.[1]

Barbados was Britain's largest military base in the Caribbean. A small group of settlers had arrived there two centuries earlier, in 1627, claiming improbably that it was an uninhabited island. In the five years between 1645 and 1650, during the English Civil War, they had been joined by 8,000 fresh settlers, an ill-assorted mixture of voluntary 'servants', political refugees and transported convicts. The settlers grew tobacco, cotton, and eventually sugar, with the essential help of slave labour.

Some 130,000 African slaves were imported to work on the plantations of Barbados in the sixty years between 1640 and 1700. They were supplied by Dutch merchants in the early years, but after the restoration of the British monarchy in 1660 they were brought across the Atlantic in the ships of the Royal African Company.[2] The Africans soon made efforts to shake off their condition of enslavement, organising rebellions and making endless individual attempts to run away. Several abortive rebellions occurred in the seventeenth century, in 1649, 1675 and 1692. The rebellion of May 1675 took place at the moment when slaves were beginning to outnumber settlers, 21,000 whites sharing the island with 33,000 blacks.[3]

Slave revolts were so brutally repressed that the eighteenth century saw no further rebellions. The planters, writes a recent historian of Barbados, devised an internal military system more effective than anything elsewhere in the English West Indies. 'With large militia regiments, plantation militia tenants, and frequent visits from imperial armies and naval fleets, the white community was able to establish and maintain a powerful island-wide system for the day-to-day control of slaves.'[4]

In such circumstances, it was not surprising that Bussa's 1816 rebellion took the whites by surprise. Unnoticed, the slaves had been preparing for some time. We wanted freedom, explained Nanny Grigg, one of the intellectual authors of the rebellion, and we knew we had 'to fight for it'. Grigg was a slave with some education: she read the local and the English papers, and kept other slaves informed of what was going on in the Caribbean and in Britain. Political debates in London about 'slave registration', current since 1812, may well have encouraged the slaves to believe that freedom was near. The Slave Registration Act, eventually promulgated in 1817, was the culmination of this campaign. All slave-owners were now obliged by law to provide a list of their slaves every two years. The London government demanded reform, but the legislation was opposed by plantation owners who saw it as a dangerous move towards emancipation. The slaves saw it as a step towards freedom.

They torched the cane on Easter Sunday, and one quarter of the sugar crop was destroyed. General Leith, a veteran of the Irish rebellion of 1798, was not on the island at the time, and the army commander, Colonel Edward Codd, declared martial law the following morning. 'A dense mob of half-armed slaves' was assembled on the heights of Christ Church, facing black troops from the 1st West India Regiment, brought in from the south of the island. As the regiment advanced with fixed bayonets, the slaves 'offered a furious resistance' and sought 'to wrench the muskets from their hands'.

The slave army was no match for the muskets, and individuals fled into the countryside with soldiers in hot pursuit. Roaming slaves were shot on sight, and villages where they might have sought refuge were burned down. The rebellion was crushed after three days. No final tally of the dead was made, but according to one contemporary source 'a little short of 1,000 slaves were killed in battle and executed at Law'. Forty-four slave rebels were killed in two days in one parish alone, and 400 were captured and imprisoned on ships to await trial.[5]

General Leith sailed in on a French schooner from Guadeloupe, nearly two weeks after the revolt had broken out. In its aftermath, according to his official figures, 144 people were executed under the terms of martial law, and seventy were subsequently sentenced to death. The colonial secretary in London, Henry Lord Bathurst, was aghast when he was told of this figure, commenting that 'the number already executed is adequate for punishment or example'. He gave orders that if other slaves were to be found guilty in future, they should be deported rather than executed.

As a result of this order, 123 survivors were sent for transportation to work as mahogany-cutters in the forests of British Honduras (later Belize). Their ship, the Frances Mary, arrived off Belize in February 1817, but was received with alarm by the colony's white settlers. They regarded it as a plague ship bearing the bacillus of rebellion, and their colonial assembly demanded that these 'dangerous characters' should 'on no account' be allowed to land. A querulous message was sent to Bathurst in London: 'Who would dare to make the experiment with wretches who do not disguise the object of their late insurrection to have been the extirpation of every white inhabitant of Barbados.'

Bathurst felt obliged to fall in with the demands of the settlers, and he gave orders for the Barbados slaves to be sent across the Atlantic to join the philanthropists' colony at Sierra Leone, which had already absorbed the Maroons of Jamaica. Yet since no action could be taken until September 1818, the slaves remained on their prison boat off the Honduran coast for more than a year. Eventually the surviving slaves, more than one hundred, arrived in Sierra Leone.

The bloody suppression of the rebellion left a cheerless legacy in Barbados. 'The disposition of the slaves in general is very bad', noted a white visitor to the island in June 1817. 'They are sullen and sulky and seem to cherish feelings of deep revenge.' The visitor concluded that Britain only held the West Indies through its 'military strength'. The settlers remained nervous. John Beckles, the speaker of the island's assembly, warned its members to be on their guard, 'to keep a watch that we may not again be caught so shamefully unprepared'.[6] Governor Leith was well out of it. He died of yellow fever soon after the rebellion ended.

In April 1820, Will and Sharper, two black slaves in a mahogany camp in the hinterland of British Honduras, organised what the white settlers in the colony described as a 'very alarming' rebellion. Forty slaves, armed with guns, had seized the logging camp, and Will and Sharper were said to be their 'captains and leaders'.

Outnumbered by slaves, both black and native, and 'surrounded by vast hordes of Indians', Britain's tiny white settler community on the shores of British Honduras had been in a barely suppressed state of panic since 'the infernal convulsion and the horrors of Santo Domingo' in the 1790s. The shadow of Haiti hung over them as it did over the rest of the Caribbean, and in 1820 they imagined that their worst fears were about to be realised.

The wealth of British Honduras came from wood. Huge logging camps, employing slave labour, had been extracting mahogany from the tropical forests for years, and shipping it to Europe. The permanent fear of the white overseers was not just that the black slaves might rebel, but that they might make common cause with the native Indian population – heirs to the traditions of the Maya – who had attacked the loggers in 1807.

The rebellion of Will and Sharper was greeted with the standard colonial remedy: a declaration of martial law. Two detachments of the 2nd West India regiment were sent upcountry from Belize with a party of locally raised militiamen. They were led by the colonial governor, Colonel George Arthur, a typical imperial representative of his time. He had fought in the Napoleonic wars and was to play a significant part in the development of empire in such diverse territories as Tasmania and Canada. Yet Arthur was also a zealous Christian, and he was appalled by the conditions he encountered at the mahogany camp.

He found that the slaves had 'good grounds for complaint', and wrote later that 'the negroes . . . had been treated with very unnecessary harshness by their owners'.[7] Reports of a rebellion had been exaggerated, he suggested. It had been more a withdrawal of labour than an armed insurrection. Those 'who had first deserted . . . had excited others to join them'. He announced that all those willing to surrender would be offered an immediate pardon. Within days of the governor's arrival, the troubles subsided.

Although the white loggers claimed to fear that their slaves would make common cause with the local Indians and turn against them, the real threat was to their economic survival. Slave desertion was commonplace in the territory, and, as in the islands of the Caribbean, British Honduras boasted several 'free territories' where former slaves could live unmolested in the bush. One of these would have been the eventual destination of Will and Sharper – a month after their rebellion they had vanished into thin air, together with eighteen other slaves who had refused to surrender. If this had become the general pattern, British Honduras would have been left without a workforce.

The rebellion led Colonel Arthur to understand more thoroughly the customs of the slave-owners. He wrote to London deploring their increasing cruelty, 'now practised with impunity', against both blacks and Indians. Cruel practices had been common in the colony. 'Retaliation against Indians has been hitherto encouraged', a lawyer told the Belize court when his white client had been accused of murdering an Indian. It had been 'sanctioned by custom and usage in this settlement, and no proclamation has been promulgated to the contrary'. The whites were justified in their actions 'on account of the many murders and other depredations committed by the same inhabitants of the woods'.

British Honduras – still not officially a British colony – was without a code of law of any kind. One result of the slave rebellion was to introduce the slave laws of Jamaica the following year, with a view to improving the conditions of the slaves, both black and Indian.[8] Colonel Arthur wrote to London to say that he had 'underrated the extent of the grievances of the slaves', and was astonished 'at the fraud and injustice so long secretly practised against them'. He had been shocked to discover that eighteen Indians, brought to Honduras from Nicaragua's Mosquito Shore in the previous century, had been illegally held in slavery for more than fifty years. Their claims for freedom having been so frequently 'denied by bench and juries, the Indians had patiently submitted to the inevitable'. Yet the rebellion of Will and Sharper was a sign that the passive attitude of the slaves was beginning to change. Both blacks and Indians began to discover that they had rights.

Colonel Arthur's sympathetic attitude towards their grievances was unfavourably received by the white settlers and the slave-owners. They demanded – and eventually secured – his removal from the colony. He was sent to run Britain's new prison gulag in Tasmania, created barely twenty years earlier, and in 1838 he arrived in Canada to crush a rather different kind of rebellion.

Three years after the rebellion in British Honduras, slaves in Guyana and Jamaica received encouraging information about the revival of an anti-slavery campaign in Britain. A new organisation, the 'London Society for Mitigating and Gradually Abolishing the State of Slavery throughout the British Dominions' had been formed in London in January 1823. Many slaves believed that this society would soon be successful and that their freedom was imminent.

The government in London, responding to political pressure at home, had already made a promise to improve the treatment of slaves in the colonies, suggesting among other things that women slaves should no longer be whipped. News of these possible changes reached the plantations of the Caribbean, relayed through the network of nonconformist churches, and slave owners grew seriously alarmed.

In August 1823, a thousand slaves on the sugar plantations of Guyana met illegally in tumultuous assembly to the east of the Demerara River. Armed with pikes and machetes, they seized their white managers and put them in the stocks. They asked for talks with the colonial government and their initial demand, having heard the news from London, was for improved conditions.

The settlements on the three rivers of the territory of Guyana – Demerara, Berbice and Essequibo – had only been under British control since 1803, though first acquired for the Empire from the Dutch in 1796. Yet many of the plantations had long been owned by English planters, who had bought land on the South American mainland whose soil was thought to be more fertile than that of the British islands of the West Indies.

The slaves in Guyana had a long history of rebellion. At Berbice, in 1763, they had seized control of the entire area for nearly a year, and again, in 1795 there had been prolonged resistance by the 'Bush Negroes' in league with Victor Hugues, the revolutionary French commissioner.[9] These early rebellions had been brutally crushed, yet as always, after a generation's pause of thirty years, resistance started up again.

The Dutch had controlled the plantations with military force, sometimes asking for assistance from the British in Barbados – as in 1763, when 200 soldiers were sent. With such methods, it was not difficult to suppress rebellion. Here there were no 'liberated areas', and no incipient friendship between imported black slaves and indigenous Native Americans. Indeed, the Dutch had introduced the custom, followed by the British, of employing the Indians – 'the inspired enemy of the Negro' – to catch runaway slaves. Social control was equally fierce. Slaves were not allowed out at night without a lantern and a pass, and dancing was only allowed on four occasions a year.

By the early nineteenth century, there were contradictions in the colonial system of repression. The arrival of nonconformist churches brought an alternative vision of empire, as well as news of changing opinions in Britain. In the Guyana capital of Georgetown, the Bethel chapel of the Reverend John Smith became a centre both of worship and of information, attended by 800 slaves each Sunday.

Well-informed about what was going on in the outside world, many of John Smith's deacons were behind the embryonic resistance movement. One of them was Quamina Gladstone, a slave on the estate of John Gladstone MP, a planter who was to be the father of William Ewart Gladstone, the future British prime minister.[10] During the revolt of 1823, Quamina was talked of as the man who would be chosen as the future king.

When the slaves on the Demerara plantations met to discuss their grievances in August 1823, they had asked to talk to the military governor, Colonel Benjamin d'Urban, and he came hurriedly from Georgetown to the central plantation with a militia detachment. D'Urban played many roles on the colonial chess-board. A veteran of the British invasion of Santo Domingo in 1796, and of the Peninsular Wars, he would later serve as governor of Barbados and, in 1834, of Cape Colony; he died in Montreal in 1849, as the military commander in Canada.

Colonel d'Urban told the assembled slaves of the rather limited improvements proposed by the London government, and the slaves immediately indicated that these changes were insufficient. 'These things they said were no comfort to them', one slave explained subsequently. 'God had made them of the same flesh and blood as the whites, and . . . they were tired of being slaves to them . . . their good king had sent orders they should be free and they would not work any more.'

During the discussions with the governor, a musket shot was fired and D'Urban abandoned further efforts at conciliation. He returned swiftly to Georgetown to declare martial law. The rebellion soon spread to other plantations, and a detachment from the West India regiment was called out. At the Adventure plantation, troops were met with fierce resistance from 2,000 slaves, and an eye-witness recorded their moderate demands: 'Some of the insurgents called out that they wanted lands and three days in the week for themselves, besides Sunday, and they would not give up their arms till they were satisfied.'[11]

Jacky Gladstone, another slave leader from the Gladstone estate, handed the troop commander a written list of demands; but with no powers to grant their requests, the officer ordered the slaves to disperse. When they refused to do so, his troops opened fire. Hundreds of slaves were shot, although many escaped into the jungle. Some were later hunted down and killed when black troops were brought in from Barbados to help in the 'mopping-up' operations. Martial law remained in force for five months.

Nor was this the end of the story. Over the next few months, some seventy-two slaves were brought to trial, and of these fifty-one were executed and sixteen received a thousand lashes. The others received lengthy prison terms. More were tried and executed later, their bodies strung up on gibbets erected outside the slave huts on several plantations. Quamina Gladstone, the would-be king of the slaves, was eventually captured and shot. His bullet-ridden body was displayed in chains at the plantation where the rebellion had begun.[12]

The white settler community called for revenge against the nonconformist priests who had given comfort to the slaves. The Reverend John Smith was charged with incitement to rebellion and sentenced to death, and Jacky Gladstone, in exchange for his life, was induced to testify against him. John Gladstone MP, the owner of Jacky, gave warm support in parliament for the death penalty for the Reverend Smith, but the London authorities refused to confirm the sentence. News of a pardon was brought back to Georgetown, but it came too late. The Reverend Smith had already died in prison of tuberculosis.

The impact of the rebellion was felt throughout the Caribbean, and planters everywhere feared trouble and directed their anger against the dissenting churches. They burned down the Wesleyan mission in Barbados in October and drove its priest into exile. They were soon examining fresh evidence of slave conspiracies in Jamaica.

Later in 1823, just before Christmas, informal slave gatherings in Jamaica, on the Balcarras estate in St George's, led plantation owners to believe that a general uprising was imminent. The colonial authorities had spies in the slave communities, and claimed to have uncovered conspiracies on other estates in the parishes of St Mary and St James.

Yet the conspiracy in St James consisted of little more than talk of freedom. Mary Turner points out that 'the antislavery campaign had stirred excitement and prompted noisy, convivial meetings, but no organisation was in evidence and no destruction of property had taken place.'[13] Seventeen slaves were arrested when drinking and raising toasts to William Wilberforce, the anti-slavery campaigner in Britain, and three were sentenced to transportation.

The slaves on the Frontier estate at St Mary were regarded by the authorities with greater suspicion. Those with long memories remembered that this had been the base of the rebellion of 1760. Eight slaves there were hanged, while seven at St George's were hanged or sentenced to transportation.

In 1824, the following year, slaves on the Argyle estate were accused of slaughtering cattle – an action feared by the plantation owners to be the prelude to rebellion. The owners claimed that their slaves were planning a general strike, to be followed by a massacre of the whites. The slaves had indeed planned 'to sit down', according to one account, and an informer claimed that if they were not given their freedom, it was their intention 'to kill the white people and take the country'.[14] Yet no evidence was provided of a wider conspiracy.

Six slaves from the Argyle estate were hanged, and four at Kingston. Others were sentenced to be flogged and transported. These hangings were much criticised in London, since the evidence had been obtained through torture. The ferocity of the repression had its effect, preventing further rebellions during the next seven years, until the great explosion of 1831.

CHAPTER 29

The Battle of Seven Oaks, Canada

In June 1816, at the white settlement of Assiniboia, on the banks of the Red River in Manitoba, a band of sixty French-speaking Métis fought back against an attack from the settlers, killing Robert Semple, the governor, and twenty-two settlers, an event remembered as the Battle of Seven Oaks. The Métis, sometimes called the Brulés, were Indians from the Canadian hinterland, intermarried over the years with French trappers. This particular group were employed by the North-West Company to guard its warehouses for the fur trade on the Red River.

The Red River settlers were part of the great wave of settlement taking place in many parts of the Empire in these years. They had arrived in Canada four years earlier, brought from Scotland under the auspices of Thomas Douglas, Lord Selkirk, a philanthropic Scottish peer with a large shareholding in the Hudson's Bay Company, a rival to the North-West Company in the backlands of Canada. With the confidence of great riches, he had dreamed up a variety of imaginative colonisation projects in the Empire for the benefit of the expropriated and disinherited peasants of the Scottish highlands.[1]

His first ambitious plan, 'a Proposal' to the British government formulated in 1802, was to send Catholic peasants from Ireland to Canada. He suggested that troublesome Irish Catholics, embittered after the rebellion of 1798 and 'a standing danger to the Empire', should be shunted off to a British colony that could be set aside solely for Catholics. Where better, Selkirk argued, than the vast territory of Canada, since this already sustained a substantial Catholic population established by its former French owners.[2] Once the Catholics had been moved out of Ireland, Selkirk's argument continued, loyal and energetic Scots settlers could be moved in, turning Catholic Ireland into an entirely Protestant country.

Since the Atlantic coast of Canada was already occupied by the farms of existing white settlers, Selkirk thought that space might be found for his project inland, near Lake Winnipeg, 'a country which the Indian traders regard as fertile'. This was fur-trading country, long familiar to the employees of the North-West Company and the Hudson's Bay Company, where Indians lived and hunted; but Selkirk made no mention of an Indian presence in his 'Proposal'.

The British government did not warm to Selkirk's scheme, and he was told that assistance would not be made available for anything so bizarre. Undeterred, he worked on a new emigration plan that he could organise himself. He would send Scottish farmers directly to Canada, and in 1803 he arranged for 800 settlers from Scotland – from Argyle, Ross-shire, Inverness and Skye – to be shipped across the Atlantic to Prince Edward Island, off the coast of Nova Scotia.

A few years later, in 1811, his agents in Scotland assembled a second group of peasant families and prepared them for emigration. Selkirk had acquired 116,000 square miles of land south of Lake Winnipeg thought to be suitable for colonisation, and a settlement was built at Assiniboia, at the junction of the Red River and the Assiniboine River.

For the settlers from Scotland, the journey was unbearably long. They came by ship to York Fort on Hudson's Bay, and then travelled up the Nelson River to Lake Winnipeg. On arrival at Assiniboia, they met strong opposition. The local Indians along the Red River were opposed to the establishment of any new settlement, as were the Métis and the employees of the North-West Company. The harsh conditions they encountered, coupled with Indian hostility, caused many settlers to give up.

The final collapse of the settlement in June 1816, at the Battle of Seven Oaks, was recorded in a contemporary account by Daniel Harmon.[3] A band of *Métis* had come down the Red River to Lake Winnipeg to guard the property of the North-West Company. When they passed close to the Assiniboia settlement, they were twice fired on by the settlers. They were unprepared for an attack, for they had few guns; but they fought back successfully, causing such damage that the surviving settlers abandoned the colony. Some went to live on the shores of Hudson's Bay, but most retreated to Canada's eastern provinces.

The indefatigable Selkirk returned to Assiniboia the following year with a fresh group of settlers capable of defending themselves, for they were all former soldiers, recruited from several different regiments. They had an easier time of it, and much of the hostility of the Métis and the Indians to their settlement evaporated when the rival trading companies merged in 1821.[4] The North-West Company was incorporated into the Hudson Bay Company, and the Red River settlement established itself permanently, soon attracting fresh settlers.

Yet the arrival of the military settlers proved catastrophic for the Assiniboine Indians, for the soldiers brought smallpox with them. 'The prairie all around is a vast field of death', wrote a German traveller, Prince Maximilian of Wied, who journeyed through the area in the early 1830s. He described a land 'covered with unburied corpses', with 'pestilence and famine' spreading for miles around.[5]

> The Assiniboines, 9,000 in number, roaming over a hunting territory to the north of the Missouri as far as the trading posts of the Hudson's Bay Company, are, in the literal sense of the expression, nearly exterminated. They, as well as the Crows and the Blackfeet, endeavoured to flee in all directions, but the disease everywhere pursued them.

Did the soldiers inadvertently bring smallpox with them, or did they actively seek to kill off the indigenous population? The records are silent. Yet the pattern of development in the nineteenth century was now established, as the more distant Indian lands of Canada were thrown open to white rule.

CHAPTER 30

Revolts and Resistance in Central India

In India in 1816, an anti-British revolt broke out in April in the streets of Bareilly, the capital of Rohilkhand. The Rohillas objected to a British decision to raise money from a house tax to pay for a municipal police force. Rohilkhand, a state on the borders of Oudh, had been controlled by the British since they had first seized it in 1774.

A large and rebellious crowd gathered when the local police set out to collect the tax. The bodyguard of the British magistrate opened fire and several people were killed. A woman was wounded, as was Mufti Mohamed Aiwaz, a respected local cleric. 'Sacrilege had been added to exaction', it was said, and the mufti retired to his mosque at Shahdara. There he unfurled the green flag of Islam as a signal to the Muslim population to assemble in defence of their religion. Angry men, armed with swords and matchlocks, poured into Bareilly from neighbouring towns.[1]

The small European population, cooped up in the military cantonment, was inadequately protected by a handful of sepoys, and one Englishman was killed. When reinforcements arrived from Moradabad, the rebellion was crushed, and more than three hundred rebels were killed, and hundreds wounded or taken prisoner. The British lost twenty soldiers.

Late in 1817, the surviving chiefs of the Maratha Confederacy in central India embarked on a final effort to drive the British out of India – the first and last rebellion since the prolonged resistance campaign against General Wellington and General Lake in the early years of the century. Their resistance then had been sufficiently powerful to cause the recall to London of the British governor, but their military defeat had left their lands diminished and their political power circumscribed. The British emasculation of the Maratha states, and the resulting dispersion of their huge armies, had caused the territories of central India to degenerate into chaos and anarchy, and the supposed benefits of Empire were conspicuous by their absence.

In November 1817, the forces of Baji Rao II,[2] the Peshwa of the Marathas, attacked the British fort at Poona and burned down the house of Mountstuart Elphinstone, the British Resident. Three weeks later, the forces of Apa Sahib, the Bhonsla of Nagpur, destroyed another British Residency at Nagpur; and in December, at the battle of Mahidpur, the soldiers of the youthful Mulhar Rao Holkar attacked the forces of General Sir Thomas

Hislop, the commander at Madras (formerly the brutal commander in Grenada and Trinidad).[3]

Baji Rao II was a survivor of the humiliations of the earlier decade. Obliged to accept the imposition of a British Resident in his home town of Poona, he had often sought ways of escaping from British tutelage. Earlier in the year, he had suggested to the Maratha chiefs and the Nizam of Hyderabad that the time had come for a final effort to unite their forces and expel the British. Aware of British plans to destroy his allies, the Pindaris, he argued that the Marathas should attack before the Pindaris were annihilated.

With the support of the three most important Maratha chiefs – Holkar, Apa Sahib and Daulat Rao Sindhia – the Peshwa planned an attack on the small British force maintained at Poona by Mountstuart Elphinstone. The destruction of such a visible target as the Residency would allow this fresh anti-British campaign to get off to a powerful start, with a victorious blow that would echo across the country.

The Peshwa's brave efforts were not crowned with success. The Residency was destroyed, but his army failed to secure further victories. Although he had over 20,000 men at his command (while the British had barely 2,000 sepoys and 800 European troops), his campaign was effectively over in ten days. At the village of Kirki, outside Poona, Baji Rao was defeated, with the loss of 500 men dead or wounded.[4] He slipped away when British reinforcements recaptured Poona a week later.

Apa Sahib, at Nagpur, was no more fortunate than the Peshwa. He too had an overwhelming preponderance of troops, and should have had an easy victory. Yet after the destruction of a second British Residency, symbol of British power, he was defeated outside Nagpur in the Sitabaldi hills. Resistance in the city itself was prolonged for a while by Arab soldiers in his army, but these were eventually bribed by the British to stop fighting.

The troops of Holkar were also defeated. Facing General Hislop at Mahidpur, they put up a tougher fight than the others. Holkar's losses were estimated at 3,000, with the surrender of sixty-three guns, while Hislop's army lost nearly 800 killed or wounded. After Mahidpur, one of Holkar's subsidiary chiefs still held out at the fort at Talner, but the gates were blown open by the British, and Hislop ordered the entire garrison of 300 to be put to death.[5] The order was obeyed, and the Maratha commander was hanged from the flagstaff tower.[6]

The force of Baji Rao was still in the field, but was finally defeated at the battle of Ashti in February 1818. Gokhale, his military commander, was killed, and the Peshwa's political and military support melted away. Baji Rao surrendered in June and was formally deposed as Peshwa. He retired to Bithur, near Cawnpore, and to make up for his loss of power and title the British provided him with a large annuity, which lasted until his death in 1851. The withdrawal of that annuity from Nana Sahib, his adopted heir, was a contributory cause of the great rebellion of 1857.

In November 1817, in the weeks before the final defeat of the Maratha rebellion, Pindaris in the lands of central India were attacked by British forces on a search-and-destroy mission in the vicinity of the Narbada River. The Pindaris were members of free-booting armies that operated in the central part of India, where the British now claimed the right to control and tax. Imperial chroniclers describe them variously as 'robbers', 'pests', 'ruffians', and 'marauders'.[7] Many Pindaris were slaughtered during these British combing operations, although a few stray bands escaped through the net to mingle with local people. Many individual Pindaris entreated the villagers 'to secrete and protect them from the vengeance of British arms'.[8]

The Pindari armies were led by chieftains in alliance with the rulers of the Maratha confederacy. The three principal chiefs, Chitu, Karim Khan and Wasil Mohammed, enjoyed a close relationship with Daulat Rao Sindhia. Amir Khan – a fourth free-ranging chief who was a Pathan and not strictly a Pindari – controlled much of the territory formerly held by Jeswant Rao Holkar. Each leader maintained regular forces of more than 30,000 men.

Chitu was the most remarkable of these rulers, a man fiercely opposed to British rule.[9] Jat by birth and sold into slavery, Chitu had been taken in by Sindhia's family, and his aim, he had once told Sindhia, was to 'ravage and destroy the country of the English'. A competent organiser and administrator, he promised to distribute British-held land to his Pindari followers, and vowed to carry fire and sword to the outskirts of Calcutta.

The Pindaris had long posed a serious threat to British hegemony. In May 1816, a Pindari band had crossed the Narbada River into British territory to engage in 'destruction, pillage, murder, and rape with the usual ferocity'. The Pindaris remained there for eleven days, and during this period 'more than 359 villages were plundered and set on fire; 182 people were put to death in a most brutal manner; innumerable women raped; hundreds of them committed suicide by drowning or burning themselves. [Five-hundred and five] people were severely wounded, and 3,603 were subjected to torture.'[10]

Such events undermined British authority, and villagers needed reassurance that the Pindaris would not re-establish themselves in British lands. Early in 1817, General Francis Hastings, the Bengali governor stationed at Calcutta and a veteran of the American wars of the 1770s, discussed a number of schemes to destroy the Pindaris. After the expensive experience of Wellesley and his generals in the Maratha wars after 1803, he was anxious to avoid a war that might also involve a clash with the Marathas. Hastings planned a pincer movement with two large armies, totalling about 120,000 men: the northern army would be under his own command, and the southern army would be led by General Hislop, the commander at Madras.[11]

By the autumn of 1817, the two armies were ready, with instructions to close in on each other and to draw a cordon around the Pindaris. Hastings took command in October, expecting the campaign to be an easy one, having – so he thought – bought off the Marathas by treaty. Then, with the Maratha attack on the Residency at Poona in November, he was faced by a Maratha rebellion before he could get to grips with the Pindaris. With the subsequent Maratha defeats at Kirki, Sitabaldi and Mahidpur, the way was clear to a resolution of the Pindari threat. Hislop was instructed not to waste time besieging forts, but to pursue the Pindaris 'as long any chance remained of overtaking and destroying them'.

The Pindaris faced a grim future, since they could no longer look to the Maratha chiefs for help. Chitu's army had some 8,000 men, both cavalry and infantry, with ten large guns; the armies of Wasil Mohammed and Karim Khan were of similar size. These were powerful forces, but no match for the troops of the British, bent on extermination.

Hastings's plan was not just to defeat the Pindaris, but to remove them for all time by physically exterminating as many of them as possible. 'Being viewed as public robbers', wrote Colonel Fitzclarence, 'their extirpation was aimed at, and not their defeat as an enemy entitled to the rights of war.'[12] The annihilation of indigenous peoples, the technique adopted in other parts of the Empire, was to be extended to India. Fitzclarence travelled through the country in this period, and left a record of the actions taken against them:

> The orders given to officers who were to move against the Pindaris – enemies who were to be considered in the light of public robbers – were as follows: individuals were to be punished capitally if fully proved to belong to these wretches, whether they were found in our territories, or those of our allies . . . It was ordered that a trial should first take place, and if conviction followed, the punishment should be summary . . . No distinction was to be made between the lowest of them and their chiefs, and every exertion was to be used to seize their families.

The first battle was joined at Beechee Tal in December 1817, with fifty Pindaris killed. Ten days later, 'Captain Tod, in command of the Rajah of Kotah's troops, fell in with a thousand Pindaris. He dispersed them with considerable loss. Thus hemmed in on all sides, the Pindaris were left in the most precarious position.' Karim Khan's army was the next to come under attack, and only 2,000 of his men survived. His wife and her female attendants were captured, as were his elephants.

More than one hundred Pindaris were killed in January 1818 by the Gujerat Field Force, commanded by General William Grant-Keir, and 1,000 were killed that month at the fort of Jawud. Soon the Pindaris were dispersed, and no longer existed as a formidable power. Many were killed by villagers in revenge for their earlier cruelties.[13]

Chitu escaped from these massacres, and in October he joined forces with Apa Sahib of Nagpur. They barricaded themselves into the great fortress of Asirgarh, often known as 'the key to the Deccan', just north of Burhanpur. With more than one hundred heavy guns, the fortress appeared impregnable, yet after heavy British bombardment for several weeks in early 1819, it fell – though at a high cost to the attackers. Chitu and Apa Sahib escaped, but Chitu's remains were later found in the forest, eaten by tigers.

With the crushing of the Marathas and the Pindaris, British control now extended over two-thirds of India.[14] An unbroken line of communication stretched through British-controlled territory – from Bombay to both Calcutta and Madras. British rule was to be military rule, enforced by military discipline imposed under martial law, and involving punishment by flogging and torture. Four decades later, in 1857, the British conquerors were to pay a substantial price for their misrule.[15]

CHAPTER 31

Revolt, Fresh Settlement and Extermination in Cape Colony

Early in January 1819, Xhosa forces crossed the Fish River into the white settler region of Albany, once the Zuurveld, and re-established their control over the entire frontier district of Cape Colony, from which they had been evicted in 1811–12. Soon they threatened the British settlement of Grahamstown itself. The Xhosa leader, Makana, was a charismatic prophet in his late thirties, known by his people as Nxele, 'the left-handed one'. The Dutch called him Links, corrupted by the British to Lynx.

The Xhosa forces made music as they advanced into settler territory, singing that they had come

> To chase the White men from the earth,
> And drive them to the sea.
> The sea that cast them up at first,
> For Ama Xhosa's curse and bane,
> Howls for the progeny she nursed
> To swallow them again.[1]

Makana had emerged among the Xhosa in 1818, with a religion to rival the Christianity of the white settlers. His god, Mdalidiphu, demanded that the whites must be driven into the sea. Makana called himself Mdalidiphu's agent, with the task of destroying the Europeans and bringing back to life all slaughtered Africans, and their cattle as well. The Xhosa considered Mdalidiphu to be vastly superior to Thixo, the white man's god; he was popular with Xhosa males, for he permitted polygamy and did not consider adultery a sin.

Makana had allied himself with Ndlambe, one of the leading Xhosa chiefs driven eastwards across the Fish River in 1811–12. Ndlambe was now an old man and Makana, who was not himself a chief, became Ndlambe's prime minister, bishop, and field-marshal. Before confronting the British, Makana's initial task was to defeat the forces of Ngqika, Ndlambe's nephew, who had collaborated with the British in the years after 1812. At a battle at Amalinde in October 1818, the forces of Makana and Ndlambe had defeated those of Ngqika, and Ngqika's son, Maqoma, was wounded.

Ngqika requested assistance from his British allies, and their troops came to his aid in December, attacking Makana's forces on the east side of the Fish River. Makana and Ndlambe retreated into the dense wooded valleys of their territory, and the British commander turned his artillery onto their hiding place, firing blindly into the bush. The Xhosa scattered and their cattle stampeded. Xhosa houses were burned down and their cattle stolen. The booty was divided between the soldiers and Ngqika.

Makana's Xhosa were soon in need not just of revenge, but of food and sustenance, to be obtained from the white farmlands of Albany. In January 1819, his armies assembled to re-cross the Fish River. Advancing swiftly, they overcame Ngqika's men and moved on towards the British base at Grahamstown. Taking advice from the Dutch frontiersman Andries Stockenstrom, the British declared martial law on the frontier, and sought reinforcements from Cape Town. Ngqika's men, Stockenstrom had told the British, were far from reliable: 'Ngqika knows that all his people will join against him the moment they see that Ndlambe gets the better of the colonial force.'[2] The best chance for the British was to take the battle into Xhosa territory on the far side of the Fish River. 'Nothing less than a repetition of the Commando of 1812', Stockenstrom said, 'will bring the Kaffirs to peace.'

On 22 April, before reinforcements could arrive from Cape Town, the Xhosa struck. Makana's army of 10,000 descended on the white settlement at Grahamstown. Yet it was an unequal struggle, for Makana's men had spears while the settlers had rifles and cannon. The Xhosa were driven back after a great slaughter; more than a thousand of them were killed.

Three months later, the Xhosa found that the British had taken Stockenstrom's advice and were advancing across the Fish River into their territory. Colonel Thomas Willshire led an army of 3,400 men as far as the river Kei. As in 1812, hundreds of Xhosa were killed, and many villages burned down. More than 30,000 cattle were driven away. The British called this the Fifth Xhosa War.

Makana surrendered, and a group of Ndlambe's councillors came to Colonel Willshire's camp to plead for his release:

> The war, British chiefs, is an unjust one. You are striving to extirpate a people whom you forced to take up arms . . . We wish for peace; we wish to rest in our huts; we wish to get milk for our children; our wives wish to till the land. But your troops cover the plains, and swarm in the thickets, where they cannot distinguish the man from the woman and shoot all.[3]

Their pleas fell on deaf ears, and Xhosa villages continued to be burned. Even the lands of Ngqika were no longer sacrosanct, for the British no longer needed Ngqika's support. Thousands of acres of his land were seized and handed over to an influx of white settlers who were to arrive from Britain two years later. 'When I look at the large piece of territory that has been taken from me', Ngqika recorded mournfully, 'I must say that, though protected, I am rather oppressed by my protectors.'

Makana was sentenced to life imprisonment on Robben Island, the prison camp off Cape Town. He soon became the leader of the slaves and other prisoners held there. A year later, on Christmas Day 1820, the prisoners rebelled, overpowering their guards and seizing a boat. They steered for the mainland, but their vessel was overloaded and capsized as they got close to Blaauwberg Beach. Most of the prisoners swam ashore to safety, but Makana was drowned. For years after his death, the Xhosa repeated a hopeful mantra to be echoed over the years: 'One day Makana will come back and help us again.'

In March 1820 the large indigenous black population of Cape Colony witnessed the arrival at Cape Town of a group of 5,000 white settlers from Britain, whose passage and settlement costs were funded by the British government. These new settlers were destined for the Albany region recently wrested from the Xhosa. Their arrival was to cause the existing Dutch settlers on the frontier to move north, pressing into the lands of the San – or Bushmen – and exterminating them.

The black population at the time (excluding the San and the Xhosa on the frontier) was made up of 25,000 Khoi-Khoi – or Hottentots – and 35,000 slaves, working for the Dutch settlers whose prosperity was largely built upon slave labour. Together they greatly outnumbered the 40,000 Europeans, of whom the great majority were still of Dutch origin.

After the war against Makana, the colonial government perceived a need to increase the British population, partly to create a human barrier against the Xhosa on the eastern border and partly to offset the influence of the Dutch settlers, with their uncertain political allegiance. The government in London wished to alleviate its own post-war unemployment situation, and agreed to fund the despatch of 5,000 settlers. These came from England, Ireland, Scotland and Wales, and were initially kept together in their individual national groups.

Stockenstrom, the old Dutch farmer, like most of the Boers, was not much impressed by the newcomers:

> There were amongst them men capable of any species of crime that can be traced in the police records of the most civilised nations. Men who may be matched, but certainly not surpassed, among the diggings of Australia or California, or anywhere else, and who have done more toward the demoralisation of South Africa than the conquest and domination of Kaffirs could have done.[4]

Some of the newcomers stayed in Cape Town, but the majority were sent to Albany.

The Dutch in South Africa, like the French in Canada, fully understood the British motive in encouraging white settlement from Britain, and, as soon as the new settlers began arriving, the Dutch farmers began looking at new territories to the north – to the lands of the San beyond the Orange River.

One interested observer was the Reverend John Phillip, a priest sent by the London Missionary Society. He kept his eyes and ears open, and in 1821 he received a letter from a correspondent in the frontier town of Beaufort that described recent 'commandos' sent out against the San. 'I have had several conversations with individuals who have been engaged on these expeditions, and they talk of shooting Bushmen with the same feelings as if the poor creatures were wild beasts.'[5]

Campaigns to exterminate the San had been underway since the turn of the century. Between 1800 and 1824, about 130,000 square kilometres of land previously occupied by hunting bands of San had been taken over by white farmers. By 1825, not one of these hunting groups remained. British officials liked to claim that the extermination of the San was chiefly the work of the Dutch, but the Reverend Philip knew that this was not so. He revealed that what had once been regarded as a purely Dutch project was also the policy of the British. The system 'which rendered the Dutch name so infamous', he wrote, was now being carried on 'in all its horrors' under the English government. 'Impatient to obtain undisturbed possession of the Bushman country, and tired of the slow method of exterminating the natives by commandoes of Boers under the field cornets, a plan was devised to employ the Cape regiments, and the British soldiers then on the frontiers of the colony, in this work of death.'

But the British were not alone. Fresh evidence of the continuing Dutch slaughter of the San came in a letter from Cape Town to the Reverend Phillip in December 1822, from a British doctor married to the daughter of a Dutch settler. The letter told of an old Khoi-Khoi, the servant of his father-in-law, who had 'just returned from the Bushman country where he had been from July last, with the commando under the command of the field cornet, Van der Merwe'. He said that 'they had killed thirty men and eighteen children, their orders being that they were not to make any prisoner'.

Phillip recorded another message he received, in July 1823, from a merchant in Cape Town who, on passing through Beaufort, 'learned that a commando had lately returned from an expedition against the Bushmen; and three Boers, who brought us across the Gamka, told me they had been on this commando, and that there were shot 26 men, 2 women, and 2 children. By such measures, the race is fast approaching annihilation.'

Though many of these stories concerned the Dutch, Phillip remained a fierce critic of the British administration and the settlers. He thought that the British behaved worse. 'Whatever may be said, on a comparative view, of English and Dutch humanity, it is evident that the mass of evil brought upon the wretched Bushmen is greater under the English government than under the Dutch.'

George Thompson, another visitor to South Africa in these years, wrote down what he had been told by Nel, a Dutch commandant. 'Within the last 32 years, he had been upon 30 commandoes against the Bushmen, in which great numbers had been shot, and their children carried into the colony. On one of these expeditions, not less than 200 Bushmen had been destroyed.'[6]

The San were not the only ones to suffer. During the same period, a violent campaign took place to deprive the Khoi-Khoi of their land. Phillip tells of the experience of one British settler, at Clan William, who had applied to the authorities for additional land:

> He was directed by the deputy landdrost of the district to take possession of a spot called Varkens-Fonteyn, a valley at the distance of some hours' ride from the place where he resided. On visiting the place, this gentleman, to his surprise, found the land promised him cultivated by some industrious Hottentots, whose ancestors had long possessed the same spot before any Europeans set their feet on the shores of South Africa.
>
> He was pleased with the land, and with the state of cultivation in which he found it; but he was so struck with the injustice which would have been done to the Hottentots in dispossessing them, that he refused to accept it on the terms on which it had been offered to him. On stating to the local authority the reasons for which he declined accepting the grant, the man in the office could not have expressed more contempt than he did at his scruples, had they been made in behalf of its ancient inhabitants, the baboons.[7]

The racism that characterised the colonial settlement in South Africa, and the desire to turn it into 'white man's country' by exterminating the existing population, were well established in its early years, and would survive over the subsequent century.

British as well as Dutch death squads were operating on the frontier of Cape Colony in the course of the 1820s, and here too nonconformist priests were present to record what was going on. The principal killer in the frontier region was the local commander, Colonel Henry Somerset – son of Lord Charles Somerset, the former governor. Henry Somerset's squad was composed of a motley collection of British and Boer settlers and military men, as well as Khoi-Khoi soldiers and Temby and Gcaleka warriors. In 1828, after eight years in South Africa, members of the 1820 generation of British settlers took part in commando operations for the first time.

In August, Matiwane, an African chief camped on the eastern borders not far from Umtata, was attacked by one of Somerset's commandoes in the battle of Mbholompho. Matiwane had escaped earlier with his followers from the warfare further north, and Stockenstrom, now the civilian commissioner on the frontier, described how Somerset had entered Matiwane's sleeping camp 'with great guns and small guns, and sabres and assegais' and made 'indiscriminate havoc before the savages were awake, or knew what had come upon them'.[8] Another version of what took place was recorded by the Reverend Stephen Kay, a Wesleyan missionary at Butterworth, who derived his information from people who witnessed the scene.

> While a great part of the people were still fast asleep, the rush of horses, the clashing of spears, and the roar of musquetry thus poured in upon them on every side . . . Very few seconds seem to have elapsed ere every hut was vacated, and thousands seen scampering off in every direction; numbers, gaunt and emaciated by hunger and age, crawled out of their miserable sheds, but with pitiable apathy sat or lay down again, as if heedless of their fate. Many of the females cast away their little ones, the more readily to effect their own escape; whilst others actually plunged into the deepest part of the adjacent river with their infants upon their backs. In this situation some were drowned, others speared, and many stoned to death by the savage throng.
>
> When the troops returned to the point whence they started, the field presented a scene indescribably shocking: old decrepit men, with their bodies pierced, and heads almost cut off; pregnant females ripped open, legs broken, and hands severed from the arms for . . . the armlets, or some trifling ornament; little children mutilated and horribly mangled.[9]

The missionary could hardly contain his indignation:

> The narrative of such atrocities committed upon a wandering tribe in search of a home, a tribe with whom we were in no respect concerned, who were so far from being at war with us that they were actually sleeping peacefully with their aged and infirm, their women and children around them, committed under the auspices of a British officer, makes one's ears tingle.

Stockenstrom recorded that the Cape governor, General Sir Richard Bourke, was shocked by the frontier massacre and planned to initiate an investigation;

but before he could do so he was withdrawn from Cape Town and transferred to New South Wales. When Stockenstrom himself sought to organise an enquiry, he was told that 'the case appeared to be of too exclusively a military character' for him to be troubled with it. Colonel Somerset continued his operations on the distant frontier for several years to come.

CHAPTER 32

The British Base and Prison on the Island of Singapore

On 30 January 1819, Abdul Rahman, the elderly Temenggong of Johore, signed a treaty with Sir Stamford Raffles, the former governor of Java, permitting the British to set up a trading post at Singapore, an island that was by no means uninhabited at the time of the British descent. Twenty gambier plantations were established there, some worked by Malays, others by Chinese. Gambier, from the gambeer tree, was harvested and sold as an essential ingredient in the dyeing and tanning industries. A few of the Temenggong's followers lived on the island, as well as a handful of Malay and Chinese fishermen. Unusually in the history of Empire, there is no record of anyone objecting to the British arrival.

Abdul Rahman was essentially a sea lord, one of the heirs to the great maritime empire of Johore that stretched across the many-islanded waters between what are now Malaysia and Indonesia. The Temenggong's principal base had been at Riau, on the island of Bentan, but he had recently been forced off the island when the Dutch, returning to the area in 1816 at the end of the European war, had given their support to a rival group, the Bugis.

Singapore was just one small participant in a large-scale 'pirate' organisation under the Temenggong's loose control, based off the island of Galang, south of Bentan. For the Malays living on this great lagoon, the sea had always been a more significant territory than the land.[1] The arrival of the British introduced a more dynamic and repressive element into their lives than they had been accustomed to during the Dutch era. The Malay 'sea gypsies', as they were sometimes called, lived off what the British chose to describe as 'piracy'; in 1819 they were about to have their age-old operations terminally disrupted.

Had these sea-going people formed a kingdom on land, they would simply have been exacting tolls and customs duties from those who travelled across their territory, though both would have been obnoxious to the free-trading British. Yet when their wholly legitimate interference with free trade took place on the 'high seas', it was described as 'piracy'. This had been the charge against the Qawasim in the Persian Gulf, and over the next thirty years, 'piracy' was to be the chief act of rebellion against British rule in the strategic waters off Singapore. British warships were soon to be based there for the sole purpose of eradicating the 'pirates'.

Raffles expressed the same optimism he had shown when seizing Java eight years earlier. The new trading post had a bright future. 'Singapore bids fair to be the next port to Calcutta', he wrote. 'This is by far the most important station in the East; and, as far as naval superiority and commercial interests are concerned, of much higher value than whole continents of territory.'

In making a deal with the British, Abdul Rahman had allied himself with two colonial servants, Raffles and Colonel William Farquhar, for many years the British Resident at Malacca, with similar interests to his own. All three men had been dislodged recently from Dutch enclaves, and all had a common interest in establishing a new base. The Temenggong had lost his headquarters at Riau; Farquhar and Raffles were ousted colonial governors looking for fresh territory. Raffles, thrown out of Java, had consoled himself with the tiny prison enclave of Bencoolen on the island of Sumatra, which he was shortly to lose to the Dutch, who had already recovered Farquhar's base at Malacca. Farquhar now took up a new position as the Resident at Singapore.

Abdul Rahman and his successors were to have an ambivalent relationship with the British. Although promised a large annual salary, he had no intention of giving up his earlier trade as a facilitator of 'piracy'. Colonel Nahuijs, a Dutch officer who visited Singapore in 1823, explained the nature of Abdul Rahman's relationship with the 'pirates': 'The Temenggong is generally said to still have good understanding with his elder brothers, the pirates, and to maintain an active correspondence with them, giving them regular news of the comings and goings in Singapore harbour, and the destination, cargo and strengths of the different ships.'[2]

In the early years, Abdul Rahman believed that his deal with the British would benefit his followers. The increased trade that the British would bring to Singapore would assist his informal tax-collectors out at sea. Formally incorporated into the Empire in 1819, Singapore remained a lawless place, as a contemporary Malay report of 1823 makes clear:

> All the inhabitants were dismayed by frequent incidents, houses catching fire, robberies taking place in the high noon, people getting stabbed. When morning came, people would be found stabbed and wounded to death. The Temenggong's men, the Sultan's men, and the foreigners of all races, went about fully armed; some of them robbed people in broad daylight, some broke into houses and stole people's property, for they were afraid of nothing . . .[3]

Slaves were still being landed and sold, in spite of the Empire-wide ban imposed in 1807. The trade continued briskly in Singapore, as in Mauritius. When Colonel Farquhar was asked if he realised that slave-dealing was now a crime, he replied that in 'a young colony' like Singapore it would be unwise to be too particular. Raffles thought otherwise, and the slave trade was formally prohibited in May 1823.

In March 1823, Sayid Yasin, a Muslim merchant from the established Malay community in Singapore, stabbed Colonel Farquhar as he walked in his gardens. The stabbing was not fatal, but the Sayid was only prevented from completing his task by the prompt arrival of the colonel's servants, who killed him immediately.

When the Resident was stabbed, the Europeans assumed immediately that the Sayid must have been acting in the name of the Temenggong Abdul Rahman, now a salaried local ruler.[4] This was not so. The Sayid and Colonel Farquhar had a semi-private dispute. When the Sayid had proved unable to pay his debts, the Resident had sent him to gaol. Such a fate was humiliating to a Sayid, and he had sought revenge.

Raffles, who had come to Singapore from Bencoolen a few months earlier, argued that an attack on an official should be met with an exemplary punishment. He called for the Sayid's corpse to be put in an iron cage and exhibited publicly for a fortnight. Yet the Sayid's grave at Tanjong Pagar soon became a shrine, and remained a place of pilgrimage for many years. Many Europeans thought that Raffles had endangered their lives by needlessly antagonising the Malays.

Farquhar was replaced as Resident by John Crawford, the old Java hand who would later turn up in Burma. Crawford forced a new treaty on the Temenggong in 1824 that effectively obliged him to leave the island. The old 'pirate' ruler died the following year.[5] He was succeeded by Ibrahim, his fifteen-year-old son, and Temenggong Ibrahim continued as an influential 'pirate' operator until the 1840s, when he moved his men into the new trade in gutta-percha.

When, in the 1830s, slavery was finally abolished throughout the Empire, Singapore became one of its many prison islands. Convicts from India provided a steady supply of cheap labour for public works, and in later years Chinese convicts were also brought in. Forced labour, that essential ingredient of empire, was now readily available.[6] Tapping the unlimited supplies of cheap labour available in Hong Kong and south China after 1840, the British entirely altered the demographic nature of their colony. Singapore went through an extraordinary transformation, and by the end of the nineteenth century its population had risen to 250,000, of whom three-quarters were Chinese.[7]

CHAPTER 33

Years of Unrest Culminate in a Fresh Revolt in Ireland

In January 1822, a band of 400 Irish peasants 'acting under crude military discipline' attacked a troop of fifty British soldiers and police in the hills above Bantry, in County Cork, forcing them to retreat to the town. Many farmworkers were said to have abandoned their homes to establish themselves in the mountains, and rumours told of an army of 'a thousand Whiteboys'.

In February, the acting British home secretary, Lord Londonderry, formerly Viscount Castlereagh, announced in parliament that 'nothing short of absolute rebellion' now prevailed over much of south-west Ireland.[1] He was not exaggerating. Accustomed to trouble further afield, the Empire found itself seriously challenged between 1821 and 1824 by rebellion nearer home. Extensive armed resistance occurred in the rural areas of Ireland, chiefly in Munster and Leinster, accompanied by a wave of millenarian excitement.

This formidable rebellion came at the end of more than twenty years of unrest in the wake of the revolt of 1798. Serious agricultural disturbance had occurred, notably in the provinces of Limerick and Tipperary. 'Rebellion was in the field', Londonderry continued in sober tones. 'It was characterised by every mark belonging to insurrection; resistance to the law, defiance of the constituted authorities, and every component principle of rebellion.' Some 300 people were detained that month for crimes committed in Munster, and ships were prepared to take them to Australian exile.

The British authorities in Dublin no longer referred to 'disturbances' or 'outrages' – the familiar words used to play down the continuing resistance. They were now obliged to admit that Munster was on the verge of open rebellion. The old tradition of the Whiteboys clearly survived, but this was something new. 'A combination of men acted together in great numbers, and with a wonderful unanimity', wrote a nineteenth-century historian. 'They appeared continually in large masses on the hills and in the vales, and might, at almost any time at night, be met with on the high roads. They were said to be under the command of Captain Rock; and all the notices of vengeance or quittance of lands were signed in his name.'[2]

'Captain Rock' was the movement's leader; but no one ever discovered who he was. His name joins the long list of pseudonyms with which Irish rebels have cloaked the identities of their hydra-headed leadership. Thomas Moore, the Irish poet, famous for his tale of *Lalla Rookh*, burnished the rebel image by writing *The Memoirs of Captain Rock* – a book, first printed in Paris in 1823, that detailed peasant grievances over the centuries.[3]

Other influences were at work in these years. The peasant Catholic rank and file had in their hands a religious tract, circulating in cheap editions, and apparently the work of an Italian, Signor Pastorini.[4] In a chapter analysing the Book of Revelation, the author claimed that all Protestant churches would be destroyed by violence in 1825. This 'revelation' was received with enthusiasm in several parts of Ireland, and credulous Catholic peasants prepared themselves for this encouraging eventuality. Signor Pastorini, commented an anonymous voice in County Limerick in January 1822, 'has done more towards the subversion of the British Empire than Bonaparte with all his legions'.[5] So strong was the belief in Pastorini's prophecy that convicts waiting at Cork to be transported to Australia were said to be glad to be leaving; they would avoid the bloody scenes that were to come. They were unaware that they would soon witness comparable events in the prison territory of New South Wales.

The chief aim of Captain Rock's men – beneficiaries of this atmosphere of prophetical fervour – was to create a climate of violence that would drive the Protestant settler landlords from their farms and their mansions. Catholic tenants would then be able to occupy their land rent-free. Fears of rebellion and massacre rose to such a peak, and so quickly, that in 1824 many Protestants were afraid to go to church on Christmas Day.

The new lord-lieutenant in Dublin in 1822 – the man in charge of repression in Ireland – was General Richard Wellesley, the elder brother of the Duke of Wellington. Last heard of as the governor-general of India at the time of the humiliation of the Maratha chiefs in 1803 and 1804, Wellesley had arrived in Dublin in December 1821 on the eve of the rural insurrection that threatened the privileges of the landlords. 'Those who dared to be obedient to the law', he complained in May 1822, were being 'punished by the control of a predominant power, exercising lawless, cruel, and savage tyranny.'

Wellesley was soon to unleash a savage tyranny of his own, pushing through parliament a series of repressive measures: the imposition of martial law, the suspension of habeas corpus, and a fresh insurrection act. The gaols were soon filled with those awaiting execution or transportation. Wellesley was less of a killer than many of his colleagues. Henry Goulburn, the chief secretary, was notably fierce, expressing the hope that 'before any amnesty is granted or any general remission of punishment takes place, sufficient example ought to have been made to prove to the deluded people that punishment will always follow crime'. However, William Gregory, the under-secretary, was less vindictive, writing despairingly in April that he did not know 'what can be done with so many persons under sentence of death. It will not be possible to execute them all.'

A special assize court sat during the period of martial law, and thirty-six death sentences were imposed. Wellesley suggested that transportation should replace hanging whenever possible, and 200 convicted prisoners to were sent off to the Australian gulag. In September, hearing that several prisoners awaiting execution in Cork had been unsafely convicted, Wellesley asked for them to be reprieved. 'I am always happy to find any reasons for respite of capital sentences', he said. Three days later, Goulburn gave him the bad news: 'the messenger did not reach Cork in time'.

Captain Rock's rebellion brought in its train a far-reaching police reform that would transform the policing of the Empire. The Irish Constables Act imposed by Wellesley established an armed police force in Ireland, county by county, with chief constables appointed by the government. Opponents of the Act perceived it as a serious threat to the constitution, which had not hitherto countenanced a large government-controlled police force.[6] The Irish Constabulary created in 1822, and reorganised in 1836 (it became 'Royal' in 1867), became the model for the colonial police forces of the Empire.

Sir Charles Jefferies, historian of the colonial police, wrote without apology in 1952 that

> from the point of view of the colonies there was much attraction in an arrangement which provided what we should now call a 'para-military' organisation . . . armed, and trained to operate as an agent of the central government, in a country where the country was predominantly rural, communities were poor, social conditions were largely primitive, and the recourse to violence by members of the public who were 'agin the government' was not infrequent.

The Royal Irish Constabulary was to provide individual recruits for the colonial system, many of whom were trained at the Constabulary depots in Ireland (and, after 1922, when it became the Royal Ulster Constabulary, in Ulster).[7]

The new paramilitary police force was in place just in time. In October 1823, the year after Captain Rock's rebellion had begun, the London government asked urgently for a reduction in the number of troops held in Ireland, since reinforcements were needed in the Caribbean. Quamina Gladstone's slave rebellion had broken out in Guyana, and repercussions were expected in Jamaica.

Captain Rock's rebellion was eventually crushed not so much through the use of repressive legislation (for the authorities had insufficient troops to enforce the insurrection act) as through the visitation of a devastating famine. Unlike the government-enforced starvation imposed on the Maroons of Dominica in 1813, the Irish peasants were the victims of the overly wet autumn of 1821, and the subsequent failure of the potato crop in 1822.

CHAPTER 34

Aborigine Resistance in Australia and White Retaliation

Aborigine resistance in New South Wales and Tasmania – the fight to prevent the settler seizure of ancestral lands – had been growing in the course of the 1820s. Sheep stations in the Bathurst area inland from Sydney came under serious attack in 1824, while Aborigine opposition to the settler occupation of the grasslands of the Hunter Valley, further north, had become more overt, with threats of direct action against the incomers. In Tasmania the Aborigines were now engaged in open warfare, as the settlers called increasingly for their extermination.

In August 1824, to combat the Aborigine resistance, General Sir Thomas Brisbane, military governor of New South Wales, imposed martial law in the ranching country west of Mount York.[1] Martial law meant that white farmers (some of whom were 'magistrates' in charge of administering the law) could shoot Aborigines with no questions asked. Brisbane, whose name was eventually associated with a great city, also created a death squad to be used against the Aborigines. This was a unit of mounted police, with two officers, two sergeants and twenty privates recruited from the colony's existing force. In September 1825, the new squad was sent out against the Aborigines in the Bathurst region.

The Reverend Lancelot Threlkeld, a sharp observer of the developing conflict who lived at a mission station further north, left a description of what took place. 'Sad was the havoc made upon the tribes at Bathurst,' he wrote in his memoirs.

> A large number were driven into a swamp, and mounted police rode round and round and shot them off indiscriminately until they were all destroyed. When one of the police enquired of the officer if a return should be made of the killed [and] wounded, there were none, all were destroyed; men, women, and children! The reply was: that there was no necessity for a return.[2]

Threlkeld was a congregationalist minister, appointed by the London Missionary Society, who had established a mission in 1823 on the banks of Lake Macquarie, in the Hunter Valley. He was a friend of Saxe Bannister, the colony's attorney-general in Sydney, and wrote regular letters to him describing the new mood of resistance among the Aborigines. Saxe Bannister was a relatively liberal lawyer, firm in the belief that the colony's laws should apply to both white and black. The two men, both new arrivals in Australia and both appalled by the frontier lawlessness and racism they encountered, soon ran into opposition from the settlers.

Threlkeld had few illusions about the whites who surrounded him. 'No man who comes to the colony, and has ground and cattle and corn, can dispassionately view the subject of the Blacks. Their interest says "Annihilate the race". I do expect that there will be a great destruction among them.' He described their hostile attitude. 'The best thing that could be done', said William Cox, one of the richest ranchers, speaking at a public meeting, 'would be to shoot all the Blacks and manure the ground with their carcasses, which was all the good they were fit for . . . the women and children should especially be shot as the most certain method of getting rid of the race.'[3]

The death squad did no paperwork after the Bathurst massacre in September 1825, but they collected up the heads of the forty-five Aborigines they had killed. The skulls were boiled down, packed up in the town, and taken back as trophies to England by the squad's commanding officer.

The rich grasslands of the Hunter Valley, where Threlkeld had established his mission station, had been occupied by Europeans earlier in the decade, as settlers and convicts pushed out into 'new' territory. A huge expanse of Aborigine land had been mapped out and sold off for sheep ranches. The Aborigine peoples – the Wonnarua and the Wiradjuri – had been vocal in their protests from the start, and in July 1826 their passive resistance broke into open rebellion. Their lands were being confiscated, and now their lives too were under threat. Direct action against the settlers was called for. 'A Black came to see me yesterday', Threlkeld wrote to Saxe Bannister in August, 'saying that a great many Blacks were coming from the mountains to burn all the houses of the whites.'[4]

Threlkeld's letter outlined the immediate cause of their anger. Resistance had been reactivated by the presence of General Brisbane's death squad, let loose in the valley in July. Brisbane had retired the previous December, to be replaced by the former governor of Mauritius, General Sir Ralph Darling.[5] Before the death squad set out, Darling had been asked by Bannister if he planned to impose martial law, as Brisbane had done. 'Martial law could not be necessary to put down a few savages', was Darling's reply.

Riding into the Hunter Valley in July, the death squad, led by Lieutenant Nathaniel Lowe, slaughtered as many Aborigines as they could find. Threlkeld gave details of its actions and of the resistance in a letter to Bannister, and the lawyer wrote to ask whether Lowe should be brought to trial for shooting the blacks. Threlkeld, who was outspoken in his writings but cautious in his actions, advised against such a move. If Lowe was removed from the area, he argued, 'this would satisfy the Blacks and the others, [but] only exasperate the settlers more . . . We [need] every support in this vile, hypocritical country.'

He gave additional news of Aborigines taking their revenge on the settlers for helping the death squad. An Aborigine group had gone to the farm of a Mr Ogilvie and demanded that two men 'who had aided the soldiers in shooting the Blacks' should be delivered up to them so that they might kill them. At another hut, the Aborigines asked for food, but were refused. 'They then threw in a volley of spears, killed two men, but a woman had the happiness to escape with her child by hiding under the bed. The settlers are all in arms. The police is out. A detachment is forwarded from Newcastle of nine soldiers, and blood will now be shed most profusely.'[6]

Threlkeld deplored the fact that all were now 'in arms and many will be slain'. Writing again in September, he announced that 'war has commenced, and still continues against the Aborigines of this land'. He also warned of a possible further development: 'If once the prisoners join the blacks, and teach them to fire the corn and wheat, what will be the result? The people despise the Blacks, and that will be their ruin, [for] they are a formidable enemy.'

Threlkeld continued to forecast gloomily that 'many lives will be lost on both sides'. He thought the cause of the trouble was 'the base, wicked, malicious report . . . that "it is the Governor's private wish to shoot all the Blacks"'. By the end of the year, Aborigine resistance in the Hunter Valley had been largely broken – by the death squad and by the ranchers taking the law into their own hands.

Threlkeld's friend in Sydney could be of no further assistance. Bannister had run into such trouble with successive governors that he was obliged to resign. He sailed home to London from Sydney in October, to become a lifelong critic of the treatment of the native races in the Empire.[7] Threlkeld, too, was under threat. There were 'many who would banish me from the colony', he had told Bannister in August, 'and prevent any attempt of a missionary nature among the Blacks – if they could'.

Yet, to the surprise of the settlers, Darling agreed that the crimes of the death squad should be looked into. Bannister's replacement, W. H. Moore, was sent to Newcastle in January 1827 to investigate. Threlkeld expected Lowe to be exonerated, since 'all the magistrates here had previously signed a letter thanking him for his conduct in taking upon himself the responsibility of shooting his prisoner while in his safe custody. The whole of the outrages may be traced to this . . .'.

Lowe was brought to trial on two occasions, but acquitted each time and cheered loudly by his friends in court. In May he was ordered to rejoin his regiment in Tasmania, where another formidable Aborigine rebellion was under way.

* * *

Proclamation to the Aborigines of Van Diemen's Land (Tasmania), 1829, authorised by the governor General George Arthur, but mistakenly attributed to an earlier governor in 1816, General Thomas Davey. Designed to create a narrative, one entirely at odds with the record, in which colonial law recognizes blacks and whites as equals.

The Aborigine struggle for land and survival in Tasmania had developed into a permanent armed conflict with the European settlers, and in June 1827 Aborigines speared and killed six Europeans. The settler retaliation was reported in *The Times* of London six months later. More than sixty Aborigines, the paper revealed, had been killed or wounded 'recently' by the military in Tasmania, noting in justification that 'the native people' brought slaughter and devastation wherever they went.[8] For a time the two sides were evenly balanced, but the gun of the European eventually proved more lethal than the Aborigine's spear.

The governor of Tasmania in these years was Colonel George Arthur, a military ruler last heard of as governor of British Honduras during the slave revolt of 1820. He had arrived on the island as a prison governor, but much of his time was taken up with the Aborigine resistance. In a single month in 1828, no less than twenty inquests were held at Oatlands into killings of British settlers by Aborigines.

Taking a leaf from the policing model of New South Wales, Colonel Arthur decreed in November 1828 that the Tasmanian Aborigines should be subject to martial law. Arthur claimed he only wanted to punish the Aborigine 'leaders', but the settlers, given a free hand without fear of retribution, aimed more widely. In one case, at Mount Victory in 1828, thirty Aborigines were massacred by convict 'servants' of the Van Diemen's Land Company, who threw the survivors over a cliff.[9] Many Aborigines were killed, and several women were axed to death. Prisoners were shot. Renewed in 1830, when Arthur came up with a yet more outlandish scheme to control the Aborigines, martial law lasted until 1832, effectively breaking Aborigine resistance in Tasmania.

CHAPTER 35

The Ashanti Defeat the British at Esamankow

The British had taken a commercial interest in the West African territory of the Gold Coast, now Ghana, since the seventeenth century. At Cape Coast Castle a private operation, the Royal African Company, had been set up in 1672, with a charter from King Charles II. Its purpose was to make money from the purchase and transport of black men and women to other parts of the world, from where they were sold. After trading for more than 150 years, the Company had sold out to the British state in 1821, after the collapse of its business in the wake of the slave trade's abolition in 1807.

Among its legacies was the Royal African Corps, a military unit traditionally recruited from the criminal element in the British army who had been banished from classier regiments. Colonel Sir Charles McCarthy, the military governor at Freetown, had reformed the Corps into what became the Royal African Colonial Corps of Light Infantry, reinforced with a smattering of additional troops brought out from England.[1] Among his responsibilities, extending along the West African coast, was the suppression of the slave trade.[2]

Cape Coast and other small forts along the West African shore had been brought under the control of the British authorities in Sierra Leone, and Cape Coast Castle was guarded with the support of a coastal people, the Fantis. The Ashanti territory inland, ruled from Kumasi, had remained free and independent; but in the early 1820s, as a result of the changing status of the Royal Africa Company, the boundaries between areas of Ashanti and British influence became a subject of contention.

Osei Bonsu – the Ashanti ruler, sometimes called Osai Tutu Quamina – had been the Asantehene, or ruler, of the Ashanti kingdom since the turn of the century. As with Kandy, Nepal and Burma, this large inland empire, with its formidable military power, posed a permanent threat to the expansionist ambitions of the British, and Ashanti resistance would continue throughout the nineteenth century. Fighting frequently broke out between the Ashantis and the British-backed Fantis, and Osei Bonsu now believed the time had come to drive the British into the sea. The Ashanti had taken note of the British capacity to mobilise the coastal groups into a coalition force that could be used against them, and they prepared their own resistance plans.

In January 1824, paying his regular annual visit to Cape Coast, Colonel McCarthy decided to lead a small force inland to Kumasi, the Ashanti capital, to curb their power. Martial law was proclaimed and, with 500 local troops and twelve European officers, McCarthy crossed the River Prah and marched towards the Ashanti capital. Only the previous year he had claimed that he 'did not entertain a very exalted idea of the skill or bravery of the Ashantees'.[3]

Underestimating the Ashanti proved a mistake; with 10,000 soldiers, they hugely outnumbered McCarthy's troops. They attacked the British column, with much singing and beating of drums, as was their custom. McCarthy ordered his own military band to strike up with 'God Save the King', but to no effect.[4] Soon his soldiers had run out of ammunition, their ordnance supplier being apparently to blame; one keg of powder was found to contain vermicelli. Colonel McCarthy was wounded during what became known as the battle of Esamankow, and then killed himself to avoid capture; his troop was almost entirely wiped out. The triumphant Ashanti cut off the colonel's head, as well as those of eight officers, and carried them in triumph to Kumasi. 'They are even to this day held in high honour', wrote the American explorer Henry Stanley, visiting the city fifty years later, 'being decorated with gold bands and jewels.' The colonel's skull was used as a royal drinking-cup.

After the battle, the victorious Ashanti marched south to the coast at Accra. They were only prevented from capturing the town by the 'newly introduced war-rockets' of the British. The Asantehene Osei Bonsu did not live long to enjoy his victory; he died on the same day as Colonel McCarthy, and was succeeded by Osei Okoto.

A second battle against the British took place two years later, in August 1826, at Akantamasu, or Dodowa, outside Accra. On this occasion the Ashanti were defeated and a peace treaty was signed. Under its terms, the Ashanti agreed to remain to the north of the River Prah, and the British retained their coastal strip.

CHAPTER 36

The Burmese Empire Fights Back

In February 1824, after a few preliminary skirmishes on the border, the British declared war on the Burmese Empire. This marked the start of a long war between the Burmese Empire, based at Ava, and Britain's Indian empire, based at Calcutta – a struggle that would remain unresolved for more than a century. Under successive rulers, the Burmese had been extending their empire to the west since the eighteenth century; and in the 1820s, with the British entrenched in Bengal, the long frontier between independent Burma and British Bengal became a flashpoint. The Burmese made probes into Assam, a zone of British influence on the borders of Bengal, while Burmese dissidents received political support from the British. Matters came to a head in 1824, and Burma's King Bagyidaw braced his countrymen to resist a British invasion.[1]

The British knew little of the Burmese Empire at the time – neither its history and geography, nor its religion and politics. Two British officers had gone on a mission to Ava in 1795,[2] a handful of merchants had travelled short distances up the Irrawaddy River, and a British 'Resident', Hiram Cox, had lived briefly at Ava for a year or two. That was all. The Burmese were not overly familiar with the British either, though a small group of Westerners had been established for some years at Ava.[3]

The Burmese were to suffer three British invasions of mounting intensity and violence in the course of the nineteenth century – in 1824, in 1852 and in 1885. On each occasion they fought back. Powerful resistance forces greeted British soldiers as they marched blithely into the jungle north of Rangoon, greeted by sickness and disease on a scale reminiscent of the Caribbean campaigns of the 1790s. The Burmese were eventually obliged to submit, but the British paid a heavy price, even jeopardising their position in India.

British strategists knew enough to understand that the invasion and conquest of Burma would be a formidable task.[4] It would clearly be foolish to march straight into the inaccessible and steeply wooded hills that marked the frontier marches with India. Their initial plan was simpler. A sea-borne invasion fleet would be sent to capture the port of Rangoon. An army of 11,000 soldiers, including Europeans and sepoys, would then move up the Irrawaddy River to confront the Burmese king at Ava – a river journey of more than 300 miles. For the first time in the history of imperial warfare, the fleet was to include a small ship powered by steam – the Diana.

The Burmese pre-empted the British plan. Their army commander, Thado Mingyi Maha Bandula (known simply by his last two names, 'Maha' meaning 'great'), had been commander under both the present king and his predecessor. He was perceived by the British to be courageous and resourceful,[5] and his strategic plan envisaged an offensive war. He would oblige the British to fight to defend India before they could attack and invade Burma.[6] His men were well-prepared,[7] and the Burmese royal family, proud of the achievements of their state, appeared eager for a war they believed they could win.

A Burmese army of 8,000 soldiers set out in May 1824 across the mountains from the royal capital at Ava, and descended into the plain of the Ganges. There they advanced on the British-held town of Chittagong, on the western side of the delta from Calcutta, and at the village of Ramu they defeated a small British detachment of 400 sepoys (and levies raised locally) led by British officers. The levies fled quickly, soon followed by the sepoys. Many were captured and sent as prisoners to Ava, and most of the British officers were killed. Panic erupted as far away as Calcutta, for Chittagong now lay wide open to a further Burmese attack. The defeat of the British in West Africa earlier in the year was now paralleled in Asia.

Dr Jonathan Price, an American Baptist missionary who had worked in Burma before the British invasion, recalled the contemptuous attitude of the court at Ava towards the British. The royal family dismissed them as the inhabitants of a small and remote island; they were particularly contemptuous of the 'black' Indians who had collapsed so easily before the attacks of the British in earlier wars. Dr Price described their reaction to the proposed invasion:[8]

> What business have they to come in ships from so great a distance to dethrone kings, and take possession of countries they have no right to? They contrive to conquer and govern the black foreigners, the peoples of castes, who have puny frames and no courage. They have never yet fought with so strong and brave a people as the Burmas, skilled in the use of sword and spear. If they once fight with us, and we have an opportunity of manifesting our bravery, it will be an example to the black nations, which are now slaves to the English, and will encourage them to throw off the yoke.

Convinced of their superiority over the Indians, the Burmese believed that they could defeat the British too.

Maha Bandula's victory over the British at Ramu in May was an important achievement, yet he had not reckoned on the strength and speed of the British fleet. He could not fight on two fronts, and news soon came of the arrival of the British invasion force far to the south, at Rangoon (today's Yangon). He was obliged to abandon his plan to invade northern India, and was ordered by the king to return to help defend the southern city.

He travelled with all possible speed, making forced marches across the mountains, but his forces arrived too late. The British armada arrived at Rangoon before he did, subjected the town to a fierce bombardment, and then came ashore to find it deserted. The entire population had withdrawn into the countryside, seeking both to ensure its own survival and to deprive the invading force of its potential food supply.

Moving into the deserted town, the British troops had gone in search of plunder. The smaller Buddhist temples were stripped of their gold and silver images by the soldiers, while the officers, led by the British commander, General Archibald Campbell, pillaged the famous Schwe-Dagon Buddhist pagoda. Soon, finding a plentiful supply of brandy in the house of a European merchant, the soldiers became extremely drunk.[9] To General Campbell, plunder was part of soldiering.[10] He was an old India hand, having fought against the armies of Tipu Sultan at Seringapatam in 1792 and 1799, and against the Dutch during the conquest of Ceylon in 1795. He was also, like so many other colonial military leaders of this period, a veteran of the Peninsular Wars.[11]

Campbell captured Rangoon with relative ease, but was soon himself a prisoner. The Burmese besieged the town for several weeks, and when Campbell's forces tried to break out in June, they met with a self-inflicted disaster – fired on by their own troops, and shot at by their ships moored in the river. More than fifty soldiers were killed.[12]

The most effective Burmese weapon was the climate.[13] Food was in short supply, malaria and dysentery set in, and the monsoon brought heavy storms. The local population refused to work as drivers or rowers. 'Few British soldiers can have spent a more miserable year . . . Unsuitably clothed, vilely fed, imperfectly tended, drenched with rain when they were not bathed in sweat, eaten up by mosquitoes, leeches and the manifold other plagues of a tropical delta, they had literally nothing but misery and death before them.'[14] Campbell's invading army remained cooped up in Rangoon, unable to move upriver. More than 3,000 soldiers died from illness.

Stymied at Rangoon, the British embarked on an alternative strategy. They would mount a two-pronged land invasion of Burma across the mountains from India. One army would start from Manipur, the other would cross the Arakan peninsula. Both invasion attempts met with failure. Cutting a road through the dense jungle from Manipur proved impossible, while the Arakan expedition provoked a mutiny before it had even begun.

Three sepoy regiments at Barrackpore, just north of Calcutta, had been earmarked for the campaign. Yet when they received orders to march to Chittagong, they proved reluctant to move. They had good historical reasons for being terrified of a war with the Burmese, and they also had specific grievances.

They had been asked to pay from their wages for the hire of bullocks to carry their kit. They were also told that they would be travelling to Burma by sea – something, as Hindus, that they were forbidden to do. (The theology was hazy, and rarely strictly enforced, since the earlier invasion force had travelled by sea without trouble.) To indicate their displeasure, the sepoys refused to appear on parade at the beginning of November 1824. Officers who came to discuss their problems were threatened with violence.

Sepoy mutinies were still frequent in British India, in spite of the fear induced by memories of 'cannonading'. Yet British power depended on a reliable mercenary army, and mutinies were invariably repressed with considerable violence. The mutiny at Barrackpore was no exception. Two British battalions arrived from Calcutta later in the day, led by General Sir Edward Paget, the commander-in-chief. Paget, most recently the governor of Ceylon, was a Peninsula veteran who had also been in Ireland. Described as 'a hard strict disciplinarian with no knowledge of the native army and a bitter prejudice against it', he was not a man to countenance sepoy insubordination.

His battalions were drawn up on the parade ground the next morning, and they fired on mutinous sepoys when they refused to put down their arms. Many were killed immediately, others were wounded and taken prisoner. Many tried to escape across the Ganges, but twenty were drowned. A court martial at Barrackpore that afternoon sentenced forty-one mutineers to death. Twelve were hanged the next morning, while the others had their sentences commuted to fourteen years' hard labour. 'It seemed an awful thing to have to mow down our own troops with our own artillery', wrote Sir Charles Metcalfe, the Resident at Delhi, 'especially those troops on whose fidelity the existence of our empire depends.' Paget's actions came under criticism in London, and he was withdrawn from India the following year.

The sepoys at Barrackpore were unavailable for action in Burma, but other British units took part in the campaign in the Arakan mountains that started in January 1825. The plan was to push over the hills and meet General Campbell's army advancing up the Irrawaddy. Yet even this apparently modest campaign had to be abandoned. A quarter of this fresh invasion force of 11,000 soldiers died of sickness, while half those remaining were soon unfit for action. The monsoon rains prevented much forward movement. An immense expenditure in lives and treasure had been incurred with little result.[15]

The extent of the Burmese resistance did not go unnoticed within India, and opponents of British rule saw an opportune moment to take action. A Jat fortress at Bharatpur, some thirty miles from Agra, raised the standard of revolt in December 1824. Bharatpur was a place of considerable symbolic importance to the anti-British struggle, for it had been the scene of earlier victories over British forces, including the defeat of General Lake in 1805.

Baldeo Singh, the rajah of the Jats, had had a tacit agreement with the British to engage in no hostile action, and on his deathbed in 1824 he had appealed to the colonial rulers to recognise his son Bulwant Singh, a boy of six, as his successor. His nephew, Durjan Singh, had other plans. He had long nursed plans to drive the British out of Rajasthan and out of India, and on the death of his uncle he seized his cousin and occupied the Bharatpur fortress.

The British also understood the symbolic importance of Bharatpur, knowing well that if the fortress remained a centre of resistance to their rule, the consequent disorder might sweep them from the country.[16] General Sir David Ochterlony, once the conqueror of Nepal and now the aged Resident at Delhi, denounced Durjan Singh as a usurper, and called on the Jats to support Bulwant Singh as their legitimate sovereign. He promised to send out a British force to recapture Bharatpur.

A serious difference of opinion now arose at the heart of the imperial machine, for no treaty justified British interference in Bharatpur's internal affairs. Lord Amherst, the governor-general at Calcutta, who had ordered the invasion of Burma, and who knew that his forces were already over-extended, ordered Ochterlony to withdraw his promise. Ochterlony resigned in protest, and died later in the year.

Yet his policy continued after new appointments had been made, for some action was clearly needed. 'All India was looking on', Sir Charles Metcalfe, Ochterlony's successor as Resident, wrote to his sister. 'From Cape Comorin to Kashmir, and further still, the name of Bharatpur was in the mouth of every native as a taunt against us.' Metcalfe had personally witnessed Lake's failure to storm the fortress in 1805, and was anxious to wipe out the memory of that humiliation. He was joined in this opinion by General Stapleton Cotton, Lord Combermere, the new commander-in-chief appointed to replace Paget, who had ordered the sepoys of Barrackpore to be shot. Combermere's previous post was as commander in Ireland from 1822 to 1825, during the rebellion of 'Captain Rock'.[17]

Metcalfe and Combermere secured Amherst's support for a march on Bharatpur, but since most British regiments were bogged down in Burma, they had to use sepoy battalions. Six sepoy regiments and sixteen sepoy battalions, accompanied by two British cavalry regiments and two battalions of British infantry, were assembled at Agra in December 1824 to prepare for an attack on the fortress. A frontal assault was impossible, for Durjan Singh had impressive artillery, directed by Sergeant Herbert, a British deserter.[18] Metcalfe ordered tunnels to be built under the fortress, and in January 1825 three mines were exploded, one using 10,000 pounds of gunpowder.[19] After some fierce fighting,

Durjan Singh's defenders were scattered and the British seized the fortress and the city, at a cost of 600 casualties.[20]

Some 8,000 of the defenders of the fortress were killed, and those who escaped were subsequently captured, including the rajah himself, who was imprisoned at Allahabad. Three British soldiers from the artillery who had joined Durjan Singh at Bharatpur, two of them from Ireland, were captured and court-martialled. Sergeant Herbert, who had once fought as a gunner at Waterloo, was hanged from the ruins of the citadel. The others were sentenced to fourteen years forced labour in New South Wales. The prize money accruing to the victors amounted to nearly £500,000, of which £60,000 was the share of General Combermere – although much of it was subsequently stolen by his banker.

The fortifications of Bharatpur were blown up and destroyed as a warning to those who sought to defy the British. Failure, wrote Metcalfe, would 'undoubtedly have encouraged disaffection'. Had a general revolt occurred, all India would have reacted against its conquerors. A torrent of hatred would have swept away 'the restraint previously imposed by Fear', and an uprising of 'tribes and nations' would have thrown off the 'detested foreign yoke'. All eyes were now on the resistance in Burma.

The besieged city of Rangoon had come under renewed attack from the Burmese forces of Maha Bandula in December 1824, and General Archibald Campbell, the British commander of the occupation forces, had sent urgent requests for reinforcements from India. Fortunately for the British, the Burmese attack proved unsuccessful, and Bandula withdrew up the river to Donabyu, fifty miles to the north, finally enabling the British to move out of Rangoon in February 1825. A small advance party led by Colonel Sir Willoughby Cotton arrived outside Donabyu in March.[21]

At this stage, disaster struck the Burmese. Bandula's army outnumbered Colonel Cotton's, and might have been expected to prevail, but a stray rocket killed the commander in April. Without Bandula, his army lost heart and his soldiers slipped away.[22] Donabyu town was quickly captured by Cotton's men.

Nothing except the climate now prevented the British from moving up the Irrawaddy towards the Burmese capital. But at Prome, a third of the way to Ava, General Campbell called a halt. He had lost nearly a sixth of his men during the rainy season, and was obliged to accept a de facto truce.

The Burmese took advantage of the truce to prepare a fresh army. Maha Nemiao, the country's oldest and most experienced general, assembled 70,000 men at Ava, and began an advance on Prome in November.[23] The British force, made up of 2,000 sepoys and 3,000 Europeans, was rather smaller than that of Maha Nemiao, but when the two armies met in December the Burmese were forced to retreat. 'All resistance collapsed and gave place to wild panic', wrote Major Snodgrass. 'Old Maha Nemiao and a few gray-haired chiefs stood nobly and fought to the last.' Their men moved to the rear of the stockade, where, the outlets being few and narrow, they were bayoneted in large numbers. Maha Nemiao was found dead, with the corpses of his attendants lying by his body.[24]

The Burmese had lost their two best generals, and were obliged to accept a truce. Peace negotiations concluded on 24 February 1826 with a treaty signed at Yandabo, some sixty miles from Ava. The British demands were severe. King Bagyidaw was forced to hand over the provinces of Arakan and Tenasserim, giving the British their first foothold in his country, and to surrender Burma's claims of sovereignty over Assam, Cachar and Manipur. He also had to accept a permanent British presence at Ava, and to open up the country to trade. John Crawfurd – formerly the henchman of Stamford Raffles in Java and Singapore – was appointed as Resident in Ava.[25] As a final insult, the king was required to pay a £1 million fine.

Unsurprisingly, the king fell into a state of acute depression after 1831; he was deposed in 1837. His successor, Prince Tharrawaddy, went mad in 1845. Yet the Burmese defeat was hardly a success story for the British. Their losses were large, and the resistance had exacted a high political cost.[26] The protracted two-year war gave many people in India the impression that the British were about to quit the continent. Metcalfe, the Resident at Delhi, noted 'an extraordinary sensation all over India, amounting to an expectation of our immediate downfall'. Brigands and tribesmen emerged again to challenge British rule, notably in the frontier territories of Assam and Manipur. 'The people everywhere would rejoice, or fancy that they would rejoice, at our destruction', wrote Metcalfe, 'and numbers are not wanting who would promote it by all means in their power.'

Burmese resistance had threatened British power in India, and it would continue to do so for years to come. Burma's rich provinces provided the British with great wealth; yet the bulk of the Burmese people never received any great benefit from imperial control, and they never accepted their incorporation into the Empire. Their rebellions were among the fiercest and most long-lasting that the Empire would ever experience.

CHAPTER 37

Tea and Strategy: The Rajahs and Hill Peoples of Assam Rebel

A rash of rebellions occurred in the decade after the Burmese war in the strategic frontier zone of Assam, where rajahs and hill tribes – the Khasis, the Singphos, the Khamtis and the Nagas – refused to accept British rule. Rajahs in the valley of the Brahmaputra and chiefs of indigenous tribes in the surrounding hills had traditionally been more in touch with the Burmese, with whom they were linked by ties of race and history, than with the Bengalis. They now made ready to resist the new foreign rulers. The rajahs did not yet know of imperial plans to bring in British settlers and establish extensive tea plantations on their land, but they were well aware that their local power was under serious threat. They sought to regain their lost lands and privileges.

In the wake of their invasion of Burma in 1824–26, the British had pushed north into the former Burmese-controlled territory of Assam, north of their base at Calcutta (and to the north of the present northern frontier of Bangladesh with India). This fertile land, lying on either side of the Brahmaputra, was acquired after the Yandabo Treaty was signed with Burma in February 1826; it became known as the North-East Frontier Territory.

The new governor of Bengal in 1828 was Lord William Bentinck, once a colonel in the Peninsular War, and an ardent reformer. He hoped that a steady flow of entrepreneurial British settlers would reinvigorate this freshly acquired territory, and he reformed the East India Company's immigration regulations to permit this to happen.[1] Hopes were briefly raised that India might rival Australia, Canada and Cape Colony as a land of colonial settlement, although the streams of British settlers never materialised. Eventually, establishing tea plantations appeared more profitable than European settlement, bringing hopes of transforming the economy of the entire region.[2]

Assam looked the most propitious place to start, and the Company soon had plans to establish commercial tea plantations throughout the Brahmaputra valley. In 1823 Robert Bruce, a Company employee, had already been given samples of the local Assam tea by Bessa Gaum, the ruler of the Singhphos, whose territory lay in the upper valley of the Brahmaputra. In the 1830s, after the death of Bruce, Chinese tea plants were brought in by his brother Charles.

British political agents working along the plains of the Brahmaputra argued that the Company should rule through the existing rajahs, since they formed the traditional ruling class that controlled the hill tribes. David Scott, chief among the agents, hoped that the British authorities would agree to subsidise a local ruler in the lands of Upper Assam, but the continuing resistance of the rajahs and the deteriorating economy made this strategy difficult.

First in the ring was Gomdhar Konwar, the rajah at Jorhat in the Brahmaputra valley, who had been deposed in the aftermath of the Burmese war. In October 1828 he assembled a large gathering of peasants and nobles and announced a plan to throw out the British invaders and re-establish his right to rule. He had received 'wonderful omens', he told the crowd, and his audience assured him he would soon again be king. He ordered them to stop paying taxes to the British revenue collectors, and to give them directly to him, their rightful ruler, as well as the 'rice, milk, and *gur*' he enjoyed according to ancient tradition. The rajah was invested with white shoes and an umbrella, the insignia of royalty, and the *bailungs* (royal priests) performed other ceremonial rituals.[3]

The rajah's rebellion gave the British a taste of what was in store. His initial aim was to seize the nearby British base at Rangpur, after securing the support of other rajahs and chiefs in recruiting soldiers and obtaining financial contributions. Some were reluctant. Pealiar Bar Gohain, known as Dhanjoy, an elderly ally from a nearby territory, sounded a note of caution: 'If you are able to succeed in the business, well and good, but it is a difficult matter . . . I see no prospect of success. Yet if you are resolved upon the trial, and will take the advice of an old man, let it not be done in a hurry.' Gomdhar Konwar told him there was no time to lose, and his army of 400 men assembled in November south of Jorhat, armed with nine muskets, ten two-edged Khamti swords, fifty spears and 'a good number of bows and arrows'.

The British were understandably alarmed. David Scott, the political agent, wrote later that, if the rajah had captured the base at Rangpur, the country would have been cast into anarchy and confusion. But the rajah's soldiers were caught unprepared, and his hopes of victory frustrated. They were faced by Scott's deputy, Captain John Bryan Neufville, who advanced with a troop of the Assam Light Infantry and attacked at night.

The rajah and his soldiers escaped into the hills of Nagaland, but he soon surrendered. Put on trial at Jorhat in December, he was charged with 'assuming the title and dignity of the King of Assam . . . without the consent of . . . the British government'. He was also accused of obstructing officers collecting revenue and of himself amassing arms 'and preparing to support his pretensions by force and rebellion'. Captain Neufville, as the presiding judge, sentenced him to death, commuted to seven years in exile. Dhanjoy, his reluctant ally, was also imprisoned, although he later escaped into the hills with his two sons to fight another day.

The optimistic Captain Neufville imagined that rebellions in Assam might now come to an end, but Scott had a firmer grip on reality. The territory's inhabitants 'are far from reconciled to our rule', he wrote; 'it may be expected that the higher classes in that country will long continue to cherish hopes and engage in schemes for the re-establishment of the ancient form of government under a Native Prince'.[4] The hills of Nagaland long remained a centre of dissent.

Pealiar Bar Gohain, known as Dhanjoy, returned to the struggle in March 1830, planning to revive the claims of another rajah, Kumar Rupchand Konwar, to be the true ruler in the valley of the Upper Brahmaputra. His plan was similar to that of Gomdhar Konmar two years earlier. He would assemble a troop of 400 men and destroy the British base at Rangpur. Together with other members of the region's surviving elite, he sent letters to the tribal chiefs of the Khamtis, the Nagas and the Khasis, and urged them to provide armed support. Some were willing, but Sadiya Khowa Gohain, chief of the Khamtis, was already in league with the British; he gave notice of Dhanjoy's plans to Captain Neufville.[5]

The treachery of the Khamti chief enabled Neufville to send reinforcements to bolster the sepoy defences at Rangpur. Dhanjoy's rebel force were confronted with a larger force than they had expected, and retreated in disarray to Galeki, where they surrendered. Most of the leaders were seized, along with their wives and families, their followers, and their weapons, but Dhanjoy again escaped into the jungle. British vengeance was swift. Two rebels were hanged in August, and five others, including Rajah Rupchand, were imprisoned. Their property was confiscated and they remained in a Bengali gaol for fourteen years. The son of the Khamti turncoat, Sadiya Khowa Gohain, was to rebel against the British a few years later, in 1839.

In the Khasi hills, in 1829, it was the turn of the tribal chiefs to rebel. Tirat Singh, the *syiem*, or chief, in the region of Nankhlao, joined by a substantial number of Khasi chiefs and armed tribesmen, surrounded the British military base there in April 1829. Two British lieutenants in charge were killed: Lieutenant Richard Bedingfield was lured out to a meeting with the Khasi leaders and summarily despatched; Lieutenant Philip Burlton escaped from the base, but was overtaken by Tirat Singh's forces as he headed north towards Gauhati on the Brahmaputra, and he too was killed.

Tirat Singh's rebellion was partly the result of the plans of Scott, the political agent, to construct a road through the Khasi and Jaintia Hills, from the Brahmaputra to Sylhet. A military guard had been provided to accompany the road-builders into the hills, and a troop of British-officered sepoys was established at Nangkhao to supervise the road's construction. A sanatorium was built there to provide rest and relaxation for the Europeans.

Tirat Singh had agreed to accept British 'protection' after the Burmese war, and he had given permission for the road to be built. But his advisers disapproved: the sole result of such a scheme, they argued, would be the eventual loss of their lands, as well as heavy taxation. With the support of the local population, which suffered from the presence of British forces, the advisers recommended resistance.[6] Tirat Singh accepted their advice.

After the base at Nankhlao had been destroyed, British punitive expeditions were sent out from Sylhet and Kamrup. Several Khasi villages were torched as a reprisal for the death of the officers, but Tirat Singh escaped. He remained free for several years, sustaining a guerrilla campaign in the hills and raiding British settlements in the Brahmaputra valley.

Yet as the British showed no signs of retreating, his support slowly ebbed away. He surrendered in January 1833, receiving a promise that he would not be executed. The British kept their promise, and he was held in prison in Dacca. Some years later, during a subsequent Khasi rebellion in 1836, they felt the need to reinstate him, and they offered him limited sovereignty under Company control. Tirat Singh refused the offer, saying that he chose to die in prison like a king rather than to 'sit on the throne of Nongkhlaw like a slave. The blood of my forefathers is still running hot in my withered veins, and here I must stay till the end.' He died in 1841.

In May 1830, soon after Tirat Singh's rebellion, the Singphos at Sadiya engaged in an act of similar resistance. The Singphos were a cross-border tribe, and sixteen of their chiefs had signed an agreement in 1826 with David Scott, the agent. Others had refused to sign, and these now joined a rebellion organised by Luttera Gaum, the principal chief. One of them, Wackum Kunjem, came with 2,000 warriors. Luttera Gaum, with 600 men of his own, prepared an attack on the British base at Sadiya, on the furthest north-eastern frontier of the North-East Frontier territory.

Hearing news of the Singpho plan, Captain Neufville advanced with a small troop from Sadiya to the village of Luttera. The party reached the village before sunset and fell upon the Singphos, according to Hemeswar Dihingia's account. The Singphos were unprepared and confused by the sudden attack, unable to withstand the British firing. Muskets against bows and arrows represented an unequal match. The Singphos fled, and Luttera Gaum disappeared into the hills.[7]

Captain Neufville was affected by his exertions, and collapsed suddenly in June 1830; David Scott died the following year, forever pessimistic about curbing these perennial rebellions: 'It would be futile to suppose that members of the ruling classes, whose ancestors had ruled in the valley for more than 500 years, would at once give up all their hopes of future greatness upon the appearance among them of a handful of strangers.'[8]

The resistance of the Singphos continued sporadically, reappearing in 1836 and 1843. Duffa Gaum, another Singpho chief who had taken refuge across the border in Burma, returned in 1835 with an army of 400 men to recover his lands. His camp was attacked by a force from the Assam Light Infantry led by Major Adam White, but after an hour's mortar attack 'the artillery could hardly break the enemy's defence'. When White ordered his troops to advance, they were 'strongly repulsed', and a British officer was seriously wounded. Eventually the superior weapons of the British obliged the Singphos to retreat, and Duffa Gaum retired across the Burmese frontier. 'Stern action' was taken against the local chiefs who had helped him, according to Hemeswar Dihingia. 'The troops burnt Singpho villages, destroyed crops, seized cattle, and released their slaves', and their actions caused 'much resentment and bitterness'.[9]

Curbing the resistance in the territory of the Upper Brahmaputra took its toll. 'Many of the finest parts of the country are now a dreary waste', wrote a Company official in 1833. 'Villages once the most flourishing are now deserted and in ruins; the inhabitants instead of finding the British government a power which would protect them with enjoyment of their hearths and homes have fled by hundreds in all directions'.

Purandar Singh, a senior rajah, was eventually installed as the local, British-backed ruler of Upper Assam, embodying Scott's original aims. He agreed to pay tribute to the East India Company, and to recognise its right to intervene in his affairs should he 'misrule'. Yet he soon found himself unable to pay the heavy tribute demanded, and developed a form of passive resistance. The experiment was abandoned after five years; with plans to establish commercial tea plantations throughout the Brahmaputra valley, the Company felt that it was useless to depend on unreliable rajahs. Formal annexation was now the plan.

The rajah was deposed and his territory annexed to the Empire; proudly, he refused the proffered compensatory pension. Smaller territories in the area suffered the same fate. Cachar was seized by the British in 1832 after its rajah had been murdered, and Jaintia was annexed in 1835 after the rajah had refused to pay tribute. Yet the resistance continued well into the 1840s as new tea plantations began to encroach on the land of others.

Far from Assam and the Brahmaputra valley, an unexpected insurrection broke out in December 1831 among the indigenous tribal peoples of Chota-Nagpur, an area of Bihar, south of Patna. This isolated and inaccessible region of hills and forests south of the Ganges had been under notional British control since the armies of the Mughal Empire had been defeated in 1764. The local people, notably the Mundas and the Oraons (described collectively by the British as the Kols), resented the gradual infiltration of their tribal lands by Hindu and Muslim *zamindaris*. These landlords had been encouraged by British policy to settle there and engage in agriculture and local commerce. Much tribal hostility was directed at the Maharaja of Chota-Nagpur, a British-backed ruler whose friends and relations were markedly hostile to the indigenous people.

The Kols began operations by seizing the cattle of the settlers in December 1831, and a large force of 700 tribesmen followed this up with a more serious attack on four settler villages. With widespread discontent at the loss of land and influence to outsiders, the attack aroused considerable popular support. Tribal peoples joined the insurrection in great numbers, and violent outbreaks occurred throughout the region. The insurgents attacked the outsiders indiscriminately, according to the *Bengal and Agra Annual Guide*.[10] They drove them 'from their homes and property, which were burnt or plundered; and sacrificed numbers of those who fell into their hands, to their excited passions, or revenge and hatred'. According to official figures, 219 Hindus and seventy-six Muslims were killed by the tribesmen; 4,086 houses were burned and 17,058 cattle seized.[11] A punitive expedition led by Captain Thomas Wilkinson took some time to crush the rebellion.

Later writers claimed that the Kol insurrection was little more than an explosion of tribal rage, but Charles Metcalfe, vice-president of the Calcutta Council at the time, was seriously alarmed. He believed that the insurrection had originated 'in the spirit of independence . . . and [in] the belief that the opportunity of throwing off our yoke had arrived'.

Subsequently, to avert such problems and to meet the special needs of the tribal peoples, the government set up a South East Frontier Agency, with a political agent responsible to the governor-general in Calcutta. Later still, in 1845, Lutheran missionaries were despatched to the region, and Christianity spread rapidly among the tribal peoples. They perceived this new faith as a way of resisting the influence of their Hindu and Muslim oppressors.

Part VII

AN END TO COLONIAL SLAVERY AND RESISTANCE TO FRESH SETTLEMENT, 1830–38

Dramatic changes occurred in the Empire in the 1830s as a result of political developments in Britain. A radical Whig government in London, influenced by liberal sentiment and evangelical Christianity, came to power in the autumn of 1830, after the death of George IV and the July Revolution in France. The conservative era that had begun with the British victory at Waterloo in 1815 came to an end: political reform and economic retrenchment were at the top of the political agenda. At home, the reform act of 1832 would change the face of British politics; abroad, the Empire came under ever-closer financial and humanitarian scrutiny. Less state money would be made available for imperial adventure; and with influential Christian evangelicals close to government, a close watch was kept on the behaviour of military governors in the colonial world.

No single decision had a greater impact on empire than the act to abolish imperial slavery in 1833. Long postponed but accelerated by the great 1831 slave rebellion in Jamaica, the end of slavery affected the entire economic basis of empire, built up with slave labour over the centuries. Once free, slaves everywhere were reluctant to work for their former masters, or even to work at all. Shortages of labour occurred throughout the Empire, and the search for workers from elsewhere was to cause great global movements of population.

The principle of slave emancipation was accepted by a cabinet committee in January 1833, and announced in parliament two months later, on 19 March. On 31 July 1834, 750,000 former slaves celebrated their freedom throughout the islands of the British West Indies. Trouble occurred in many other places, especially in territories where the white settler slave-owners had formerly owed allegiance to another European power, like the Dutch in South Africa and the French in Mauritius. But the British government had been careful to promise financial compensation to the tune of some £20 million, and this lessened the prospect of white settler rebellion.

The slaves were freed, but the resistance of other subject peoples within the Empire remained formidable. The Aborigines in New South Wales and Tasmania fought back against the inroads of white settlement, as they did in the freshly occupied territories of Western Australia. Sustained resistance came from the Xhosa in South Africa and from the landless peasants of Ireland. As the Empire grew larger, so too did the numbers of those who rejected it.

New possessions saw scenes of open hostility from traditional rulers and tribal chiefs that would continue for decades. The Maoris of New Zealand, even before the formal colonisation of the islands in 1840, gave a strong indication of their hostility to outside exploiters. In the seas off Malacca and Singapore, the sea-farers the British called 'pirates' sought to maintain their tax-raising traditions over waters now subject to European predators, taking on the British navy in the process.

The existence and strength of this imperial resistance brought the plight of the indigenous peoples of the Empire to the sustained attention of the imperial parliament in London for the first time. Imperial soldiers and white settlers continued their task of repression, destruction and annihilation of native communities, but news of their activities began to percolate back to Britain. The leaders of imperial rebellions discovered that they had allies in London, and not just in the missionary orders, though the promotion of a reformist model of Christianity was to be a significant element in the new imperial mood.

The House of Commons established a select committee on Aborigines in 1835, concerned above all with the treatment of indigenous peoples throughout the Empire. The committee's stated purpose was to secure for indigenous peoples 'the due observance of Justice and the protection of their Rights'. A further aim was to promote 'the spread of civilisation' among indigenous peoples 'and to lead them to the peaceful and voluntary reception of the Christian religion'. This was a two-edged sword, since the 'reception' of Christianity in some places was often forced as much as voluntary.

The chairman of the select committee was Thomas Fowell Buxton, MP for Weymouth and a prominent campaigner against slavery and the slave trade. 'I think England is a deep offender in the sight of God for the enormities she permits to be practised upon these poor ignorant, defenceless creatures', he told the committee. 'We Englishmen are, by our own account, fine fellows at home! Who among us doubts that we surpass the world in religion, justice, knowledge, refinement, and practical honesty? But such a set of miscreants and wolves as we prove when we escape from the range of laws, the earth does not contain.'[1] Buxton's committee was concerned chiefly with Aborigines in New Zealand, New South Wales, Tasmania, North America and the Pacific islands, but many of its hearings were dominated by events in South Africa resulting from the Xhosa rebellion of 1834. Humanitarian issues were on the agenda, but the perceived cost of Empire was also of major concern. Members of parliament wanted to know 'how to brake the inner momentum of overseas settlements when they appeared to be heading recklessly towards disastrously expensive confrontation with indigenous peoples'.[2]

The committee's first report, in June 1837, pulled many of its punches. No villains were found. It was 'not against individuals', the committee noted, 'much less against the colonists or the military as bodies, that we would direct our reprehension'. The MPs were 'convinced that a large proportion of both are well and kindly disposed towards the natives'.[3] Yet their document was an early statement of imperial unease about what was known to be happening, and what was thought to be wrong. It called for change, describing imperial rule as 'a system that . . . requires a complete alteration . . . a system which puts it in the power of the few who are rash, reckless or greedy, to hazard the peace and welfare of the whole community'.

The committee's report did little to halt the expansion of empire, nor even to improve the lot of indigenous peoples, but it helped to create a lasting concern in Britain about conditions in faraway countries. The committee's work was continued by the Aborigines' Protection Society, set up in 1837 by Thomas Hodgkin, a Quaker physician.

Ireland was one area of the Empire that remained impervious to the wave of imperial humanitarianism in the 1830s, although it too spawned a select committee to look into its affairs. 'Oh! I wish we were blacks!'[4] cried the Irish Catholic reformer Daniel O'Connell, pointing out that 'if the Irish people were but black, we should have the Honourable Member for Weymouth [Fowell Buxton] coming down as large as life . . . to advocate their cause.'

Some of the bloodiest encounters of the century in Ireland took place in the early 1830s, between peasants and the newly established paramilitary police force, often backed by British soldiers or by the local Protestant yeomanry. Violent encounters were sparked off by the campaign of resistance to the payment of a tithe tax to local clergymen. The campaign, initially backed by O'Connell and by Catholic bishops, was perceived by the English as a Catholic conspiracy against the revenues of the Protestant Church – and against its very existence. It took place against an upsurge in the insurrectionary activities of Ireland's various secret peasant societies – the Whitefeet, the Blackfeet and the Ribbonmen – and soon became a generalised struggle for land.

Throughout the Empire, land, and the imminent loss of it to settler advance, became the battle cry of rebels everywhere – the Irish, the Aborigines, the Maoris, the tribesmen in Assam, the Kols in Bihar, the Xhosa in Cape Colony.

While the Empire faced endless resistance from indigenous peoples, it was also frequently confronted in this decade by serious threats from white settlers, slave-owners or businessmen, who feared that what they perceived as their historic rights were under attack from some new reformist fad in London. While it was the task and the duty of military governors to keep settler rebellions under control, they were sometimes obliged to do so by giving in to settler demands.

These rebellions often came from small groups of settlers seeking the right to have a greater say in their individual destinies, but occasionally, and notably in provinces which had been acquired through treaty or as a byproduct of treaty arrangements with some other European power, the settlers sought freedom and independence from imperial control. First in South Africa and then in Canada, the minority Dutch and French populations rebelled in the 1830s. The Dutch rebellion in South Africa took the form of a 'Great Trek' – a simple if desperate decision by Dutch settlers to move out of the British colony and establish themselves in African territories beyond. In Canada, the French in Quebec rebelled against their British overlords, and were then joined by Republican elements within the British population in Ontario.

North America had always been a cause for imperial concern. The white settlers in the American colonies, regardless of the interests of the Native Americans, had fought successfully for independence in the 1770s, and the British often feared that Canada might go the same way. While most settlers in Canada had supported the British cause in the 1770s (and their numbers had been swelled after 1783 by the 'Empire Loyalists', the pro-English refugees from the south), no tacit contract existed between the colony and the motherland that could not be disrupted by incompetent or prejudiced administration; the loyalty of the French settlers in Quebec could never be relied on. At the end of the 1830s, both the French and the English settler populations were to register their dissatisfaction through open rebellion.

CHAPTER 38

Slave Rebellions in the Caribbean Hasten the End of Slavery

In Christmas week in 1831, slaves in Jamaica organised a strike that swiftly developed into the largest rebellion the island had ever seen. The slaves were convinced that the British king had granted their freedom, and they were led to believe that a new era would start in the New Year. Their plan was to refuse to return to the sugar plantations after the Christmas holiday. 'We have worked enough already', a slave told a missionary who argued with him not to stay away from work. 'The life we lead is . . . the life of a dog. We won't be slaves no more; we won't lift hoe no more; we won't take flog no more. We free now; no more slaves again.'[1]

The strike was chiefly due to the work of Sam Sharpe, a black slave who worked as a domestic servant in Montego Bay. Sometimes called 'Daddy Sharpe', he was well-known as an impassioned Baptist deacon and preacher. The Reverend Henry Bleby, a Wesleyan missionary, described him as the most remarkable and intelligent slave he had ever come across.[2] Sharpe's involvement led the whites to remember the rebellion as the 'Baptist War'.

More than 20,000 slaves took part in this final revolt, the last of the almost continuous slave uprisings within the Empire since the successful revolution in Haiti in 1791. The cumulative effect of these rebellions, and the shock of the final explosion in Jamaica, obliged a reluctant British government to abolish slavery altogether. Its formal ending came two years later, in August 1833.[3]

Simmerings of slave unrest had erupted in Jamaica during the previous decade, and in the 1830s a new generation of impatient slave rebels sprang up elsewhere in the Caribbean.[4] In Jamaica the slaves secretly formed a 'Black Regiment', commanded by a 'Colonel Johnson', seemingly with the hope of defeating the island's meagre armed forces in a direct confrontation.

The rebellion that broke out over Christmas 1831 had started with the familiar incendiary pattern. The great house and sugar works at Kensington Estate, in the parish of St James, were set ablaze on the evening of 27 December, and other plantation houses in the neighbourhood were soon on fire. Looking out from his house in the parish the next day, the Reverend George Blyth counted sixteen incendiary fires.

The whites had had some inkling of what was coming, and might reasonably have been more prepared, but the rebellion lasted for an unprecedented two weeks. Slaves on an estate near Montego Bay had been provoked into showing their hand early in the week before Christmas. An officer, Colonel James Grignon, had ordered a woman slave to be whipped, and several slaves protested vigorously. When police arrived to discipline the offenders, 'the whole body of slaves on the plantation resisted the constables, menacing them with their cutlasses'. The slaves seized the constables' pistols and disappeared into the woods.

The slaves now feared that the whites might take the law into their own hands if they did not act first. Some said that Colonel Grignon and his friends were planning to take out the slave men and 'shoot them like pigeons', while keeping slave women and children in slavery.

The various military encounters of the rebellion have been detailed by Mary Turner in her book, *Slaves and Missionaries*.[5] The military core of the rebellion, the Black Regiment, had some 150 slaves, with fifty guns among them. They were assisted by slaves recruited from the surrounding estates, commanded by 'Colonel Johnson' from the Retrieve estate. On 28 December, at the Old Montpelier estate, they confronted the island's white militia that advanced from their barracks at Shettlewood.

'Colonel Johnson' was killed in the first clash, but a new leader, Colonel Robert Gardner from the Greenwich estate, took over; he forced the militia to retreat to Montego Bay. 'Elated with success, the slaves carried rebellion into the hills, rousing support, burning properties, and setting off a train of fires through the Great River Valley in Westmoreland and St Elizabeth. The country between Montego Bay, Lucea, and Savanna-la-Mar was in rebel hands.'[6]

The Greenwich estate had long been a centre of Native Baptist preaching. It was now to be one of the headquarters of the rebellion:

> From Greenwich a sketchy organisation held sway over the surrounding country. On rebel estates slaves were organised into companies, each responsible for guarding its boundaries and holding allegiance to Gardner at Greenwich . . . Their work was supplemented by self-appointed leaders who organised their own estates, or roamed the country collecting recruits to resist the whites, destroying property, proclaiming freedom, and blocking roads against the military.[7]

The white plantation-owners were genuinely terrified. The moment they had been dreading for more than half a century had arrived. Some of their worst fears were being realised. Some called for bloodhounds to be brought over from Cuba, as had happened during the Maroon war of 1795. Others demanded the imposition of martial law, and this was proclaimed on 30 December. General Sir Willoughby Cotton,[8] the British commander-in-chief, established his headquarters at Montego Bay, and the slaves received a blunt message from him on 2

January 1832. They were told that the notion that the British king had ordered their freedom was wholly without foundation. Resistance was folly, the general said, but mercy would be shown to all except the ringleaders. They would be singled out for punishment, and a reward of $300 was offered for the capture of four of them: Colonel Johnson, Colonel Gardner, Captain Dove and Samuel Sharpe.

During January, scattered groups of slaves were slowly corralled in the hills by General Cotton's forces. They tried to persuade the Maroons to join them, but without success. Resistance was eventually crushed, and with their military defeat the slaves faced a brutal campaign of repression by the settler regime.

Martial law was extended for a further month, and captured prisoners were executed without trial. In the weeks before 4 February, ninety-four rebel slaves were hanged in Montego Bay, and twenty-five were shot or hanged in Falmouth. Each day some fifteen to twenty slave prisoners were flogged.[9] Some of those present noted the courageous bearing of those destined for execution. They walked to the scaffold 'calm and undismayed . . . as if they had been proceeding to their daily toil . . . With the dignified bearing of men untroubled as to the justice of their cause, they yielded themselves to their doom.'[10] Samuel Sharpe, the Baptist preacher, was among those captured and hanged.

More than 300 slaves were killed during the fighting, and the final toll was much higher. A further 300 were executed in the immediate aftermath of the rebellion's collapse, and trials continued over the next two years. More than 140 of those indicted for 'murder, rebellion, arson, etc.' were shipped off to the Empire's convict settlements in New South Wales.[11] It was a long journey – first to Britain, and then on to Australia. British colonialism had an unusual capacity to disrupt people's lives by shipping them around the globe. Slaves seized in Africa and taken to the West Indies might subsequently find themselves taken, via Britain, to Australia.

The panicking white settlers suffered rather less than they had feared. Only fourteen of them were killed during the rebellion. Yet the whites still wanted revenge. In February, as the gibbets worked overtime in Falmouth and Montego Bay, white mobs took out their anger on the Christian chapels which they believed had nurtured the rebellion. The mob at Montego Bay was a cross-section of white society: book-keepers and overseers joined hands with lawyers and landowners; some of them were magistrates. Chapels were destroyed all over the island.

The planters were seriously affected in their pockets, and the government in London lent them £200,000 to re-establish their businesses. The economic cost of the uprising was estimated at over £1 million, and things would soon get worse. The effect of the rebellion was to speed up the end of slavery, decreed in 1833. Many of the settlers could not accept this diktat from London. When a new governor, Constantine Henry Philips, the Earl of Mulgrave, arrived that year, his first task was to crush a mutiny by the officers of the white militia. His second was to order that the heads of executed slaves should be removed from poles at the entrance to sugar estates; he complained about 'the revolting nature of such a spectacle'.

Although slavery had been declared illegal in the British Empire, and although the slave trade had long been formally abolished, the seizure of Africans for the armed forces from slave ships captured in the Atlantic still continued. Desperate for recruits to serve in their armies in the West Indies, the British would enrol them into their West Indian regiments. In September 1836, 112 potential soldiers were recruited in this way; in January 1837, 109; and in May, from two ships, 205. Over a period of eight months, the First West India Regiment, based at Trinidad, received more than 400 not-very-willing African recruits.

'The formality of asking these men whether they were willing to serve was never gone through', wrote A. B. Ellis, an historian of the regiment, in 1885.[12] 'Many of them did so unwillingly.' Ellis justified the practice on the grounds that 'they were all savages in the strictest sense of the word, entirely unacquainted with civilisation, and with no knowledge of the English language.'

Many slave soldiers recruited in this way were not loth to mutiny, and on 18 June 1837, at Trinidad's San Josef barracks, outside Port of Spain, 300 black soldiers took this course, mostly fresh recruits to the First West India Regiment. Their mutiny was organised by an African chief called Daaga, also known as Donald Stewart. The mutineers, according to the regimental account of the mutiny, were mostly Popos, Longos and Ibos, with a few of the Yoruba that Daaga had himself recruited. The citizens around the barracks were kept awake that night by the sound of the mutineers singing the war chant of the Popos:

> Dangkarree,
> Au fey
> Oluu werrei
> Au lay.
> Come to plunder, come to slay,
> We are ready to obey.

Daaga was not himself a slave, but a slaver. His story was unusual. At home on the Nigerian coast, he had collected a number of Yoruba to sell, and had delivered them to a Portuguese slaving ship. Once on board, the Portuguese crew had seized him to add to their cargo. Subsequently, during the Atlantic crossing, the Portuguese ship was captured by a British cruiser. Daaga and the slaves were taken back to the African coast, landed at Sierra Leone, and recruited into the First West India Regiment. They were then sent over to Trinidad.

No favours were done to a captured slave by turning him into a soldier, argued Edward Joseph, a Trinidad historian of the time. 'Formerly it was most true that a soldier in a black regiment was better off than a slave; but certainly a free African in the West Indies now is infinitely in a better situation than a soldier, not only in a pecuniary point of view, but in almost every respect.'[13]

Daaga's mutiny began with the torching of their barrack block and the seizure of the armoury. The mutineers set off into the countryside in the belief that they would be able to walk back to Guinea.[14] They did not get far. Forty were killed by the militia and the rest were rounded up. The three organisers were sentenced to death, and Edward Joseph gave an account of their execution:

> Donald Stewart [Daaga], Maurice Ogston and Edward Coffin were executed on August 16, 1837 at the San Josef barracks. Nothing seemed to have been neglected which could render the execution solemn and impressive . . . The condemned men displayed no unmanly fear. On the contrary, they steadily kept step to the Dead March which the band played . . .

When the provost-marshal cried out 'Ready, Present', Daaga removed the bandage from his eyes, and his deep, metallic voice sounded out in anger: 'The curse of the Holloloo on white men. Do they think that Daaga fears to fix his eyeballs on death?'[15] Contemptuous of his executioners, the Nigerian chief turned his back on them.

CHAPTER 39

White Settlers Devise New Ways to Hunt the Australian Aborigines

In October 1830 the surviving Aborigines of Tasmania were threatened with annihilation. Colonel George Arthur, the military governor, conceived a surreal plan to use the white settlers and the convicts as a broom to sweep the Aborigines off the island. Mobilising 3,000 people – nearly one quarter of the European population – he spread them out in a long 'Black Line' across the south-east region of the country. The aim was to drive the Aborigines southwards in front of the line and then to corral and secure them on Tasman's Peninsula, south of Hobart.

Martial law, imposed in November 1828, was still in force, so mobilisation was simple. Present on parade on 7 October were policemen, rural settlers and urban inhabitants, as well as the island's military force of 1,000 soldiers. Some 700 convicts on parole, referred to as 'servants', who worked as slave labour for the settlers, were also summoned. Only those held permanently behind bars were exempt from the general mobilisation. The costs of the expedition, some £30,000, or £100 for each of those who took part, were paid by the British exchequer.

Projects for removing Aborigines from 'settled' areas occupied by the whites had been discussed through the years of resistance in the 1820s. Proposals had been made to drive them into controlled reservations, or to move them from the island entirely. If they are not removed, the *Colonial Times*, the settler newspaper, had suggested in 1824, 'they will be hunted down like beasts and destroyed'. Colonel Arthur's 'Black Line' was designed to test this proposal.

The Aborigines of Tasmania had already been decimated by the actions of the settlers during three decades of military occupation. Three-quarters of the original population had been exterminated by the 1820s. A native presence of some 7,000 people in 1803 had dwindled to barely more than a thousand. Yet the survivors courageously maintained their resistance to the seizure of their land, and to some effect. 'The total ruin of every establishment' was likely, according to a government report in 1830, unless something dramatic was done to halt Aborigine attacks on settlers. The report referred bleakly to the island's 'unparalleled' devastation.

Colonel Arthur, a veteran of colonial law enforcement in British Honduras during the rebellion of 1820, felt called upon to act. 'The hostile spirit of the natives' was on the increase, he wrote to London in April 1830. 'Their exploits in the pursuit of plunder have rendered them much more daring and robust during the last two years.' He requested reinforcements from Britain to deal with the increased threat, asking for more soldiers and at least 2,000 more convicts. In a subsequent note, expanding on his theme, he described how 'the savages' had become 'more expert', and 'more bold and sanguinary'. They would undoubtedly 'murder every white inhabitant, if they could do so with safety to themselves'.[1]

The colonial secretary in London since 1828 was General Sir George Murray, an officer and a Tory politician, with an extensive military career in the West Indies, the Peninsular War, Canada, and most recently in Ireland as commander-in-chief. Yet he was more cautious than Colonel Arthur, and expressed concern about the eventual fate of the natives. 'The great decrease' in the Aboriginal population, he argued, might mean that 'the whole race of these people may at no distant period become extinct.' Whatever the settlers might think, wrote Murray, 'it is impossible not to contemplate such a result of our occupation of the island as one very difficult to be reconciled with feelings of humanity, or even with principles of justice and sound policy'. Any line of conduct leading to 'the extinction of the native race', General Murray continued, could not fail to leave 'an indelible stain on the character of the British government'. He told Arthur he had no troops to spare, but promised to send out more 'criminals' sentenced to forced labour.

Colonel Arthur had to make do with the forces he had at hand and, in spite of Murray's warnings, he went ahead with his ambitious plan to drive the Aborigines into the sea. The initial 'line' was formed a third of the way down the island, from St Patrick's Head on the east coast to the Great Lake in the centre. In October 1830, the 3,000 marchers were assembled and positioned forty-five yards apart. Moving slowly forward, they advanced over the next two months towards the south-eastern corner of the island. When their 'Black Line' finally reached the neck of Tasman's Peninsula, their expectations of a large haul of Aborigines were high.

Yet the Aborigines had conducted their retreat across the island with considerable skill, taking advantage of hill and forest and the protection of darkness. During the course of the long trek south, only one small Aborigine band, five men and a boy asleep in their camp, was found by the marchers. Two of the five men were shot, and the boy was taken prisoner by the settlers. 'Plenty more black fellows in scrub', said the boy as he begged to be released, and indeed there were. The Aborigines had all passed silently through the advancing line – and lived to fight another day. When the settlers arrived at the furthest end of the peninsula, 'not a native was to be seen; not a sound was heard; all was as silent as the grave'.

The Conciliation, a painting by Benjamin Duterrau of Aborigines in Tasmania in 1835 with George Augustus Robinson, a settler charged with looking after them and transferring them to Flinders Island.

The Black Line had proved a failure, and Colonel Arthur now put a second and more successful plan into operation. Where force had failed, the blandishments of a religious leader might succeed. George Augustus Robinson, a Methodist settler, was asked if he could persuade the surviving Aborigines to leave Tasmania peacefully. The plan was to transfer them to a small concentration camp on Flinders Island, off Tasmania's north-east coast. Robinson went to work, and by the end of 1834 he had rounded up most of the Aborigine population. One hundred were eventually relocated on the island, although many died in makeshift transit camps. The conditions on Flinders Island were so bleak that Robinson transferred the survivors to the Australian mainland four years later, in 1838. Some forty years after the white settlers had first arrived, Tasmania had become an Aborigine-free zone.

Far to the west of mainland Australia, close to the new white settlement at Pinjarra, in the Murray River district of Western Australia, a group of seventy

Aborigines were gathered in October 1834 to protest against the invasion of their tribal lands. They were attacked by an expedition of twenty-five settlers and soldiers organised by Captain James Stirling, the military governor of the new colony. A naval officer by origin, Stirling had taken part in the recapture of Cape Colony in 1806 and the failed expedition to Buenos Aires in 1807. He was now an ambitious landowner, and his military skills were to be deployed against the Aborigines.

Earlier, in the 1820s, Stirling had explored the region of the Swan River, and had persuaded the London government to allow him to establish Australia's first non-convict colony, with him as the governor. Arriving at Fremantle in 1829, he established a capital at Perth, a few miles inland. Some 3,000 British settlers arrived in the first two years, but in taking over what they thought of as 'virgin' lands they had immediately encountered Aborigine resistance. The Aborigines, rightly, saw the settlers as a threat to their survival, and they forced half the settlers to abandon their farms in the first year of settlement.

Stirling knew exactly what had to be done. 'The one way for 2,000 white people in those scattered settlements to prevent 50,000 Aborigines waging a bloody war of attrition with their primitive weapons was for the white man to display and make use of his superior firepower until such time as he outnumbered the Aborigines.'

Faced with the Aborigine crowd at Pinjarra, Stirling embarked on a vicious attack. It was an unequal battle, for although the Aborigines killed Captain Ellis from Stirling's squad, more than thirty of them were killed. British war veterans among the settlers in Western Australia were notably merciless. Captain Richard Meares, one of Stirling's killer party and a survivor of Waterloo, had a mural of the 'battle of Pinjarra' hung on his dining room wall, opposite one that depicted the battle of Waterloo.[2]

Having slaughtered the Aborigines, the new settlers in Western Australia were soon short of labour. Although established as a non-convict colony, the settlers were forced to ask London to send out some prisoners. Later, in the years between 1850 and 1868, when the rest of Australia had turned against the use of convict labour, Western Australia was pleased to receive no less than 10,000 male convicts from Britain, to people the land seized from its indigenous inhabitants.

In New South Wales throughout the 1830s, the sheep and cattle of the settlers had been moving far beyond the frontiers of established settlement in search of fresh pasture. 'While nature presents all round an unlimited supply of the most wholesome nutriment', wrote the governor, Sir Richard Bourke, in 1835, it would be 'a perverse rejection of the bounty of providence' to prevent this development. Yet he knew well that this land of 'unlimited supply' was the territory of

Aborigines who maintained a steady resistance, constantly coming into conflict with the invading shepherds and cattle hands.

Cattle stations had been established on a branch of the Big River, near Inverell, some 350 miles north of Sydney, and on Sunday 10 June 1838 the cattle hands engaged in what became an emblematic slaughter of the local people. A group of Aborigine families were camped that day on the banks of Myall Creek, mostly women and children and a man known as Daddy. The Aborigine men had left the camp that morning. In the afternoon, a dozen white labourers on a farm owned by Henry Dangar, all but one former convicts, set out to attack the camp. One of them, John Johnstone, was not white at all, but a former black slave transported from the West Indies. The gang rounded up the thirty-three Aborigines they found at the camp, 'of all ages and sexes, though for the most part women and children'.

The labourers 'tied them all to a rope', Major-General Sir George Gipps, the new governor, subsequently reported to London, 'in the way that convicts are sometimes tied in order to be taken from place to place in the colony'.[3] The Aborigines were slaughtered with cutlasses and musket fire, and their corpses were burned on a fire. Only four children and one woman escaped. The convict gang scoured the country on horseback, searching for the dozen survivors. 'It is doubtful to this day', recorded the governor, 'whether they were not overtaken and murdered also.'

Gipps was a recent arrival, from Canada. He momentarily brought a change of attitude towards the decimation of the Aborigines, hitherto tacitly approved. Another veteran of the Peninsular Wars (he had gone on in the 1820s to serve in the West Indies), he hoped to abolish 'lawlessness' on the frontier, and to curb the appetite of the frontier settlers for massacre.

Eleven convict labourers were brought to trial in Sydney in November, charged with 'the murder of an Aboriginal black called Daddy', the only adult male who could be identified out of those slaughtered at Myall Creek. One of the original dozen labourers had turned informer and testified against the others. The labourers were acquitted and a second trial took place. This time only seven men were charged, with the murder of women and children and 'an Aboriginal child called Charley'. They were nearly acquitted a second time, on the grounds that proof was lacking of the child's name; but eventually all seven were found guilty and sentenced to death.

In prison, awaiting execution, they admitted their guilt, though 'they all stated that they thought it extremely hard that white men should be put to death for killing blacks'. Seven men were hanged on 18 December, while the four who had survived the first trial were never brought to justice. 'It is now pretty certain', Gipps recorded regretfully, 'that one of the four men, who have for the present escaped, was the most guilty of the whole.'

The Myall Creek massacre led the government to reconsider its policy of benign neglect of the frontier. 'The only question', noted Gipps in 1839, 'is whether we will abandon all control over these distant regions – and leave the occupiers of them unrestrained in their lawless aggressions upon each other and upon the Aborigines – or make such efforts as are in our power to preserve order amongst all classes.'[4]

The chief 'effort' made was to establish a Border Police Force. Yet its aim was to assist the settlers, not to protect the Aborigines from settler attack. This was the pattern when colonisation was extended into the neighbouring territory of Queensland in the 1840s. Some thought was given to the formation of a 'Native' police force, recruiting Aborigines for use in frontier policing against the resistance struggles of their own people. Some civilian bureaucrat remembered that Cape Colony in South Africa had had some experience of this, and the police magistrate in Melbourne, Captain Lonsdale, had tried an experiment in 1837. He engaged a South African, Christian de Villiers, who had served previously with the Khoi-Khoi regiment, to organise such an Aborigine force.

These were the new means of Aborigine control introduced in the wake of the Myall Creek massacre. Another one was yet more effective, echoing the experience of British officers in North America in the eighteenth century. 'Many pastoralists and labourers', writes Jan Kociumbas, 'now turned to the distribution of poisoned flour, a deadly technique that was almost impossible to prove in court.'[5] This was to become a favoured method of ensuring Aborigine destruction.

CHAPTER 40

The Whitefeet in Ireland Oppose the Payment of Tithes and Rent

The system of collecting tithes to fund the alien Protestant church in Ireland had been imposed on the country by the British occupying power since the sixteenth century. The tithe levied was traditionally a tenth part of a peasant's annual agricultural production. One of the giant evils under which 'Ireland has long heaved and groaned', noted George Poulett Scrope, an English MP with a close interest in Irish affairs, is 'the domination of a Protestant Church, imposed by right of conquest on a Catholic people [and] maintained on the spoils of the ancient Catholic establishment'. This, he reported, was 'necessarily looked upon by the people both as a badge of their servitude and a sacrilegious usurpation of the rights of their own church'.[1]

The British had always insisted that the cost of maintaining the clergymen who sustained the Protestant ideology, alien and anti-Roman, should be raised through a tithe taken from the Catholic Irish peasants who formed the great majority of the country's population. Degraded for centuries on the score of race and religion, writes Angus Macintyre, and dispossessed of their tribal lands by an alien landlord class, 'the peasants formed a virtually autonomous community, cut off by its differences of language, customs, lack of education and above all by its economic position, from the rest of Ireland'.[2]

In the 1830s peasants began fresh campaigns of resistance, demonstrating against tithe-collection not just in County Waterford but throughout West Meath, Kilkenny and County Cork. 'The country is at this moment all but in a state of rebellion', wrote General Henry Paget, Lord Anglesey, the lord-lieutenant of Ireland. A soldier who had lost a leg at Waterloo, the noble lord found himself bleakly contemplating the difficult choices ahead. 'I tremble at every day's post', he wrote. 'I cannot cover the whole country, and can only subdue two or three counties at a time'.[3]

One immediate cause of the rebellious atmosphere came from the unfulfilled expectations aroused by the passing of a Catholic Emancipation Act in 1829. This, for the first time, had allowed the Catholic Irish to take up official positions in the British state. Ever since the reign of Henry VIII in the sixteenth century, when England had rejected the authority of the Roman pope overnight, the English had tried to force the Irish Catholics to do the same. Yet when the Irish remained stubbornly attached to Roman Catholicism, the

British authorities regarded those who failed to convert as a potential security risk. Catholics who refused to take the Protestant oath of loyalty, a requirement for state employment, were refused jobs.

Daniel O'Connell, a Catholic lawyer elected as MP for County Clare in 1828, had stormed the country arousing popular opposition – both against the security oath, which prevented him and other Irish Catholic politicians from sitting in the Westminster parliament, and against the payment of the Protestant tithe.[4] When his campaign was victorious, with the passing in 1829 of the Emancipation Act, many Irish people believed this would lead to an improvement in their lot, as well as an end to the unpopular tithe. They were soon to be disabused.

Peasants turned for help to their own dormant secret societies – the Whitefeet, the Blackfeet and the Ribbonmen, the successor organisations to the Whiteboys of the 1760s and the Defenders of the 1790s. All over the country ancient weapons were dusted down as a new generation prepared to renew the struggle of their grandfathers. The second of twelve separate oaths taken by Whitefeet recruits (an updated version of the Whiteboys' oath at the end of the eighteenth century) emphasised the republican and anti-imperial aspirations of the organisation: 'I sware, I will to the best of my power, Cut Down Kings, Queens and Princes, Dukes, Earls, Lords, and all such with Land Jobin and herrisy.'[5] Enraged and revived by the failure of the Emancipation Act to address the problem of the Irish poor, the Whitefeet became the principal political force in the rural areas. 'Emancipation has done nothing for us', a Whitefeet leader told the Reverend Nicholas O'Connor, parish priest of Maryborough, in Leinster's Queen's County, a centre of resistance. 'Mr O'Connell and the rich Catholics go to parliament; we die of starvation just the same.' Father O'Connor was explaining to a House of Commons committee in 1832 what he knew of the peasants' attitudes: 'I have often heard their conversation when they say "What good did the Emancipation do us? Are we better clothed or fed? Or our children better clothed or fed? Are we not naked as we were, and eating dry potatoes when we can get them".'[6] Poulett Scrope MP wrote that the Whitefeet gave the peasants 'that essential protection to their existence which the established law of the country refuses to afford.'[7]

The anti-tithe campaign of the Whitefeet had first exploded in County Wexford, in June 1831.[8] Peasants at Newtonbarry had tried to prevent the sale of cattle seized for tithe by the Reverend Alexander McClintock, the local rector. After an initial struggle between the peasants and the police, 200 members of the Protestant yeomanry were summoned by a magistrate, and there followed 'a most sanguinary conflict', with the yeoman coming under attack from stones and sticks. The peasants prevented the sale of the cattle for tithe, but at a heavy cost. Twelve were shot dead, and twenty wounded. The massacre caused considerable public outcry, but a jury of landowners refused to convict the police captain of murder.

A similar affray took place in December at Carrickshock, in Kilkenny. A 'hedge schoolmaster', an old United Irishman from the 1790s, led more than 2,000 peasants against a police unit commanded by Lieutenant Gibbons, sent out to protect a man serving notice of the tithe collection. The peasants refused to yield, declaring their intention to finish off the tithe system. The peasant leader was killed when Gibbons ordered his men to fire. Police fire was returned by a volley of stones, and one struck the lieutenant on the temple; he dropped dead from his horse. A hand-to-hand conflict followed, the peasants with scythes and pitchforks, the police with bayonets. Eleven policemen were killed and seventeen wounded; the peasant casualties were also considerable. Six months later the area was still organised for rebellion, with more than 100,000 peasants gathered near Carrickshock in July 1832. 'The men marched from the various outlying districts in divisions, moving in military style, and in obedience to commands given by chosen leaders in military phraseology.'

A further serious incident occurred in September at Wallstown, in County Cork. The Reverend Gavin, the local rector, had sought to survey the lands of his parish with a staff of valuers, with a view to establishing the tithe. He arrived with a party of police, a detachment of the 92nd Highland Regiment, and a number of foot soldiers. The chronicler records that although the entire population of Wallstown consisted of barely 3,000 Catholics and a single Protestant, the rector's force was commanded by an admiral, two generals and three magistrates. The peasants had been well prepared by the Whitefeet. The fields of James Blake still had crops on the ground, and he believed that this gave him a legal right to resist valuation. A peasant leader called Doyle assembled 500 peasants armed with reaping hooks and pitchforks, and prepared to resist the military attack. The soldiers broke down the gate of Blake's farm and the admiral read out the words of the Riot Act, concluding with the traditional sentence: 'I now call upon you in the name of the law to disperse.' 'We won't!' the peasants shouted back. 'No tithes! No Church! No minister! No by-laws!' The admiral ordered his men to load and fire; four peasants were killed and many wounded.

The incident caused settler newspapers to print editorials supporting Protestant supremacy. The *Standard* outlined what was at stake: 'Ireland must be made Protestant, essentially Protestant, or Ireland will be lost to England.' Another paper pointed out that 12,000 'attachments for arrears of tithes' had now been issued, and it would be the government's task to collect them, 'at the point of the bayonet if necessary'.

Peasants assembled in October in a field near Rathkeeran, in County Waterford, to protest against the tithe. The hostility of the peasants was such that the local police inspector and his posse of armed police, out attempting to post notices about the tax, were unable to do so. The confrontation ended in a murderous battle.

According to an account written down fifty years later from court records, the inspector, a man called Burke, called on the protesters three times to withdraw; three times they refused.[9] When his men were ordered to load their guns, Catherine Foley, a young peasant woman, sprang forward to the front of the crowd, shouting, 'Now boys is your time. Attack them and don't spare a man.' The crowd surged across the field, forcing the police back with stones, sticks and slanes. The police opened fire and charged with their bayonets fixed. Catherine Foley was hit in the face by a musket-ball and died at once, and twelve other peasants were killed; many were wounded. Inspector Burke was found guilty of Foley's 'wilful murder', but received no punishment.

The agitation against tithe-collection was still going on two years later. Peasants in the village of Rathcormac, in County Cork, were ready with their usual weapons in December 1834, confronting a troop of cavalry sent to collect the tithes due to Archdeacon Ryder, JP, of the parish of Gortroe. The Riot Act was read, and Lieutenant Shepherd turned to the peasants, saying, 'Now if you do not give way, I must fire.'

'We are not afraid to die', replied their leader. 'Lives must be lost on either side before ye come in.' The lieutenant gave the order to fire, and the crowd first dispersed and then rushed back. 'Never flinch, my boys!' cried the leader. 'Close up, and at them again.' The peasants were obliged to retreat after twelve had been killed and forty-two wounded. The lieutenant noted later that he had never seen 'such determined bravery.'

The agitation against the tithe was only one aspect of the resistance war in Ireland in the 1830s. It was superimposed on the longstanding agrarian unrest that had exploded ten years earlier, during the rebellion of 'Captain Rock', and extended to the collieries of Leinster. With the organisation and direction of the Whitefeet, the resistance grew stronger – 'this midnight war of poverty against property', as Colonel Henry Hardinge, the Irish chief secretary in Dublin in 1830, had perceptively described it.

Paradoxically, the peasant agitators had some support from Hardinge. A Peninsula veteran (and later to be governor in India and a significant participant in the crushing of Sikh resistance in the Punjab in 1845), Hardinge was an outspoken critic of the landlords. Writing to Sir Robert Peel in October 1830, he cited the case of Sir Robert Hudson, a Protestant gentleman who had ejected 400 Catholics from his estate in County Cavan 'in the depth of winter'. Hudson had sent them 'into the mountains, having no means of lawful existence from the difficulty of obtaining work', and their farms had been rented out to Protestants. 'Can we be surprised', wrote Hardinge, 'at the burnings of houses and the maiming of cattle?'[10]

The peasants had originally been mobilised against the payment of tithes; now they were questioning the payment of rent. Groups of peasants in Clare and Galway had already begun to challenge the rent collectors in 1831. They assembled in their thousands in Donegal, vowing 'to pay neither rent nor taxes until O'Connell got new laws for them'. Soon they were in open rebellion, and a wealthy landlord in Galway thought the country to be 'very near revolution'. Lord Clanricarde, the lord-lieutenant of Galway, noted in April 1831 that 'the lower orders' were convinced 'of the supremacy of the power of the people', and believed 'there is to be a general revolution accomplished all over Ireland'. Clanricarde had no immediate concern, for he knew there were 'troops and police in the county more than sufficient to overcome any open insurrection'. The British had an army of 25,000 men in Ireland, organised in flying columns and supported by an armed police force. Yet even these might not be sufficient, Clanricarde feared, since 'to prevent outrages the whole country must be incessantly patrolled'.

The state of the country had become desperate', wrote Barry O'Brien half a century later.

> Side by side, as it were, with the tithe war, the eternal land war was being waged. Landlords, agents, or bailiffs were habitually shot; tenants were terrorised, and merchants and traders appalled at the awful doings of the secret societies. Raids for arms were constantly made on the houses of the gentry, and parties of police were not infrequently attacked in the open day by bands of Whitefeet, Blackfeet, Terry Alts, Rockites, or Molly Maguires, and put to flight.[11]

Behind the peasant agitation for land was the efficient operation of the Whitefeet organisation. Their chief aim, Father O'Connor told the House of Commons committee in 1832, was 'to keep themselves upon their lands' – a view echoed by Wellesley Despard, a magistrate in Queen's County. Their objective, he told the committee, 'is a complete resistance to the existing laws; some of them say they will have all the lands in the country in their hands again'.

'The Whitefoot system', Poulett Scrope MP wrote in 1834, 'is the practical and efficient check upon the Ejectment system. It cannot be denied that but for the salutary terror inspired by the Whitefeet, the clearance of estates . . . would proceed with a rapidity and to an extent that must occasion the most horrible sufferings to hundreds and thousands of the ejected tenantry.'[12]

Peasants faced with eviction for non-payment of rent had found their politicians to be ineffective, and had turned to the Whitefeet for support. Daniel O'Connell had taken up the cause of tithe reform, but he was opposed to insurrectionary outbreaks aimed at the landlords; he made stinging attacks on the Whitefeet and the other organisers of rural protest. He believed in 'legitimate agitation', he said, but deplored the fact that 'all the poverty of our counties is being organised', arguing that no man 'in the rank of comfortable farmer' was likely to be engaged in the Whitefeet organisation. He feared that his own constitutional movement was in danger of being swallowed up by social revolution.

O'Connell became more hostile to peasant agitation as the months passed. 'Our first concern is to put down the Whitefeet', he declared in April 1833. Thomas Steele, his close collaborator, had a similar view, made clear two years earlier in an open letter addressed to the Whitefeet leaders: 'Unless you desist, I denounce you as traitors to the cause of the liberty of Ireland. I and other friends of the people will advise you no more, since you follow the councils of miscreant villains . . . I leave you to the Government and the fire and bayonets of the military.'[13]

With serious division in the Irish ranks, and with the Whitefeet receiving little political support outside the peasantry, the British remained convinced that law and order had broken down in many parts of Ireland. Additional repressive legislation was drafted, and the Coercion Act of April 1833 effectively established martial law on a permanent basis. The lord-lieutenant was empowered to 'proclaim' any area deemed to be 'disturbed', and within the counties so 'proclaimed' no meetings of any kind could be held, habeas corpus was suspended, and ordinary courts were replaced by courts martial. General Hussey Vivian, the commander-in-chief in Ireland (and another veteran of the Peninsular Wars and Waterloo), was optimistic about the Act's potential. 'Such is the terror it has inspired in the offenders', he declared, 'that many of the worst characters have taken their departure for America or elsewhere.'

Yet initially the new legislation had little impact, and in the autumn and winter of 1833, the Whitefeet continued to hold the country in thrall. 'Houses were burned, cattle were houghed, and daring murders perpetrated. Such was the religious feeling infused into the land movement by the circumstance of the tithe agitation, that – a rare thing in the Irish agrarian war – Protestants were attacked and in some places forced to fly from the country in terror and despair.'[14]

In Leinster and in Connaught, the Whitefeet refused to be intimidated. The veteran General Richard Wellesley, who had returned to Ireland as the lord-lieutenant at the age of seventy-four, wrote that 'secret combination, concealed organisation, intimidation, suppression of all evidence of crime, and ruling society by the authority of the common people, and of superseding the law by decrees of illegal associations – all these have prevailed to a great extent in Connaught.'[15]

Eventually the Coercion Act had a deeper impact. Joseph Greene, a magistrate in Kilkenny, noted in May 1834 that the Act had prevented 'nearly all combination of outrage, inasmuch as evil doers are afraid to meet by night from the number of patrols that are kept up, and the occasional calling over the rolls of suspicious characters keeps them at home and also prevents them frequenting public houses'.

Sir Edward Bulwer-Lytton MP had spoken of his concern during a debate on the Coercion Bill in March 1833: 'I do not fear an open rebellion against the armed force and discipline of England; but if you madden the people, it is impossible to calculate the strength of insanity. Indeed, I think that an open rebellion is the least evil to be feared.' What he feared more was 'a sullen, bitter, unforgiving recollection, which will distrust all our kindness and misinterpret all our intentions; which will take all grace from our gifts; which will ripen a partial into a general desire for a separate legislature, by a settled conviction of the injustice of this'.

Sir Edward envisaged a yet bleaker prospect: an end to political support for empire. There was a danger, he warned, that 'the English people themselves, worn out with unavailing experiments, wearied with an expensive and thankless charge, and dissatisfied with a companionship which gives them nothing but the contagion of its own diseases, will be the first to ask for that very dismemberment of the empire which we are now attempting to prevent'.

It was an early point at which to imagine that the English themselves might start to dismantle the Empire that they had only just begun to construct. One outcome of the Coercion Act was an increase in the number of Irish convicts sent off to help populate the colony of New South Wales and to combat the Aborigines. Further rebellions were required in Ireland before the British tired of their imperial adventure.

CHAPTER 41

White Settler Rebellions and Buddhist Resistance in the East

Few of their island colonies caused the British so much trouble as Mauritius, seized from France in 1810. The white settlers established there, mostly of French origin, were chiefly planters, merchants, lawyers and shopkeepers – not more than 8,000 in total. Hostile to almost every aspect of British rule, they were especially concerned about policies developed in London that might affect their slave plantations – their principal economic activity and the source of their wealth. The anti-slavery lobby in Britain, now active in the Anti-Slavery Society, set up in 1823, was well informed about the bleak situation of the 68,000 slaves in Mauritius, and in 1826 it had secured the island's inclusion in the work of the British government's Commission of Eastern Inquiry, set up originally to examine the affairs of Cape Colony.[1]

The Commission concluded that illegal slave-trading had continued in Mauritius until 1820, and it listed the steps that would be needed to improve conditions for the tens of thousands of people still enslaved. An Order in Council in 1830 reinforced earlier demands for the forbidding of the whipping of female slaves – a punishment that had provoked large protest meetings in London.

Concerned about the hostile publicity the settlers were receiving in London, their leader, Adrien d'Épinay, travelled to England. His purpose was to bring their grievances to the government's attention. D'Épinay was an archetypal leader of white settler rebellions. A lawyer and a banker, rather than a plantation owner, he was also the publisher of a newspaper that sustained a hostile attitude towards anti-slavery campaigners. Among other things, his paper had supported the settlers' revival of the old militia – their own small army dressed in the uniform of the French National Guard – re-established with the permission of the governor, General Sir Charles Colville, formerly the army commander in Bombay.

D'Épinay told the government of the islanders' discontents, but his mission was unsuccessful. The British government did not wish to give in to the settlers. On his return to Mauritius the settlers rebelled. The immediate cause of the rebellion in June 1832 was the arrival at Port Louis of a new procureur général, John Jeremie, a lawyer sent out to enforce the new laws designed to improve conditions for the thousands of plantation slaves.

Jeremie was known to be a supporter of the Anti-Slavery Society, and his presence was most unwelcome to the settlers. They greeted his arrival with a general strike, and he was held under virtual house arrest in the home of General Colville. The settler assembly demanded his immediate expulsion, and stirred up protest across the island. After two months' agitation, the governor gave in to settler pressure. He agreed that Jeremie should leave the country to save 'the subjects of Mauritius from fire and sword, and the horrors of internal warfare'. He was also anxious to avoid a possible slave uprising.

A colonial civil servant in London noted that if the governor 'had acted in his military capacity in the same spirit which has characterised his civil proceedings, no court martial of British officers could have done otherwise than [have] condemned him to be shot'.[2] There was no such penalty for the inadequate governor, but after Jeremie's expulsion a new Whig government in London ordered the governor to be replaced. It also insisted that Jeremie should return to Mauritius.

Yet nothing changed on the island. On his return in May 1833, Jeremie was subjected to the same treatment he had received the previous year. He was forced out again in October, although by this time the circumstances had changed somewhat. The formal end of slavery had been decreed in London that year, and the planters felt obliged to accept the decision. They were partly influenced by the British government's decision to buy them off. They received substantial compensation for the loss of their slaves: £2 million was divided among 6,874 owners of 68,613 slaves. D'Épinay himself fell victim to settler politics, and suffered the same fate as Jeremie; he was driven out of the island and went into exile in Paris, where he died in 1839. Jeremie was appointed to be governor of Sierra Leone, and died there in 1841.

James Stephen, the colonial secretary's legal adviser, admitted in October 1834 that the settlers of Mauritius had been a tough nut to crack:

> On the subject of slavery and the slave trade, the people of Mauritius have been too strong for the people of Great Britain. Neither acts of parliament, nor orders in council, nor local ordinances, have been of force to secure the obedience of the handful of white inhabitants of that small island, or even to induce them to mask their disobedience under the ordinary forms of decorous and respectful courtesy.[3]

Imperial irritation with settler intransigence was rarely expressed so eloquently.

Another British island in the Indian Ocean caused trouble in 1834. In Kandy, the inland kingdom of Ceylon, the old ruling elite had been defeated in 1818, and their country had been incorporated into the Maritime Provinces of Ceylon. But the elite retained their hostility to British rule and resented their lack of independence. They lamented the loss of their traditional source of economic power – the use of forced labour. This was now available solely to the British, a crucial element in their strategy of road-building, designed to curb future outbreaks of guerrilla resistance.

In July 1834, Buddhist priests and senior figures from the Kandy nobility organised a rebellion against the occupation of their upland kingdom. Their plan was to poison the governor and destroy the British garrison, with the support of the government's Malay mercenaries. The objective of the rebellion was to restore the independence of Kandy, but it was crushed before it got off the ground.

Several suspects were arrested and brought to trial in Kandy in January 1835. They were acquitted 'in direct opposition to the summing up of the judge'. Whether there had really been much of a conspiracy remains uncertain, but Major Thomas Skinner, the commissioner of roads, noted that the effect of the trial was 'to seriously impair the influence and authority of government in the minds and affections of the people'.[4] Simmering resentment continued until a further popular explosion in 1848.

CHAPTER 42

Resistance in the Strait of Malacca

Earlier, in June 1831, Abdul Said, the Penghulu of Naning, had prepared to defend his small Muslim state against a British military expedition. Naning, with a population of barely 5,000, lay inland from the port of Malacca and had long enjoyed a treaty relationship with representatives of the Dutch Empire at that city. The Dutch and the British had argued about Malacca over the years, but in 1824 Britain was permitted to add it to the Empire – it joined Penang, acquired in 1786, and Singapore, occupied in 1819. Together, these small but strategically significant territories became known as the Straits Settlements.

A question mark hovered over Malacca's hinterland of Naning, although the British assumed that an arrangement with the Penghulu, similar to the one he had had with the Dutch, would continue under their rule. The Penghulu had previously channelled his state's tin production through Malacca, for which he had paid the Dutch a peppercorn transit tax. Now he was expected to pay the British, and this he refused to do.

He was soon faced with a military expedition prepared by Robert Fullerton, governor of Malacca, and made up from sepoys employed by the East India Company and a few locally recruited porters. The expedition's British officers thought the march from Malacca to the Penghulu's capital at Taboh would be a 'picnic', and they pictured the welcome they would receive from the Naning peasants, thought to be hoping for liberation from the alleged oppression of the Penghulu.

This was not so. The Penghulu was a popular ruler, believed by his subjects to have supernatural powers. The peasants showed no sign of welcoming the invading army; indeed they fled at the sight of it. Village leaders refused to provide messengers or porters to the advancing troops who came with fire and the sword. Lieutenant Peter Begbie, one of the participants, wrote of 'the unsparing manner in which house after house had been subjected to the flames', a measure 'more calculated to exasperate, than conciliate, the population'.[1]

Morale was low among the sepoys, wrote Constance Turnbull in her history of the war, and even worse among the camp followers: 'The porters took to wearing white flowers in their hair as a secret sign to the Naningites that they were friendly towards them, and gradually they slipped off into the jungle.'[2] The British faced further trouble when their supply boats tried to move upriver. The channel was too shallow; the boats were obliged to return to Malacca.

When the sepoys came within striking distance of the capital at Taboh, only a handful of porters remained. The officers abandoned the campaign and began a humiliating retreat. The Penghulu's soldiers retreated into the jungle to wage a guerrilla war, and Begbie described how they evaporated whenever the British approached and 'poured unseen shots upon them from the jungle'. To block the road back to Malacca, they cut down trees across the track; guns and heavy baggage had to be left behind. Returning eventually to Malacca, the British found the town fearful of attack, with the inhabitants polishing rusty swords behind closed doors.

A year later, in March 1832, the defenders of the Penghulu at Taboh faced a second, better-planned expedition. A fresh sepoy regiment was brought in from Madras, with two companies of sappers and miners and some additional European help. Two British naval officers, Lieutenant Henry Keppel in HMS *Magicienne* and Captain Stanley Congalton in HMS *Zephyr*, were charged with blockading the river Lingy to prevent the Penghulu receiving reinforcements.[3] Two months were spent in building twelve miles of military road through the jungle, eighty yards wide.

The Naningites harassed the road-builders and killed two officers, but victory eluded them. Taboh was captured by the British in June, although, as Turnbull notes caustically, 'it had taken two campaigns with an army of some 1,200 to 1,400 men and an expenditure of £100,000 to capture this miserable disease-ridden village of some thirty houses'.

Abdul Said fled before the advancing army and surrendered in February 1834. He was eventually enticed to Malacca and provided with a house, an orchard, and a pension.[4] He retained his reputation as a healer, and died there in 1849.

At the end of May 1836, three large *prahus* (boats) manned by sailors from the Arroa islands, off the coast of Sumatra, came under attack from a British war party sent out from HMS *Andromache*, commanded by Captain Henry Chads. 'Refusing all quarter, and even using their arms in the water, [they] were destroyed, excepting a few that reached the island', wrote Montagu Burrows, a young midshipman on board the *Andromache*.[5] More than a hundred of those on the *prahus* were killed.

Another witness, Lieutenant Colin Mackenzie, described the encounter in a letter to his wife:

> The whole crew having in their desperation jumped into the sea, the work of slaughter began, with muskets, pikes, pistols, and cutlasses. I sickened at the sight, but it was dire necessity. They asked for no quarter, and received none; but the expression of despair on some of their faces, as, exhausted with diving and swimming, they

turned them up towards us merely to receive the death-shot or thrust, froze my blood . . . The most pitiable circumstance of the whole was that two male children were killed by our fire.[6]

These off-shore peoples that British sailors disturbed that day had lived on the waters of the great archipelago south of Singapore for centuries. Sometimes they were described as 'sea gypsies', but the British called them 'pirates'. They lived off the taxes they collected from passing ships, some operating independently, others provided with a licence to operate by the sultan of Johore, or other minor sultans controlling limited stretches of coastline.[7]

Their way of life and their means of sustenance, historically legitimated, involved exacting tolls from the passing trade. They 'had been taught by long immunity to regard themselves as employed in a perfectly legitimate calling', noted Burrows. They lived on and by the sea, and they certainly did not perceive it as a free channel through which anyone could pass at will. They saw it as a marine territory that they, as a nation, were fully entitled to possess and exploit. 'The scanty literature' of their nation, wrote Peter Begbie, another contemporary observer, 'turns wholly upon . . . the exploits of some noted pirate of either ancient or more modern times, forming the theme of their legends or romances.' The crew of their boats would be 'nerved by songs of a similar description as they pull their long oar in chase of the trading boat, which passes their lurking place.'[8]

Their *prahus* were impressive constructions, designed to be fast and manoeuvrable. Usually over fifty feet long and fifteen wide, they were double-banked with thirty-six oars, eighteen on either side. Simply rigged, with two sails, they could carry as many as six brass guns. The boats served as the semi-permanent homes of the crew, as well as a kind of customs control mechanism. Entire families often lived on board, sometimes accompanied by a Muslim priest. Mackenzie told his wife of the books and papers he had found, including 'scraps of the Koran, love-letters, charms, accounts, and Malay poetry recounting the heroic exploits of the pirates of former times'. These, he explained, were 'a sort of poetical history of the Malay islands and peninsula, proving that piracy is esteemed among that race quite as laudable a mode of obtaining a livelihood as it formerly was among more northern nations'.

Yet, however much British officers might honour the similarity between a Malay pirate nation and the Vikings of their own tradition, this age-old activity clashed with the trading ambitions of the British Empire and its need to have free seas on which to sail. 'Piracy', however defined, would have to be stopped, and the 'sea gypsies' would have to be killed, at whatever cost.

The participant-observers on the *Andromache* could not fail to notice that they were often obliged to fire indiscriminately on men, women and children.

'There is an unpleasant circumstance connected with our pursuit of these Malays', Mackenzie explained to his wife. Since it was difficult to discover whether an individual *prahu* was a pirate ship, the sailors took no chances. Their practice was to force the crew of suspect *prahus* out of their boats and into the water, and there they would be slaughtered. These were Chads' orders, according to Burrows, and sailors were forbidden to board the *prahus*. 'They were to be conquered by our guns and muskets, and destroyed like vermin' noted Burrows, though adding with some relief that these 'ghastly orders' did not apply 'to non-resisting captives taken on shore'.

The mission of HMS *Andromache* was to exterminate the 'pirates' who lived on and around the Strait of Malacca, offshore from Singapore – a task perceived as an unavoidable necessity. 'Nothing but the most rigorous measures . . . will tend to check the evil', wrote a contemporary traveller through these seas, 'even to the utter annihilation of those who may be caught in the act.'[9] Captain Chads, formerly one of Nelson's sailors, had commanded the naval expedition up the Irrawaddy River during the Burmese War of 1824. An observing Christian, he spent part of each morning and evening in Bible study and prayer.

Chads and George Bonham, the governor of Singapore, had been charged by the British authorities in India to crush the sea rebels operating in the waters around the town, and they set sail together. Chads was to deal with naval matters, while Bonham was involved in onshore politics, signing treaties of cooperation with minor Malay chiefs, and checking on the secret activities of Temenggong Ibrahim of Singapore, who had been favoured with a treaty relationship.

Before sailing from Singapore, Chads had issued a 'proclamation' informing all Malay chiefs that a British system of licences would operate in future on their seas, enabling all trading vessels to be readily identified. Boats without a British pass would be treated as 'pirate' vessels. The old system, whereby the local rajahs issued licences to the *prahu* operators, was now under threat.

The *Andromache* sailed down to Singapore from Madras to give support to two other British ships already working in the area: one of them, HMS *Wolf*, under Captain Edward Stanley, had already rendered 'useful assistance' to the military during Maqoma's Xhosa rebellion in Cape Colony in 1835 (see Chapter 44 following); the other, HMS *Zephyr*, was commanded by Samuel Congalton, another veteran of the Burmese War and of the campaign against the Penghulu of Naning in 1831. HMS *Wolf* had been engaged in the task of exterminating 'pirates' before the arrival of the *Andromache*, as Mackenzie explained to his wife: 'She had had a good deal of boat fighting with the pirates, and contrived to slay a good number without any loss.'

The previous year, in March 1835, a large group of eighteen *prahus*, with a total of 700 people on board, had been attacked off the Dinding Islands by the *Wolf* and the *Zephyr*. Lieutenant Henry James on the Wolf noted in his diary that 'the grape and musket shot fired from the pinnace must have killed many . . . Captain Congalton says that they have not had such a thrashing for years.'[10]

Part of the reason for the excessive violence lay in the fact that the British found it difficult to arrange a trial for captured pirates, let alone to secure a conviction. There was no Admiralty Court in Singapore capable of dealing with captured naval prisoners, and captured 'pirates' had to be sent on to Madras. Commanders often took the law into their hands. Lieutenant James noted the action of a boat commander of HMS *Wolf* who, knowing 'he would not get them punished if he took them to the Government . . . coolly put stones about them and drowned them'.[11] Congalton of the *Zephyr*, wrote James, 'always kills all, and his Malay crew glory in it'. Killing 'pirates' was easy money. Since 1825 the British had operated a bounty system. Anyone on board a ship sent on extermination duty received £20 for every 'pirate' destroyed, whether captured or killed.

After its action off the Aru islands, HMS *Andromache* continued south past Singapore, destroying villages, burning boats, and killing people. Towards the end of June 1836, she arrived off Galang, an island in the jurisdiction of the Dutch Resident at Riau, and the sailors spotted a 'pirate' encampment. 'We found it had been deserted on our approach', Burrows recalled. 'It was beautifully situated on a cleared space, with dense jungle behind, from whence there was some ineffectual firing; but we soon burnt the village and all the boats which were building.'

The presence of these boats, wrote Burrows, 'and the number of houses (all on piles) confirmed our information that it was the centre of the pirates on this coast'. It lay at the mouth of a river, and soon the crew had found and destroyed another 'very populous settlement'. The Dutch Resident at Riau complained at this high-handed British action, but to no avail. 'As they sailed back to Singapore from Galang', noted a contemporary Malay report, 'they kept watch for native craft and, whenever they met one, it would be destroyed by cannon fire.'

Like tourists of a later era, the British officers could not resist collecting souvenirs. After an encounter with 'pirates' near Point Romania, Mackenzie wrote to his wife to describe how he had secured the severed head of a Malay chief to send to his friend, the editor of the *Journal of the Asiatic Society of Bengal*:

> I then remembered my promise to James Prinsep touching a specimen of a Malay caput mortuum. I accordingly got into a small canoe with three Malays belonging to the gunboats and rowed away to the first prahu, which had drifted a little out to sea. On getting on board, I found, among other relics of mortality, the body of the Pangleemah, or chief of the Prahu, lying still warm on the poop, his arms beside him.
>
> Not choosing to defile my own sabre – after admiring the corpse which was that of a splendid young fellow, symmetry itself – I made a Malay carefully cut off the

> head with the defunct's own sword and wrap it up in a basket. I then possessed myself of his sword, spear, and dagger, which I send with his head. The human hair on the handle of the sword denotes the rank of the owner, and, I believe, is that of a victim. I am sorry I could not take the fellow's immense shield, my canoe being too small.

Returning to the Andromache, Mackenzie found Captain Chads 'overjoyed at our complete success. The pirates, who numbered nearly 130 men, lost at least one-third of their number, many more being so severely wounded as to be scarcely able to crawl to the jungle.'[12]

The campaigning continued, and at Siak, in the middle of July, on Bucalisse island off the coast of Sumatra, the 'pirates' fought back with determination. 'Commanded by some unusually brave chiefs', noted Burrows, 'they made a stout resistance which cost our force the loss of seventeen men killed and wounded.' The wounded chief of one of the *prahus* refused to surrender and had his boat deliberately blown up.

Yet stout resistance was at best suicidal, for British terror tactics carried all before them. The boats of Captain Chads, wrote Burrows, 'struck terror into the whole population of either side of the Malay peninsula'. At the Aru islands, at Galang, at Point Romania and at Siak, they had 'completely destroyed every piratical squadron they came across', as well as 'one important nest of these people'.

By the middle of September, Governor Bonham was ready to go ashore, leaving Chads to continue alone. The bloody work of the British ships was nearly done. 'We had made treaties with some of these little Malay potentates, frightened others, and destroyed many pirates and their headquarters', wrote Burrows. 'The neck of the general enemy of mankind was broken, at least for a time.'[13]

The following year, 1837, the inhabitants of the inland rivers faced a new terror weapon. Charles Buckley, the Singapore chronicler, recorded their shock when six large *prahus* were first confronted by a steamship. Seeing the smoke, they 'thought it was a sailing ship on fire', and they 'left the Chinese junk which they were attacking, and bore down on the steamer, firing on her as they approached'. To their amazement, 'the vessel came close up against the wind, and then suddenly stopped opposite each *praha*, and poured in a destructive fire, turning and backing quite against the wind, stretching the pirates in numbers on their decks'. The ship, HMS *Diana*, was Captain Congalton's new command, a steamship whose name commemorated the steamer that had first seen service on the Irrawaddy in 1824.

The campaign Britain undertook in the 1830s to suppress 'piracy' in the seas around Singapore continued for a quarter of a century, and was to seal the fate of the sea peoples; their political and economic importance began to decline. 'By 1860, the once proud sea rovers of the archipelago were reduced to a few scattered tribes of shy, nomadic peoples.'[14] Britannia now ruled the waves, and no Malay ruler would ever again build a state based on the seafaring society of the archipelago. The pirates had been literally blown out of their island strongholds.

CHAPTER 43

Resistance on the Gambia River in West Africa

The British had established a foothold on the coast of West Africa at the end of the eighteenth century, notably at Sierra Leone. In 1816 they built a military base at the mouth of the Gambia River, to assist in the campaign against the slave trade and to protect commercial traders from French-occupied Senegal.[1] They called it Bathurst, after Henry Bathurst, the colonial secretary at the time (today it is called Banjul). Captain Alexander Grant, the governor, laid out a town and built barracks, erecting an artillery battery to control access to the river. The local chief of Kombo had agreed to 'cede' the land for the base, but both at the mouth of the river and in territories inland, the British soon found that they were not welcome.

On 22 August 1831, Burungai Sonko, chief of Barra, a territory on the northern shores of the Gambia River, defeated 'a medley of soldiers, merchant seamen and civilians' who had crossed the river from Bathurst to reinforce a small fort built at Esau. Ten of them were killed, including the English captain. 'Because he was a white man', wrote the local Wesleyan minister, 'they cut off his head, raised it upon a pole as a monument of their achievements, and burned his body to ashes'.[2]

Burungai Sonko had been king of Barra since 1823, and although hostile to the settlement of the Europeans across the river, he had been forced to sign an agreement in 1826. The 'Ceded Mile Treaty' gave the British the right to occupy the northern shore and to build Fort Esau. The king received a small annual subsidy in return. Dismissed in colonial records as 'an insane drunkard', he maintained his resentment at the presence of the British intruders, and refused any cooperation.

Conflicts within the territory occurred over the years, and the Reverend William Moister, the minister at Bathurst, wrote of a 'war with the neighbouring native tribes, the Mandingoes', who sought 'to accomplish the entire destruction of this settlement'.[3] The British attempt to reinforce Fort Esau in 1831 cannot have been altogether unexpected by the Barra chief, and when the military party sailed across the river, Burungai Sonko's men were ready.

The Africans 'poured heavy fire' onto the attacking force from well-prepared positions in the long grass. Outnumbered and in great confusion, the British were driven back to their boats; the captain and several others were killed. The

Africans waded into the water when the boats tried to move away, and inflicted further casualties. 'Twenty-three soldiers and a number of civilians were killed in this lamentable affair', the Reverend Moister recorded.[4]

The actions of Burungai Sonko aroused the possibility of a wider war, and the British in Bathurst sent appeals for help to the British in Freetown, and even to the French in Senegal – at Gorée island and St Louis. The French officer at Gorée, evincing unusual inter-imperial solidarity, despatched a ship, the *Bordelaise*, commanded by Commandant Louvel. The Africans watched as the French ship crossed to the north bank of the Gambia River on 15 September, 'accompanied by some schooners, with men of the West India Regiment and the local militia on board'. It had the clear intention of seizing Barra Point.[5] Burungai Sonko was ready, and the French found the Africans 'strongly entrenched'. An explosion of gunpowder caused casualties among the seamen and, since his forces were limited, Louvel retreated across the river to Bathurst.

The Barra king was faced by fresh French units in October of the same year, when the Senegal governor sent a troop of marines. More soldiers came in November from Freetown. 'Heavy fire' from the African trenches greeted the troops from this combined force as they landed at Barra Point, after a powerful bombardment from the sea. The Africans continued to maintain 'a vigorous fire' after the European force had advanced on the fort at Esau and attacked it 'with some small field pieces'. The invaders' ammunition ran out after five hours, and they were forced back to Barra Point. Once again, the Africans had triumphed.

Yet Burungai Sonko now decided to abandon his resistance, and peace talks took place. Doubtless he had received another large bribe. One chronicler records that he and the Barra people 'publicly declared their sorrow for the outrages they have committed in an unjust and cruel war',[6] while the Reverend Moister crowed with pleasure that 'the warlike natives were subdued by the force of British arms'. But the record suggests that the battle on the Gambia River was a close-run affair.

Kemintang was a chief on the upper reaches of the River Gambia. In June 1835, he defeated a British naval expedition sent to crush his independent state. The Africans captured several heavy guns and positioned them at the entrance to the chief's town of Dungassen, some 200 miles upriver, near a creek that led up from the Gambia River. Kemintang had had innumerable run-ins with the traders located at Britain's military base at Bathurst, and was regarded by the British as a permanent irritation. So when HMS *Brisk* sailed into Bathurst in June 1835, carrying troops from the Royal African Corps, he would have known that George Rendal, the governor of the Gambia, was preparing an expedition to attack him.

Rendal selected 120 men drawn from the crew of the *Brisk*, some additional soldiers from the Royal African Corps, and fifty members of the MacCarthy

Island militia. The militia consisted of slaves taken off slaving ships by the Royal Navy – described as 'liberated Africans' – and dumped on islands in the Gambia River. Rendal's expeditionary force set off up the river with an additional number of 'native allies'. Arriving at the Dungassen creek, they transferred to small boats and embarked on a cross-country march of fifteen miles to Chief Kemintang's town.

Things did not go well for the British. Ammunition boxes had been given to native porters to carry, but most soon deserted, abandoning their loads or carrying them away with them. After an eight-hour trek, covering only half the distance, the force halted for the night. The following morning, they found they had run out of water. Arriving at Dungassen, their heavy guns were brought into action, but a four-hour bombardment made little impression on the defenders' position. Since most of their 'native allies' had vanished into the bush, a decision was taken to retreat to the boats. The withdrawal was carried out in great disorder. Three of the heavy guns were abandoned, one was spiked, and the remaining two were left behind.[7]

Chief Kemintang's men recovered the guns and dragged them in triumph to their fort, dealing a severe blow to British prestige on the river. Kemintang maintained his independence for another decade without being further molested, and he died in 1843 with the guns still in his possession.

CHAPTER 44

The End of Slavery in Cape Colony, the Rebellion of Maqoma, and the Flight of the Boer Farmers

The troubled Cape Colony – with its divided groups of white settlers (Dutch and English), its large slave population, and with the enraged Xhosa permanently installed on its eastern border – forced its way to the top of the agenda of the new reformist governments in London in the early 1830s. General Benjamin d'Urban was sent out to Cape Town in 1834 as the new governor. Another veteran of the Peninsular Wars and the Caribbean battles of the 1790s, D'Urban had considerable colonial experience, having been responsible as governor for the suppression of the slave rebellion in Guyana in 1823. Slaves were again to be his immediate consideration in South Africa, for his first task was to prepare the colony for their freedom, decreed in London to be achieved throughout the Empire. In Cape Colony the date was fixed for December 1834.

Most of South Africa's large slave population lived in and around Cape Town, but the Dutch farms on the frontier depended on slave labour for their economic survival. They had already been deprived of their Khoi-Khoi (Hottentot) labour after pressure from English missionaries. The enactment in 1828 of Ordinance 50 had given the Khoi-Khoi the same rights as the whites. They could now travel without passes and were granted the freedom to own land. This historic decision had been deplored by the settlers, and now they were faced with the loss of their slaves as well. D'Urban's first task was to decide on the compensation payable to each slave-owner, and, although farmers were notionally compensated for the loss of their slaves, they were only to receive one-third of a slave's value, payable in London.

The old Dutch settlers were not happy with this outcome. How could they farm without slaves? Groups of them soon began contemplating an exodus from the British colony, to make a new life for themselves in African territories further to the north. Such thoughts were an indication of the mood within sections of the settler community that had never been reconciled to British rule. Soon some of the Boer farmers were to vote with their feet, travelling out of the British colony across the Orange River, to the banks of the Vaal.

After supervising the end of slavery, General D'Urban's second task was to address the future of the frontier provinces and their Xhosa population.

Officials in London were aware of the problems, and advised D'Urban to make a permanent settlement with the Xhosa. They planned to copy the imperial system pioneered in India that encouraged local chiefs to take on a significant subordinate role within the administrative structure of empire. Xhosa chiefs on the frontier would receive handsome gifts and a small annual wage, and in return they would be expected to keep their followers under strict control.

This was a controversial policy, far from being accepted by either the Dutch or English settler communities. The fear of the Boers that the British would eventually make a deal with the Xhosa was a further cause of their desire to abandon the colony. Many officers on the frontier preferred the politics of confrontation. Some would have chosen the path taken by settlers in Australia, wiping out the indigenous inhabitants whenever possible. John Philip, the combative missionary, wrote of how painful it was 'to observe how easily and imperceptibly even many well-bred Englishmen imbibe the colonial prejudices against the natives, how often they drop all the ordinary marks of common civility towards them'.[1]

Maqoma, the Xhosa leader, was exactly the kind of chief with whom the British might have done a deal. Born in 1798, he was the son of Ngqika, once the ally of the British.[2] Of all the Xhosa chiefs in this period, writes Noël Mostert, he was seen as 'indisputably the greatest leader, the potential organiser of Xhosa military power, and the likeliest indigenous victor, if ever there was to be one'.[3] Yet, like Ngqika before him, he had gone a long way towards accommodating British demands. In effect, he had already accepted a position as a chief whose interests were subordinate to those of the settlers, and he had allowed Christian missionaries to establish mission stations on his territory.

Yet in spite of his willingness to compromise, he had been endlessly ill-treated by the settler regime, and forcibly expelled from his lands by settler commandos in May 1829. Colonel Henry Somerset had taken the necessary steps in the familiar fashion, impounding cattle and burning kraals. His instructions were to punish Maqoma's 'insolence' and to rid the colony of 'this most troublesome and dishonest chief'; but the underlying reason for his attack was different. The British needed his land, to plant it with other Africans deemed more friendly to their cause.

Maqoma's country between the Fish River and the Keiskamma River, known since its conquest in 1819 as the 'Ceded Territory', had originally been designated as a frontier area in which Xhosa would not be allowed to settle. The first British plan, according to Andries Stockenstrom, the old Dutch frontiersman, was to place 'a dense European population' in the territory.[4] Yet Maqoma had been allowed to remain, in the belief that he was friendly and pliable. Missionaries established a mission station at Balfour to keep an eye on him, and relative peace was maintained on the frontier for six years. The plan to open up the area to white settlement was dropped.

In 1829 the British had a fresh use for Maqoma's land. Missionaries had long campaigned for an improvement in the conditions of the Khoi-Khoi, the largest group of indigenous blacks within the colony. Many worked in near-slave conditions on settler farms. Missionary pressure produced the government's Ordinance 50 of 1828 which gave the Khoi-Khoi the same rights as whites. The governor at the Cape at that time, General Sir Lowry Cole, an aristocratic officer with experience in Ireland, in the Peninsula, and most recently in Mauritius, suggested that the Khoi-Khoi should now be given land to settle on, and it was thought that Maqoma's 'Ceded Territory' would be suitable. Stockenstrom expressed his delight: this was an opportunity to provide 'the forlorn remnants of the former possessors of South Africa' with their own land; they would create a barrier against the Xhosa, 'a breastwork against an exasperated, powerful enemy in the most vulnerable and dangerous part of our frontier'.[5] Yet since the Xhosa already occupied the land, they would have to be expelled before several thousand Khoi-Khoi could be moved in.

Colonel Somerset's task was to tell Maqoma and his people to leave. 'The teacher has told me that God will judge all men according to their deeds', he was told by Maqoma, well-schooled by the missionaries. 'You have overcome me by the weapons that are in your hands. But you must answer for this. You and I must stand before God. He will judge us. I am a man who does not know God. Yet I rejoice he will be the judge.'

To the dismay of the missionaries, the British troop began burning down the homes of the Xhosa on a Sunday. Maqoma withdrew across the Keiskamma River, quickly followed by the missionaries. In his new lands, wrote the officer in charge of the expulsion, 'there was not a morsel of grass . . . it was as bare as a parade'. Where Maqoma used to live was 'better for [both] water and grass than the one they were removed to, which was already thickly inhabited'.

Within a year, the old 'Ceded Territory' of 400 square miles had been settled by 4,000 Khoi-Khoi, each with a plot of six acres. The British made them into a permanent and indispensable part of their military establishment, playing a similar role to the sepoys in India. Formed into the Cape Mounted Rifles, commanded by Somerset for thirty years, they became the mainstay of frontier defence.[6] 'Patrols' and military 'commandos' were sent out in the early 1830s on the pretext of capturing stolen cattle, but their real purpose was intimidation. Xhosa land was seized and homes burned. Further punitive commando expeditions took place in 1834, and the Reverend Philip, visiting Maqoma in his barren new territory in September, found the Xhosa 'in a state of continual alarm'. He described how 'the complaints of the men were almost forgotten in the distress of the women and children . . . literally perishing . . . for want of the fruits of the field and the milk that had been the means of their support, their cows having been carried away by the patrols'.[7]

Philip suggested to Maqoma that he might like to send his children to the mission school. 'Yes', Maqoma replied, 'all this is very good, but I am shot at every day; my huts are set fire to, and I can only sleep with one eye open and the other shut. I do not know where my place is, and how can I get my children to be instructed?'

Colonel Francis Wade, acting governor of the colony before D'Urban's arrival, was also shocked by the sight of the continuing intimidation of the Xhosa. After a visit to the frontier, he reported how 'these valleys were swarming with Caffres, as was the whole country in our front . . . the people were all in motion, carrying off their effects, and driving away their cattle . . . and to my utter amazement, the whole country around and before us was ablaze'.

Somerset had remained the commander on the frontier, and the shooting of Xoxo, Maqoma's nephew, during one of his commando raids was a particular cause of Xhosa outrage. 'It is better that we die than to be treated thus', one Xhosa told a missionary. 'Life is of no use to us if they shoot our chiefs.' Xoxo was not the first Xhosa chief to have been shot at. Sigcawu, younger brother of Ndlambe, had been killed by a military patrol in June 1830; another chief had been detained at Fort Willshire.

'Several of our chiefs have been shot, and we have remained quiet', a Xhosa councillor told a missionary in 1834, 'but now we are determined to fight.' By the end of that year, the Xhosa had reached breaking point. Maqoma's expulsion had become the spur to his own anti-colonial militancy, writes Mostert. 'It rankled to the end of his life, never forgotten, never forgiven.'[8] Maqoma could no longer restrain the anger of the people. Far from submitting to enrolment as a British chief, he and his brother Tyali became formidable opponents of British expansion.

An immense army of Xhosa warriors erupted without warning across the eastern frontier on 21 December 1834, with the stated aim of driving the settlers into the sea. Maqoma was forced into action by pressure from his people. 'The fire is burning', he told a missionary, 'and I cannot quench it.' This great Xhosa rebellion, known to the British as the 'Sixth Kaffir War', lasted for nearly a year, the first major uprising in Cape Colony since Makana's great revolt of 1819. It placed the white settlers in southern Africa under serious threat.

Pouring westwards across the Great Fish River, several thousand Xhosa reclaimed large areas of Albany (the territory formerly known as the Zuurveld), catching the few hundred soldiers in the area by surprise. Their immediate aim was to capture and kill Colonel Somerset, the officer seen as the principal author of their oppression. They were soon lapping around the white settlement of Grahamstown, now with a population of 3,000 British settlers. They moved forward with little resistance, slaughtering the settlers and burning their houses. The old Dutch settlers and the British who had arrived in 1820 suffered in equal measure.[9]

Within a week, having occupied most of the Zuurveld, the Xhosa declared a unilateral ceasefire and requested negotiations. Maqoma put his faith in the new governor, and sent a message to Cape Town through a missionary intermediary. General D'Urban was handed Maqoma's complaints about settler behaviour:

> No one has told Your Excellency how the colonists have been accustomed to deal with the [Xhosa] . . . Colonel Somerset communicates with you . . . but he tells you only one side of the story. Colonel Somerset for a long time has killed the [Xhosa], he has disturbed the peace of the land, and torn it in pieces, and matters are now come to such a crisis that you alone are able to rectify them.

Governor D'Urban's reply came in the form of a new commander, Colonel Harry Smith, despatched at speed to the frontier. A change of government had taken place in London, and a tough military response to the Xhosa rebellion might now be welcomed. The Whigs of Earl Grey and Lord Melbourne had been replaced by the Tories, led by the creator of the Irish paramilitary police force, Sir Robert Peel, and briefly by the aged Duke of Wellington.

Colonel Smith was an officer destined to play a major role in the extension of empire in India and Africa over the next fifteen years. A veteran of the occupation of Buenos Aires and of Waterloo, he had been stationed at the Cape since 1828. Arriving at the frontier in January 1835, he rejected out of hand the Xhosa request for peace talks. He declared martial law and made plans for an immediate counter-offensive. The Xhosa would be pushed back from the Zuurveld, and then face an invasion of their territory to the east of the Keiskamma River – the territory the British had labelled 'Kaffirland'. Smith aimed to clear the Xhosa first from the region of the Great Fish River, and then from the Amatolas mountains to the north. Martial law would remain in force for the next eighteen months.

The Xhosa put up considerable resistance when Smith crossed the Great Fish River in February. 'It is certainly not child's play tracking through the dense bush', noted one of Smith's officers, 'having a volley of musquetry suddenly poured on the party from above, and stalwart and naked warriors rushing with yells and stabbing asegais from the elephant grass around.' The Xhosa fell upon the white soldiers 'like mad fiends, yelling and shrieking "stab the white man"', according to a British settler's report.

Xhosa resistance slowly crumbled before the brutal sweep of Smith's army and its Khoi-Khoi auxiliaries. Smith described the nature of their war-making in a letter to his Spanish wife, Juana: 'You gallop in, and half by force, half by stratagem, pounce upon them wherever you can find them; frighten their wives, burn their homes, lift their cattle, and return home quite triumphant.' Within a matter of weeks, the Xhosa had been driven beyond the Keiskamma River.

Governor D'Urban himself came up to Grahamstown in January 1835 and witnessed the devastation caused by the 'eruption' of Maqoma's Xhosa. He realised that it would be impossible to defend the white settlers on the frontier unless all the Xhosa population was driven out of the lands between the Great Fish River and the Great Kei River, and the territory permanently annexed to the British colony. Yet these were the lands of Hintsa, the paramount chief of the Xhosa. Although Maqoma was their military leader, their supreme ruler was Hintsa.

A man of about forty-five, born around 1790, Hintsa was regarded with awe by many settlers. 'Marvellously clever', said one, 'the greatest black man I ever knew'. He was now to be the victim of an ambitious scheme devised by D'Urban. On 24 April, after skirting the Amatolas mountains and acquiring some African allies, D'Urban crossed over to the east of the Great Kei River and fired a ceremonial salute, to mark his formal declaration of war on Hintsa.

Hintsa had not taken part in Maqoma's frontier rebellion in 1834, living far from the action at that time. 'You have been badly used by the English', he had told Maqoma, 'and as you have already begun to fight, go on; I shall remain neutral'. He had long been acquainted with the British, and with British perfidy, ever since his 'Great Place' had been visited by Colonel Richard Collins in 1809. Even the friendliest of the old Xhosa chiefs had been treated badly in subsequent decades: Ndlambe had been outlawed; Makana had been tricked into surrender and imprisoned on Robben Island; Ngqika, Maqoma's father, had been kidnapped. Hintsa's fears of British treachery had grown in the 1820s after several chiefs had died in rapid succession. Ostensibly Ndlambe had died from old age, his son Mdushane from syphilis, and Ngqika from complications caused by heavy drinking. Hintsa suspected that all three had been poisoned; he would always refuse to eat with white men.

When D'Urban arrived at the Great Kei River, he found that others had arrived there first. Hintsa's kraal had been attacked by a white settler patrol, and Hintsa, fleeing from its ruins, appeared at D'Urban's camp to negotiate. He was presented with a series of humiliating demands impossible to fulfil: a fine of 50,000 cattle; the surrender for execution of Xhosa found guilty of murder; a requirement to put pressure on his people and on other chiefs to surrender. Hintsa agreed to the demands, well aware, as were the British, that he was making promises he would be unable to deliver. The British detained him in their camp, threatening to send him to Cape Town and on to Robben Island – the fate of Makana sixteen years earlier.

With Hintsa in his power, D'Urban now announced the formal incorporation into the British Empire of that part of Hintsa's territory that lay between the Keiskamma and the Great Kei rivers. In homage to the wife of the current British king, the land once known as 'Kaffirland' would be called the Province of Queen Adelaide. A new military headquarters was to be established at its centre with the name of King William's Town. Innumerable smaller forts were to be erected along the road east to the Great Kei River. The Xhosa, described by D'Urban as 'treacherous and irreclaimable savages', would be driven out.

Indeed, D'Urban went further. The Xhosa were to be 'exterminated'. Later historians have sought to exculpate D'Urban for his use of this emotive word, and some have argued that word was used in its classic meaning of 'to thrust beyond the boundaries' rather than 'to extirpate'. Yet Sir Charles Bunbury, a visitor to Cape Colony at the time, wrote of a British officer who talked of 'the imperious necessity, dictated alike by reason, justice, and humanity, of exterminating, from off the face of the earth, a race of monsters'.[10]

Hintsa was the first casualty. Early in May, fulfilling promises made to assist in the recovery of stolen cattle, Hintsa travelled across the territory with Colonel Smith. After riding away from the British column on 12 May, in an effort to escape, he was pursued and shot at, but he found a hiding place on a river bank. When his British pursuers caught up with him, and saw him hiding in the water, he stood up and called out several times in Xhosa, 'Mercy'. He was promptly shot by George Southey, a Xhosa-speaking settler. His head was shattered, and soldiers fell on his lifeless body, cutting off his ears and removing his teeth.

'Thus terminated the career of the Chief Hintsa', wrote Smith in his official report, 'whose treachery, perfidy and want of faith made him worthy of the nation of atrocious and indomitable savages over whom he was the acknowledged chieftain.'[11] D'Urban was of a similar view. 'I have come deliberately to the conclusion', he wrote in a letter to a military underling, 'that the Kafir is the worst specimen of the human race that I have ever had to deal with.'[12]

In the climate of Britain's settler colonies, formerly decent liberal officers easily turned into racist killers. Yet one settler, William Gilfillan, present at the killing and despoiling of the Xhosa chief, wrote that night in his diary of his regret that Hintsa's captors had allowed 'their insatiable thirst of possessing a relic of so great a man to get the better of their humanity and better feeling, which teaches us not to trample on a fallen foe'.[13] Such expressions of humility were rare in colonial South Africa.

In the Amatolas mountains, meanwhile, the Xhosa had begun a tactical withdrawal in April 1835, aware that Colonel Smith would soon attack. Smith's troops 'moved through an apparently abandoned world', writes Noël Mostert, 'whose considerable population had suddenly decamped. The huts and crops were set to the torch, and then suddenly the Xhosa appeared, on opposite ridges, beyond cannon shot, the tall figures moving in their flowing karosses, gesturing with their assegais and shouting to their own people concealed in the forests below.'[14]

The Xhosa warriors eluded capture for months, but their homes and families suffered severely in their absence. 'You burn our houses and destroy our cornfields. What shall we live on when this war is over?' a group of them were heard to call out in early May. 'They had lost a huge quantity of cattle', writes Mostert, 'and seen crops and homes destroyed and, anathema to their style of warfare, had seen their women killed. Unable to come to close quarters, the British had simply fired indiscriminately into the bush whenever their presence was suspected, or directed their destructive shellfire on to the Xhosa.'

One of Maqoma's wives was a victim of this form of warfare. Discovered lying on the ground, wounded, by Captain Charles Stretch, a frontier farmer, he found her expression of fear and pain 'was so truly distressing' that he felt 'ashamed of being in command'. It was too much for him, 'and as I could render no assistance I hurried from the melancholy scene, lamenting I was ever employed on such duty'.

The Xhosa in the Amatolas faced a fresh attack in June, when Smith's forces were reinforced by 2,000 British regular soldiers, as well as a handful of settler militia and some Khoi-Khoi. More than a thousand huts were burned during this new campaign, and immense stores of corn destroyed. Now facing imminent extermination, the reticent Xhosa began to fight back. While still avoiding a frontal collision with the colonial forces, they struck whenever opportunity presented. At the end of June they wiped out a British patrol that had run out of ammunition – the largest single British disaster of the war.

The British slowly came to understand that they could not entirely destroy the Xhosa in the Amatolas. 'The unpleasant truth for a man like Harry Smith to accept', writes Mostert, 'was that the British army and its auxiliaries were themselves in a very bad way.' Indeed they may have been worse off than the Xhosa. 'Although their homes had been burned, their crops destroyed and their cattle taken, the Xhosa remained in possession of the areas they occupied when the war broke out.'

The Xhosa now obliged the British to contemplate negotiations, which had been on offer since the beginning of the year. D'Urban told Smith that if he were to meet Maqoma he was to tell him that the British no longer planned to expel the Xhosa to the east of the Great Kei River. They would be granted land 'in what was their own country'. Maqoma sent an assegai to D'Urban as a gesture of friendship, and a final peace agreement was signed on 17 September. Some 2,000 Xhosa had been killed in the war, and 100 settlers. D'Urban decided that 70,000 Xhosa should be granted land both in the Amatolas and to the west of the Great Kei River. They would henceforward be considered British subjects. It was a victory of sorts for Maqoma.

The resistance of the Xhosa and the cruel death of Hintsa had entirely changed the climate of opinion. In London, news of D'Urban's treatment of the Xhosa was described by the missionary John Philip as 'equal in horror' to the French Revolutionary 'Reign of Terror'. This had not been a war, he said, but 'a massacre'. Even in Cape Town, Hintsa's killing was regarded as 'a most atrocious murder'.

D'Urban had over-reached himself. Not only was he unsuccessful in his campaign to exterminate the Xhosa; his project to extend the borders of the British Empire was soon to be thwarted. A new government had been in power in Britain since April 1835. Lord Glenelg, formerly Charles Grant, the Irish secretary from 1819 to 1823, replaced the Tory Lord Aberdeen as colonial secretary. Glenelg was a close friend of the Radical MP Thomas Fowell Buxton. As he listened to the news from Cape Town brought by the Reverend Philip and other missionaries opposed to D'Urban's annexation project, he set about formulating a new policy.

In August, Fowell Buxton's parliamentary Committee on Aborigines began to hear evidence; several witnesses, including the old Dutch settler Andries Stockenstrom, spoke up for the Xhosa. The conclusive argument against D'Urban's plans came from Major William Dundas, an officer from Grahamstown with no brief for the Xhosa. He opposed the annexation scheme on the grounds of cost. 'The expense of keeping that country will be enormous', he told the Committee. 'A vast population from England' would have to be sent to occupy the new province, involving a large army to defend it. 'Unless it is occupied, it will be the constant cause of warfare between us and the Caffres; it must be occupied in force or be given up.'

Glenelg listened to the evidence and came down on the side of the Xhosa. D'Urban was ordered to reverse his programme of annexation. Writing from Downing Street in December, Glenelg instructed him to withdraw from the new province dedicated to Queen Adelaide. Much of his letter was taken up with criticism of D'Urban's actions, and the treatment of Hintsa was singled out for particular criticism: '[H]e was slain when he had no longer the means of resistance . . . the dead body of the fallen chief was basely and inhumanely mutilated'. A conclusive rebuke came at the end: it was the opinion of His Majesty's advisers, Glenelg wrote, that 'the original justice was on the side of the conquered, not of the victorious party'.

The Radicals at Westminster were overjoyed. 'I have to tell you a piece of news which has made me sing ever since I heard it', Fowell Buxton wrote to a friend. 'A whole nation, doomed to ruin, exile, and death, has been delivered and restored to its rights . . . Only think how delightful our savage friends must be . . . surely we must make a party and pay King Maqomo a visit.'

The celebration of the Radicals was a trifle premature. Glenelg had written of 'the opinion of His Majesty's advisers', but it was not the opinion of His Majesty himself. William IV, a naval officer who had fought in the anti-French wars at the turn of the century, had no intention of surrendering territory conquered in war, and indicated his royal displeasure. Glenelg was obliged to add a rider to his letter to D'Urban stating that no final decision would be taken until he had received a full report from the governor.

Glenelg's letter did not arrive at Cape Town until March 1836, by which time Colonel Smith had spent nearly a year in charge of the Queen Adelaide territory, building forts and humiliating Xhosa chiefs. Smith was appalled by the letter, and he sat down to write a long defence of the right of conquest: 'that right by which the British dominions have been extended to their present magnitude, by which they are extending at this moment in Australia, that right which has ejected the Aborigines from the vast territory of America, the West Indies, the ancient Oriental world . . .'. Were the Kaffirs not to be ejected by the same right? 'Are they alone of all the rest of the Aborigines from whom England has wrested her possessions to be thus favoured?'[15]

D'Urban was of the same opinion, yet he realised that even the support in London of William IV and the Duke of Wellington would be insufficient, and in October 1836 he ordered the evacuation of Queen Adelaide's province, formally renouncing British sovereignty over the area in February 1837. He himself was sacked as governor by Glenelg in May 1837, although he remained in Cape Town until he was replaced at the end of the year.

Andries Stockenstrom was left in charge on the frontier, once more on the Great Fish River, to negotiate treaties with the Xhosa chiefs beyond it. After the death of Hintsa, his son Sarile became the new paramount chief of all the Xhosa, called upon to agree to the treaties to which his father had put his name. Stockenstrom was effectively withdrawn in 1838. The Xhosa victory was complete.

Their victory also had an effect of stiffening resistance further to the north. In Basutoland, the Basuto King Moshoeshoe and his followers had assumed that the British would defeat the Xhosa, and indeed had 'entertained no doubts as to the issue . . . they expected to hear every day that the Caffres were subdued . . . They said there was no standing against the white men . . . the colony was looked upon as invulnerable.' Yet suddenly all was changed. The spell had been broken 'by the resistance of the Caffres'.

What now took place in Cape Colony was not so much a rebellion as a vote of no confidence in the British Empire itself. Hundreds of Dutch families rejected their British citizenship and headed out of the territory. As early as December 1833, Carel Johannes Trichard, a Dutch farmer long settled in the district of

Somerset, had set off with his family and a handful of others towards the Orange River, to the north, following in the footsteps of earlier Dutch farmers unhappy with British rule, who had moved east or north into African territory. Most had disappeared, or survived leaving little trace. Trichard's expedition also ended in disaster.[16] Yet in Boer mythology these epic 'voortrekkers' were perceived as the forerunners of the people who would eventually set up new settler states independent of the British Empire. They, like the burghers of Graaff Reinet and its adjacent districts – Jacobin rebels since 1795 – remained convinced that the cause of their suffering was 'the existence of the British Government in the country'.

Maqoma's revolt in 1834 had been an important factor in Boer discontent, as had the British decision to end slavery; but for many the final straw came in 1835, when Glenelg revoked D'Urban's decision to extend the colony eastward into Xhosa territory, largely on the grounds of expense: 'We should be engaged in a series of contests desolating to Africa and ruinous to ourselves.' The Dutch settlers realised that they would receive no further support from the British for their territorial ambitions, and they now embarked on what became known to history as the 'Great Trek' – a fresh and different kind of white settler rebellion. Between 1835 and 1837, some 5,000 European settlers of Dutch origin moved north out of Cape Colony across the River Orange, to set up an independent country of their own – the Orange Free State. Within twenty years, a further 20,000 settlers had followed them out of the British Empire.

The British had no way of stopping their departure, and were to some extent pleased to see the back of such disruptive citizens, despite the loss of a significant element in their frontier defence system. The trekkers were now someone else's problem – notably that of the African nations whose territories they seized or passed through. Yet the binding links between the British and their Dutch subjects were never entirely broken, creating endless conflicts throughout the century.

What would have happened in Cape Colony if there had been no migration, asked Robert Godlonton, the editor of the *Grahamstown Journal*, in August 1838. 'In all probability, a similar scene would have been presented here to that which has been witnessed in the Canadas. The whole country might . . . have been torn to pieces by intestine commotion; and the British government . . . might have been necessitated to send hither an expensive armament to put down rebellion.'[17]

By allowing the Boers to migrate, the British turned them loose on the Africans, and they were soon to meet with African resistance – from the Zulus in Natal and from the Ndebele further to the north. A small army of the Ndebele were hunted down for ten days by a commando of 135 trekkers under Hendrik Potgieter, killing 'an estimated 9,000 warriors without the loss of a man themselves'. The surviving Ndebele retreated northwards to the territory that became Matabeleland, then Rhodesia, and eventually Zimbabwe.

Piet Retief was one of the participants in the Boer 'Great Trek' that set off towards Natal in 1837. He had formally renounced his British allegiance: 'We quit this colony under the full assurance that the British government has nothing more to require of us, and will allow us to govern ourselves without its interference in future.' In October, he arrived at Port Natal, in the lands of Dingaan, the great chief of the Zulus of Natal.

Dingaan occupied a large territory north of Port Natal, a harbour where a small English trading population had been established since 1824. It had recently been re-named D'Urban in honour of the Cape governor, and perhaps in the hope that he would extend British protection to it. Dingaan, traditionally demonised by white historians, was the half-brother of Shaka Zulu, who he had killed in 1828.[18] Like Shaka before him, Dingaan had tolerated the informal British settlement on the coast, but he was aware of the dangers involved and made considerable efforts to secure modern weapons for his armies.

Dingaan had been informed years earlier by his Xhosa contacts of the expansionist activities of the white settlers: 'First the white people came and took a part of the [Xhosa] land, then they encroached and drove them further back, and have repeatedly taken more land as well as cattle.' Dutch farmers who had penetrated far into Dingaan's lands brought back enthusiastic reports. 'I have never in my life seen such a fine place', one of them noted. Andrew Smith, a Scottish doctor, was sent by the Cape Colony governor in 1832 to see whether Natal would make a suitable British colony, and arrived at Dingaan's splendid kraal at Umgungundhlovu. Fortunately for Dingaan, the British had other things on their minds at that time.

In 1837 Dingaan was faced with the arrival of Retief and his cohort of Dutch settlers, who planned to occupy his territory inland. He was well aware that they had few scruples about slaughtering and humiliating the local population. Johan Wahlberg, a Swedish naturalist, had described a typical plundering expedition by the Dutch at this time. 'Not so many Kaffers' had been killed, about 130, but others 'were beaten with the sjambok in the most frightful manner'. Wahlberg wrote that, on one occasion, a whole party 'from terror and pain could not keep back their excrements, so that the ground all round the place where this devilish deed was committed was covered with them'.[19]

In October Retief made his way up to Dingaan's kraal at Umgungundhlovu, and at first Dingaan appears to have thought that he could control the Dutch settlers. He signed a document in February 1838, drafted by Retief, that would have granted a right to the settlers to establish farms in Natal. Soon he thought better of this decision, determined to smash the settlers' vanguard before they turned on him.

On 6 February 1838, Dingaan's Zulu forces attacked Retief and an advance group of sixty settlers, and slaughtered them all. A week later, Dingaan's troops killed a further 600 Dutch settlers who had been hoping to seize land. 'No comparable disaster had ever been experienced by whites in southern Africa', writes Stephen Taylor in his history of the Zulus.[20] Dingaan's men then turned their attention to the British settlement on the coast, which had sent out a militia troop to assist the Dutch. The Zulus overwhelmed the English at a battle on 17 April, and only four Europeans escaped back to Durban. The surviving inhabitants of the settlement took refuge on boats offshore, and only a handful ever returned to the town. Most of the missionaries, hunters and traders fled to the Cape.[21]

The British authorities, at the Cape and in London, shed few tears for the dead Dutch settlers who had trekked out of the colony and caused havoc beyond. 'Much as I lament the fate of these misguided men', wrote Lord Glenelg, 'it was not to be expected that the natives of the countries adjacent to the colony would suffer themselves to be overrun by those invaders.' Strong action should be taken, wrote Andries Stockenstrom, 'against those of His Majesty's subjects who had exterminated whole tribes of blacks'.

Yet since the Dutch survivors who had arrived in Natal could hardly return to Cape Colony, they were obliged to press on. By the end of 1838 they had been reinforced by a new group of nearly 500, led by Andries Pretorius, a farmer from Graaff Reinet. Dingaan's Zulus again sought to beat them off, in a fight on 16 December remembered as the battle of Blood River; but this time the victory went to the Dutch. Dingaan fled, and the victorious Boers entered the royal kraal to claim themselves masters of Natal and to bury the skeletons of Retief and his party.

Mpande, Dingaan's brother, joined forces with the Dutch a year later, and their joint forces moved against Dingaan himself. The Zulu leader who had tried to resist this new encroachment of white settlers was killed. With Dingaan's defeat, the Dutch established their own inland town at Pietermaritzburg. Yet they still had to settle old scores with the British, still nominally their colonial overlords. The authorities at Cape Town could not tolerate the idea of white settlers, perceived as British citizens, setting up an independent state in Natal. In 1841, Captain Thomas Smith was sent to the borders of Natal 'to afford the native tribes of Africa the protection of British arms against the aggression of Her Majesty's subjects'.[22] In 1843, after some sporadic resistance from the Dutch settlers, Natal became a British colony and was incorporated into the Empire.

CHAPTER 45

White Settler Rebellions in Canada

The autumn of 1837 saw the start of a series of stuttering white settler rebellions against British rule in both the French and English provinces of British North America, eventually to be known as Canada. They were to last, with interruptions, for more than a year. The settlers of French-speaking Quebec (Lower Canada) and the English-speaking settlers of Ontario (Upper Canada) both sought independence from the British Empire. The indigenous peoples of the territory, the Mohawk Indians, some of whom lived at Kahnawake, across the river to the south of Montreal, were largely uninvolved, remaining loyal to Britain. Trouble among the French settlers in Quebec bore some resemblance to that among Dutch settlers in Cape Colony, who sought independence earlier in the 1830s by starting their 'great trek' out of the colony.

Since the 1760s, British North America had been two countries in one: half French by original French conquest; half British by military victory, settlement and immigration.[1] The French in Quebec and the British in Ontario had continued their existence as separate societies after 1760, with different religions, legal traditions, and cultures. Yet both were affected by the deteriorating economic crisis of the 1830s. Radical elements in the two provinces rebelled against the conservative rule of the imperial *ancien régime*.

A successful insurrection against the Empire seemed possible at that moment, both to the settlers and to the British authorities. In French-speaking Lower Canada, the French population of 400,000, formed largely of smallholders known as habitants, had long been disaffected from British rule. The total number of British settlers in the province was half that – less than 200,000; and only 1,700 British soldiers were stationed there, mostly in the towns of Quebec and Montreal. The situation was similar in English-speaking Upper Canada, where a British settler population of some 400,000 was protected by only 1,300 regular soldiers.

In both provinces, weapons and fortifications were crumbling away, 'the cankered remains of a long period of military inaction'.[2] Years of peace 'had made sad havoc with gun carriages, harness, limber wheels, and all manner of warlike munitions. The powder in the musty magazines was damp; muskets, swords and bayonets, had long rusted in inglorious ease; and bedding and blankets had disappeared before successive generations of moths.' Quite suddenly, the British military were challenged by unexpected rebellions.

Dr Wolfred Nelson, French rebel commander in Canada.

On the morning of 23 November 1837, groups of well-armed French settlers assembled in the village of St Denis on the River Richelieu, east of Montreal, in the strategic territory of Lower Canada close to the United States frontier. The French-speaking habitants, small farmers for the most part, had come in from the surrounding countryside to lend their moral and military support to the political leadership of the growing independence movement of Quebec. Its principal leaders, Wolfred Nelson and Louis Papineau, had been issued with arrest warrants in Montreal, and had fled to the safety of St Denis. The small force of 300 armed habitants prepared for an attack by British troops advancing from the St Lawrence River.

Their commander was Nelson, a doctor of English origin who spoke fluent French. A prominent politician in Lower Canada's assembly, he was also a wealthy local brewer. Papineau was the intellectual author and inspiration of the rebellion. A lawyer and landowner, he was a former president of the assembly. The rebellion drew strength from the inherited enmities between the French and the British, but it was more immediately the result of a long political conflict that had pitted the colony's military rulers sent out from London, and their hand-picked legislative council, against Papineau's assembly, elected by popular vote. Quebec was ruled by British military governors, but French Canadians were the majority population, represented by Papineau's Parti Patriote.

The colonial authorities had ignored Papineau's calls for reform, and the French settlers felt that time was now against them. Successive British governors had called for increased immigration from Britain, and the new population stream was changing the balance in favour of the British. Anti-British sentiment in Quebec reached fresh peaks in the mid-1830s, when Irish immigrants brought cholera with them, causing the death of thousands of French Canadians. Papineau might once have been satisfied with reform; now he sought independence, a clear break with Britain. His party's programme was modelled on that of America's settler rebels of 1776 and inspired by distant memories of the French Revolution. Its popularity was fuelled by his splendid rhetorical skills.

With the parliamentary road to reform exhausted, Papineau argued that armed rebellion was the only way forward. In Toronto, in English-speaking Upper Canada, a radical English politician had come to a similar conclusion. William Lyon Mackenzie, leader of the Reform Party, was also preparing for an armed rebellion, to start in December (see below, p. 312). Together with Papineau, he had made the necessary plans and contacts.

Papineau's supporters in Quebec formed small paramilitary groups to mobilise opinion for independence, the largest being Les Fils de la Liberté – the 'Sons of Liberty'. Sections of the British community opposed to independence soon began organising in opposition to the French, enrolling themselves in the Doric Club. The two groups armed and drilled their supporters, and made ready for war. By the autumn of 1837 the atmosphere in Montreal was rebellious and anarchic. The French groups, perceived by the British as 'seditious mobs', sang the Marseillaise in the streets; in the French-speaking villages to the east of the city, at St Denis and St Charles, taverns displayed eagles instead of the usual pub signs; at St Hyacinthe the tricolour flag flew from the windows; and in Montreal, the *Vindicator*, an English-language newspaper, came out in support of Papineau's demands, publishing an incendiary declaration from Les Fils de la Liberté in September. Edited by Dr Edmund Bailey O'Callaghan, a Catholic from Ireland and an assembly member, the paper proclaimed the need to free the province 'from all human authority except that of the bold democracy residing within its bosom'.

In October Papineau addressed a large open-air meeting at St Charles, on the banks of the Richelieu River; delegates came from most of the frontier counties. When he called for independence, the crowd cried out 'Vive Papineau!', 'Vive la liberté!' and 'Point de despotisme!' The atmosphere of impending civil war intensified in November, when the British settler militia began to mobilise.

An anti-French riot in Montreal ended in the sacking of the *Vindicator*'s offices, while across the river at Longueuil a group of 300 habitants, armed with shotguns and muskets, beat off an attack by British settlers. The habitants formally joined the rebellion in other towns and villages.

British forces in both Canadian provinces were under the command of General Sir John Colborne, another veteran of the Peninsular Wars and of Waterloo, stationed in Canada throughout the 1830s. With the situation deteriorating in Lower Canada, Colborne moved his headquarters from Toronto to Montreal and took decisive action: the local militia was called out, political meetings were banned, and warrants were issued for the arrest of Papineau and other leaders of the Parti Patriote. Papineau, Nelson and O'Callaghan escaped from the city and sought refuge with the habitants at St Denis.

On 23 November the habitants came under attack from a squad of British soldiers sent down the St Lawrence River from Montreal, and led by Colonel Francis Gore. Colborne had ordered them to advance on the Richelieu valley from the north, via Sorel; they dragged a brass field gun with them through the autumn mud. The village's defences held out well against the British gun, and after sporadic attacks throughout the afternoon, Colonel Gore retreated. He abandoned the gun, now spiked and useless, to the rebels. This was a victory of sorts for the rebels, though it was not won without casualties, and several unfortunate developments affected their position.

In an incident whose details were unclear, Lieutenant George Weir, a British officer captured by the rebels, was shot 'while trying to escape'. Also without explanation was the decision by Papineau and O'Callaghan to slip away from St Denis that day, and to cross the frontier to the United States. Their absence was to have a baleful effect on rebel morale in the weeks ahead.

The rebel victory at St Denis was an isolated event. Three days later a second British force, commanded by Lieutenant Charles Wetherall, advanced from the south to the nearby rebel village of St Charles. With superior guns, they were swiftly victorious. Poorly constructed trenches around the village were breached by Wetherall's guns, and the habitants were scattered by a bayonet charge; fifty-six were killed, their houses set on fire, and 'several died miserably in the burned houses'. British troops took their revenge on those they believed responsible for the death of Lieutenant Weir.

The tide had turned against the rebels. Martial law was declared in the Montreal area on 5 December, and resistance around the city was mopped up by Colborne's troops. St Denis was attacked again in December, and captured without difficulty. Nelson and his men had already withdrawn. Five hundred houses were burned down.

ADVANCE OF THE BRITISH TROOPS ON THE VILLAGE OF ST DENIS, 1837
From a colour drawing by C. W. Jefferys

French settlers in Canada, commanded by Wolfred Nelson, come under attack from British troops at St Denis, east of Montreal, 23 November 1837.

St Eustache, a rebel stronghold to the west of Montreal, was now in the sights of General Colborne. The habitants there had been organised by Amury Girod, appointed by Papineau to direct the rebellion in the territory north of the St Lawrence River. The rebels assembled to defend the church, but could do nothing against superior artillery. A fresh wind blew at the time, and sixty buildings in the vicinity of the church were soon ablaze. Rebels who had taken refuge in the steeple perished in the flames.[3] Colborne's enthusiasm for burning houses (he personally directed the attack on St Eustache) earned him the nickname of *le vieux brulot*. Comparable horrors took place at St Benoit, further to the west, where 300 rebels surrendered and watched while the settler militia burned their church and every house.

This, the first of the rebellions against British rule in Canada, lasted barely a month. Its leaders were dispersed, captured or dead: Papineau had left the country; Amury Girod had escaped from St Eustache and shot himself when facing capture; while Nelson and other leaders were captured and imprisoned in

French settler forces flee the burning town of St Eustache, west of Montreal, destroyed by the British in December 1837.

Montreal.[4] The rebellion's failure was due partly to Papineau's precipitate flight, partly to the lack of assistance that the rebels had hoped for from the United States, and partly to the decision of the local Catholic hierarchy to oppose it. General Colborne's prompt military response also counted against its success. Martial law remained in force until April 1838.

Yet the threat of rebellion remained, and the embers of this first bid for independence were coaxed into flame in 1838 by Nelson's younger brother Robert. He had escaped across the frontier to the United States in December 1837, taking many supporters with him, and returned in 1838 to fight again, in February and November. But the banner of independence was first raised for English Canada, by the English-speaking rebels in Toronto.

In the evening of 5 December 1837, just two weeks after the brief French settler victory at St Denis outside Montreal, a group of 800 English-speaking rebels in Toronto assembled at Montgomery's Tavern outside the city and prepared to capture it. Their aim was to seize the capital of Upper Canada and establish an independent republic. Some 200 men armed with rifles marched in front, while behind came a larger number of pikemen; others had muskets and shotguns.

Advancing into the outskirts of the city, they unexpectedly came under fire from a militia group hidden behind a fence. Astonished at this reverse, they retreated rapidly, firing scattered shots in return and leaving their dead and wounded behind. The militia were equally fearful, and also fled in panic.

The rebel march was led by Peter Matthews, a blacksmith by trade, and Samuel Lount, a wealthy farmer and radical politician. The rebellion's chief organiser was William Lyon Mackenzie, an immigrant from Scotland, a politician and newspaper publisher, and the leader of the Reform Party. He had long been an advocate of independence for Canada, and in May 1834 he had exchanged views on the subject with Joseph Hume, the Radical MP for Middlesex in England. Hume had suggested, on the first occasion when 'independence' for Canada was publicly mentioned, that Canada's long political crisis might well end 'in independence and freedom from the baneful domination of the mother country',

In 1837 the British population of Upper Canada was almost entirely confined to a strip of land along the shores of the St Lawrence, and of Lake Ontario and Lake Erie. The country to the north and to the west, along the shores of Georgian Bay and Lake Superior, was a *terra incognita* to most British settlers, and virtually inaccessible, inhabited solely by Indians and a few white hunters. The fertile prairies to the west, the habitat of millions of buffaloes, were under the administration of the Hudson's Bay Company, and there too the only inhabitants, apart from those at the Company posts, were Indians and hunters.

The government of Upper Canada, like that of Lower Canada, had for years been in military hands. 'Their stern military habits', wrote the nineteenth-century historian John McMullen, 'their stiff and unbending manners, their natural desire to rule the people a good deal as they ruled their own commands, made them, to no small degree, unfitted to win favour with a community verging towards pure democracy'. A new governor, Major Sir Francis Bond Head, had arrived in January 1836, having almost certainly been appointed by mistake – the bureaucracy having confounded him with his more talented cousin, Edmund Bond. He proved to be unusually incompetent, and ignored the demands for reform.

Secret meetings of radical politicians produced a 'Declaration of Independence of Upper Canada' in August 1837, with a pledge to make common cause with the French radicals of Louis Papineau in Lower Canada. Detailing a long list of grievances, the Declaration called for a convention to be held in Toronto in 1838 'to seek an effectual remedy for the grievances of the colonists'. Mackenzie believed the government would accept the reform proposals, and he imagined that the proposed convention would be the occasion for a new Magna Carta for Canada.

He had other more subversive plans if the government were to reject his proposals: the governor and his non-elected council would be seized, and a provisional government would take over, headed by Dr John Rolph, one of his leading supporters. A rebel force began to train and drill secretly in the course of 1837, under the command of Colonel Anthony Van Egmond, a sixty-seven-year-old Dutch soldier who had served with Napoleon.[5] In December, just after the Quebec rebellion, the rebels in Upper Canada were ready, and assembled at Montgomery's Tavern.

Their advance on Toronto, ill-planned and poorly coordinated, was more in the nature of a putsch than a rebellion. Many were religious dissenters, others were of American origin, and all were recruited in the belief that a show of force would be sufficient to topple the Toronto government. Mackenzie himself seems to have assumed that this would be enough. After the initial clash with the militia, Lount rallied the survivors who drifted back to Montgomery's Tavern, but to no purpose. The numbers dwindled, and most went home; those left at the tavern were soon scattered by the militia. Lount and Matthews were captured; John Rolph, the proposed president of the new Canadian republic, despaired of success and, taking a leaf from Papineau's book, escaped across the Niagara River to the United States.

Mackenzie had arrived belatedly at Montgomery's Tavern and, realising the futility of the attack, had retreated to Navy Island in the Niagara River. On 13 December he formally proclaimed the establishment of an independent Republic of Upper Canada, and published the names of those to be in a future government. It was a vain gesture. He claimed to be preparing for an invasion of Canada from the United States, but after a militia force had captured and burned his supply ship he was forced to follow Dr Rolph to the American mainland, where he settled in New York.[6]

Others were less fortunate. Lount and Matthews had been captured, and they now faced justice from a new military governor of Upper Canada – none other than Colonel George Arthur, the promoter of the 'Black Line' across Tasmania in 1830. Arthur arrived in Toronto in March 1838, and his first task was to decide the fate of the captured rebels. They were both found guilty, and Arthur upheld the death sentence by hanging. Both men were Methodist Episcopalians, and on 12 April, at the King Street prison in Toronto, they were accompanied by Methodist ministers to the scaffold.

That same year, in February 1838, the 'patriot army' of the Quebecquois revived the earlier French Canadian rebellion of November 1837. The army, 600 strong, crossed Lake Champlain from the United States. It was commanded by Wolfred Nelson's brother, Robert, a Presbyterian doctor. Armed with weapons and ammunition stolen from American arsenals, he had high hopes of success. 'We have been oppressed by the hand of a transatlantic power', he proclaimed, 'and unjustly and cruelly castigated with the rod of unrelenting misrule for a long series of years – so long, that the measure of Tyranny has filled to overflowing.'

Robert Nelson issued a radical and far-reaching declaration of independence, granting civil rights to the Indian population, separating church and state, providing for extensive land reform, abolishing the death penalty except for murder, and introducing universal adult male suffrage.[7] His liberal message evoked little initial response in Lower Canada, and his invasion proved premature. In their first clash with the local militia at Missisquoi, on the north bank of Lake Champlain, his force was defeated. Nelson and the other survivors withdrew to US territory.

Later that year, in November, the French Canadians embarked on their third attempt to secure independence. Robert Nelson was again the moving spirit behind this new revolt, and he crossed the US frontier from Vermont on 4 November. Advancing with 300 men into Canada, he halted his troop at the village of Napierville, twenty-seven miles south-east of Montreal, while a second invasion force headed for Hemmingford. Nelson described himself as the 'President of the Provisional Government of Lower Canada', and the white ensign of the new Republic, emblazoned with two blue stars, was flown from the village flagpole. His declaration of independence, first issued in February, had continued to circulate among the habitants, and the rebels were optimistic about their chances.

A day earlier, Pierre-Paul Desmarais, the leader of the French habitants in the territory south of Montreal, had seized the town of Beauharnois, across the river from the city. Leading 500 men armed with muskets, shotguns and pikes, he captured the great house of the Seignior of Beauharnois, securing additional arms and ammunition. His strategic aim was to cut the military communications between Montreal and the territory south of the St Lawrence River, and to prevent British soldiers being mobilised to crush the habitants in the Richelieu valley, as they had done successfully the previous year.

The capture of Beauharnois was the signal for a general uprising against the British in the largely French-speaking area between the St Lawrence and the border with the United States. 'The hated British settlers were to be certainly driven out of the country this time', wrote the historian John McMullen, 'and independently of the acquisition of their deserted homesteads, the deluded habitants saw visions of future prosperity in the promises of their leaders, that seignorial dues and rights, and tithes as well, would be forever abolished.'[8]

The backbone of this new independence movement were 'the Freres Chasseurs', a radical society of 'Brother Hunters' created on Masonic lines, with rituals and loyalty oaths designed both to ensure secrecy and to emphasise the link with Britain. Women joined the Chasseur lodges as well as men. They were active throughout the province, organising the habitants and preparing them for war. More than 3,000 members were enrolled in Montreal. So secret was their plotting that the English-speaking farmers and shopkeepers in the rural districts were thrown off their guard, and continued to believe that the French Canadians had abandoned their dreams of independence.[9] Yet throughout the district of Montreal, the habitants polished up their old muskets and kept village blacksmiths busy forging pike-heads and daggers.

Desmarais ensured that the preparations for the rising were well organised in each locality, and developed a strategic plan: the British settlers were to be disarmed and held captive; the barracks at Laprairie, close to Montreal, were to be occupied; and the muskets and ammunition of the Mohawk Indian community at Caughnawaga (Kahnawake), south of the river opposite Montreal, were to be seized.

This was a miscalculation. Desmarais's habitants were unaware of the extreme hostility of the Mohawk to their rebellion. The Mohawk were firmly enrolled on the British side, having been provided with weapons by the British during the rebellion of the previous year. When Desmarais's men advanced into the Mohawk village, they had lost the element of surprise: 'The Indians sounded their warwhoop, suddenly surrounded the insurgents, and disarmed them in a few moments.' Some seventy-five habitants were captured, and Desmarais and the others fled into the bush. The Mohawk obliged their prisoners to row over to Montreal, where they were handed over to the British authorities and imprisoned. The sight of captive rebels put paid to the plans of the urban Chasseur lodges to join the insurrection.

Lest they should do so, General Colborne declared martial law in the Montreal district that day, as he had done in 1837. He ordered a pincer movement against the rebels in the countryside. Colonel Carmichael at Cornwall was to move downriver and attack Beauharnois, while Captain Campbell at Lachine was to cross over to Caughnawaga to assist the Mohawks, and then to move to break up the rebel camp at Chateaugay. Both British units found that Desmarais's forces had withdrawn by the time they arrived, and at Chateaugay the Mohawks, with Campbell's column, set fire to several houses and barns, looting everything they could lay their hands on.

Further to the south, at his headquarters at Napierville, Robert Nelson was also in trouble. The second invasion force at Hemmingford had been crushed by a militia of anti-Catholic settlers from Ulster, and news of the setback had an adverse effect on Nelson's own makeshift army. Many abandoned the struggle and returned home.

Colborne advanced from Montreal, with an army of 5,000 soldiers, 400 Indians and 500 volunteers. He arrived at Napierville on 10 November and found the town deserted. Nelson's depleted band had retreated across the US frontier, and Nelson himself had returned to Vermont.

British troops now exacted vengeance on the defenceless habitants. 'Sentiments of humanity and a horror of bloodshed had no place in the breast of a soldier such as Colborne, the old "Firebrand", as he was called, who set fire to so many villages that in some districts the sky became, as it were, a sea of fire from the reflection of the fateful flames.' John McMullen described it as 'a cruel civil war of races while it lasted, and the destruction of property was very great'.[10]

Clemency had been the characteristic of the previous year, but Colborne was now in sole charge in Canada as acting governor, and this time things were different. Colborne was determined there would be no amnesty for the rebels responsible for the latest rebellion and, with martial law still in force, he made an immediate example of the rebels in his hands.

A court martial began work on 20 November, and the first prisoners were sentenced to death and executed on 23 December. Four more followed on 18 January 1839, and another five on 25 February. The court martial continued its sittings throughout the winter, and a further seventy-six prisoners were sentenced to death. Their sentences were commuted to transportation to Australia – a fate awaiting forty-seven others found guilty of lesser crimes. They joined a large number of other rebels, from both Upper and Lower Canada, sentenced after the earlier rebellions.

Early in 1840, the British frigate *Buffalo* docked at Sydney to unload fifty-eight French Canadian prisoners, before sailing on to the Tasmanian port of Hobart with ninety-five English Canadians from Toronto. The English rebels received rather better treatment than the French, and Sir John Franklin, the governor of Tasmania, wrote to describe how he had not allowed them 'to pass through the usual ordeal of the convicts' barracks, not wishing them to be thrown among the usual class of thieves and rogues who are kept in such places of punishment'.

Reforms of the constitutional arrangements of the two Canadas were now made with no input from the French Canadians, judged to have forfeited their right to an opinion. Lord Durham composed a report outlining a possible solution to the underlying problems highlighted by the rebellions of 1837 and 1838, and the union of the two Canadas he suggested was soon established. Approved by the British in Upper Canada, it was bitterly opposed by the French Canadians, whose opposition would reverberate over succeeding decades.

Part VIII

IMPERIAL HUMILIATION AND FURTHER EXPANSION, 1839–47

China and Afghanistan both came under attack from British forces in the course of 1839 in ambitious undertakings that would change the face of empire. The Afghan city of Kabul was captured in August by the British Army of the Indus, while the Chinese island of Hong Kong was seized in the same month. In November a fleet of Chinese junks was sunk by the British navy off Canton – an event that marked the opening of the first 'opium war', designed to open Chinese ports to British trade. In January of the same year, the port of Aden was captured by a British naval force. The imperial strategy of seizing useful harbours while avoiding an occupation of the hinterland would become a hallmark of empire.

The Chinese war was a relative success for the British, the Afghan invasion a huge disaster. The two events ran in parallel. In 1840, a British force of 4,000 men, half British soldiers and half sepoys, commanded by General Sir Hugh Gough, occupied Chusan at the entrance to Hangchow Bay, blockading both Canton and Hong Kong. Canton itself was occupied in May 1841, and Gough's fleet then moved slowly up the coast, to capture Shanghai in 1842. Nanking came under threat, but hostilities were formally concluded there with the Treaty of Nanking. Five 'treaty ports' were established on shore, giving the British unparalleled trading opportunities, while Hong Kong was formally incorporated into the Empire, to be retained by Britain until the end of the twentieth century.[1]

The attempt to include Muslim Afghanistan in the imperial fold was less successful. Dreamed up in London but executed by the authorities in India, the policy envisaged the establishment of temporary, and then permanent, control over the intervening independent states of Sind and Baluchistan, and the eventual occupation of the Punjab. Sind, in the lower Indus valley, was seized by British armies in 1843, and the Sikh rulers of the Punjab were forced into subjection after battles in 1846 and 1849. But the British capture of Kabul and other southern Afghan cities in 1839 soon proved to be a catastrophe.

For a brief moment, Britain's triumphant occupation of Kabul appeared to be a striking and significant geopolitical achievement, yet the project unravelled almost immediately. Afghan resistance to the British presence was sustained throughout 1840, and in November 1841 crowds of angry Afghans surrounded the British garrison, and several officers were killed. News of the subsequent disastrous British retreat to Jalalabad, through the snowy mountain passes of the frontier region, echoed around the Empire, putting fresh heart into resistance movements everywhere. The British defeat showed that imperial forces were enfeebled, vulnerable and overstretched – and might now be challenged.

The impact of this British humiliation was felt initially in India itself, whose population bore the cost of this unsuccessful conquest. As with the war against China, sepoys from India played a leading role in the invasion of Afghanistan, and the subsequent debacle had a particular impact on these imperial legions. Hundreds of frost-bitten sepoys from the defeated army survived to tell the story of the demoralisation of British officers and soldiers they had witnessed during the retreat. Some believed that this humiliation was the fatal seed from which the Mutiny was to spring fifteen years later.[2]

In spite of the Afghan setback, the British continued to expand their empire in India throughout the 1840s. Yet the retreat from Kabul had shown that the Empire was not as powerful as it imagined itself to be, and the populations of the freshly invaded regions of Sind and the Punjab took heart from the Afghan resistance. Baluchi soldiers sought to repel the British invasion of Sind in 1843, as did the Sikh soldiers of the Punjab – heirs to the armies of Ranjit Singh – in 1845. Both Sind and the Punjab eventually succumbed to British firepower, but the battles were fierce and not without cost to the British. The Sikh victory at Chilianwala in 1849 sent a further tremor through the Empire, in another premonition of the events of 1857.

In other sections of the colonial portfolio, the period inaugurated by the Kabul disaster saw the creation of fresh zones of white settlement and the renewed growth of the indigenous opposition. In New Zealand, the Maoris showed immediate hostility in 1840 to new British settlement schemes, provoking the first of a series of resistance wars in 1843 that continued sporadically throughout the 1840s and beyond. Elsewhere, local peoples raised vigorous objections to the expansion of existing areas open to British pioneers in Australia, South Africa and Canada. The flow of migrants leaving Britain grew to tidal proportions in these years, though short of the huge scale it would achieve later in the century.[3]

These newcomers were met by the growing hostility of the Aborigines in Australia, while in Cape Colony the Xhosa maintained their long-term commitment to drive white settlers into the sea. The Xhosa were no longer the sole enemy of the British, for the heirs to the former Dutch settlers of South Africa, now established in independent Boer territories beyond Cape Colony, were embarked on the first of many wars against the Empire.

The white populations of Europe were not the only peoples forced onto the move by the expansion of the Empire. The formal abolition of slavery within the Empire in 1834 had obliged settlers everywhere to search for new sources of cheap labour, and the end of the apprenticeship system in 1838, in practice a brief extension of slavery, accelerated the process. Workers had to be brought from elsewhere, since freed slaves and most indigenous peoples refused to work for the imperial settlers. They came chiefly from the seemingly inexhaustible pools of labour in India, and later from China, many of them travelling through the new port facilities at Hong Kong. Just as the British used sepoys in India and Khoi-Khoi in South Africa to man their imperial armies, so the imperial outposts in the Caribbean and elsewhere were able to use this cheap Indian and Chinese labour to replace their slaves from Africa, and to provide a fresh economic resource for the Empire.

A flow of Indian 'indentured' labourers to the colony of British Guiana on the South American mainland began in 1838, and private recruiters sent thousands of Indians to Mauritius in 1839. An initial shipload of workers (described as 'coolies') sailed from Calcutta for the West Indies in 1845, disembarking at Trinidad and Jamaica. Earlier, in 1841, a parliamentary commission of enquiry into 'the abuses alleged to exist in exporting Bengal Hill Coolies and Indian labourers' had denounced a new system of slavery: 'If West Indian voyages be permitted, the waste of human life and misery that will fall on the Coolies under the name of free labourers will approach to those inflicted on the negro in the middle passage by the slave trade.'[4]

Yet economic necessity drove workers along these new channels of migration, and over the next eighty years Indians became the majority population of Mauritius, outnumbered the Europeans in Natal, and grew to form one-third of the population of Trinidad. They also became a substantial minority in British Guiana and Fiji.[5] Many in the early years received the harsh treatment reminiscent of the centuries of slavery. On John Gladstone's estate in British Guiana, salt pickle was rubbed into the backs of 'coolies' who had been flogged. Yet Indian labour was relatively quiescent until the development of active trade unionism in the twentieth century. Chinese migrants, on the other hand – notably in Singapore, Sarawak, Australia, and Hong Kong itself – rebelled frequently, creating difficulties for the imperial authorities later in the century.

Slaves were no longer available in the 1840s, and soldiers to conquer and control the Empire were also in short supply. When a British ship arrived at New Zealand in January 1840 to establish a new colony, the captain was warned beforehand that no spare troops were available to assist his conquest. The British were hard-pressed militarily at the end of the 1830s on many fronts – notably at home, where the Chartists had embarked on campaigns of civil disobedience. In the northern counties of England, General Sir Charles Napier, a veteran of the Peninsular Wars, had been sent out with 6,000 troops to frighten the Chartists, while the Colonial Office warned that no additional troops would be available for foreign conquest, or even for police work, when 'the most pressing demand for troops' existed in every part of Britain itself.[6]

Soldiers were also needed in India and North America, where the Canadian rebellions of 1837–38 had necessitated rapid fresh redeployments. The London authorities noted with irritation that Australian governors in New South Wales and Van Diemen's Land were constantly complaining about 'the inadequacy of their forces'. The governors were bluntly told that 'not a spare regiment' could be found anywhere. Yet in New Zealand the fierce Maori resistance to settlement throughout the 1840s was so strong that the British government was obliged to pay attention. Its reluctance to find extra troops was eventually overcome, and the Maori resistance was invariably met with the harsh conditions of martial law.

While Britain's stretched forces were extending the Empire in New Zealand, Australia and India, they were also moving into the South China Sea, in the waters of Hong Kong, and pushing eastward from Singapore along the coast of Borneo. A renewed campaign to exterminate 'pirates', who had been picked off spasmodically in the 1830s, was launched in the archipelago south of the Strait of Malacca. The 'piratical' tax-collectors who made their living from exacting tolls on those who passed through their waters were now engaged in a long rearguard struggle. After 1842, with an end to the China war, the British sent their spare ships to attend to the suppression of 'piracy' further south. An added attraction for the sailors was the payment of a £25 bounty for every 'pirate' head brought in.

Pangeran Makhota, a Muslim ruler on the island of Borneo, became a fierce opponent of the encroachments into Sarawak and Brunei of Lieutenant James Brooke, a freelance British naval operative who imposed himself on the region in the decade after 1841, with the official connivance of Captain Henry Keppel and HMS *Dido*.[7] The Dayak 'pirates' were attacked along the northern Borneo coast in 1843, and their homes and villages were burned; but in 1844, they struck back, plundering passing British trading ships. This form of imperial warfare – attacks by British warships and retaliation by 'pirates' – continued throughout the 1840s.

The resistance of native peoples, and the arrival in London of information about British atrocities, often provided by missionaries, began to chip away at Britain's self-confidence in its imperial project. William Gladstone, colonial secretary in 1846, outlined his distrust of imperial expansion:

> The multiplication of colonies at the other end of the world must at all times be a matter for serious consideration; but especially at a time when we have already land almost infinite to defend that we cannot occupy, people to reduce to order

> whom we have not been able to keep in friendly relations, and questions in so many departments of government to manage.[8]

The distant resistance struggles of the 1840s helped to create serious doubts at home about the imperial mission abroad.

CHAPTER 46

The Capture of Useful Imperial Harbours

Early on a January morning in 1839, Mahsin bin Fadhul, sultan of Lahij and the Muslim ruler of the port town of Aden, perceived a small squadron of British ships standing offshore, poised for attack. Aden, on the shores of south-west Arabia, had been in British sights for some years, and the sultan had been engaged in desultory negotiations about a possible lease of the port with Commander Stafford Haines, a naval officer employed by the East India Company. The sultan had received a verbal offer from Haines, but on this particular morning the British officer was more interested in action than words.

Mahsin had been sultan of Lahij, a town in the desert some thirty miles inland of the port, for more than a decade. The defence of Aden was concentrated on the island of Sirah, a natural fortress overlooking the harbour entrance, and on it stood a sixty-foot tower, built at the sultan's command. The sultan had 1,000 soldiers armed with matchlocks and thirty cannons.

Yet, as so often in the imperial story, this was an unequal struggle. The sultan was faced by several British warships, and transports with 700 British and Indian troops on board. If bombardment from the sea failed to secure his surrender, the sepoys would land and seize the town. Early that January morning, the defenders on Sirah were fired on by the British flagship, which had moved close to the shore. Neither the sultan's proud tower nor his soldiers armed with matchlocks could offer an adequate response to the British cannonade, and the tower was toppled within the hour. British troops landed at Aden in the late morning, and made their way through the corpses of the defenders.[1] The sultan's palace soon flew the British flag, and the mullah at the principal mosque was asked to keep women and children within its walls while British 'mopping-up' operations took place in the town. The casualties among the defenders amounted to 150, and a serious incident occurred when twelve released prisoners were mown down by sentries. The sultan's thirty guns were surrendered, and three fine specimens were sent to Queen Victoria, later to be placed in the Tower of London.

Sultan Mahsin did not accept British occupation gracefully, and 4,000 of his soldiers attacked the Aden garrison in December. They were fought off, and 200 were killed. Further unsuccessful attacks occurred in 1840. Sultan Mahsin abdicated that year in favour of his son Hamed, and he died in 1847. Commander Haines became the first ruler of British Aden, and ran the port town for fifteen years before ending his career in disgrace, accused of corruption. Put on trial in

1854, he died in prison in Bombay in 1860, aged fifty-eight. The British remained in Aden for more than a century and had nothing but trouble throughout their rule, which finally ended in 1967.

In August 1839, the 4,000 Chinese inhabitants of the island of Hong Kong observed the arrival of soldiers from a British fleet, a few months before the start of Britain's 'Opium War' with China. No record exists of their reaction to this occupation, but they had witnessed the comings and goings of British ships for many years before their island was formally acquired and incorporated into the Empire. Lying at the entrance to the Pearl River, the route from the South China Sea to the major Chinese trading port of Canton [Guangdong], Hong Kong had long provided British fleets with a convenient and familiar anchorage. Cargoes were often unloaded there, and stowed into smaller coastal vessels for onward passage up the rivers of the Chinese mainland.

The original purpose of the occupation of Hong Kong, made permanent in 1842, was to safeguard the rearguard of the British forces engaged in punitive actions against Chinese cities. The sinking of Chinese junks off Canton in November 1839 marked the beginning of the first Opium War – a war brought to a formal conclusion three years later with the signing of the Nanking treaty in August 1842. Hong Kong was then ceded to Britain in perpetuity, and the Chinese were forced to accept that the cities of Canton and Shanghai, and three other towns designated as 'treaty ports' – Ningpo, Foochow, and Amoy – would be open for trade, with 'reasonable' tariffs. The first British governor of the new colony was General Sir Henry Pottinger, an officer who had spent much of his life in India, notably as the political agent in Sind during the invasion of Afghanistan. Later, in 1846, he became the governor at Cape Town.

Until the British occupation, Hong Kong island had only a population of a few thousand, but during the wartime upheaval many Canton traders moved to Hong Kong, to be followed by flocks of boatmen and artisans. The population trebled in three years, and by 1845 the island was home to more than 20,000 people 'mostly of the lower classes: coolies, boat people, stone-cutters, domestic servants, craftsmen, small traders; in addition to Triads, pirates, outlaws, opium smugglers, brothel keepers, gamblers and like adventurers'.[2] Few of the newcomers were women; adult males from the mainland left their families behind.

While the mainland traders came to Hong Kong largely because of the economic disruption caused by the British war, the island's dramatic growth had other causes. The global need for labour, in the wake of the abolition of the African slave trade, was soon to have an important impact on the colony. Hong Kong became the principal centre for the vast Chinese emigration abroad in the middle of the nineteenth century. In the half-century before 1900, nearly 2 million Chinese labourers embarked from Hong Kong for a variety of different destinations. Much of this trade in 'coolies' went to North America, but much was destined for parts of the British Empire.[3]

While some migrants went to replace the freed slaves, others supplied the demand for labour in territories where the indigenous inhabitants were being exterminated. As poisoned 'damper' took its toll of the Aborigines, and as the supply of Irish convicts tailed off, Chinese labourers were sent to take their place. In one year alone, 1857, more than 17,000 'coolies' left Hong Kong for Australia. Racial animosity towards the Chinese eventually caused the trade to decline, yet a further 17,000 were sent out in the years between 1860 and 1874. Earlier the flow of migrants, often carried in Chinese-owned ships flying the British flag, was the partial cause of the second British war against China, in 1857, which concluded with a march on Peking and the burning of the emperor's Summer Palace in September 1860.

CHAPTER 47

Revolts among the Hill Tribes of Assam

The Sadiya cantonment – the principal British base in the north-east of Upper Assam, on the Burmese frontier – had been established in the 1830s to police the rebellious tribal groups that lived in the surrounding mountains. In January 1839, the base was attacked by 500 Khamtis who descended from the hills above the Tengapani River. Their leader, Sadiya Khowa Gowain, was the son of an earlier chief of the Khamtis, who had cooperated with the British in crushing a tribal rebellion in 1830. Armed with spears and muskets, the Khamtis singled out the sepoys for special attention, killing seventy and setting the barracks and the ammunition store on fire.

The Khamtis had come originally from the mountains between Assam and the Irrawaddy River. They were Buddhists of Shan descent, and had been encouraged by the British to remain in Upper Assam. The arrival of tea-planters had caused them to change sides. 'The government seems at this period', wrote Alexander Mackenzie half a century later, 'to have been much impressed with the advisability of inducing colonists to take up land at the head of the Assam valley . . . What was wanted was a cheap and effective barrier against future invasion from Burma, dread of which long continued to trouble the Government'.[1] The Khamtis were welcome to remain, as long as they did not interfere with the area reserved for new settlers to cultivate tea.

Unlike his father, Khowa Gowain did not trust British intentions. The Khamti attack was swift and unexpected – one of the boldest ever made by the hill tribes of the North-East Frontier against the British occupiers – and for several hours the entire cantonment was at their mercy.[2] Among those killed was Colonel Adam White, a political agent with long experience in the region who had organised the repression of earlier rebellions.[3]

After the death of the colonel and of such a large body of sepoys, the British sent up reinforcements from the Assam Light Infantry. Khowa Gowain retreated into the hills, pursued by a troop led by Captain S. F. Hannay, whose soldiers burned villages and destroyed crops. The repression was effective at the time, but the Khamtis continued to harass the expeditions that were sent out against them over the following years.

Another well-organised rebellion erupted in February 1843 on several fronts along Assam's border with Burma. Several Singpho chiefs, formerly loyal to the British, decided to join forces with others across the border who were living in exile in the Hookong province of Burma. The disaffected Singpho were encouraged to rebel by the Tipam Rajah, a relative of a former Assam Rajah who lived across the frontier. The main reason for their rebellion was their hope of recovering their ancestral land, seized by the British for tea plantations.[4]

One group of Singpho, led by Set Gaum and armed with firearms, spears and long knives, captured the village of Ningrang. The British sent out a troop of the Assam Light Infantry commanded by Captain Mainwaring, and it reached the village at nightfall. The Singphos were wholly unprepared for the British attack, and thirty were killed and forty wounded. All the minor chiefs were detained, but Set Gaum escaped into the hills. He was captured a few days later.

In the same month a second group of 1,000 Singphos, led by Beesa Gaum and Ningrula Gaum, surrounded the British base at Beesa. The small garrison of sepoys surrendered in the face of such overwhelming numbers, and were killed. A British rescue force arrived too late to save them, but they drove the Singphos back into the jungle. 'We shall not go without the lands being restored to us', a group of captured Singphos told Jenkins, the political agent, 'and you shall have an opportunity of burning down our villages as we have made up our minds to give trouble – you shall have enough of it'. The unrest in India's North-East Frontier territory continued over many more years, as they promised.

On 10 December 1850, in the Naga hills between Assam and Burma, Netholey, a chief of the Nagas, sought to defend his jungle headquarters at Khonomah against a substantial British attack. Khonomah, ten miles west of Kohima, was a powerful Naga fortress in the Angami country. A British unit of 500 soldiers from the Assam Light Infantry, led by Major Foquett and Captain Reid, encircled it from a safe distance before launching a barrage of mortar shells. Netholey's Nagas retaliated by showering spears and rocks on the attackers. An unequal struggle, it lasted for sixteen hours, with more than 200 Nagas killed. The rest escaped into the hills while the British force torched the town.

The Nagas occupied a strategic position between the princely state of Manipur, acquired from Burma in 1826, and the fertile valley of Assam. Here the British, with a military base at Nowgong, had established tea plantations in the 1830s. The first encounter of the Nagas with the British had occurred in 1832, when a large military expedition led by Captains Jenkins and Pemberton sought to open a road between Imphal in Manipur to Nowgong. Naga tribesmen attacked this force all the way along the route to Dimapur and Samaguting, on the Assam frontier.[5]

The authorities in Calcutta had two preoccupations. They were concerned that the tea plantations might come under attack, yet at the same time they needed labourers from Nagaland to work on them. Military expeditions were sent out almost every year in the 1830s and 1840s to enforce British control of the hills and to tax the chiefs.

The destruction of Khonomah came at the end of this long period of inconclusive violence along the frontier, in which the British used ever more coercive forms of warfare. British relations with the Nagas, wrote Colonel Robert Woodthorpe in 1877, stretching over fifty years, 'have been one long sickening story of open insult and defiance; of bold and outrageous and cold-blooded murder on one side, and of long-suffering forbearance, forgiveness, concession, and unlooked-for favour on the other'.[6]

The Nagas chased out a tribute-seeking officer in 1844, but the British exacted retribution with another expedition, sent to burn their villages. When a further expedition, led by Captain John Butler, came in 1845, securing tribute of ivory and spears, the Nagas confronted a new and more permanent threat.[7] The British established a force in the hills, led by a sepoy called Bhogchand, with a mandate to collect tribute and settle inter-tribal disputes. Yet he was almost immediately killed by the tribesmen. The British agent at Nowgong advised Calcutta that if they wished to recover their influence in the Naga hills, they would have to 'systematically burn granaries and crops' to secure 'the surrender of those concerned in Bhogchand's murder'.

'The government of India', a Calcutta official replied judiciously, 'has certainly been always most averse to resort to such extreme measures as burning villages, destroying crops, granaries, and the like; and as respects these Naga tribes in particular, very great forbearance has been shewn'. Yet after Bhogchand's death, the government decided that more severe measures should be taken. The agent was told that 'as far as it may be possible so to arrange, no village should be burnt, nor the crops of any village destroyed, except those which you may yourself point out to be so dealt with'.[8]

When a fresh expedition was sent out in December 1849, led by Captain Vincent, he was given 'plenary powers of granary burning'.[9] Vincent fell ill and had to retreat, but he returned in March 1850 to burn down part of Khonomah and to punish the surrounding villages. Yet, 'after holding his own for some months, the steady hostility of the Nagas became so formidable that he felt compelled to concentrate all his forces at Mozemah itself, and to call for assistance from the plains'.[10] This was the moment in December, discussed above, when Netholey sought to resist the fresh attacks of the Assam Light Infantry sent out from Nowgong.

Although defeated, Netholey's resistance had had its effect. Early in 1851, Captain Butler, now the principal officer at Nowgong, advocated withdrawal from Nagaland. He sought 'the immediate and complete abandonment of the hills, our interference with the internal feuds of the enemy having in his opinion proved a complete failure'. Lord Dalhousie, the governor-general in Calcutta, agreed with him. The position of the troops 'during last season appeared to me far from satisfactory', he wrote. 'I should be very reluctant to continue that state of things in another season. The troops so placed are isolated; they are dependent . . . on the Naga tribes for their food, and for the carriage of supplies of every description.'[11] He also noted that the expeditions cost money that his government could ill afford.

The British decision to abandon the hills caused jubilation among the Nagas. Understanding that they were now going to be left alone, they celebrated by organising twenty-two serious raids into the tea plantations in the Assam valley in a single year.[12] The British may have regretted their decision, but they kept out of the Naga hills for fifteen years. They would return in force in 1866.

CHAPTER 48

Resistance to the British Invasion of Afghanistan

The British launched an invasion of Afghanistan in 1839 – a strategy that ended in disaster two years later, with a humiliating retreat and the destruction of their expeditionary force by Afghan tribesmen. Dost Mohammed Khan, the Amir of Kabul, was the target of the British attack, for it was suggested by faulty intelligence that he was overly favourable to the Russians hovering on the northern frontiers of Afghanistan. The British imagined that their interests in this frontier zone of British India would be advanced through the return to power of Shah Shuja, a former ruler who it was hoped might become a willing puppet. Some visionaries even foresaw the possibility of opening up Central Asia to British trade via the Indus River. Shuja had been overthrown by Dost's family in 1818, after long periods of civil war, and he had subsequently lived quietly in exile in the Punjabi town of Ludhiana. Britain's mistaken and ill-judged analysis led to the disastrous invasion in Shah Shuja's support.

The southern cities of Afghanistan seized by the British in the early months of 1839 were controlled by Dost's extended family. Dost's son Akhbar Khan held Jalalabad, while among his relatives Kohun-dil-Khan was in charge of Kandahar, and the great fortress of Ghazni was controlled by Hyder Khan. All of Dost's clan ruled in close collaboration with the Ghilzai tribesmen in the mountainous parts of their area (and at the end of the twentieth century became the chief supporters of the Taliban government). A spirited and eventually successful resistance by Dost's family and the Ghilzai led to Britain's dramatic defeat.

Dost Mohammed in Kabul was aware of the impending British invasion, and had several months to prepare. The invasion force, the Army of the Indus, was formed in the Punjab from an army of 21,000 men, most of them sepoys. The British had sought the cooperation of Ranjit Singh, ruler of the Punjab, but this was not forthcoming. This meant that they were not able to take the short route to Kabul via the Khyber Pass and Jalalabad. Instead, the army, commanded by General Sir John Keane, a veteran of wars in Egypt and Spain, was obliged to take a more southerly route through Sind. Here it encountered considerable opposition from the local amirs and from Baluchi tribesmen as it advanced through the mountain passes towards Kandahar.

Dost Mohammed, king of Cabual, and his youngest son.
Lithograph by E. Walker after James Rattray, printed in 1848.

News of the arrival of Keane's army in the plains of Kandahar in April led Kohun-dil-Khan, Dost's brother, to withdraw to Helmand, allowing Shah Shuja and the British forces to enter the city unopposed, but to an unenthusiastic welcome. The British moved on towards Ghazni in July, coming under attack from thousands of Ghilzai tribesmen before capturing the fortress. They sustained serious losses, but Hyder Khan, the governor, was captured.

Hearing of the loss of Ghazni, and learning that the British were offering him nothing more than 'an honourable asylum' in India, Dost Mohammed summoned his son Akhbar Khan from Jalalabad. Together they advanced with 13,000 men to confront the British force now advancing on Kabul. Yet the Afghan troops were unnerved by the British victories, and proved reluctant to fight. Dost rode among them 'Koran in hand', to try to retain their allegiance, but they turned against him. He retired north, towards Bamian, and eventually to Bokhara, leaving Akhbar Khan to cover his retreat.

* * *

Kabul was seized and occupied by General Keane's troops in August, but most of the city's population were reluctant to be included within the imperial orbit, and showed their opposition to Shah Shuja's return from the first day. He was greeted by silent crowds as he rode up to the palace. Accompanied by 'British officers in their gayest uniforms' and 'seated upon a white horse, gorgeously clad, and sparkling with jewels', he was surrounded 'by splendidly-dressed servants', yet 'as the glittering procession passed through the streets, there was never a cheer'.[1] They were right to refrain from celebration, for Shah Shuja was soon to levy fresh and extortionate taxes – one of the causes of his eventual overthrow.

To defend Shah Shuja's unpopular regime, the British kept 10,000 soldiers in Kabul as a permanent occupation force. Garrisons were also maintained at Kandahar, Ghazni and Jalalabad, and for a while further north, at Charikar and Bamian. The wives and sisters of British officers were brought up from India to keep house for them, and thousands of camp followers did the same for the sepoys. Their presence was an additional cause of Afghan resentment.

Political control over Shah Shuja was in the hands of Sir William Hay Macnaghten, a senior political adviser from Calcutta, appointed British Resident. Macnaghten and his assistant Sir William Burnes were aware that the British occupation force had few friends or allies, and they spent much time and treasure on a search for cooperative Afghan chiefs. Those who might help were given substantial funds; those who resisted were earmarked for assassination. The Ghilzai chiefs who controlled the territory between Kabul and Kandahar, and south to Jalalabad, were paid £600 a year to keep the roads clear. Money was also found to pay off the Afridis, a tribe that traditionally demanded money with menaces from those seeking to travel through the Khyber Pass, the nearest and quickest route from India to Kabul.

Dost Mohammed and his son refused to accept the British conquest of Kabul, and they returned from exile in Bokhara in July 1840. Dost advanced on Bamian in September with an army of Uzbeks, but he was fought off by a British force. Moving east, he advanced into the region of Kohistan, north of Kabul, where local chiefs supported him; they had turned against Shah Shuja after his demand for fresh taxes. Dost defeated a British troop sent out against him in November.

In spite of this relative success, Dost perceived that further armed resistance would be unwise; he felt that an honourable surrender would save the country much misery. He came of his own accord to Kabul, where Macnaghten greeted him warmly and granted him asylum in India. Had the British backed Dost in the first place, they might have saved themselves considerable trouble.

It fell to Akhbar Khan to revive the resistance campaign the following year, and Ghilzai tribesmen were soon attacking British forces around Kandahar in the south. Major battles took place in the neighbourhood of Khelat-i-Ghilzai in May 1841. Opinion among the British occupiers about the future of the country was divided. Macnaghten in Kabul claimed that 'all is content and tranquillity' and that 'wherever we Europeans go, we are received with respect, attention and welcome'. General Sir William Nott, in charge in Kandahar, had a different view: the strategy of Macnaghten and other political advisers, he warned, had 'bared the throat of every European in this country to the sword and knife of the revengeful Afghan and bloody Belooch'. Nott added that 'unless several regiments be quickly sent, not a man will be left to describe the fate of his comrades'.[2] His premonitions proved correct.

Rebellion became more probable in September 1841 after Macnaghten had come under pressure from London to spend less money. Paying large bribes to Afghan chiefs to win their support, he was told, was too expensive, and he summoned several chiefs to Kabul to inform them of this unwelcome news. The Ghilzai chiefs were the first to react, seizing the mountain passes between Kabul and Jalalabad, and effectively blocking communication with India via the Khyber Pass. An uprising in Kohistan by Akhbar Khan was thought to be imminent.

The Ghilzai faced a brigade led by Colonel Robert Sale that had long been scheduled to leave Kabul for Jalalabad and India. They attacked this force in October as it pushed over the mountains into the Tesin valley on the road to Jalalabad. They remained in control of their fortifications and obliged the British to restore their former financial subsidy before allowing Colonel Sale's troop to travel through their territory. It arrived at Jalalabad on 14 November.

Early in November, the Afghans rebelled in Kabul. Large crowds gathered in the centre on 2 November, surrounding the homes of British officers and their families. Alexander Burnes, the agent responsible for funding the tribesmen, was killed, and several officers were held hostage. Fighting in and around Kabul continued for several weeks, and the British withdrew from their northern camp at Charikar. Eventually, in December, Osman Khan, a senior rebel leader, called a halt. He wrote to Macnaghten pointing out that the final destruction of the British cantonments was now inevitable. The sole desire of the Afghans, he said, was for the British to quietly evacuate the country. They should allow the chiefs to govern the country according to their customs, with a ruler of their own choosing.

Akhbar Khan, who had arrived in the city late in November, outlined to the humiliated Macnaghten the conditions for a British retreat. Macnaghten told Colonel Sale to return with his brigade from Jalalabad to Kabul, but Sale was reluctant to return through the Ghilzai-dominated mountain passes through which he had just travelled, and he refused to move. The British force in Kandahar tried to respond to a similar request, but were defeated by the weather.

Macnaghten, foreseeing no possibility of rescue from outside, accepted Akhbar's invitation to meet to discuss the details of a British withdrawal. Hardly had he dismounted from his horse on 23 December before he was seized by tribesmen. Akhbar had planned to hold him as an additional hostage, believing he was still engaged in secret negotiations with the tribesmen suborned by Burnes, but in the ensuing scrimmage Macnaghten was killed. His severed head was paraded in triumph through the central bazaar.

Akhbar reopened negotiations with General Sir William Elphinstone, an officer sent to take charge in Kabul earlier in the year. The British agreed to withdraw from Kabul and from their remaining garrisons at Kandahar, Ghazni and Jalalabad. They would retreat down the Khyber Pass to Peshawar, and the Afghans agreed to provide the surviving British contingent with a safe-conduct order across the mountains to Jalalabad. They had no choice but to surrender their artillery before leaving.

Since he did not trust the British to fulfil their side of the bargain, Akhbar required further hostages. Four British officers were handed over with their wives and families. The surviving British contingent in Kabul now consisted of 690 British soldiers, 3,800 Indian sepoys and 12,000 camp followers – wives, children and servants. They began the long retreat towards Jalalabad, some ninety miles away, in January 1842. Shah Shuja was left behind, to be assassinated in April.

Akhbar's safe-conduct permit was ignored by the Ghilzai tribesmen along the route, and the British caravan was attacked throughout its journey. Some 3,000 died in the first week, some from the cold, others shot by tribesmen.

Akhbar was supposed to be accompanying the British to guarantee a safe passage, but some time elapsed before he caught up with them. He complained that they had left Kabul prematurely, which was true; he also pointed out that neither he nor his chiefs could control the Ghilzai in the hills, but he offered to place the surviving women and children, and the married officers, under his personal protection. This was agreed, and a fresh group now joined the hostages taken earlier in Kabul. Akhbar was true to his word, and the hostages survived, to be liberated later in the year.

The British were less conscientious. Although Sale had had orders from Elphinstone in Kabul to abandon Jalalabad and retreat with his brigade through the Khyber Pass, and to hand over the fort to an Afghan governor, he refused to move unless ordered to do so by the government. His decision to remain, much debated within the small band of officers at the fort, may have been affected by the fact that his wife, Florentia, was among the hostages.[3] While the hostages survived, the remnants of the retreat from Kabul were almost all dead by mid-January. Dr William Brydon, an army surgeon, was famously one of the very few who reached Jalalabad alive.

Akhbar now advanced on the fort, where Sale was preparing to make a last stand, and early in April his troops were defeated. Akhbar retreated to Kabul, taking the large crowd of British hostages with him.

The British could not allow their humiliation in Kabul to go unchallenged. A relief expedition, called the 'Army of Retribution' was assembled at Peshawar in February 1842, commanded by General Sir George Pollock, who had served in the Gurkha and Burmese wars. The army travelled through the Khyber Pass and arrived in Jalalabad in April, just two weeks after Akhbar's forces had been defeated.

Akhbar came out from Kabul to meet Pollock's army in September, and the two armies clashed at Tesin. Akhbar's forces were defeated, and Pollock finally reached Kabul on 15 September and recovered the ninety-five surviving hostages. Pollock then set about the work of 'retribution'. He destroyed the city's central bazaar, where Burnes's corpse had once been displayed, as well as the towns of Charikar and Istalif.[4] Yet this second seizure of Kabul was only for show. The British could not afford to remain in Afghanistan, and in December 1842 Pollock withdrew his forces from the city and returned to Peshawar. The Afghans were left to run their country on their own. Dost Mohammed returned to power, remaining as ruler until his death in 1863. Akhbar Khan was his chief minister until he died in 1847.

The occupation of Afghanistan had been an almost unparalleled disaster for the British. The policy was not only unjust, but 'so idiotic in conception and so inept in execution', wrote Penderel Moon, that 'the reader may wonder how a nation capable of such blunders should have succeeded for a further century in retaining and enlarging its empire'.[5] The British learned nothing from their mistakes, returning to Afghanistan again and again in succeeding centuries.

CHAPTER 49

The Resistance of the Amirs of Sind Is Reinforced by Their Baluchi Soldiers

The lowland territory of Sind, bordering on the Arabian Sea and made fertile by the waters of the Indus, lay far to the south of the mountains of Afghanistan, where the British had been so humiliated in 1842. Largely Muslim, the country had been ruled since the eighteenth century by the Baluchi Talpurs, an extended family of amirs, or princes, from the western hills of Baluchistan. They ran a competent administration, devoting themselves to an impressive system of canal-building, and internal peace had long prevailed.

The amirs at Hyderabad, in Lower Sind, had been visited in 1827 by Dr James Burnes, an officer adventurer, who wrote enthusiastically about the potential value of the Indus as the high road to Central Asia, and in 1831 they had allowed his brother, Alexander, to pass through their territory to take a gift of horses to Ranjit Singh in the Punjab. The amirs signed a commercial treaty with the British in the 1830s, and allowed access to the Indus by British traders, many of whom brought opium down to Karachi from the fields of Rajputana. The amirs also allowed Colonel Henry Pottinger to set up an office in Hyderabad and call himself the British Resident, but they refused to countenance a British military presence.[1]

When the commercial treaties came to be renewed in 1838, Pottinger requested the right to march soldiers through Sind on the way to Kabul, and to garrison a number of intervening towns. His request went beyond any clause of the existing treaties, and the amirs were loth to agree, but when the British threatened them with the sack of Hyderabad they bent over backwards to be accommodating. They ordered boats, camels and timber to be made available to the British army, and paid large sums to defray the expenses of the troops. While individual amirs perceived that they might secure some benefit from a close if unequal friendship with the British, their Baluchi soldiers took a more nationalistic position. Many opposed the decision of the amirs, and there were frequent attacks on British supply lines during the occupation of Kabul.

Sind in the 1840s was ruled by six senior amirs, each controlling a different area of the country. Mir Rustam Khan, who lived at Khairpur in Upper Sind, was the oldest. A man in his seventies, he was long wary of too close a relationship with the British. Mir Ali Murad, his younger brother, looked more favourably on the new power in the land, and had hopes that the British would support his claim to succeed his father. Four amirs perceived as the most powerful and influential – Mir Nasir Khan, Mir Mahmood Khan, Mir Shahdad Khan and Mir Sobdar Khan – ruled in partnership at Hyderabad. A sixth amir, Sher Mohammed Khan, enjoyed considerable independence from the others, and controlled the south-east of the country from his base at Mirpur.

After the British retreat from Kabul, several amirs felt that the unequal treaties had brought them little benefit. Mir Nasir suggested sending an envoy to London to outline their complaints, while others contacted the Sikh rulers of the Punjab to see whether joint action might be taken against the British. Alarmed by this possibility, Lord Ellenborough, the governor-general in Delhi, decided to deal with the amirs in a new way. For years they had been cajoled into friendship; now he decided to enforce fresh treaties through military threats, entrusting the task to General Charles Napier, lately in charge of the repression of the Chartists in northern Britain. Napier was an ageing newcomer, an officer with no previous service in India.

The relative merits of the rule of the amirs became the subject of bitter argument within the British ruling elite. Some with long experience in India believed that the amirs were useful allies who should be left in control; they spoke out firmly against the policy of military intervention. Major James Outram believed that 'all classes in the country were as happy as those under any government in Asia', and he described how the sense of amity among the Amirs 'was dwelt upon by all who visited these countries with wonder and admiration'.[2]

Late in 1842 the amirs held meetings with Napier, both in Karachi and in Hyderabad, and 'prepared all things requisite for receiving him with honour; they despatched a palanquin ornamented with gold for his conveyance, and dromedaries equipped with gold and silver furniture for the officers who attended him'. Yet it was all to no purpose. They were presented with draft treaties that even the most pro-British among them found difficult to accept. When they rejected them, Napier vented his displeasure, describing them as 'tyrannical, drunken, debauched, cheating, intriguing, and contemptible'. Faced with 'such atrocious scoundrels', he wrote, it would be 'virtuous to roll them over like ninepins'.

The first to be rolled over was the ageing Mir Rustam. Deposed by Napier, he was replaced by Mir Ali Murad, his pliant younger brother, and then, as a warning to the other amirs to refrain from resistance, Napier's forces destroyed the abandoned desert fortress of Imamgarh in Upper Sind.

Some of the amirs might have wished to continue to appease the British general, but matters were taken out of their hands. Their Baluchi soldiers were determined to resist, and 5,000 of them assembled outside Hyderabad. They were convinced that Napier planned to seize the country: 'Let Napier slay us, and after that let him plunder our houses, which shall not be available to the spoiler but over our dead bodies.'

Mir Shahdad Khan, one of the four powerful amirs, was persuaded to join the Baluchis, and in February 1843 they attacked and destroyed the British Residency at Hyderabad. Its defenders made a humiliating escape to boats on the Indus. Napier now had the excuse he had been hoping for; the way was open to attack and destroy the army of the amirs.

Two days later, in a dry river bed outside Hyderabad, 35,000 Baluchi soldiers came under attack by Napier's force and were defeated at the battle of Miani, a decisive encounter that brought Sind into the British Empire. The Baluchi artillery was overwhelmed by British guns, and their soldiers were mown down. The Baluchis retreated, leaving 5,000 corpses behind in the river bed; the British casualties were counted at 256. Napier had put his faith in the Irish soldiers in his army, 'strong of body, high-blooded, fierce, impetuous soldiers', and they had not disappointed him.

After the battle, Napier advanced towards the fort at Hyderabad and, according to the amirs' own account, Mir Nasir Khan rode into Napier's camp of his own free will, and surrendered his sword to the general. Napier returned the sword 'and said some words of encouragement to the effect that in twenty-five days time the Amirs' affairs should be settled to their satisfaction, and that they should retain their country'.

It was not to be, and any hope that the amirs might have entertained that they would be allowed to remain in power was rudely removed a few days later, when they were obliged to surrender their fort. The principal amirs were detained and imprisoned, and the apartments of their women were broken into. The soldiers 'plundered them of all the female ornaments of gold and silver, dresses, etc., that they contained, and tore off the ornaments that the ladies wore on their legs and feet. The unhappy ladies, overwhelmed with shame and terror, fled from the city'. The British needed every jewel they could lay their hands on to pay their soldiers. The personal property and the household effects of the amirs was put up for auction, and Napier himself received £50,000 in prize money. The captured amirs were sent first to Bombay, and then, a year later, to exile in Bengal.

Sher Mohammed Khan was the last surviving amir, a relatively independent ruler based at Mirpur. Escaping after the battle of Miani, he decided to fight on. He was a popular figure, and many Baluchis rallied to his standard. His troops clashed with Napier's in March at Dubba, east of Hyderabad. The battle was a repetition of Miani, although the numbers involved were smaller. Sher Mohammed had 15,000 men, Napier had 5,000. After some stiff fighting, the

Baluchis abandoned the struggle, losing about 2,000 killed and wounded. The British casualties were 270.

Although defeated, Sher Mohammed continued to pose a threat to Napier's force. He moved around the country with an army of several thousand; local people provided food and kept him informed of Napier's movements. The Baluchis were helped by the hot weather, which made active operations difficult for the British; several soldiers died of heat stroke, and Napier himself was incapacitated for a time. Eventually, in June, Sher Mohammed's forces were surprised near the village of Shahdadpur by a British troop that captured three of their guns and won an almost bloodless victory. Sher Mohammed slipped away to the north, to take refuge in Afghanistan.

As governor of the new imperial province of Sind, Napier called, with typical pomposity, for the creation of 'a new Egypt'. It was meant as a tribute to the achievements of Mohammed Ali Pasha, the progressive Ottoman viceroy established by British treaty in 1840 as the hereditary ruler of Egypt. The Baluchis were unimpressed by Napier's promises, and referred to him as *shaitan-ka-bhai* – 'Satan's brother'.

The British conquest of the large Muslim territory of Sind did not go unnoticed elsewhere. James Richardson, the great African traveller who journeyed across the Sahara in 1845, arrived at Ghadamis in Libya and encountered Haji bin Musa Ethani, the aged chief of the most influential local families.[3]

> After a short silence he addressed me: 'Christian! do you know Sindh?'
>
> I replied, 'I know it.'
>
> 'Are not the English there?'
>
> 'Yes', I said.
>
> He then turned . . . abruptly to me, 'Why do the English go there and eat up all the Musulman? Afterwards you will come here.'
>
> I replied, 'The Amirs were foolish and engaged in a conspiracy against the English of India; but the Musulman in Sindh enjoyed the same rights and privileges as the English themselves.'
>
> 'That is what you say", he rejoined, and then continued: 'Why do you go so far from home to take other people's countries from them[?]'
>
> I replied, 'The Turks do the same; they come here in the Desert.'
>
> 'Ah! you wish to be such oppressors as the Turks', he continued very bitterly, and then told me not to talk anymore.

General Napier's treatment of the amirs was 'the most unprincipled and disgraceful that has ever stained the annals of our empire in India', wrote Henry Pottinger, long the champion of the amirs.[4] For several months Napier ruled the country under martial law, reintroducing the practice of flogging prisoners, abandoned by earlier rulers. He also organised a local police force, modelled on the paramilitary Irish constabulary established in the 1820s.

The more recalcitrant Baluchi prisoners were exiled to the new colony at Aden, and several amirs died soon after in captivity: Mir Rustam in Poona in 1844, Mir Nasir in Bengal in 1845, and Mir Sobdar in 1846. Only Sher Mohammed, who had taken refuge in Afghanistan, was permitted to return to Sind, in 1853.[5]

Far from Sind, in Kolhapur, a small princely state south of Bombay, close to the Portuguese territory of Goa, a rebellion broke out in September 1844. There had been 'a spirit of uneasiness' in the region ever since Napier's campaign in Sind, noted the governor of Bombay, the ubiquitous General Sir George Arthur. 'Many Indians' hoped, he suggested, to be able to 'turn out' the British, with the bulk of the army away on a distant frontier across the sea. The 'long unquiet' country of the south Marathas, with its 'petty independent chiefs' and its 'volatile population', was quick to seize its chance.

Kolhapur had remained aloof from the earlier Maratha wars against the British, and its rajah had steadily resisted British encroachments in the 1820s. Things changed in 1843 when, during the minority of the rajah, the British imposed a Brahmin regent, Daji Krishna Pandit, controlled by a political agent sent down from Bombay. The reforms of the land tax introduced by this new regime stirred memories of earlier rebellions, and a widespread revolt was sparked off in 1844.

The first to rebel were the troops in the garrisons of the hill forts surrounding Kolhapur, including Bhudargad, Samangad, Panhala and Vishalgad. At these historic forts, the soldiers rejected British rule and locked themselves behind closed gates.

'The hill chiefs took up arms', according to the near-contemporary account by Cooke Taylor, and Daji Pandit showed every sign of giving in to the rebels. Mr Reeves, the British political agent, was in favour of a firm response, and troops were sent down from Bombay. But they 'bungled the business of fighting, and for several months confusion and alarm prevailed'.[6]

The defenders of the hill forts repulsed the soldiers sent to besiege them, and the revolt soon spread to Kolhapur itself. Babaji Ahirekar emerged as the rebel leader, and his militia seized Daji Pandit and the British regent, and established their own independent government. Now seriously alarmed, the British sent out Colonel James Outram from Bombay. Outram recommended a peaceful strategy, suggesting that rebels who surrendered should be granted a free pardon, but this was vetoed by General Arthur, who favoured tougher measures.[7] The fort at Samangad was recaptured in October by General Delamotte.

The rebels at Kohlapur negotiated with Outram, and Daji Pandit was released, but Babaji Ahirekar escaped with 500 militiamen to the fort at Bhudargad. Delamotte surrounded the fort in November, but Babaji Ahirekar escaped to Panhala. Here the rebels seized Colonel Ovans as a hostage. Ovans, the British Resident at Satara, had been on a tour of the area. Outram secured his release, and the fort came under attack from Delamotte's troop in December. Babaji Ahirekar was killed, and many rebels were captured.

The country then 'swarmed with British troops', but resistance continued in the district of Concan, between the mountains and the sea. Here the rebels 'kept the Bombay troops busy by guerrilla warfare and bush-fighting'.[8] Several rebel chiefs escaped across the frontier into Goa, but the Portuguese authorities, fearing a British invasion, returned them to India. General Arthur commented peevishly that it was 'impossible to tolerate this petty state receiving marauders and brigands who fly from justice'. The cost of crushing the rebellion was charged to the local administration of Kolhapur, and was paid to the Bombay government in instalments.

CHAPTER 50

The Long Struggle of the Sikhs in the Punjab

In the autumn of 1845, the British in India reinforced their small cantonments at Ferozepur and Ludhiana, on the south side of the Sutlej River – on the frontier of the Punjab fifty miles from Lahore. They anticipated a possible attack by the Sikh army of the Punjab, known as the Khalsa. Yet when the Khalsa observed the increase of foreign troops along their frontier, the boats assembled along the Sutlej, and the preparations made to create a bridge across, they foresaw a British attack. The yeomen and peasants who formed the bulk of the Khalsa, rather more patriotic than their leaders, determined to defend the Punjab.[1]

Ranjit Singh, the great Maharajah of the Punjab since the beginning of the nineteenth century, had long maintained a policy of both friendship and rivalry with the British, but he had died in 1839. His success in maintaining his independent and expansionist state had irritated successive governors of British India, yet all had recognised the Punjab's value as a buffer against Afghanistan and the tribesmen in the mountains along the Afghan border. Now, in the mid-1840s, the British were reconsidering their policy, for after Ranjit's death the Punjab had entered a long period of instability. An extensive succession struggle was punctured by several assassinations – and the deaths of many wives and concubines on the resulting funeral pyres.

This unstable period saw the emergence of the Sikh army, the Khalsa, as the principal player in an increasingly troubled state. In origin, the word 'Khalsa' referred to the five 'pure' men at the heart of the Sikh religion, but Ranjit's army, in recognition of its service to the Punjabi state, had claimed the privilege of representing the Khalsa and acquired the title for itself. An inherently democratic institution, controlled by its rank-and-file *punchayats* (committees of regimental delegates), the Khalsa was the country's most influential political force. Attempts to create an alternative to Khalsa rule, or a failure to pay its soldiers' wages, was always met with steely opposition.

In 1843 – with the general recognition that Ranjit's youngest son, Dalip Singh, aged four, was the new Maharajah – a marginally more stable government emerged. The Maharani Jindan Kaur, the mother of Dalip and a woman who benefitted from her status as the widow and queen of Ranjit Singh, emerged as the power behind the throne. She was an impressive woman, said by one British officer to have 'more wit and daring than any man of her nation'.[2]

Rani Jindan and her brother Jawahir Singh were hostile to British ambitions. Her character was subsequently blackened by the British, who like to emphasise the incidence of wife-burning and daughter-infanticide in the Punjab. Yet women were by no means uniquely oppressed in the era of Sikh rule. Lahore had sixteen elementary schools for girls in the 1840s. Upper-class women, or those who slept their way into the elite, played politics as competently as men, and Rani Jindan herself had powerful survival skills. On Ranjit's death, she had avoided performing suttee – refusing to cast herself on his funeral pyre – by attaching herself to Lal Singh Morareea, an important noble at Ranjit's court. 'She was a woman of great capacity and strong will', wrote Lady Lena Login, as well as being 'a skilful intriguer'.[3]

The political instability in Lahore continued, and in November 1844 Hira Singh, the Punjabi *wazir*, or chief minister, was murdered after he had failed to raise the Khalsa's wages. Rani Jindan was the beneficiary of his death, not just as the mother of Dalip but also because her brother Jawahir Singh became the new *wazir*. When she increased the soldiers' pay to double that paid to the Bengali sepoys working for the British, the decision alarmed the British, since a string of mutinies soon affected the sepoy regiments serving in Sind.

Rani Jindan's populist move had only a short-lived impact, for Jawahir Singh was himself murdered in September 1845. He had not been unwilling to pay the wage increase; he had simply run out of money. He had had plans for the Khalsa to recoup their wages by waging war against the British forces across the Sutlej, and had advocated an immediate attack. The decision was not popular, and fresh disputes within the Khalsa had led to his murder. Some senior Sikhs, including Rani Jindan and her advisers, noting the British disaster in Afghanistan, thought the time was ripe to take a more hostile position towards the British. Others, looking to the future, hoped that a British defeat of the Khalsa would enable them to enhance their status in a British-controlled Punjab.

Militarily, the Sikhs and the British were evenly matched, but politically the Sikhs were at a disadvantage. Divided among themselves, with their leaders often in secret contact with the British, a succession of Sikh rulers had been unable to decide whether to appease or confront the imperial power. For their part, the British had been participant-observers in the unfolding political drama in Lahore, bribing some factions and making honeyed promises to others. The directors of the East India Company received a letter from the governor-general, Colonel Henry Hardinge, in September 1845, warning that the 'most influential' figures in Lahore had felt their personal interests endangered 'by the democratic revolution so successfully accomplished by the Sikh army'. Even the Rani Jindan, he noted, had seen her brother Jawahir 'shot down before her own eyes, by the sentence of this armed Inquisition'. The governor rightly foresaw trouble ahead.

* * *

In December 1845, some 10,000 Sikh soldiers moved south across the Sutlej River to attack the British at their military bases at Ferozepur and Ludhiana. They may even have had larger ambitions; a rumour reached Colonel Harry Smith, based at Ludhiana, that they hoped to sweep on to Delhi, to place Rani Jindan and Dalip Singh on the imperial throne. Smith, the curse of the Xhosa in South Africa in the 1830s, had come to fight in another part of the Empire. The more immediate aim of the Khalsa was to keep the British from crossing the Sutlej, then the agreed eastern boundary of the Punjab. The Sikh forces assembled at the village of Mudki, in an area of dense jungle, and they spent the first day of battle trying to prevent the British from moving through this natural barrier. They were led by Tej Singh, the military commander, and by Lal Singh, the *wazir* of the Punjab. The British forces were commanded by Colonel Sir Hugh Gough, the commander-in-chief, recently in China.

The Sikhs picked off the British with 'demoralising accuracy', while British gunners and horses received a blast of grapeshot and musket fire.[4] The sepoys, traditionally frightened of the Sikhs, began to hang back. But the Sikhs were soon exhausted, and the British chalked up the battle as a victory. Yet their losses were severe: half the casualties were European, and many were senior officers. The Sikhs, too, had serious losses.

A second battle took place three days later, at Ferozeshah. Tej Singh launched an artillery attack on the British infantry, who were weary and short of ammunition. Hardinge, governor of India, was so uncertain of victory that he gave orders for the sword that commemorated his participation in the campaigns against Napoleon, once received from the hands of the Duke of Wellington, to be sent into safe-keeping.[5] The Sikhs were again on the verge of success, but their commander's loyalty was paper-thin, and Tej Singh withdrew his forces to fight another day. Many men had been lost, and the Khalsa forces drew back across the Sutlej at Sobraon. Colonel Gough's forces had more than 2,000 casualties, of whom a hundred were officers.

The Sikhs had been worsted by the British at Mudki and Ferozeshah, but the two armies were evenly matched, and battle was joined again in January 1846. The Sikh army, led this time by Sham Singh Attariwala and Ranjur Singh Majithia, recrossed the Sutlej and advanced towards the British base at Ludhiana. Sham Singh Attariwala was a veteran of Ranjit Singh's armies, the son of Nihal Singh, one of Ranjit's generals; his daughter was married to Ranjit's grandson, Nau Nihal Singh. It was said of him that he squeezed 'blood out of the whites as one squeezes juice out of a lemon'; his memory is revered to this day.

At the village of Aliwal, the Sikhs 'opened a heavy fire of cannon' on a British troop led by Colonel Harry Smith. The Sikhs initially had the upper hand, but the British ended the day triumphant.[6] British losses were severe, about 2,400 in all, but half the 20,000 men who had manned the Sikh entrenchments were killed or drowned, and the sixty-seven large guns they had brought across the Sutlej were captured. This was a crushing defeat for the Khalsa, who again retreated across the Sutlej.

The Sikhs now faced British forces at a final battle at Sobraon. Faced with divided counsels at home, and the prospect of a future dominated by the invader, Sham Singh Attariwala vowed not to give himself up alive. Dressed in white and mounted on a white mare, he continuously sought to rally the Khalsa, until he was killed in a last stand, along with fifty others.[7] His wife knew that he would die according to his vow and, without waiting for his body to be brought in, she burned herself to death.

At Sobraon the losses were huge on both sides, the Sikhs losing up to 10,000 men. British casualties were also severe, with a total of 6,000 at Mudki, Ferozeshah, Aliwal and Sobraon, of which at least 3,400 were European soldiers – nearly half their number. The loss of officers was especially severe.[8] The principal cause of the losses, outlined by Colonel Gough in a letter to his son, was the sepoy reluctance to fight: they had not recovered from the Afghan disaster, they considered the Sikhs to be invincible, and they shared the feeling throughout India that the British should not be allowed to overthrow the last independent government.

After the battle, the Sikhs presented no further opposition to the British advance on Lahore. Golab Singh, a wealthy Sikh noble favourable to the British, came out to negotiate a peace, and signed the Treaty of Lahore on 9 March. Hardinge hoped to annex the Punjab outright, but he knew that the Khalsa was still a powerful force. The British seized the rich territory of Jullundur Doab instead, and obliged the Punjabis to pay a large indemnity. The Punjabis also agreed to reduce the size of the Khalsa, and to give up their heavy guns. Golab Singh was rewarded with the immense territory of Kashmir.

The *wazir* Lal Singh and other Sikh nobles requested the British to keep a force at Lahore to protect the Maharajah Dalip. Presents were exchanged, and British guns fired a salute to the maharajah, now aged seven. An independent Punjab, severely truncated, was allowed briefly to survive; Lal Singh remained the *wazir*, and Rani Jindan continued to act as regent for Dalip; but effective power lay with Colonel Henry Lawrence, appointed as the British Resident in Lahore. The new arrangement did not last long. Lal Singh, who had opposed the cession of Kashmir to Golab Singh, was accused by the British of 'duplicity' and put on trial. Exiled to Dehra Dun, he died in 1867.

A fresh treaty was signed at Bhairowal in December 1846. This time, the Punjab was placed under the complete control of the British Resident, with the pro-British Tej Singh as the nominal *wazir*. A British force would remain at

Lahore until 1854, when Dalip Singh would be sixteen. Hardinge outlined the new rules. 'The chief of the state', he wrote,

> can neither make war nor peace nor exchange nor sell an acre of territory, nor admit an European officer, nor refuse us thoroughfare through his territories, nor, in fact, perform any act (except its own internal administration) without our permission. In fact, the native Prince is in fetters, and under our protection, and must do our bidding.

The treaty deprived Rani Jindan of all formal power, and pensioned her off with an annuity. Yet she was not a woman to be thus humiliated, and within months she began organising resistance to this British experiment in indirect rule.

The Rani Jindan's opposition to the British, evoking echoes within the court at Lahore, reflected the wider discontent of the population at the British occupation of the Punjab. The insolence of individual Englishmen did not endear them to the people, and the religious sentiments of the non-Muslim population were outraged by the slaughter of cattle. Sikhs resented the British entering their gurdwaras with their shoes on. Abuse, mistreatment and the molesting of women by English soldiers were common grievances.[9]

The Rani Jindan brought the infighting within the Lahore court into the open in August 1847, by organising the public humiliation of the *wazir* Tej Singh. At a ceremony held ostensibly to honour the child maharajah, Dalip Singh, well coached by his mother, refused to mark the forehead of the *wazir* with the saffron sign of nobility. 'His Highness shrank back into his velvet chair', wrote the irritated Lawrence, 'with a determination foreign both to his age [nine] and gentle disposition.'

Hardinge had already noted 'the baneful influence' that the Rani had on the maharajah, accusing her of 'breeding him up systematically to thwart the government and the English connection'. He decided to remove her from the city. Accused of participation in a plot to poison both Tej Singh and Lawrence, she was exiled to Sheikhupura, twenty miles outside Lahore – 'dragged out by the hair', according to her own account. 'Surely royalty was never treated the way you are treating us! Instead of being secretly king of the country, why don't you declare yourself so? You talk about friendship and then put us in prison. You establish traitors in Lahore, and then at their bidding you are going to kill the whole of the Punjab.'

After a Sikh mutiny in May 1848, led by General Kahan Singh, the Rani was banished from the Punjab altogether. She was sent under guard to Benares, while the general was arrested and hanged. Exiled later to the Chunar fortress, she escaped to Nepal in April 1849. She travelled to England in 1861, where she died in 1863. Yet her harsh treatment continued to serve as an inspiration to others to resist.

Another Sikh garrison mutinied in 1848 at the fortress of Multan, south of Lahore, in support of Diwan Mulraj – the former Muslim governor of the city, who pledged to wage a jihad against the British. The mutiny, remembered by imperial historians as 'the second Sikh war', sparked off a resistance war that mobilised the population of the Punjab over the following year.

Mulraj, an administrator with a reputation for justice and honesty, had become a focus of opposition in the Punjab, attracting those suffering under the new British regime.[10] Those hostile to British rule included the extended family of Ranjit Singh, as well as sacked officials and thousands of Khalsa soldiers discharged without pay.

Mulraj's rebellion prospered, and he was soon joined by Bhai Maharaj Singh, a religious leader with the support of both peasants and nobles. Bhai Maharaj had been travelling around the country in the course of 1847, speaking out against the British occupation and urging people to rise up and expel the *feringhis* (foreigners). He joined Mulraj with some 5,000 soldiers raised near Lahore, and although the British soon defeated his force, driving it into the Chenab River, the guru himself was able to travel on to Multan.

Mulraj's rebels were besieged by a large Sikh force sent out by the British and commanded by Sher Singh Attariwala, a Sikh collaborator. But in August Sher Singh defected to the rebels and forced the British to abandon the siege. Later the Sikh victor at Chilianwala in 1849, Sher Singh was a member of the court circle at Lahore associated with the Rani Jindan: his father, Chattar Singh, was an adviser of the young maharajah, while his sister was scheduled to be Dalip Singh's bride.

Abandoning Multan, Sher Singh established himself at Gujrat, on the Chenab River far to the north of Lahore, and called on the people of the Punjab to expel the *feringhis*:

> It is well known to all the inhabitants of the Punjab, to all the Sikhs, and those who have cherished the Khalsa, and, in fact, the world at large, with what oppression, tyranny and violence the *feringhis* have treated the widow of the great Maharajah Ranjit Singh, and what cruelty they have shown towards the people of the country.[11]

The Sikh rebels had little time to organise, and later in the year they were faced by two British armies – one sent out to capture Mulraj's redoubt at Multan, the other advancing on Sher Singh's headquarters at Gujrat. General Gough moved towards Ferozepur in early November, with a force of nearly 20,000 men and sixty guns. Mulraj held out at Multan until January 1849, a week after Chilianwala, when his fortress fell finally to a British attack. Mulraj himself was put on trial in Lahore and sentenced to death. 'I cannot hang him', Dalhousie wrote, 'but I will do what he will think a thousand times worse: I will send him across the sea.'[12] Mulraj fell ill while waiting for a boat at Calcutta and was taken to Benares. He died there in August 1851, aged thirty-six.

At the centre of the lush lawns stretching down from London's Royal Hospital to the Thames at Chelsea Bridge stands a tall stone obelisk. The carved tablet below records its dedication 'to the memory of 255 officers, non-commissioned officers and privates of the XXIV Regiment who fell at Chilianwala, 13 January 1849'.

British forces in the Punjab were defeated that day near the village of Chilianwala by a large Sikh army under the command of Sher Singh Attariwala; the next morning the Sikhs fired a twenty-one-gun salute to celebrate their success. The Sikh victory appeared so decisive that Lord Dalhousie, the governor-general, demanded the recall of General Gough, the commander-in-chief.

The British also claimed victory, but no one was deceived. The battle was perceived as a disaster in England, creating a tremendous outcry. 'The impression made on the public mind', wrote Sir John Hobhouse, a radical MP and the chairman of the East India Company, was 'stronger than that caused by the Kabul massacre' of 1842. The poet and novelist George Meredith composed several suitably morose stanzas:

> Chillianwallah, Chillianwallah!
>   'Tis a wild and dreary plain,
> Strewn with plots of thickest jungle,
>   Matted with the gory stain.
> There the murder-mouthed artillery,
>   In the deadly ambuscade,
> Wrought the thunder of its treachery
>   On the skeleton brigade.

'In public, of course', Dalhousie wrote to the Duke of Wellington, he made the best of things.

> I treat it as a great victory. But writing to you confidentially I do not hesitate to say that I consider my position grave. I have put into the field in the Punjab a force fit to match all India. In the hands of the commander-in-chief, I do not now consider that force safe, or free from the risk of disaster. There is not a man in that army, from his generals of division to the sepoys, who does not proclaim the same thing, and write it to his friends. They do not feel themselves safe in his hands.[13]

The chief British concern was military: a cavalry regiment had flinched under fire. General Gough had planned an attack at Chilianwala for the following day, but, irritated by the Sikh resistance, he launched his men prematurely into the thick brushwood jungle where the Sikh artillery were entrenched. The British units lost touch with one another and suffered large casualties. A troop of cavalry, entangled in the scrub, was put to flight and charged backwards through its own artillery, enabling the Sikhs to capture four British guns.[14]

By evening, the British were obliged to retreat, having lost nearly 3,000 officers and men. They claimed victory because the Sikhs, too, had retired, abandoning a dozen of their heavy guns. Yet the principal loser was General Gough, veteran of many imperial wars. He was replaced as commander in India by General Napier, organiser of the wars in Sind, although the change-over did not take place until the Sikhs were finally crushed.

A month after Chilianwala, on 21 February, the Sikhs grappled with General Gough's army in a final, decisive battle not far from Gujrat. Their guns were soon silenced and their positions subjected to a tremendous cannonade. Gough's infantry and cavalry advanced, and the Sikhs, badly battered, retreated in some disorder. They abandoned their camp equipment, much ammunition, and most of their guns. The battle at Gujrat was the final Sikh defeat. Three weeks later, the entire Sikh army laid down its arms, and one Sikh warrior cried out: *Ay Ranjit Singh mar gaya* – 'Today Ranjit Singh is indeed dead'.

In March the advisers to the Maharajah Dalip (including Tej Singh) signed a fresh treaty at Lahore making permanent the British annexation of the Punjab. Dalhousie announced a new era: 'The kingdom of the Punjab is at an end, and . . . all the territories of the Maharajah Dhulip Singh are now, and henceforth, a portion of the British Empire in India.' The properties of the Sikh leaders were confiscated, the population was disarmed, and capital punishment was introduced for robbery. More than a hundred dacoits were hanged during the first year of British rule.

The Maharajah was obliged to resign 'for himself, his heirs and successors, all right, title, and claim to the sovereignty of the Punjab', and 'all property of the state' was to be confiscated by the East India Company to pay for the cost of the war.

Dulip Singh, the maharajah, with his mother Rani Jindan, was handed over to the care of Dr John Login, a former medical officer in the Bengal Army, who was also left in charge of the royal treasury at Lahore – 'a profusion of gold and silver, religious relics, jewels of immense size, golden thrones, cashmere shawls, magnificent armour and weapons, embroidered tents, bejewelled saddles'. Among the trophies seized by the British was the Koh-i-noor diamond, once given to Ranjit Singh by Shah Shuja-ul-mulk of Afghanistan.[15]

The Sikh humiliation at Gujrat was not the end of their story. The struggle for freedom continued. Bhai Maharaj Singh, the religious leader who had made common cause with Mulraj at Multan in 1848, went from village to village to try to persuade the peasants not to give in to the foreigner.[16] The British promised handsome rewards for his capture, and eventually, in December 1849, he was detained. When brought to Jullundur prison, the guards bowed before him, and people from neighbouring villages – Hindus, Muslims and Sikhs – came to worship at the walls within which he was imprisoned. 'The Guru is no ordinary man', wrote Mr Vansittart, who had arrested him. 'He is to the natives what Jesus is to the most zealous of Christians.' Unwilling to risk a public trial in India, the British deported him to Singapore, where, kept for three years in a solitary cell, he died in July 1856.

Chattar Singh and Sher Singh Attariwala were initially treated as prisoners of war, but once the British were firmly in control, they were released on parole to their home village of Attari. They kept alive the hope of rebellion, and the British were eventually obliged to send them into exile. Sher Singh subsequently expressed a desire to join the detachment of Sikh troops sent to invade Burma in 1852, but Dalhousie refused permission, perceiving him correctly as 'a faithless friend' to the British government.

After nearly a hundred years since the early resistance of Siraj-ud-Daula in Bengal in 1756, the British had finally rolled up the entire map of India as far as the Indus River. 'That which Alexander attempted', General Gough announced to his soldiers with a classical flourish, 'the British army have accomplished.' Yet within ten years, as Indian resentment turned to revolt and mutiny, the British victory turned to ashes.

CHAPTER 51

Aborigine Resistance in Victoria and Queensland

In the 1840s, as white settlers opened up new tracts of land in the future Australian territories of both Queensland and Victoria, Aborigines organised themselves to resist. In 1843, Yagan, an Aborigine in Victoria, told George Moore, the state's advocate-general, what was on his mind: 'Why do you white people come in ships to our country and shoot down poor black fellows who do not understand you? You listen to me! The wild black fellows do not understand your laws.'[1] In his land, Yagan continued, 'every living animal that roams the country, and every edible root that grows in the ground are common property. A black man claims nothing as his own but his cloak, his weapons, and his name . . . He does not understand that animals or plants can belong to one person more than to another.' Sometimes, Yagan explained, 'a party of natives come down from the hills tired and hungry, and fall in with strange animals you call sheep. Of course, away flies the spear and presently they have a feast. Then you white man come and shoot the poor black fellows!' Yagan finished with a warning for the lawyer: '[F]or every black man you white fellows shoot, I will kill a white man! . . . I will take life for life.'[2] The Aborigine war against the settlers was already well under way.

In 1840, a group of Aborigines in the territory about to be called Queensland attacked a party of government surveyors measuring out land for new settlement. Aborigine territory in the northern part of New South Wales had long been under threat, while Moreton Bay (soon to become Brisbane, Queensland's capital) had earlier been recognised as land set aside for Aborigines. General Sir George Gipps, the military governor, now wanted it thrown open to white settlement. He reckoned that if labour were obtained from the local colony of transported convicts, the economic prospects for the region looked good. In June 1840, he ordered a land survey to be made. G. C. Stapylton and several settlers – as well as William Tuck, a convict – were employed on the survey team.

Recognising that the surveyors' arrival was the first step that would lead to the seizure of their land, the Aborigines planned to stop them. A group including two men called Merridio and Neugavil attacked the surveying party, and Stapylton and Tuck were killed. The Aborigine attack was so successful that the governor suspended the survey.[3]

The British setback was only temporary, and retribution came the following year. Merridio and Neugavil were captured and taken to Sydney for trial, but no evidence was provided to indicate that they had been directly involved in the attack. They were certainly not the only Aborigines present, and they may have been wholly innocent. Tried for Tuck's murder, they were found guilty in May 1841 and hanged at Moreton Bay – an event recorded as Brisbane's first execution. It was not the last, nor did it halt the Aborigine resistance.

A small Aborigine resistance group in the state of Victoria attacked white settlers in October 1841, killing two sealers near Westernport. A newspaper report recorded that women rebels were 'as well skilled in the use of firearms as the males'.[4] The group's leaders were Timninaparewa, known as Jack Napoleon, and Jemmy Smallboy, known as Bob. Timninaparewa came originally from Tasmania, and was once a protégé of George Robinson, the missionary who had rounded up the Aborigines in the early 1830s and confined them on Flinders Island.[5] He had been brought to the Australian mainland in 1837 to assist in Robinson's campaign to 'civilise' the Aborigines of Victoria. The British authorities had hoped that the surviving Tasmanian Aborigines, suitably 'tamed', might somehow induce those on the mainland to be more friendly towards the white invader. A difficult task.

Timninaparewa had been brought over with four others, including Truganini, a woman sometimes called Lalla Rookh. His small band of two women and three men had no intention of helping the settler cause, and he gave vivid details of his Tasmanian experiences to the Aborigines in the area around Port Phillip (later to be called Melbourne, the capital of Victoria). He told them, according to a contemporary account, of 'what they had suffered at the hands of the white man, how many of their tribe had been slain, how they had been hunted down in Tasmania'. Now, he said, 'was the time for revenge.'

So instead of 'civilising' the local Aborigines, Timninaparewa enlisted their support for an armed resistance campaign against the embryonic white settlements of Victoria. A report on Timninaparewa's group written by Charles La Trobe could not explain 'why they left Mr Robinson's service and much less . . . their suddenly betaking themselves to the Bush'. Yet in the course of about six weeks, 'they committed two murders, fired at and wounded four men, and robbed seven [sheep] stations with arms in their hands'.

Their resistance was short-lived; they were captured in November while asleep. Timninaparewa and Jemmy Smallboy were tried and executed in January 1842, while Lalla Rookh and the two other women were sent back to Tasmania.

White settlers in Australia were soon experimenting with new ways of destroying the native population. A settler expedition exploring to the north of Brisbane in 1842 found a white man living with the Aborigines. He told them the story of a white shepherd killed by Aborigines at a sheep station at Kilcoy Creek. The white farmhands had decided to retaliate, giving flour to the Aborigines with which strychnine had been mixed. Some fifty or sixty of them were killed.[6] Extermination of the Aborigines became a commonplace on the expanding frontier for many years to come. Strychnine, a component of sheep-dip, was readily available, and became a favoured murder weapon.[7]

CHAPTER 52

Maori Resistance in New Zealand

In June 1840, the first stirrings of Maori resistance to British settlement on the North Island of New Zealand were crushed by military force. The Maoris – perhaps 100,000 people in the 1830s – had never welcomed outsiders very warmly. 'The first Maori reaction to contact with Europeans', writes one historian, 'was, unambiguously enough, to kill and eat them.'[1] Abel Tasman, a Dutch explorer who visited the coast in 1642, had his boats attacked and four men killed. By the early nineteenth century the Maoris had grown accustomed to the comings and goings of European traders. Sepoys from India had chopped down trees to repair their ships in 1795. British missionaries from New South Wales had settled at Bay of Islands on North Island in 1814. A tiny British settlement established there, at Kororareka, depended entirely on the good will of the local Maoris for its survival, and in 1831 a British 'Resident' had been appointed to watch over Maori interests.

Trading ships came frequently, both from Australia and from the Americas, and the Maoris bought muskets from them in the 1820s. Happy to trade, the Maoris were fiercely resistant to efforts made to patronise or subdue them. Numerous beach massacres occurred, as well as incidents of cannibalism. Travellers told of the Maori custom of head 'smoking'.[2] In 1831, General Ralph Darling, British governor of New South Wales, forbade the introduction into his territory of smoked Maori heads, a favourite trophy among tourists at the time.

An early incident gave an indication of what was to come. In April 1834, the trading barque *Harriet*, sailing from Sydney, was wrecked off Cape Egmont, north of Wellington, on the North Island. A Maori group captured twenty-four survivors and killed twelve of them. For an indigenous people on the brink of being conquered and colonised, this was a wise precaution. The *Harriet*'s captain, John Guard, was a former convict, transported to Australia, with outspoken views about Aborigines. How would he civilise the Maoris, he asked rhetorically. 'Shoot them to be sure! A musket ball for every New Zealander is the only way of civilising their country.' The Maoris on shore released the captain, to make the return voyage to Sydney to find the wherewithal for a ransom, but they kept his wife Betty and their two children as hostages.[3]

Returning to Sydney after the wreck of his ship, Captain Guard persuaded the authorities there to send a British warship to rescue his wife and family. The Maoris were faced with a small punitive expedition, led by Captain Lambert of HMS *Alligator*, which arrived off their coast in September. Soon their cliff-top fort of Waimati, on the south side of the Kapuni River, was under shell-fire. A small party of soldiers and sailors landed a week later, and, although flying a flag of truce, 'the troops got out of hand'. The Maoris were fired on, and the British seized Jack Guard, one of the captain's two children. His wife and the other child were subsequently delivered up safely.

The British 'Resident' reported later that the rescue was only effected 'after a most severe punishment, inflicted on the said tribes, by burning their *pa*'s [fortified villages], and killing and wounding many of them'. Two Maori forts, evacuated after the initial shelling, were destroyed. The attack by the crew of HMS *Alligator* marked the first occasion since the voyages of Captain Cook in the eighteenth century when Maoris had come into serious conflict with British troops. It was not the last.

Six years later, in January 1840, Captain William Hobson, a British trader already familiar with the coastline, landed at Kororareka. He had the authority of the British government to annex the territory to the Empire. A group of Maori chiefs were assembled to meet Hobson at Waitangi, on the far side of the Bay of Islands. They gave their tentative support, on 6 February 1840, to the terms of an agreement that became known as the 'Treaty of Waitangi'.

The chiefs obtained a guarantee that they would remain in possession of their forests and lands, in exchange for surrendering their sovereign rights over the territory to Queen Victoria. Should they wish to sell their lands, it was further agreed, the Crown alone would have the right to buy them.

This unequal treaty, foisted on the Maoris by Captain Hobson, was contested at the time and has been ever since, for the signature or mark of a particular chief was no guarantee that the Maoris as a whole would accept this British diktat. The first large group of British settlers arrived later that year, and in May 1841 New Zealand was formally declared to be a British colony. By 1843, some 6,000 settlers were established on the island. Yet armed resistance by the Maoris took place at the start, and continued in a series of bitter colonial wars for another thirty years.

On 23 June 1843, those Maoris living close to the newly established British settlement of Cloudy Bay, in the north of the South Island, prepared for an attack by a group of armed white settlers. Cloudy Bay, in the fertile plains of the Wairau valley, was the headquarters of a party of land surveyors employed by the New Zealand Company to map the lineaments of new farms.

Maoris in the valley had already expressed their opposition to white settlement, but the British authorities needed land for the influx of settlers they were enticing to the area. Surveyors had arrived in May to measure up the valley floor. They were guarded by a troop led by Captain Arthur Wakefield, the brother of Edward Gibbon Wakefield, one of the founders of the Company. Soon, as

Te Rangihaeata, chief of Ngati Toa. Watercolour by Captain Richard Oliver. .

the Australian settlers had discovered when surveying in the Brisbane area, the surveyors ran into considerable local resistance.

Te Here Rangihaeata was the local Maori chief in the valley. In his view, the Company had no land rights in his territory, and he took immediate steps to halt the survey. Maoris blocked the tracks across the valley, and destroyed the houses of the surveyors at Cloudy Bay, as well as those of some premature settlers.[4]

A magistrate at the settlers' town of Nelson issued a warrant for Te Rangihaeata's arrest, and the Maoris were confronted in June by Wakefield's troop. Maoris and settlers exchanged fire, and Te Rongo, Te Rangihaeata's wife, was killed. Many of the Maoris were concealed in the bush, and their accurate firing unnerved the settlers' untrained militia troop.

Wakefield surrendered, and called on his men to do likewise, although some stationed on a hilltop continued to fire over the heads of those who were giving themselves up. Enraged by the death of his wife, and further angered by the militia's continued firing after the formal surrender, Te Rangihaeata seized

Captain Wakefield and tomahawked him with his own hand, as *utu*, or revenge. More than twenty members of the settler troop were killed.

Faced with an ill-organised posse of armed settlers, the forces of the Maoris in the South Island had proved superior, although in the popular mythology of white New Zealanders the settlers' defeat became remembered as 'the Wairau massacre', since Wakefield and several settlers had been killed after their formal surrender.

The two sides learned important lessons. Te Rangihaeata recognised the seriousness of the settler threat, while the settlers realised how weak and disorganised they were in the face of this strong Maori resistance. Many had arrived in New Zealand without understanding that they would face strong local opposition to their settlement schemes, or that one day they would be obliged to summon British soldiers to their assistance.

Te Rangihaeata saw the need to secure the unity of the Maori tribes, and he travelled across to the North Island to rouse other tribes to the resistance struggle. He warned them to understand 'that tyranny and injustice is all you can expect from the *Pakeha* (white settlers)', and called on them to sweep the settlers 'from the land which they have sought to bedew with our blood'. He reappeared in 1846, to take part in the land struggle in the Hutt valley, north of Wellington.

Maori chiefs in the Bay of Islands had benefitted over the years from the visits of foreign ships to their anchorages. Traders and whalers from the United States and France, as well as Britain, often stopped for food and water at this, the northernmost point of New Zealand's North Island; and they paid customs duties or tax to the Maoris for the services they received onshore. As white settlers arrived from Britain in the 1840s to establish themselves on Maori land, this beneficial arrangement came to a halt. Customs dues and tolls were now collected by a British customs officer rather than by Maori chiefs. These had good and immediate cause to feel aggrieved by the presence of the settlers, and in 1845 they fought back, securing the first in a string of military victories familiar to New Zealand historians as the 'Northern War'.[5]

On 10 January 1845, Hone Heke, a thirty-five-year-old Maori chief, made a symbolic attack on the first white settlement established in the Bay of Islands. A flagpole had been erected by settlers at the top of Maiki Hill at Kororareka, and Hone Heke ordered his men to chop it down – an action designed to alarm the settlers. Born into the Ngapuhi tribe, Hone Heke had participated in the intertribal wars in the years when the British had first traded along the shores of New Zealand; he lived in the 1830s at Paihia and came under the influence of the Reverend Henry Williams, a British missionary. He had acquired a considerable knowledge of the wider world, and knew of the fate of the aboriginal peoples in other areas of European colonisation.[6]

The settlement at Kororareka in the Bay of Islands, New Zealand, sketched by Captain George Clayton, 10 March 1845, on the morning before it was attacked and destroyed by Hone Heke and Kawiti. HMS *Hazard* is on the left.

The flagpole had been removed on an earlier occasion in the previous July, but Captain Robert Fitzroy, the British governor, had been unable to take action since no soldiers were available at the Bay of Islands, and only ninety were stationed further south, at Auckland. Fitzroy had sent an urgent appeal for help to the military authorities in Sydney, but no British ships arrived until August 1844. After negotiations, Hone Heke agreed to replace the settlers' flagpole if the British would cease exacting customs duties from visiting ships.

When the Maoris cut down the flagpole for a second time, Fitzroy deployed a small detachment of British troops, sent from Auckland by ship, to re-erect it. When the soldiers arrived in February 1845, the Reverend Williams warned that it would prove a mistake to flaunt the flag in the face of the Maoris. If it could not be properly and permanently defended, the Maoris would surely remove it again. He was right. The flagpole was chopped down for the third time on the night after it had been re-erected, and the Maoris seized the British flag and danced with it on the beach.

This time, the Maoris were at war, and war canoes soon swept up to the settlement. After a battle lasting several days, the settlers surrendered and the Maoris ordered them to board the British warship, HMS *Hazard*, anchored offshore. Yet with their settlers safely on board, the British hit back and the Maoris came under shell-fire on the beach. Years later, a Maori told the bitter story of what had happened:

> We treated the women and children kindly, and took those of them who remained late off to the ships in our canoes. But as soon as all the refugees were on board – and even before that – the man-of-war set to and opened fire on our people on the beach. It was an act of treachery to shell us after the town had been given up to us by the whites. When the firing began, some of us were sorry we had not tomahawked all the *pakehas* we could find.

The Maoris exacted their revenge for this betrayal, burning every house in the Kororareka settlement and destroying its food stocks. The loss of the town was a demoralising blow to the British, for the seizure by the Maoris of a settlement protected by British soldiers was an unusual event. Fitzroy ordered reinforcements from New South Wales, and 200 soldiers arriving at Auckland in April were swiftly sent on to the Bay of Islands. Martial law was declared, and not lifted until the following year. All legal restraint on the action of troops sent to search for Hone Heke was set aside.

Kawiti, one of Hone Heke's most important allies, controlled an inland *pa* up the Waitangi River, at Puketutu. He prepared for the arrival of the British expedition that moved in from the coast, consisting of 300 regular soldiers, 40 European 'volunteers' and 150 seamen and marines. His village came under attack from a British storming party early in May, but fierce Maori resistance forced it to withdraw. Possibly fifty men were killed on both sides combined, although the number wounded was disproportionately low, since the British killed some of Kawiti's men as they lay injured.[7]

This further Maori victory caused considerable despair among the settlers. 'Until a complete overthrow is given to Heke', wrote one government official, 'the British possessions in New Zealand are not worth having . . . The attention of the whole island is drawn to this struggle, and the future state of the colony depends on the result.'[8]

The effect of the Maori victories on settler morale being clear to the British, a *pa* being built by Kawiti at Ohaeawai came under further attack from a British military expedition in June. Again the Maoris were victorious, and again the British were forced to retreat, leaving more than a hundred dead or wounded. A British officer noted that his men were 'tired and dispirited and disgusted beyond expression at having been defeated by a mob of savages and with such fearful cost too'.[9]

After the British defeat at Ohaeawai, the Maoris sang a victory chant:

> Oh sons of warrior strength,
> Behold the trophy in my hand,
> Fruit of the battle strife –
> The head of the greedy cormorant
> That haunts the ocean shore! . . .
> We shall fight, we shall fight!
> Ah! You did not remain
> In your homeland in Europe.
> [Here] you lie overwhelmed
> By the swift driving wave of the battle.

The Reverend Henry Williams, a missionary, reflected the despair of many settlers when he wrote after the battle that 'everything is uncertain around even the very existence of the country as a colony of Great Britain'.

The settler newspaper, the *New-Zealander*, noted that 'there is not a native throughout the island but considers – and most true it is – that his countrymen have been victorious, and that the former halo of European superiority is completely dispelled'.

The first political casualty of these Maori victories was the British governor. Captain Fitzroy was withdrawn in October, to be replaced by Captain George Grey, the governor of South Australia. Sailing into Auckland in November, Grey travelled immediately to the Bay of Islands to make contact with Hone Heke. He offered impossible terms: the Maoris were to regard the Treaty of Waitangi of 1840 as binding; they were to respect the British flag and to restore the plunder taken in March; and they were to give up the lands they had seized.

'We will not give up our lands', Hone Heke told Grey. 'If the white man wants our country, he will have to fight for it, for we will die upon our lands.' Hone Heke made his views even more explicit in December: 'God made this country for us. It cannot be sliced; if it were a whale it might be sliced. Do you return to your own country, to England which was made by God for you. God made this land for us; it is not for any stranger or foreign nation to meddle with this sacred country.'

Having made no headway, Grey sailed back to Auckland. He announced that it would be 'absolutely necessary to crush either Heke or Kawiti before tranquillity could be restored to the country', and he summoned up all the forces available to him: ships, soldiers and artillery.

With a makeshift armada, and an army of more than 1,300 men – including eighty European soldiers from India – Grey sailed back to the Bay of Islands, the fourth British expedition sent out in a single year. Kawiti was now in charge of a village at Ruapekapeka, and the British advanced towards it, up the Kawakawa River. It was hard going, crawling over miles of hill and bush, river and ravine. They brought thirty tons of artillery with them, cutting a road as they went.[10]

Kawiti's *pa* was bombarded by the British force for two weeks, day and night, in January 1846. Kawiti was advised by Hone Heke to evacuate his troops and to fight in the woods, where they would have an advantage. 'You are foolish to remain in this *pa* to be pounded by cannon balls', Hone Heke told Kawiti, 'let us leave it. Let the soldiers have it, and we will retire into the forest and draw them after us, where they cannot bring the big guns. The soldiers . . . will be as easily killed amongst the canes as if they were wood pigeons.' Kawiti agreed, and when the soldiers seized the *pa*, they found that the defenders had melted away into the forest. The Maori forces harassed the British all the way back to the coast.

This was the end of the 'Northern War', and peace negotiations took place. The settlers trickled back to the Bay of Islands, although many years passed before the contentious flagpole at Kororakeka was replaced. Grey announced that the North Island would be renamed 'New Ulster', suggesting that the settlers would be as secure there as those in the plantation in northern Ireland.

Grey had learned an important lesson. British soldiers would never again be employed in hilly bush country, unless they could secure the support of *kupapa* – the Maori native contingents prepared to fight with the British. If such support was available, siege guns could be hauled into place. With adequate artillery, the Maori strategic villages could be bombarded.

The British claimed the capture of Ruapekapeka as a victory, but it was not perceived as such by observers on the ground. 'It cannot be said that we have peace of a healthy character', the Reverend Williams noted later that year, pointing out that Hone Heke was 'moving from place to place exciting much sympathy'. According to the missionary, 'Heke's cause is by no means extinguished, he is at large and could command as large a force as ever.' Williams also reported that 'the flagstaff in the Bay is still prostrate, and the natives here rule. These are humiliating facts to the proud Englishman'.

Hone Heke's resistance was at an end, although other leaders continued the struggle against the settlers in other parts of the North Island. He died in 1850, and some of the descendants of his Ngapuhi warriors, who had fought so fiercely in 1845, were eventually to become *kupapa*. Many died fighting for the Empire seventy years later, at Gallipoli.

* * *

Topine Te Mamaku, resistance leader in New Zealand in 1846–47, first in the Hutt Valley, north of Wellington, and later on the Wanganui River. Photograph taken May 1885 by Alfred Burton when Te Mamaku was 100. He died two years later.

In March 1846, Maoris in the Hutt valley, north of Wellington, destroyed the farms of white settlers who were squatting there. The resistance was led by Te Rangihaeata and Topine Te Mamaku, two experienced and charismatic leaders. Te Rangihaeata had already clashed with the British in the Wairau valley in the South Island in 1843. Te Mamaku, chief of the Ngati-Haua-te-Rangi tribe, living in the region of the upper Wanganui, was described by a British officer as the most intelligent Maori he had ever met.

The settlers in the Hutt valley had received land grants, purchased by their government from Maori chiefs, but many Maoris remained hostile to their presence. The Maoris had the law on their side, for the British purchase of the valley had specifically excluded all native homes and cultivations. Governor Grey's legal adviser argued that the Maoris were justified in resisting eviction by force.

The 'Northern War' waged against settlers in the Bay of Islands had ended with a Maori defeat in January 1846. With the 'pacification' of much territory to the north of Auckland, Grey now had time and troops to spare to deal with the Maoris resisting white settlement around Wellington and along the Cook Straits. British troops were ordered to regroup at Wellington.

Between them, the two Maori leaders had an active force of some 200 men. Grey had a troop of 700 British soldiers, reinforced by a local white militia of 200 settlers. He also commanded two warships, HMS *Calliope* and HMS *Driver* – a steamship – both recently involved in the drive to exterminate 'pirates' off the coast of Borneo. Now they had come to assist in the extermination of the Maoris.

Other echoes of imperial themes could be found in the stockaded fort the settlers constructed in the Hutt valley. Designed by Captain George Compton, a militia captain who had once lived in North America, it was patterned on the military forts built there to withstand the attacks of Native Americans. Scores of these military posts were built in succeeding years to control the Maori frontier on the North Island, and many remained with their garrisons over the next 40 years.

The Maoris attacked the settlements in the Hutt Valley in March, but the conflict began a month earlier when the homes and crops of a Maori village were destroyed by a British posse from Wellington. The Maoris were not slow to retaliate. Divided into small armed parties, and moving rapidly along the rivers, they visited each home separately, destroying furniture and smashing windows. They killed the settlers' pigs, and took away what they could carry. Bands of distressed settlers, robbed of their possessions, took refuge in Wellington.[11] Early in April, Maoris killed two settlers, and Te Rangihaeata refused to surrender the killers. Grey declared martial law and sent additional troops to the valley.

After a pause in the fighting, Te Mamaku and Te Rangihaeata ordered a surprise attack on Boulcott's Farm in May and a second one in June, causing fresh dismay in the settler ranks. Te Rangihaeata then withdrew north to a well-fortified *pa* close to the shore at Pauatahanui, in the Porirua harbour, while Te Mamaku returned to Wanganui. Grey's forces attacked the *pa* at Pauatahanui in July. Short of food and ammunition, and lacking support, Te Rangihaeata retreated, retiring with a hundred men to a well-defended *pa* south of the Manawatu River. The soldiers would be unable to capture him in this region, 'all but surrounded by miles of deep flax-swamps, threaded with slow-running watercourses, and dotted with lagoons swarming with wild ducks'.[12] He discouraged European penetration of the area for several years, and died in Otaki in 1856 after contracting measles, aggravated by bathing in a cold river.

Topine Te Mamaku began a new struggle in April 1847 against a white settlement on the banks of the Wanganui River. Ultimately inconclusive, this war left the settlers in considerable doubt about their future in New Zealand. Wanganui lies in the great bay that stretches north of Wellington, at the estuary of the

Wanganui river. The settlement there, first planted by Edward Wakefield in 1841, was a colony of the New Zealand Company. Some sixty houses with a population of 200 Europeans were surrounded by Maori villages with a population of 4,000, living under the watchful eye of a missionary, the Reverend Richard Taylor. Many Maoris had been on friendly terms with the settlers, and some proved more enthusiastic church-goers than the incomers. On Christmas Day 1846, in a community where settlers and soldiers together totalled 400, the Reverend Taylor had a congregation of 2,000 at the Maori church, and barely twenty at the European one.

Yet however friendly some Maoris might appear on the surface, many others had contested the right of the settlers to be there from the earliest moment. Prolonged Maori opposition meant that many settlers, who had paid for their title deeds before leaving London, were unable to secure their promised land. The authorities in Wellington, anticipating trouble at Wanganui, sent out a force of 200 soldiers in December 1846. The settlers, never guilty of missing a trick, had immediately doubled the price of their beef and mutton. The soldiers were soon reinforced by the arrival of HMS *Calliope*.

The war started almost by accident. A group of six Maoris attacked the home of a settler called Gilfillan, two days after an incident in which a midshipman from the *Calliope* had accidentally wounded Hapurona Ngarangi, a sixty-year-old chief. The Maoris attacked Gilfillan in retaliation, wounding him and tomahawking his wife and three children. They were captured almost immediately by *kupapa*, Maoris loyal to the British; with martial law in force, they were hurried before a court martial. Within the week, four had been hanged.

Their execution was the signal for war. On a wintry May morning, Topine Te Mamaku and a small army came sweeping down the Wanganui River in their war canoes, chanting their paddling time-songs and their war-cries. Their fleet halted a few miles above the Wanganui settlement, landing 500 men armed with muskets. They attacked the settlement the following day but were driven off by the British gunboat. For some days, the Maoris stayed out of sight, but burned down isolated settler houses and killed their cattle. A soldier caught out in the open was tomahawked.[13]

After the execution of the four Maoris, the authorities in Wellington sent an additional contingent of 100 soldiers to Wanganui. Grey arrived on board HMS *Inflexible* on 24 May, bringing with him several Maori chiefs loyal to the British, including the Waikato chief Potatau Te Wherowhero. Inconclusive fighting took place from May until July, with the Wanganui settlers remaining nervous. Some asked to be moved elsewhere. The Maoris repelled the military probes made towards their forest positions with ease. 'I do trust the soldiers may be able to do something', wrote the Reverend Taylor on 8 June, 'as these natives really deserve to be punished.' If his flock was to be suitably 'punished', the missionary hoped that this would be 'the last war of any consequence in New Zealand' – a hope that was far from fulfilment.

The Maoris besieging Wanganui were just as preoccupied as the settlers by the inconclusive nature of the war. The season for planting potatoes was approaching, and they needed to attend to their crops. In July, some 400 Maoris moved to St John's Wood, a ridge above the town, to try to break the stalemate. An inconclusive battle followed, with casualties on both sides, and the Maoris withdrew upriver, their siege of Wanganui at an end. Early in 1848 they concluded a deal with Grey: the settlers would remain, and pay a small sum for the return of their cattle; the beasts that had not been eaten were handed back.

Governor Grey remained in his post until 1853, when he was transferred to Cape Colony, returning to New Zealand in 1861. Maoris and settlers lived in relative harmony on the Wanganui river until 1864, when Topine Te Mamaku was among those who lived to fight again in the Hauhau wars of the 1860s; he died at Tawhata in 1887.

CHAPTER 53

Muslim Resistance in Sarawak

In September 1841, Pangeran Makhota, one of the Muslim rulers of Sarawak based at the port of Kuching, on the Sarawak River, was forced from power by the guns of Lieutenant James Brooke, a bizarre and unlicensed British adventurer. Taking advantage of dissension within the extended family of the sultan of Brunei, Brooke had established himself at Kuching a year earlier, allying himself with Pangeran Muda Hassim, Makhota's nominal overlord and rival for the fruits of the antimony trade. Brooke had then sought to encompass Makhota's downfall, landing troops and declaring himself on 24 September 1841, at the invitation of Muda Hassim, the 'rajah of Sarawak'.

Pangeran Makhota, or Prince Makhota, was one of many chiefs who traded along the rivers of northern Borneo. Sometimes calling themselves 'rajahs' or 'sultans', they governed statelets that were often at war with each other or with the 'pirate' states that occupied the shore line and the river banks. Muslim by religion and interrelated through family ties, these sultans would make both war and peace, and then engage in small-scale trade and barter. Some of them, some of the time, would engage in the semi-piratical task of exacting tolls from passing traffic. Others were involved in the mining and trading of antimony ore.

Makhota belonged to the family of the sultan of Brunei, a small sultanate to the east of Kuching that laid claim to several territories along the coast. After the establishment of a British settlement at Singapore in 1819, the Brunei sultan perceived that money could be made there by selling antimony ore, collected cheaply by Dayaks in the Sarawak rivers. In 1827 he had sent Makhota to be a governor on the Sarawak River – and to organise the antimony trade.

Makhota settled on the river, built the town of Kuching some twenty miles from the sea, and became the overseer of the Dayak antimony producers. He was a skilled international operative, and he needed to be. The trade was organised through British Singapore, but the Dutch in Java, the older and more experienced colonial power, were still active in the area. After the brief occupation by Stamford Raffles, the Dutch had returned to Java in 1816 and retained their position at the port of Rhio. They also had influence, on the western side of Sarawak, with the sultan of Sambas, another small-time operative active in the antimony trade. Makhota, who had been educated in Dutch Batavia (Jakarta), had a sharp eye for inter-imperial conflict, and understood the advantages of playing off the Dutch in Java against the British in Singapore, and vice versa.

Makhota was a strong ruler, tough on the Dayak producers who mined antimony in conditions of virtual slavery. But in the mid-1830s Pangeran Yusuf, another relative of the sultan of Brunei, took up the leadership of the Dayaks and rebelled against Makhota. Their revolt was organised by the sultan of Sambas and funded by the Dutch, the sultan hoping that the Dutch would incorporate the Dayak territory within their empire. Makhota proved unable to crush Yusuf's rebellion, and in 1837 Omar Ali, a new sultan of Brunei, sent another relative to Kuching, Pangeran Muda Hassim, to investigate. Makhota remained governor of Sarawak, but Muda Hassim became his nominal superior. Yet since Makhota had been appointed by the previous sultan and had local experience, he had a more privileged position.

James Brooke had first entered this fractious scene in August 1839, sailing up the Sarawak River to Kuching. A wealthy former officer, born in Benares, he had been wounded during the British war against the Burmese Empire in 1824. Beguiled by the area, and by its commercial possibilities, he had returned as a private citizen, sailing in his own 142-ton yacht, *The Royalist*, from Singapore to Sarawak. On arrival at Kuching, he had established a relationship with Muda Hassim, perceiving him to be the senior ruler and finding him to be 'greatly inclined to the English'. He had come loaded with gifts, the traditional way of coaxing the native rulers of India into the imperial web.[1] He foresaw that the technique would work well in Sarawak as well.

Muda Hassim and Makhota were still trying to quell the Dutch-backed rebellion of Yusuf and the Dayak miners upriver when Brooke first anchored at Kuching. Brooke, with his impressive-looking British ship, had arrived at an opportune moment; 'hints have been thrown out', he noted in his diary, that Muda Hassim 'wishes me to stay here *as a demonstration* to intimidate the rebels'.

Makhota came one night to visit Brooke on his ship, and told him of the interest the Dutch had shown in seizing the mines of Sarawak, explaining how Yusuf's rebels had asked the Dutch Resident at Sambas for protection. Brooke assumed that Makhota was Muda Hassim's chief minister and thought he was the more interesting of the two, describing him as 'a man of much ability', whose manners were 'lively, frank and engaging'.[2]

Brooke did not remain long in Kuching, but returned the following year, in August 1840, when Makhota was making a final effort to crush Yusuf and the Dayaks with a small army of Malays and loyal Dayaks. Brooke sailed upriver to visit Makhota's campaign headquarters, noting in his diary in September that a few hundred men still held out at a handful of forts, 'and it now remained to drive them from their last stronghold of resistance'.[3]

Victory over the rebels was imminent, leaving the two rival pangerans (or princes) in power in Kuching. Muda Hassim knew that Makhota's enlarged and now victorious army could be deployed to get rid of him, or to banish him to Brunei, and suddenly the presence there of Brooke and his well-armed ship seemed providential. He suggested to Brooke in December that he, Brooke, should take over as the 'rajah' of Sarawak, and replace Makhota as the governor at Kuching. Flattered, Brooke accepted the offer, and *The Royalist* took part in the final weeks of fighting against the Dayaks. Seriff Muhammad Husain, a Dayak leader, agreed to surrender if Brooke became the new rajah, thus ensuring that the Dayaks would no longer come under Makhota's rule.

Makhota made efforts throughout 1841 to undermine Muda Hassim's alliance with the English adventurer, but in September he was faced with military action by Brooke, who had sent troops ashore to reinforce Muda Hassim. 'I determined to bring matters to a crisis', wrote Brooke.

> I landed a party of men, fully armed, and loaded the ship's guns with grape and canister; after which I once more proceeded to Muda Hassim, and whilst I protested my kindness towards him, exposed Macota's machinations and crimes, his oppressions and deceit, and threatened him with an attack, as neither Muda Hassim nor myself were safe whilst he continued practising these arts.

Impressed by the presence of Brooke's soldiers, Muda Hassim agreed to keep his promise that Brooke should become the new rajah. Brooke recorded that 'affairs proceeded cheerily to a conclusion' and an agreement was signed: 'Guns fired, flags waved; and on September 24, 1841, I became the governor of Sarawak, with the fullest powers.'

Brooke had effectively seized power from Makhota, who had no troops and was deserted at this crucial moment by everyone except his twenty household slaves. Stripped of his governorship, Makhota stayed in Kuching for a few months, but was eventually forced out. 'I have given Pangeran Macota orders to leave', Brooke noted firmly in his diary on 1 January 1842.

Driven from Kuching, Makhota withdrew in early 1842 up the Batang Lupar River to Sadong, to stay with his ally Seriff Sahab, the Arab governor of the region. Makhota and Sahab now sought to undermine Brooke's position by stimulating resistance with the means at their disposal. Some 10,000 Dayaks along the coastline worked as freelance tax-collectors or 'pirates', and Makhota mobilised them against the trading fleets organised by Brooke. They soon threatened the new political structure in Sarawak as well as Brooke's business ventures.

As the self-styled 'rajah' of Sarawak, Brooke had secured control of a sizeable territory, and was able to exploit the gold and antimony mines once operated by Makhota. Yet he was militarily weak, protected only by a small retinue of hired sepoys. These were not sufficient to confront, let alone to exterminate, Makhota's Dayak 'pirates' in the neighbouring river.

To undermine Makhota's strategy, Brooke perceived that he would need assistance from the British state, and he dreamed of reviving the British anti-piracy campaigns that had proved so effective in the 1830s in the waters around Singapore. The permanent establishment of a colonial enclave at Hong Kong in 1842, and the growth in shipping between Singapore and Hong Kong, meant there was a fresh need to sweep the channel along the north Borneo coast. The war with China having come to an end, spare ships were now available from the China station to suppress the 'piracy' further south.

After discussions with Brooke, Admiral Thomas Cochrane, the commander-in-chief on the China station, requested Captain Henry Keppel of HMS *Dido* to go to Brooke's assistance. Keppel was an old hand in these waters, having taken part in the attack on the Penghulu of Naning in 1832. Early in 1843, Keppel and Brooke met in Singapore to discuss their strategy. Brooke told Keppel that he saw himself as the linear descendant of Stamford Raffles, who had died twenty years earlier, and he declared his ambition 'to carry Sir Stamford Raffles' views in Java over the whole archipelago'. Telling Keppel of 'the mysteries, depths, and horrors of pirates' in the seas off the Malay Peninsula, the two men agreed that 'the only way to strike at the root of the evil would be to destroy the piratical strongholds in the interior'.

Makhota and Seriff Sahap were based that year on the River Sarebus, a waterway to the north of Batang Lupar, and Keppel and Brooke sailed up to confront them in HMS *Dido* in June. Some eighty men were despatched upriver in five boats to the villages of Rembas, Pakoo and Paddi, and destroyed the homes and 'pirate' boats of the villagers. This was a heavy blow to the Dayak communities on the coast, but a few months later, in February 1844, the 'pirates' struck back, attacking and plundering two British trading ships.

This form of imperial warfare – attacks by British warships and retaliation by Dayak 'pirates' – continued for several years. Makhota and Sahab were attacked again by HMS *Dido* in August 1844, at their stronghold of Patusen. Brooke was on board, as before, and the *Dido* was joined on this occasion by HMS *Samarang*, a naval survey vessel commanded by Captain Sir Edward Belcher.[4] Five of their river forts came under fire, and British sailors, according to the account in William Clowes's history of the British navy, marched ashore:

> No fewer than sixty-four brass guns, besides iron ones, were found in the place, which was looted and burnt. Hundreds of *prahus* were also destroyed . . . A very serious blow was dealt at a chief who, for twenty years, had been a leading patron of pirates, but who now found himself without warboats, guns, ammunition, or shelter for his followers.[5]

After HMS *Dido*'s guns had destroyed the forts, Frank Marryat, a midshipman on HMS *Samarang*, wrote of 'the smoking ruins of what had been a Malay town', while Captain Keppel recorded that Patusen made 'a glorious blaze' that went on for three days.

The sacking of Patusen changed the history of Borneo, for the independent northern sultanates were now to come under British control. It also marked a new stage in the British campaign of extermination – the wiping out of the riverine communities along the coast – that lasted until the end of the decade. Makhota was among those captured by the British, but, as an influential relative of the sultan of Brunei, he was eventually set free and allowed to make his way to Brunei. Seriff Sahab escaped to Pontianak in Dutch Borneo, where he died.

The *Dido* and the *Samarang* returned to Kuching, where Pangeran Muda Hassim was still nominally in control. Brooke realised that he no longer had need of the pangeran and his expensive entourage, described by Captain Belcher as 'a dead clog' on the advancement of the inhabitants of Sarawak, and Belcher was charged with escorting him to Brunei. Brooke went with him, for he now had wider ambitions. Having brought Sarawak into the British sphere of influence, he intended to seize Brunei, also regarded as a centre of 'piracy'.

Sultan Omar Ali was still the ruler at Brunei, with Pangeran Yusuf as his chief minister. When Brooke and Belcher arrived, the sultan was told that Yusuf, known to be hostile to British ambitions, should be replaced by the pliable Muda Hassim. He was also told of the British intention to establish a naval base on the island of Labuan.[6]

Under threat of hostile action, the sultan did what he was told, and Yusuf left Brunei to make common cause with Seriff Osman, the chief of the Lanun 'pirates' in Malludu Bay, to the north. Muda Hassim, now chief minister at Brunei, told his British advisers that the pirates were 'exceedingly displeased' with his British alliance, and in consequence he strongly recommended an attack on Malludu 'with a view to destroying the pirates'.

Brooke approved the idea, and in March 1845, he sent a memo to Admiral Cochrane outlining 'the best mode for the suppression of piracy' in the areas for which he had made himself responsible. 'A blow should be struck', he said, 'at the piratical communities with which we are already acquainted, and struck with a force which should convince all other pirates of the hopelessness of resistance.' He emphasised the need to strike at the communities themselves – the places where the pirates lived: 'the pirate haunts must be burnt and destroyed, and the communities dispersed . . . What pirate would venture to pursue his vocation if his home be endangered?' Brooke sought to avoid a discussion about the rights and wrongs of what he was doing, adding, 'we must carefully avoid introducing the refinements of European international law amongst a rude and semi-civilised people, who will make our delicacy a cloak for crime'.

In August 1845, Admiral Cochrane followed Brooke's advice to the letter, sailing to Brunei with six ships and 150 marines. In the course of the previous year, Pangeran Yusuf had returned to Brunei and ousted Muda Hassim as chief minister. Sultan Omar Ali was now ordered by Cochrane to surrender Yusuf, and when the pangeran failed to appear, his house was bombarded from the river.

Cochrane sailed on to Malludu Bay to attack Seriff Osman's upriver fort. When the 'pirates' called for peace talks, Cochrane demanded unconditional surrender. Osman refused, and the British force cut through the boom across the river that protected his fort. Six men were killed on the British side in the ensuing battle, but Osman's forces and the 'pirate' town were destroyed. Osman himself was mortally wounded, and carried away into the jungle to die. Malludu, Brooke boasted in his diary, has ceased to exist.

Makhota and Sultan Omar Ali prepared to resist a fresh British attack on Brunei in July 1846. Makhota had returned there late in 1845 after his capture at Patusen in 1844, and in the absence of Pangeran Yusuf he became the sultan's chief adviser. He had plans to stir up rebellion against Brooke's base in Kuching, but first he struck at British influence in Brunei itself. In January 1846 he prevailed on the sultan to order the execution of Pangeran Muda Hassim, who stood accused of knowing in advance about the British attack on Malludu Bay, and of favouring the British plan to seize the island of Labuan. Armed men surrounded the house of Muda Hassim, but the pangeran blew himself up with a keg of gunpowder before he could be captured. His last request was for Brooke to 'tell the Queen of England how he had perished'. His entire clan, comprising the pro-British party in Brunei, was killed.

Makhota and the sultan ordered new forts to be built on the river to defend Brunei against future attacks by 'Rajah' Brooke. Their threat to his hegemony was something that Brooke could not ignore, and he determined to 'depose the Sultan, destroy Brunei, [and] reinstate Muda Hassim's family'. Turning again to Admiral Cochrane, he requested his help to 'act against this atrocious Sultan', and Cochrane sailed from Singapore in July 1846, with Brooke on board.

Makhota and the sultan were outgunned, and their new forts were soon captured. The two men withdrew upriver, beyond the reach of the British ships. Cochrane then sailed on to China, leaving Captain Rodney Mundy, the captain of HMS *Iris*, to attack Makhota's piratical allies in the rivers to the north. Omar Ali reoccupied his palace in Brunei later in the year, and concluded a formal treaty with Mundy in December. The conditions were harsh: the sultan was required to give up 'piracy' and the slave trade, effectively depriving him of his income, and he was forced to cede 'for ever' the strategic island of Labuan at the mouth of his river. The British takeover of the island was not popular with its inhabitants. 'As we approached Labuan', noted Midshipman Marryat, 'we found it necessary to be on the *qui vive*, as all the natives were hostile to us, and would have cut off our surveying parties if they had had a chance.'[7]

Makhota and Omar Ali had struggled to maintain their independence, but their resistance was now almost at an end, overcome by the firepower of the British navy. Makhota continued to foment rebellions against the British, notably among the Sarebus and the Sakarran towards the end of 1846, as Brooke imagined they would. 'I cannot expect these men . . . to forgive me for having dethroned them from their high places', he wrote sourly in December. 'They are wicked and unforgiving – they regret their loss of power – blush at their defeat, and would do me a mischief if they knew how.' But resistance eventually proved impossible, and Makhota and Omar Ali made a final peace agreement, ceding Labuan but securing their right to remain at Brunei. Omar Ali died there in 1852. On landing on Labuan, and formally claiming it for the Empire, Captain Mundy outlined his intention of ordering 'his steamers and ships to destroy all pirates by land or by sea, killing them and burning their villages'.

The campaign to exterminate 'pirates' and their communities in the neighbouring rivers continued for several years, until the scale of the killings reached the ears of Radical MPs in parliament in 1849. The excesses of the navy in its support of the territorial and trading ambitions of Brooke were condemned, and some of the worst aspects of the anti-piracy campaign – the payment of 'head-money' to sailors for exterminating people – were curbed.

In July 1849, in waters to the east of Sarawak, a Dayak flotilla was intercepted and attacked by three British ships – an event later dubbed the Battle of Batang Marau. The British expedition was led by Captain Arthur Farquhar of HMS *Albatross*. James Brooke's ship, *The Royalist*, and HMS *Nemesis*, an armed paddle-steamer belonging to the East India Company, were also involved, as well as boats from the Albatross.

Captain Farquhar's flotilla had taken up a position at the mouth of the Sarebas and the Si Marang rivers, and on the night of 31 July the battle began. Numerous *prahus* were sunk, the crew of one being cut up by the paddles of the *Nemesis*. Dawn revealed a tangle of wreckage in the bay. More than seventy *prahus* were ashore, and of the 120 that had been in the Si Maring River, eighty were destroyed, together with nearly 1,200 of their Malay crews. Farquhar went on to burn other *prahus* and villages in the Sarebas, teaching 'a lesson so severe and wholesome that it was not forgotten for many years'.[8]

There was indeed a tremendous slaughter, denounced in a speech to the House of Commons in July 1851 by the British Radical MP Richard Cobden: 'The loss of life was greater than in the case of the English at Trafalgar, Copenhagen, or Algiers, and yet it was thought to pass over such a loss of human life as if they were so many dogs; and worse, to mix up professions of religion and adhesions to Christianity with the massacre.'

Years later, speaking about the Turkish atrocities in Bulgaria in June 1877, William Gladstone recalled the massacre at Batang Marau in 1849: 'I cannot recollect a more shameful proceeding on the part of any country than the slaughter of the Dayaks by Her Majesty's forces and Sir James Brooke.' The crews of the ships participating in the slaughter of the Dayaks were paid 'head money' for the 'pirates' they killed, and the figure paid out by the British government amounted to more than £20,000 – with 500 people 'destroyed' at £20 a head and 2,000 'dispersed' at £5 a head.

The crew of the armed paddle-steamer HMS *Nemesis* had been engaged in this kind of fundraising for some time, having participated in earlier attacks on Dayak settlements at Saribas and Sekrang. These had produced 'head-money', but they were not simple attacks on 'pirates'; they were attempts by Brooke to exact revenge on his old enemy Pangeran Makhota, whose political strength now rested with the Dayaks. After 1846, revolutionary groups in Brunei naturally turned to the pirates as a means of dislodging Brooke.[9]

Some years later, in February 1853, the Dayaks hit back. Rentap, a Dayak chief, attacked the British fort at Lingga, built the previous year, killing its commander, Alan Lee – one of Brooke's men. William Brereton, in command of a Brooke fort at Sekrang, escaped, and an expedition was mounted against Rentap in 1854. He was wounded in this encounter, but fought on for many years.

Brooke blamed the catastrophe at Lingga on the failure of British naval steamers to visit the new forts. Yet the rules of engagement had changed. The slaughter at Batang Marau had aroused such a political storm in Britain that payments of 'head-money' were made 'discretionary' after 1850. The British Radical MP, Joseph Hume, said he expected the Sea Dayaks to take revenge for Batang Marau, since the British navy would no longer support the marauding expeditions of Rajah Brooke.

Makhota drowned in 1858, after trying to crush a Dayak revolt at Limbang.[10] James Brooke was to die in his bed of a stroke ten years later. 'A greater villain it would be impossible to conceive, with heart blacker, head more cunning, and passions more unrestrained.' These words, written by Brooke when he heard of the death of Makhota, would have provided a suitable obituary for Brooke himself.

CHAPTER 54

The Penultimate Battles of the Xhosa in Cape Colony

Ever since the great Xhosa resistance war of 1835–36, the white settlers in Cape Colony had been forbidden by the government to move into Xhosa land to the east of the territory; but a decade later, driven by the high world price for wool, the settlers again raised a clamour for fresh land. A new governor at the Cape, General Sir Peregrine Maitland – a veteran of Waterloo, Madras, and Canada – announced a policy of expansion into the contested and Xhosa-occupied frontier zone in September 1844. Survey parties similar to those in New Zealand and Australia moved in, backed by the settlers and protected by the construction of new forts, creating a permanent military presence. 'Is it just', asked John Mitford Bowker, a settler at Grahamstown, 'that a few thousands of ruthless worthless savages are to sit like a nightmare upon a land that would support millions of civilised men happily?'

The Xhosa were well aware that the surveyors and soldiers would soon be followed by settlers. Their leader in the 1840s was Sandile, a man in his twenties with a pronounced limp. Successor to Ngqika and half-brother of Maqoma, Sandile perceived the need for action. Coming upon a surveyors' camp in January 1846, at Block Drift, east of the Keiskammer River, he ordered the mapping party to leave. His request alarmed the officer in charge, who summoned reinforcements from Fort Beaufort, but accepted a temporary truce. The British surveyors and soldiers withdrew, to return in April with a larger force – and to meet an unexpected defeat.

In April 1846, Xhosa forces attacked the British column invading their territory in the Amatolas mountains, in Hintsa's former territory between the Keiskammer and Kei rivers. They forced it to retreat: the soldiers abandoned their kit and a long trail of wagons was set on fire. The subsequent conflict – referred to by imperial historians as the 'war of the axe' and by the Xhosa as the 'war of the boundary' – was the worst humiliation suffered by the British in South Africa up to that time.[1]

The British could not defend the surveyors in Xhosa territory without making war on their ancient frontier enemy, and they soon found a pretext. A Xhosa worker had been detained at Fort Beaufort in March, charged with stealing an axe – an otherwise trifling event; a group of Xhosa rescued him on the road to Grahamstown as he was being taken for trial. Outraged by this incident, Colonel John Hare, long the governor of the eastern province, declared his intention to invade Xhosa territory to exact punishment. He had 1,000 regular soldiers at his command, as well as Khoi-Khoi troops enrolled in the Cape Mounted Rifles. The Xhosa forces numbered more than 12,000.

Governor Maitland supported Hare's move and travelled up to Grahamstown to take personal charge of the campaign, commanding the largest military force ever assembled by the British in South Africa, with 14,000 men in arms. Some 3,000 were British regular soldiers, and, as one young private recorded, they 'looked on the commencement of this war as the beginning of a glorious succession of picnic parties'. Yet as they moved into the Amatolas hills, camping at Burnshill, they were surprised to be confronted not with assegais but with rifle fire. 'It's a new thing for me', noted Bowker, the Grahamstown settler, 'to be running on foot, before Kaffirs mounted on horseback, and the balls whistling like hail about me.' For the first time in the long history of their defence of their land, the Xhosa had firearms, provided by gun-runners operating on behalf of merchants in Grahamstown.

A huge Xhosa force pursued the retreating British, streaming across the colony on a wide front. They burned farms and mission stations, and even threatened Grahamstown, with its garrison of inexperienced soldiers shipped in from Ceylon. The Xhosa gave warning that they would not stop until they had 'driven out the last Englishman at the point of the Cape'.

General Maitland declared martial law, soon in force throughout the colony, but the Xhosa continued their sweeping advance, securing another humiliating British retreat from a settlement outside Fort Peddie. The commander was arrested and sent for court martial. The Xhosa attacked the fort again in May, capturing much cattle, but this was the summit of their achievement. The British brought up artillery and prevented them from seizing the fort.

The Xhosa fought a rearguard action for several months, eventually adopting a policy of non-resistance and then patching up an impermanent peace. Sandile reluctantly handed over the man who had stolen the axe – the notional excuse for the war – and Maitland informed London of the stalemate: 'We are at this moment neither at war or at peace, nor is there even a defined truce between us; but no hostilities take place.'[2]

Many local observers considered this to be a victory for the Xhosa. Richard Birt, a missionary, noted that 'the Caffres have not been humbled by anything our force had done, and they are as unsubdued as at the commencement of hostilities . . . their loss by actual war . . . is not sufficient to remove from their minds the idea that we have had the worst of it.'[3]

In the wake of this debacle, the British officers and politicians associated with the war were forced out of office. Colonel Hare resigned, dying on board ship shortly after leaving the Cape; General Maitland was prematurely retired in January 1847 and sent back to London. He died in 1854.

In September 1847, the Xhosa were faced with a fresh British military offensive after another insignificant frontier incident – the theft of some goats – again provoked a war. On this occasion, Sandile was himself under threat: the British invaded the Amatolas to seize him in his home.

The Xhosa were confronted with a new opponent that year. Maitland's replacement was General Sir Henry Pottinger, the veteran of Indian wars who had made his reputation in Hong Kong, the Punjab and Baluchistan. Pottinger arrived in Cape Town in January with plenipotentiary powers as 'High Commissioner'. He was required by Earl Grey, the colonial secretary in London, to 'settle and adjust' the affairs of the territories 'adjacent or contiguous to the Eastern and Northern border' of Cape Colony, and he was further instructed to promote 'the good order, civilisation and moral and religious instructions of the tribes'.

With his experience of the system of indirect rule introduced into India, Pottinger envisaged incorporating the Xhosa into the Empire by allowing the chiefs to remain in command with the assistance of a British political agent. He was contemptuous of white settler society at the Cape, and declared that he had never seen such extensive corruption and idleness, 'even in an Indian native state'. His immediate task was to re-launch the war against Sandile, perceived as the single most recalcitrant chief. Sandile's supporters would be reduced to submission 'by devastating their country, destroying their kraals, crops and cattle, and letting them finally understand that, cost what it may, they must be humbled and subdued'.

The Xhosa were faced with a three-pronged British offensive in the Amatolas in September, with General Sir George Berkeley, another Waterloo veteran, as the new commander-in-chief. Among his officers was Henry Somerset, the old frontier expert. The strategy was ruthless: the homes of the Xhosa were burned and their cattle seized. Sir John Hall, the army's medical officer, noted that 'this system of cattle stealing and hut burning is a disgrace to the age we live in, and, if the savages retaliate hereafter, no one can blame them, after the example of pillage and destruction that has been set them by the army on the present occasion'.[4]

The war was brought to an end by a typical act of British perfidy. Sandile was prevailed upon to consider negotiations at the British camp, and in October, believing that this was possible, he agreed to travel under escort to King William's Town. Yet instead of attending a meeting to discuss peace terms, he was promptly sent on to Grahamstown and imprisoned. 'A miserable starving chief has surrendered', Andries Stockenstrom, the old frontier hand, wrote to Grey in London, 'and we are as elated as if the battle of Waterloo had been fought and won again.'[5] Sandile regarded his involuntary imprisonment as an act of gross treachery, declaring sadly that he would never again trust the word of a white man.

Sandile was taken from his prison in December 1847 and brought before the new governor, sent out to replace Pottinger. The new ruler of Cape Colony was none other than General Sir Harry Smith, recently appointed Baronet of Aliwal on the Sutlej, for his successful campaign against the Sikhs in the Punjab. Smith had had long experience of the Xhosa frontier, having fought there in the 1830s. Now he was back on his old territory, with a new agenda.

'Who is the great chief of the Xhosa?' Sandile was asked by Smith.

'Sarili', replied Sandile, referring to the man who had become the paramount chief in 1835, after Hintsa had been murdered while in Smith's charge.

'No', said Smith. 'I am your Paramount Chief, and the Kaffirs are my dogs. I am come to punish you for your misdoings and treachery. You may approach my foot and kiss it, but not until you repent the past will I allow you to touch my hand.' To show his magnanimity, Smith ordered Sandile's release.

A week earlier, the new ruler had landed at Algoa Bay (Port Elizabeth) and seen his old Xhosa adversary, Maqoma, standing in the welcoming crowd. Maqoma had come forward to shake Smith's hand, but the governor had other ideas. Maqoma was forced to get down on the ground, and the governor put his foot on his neck, saying, 'This is to teach you that I have come to teach Kaffirland that I am chief and master here, and this is the way I shall treat the enemies of the Queen of England.'

This charming encounter – a form of imperial greeting possibly brought to Africa from India – was to be endlessly repeated throughout the rest of the century, storing up wells of fury among those subject to such humiliation. 'I always thought you were a great man until this day', was Maqoma's icy reply when he got to his feet, and, according to oral legend, he had a further remark for Smith. 'You are a dog, and so you behave like a dog. This thing was not sent by Victoria who knows that I am of royal blood like herself.'[6]

Finally, at King William's Town, the frontier chiefs and thousands of Xhosa took part in a dramatic ceremony staged by Smith. Sandile was there, but Maqoma was absent. Smith declared himself to be the supreme chief, the Inkosi Inkhulu, and each African chief was summoned forward in turn to kiss his boot and stirrup. The chiefs listened to the governor as he tore up the treaty of 1835, which the Xhosa still held to, and shouted, 'No more treaties!', before announcing the formal annexation of the Xhosa land between the Fish and Keiskammer rivers as an integral part of Cape Colony apt for white settlement. The Xhosa would be shepherded into the land further east, between the Keiskammer and the Kei, in a territory to be called 'British Kaffraria', the region that Benjamin D'Urban in the 1830s had named 'Queen Adelaide's Land'. British Kaffraria was to be constructed as a purely military colony, to be ruled under the harsh and arbitrary terms of martial law, and the Xhosa chiefs were required to swear allegiance to Queen Victoria. Their land was lost forever.

The Xhosa were not alone. In August 1848 it was the turn of the rebel Boers living beyond the Orange River to come under British attack at Boomplatz, south-west of Bloemfontein. Led by Andries Pretorius, the Boers sought to oppose the British annexation of the land they had settled during the years since the 'Great Trek' out of Cape Colony in 1836. Fresh from the creation of Kaffraria, Harry Smith declared that this Boer-occupied land between the Orange and Vaal rivers should also be British, calling it the 'Orange River Sovereignty'. It would in future be open for settlement by British and Boer settlers from Cape Colony. Pretorius's Boer army was defeated by British forces in August at Boomplatz, and retreated across the Vaal, where Pretorius set up the independent republic of the Transvaal. This was eventually recognised by the British in 1852, and Pretorius died the following year.

Six years after Boomplatz, the Boer settlers in the new Orange River Sovereignty campaigned for self-rule. The British, faced with such powerful opposition, decided to abandon the territory to the Boers. Sir George Clerk, a special commissioner sent from England, formerly the governor of Bombay, signed the Convention of Bloemfontein, and the 'Orange Free State' was finally created as an independent Boer Republic.

Part IX

PRELUDE TO THE MUTINY, 1848–53

In the six years between 1848 and 1854, between the revolutions that broke out in the imperial capitals of Europe in 1848 and the inter-imperial war that began in the Crimea in March 1854, the incidence of rebellion and resistance intensified in many parts of the Empire. In February 1848 the monarchy was overthrown in France, and radical uprisings took place in other European cities. The repercussions were felt throughout the colonial world, as the apparent fragility of government in the imperial heartland became apparent to those resisting colonial rule.

By the middle of the year, from Ireland to Ceylon, rebels took their cue from events in Paris, while in the Punjab the Sikhs embarked on their final resistance to the imposition of British rule, culminating in their great victory at Chilianwala in 1849 (see p. 351–2). British interventions in the Muslim provinces that now form Pakistan led to the establishment of a new imperial borderland in the mountains east of Afghanistan, and from the 1850s onwards the so-called North-West Frontier of India became a scene of epic confrontation. A succession of Muslim tribal chieftains presented a continuing challenge to the Empire throughout the nineteenth century and on into the Empire's final years – and beyond. To the west of India, in the so-called North-East Frontier territories, the Naga tribesmen presented a comparable and enduring threat.

Elsewhere in Asia, the Burmese rebelled in what became known as the Second Burmese War, while along the shores of Sarawak, the local 'pirates' resisted the encroachments of James Brooke, culminating in the brutal massacre at Batang Marau in 1849 (see p. 375–6) that reached the ears of attentive MPs in London, already concerned about the prolonged period of martial law in Ceylon.

In Africa, the continuing struggle with the breakaway Boer settlers beyond the frontiers of Cape Colony was a significant feature of this period, as well as the revived and final episodes of Xhosa resistance by Maqoma and Sandile in 1851. In West Africa, opposition emerged to the steady advance of British traders and naval gunboats, often cloaked in their apparently humanitarian ambition to end the slave trade.

At this same moment, in the middle of the nineteenth century, a fresh crisis blew up in the Empire's policing and prison system, similar to the problems that had arisen some seventy years earlier that had seen the development of the Australian gulag. In the 1780s the British had only to consider the fate of British convicts; in 1850, the entire Empire needed prison space.

Trouble began in 1848, when the settlers in Tasmania heard rumours that their island was to become the sole receptacle for the criminals of the Empire. The convict population there had already increased rapidly in the 1840s to more than 30,000 – nearly half the population. A convict cargo ship, the Ratcliff, sailed from Portsmouth into the Tasmanian harbour of Hobart with 248 male prisoners on board in November 1848. A group of influential local citizens presented a petition to the governor requesting an end to any further shipments, but no action was taken.

Convicts continued to arrive in ever-greater numbers. Some twenty ships with prisoners on board arrived at Hobart in 1849, sailing from different parts of the Empire: 'six from Ireland, with 884 male and 555 female prisoners; three from England, with 33 male and 313 females; five from New Zealand, with 16 males; two from Adelaide, with 23 males; one from Sydney, with 5; one from Port Philip, with 10; and two from India, with 21' – a grand total of 1,860 convicts.[1] So great was the outrage in Hobart that the London authorities began to take note. The transport of imperial convicts to Tasmania was brought to an end in 1853, although convict ships continued to sail to Australia until 1868.

Britain had other convict gulags where local people sought an end to these trans-shipments. Singapore, like Penang and Malacca, had been used for years as a workhouse for prisoners from India and China, and cheap convict labour lay at the root of the prosperity of these colonial outposts. Some 1,500 Indian convicts were working in Singapore in 1845, some employed in building up-country police stations. Convicts from China were less well received by the local authorities, since they could more easily defect and disappear into the population, but they continued to arrive.

In January 1848, one event in particular drew attention to the convict drama. A British passenger vessel, the *General Wood*, had sailed from Hong Kong to Singapore with ninety-three Chinese convicts on board, and then, within sight of their destination, the convicts rebelled. The ship was seized by the prisoners, and they killed the captain. The European passengers were held hostage, and the ship set course for China. The freedom of the rebels was brief, for their ship ran aground. They were recaptured and sent back to Singapore, and again put on trial.

Yet the scandal was sufficient to oil the wheels of protest, both in Singapore and in London. The transport of Chinese convicts was stopped in 1856, while Indian convicts ceased to be sent to Singapore after 1860.

In the light of the continuing resistance to empire, fresh doubts were expressed in Britain at mid-century about its purpose and utility. A handful of Radical MPs in the House of Commons were the chief critics of empire, but their arguments were stoutly rejected by Henry Earl Grey, the politician in charge of the Colonial Office since 1846 and the author of an influential account of his stewardship. In his book, *The Colonial Policy of Lord Russell's Administration*, published in 1853, Grey placed particular emphasis on the need for Britain to spread the benefits of Christianity throughout the world. 'The authority of the British Crown is at this moment the most powerful instrument, under Providence, of maintaining peace and order in many extensive regions of the earth, and thereby assists in diffusing amongst millions of the human race the blessings of Christianity and civilisation.' Yet the increasing activity of British missionaries and evangelical soldiers aroused considerable opposition, notably in the colonial territories that were already beholden to Islam.

Grey believed firmly in the imperial mission. If Britain was to abandon its colonies, he argued, the West Indies would see 'a fearful war of colour', and so too would Ceylon. The 'most hopeless anarchy' would result, even in New Zealand. The African slave trade would revive.

Without its empire, Grey foresaw an even gloomier prospect for Britain itself: it would see the 'annihilation of lucrative branches' of its commerce, 'which now creates the means of paying for British goods consumed daily in larger quantities by the numerous and various populations now emerging from barbarism under our protection.' Grey's Christian mission to bring peace and order was closely linked to the expansion of British commerce.

CHAPTER 55

William Smith O'Brien and the Rising of the Young Irelanders

In July 1848 a rebellious Irish movement known as 'Young Ireland' stumbled into an insurrection in the mountainous area between Kilkenny and Tipperary, in the aftermath of the worst famine ever experienced in Ireland. The rebellion was ill-organised and easily suppressed within ten days, for many of its leaders had been imprisoned earlier in the year. Yet its repercussions were to echo through the rest of the century; among the young men who took part were those who would later establish the revolutionary movement known as the 'Fenians'.

The situation in the countryside in the mid-1840s had become increasingly desperate. The potato crop had failed throughout much of the island in 1846, and by the spring of 1847, after a bitter winter, a million had died, another million had emigrated, and 3 million were on relief. One small group argued that independence from Britain would improve the situation. Set up in January 1847, the group called itself the 'Irish Confederation', although the 'Young Irelanders' was their unofficial name, recognised by history. Their leader was William Smith O'Brien, a landlord MP from Limerick, not a Catholic but a Protestant.

Their moderate programme was soon outbid by more radical voices: by John Mitchel, a Protestant newspaper editor from Ulster, and by James Fintan Lalor, a member of a prosperous Catholic farming family. Lalor was among the first to link political action with peasant protest; he called both for independence and for peasants to recover control of their land. 'I acknowledge no right of property in eight thousand persons', wrote Lalor, 'which takes away all rights of property, security, independence, and existence itself, from a population of eight millions . . . I acknowledge no right of property which takes the food of millions and gives them a famine'.[1]

Lalor argued that 'the entire ownership of Ireland . . . is vested of right in the people of Ireland'. Mitchel took up these ideas, and, moving to the left, he withdrew from Smith O'Brien's Irish Confederation early in 1848. In his newspaper, the *United Irishman*, he called openly for rebellion against the British.

Then, as in the 1790s, news came from Paris in February 1848 of the overthrow of the French monarchy. Radical uprisings followed in cities

William Smith O'Brien,
political leader of Young Ireland.
Lithograph by Henry O'Neil.

Thomas Francis Meagher,
Irish rebel, in the United States
in 1864.

throughout Europe, and the Irish began to imagine that their hour might again have come. Several groups began serious plotting. One, led by Thomas Francis Meagher, sought to ally itself with the Chartists in Britain. Another travelled to France to try to secure support from the French (although the British became aware of their plans, and scotched them before they were far advanced).

The British prime minister, Lord John Russell, was convinced that Ireland was on the verge of an armed insurrection. The Treason Felony Act, introduced originally to crush the Chartists, was now used against the Irish, and the first victim was the editor Mitchel. Arrested in May and found guilty of treason, he was sentenced to fourteen years' transportation. In July, Russell suspended habeas corpus in Ireland for seven months, and warrants were issued for the Young Irelanders still at liberty, notably Smith O'Brien.

Their paper, the *Nation*, published in Dublin, printed an editorial that sought to rally the Irish to the coming struggle, and called for the capture of Dublin Castle: 'Oh! for a hundred thousand muskets glittering brightly in the light of Heaven, and the monumental barricades stretching across each of our noble streets, made desolate by England . . . The Castle is the keystone of English power; take it, destroy it, burn it'. Yet no real possibility existed of an uprising in Dublin; its garrison had already been powerfully reinforced. General Henry Hardinge – the Irish secretary in the 1830s, the recent victor over the Sikhs, and the governor-general of India – had been sent there to keep an eye on things.

Two leaders of the Young Irelanders still at large, Meagher and John Dillon, met in July to consider an alternative uprising outside the capital. If Smith O'Brien would only give the word, they would throw themselves 'into Kilkenny, call the people to arms, barricade the streets, and proclaim the separation of the country'. The two men travelled south to visit O'Brien at the town of Enniscorthy, beside Vinegar Hill, in County Wexford. Inevitably they fell to discussing the events that had happened there fifty years earlier, during the rebellion of 1898. They were greeted by enthusiastic supporters who pledged themselves 'to obtain arms and to be ready to join in a national rising'.

The assembled crowd added an important caveat. They would only do so 'as soon as they heard of its having begun in any adjacent county'. In spite of the large gathering at Enniscorthy, County Wexford was not ready to take armed action. The memory of the repression after 1798 was still green. 'Tens of thousands of people still lived in the county who had vivid recollections of the brutalities and the tragic bloodshed of fifty years ago, and of the merciless reprisals that had followed upon that abortive rising.'[2]

The revolutionaries of 1848 were obliged to turn their attention elsewhere, and they looked first to the mountains of Kilkenny to the west. At Graiguenamana they exhorted the crowds to prepare to assist an uprising in Kilkenny, while at Kilkenny itself, Smith O'Brien appealed to people to collect arms 'within the next few days'.

At Callan, things looked more promising. Crowds were waiting for them with a bonfire in the main street and music played by the Temperance Band. Houses were decked with laurel branches; flags and ribbons hung from the windows. At Carrick, they were joined by John O'Mahony and assured that 'the country all about Carrick, on towards Clonmel, and along the Suir on the Tipperary side, was thoroughly alive and ready to take the field at once'. Meagher was now exhilarated by what he perceived as a revolutionary atmosphere, and he outlined a programme for the future independent Irish Republic.[3]

Yet in spite of the apparent popular enthusiasm for the rebellion, local leaders were uniformly pessimistic, and Catholic priests were reluctant to take part. At Killenaule, Father Corcoran protested against any attempt to start a rising before the harvest, while at Templederry, Father Kenyon – once an outspoken

Young Ireland supporter – refused any assistance at all. 'Yes, of course he would fight if the people showed themselves prepared for revolution', he said, 'but it was not becoming for a priest to begin a bootless struggle.' What, he asked rhetorically of the messengers who came from Smith O'Brien, did they want him to do?

He was told that 'they wished him to summon the congregation by ringing the chapel bells, and march at its head to the aid of Smith O'Brien'. This Father Kenyon resolutely refused to do. 'If they thought his people were in the necessary disposition for such an adventure', he suggested, then they might perhaps 'raise a green flag on a pole anywhere in the district, and see how many men would rally round it.' To this he would have no objection. The clergy were clearly reluctant to join the struggle; a further blow came with the arrest of Lalor, awaiting developments in Templederry.

Smith O'Brien, as a landlord, appears to have been seriously out of touch with the mood of the peasants who flocked to his banner. In the wake of the famine, they were still close to destitution. Indeed, their enthusiasm for rebellion was allied to their hope that the rebel leader might soon be able to provide them with food, or at the very least encourage them to steal – something the priests had discouraged them from doing.

Smith O'Brien's opening speech to the assembled volunteers at Kilkenny was a disappointment. He told them to go home and to return the next morning, bringing 'provisions for at least four days'. He suggested optimistically that oatmeal bread and hard-boiled eggs would be suitable. The meeting was then addressed by Dillon, who 'at once perceived that his words found no response in the hearts of his hearers'. He well understood that many peasants had only joined the movement in the hope of being fed. The chronicler records that 'the people dispersed downcast, and from this day forward never again came together in such numbers.'

Serious differences now arose among the rebel leaders. Radicals like Dillon demanded that 'the property of the country' should be seized to support their movement. Michael Doheny argued that the banks in Carrick and other towns should be seized. But Smith O'Brien refused to contemplate such radical proposals; he specifically warned the peasants assembled at Ballingarry against looting. 'As their cause was a holy one, it should not be disgraced by any outrage on person or property . . . He would punish with death any one of his followers who would injure the property of any man.'

Father Kenyon, at Templederry, thought that it was 'utopian to attempt revolutionising a country' with the conservative methods advocated by Smith O'Brien. The priest, most reluctant to participate, had a bolder idea of what would be necessary:

> If you are in earnest, you must engage the very passions of the people, nay, you must work on their worst passions . . . You should seize on all the property of the country – the corn, the cattle, nay, the very plate of the enemy should be secured and converted into cash for the payment of foreign officers, who will hereby discipline your army. You should seize on the person of every aristocrat; and every other friend of the government, and hold them as hostages, and should the enemy, brutal as he probably would be, so forget the usages of legitimate warfare, as to shoot all the prisoners taken by them, on the plea of their being rebels, you will have it in your power to retaliate by executing one of their friends and allies for every man of yours so treated by them.

This was very far from being the programme of Smith O'Brien and his immediate entourage. 'Whatever hopes they might have had of posing a serious threat to the regime,' writes F. S. L. Lyons, 'vanished in the face of their own inefficiency and the vast indifference of a population too confused by faction and demoralised by hunger and disease to have any will to fight.'[4]

Yet out in the country, handfuls of peasants were beginning to mobilise. On 25 July, at Mullinahone, 'towards night, there were at least 2,000 men armed with guns, pikes, and pitchforks'. At Ballingarry, the next night, some 600 peasants had assembled on the common, fifty armed with muskets and 150 with scythes, pitchforks and pikes. Smith O'Brien drilled the men with muskets, but when news came that the British had gathered 'a large military and constabulary force' nearby, at Callan, and were assembling reinforcements, he ordered a retreat towards the mountain of Slievenamon. The retreat soon turned into a rout.

Stopping at Mullinahone for provisions, Smith O'Brien provided each man with a two-penny loaf at his own expense, but his generosity proved misplaced. After the local priest had warned everyone of the 'terrible consequences that were sure to befall them' if they did not go home, all but a hundred of the rebel band evaporated. When they resumed their march, a further eighty disappeared. Smith O'Brien was left with just twenty men.

A few days later, on 30 July, he surrendered to a body of armed police in a muddy field – 'on Widow MacCormick's cabbage patch', as the legend has it. Together with Meagher and two others, O'Donoghue and McManus, he was tried at Clonmel in October and found guilty of high treason. All four men were sentenced to death.

Both Russell, the prime minister, and the lord-lieutenant of Ireland, George Villiers, Lord Clarendon, were anxious to avoid executions, considering them to be unnecessary and politically unwise. Executing Smith O'Brien, Clarendon believed, would merely 'convert the little feeling now exhibited for him into general sympathy'.

Russell was equally reluctant: 'All I can say is that executions for political offences, though justifiable, are seldom politic – a martyr transported is not nearly so interesting as a martyr hanged.' As a result of their reluctance, judicial repression was kept to a minimum. The sentences were commuted in February 1849 to transportation for life, and in July that year they were shipped off to Tasmania. Later they escaped to America, and Smith O'Brien was even able to return to Ireland in 1856, where he died in 1864.

The fate of John Mitchel, who had been arrested earlier, was slightly different. Transported on HMS *Neptune*, he was among the first cargo of 300 convicts (of whom two-thirds were Irish) that the British had hopes of putting ashore in South Africa, after so much resistance to the continuing arrival of prisoners had been raised in Australia. The *Neptune* took five months to reach Cape Town and sat at anchor there for a further five months, while a near revolution was averted ashore. Mitchel was eventually sent on to Tasmania, but he too escaped in 1853 and made his way to the United States. He lived there for a further twenty years as a journalist, supporting the cause of the South – and slavery – during the Civil War.

The Young Irelander rising was a flop, and the London government had wisely refused to make martyrs of its protagonists. Yet the event raised interesting questions for the British, as an editorial in the London *Times* of 16 August rhetorically pointed out:

> There are a few grave facts and one grave question for the English people and government to ponder on. Is Ireland worth keeping? Shall we retain this diseased and feverish member of our common empire, or shall we fling it from us for ever? Is the benefit that we derive from the possession of Ireland, or the loss that we should sustain from its secession, so great as to make us anxious about keeping it? This is a grave question, and involves manifold considerations. It enters into all and every reflection respecting the future fortunes of the British Empire. Is Ireland linked to us forever by an inevitable destiny? Cannot we in justice, in honour, and without ignominy or detriment, shake it off? . . . We cannot go on with a fresh rebellion every year.

The Times did not answer its rhetorical questions, concluding only that the Irish were 'best governed by martial law'.

Meagher wrote later that 'the defeat of 1848 was not the defeat of a whole people. It was nothing more than the rout of a few peasants, hastily collected, badly armed, half-starved, and miserably clad. The country did not turn out.'[5] Yet despite the government's best endeavours, the Young Irelanders did in fact become popular heroes, as Virginia Crossmann has pointed out: 'Their attempt, however ineffectual, to overthrow a government which had so clearly failed to protect the lives of Irish people, was to encourage and, in some degree, to legitimate the activities of subsequent agitators.'[6] The uprising of 1848 joined that of 1798 as a significant mythmaker in the development of Ireland's long rebellious tradition.

CHAPTER 56

Dr Christopher Elliott, Wikrama Sardawa Siddhapa and the Rebellion of the Kandy Pretenders

In July 1848, an Irish doctor played a prominent role in a rebellion in Ceylon that led to the imposition of martial law, the slaughter of scores of peasants, and the execution of its nine ringleaders. Born in County Kilkenny in 1810, Dr Christopher Elliott was a medical doctor and a Baptist who had come to Ceylon in 1834. While in practice at Badulla he had purchased the *Colombo Observer*, and he used it over the years to campaign for political reform – for adult suffrage and representative government. His campaign against the government's introduction of new taxes and his endorsement of the constitutional aims of the 1848 Revolution in France helped spark off a rebellion in both Kandy and Colombo that took place on the anniversary of the great revolt of 1818. An additional cause, noted nervously by the imperial authorities, was the belief held by chiefs and priests in Kandy that the Empire had been weakened by that year's fierce resistance by the Sikhs in the Punjab.[1]

The first signs of trouble arose in Kandy on 6 July, when several thousand peasants assembled to protest against the new taxes. The crowd got out of hand, the police lost control, and the military was called in. Two days later, Sir James Tennent, the colonial secretary of Ceylon, met the Kandy chiefs at the King's Pavilion and listened to a recitation of their complaints. Tennent, who hailed from Belfast, told them that the government would not be deflected from its programme.

The July rebellion was the work of four 'Pretenders' to the throne of Kandy. Sri Wikrama Sardawa Siddhapa was the principal figure, described as 'the illustrious, heroic, pious, divinely accomplished prince', and sometimes referred to as 'King David'. The British called him Gongalagodde Banda. For several years, according to the memoirs of Captain John Henderson, an officer who participated in the repression of the rebellion, 'he appears to have been living on the charity of the credulous Kandians to whom he proclaimed himself as a member of the royal family of Raja Singha'. He hoped to see again 'a native king on the throne of Singhala'.[2]

All four Pretenders had been active during an earlier rebellion in 1843 that had sought to restore the traditional Kandyan monarchy. Sri Wikrama's brother Jawa, called King Dinis, was described as 'a most dangerous and active person', whose task at that time was to infiltrate and subvert the armed forces. A third Pretender, Purang Appu, was appointed as the sword-bearer to 'King David' and considered one of his 'most active, formidable and zealous' supporters. The fourth Pretender was named Dingeralle.

Henderson explained to his readers how the system of 'Pretenders' worked. 'With Orientals', he wrote, 'no insurrection can be carried on without a king. A cloth is tied to a spear for a banner, and a monarch improvised on the spot.' He is merely 'a puppet in the hands of the real leaders of the movement, who, should success light upon their arms, speedily dispose of the sovereign of the day, to make room for him who they intend should rule over them'.[3]

Prior to the rebellion (according to information received from a government agent at Kaigalle in June 1848), Sri Wikrama 'had been actively engaged in perambulating the country, using seditious language at the temples and houses of the chiefs, and collecting money, and announcing that his intention was to create a disturbance against the Government'. His expeditions had taken place over several years and 'had extended over the length and breadth of the Kandyan kingdom'.

According to a letter received by the government in August from Mr Dunewelle, a family member of a Kandyan chief, 'the pretended king and his younger brother have been, it seems, busy for the last five or six years in fomenting disaffection in the minds of the Kandyans who live far away from the town'. Dunewelle concluded that 'the recent transactions in France, and all over Europe, must have been represented to the poorer classes of the Kandyans in such a light as to have induced a belief that it was right to enlist themselves in behalf of the designing Pretender and his brother'.

There were additional reasons for rebellion closer to home. New taxes – on guns, shops and dogs – had been imposed by the island's governor, George Byng, Viscount Torrington. A new road ordinance had also been introduced, requiring all able-bodied males between the ages of sixteen and sixty to work on the roads for six days in the year, or to pay the equivalent in cash. The government had planned these changes for some time, seeking revenue from a new land tax rather than from import and export duties, but their implementation was accelerated by an impending economic crisis.

Particularly affected were the workers on the European coffee plantations, now established on the island for more than twenty years. The peasants had been hostile to these settlers from the start; their obligation to provide labour to build roads through to the coffee plantations was itself a cause for rebellion, and the new taxes were the final straw. According to Colonel Jonathan Forbes, one of the first coffee planters who had lived in the Kandyan town of Matale since the 1830s, the new laws removed 'a moderate indirect taxation from the European capitalist to inflict large direct taxation on the native'.[4]

The authorities were aware of the unpopularity of the plantations. 'Our coffee estates are a source of deadly hatred to the Kandians', was Torrington's comment, and he held no brief for the settlers either: 'The mass of the coffee planters, many of the worst *class* of Englishmen, has very much tended to lower and degrade our *cast* and character in the eyes of the natives'.

One further complaint raised by the nobles of Kandy was that British rule had brought the introduction of hard liquor and the subsequent demoralisation of the native population. Tennant argued the government secured so much money from the arrack tax that it could not abandon the scheme. 'The income we derive from this source', he noted, 'is so very large [upwards of 50,000 pounds a year], that it becomes a matter of difficulty to deal with it in the present state of the colonial finances.'[5]

Complaints about alcohol and the imposition of new taxes provided the background to the Kandy rebellion, but the more immediate cause was Dr Elliott's enthusiasm for the revolution in France. Elliott's *Colombo Observer* published a letter on 3 July 1848, signed by 'An Englishman', which was read by many as a call to arms: 'The principle is now pretty generally realised that all *who pay taxes* should have a voice in the government of their country and in the imposition of taxes. Millions in Europe have lately acquired these rights and enlightened Ceylonese who have heard of the onward movement were in hopes of sharing in the boom'.

The letter, translated into Sinhalese and circulated in Kandy, argued that the people of Ceylon were now called upon 'to follow the example of the French, to refuse to pay the new taxes and to agitate for the establishment of a radical democratic society based on racial equality and universal suffrage'.

The press had not objected to the taxes, according to Tennent, until the arrival of 'the intelligence of the French revolution, and the insurrectionary movements throughout Europe that followed it'. Immediately 'there was a very distinct alteration in the tone of the press', he said. Several articles 'singled out the recent taxes, and . . . recommended resistance to them in very strong and unmistakeable terms'.

News had arrived at the same time, he said, of 'disasters to our army in India', and he recalled being 'assured by intelligent Kandyans that those two circumstances had a very material effect on the minds of the Kandyans, and that they were made an improper use of to incite them to rebellion'.

In the weeks after the initial trouble in Kandy at the start of July, signs of further trouble were not lacking. Salt and paddy disappeared from the bazaars, according to the memoirs of one coffee planter, P. D. Millie:

> Large numbers of villagers commenced to flock into Kandy, on various pretences, and it was quite evident that something unusual was in contemplation; a number

> of planters, who were in town on private business, were detained there by the Government to help, if need be, in preserving the public security. Sentry guard was kept at the bank and public offices.[6]

There were two centres of disturbance, one in the Kandyan provinces and the other in Colombo, and both erupted on 26 July. The Kandyan rebellion took place in Matale, sixteen miles from Kandy, and in Kurunegalle, twenty-seven miles to the west of the town. Tennent considered the district of Matale to have been 'the focus of sedition on all previous occasions of insurrection'.

In Colombo, a protest meeting of townsfolk and peasants was held on 26 July, in the Cinnamon Gardens at Borella, about two miles from the centre. The demonstrators brought a petition about the taxes to present to the governor, saying that if he did not give a favourable reply, 'we certainly will not obey any of these new laws'.

'Blows were given and returned, several of the police and the superintendent being injured', according to Captain Henderson's account, and troops were summoned. But when Dr Elliott arrived, he asked people to remain quiet. 'So great was the influence which this gentleman possessed over the natives, in consequence of his uniformly advocating their cause, and from his always giving them medical attention gratis, that his request was immediately attended to, and the military on their arrival found that their services happily were not required.'[7]

Dr Elliott persuaded those present to present their petition to the governor by signing their names on separate sheets of paper, and these were duly handed in. The assembly dispersed peacefully, but a subsequent gathering later in the week, called to listen to the governor's reply, was banned.

By that time, the revolt had exploded inland. Thousands of people had gathered at Dambulla, the site of the principal rock temples in the island, some forty miles north of Kandy. Sri Wikrama was crowned as the new monarch by the priests, receiving 'the homage of some headmen and of several thousand armed natives'. Then, according to a subsequent account by Henry Earl Grey, the colonial secretary in London, 'large numbers of men assembled in arms in different places'.[8] One group attacked the town of Matale, sacking and plundering various public buildings; another attacked Kurunegalle, which was 'for a short time in the hands of the insurgents'.

Some on the spot were less than impressed. The crowd at Matale, according to the planter Millie, was 'merely a mass, a mob, with not the slightest pretension to military discipline, display or armament; the men were armed with old flint guns, crude spears, knives . . . The only source of danger was in their numbers, but even that, without a trained military leader, was of little use.'[9]

The British military authorities took a more serious view of the potential threat. Martial law was proclaimed in Kandy on 29 July and in Kurunegalle on 31 July. It would last for ten weeks. Detachments of European and Malay troops were marched out from Kandy to Matale, and telegrams were sent to Madras for military reinforcements.

The British authorities clearly panicked, fearing that the events of 1817–18 were about to be repeated. Brought to defend themselves subsequently before the House of Commons, they sought to inflate the size and importance of the rebellion. The British commander in the Central Province, Colonel Henry Drought, gave his version of events to the parliamentary select committee in December 1849, explaining that he had sent 200 soldiers to Matale on the evening of 28 July.

> When only five miles on their march, shots were fired near them, and at Warriapolle, a place a mile and a half from Matale, the troops were opposed and fired on by a very large body of natives, a comparatively small number showing themselves on the road, supported by many thousands under cover of the jungle . . . At this spot many prisoners were made, upwards of 100 stand of arms and a considerable quantity of ammunition were seized, and the pretender's palanquin was also taken.[10]

Quoting a statement by one of the Pretenders, Colonel Drought suggested that 'the whole force amounted to 18,000 men', and that their leaders planned to seize the town of Kandy. He said that Purang Appoo, their commander-in-chief, who was subsequently captured, had 'gloried in the project', and had told an officer that 'had our king but three men like me, we should now have been in possession of Kandy'. Another prisoner, Drought claimed, said the rebel aim was to march on Kandy and, 'with the aid of the Malays, to surprise the garrison and the Europeans whilst at church'. Drought also claimed that the Pretender Dinis had expected to arrive at Kandy with 'at least 80,000 men, and with every prospect of succeeding in its capture'.

Other observers and later historians have been less inclined to accept these figures. Although a large crowd attacked Matale on 29 July and sacked government buildings, and some 4,000 people attacked Kurunegalle on 31 July, the rebels were easily suppressed. A subaltern with thirty men proved more than a match for the rebels at Kurunegalle, while the rebels at Matale were routed at an abandoned coffee estate at the village of Wariyapola. Order was restored in both districts in less than a week.[11] Some 200 Kandyans were killed or wounded.[12] Torrington reported to London on 14 September that the rebels had been subdued by 'a wholesome terror inspired by martial law'.

The Pretender Dingeralle was captured almost at once and brought before a court martial at Kurunegalle on 4 August. Sentenced to death, he was shot with seventeen others, including Purang Appoo and a Buddhist priest. Dingeralle, according to Captain Henderson, 'was sentenced not only to be shot, but to be hanged on a tree in a public place in the neighbourhood of Kornegalle for four days!'

Two other Pretenders, Sri Wikrama and Dinis, escaped, hiding for a month in a cave at Elkaduwa, some miles from Matale. They were both arrested on 21 September, and charged with high treason on 27 November. Found guilty of waging war against Britain, they were scheduled to be hanged on 1 January 1849, but their sentences were commuted to one hundred lashes and exile to Malacca. Sri Wikrama died there in December.

Order was restored, but at a price. 'Did not hundreds of persons fall by the rifle bullet, or sink below the Malay *cris* [dagger]?' wrote Colonel Forbes, and, according to a letter from Dr Elliott, 'the day alone will reveal the extent and atrocity of the proceedings under martial law'.

When the Malay soldiers reached Matale, wrote Elliott,

> they found the people sacking some houses, and surrounded one[;] they never ceased firing into it until they shot 23 poor creatures (every man in it, I understand), although they made no resistance. Upwards of 200 were killed near and at Matale. The European soldiers behaved well; did not fire after the first volley; but the Malays shot and creesed the men after they had thrown away their guns, and were standing still. Things were little better in Kornegalle. Sims, the police magistrate, told me there were 47 laid in one hole, over which a vine has been planted . . .
>
> Such were the atrocities perpetrated in what ought to have been considered little more than a row. At all events, after the first volley, and the dispersion of the mob, there was no necessity for such barbarities. Officers in command of parties went out plundering the country, sacking houses, digging up the floors for money and jewellery, and finally setting fire to the premises.

According to the evidence of Thomas Young McChristie, a radical lawyer in London, describing events at Matale, 'they say that the troops went among the people, and shot them like birds before sportsmen . . . At Kornegalle, they complain also that there was undue pressure upon the people by the troops.'[13]

The prolonged imposition of martial law was to be severely criticised by the parliamentary select committee. 'Whatever the necessity which may have existed for the proclamation of martial law in the Kandyan provinces on July 29 and 31', declared Sir Joshua Walmsley MP in a draft report on 18 July 1850, 'the continuance and protracted operation of that law until October 10 of that year, to the sequestration and destruction of property and the sacrifice of life, were proceedings for which the Committee can find no sufficient justification, notwithstanding they were supported by many of the civil and military authorities.'[14]

The 'council of war' that implemented the decisions concerning martial law was made up of three men: Colonel Drought; Captain Charles Bird of the Ceylon Rifles; and General Herbert Maddock, a retired East India Company official with a coffee plantation at Matale, later described as 'the evil genius behind the whole policy of repression' (his coffee store in Matale was burned down by the rebels). The imposition of martial law was attributed to the influence of another coffee planter, General John 'Tiger' Fraser, formerly the colonel of the 37th Regiment, who had taken part in the repression of the rebellion in 1818.

The court martial assembled at Matale on 13 August sat for six weeks. Nine prisoners were shot, and 'scores of others were sentenced to be flogged, transported, imprisoned with hard labour etc.'. Colonel Forbes noted that it was

> considered by most people a very unnecessary piece of severity, to shoot men, and men of the lowest order, too, not ringleaders, six weeks or more after anyone had been found in arms; more especially as the outbreak has been so ridiculously unsuccessful, and not a single life has been lost on the part of the Europeans.[15]

Later in the month, on 28 August, with martial law still in operation, the Supreme Court met in special session at Kandy to try more than 250 prisoners. Seventeen were convicted of high treason and condemned to death. The chief justice, Sir Anthony Oliphant, recommending mercy, pointed out how little fighting there had been, and that eighteen people had already been shot under martial law. 'The blood which has been already spilt is sufficient', he said. Governor Torrington was opposed to such clemency, but he eventually commuted the death sentences to terms of imprisonment, ordering an additional punishment of flogging.

Martial law had a serious impact on the population at large, causing much of the rural population to abandon their homes. Asked to account for this phenomenon by the select committee, Colonel Samuel Braybrooke of the Ceylon Rifles said that people fled 'from their timidity, and dread of having the military let loose upon them, and not the military only, but the marauders who accompany a military force, servants of the officers and servants of the soldiers, and their followers, who commit much more mischief than the military themselves'. After martial law had been in effect for three weeks, Torrington ordered everyone to return home, adding that if they failed to do so within twenty days their property would be sequestered. Expropriation was then 'extensively enforced, partly as a measure of terror and partly as one of protection'.

There was a further purpose. General Maddock suggested to Tennent that if lands were to be confiscated from the rebels, 'colonies' of imported Indians could be established on them. These Indians would then be available to work on the European coffee plantations. A letter was then sent from Tennent to Torrington (according to Colonel Forbes's account) 'recommending that the Malabars (the class who labour on the coffee estates, and come from the continent of India) should be located at Kurunegalle and Matale, on the lands to be forfeited from the rebels'. Tennent later reported that Maddock's proposed 'colonies' were not established because the sequestration of land 'had fallen far short of expectation'.[16]

There are few more revealing insights into imperial disaffection than those provided by Sir James Tennent during his interrogation by the select committee in March 1850. Since 1815, he said,

> there have been six treasonable movements of considerable importance against the Government. There has been on the average one such movement in every six years. There was open rebellion in 1817, in 1823, and in 1848. There were three conspiracies detected before their explosion, in 1820, 1834, and 1843, and those are independent of the treasonable plots which were detected and arrests which took place in 1816, 1819, 1820, 1824, 1830, and 1842.

On all these occasions, said Tennent, 'the manifestations of insurrection on the part of the Kandyans have originated in their impatience of British supremacy and their desire to restore a native sovereignty'. Disaffection was not confined to religious causes, Tennent suggested, but existed generally 'among the natives'.

Tennent knew exactly what was wrong. He argued that the British judicial system had been prematurely introduced and was 'unsuitable to the state of the Kandyan country'; he thought that 'the system under which our revenue has been collected has been oppressive'. Yet the principal error of British policy, he thought, had been to force upon 'a purely Oriental people European and British institutions which they have neither appreciated nor enjoyed'.

Philip Anstruther, an earlier colonial secretary, from 1830 to 1845, and subsequently a coffee farmer, pointed out other imperial failings, in evidence given to the select committee on 24 July 1849:

> There is a complete curtain drawn in Ceylon between the Government and the governed; no person connected with the Government understands the language; very few of them have the remotest idea of the customs of the natives; they are perfectly ignorant of the people, as ignorant as any gentleman in London could be of the people over whom they rule.

As a result of the findings of the select committee in London, Governor Torrington was recalled in 1850, and the colonial secretary, Tennent, was dismissed. London felt that the two leading local authorities were largely responsible for what had happened, and they paid the price.

Dr Elliott, the Irish Baptist inspired by the revolution in France to seek reform in Ceylon, lived on there until his death in 1859. 'As a journalist', his obituary notice recorded, 'he may, like the rest of us, have sometimes erred, but he was always honestly anxious for the welfare of his adopted country and the cause of justice, truth, and pure Christianity.'

CHAPTER 57

The Final Rebellion of the Xhosa in Cape Colony

In December 1850, the Xhosa in British Kaffraria prepared to renew their rebellion. British Kaffraria was now a frontier zone, controlled permanently under martial law. A new young prophet, Mlanjeni the Riverman, now came forward to echo the old prophecy that the former heroes of the nation would live again, to assist the new generation to defeat the white oppressors. The leaders of the Xhosa, Sandile and Maqoma, lived in the Amatolas mountains, surrounded by a ring of British forts: Fort Murray, Fort White, Fort Cox, Fort Hare, Fort Beaufort and Fort Armstrong. In the valley of the Tyumie River, which ran into the Keiskammer, General Sir Harry Smith, the governor, had established military villages where retired British soldiers had each been given a twelve-acre plot.

Mlanjeni, barely out of his teens, lived near the Keiskammer river and was to follow in the footsteps of Makana, who had led the great rebellion of 1819. Since those days, the Xhosa had often repeated the hope that Makana would come back to help them. Mlenjeni began as a simple exponent of witchcraft, but soon the British perceived him as a potential threat to their rule, and sought to detain him. His fame grew after he eluded capture, and he was visited by Sandile and his councillors in November 1850. They were told to prepare for war; each Xhosa warrior was required to slaughter one among their cattle, while Mlangeni himself would ensure that the warriors would be invulnerable in battle. The guns of the British, Mlanjeni said, would only fire hot water; he provided the warriors with special roots that would ward off the bullets.

Sandile was inspired by the young prophet and sent out an urgent message: 'Arise, clans of the nation! The white man has wearied us; let us fight for our country; they are depriving us of our rights which we inherit from our forefathers.'

Harry Smith, for his part, hearing of Mlanjeni's threats and recalling that Makana had been defeated in 1819 and imprisoned on Robben Island, told his officers to seek his capture. 'If you catch this Mahomet', he said, 'let him be right well secured, and he shall speedily find himself on Robben Island.'

At the end of December 1850, urged on by Mlanjeni, Maqoma's Xhosa forces attacked and decimated a British troop on the frontiers of Cape Colony not far from Fort Hare, south-west of the Amatolas mountains. This new battle marked the start of the second-longest war in nineteenth-century South Africa, and the largest single conflict between black and white south of the Sahara.[1]

'The military power of England', wrote Sir John Fortescue in 1913, 'was strained almost to breaking point by three thousand savages.'[2]

Sandile had been the Xhosa leader in the battles of the 1840s, but Maqoma now came out of retirement to take the lead, fighting for the first time since the resistance war in 1835. To British surprise, the Khoi-Khoi of the Kat River settlement also joined in, fighting together with the Xhosa. Long perceived as the sepoys of South Africa, the Khoi-Khoi were regarded as Britain's most loyal allies. Now, for the first time, there was a degree of unity among the African population and a willingness to resist the British, led yet again by Smith and Colonel Jack Somerset.

A large Xhosa force assembled in the hills and attacked Somerset's battalion of 150 soldiers as they made their way from Fort Hare to Fort Cox, accompanied by seventy Khoi-Khoi cavalry from the Cape Mounted Rifles. Somerset was forced to retreat, while thousands of Xhosa 'swarmed out of every valley along the way, and across every ridge, densely massed, and with the dispositions arranged with evident skill and prompt, shrewd observation by Maqoma'.[3]

The Xhosa had soon surrounded the British force, and Smith was blockaded within Fort Cox. 'Now commenced the work of death', wrote one of the British survivors of the attack, in which two officers and twenty soldiers were killed. It was a severe humiliation for the British, writes Noël Mostert: 'Not until Rorke's Drift some eighteen years on would the British army again fight and die in such a brave, cruel and intimate scuffle on the African veld.'[4] This was a significant triumph for Maqoma, for he had humiliated Somerset and Smith, his two oldest enemies.

The Xhosa were assisted by a rebellion of the Khoi-Khoi at the Kat River settlement. For the military and civil establishment of Cape Colony, the revolt of the formerly loyal Khoi-Khoi was an unforgivable act of treason, 'a military mutiny as well as a social insurrection'.[5] It created a dangerous precedent and had to be put down at once. 'The people of the Kat River were, after all, full subjects of the Queen, against whom they had taken up arms.'[6] The Khoi-Khoi appeared to hate the English settlers even more than they had once hated the Dutch. According to one close observer, the substance of many remarks being made by the rebellious Khoi-Khoi was: 'The English must leave the country and go away in ships.'[7]

The Xhosa triumph of December 1850 was short-lived, for Maqoma could not prevent Harry Smith's escape from Fort Cox, or his safe return to his headquarters at King William's Town. The Xhosa were now to be faced by something entirely different: an enemy intent on their physical destruction. Smith decided that famine and the torch provided the only means to defeat the Xhosa. He issued a 'notice' in which he expressed a hope 'that the colonists will rise en masse . . . to destroy and exterminate these most barbarous and treacherous savages, for the moment formidable'.

Smith wrote to Robert Godlonton, editor of the *Grahamstown Journal*, to say that they must now make 'an attempt at extermination' – a phrase he was to use repeatedly in the following weeks. The troops should 'give no quarter to any Kaffir', said one British colonel, 'but rather put a price upon them, as you would upon so many beasts of prey, and honestly pay the same, for every Kaffir head brought in'. No prisoners should be taken, and all should be 'hanged or shot "without benefit of clergy"'.

Sarili, paramount chief of the Xhosa, sought an honourable end to the conflict, promising to put pressure on Sandile:

> We beg for peace over the whole land . . . If the Governor Smith, our Father, does not like to send to Sandile to tell him to put down his assegais and stop the war, then, if Smith, my Father, will send to me, I will send to Sandile to tell him to put down his assegais.[8]

Smith ignored these peace feelers, and the Xhosa fought back in a prolonged and furious campaign. One of their chiefs, Siyolo, was described by a later governor as 'personally the most active, warlike and inveterate enemy we have to contend with'.[9] Fighting in the territory along the Fish River in November 1851, Siyolo's men killed sixty British soldiers – the greatest Xhosa triumph in the war. A senior British officer, Colonel Thomas Fordyce, was also killed.

Colonel Smith's words and actions had not gone unnoticed in London. He had finally over-reached himself, and in November 1851 he was recalled to London, just as Torrington and Tennent had been summoned home from Ceylon a year earlier. 'You have failed in showing that foresight, energy and judgement which your very difficult position required', wrote Earl Grey, telling him that the conduct of the war would be placed in other hands. Smith was replaced by General George Cathcart, one of Wellington's generals, and reinforcements were sent out. The HMS *Birkenhead* sailed for Cape Colony with some 500 soldiers drafted from Ireland. The ship arrived safely at Simonstown, near Cape Town, but when bound in February 1852 for Alagoa Bay (Port Elizabeth), the nearest port to Grahamstown, it hit a reef. Fewer than 200 of those aboard survived the shipwreck.

The Xhosa were jubilant. The forced departure of General Smith and the sinking of the *Birkenhead* revived their spirits. The magic spells of Mlanjeni had worked well. Maqoma and Sandile had won their long struggle with Harry Smith, but it was a pyrrhic victory. Soon they were fighting battles on several fronts. Early in 1852, the Xhosa in the Amatolas were faced by seven military columns that came to cut down the standing crops of maize and millet. British soldiers were equipped with scythes and sickles, and the work of destruction began – levelling crops, seizing cattle and burning huts. This had long been a feature of war on the frontier. 'What made the campaign of January–March 1852 so different', writes J. B. Peiris, 'was that it was a coordinated, deliberate plan aimed exclusively at the Xhosa fields and gardens.'[10]

With their crops and gardens gone, the Xhosa were now systematically hunted down. Half starving, they lost the will to resist. One colonial volunteer described their retreat: 'They made no stand and offered no resistance, neither did they beg for mercy or show any fear, but kept on at a steady pace while our people rode up to them and shot them down.'[11] The British hanged the Xhosa from trees, and boiled down their skulls for despatch to Britain as souvenirs, and for the attention of phrenologists.

By the autumn of 1852 the Xhosa were seeking peace negotiations, and Governor Cathcart brought the war to a close. Siyolo was seized in October 1852, after agreeing to discuss negotiations, and imprisoned on Robben Island for seventeen years. Mlanjeni died of tuberculosis in August 1853, promising before his death that all those killed in the war would one day rise up again.

After the great slaughter, vast tracts of land were left deserted. Fresh cohorts of white settlers were sent in, and the boundaries of the colony were extended. After the end of the Crimean War, many of the new settlers were Germans who had been recruited into the British army during that war, and were now given their reward with farms in British Kaffraria. Some years later, in 1865, the territory was formally incorporated into Cape Colony.

In the middle of Mlanjeni's war, on 30 June 1851, Moshoeshoe, king of the Sotho, secured a notable victory against a small British force. The composite force of British soldiers, Dutch farmers, Africans and coloureds, led by Major Henry Warden, the Resident at Bloemfontein, suffered a crushing defeat at the battle of Tihela, near Ladybrand, and lost 150 men. Moshoeshoe's country, today Lesotho, lay between the Orange and Celadon rivers. Moshoeshoe had sought the protection of the British in 1843 when threatened by the advance of Boer settlers across the Orange. Under a treaty signed with George Napier, the governor at the Cape, Moshoeshoe had been recognised as an ally, paid £75 a year, and required to keep order in the territory north of the Orange.

Five years later, in 1848, the British had moved the imperial frontier north to the Vaal, proclaiming the land between the Vaal and the Orange as the Orange River Sovereignty. Major Warden was established at Bloemfontein with the task of marking out the boundaries between the territories of rival groups, including the Sotho, the Griqua, and the Dutch farmers.

In 1851, Moshoeshoe had come to assist his ally Chief Moletsane of the Bataung, whose villages, on the Viervoet mountain near Thaba Nchu, had been attacked by the British. Chief Moletsane had been seeking to resist the settler advance. To crush Moshoeshoe's resistance, George Cathcart, the new governor at the Cape, moved 2,000 troops to a spot near Maseru in December 1852, and ordered Moshoeshoe to pay a fine of 10,000 cattle and 1,000 horses within three days. Moshoeshoe refused, and when the deadline expired he was attacked by Cathcart's forces. These in turn were attacked successfully by Moshoeshoe's son Molapo, and the British retreated. It was a Sotho victory.

Cathcart returned to London to fight and die in the Crimean War, and was replaced by George Grey from New Zealand. In 1854 the British transferred the territory to the Boers, who renamed it the Orange Free State. The Boers had continuing troubled relations with the Sotho enclave of Moshoeshoe, and in 1861 he again requested British protection.[12] Eventually the British government agreed to annex his country of Lesotho, and it was incorporated into the Empire in March 1868. Moshoeshoe was born in 1786 and died in 1870, having ruled over the Sotho for more than fifty years.

CHAPTER 58

West African Resistance

On 25 November 1851, King Kosoko, an African ruler based at the town of Lagos on the west coast of Africa, came under attack from British naval forces. His men repelled the attack, killing two officers and wounding sixteen sailors, but in a second attack a few days later, the British landed on the eastern spit of Lagos island and burned down the slave barracoons belonging to three Portuguese slave-traders. Yet they were still unable to capture the town. They returned a month later.

Kosoko had been warned of trouble when he received an ultimatum from John Beecroft, the British consul resident at Fernando Po. Sailing to Lagos a few weeks earlier, accompanied by three naval officers, Beecroft had demanded of Kosoko that he should sign a 'protection' treaty with Britain. Kosoko refused, declaring that he had no need of protection and no desire for friendship with Britain.

The attack on Lagos marked another episode in Britain's prolonged period of intervention along the coast of West Africa. 'At no period has the British Navy been more continuously engaged . . . in small wars', wrote Sir William Laird Clowes, in a history of the navy that recorded 'hundreds of minor operations' that took place in the last half of the nineteenth century.[1] The excuse for British intervention was the campaign to eradicate the slave trade that had so enflamed opinion in Britain, but behind the humanitarian impulse came the need to open up markets and to spread the ideology of Christianity.

The navy needed bases from which to operate, and one of the places chosen was Fernando Po, nominally a Spanish island in the nineteenth century. Between 1827 and 1843 the British leased two naval ports there from the local chief, and Beecroft, a trader and explorer-adventurer, was appointed as the British consul. In the 1840s, when engaged in exploring the creeks and rivers of the West African coast, he was made consul for the Bights of Biafra and Benin, to advance British commercial interests and to help regulate relations with local rulers.

Irritated by Kosoko's resistance in November 1851, Beecroft and Commodore H. W. Bruce, the British naval commander, summoned Akitoye, a rival claimant to the throne of Lagos, to a meeting on their ship. In return for British support for his claim, Akitoye promised to stop the local slave traffic and to abolish the practice of human sacrifice that Kosoko was alleged to practice. The British naval force returned to Lagos on Christmas Eve, with four ships, 357 soldiers, and a locally recruited African army of 650 men loyal to Akitoye. While the British sailors rested on Christmas Day and held church services, Akitoye's non-Christian army erected gun batteries onshore. Yet when the British force tried to land on 26 December, the resistance of Kosoko's men was so effective that they were obliged to retreat. HMS *Teazer* ran aground in range of Kosoko's guns, and a landing party was sent to destroy the battery – though at a heavy cost.

Lagos was bombarded and set alight on the following day, and much of the town was destroyed in the flames. Kosoko abandoned the town in the evening, but his followers fought on, resisting the British attempt to land their troops. The British suffered fifteen killed and seventy-five wounded, but eventually claimed victory. Akitoye was installed as the new king.

Kosoko retreated to a base at Epe, some thirty miles away, and remained a thorn in Britain's side, landing at Lagos two years later, in August 1853, in an attempt to overthrow Akitoye. A fresh battle for the city began, and British naval forces again intervened. Kosoko's men were driven off.

Akitoye had never been popular, and when he died later that month the British installed his son Dosumo as the new king. Kosoko was eventually bribed to abandon his resistance, and he signed a treaty with the British the following year. Lagos was formally annexed to the British Empire in 1861.

William Dappa Pepple, King of Bonny in the delta of the rivers of Biafra, was the next African ruler in the sights of John Beecroft. Pepple had been one of the first to sign a treaty with the British, as long ago as 1839. Promised a £2,000 subsidy payable annually for five years, he had agreed to abolish the slave trade, but the money was not forthcoming. The king complained bitterly about 'the bad faith of the English government', for he needed the money to buy off rival chiefs. The trade continued through Spanish vessels, and British ships and traders had a rough time in the waters of Bonny. Fresh treaties were signed in 1848 and 1850, but proved as ineffective as the first.

In 1854 King Pepple had antagonised both local chiefs and foreign traders, and they turned to Beecroft, asking him to intervene. Pepple had become seriously ill and was partially paralysed, and in January he was persuaded by Beecroft to retire in exile to Fernando Po. Considerable controversy arose as to whether the king had chosen to leave of his own accord. Beecroft died in June, but King Pepple's case was raised in the British parliament, and he was repatriated in 1861 and given £4,000 in compensation. He became a convert to Christianity and sought to spread it among his people.[2]

In May 1855, Bamba Mina Lahai, the Muslim chief of Maligia, a town on the shores of the Melakori River north of Freetown, caused the British to suffer their worst military disaster in Sierra Leone during more than half a century of occupation. HMS *Teazer* lost seventy-seven men from the West India Regiment, shot, drowned or taken prisoner.[3]

The Melakori River had long been a centre of the lucrative groundnut business, controlled by English and French traders. In 1854, unhappy with their activity, the Maligia chief gave the traders ten days to leave, and three British gunboats arrived in December with 400 troops to persuade him to reverse his decision. Bamba Mina Lahai initially caved in to this pressure and agreed to pay compensation to the traders, but the promised money was not forthcoming; HMS *Teazer* returned in May 1855 on a follow-up mission to secure what was due.

Following established tradition on the west coast of Africa, the British ship would indicate its presence by attacking the town from a safe distance with Congreve rockets. On this occasion the ship had none available, and 200 soldiers went ashore to collect the money. Initially the chief's men offered no resistance, but the town's mosque and Bamba Minha Lahai's house was burned down and the chief's men fired at the re-embarking soldiers. On the following day, as the British set fire to other houses with Lucifer matches, they were shot at from the bush. Retreating to the shore, the soldiers escaped in a small boat, to return to the *Teazer*. The boat capsized, and although the Teazer picked up a handful of survivors, nearly eighty men were lost. It had been a disastrous expedition for the British.

CHAPTER 59

The Start of an Endless Saga: The North-West Frontier Territories of India

The flickering resistance struggle against the British on India's border with Afghanistan, which had continued throughout the 1840s, burst into flame in November 1851. It marked the start of the recurring problems that the Muslim inhabitants of India's North-West Frontier territories were to have with the British in the wake of the latter's seizure of the Punjab in 1849. The frontier was to make a lasting impact on the British too, for, as Penderel Moon has recorded, the frontier and its turbulent tribes were to acquire a certain romance for the British public: 'For British military officers it had a special attraction, offering many of them, among others Wavell and Churchill, a chance of getting away from peace-time soldiering and enjoying the excitement of active service. But it took up more time and attention and provoked more controversy than it really deserved.'[1] The problems that began in the 1850s were to survive well into the twenty-first century.

The old frontier administration set up in the era of Ranjit Singh had been loose, barbarous, and relatively effective. The old ruler of the Punjab built forts on the narrow strip of the trans-Indus plain that he claimed as his territory, and marked out a rough boundary along the foothills of the mountains. His toughest generals were sent there to keep order by whatever ruthless methods they might choose.

The British imagined they were continuing the good work. They accepted Ranjit Singh's frontier, they built a road along it with a protective chain of forts, and they made efforts to conciliate and bribe the frontier chiefs. Yet the lasting phenomena over the next hundred years – and more – were tribal resistance and imperial punishment.

Resistance to British rule took the form of endless raids and rebellions. Some sixty tribal rebellions took place on the North-West Frontier in the sixty years between 1847 and 1908, while the British launched twenty-six large-scale 'punitive expeditions' in the twenty years between 1850 and 1870. Many involved forces of more than 5,000 men, and the casualties on the British side were often in the hundreds.

The most rebellious tribesmen came from Waziristan, south of the Khyber Pass – the Wazirs and the Darwesh Khel, the Dawaris, and the Mahsuds. They were to rebel against the British in 1852, 1859, 1860, 1880, 1881, 1894, 1897,

1900 and 1908. Indeed their rebellions were to continue until independence in 1947, and beyond.

The Afridis, west of Peshawar, were equally formidable rebels, and the largest British military expedition – with an army of over 34,000 soldiers – was deployed against them in 1897, resulting in the most severe casualties, with nearly 300 dead and nearly 1,000 wounded. The Afridis were to rebel in 1850, 1853, 1855, 1877, 1878, 1897 and 1908. The Ambela expedition of 1863 against the so-called 'Hindustani fanatics' deployed over 9,000 soldiers, and also took large casualties – 238 killed and 670 wounded.

The Mohmands, in the hills and plains between Peshawar and the Afghan border, were also frequent rebels. They were subjected to 'punitive expeditions' sent out against them in 1851, 1854, 1864, 1878, 1880, 1897 and 1908. According to a British officer writing in 1912, the Mohmands 'have gained for themselves of more recent years a reputation as brave fighters as well as troublesome raiders, but are thoroughly mistrusted and detested by their neighbours, who accuse them of the grossest treachery'.[2]

Saadat Khan, the leader of the Mohmand rebels at mid-century, was based at Lalpura. In November 1851 he attacked a number of British-protected villages in the valley of the Kabul River, and soon he was preparing to fight off a British expeditionary force sent out from Peshawar. Mohmand resistance had started a year earlier, in December 1850, when Saadat Khan's son Fateh had led a group of tribesmen in an attack on the British fort at Shabkadar, in the Kabul River valley to the north of Peshawar. Further attacks on British-controlled villages had occurred in the course of 1851, and eventually the British felt obliged to respond. A force of 1,600 men marched out of Peshawar on 25 October led by Brigadier Colin Campbell, a Peninsular War veteran who would become the commander-in-chief in India during the Mutiny in 1857.

Saadat Khan had first been in contact with the British in 1838, when their invading army came through his territory on its way to Afghanistan. He had tried to oppose the invasion, but the British had simply removed him as chief, replacing him with Turabaz Khan, a more pliable cousin. Recovering his position as Mohmand leader after the British disaster at Kabul in 1842, Saadat Khan refused to recognise the British occupation of the Peshawar valley. As the British gave strength and structure to their presence, after absorbing the Punjab in 1849, Saadat Khan became a bitter opponent, protesting against the seizure of Mohmand lands and refusing to pay the taxes that British occupation forces required. Over many years, he and the Mohmands gave the British more trouble than any other group in the region.

Saadat Khan's chief grievance was the British support given to the villagers in the fertile valley land, leaving other Mohmands with little but barren mountainsides on which to feed their animals and grow their crops. When attacking British-protected villages in 1851, he gathered allies from other tribes in a concerted effort to drive the British out.

Early in December, more than 4,000 men occupied the hills around the camp that Brigadier Campbell's men had constructed at Michni. The British plan was to destroy Saadat Khan's hill villages and reinforce Fort Shabkadar, but initially they were too few. When reinforcements arrived from Peshawar, it was the turn of Saadat Khan to be outnumbered. He retired to his home base of Lalpura in the west, while the British retreated to Peshawar.

In March 1852, the Mohmands again fired on the Shabkadar fort, and another British punitive expedition was sent out from Peshawar. This time the outcome was more favourable to the Mohmands. The rebel tribesmen abandoned their villages, but a troop of the 7th Bengal Light Cavalry ordered to pursue them refused to obey orders. Lieutenant F. R. Tottenham ordered his men to charge, but was faced with a mutiny: 'Not a man followed him. Riding back, he entreated his men to follow him as the enemy passed their flank, but in vain . . . No order, no entreaty, no example could get them to charge.' Unable to fight the Mohmands, the British force retreated to Peshawar, setting fire to their villages before they left.[3]

In December 1852, the Hassanzai tribesmen to the north-east of Peshawar came under attack from a British punitive expedition led by Colonel F. Mackeson, the commissioner at Peshawar. The Hassanzai, a group of Pathans living on either side of the Indus River on the slopes of the Black Mountain, earned money by shipping salt across the Indus into the Punjab. Since salt was traditionally an item whose sale was controlled by the state, the Hassanzai were regarded, both by the Sikhs and by the British, as smugglers. In the period after the new British frontier line had been defined and extended, in the wake of the Sikh wars and the annexation of the Punjab, the Hassanzai smugglers had killed two British customs officers trying to stop what they perceived as an illegal trade.

The British officers had been operating in the territory of the Nawab of Amb, a chief of Hazara to whom they paid a regular subsidy. The authorities at Peshawar complained to the Nawab about the death of the officers, and asked him to hand over the killers. The Nawab surrendered a few Hassanzai, whereupon the Hassanzai leaders attacked the Nawab's border villages and seized two of his forts, one at Shingli.

With such an attack on their ally the Nawab, the British felt obliged to act, although the Hassanzai had some 2,000 men under arms and strong alliances with neighbouring tribes, including the 'Hindustani fanatics' based at Sitana (a group of fundamentalist Pathans), who seized the Nawab's fort at Kotla, on the right bank of the Indus. The Hassanzai were faced by Colonel Mackeson's punitive expedition, assembled at Shergarh, with cavalry, sappers, guides and local levies, as well as hundreds of camels and quantities of baggage. The expedition took three days to travel seventeen miles, and within the month the Hassanzai had disappeared. In their absence, the British recaptured Shingli and restored it to the Nawab, with minimal casualties. They went on to destroy the local Hassanzai villages and their grain stocks.

In January 1853 the 'Hindustani fanatics' at Kotla came under British attack. Established on the Yusafzai border of Peshawar since 1823, their continuing resistance posed a threat to the British, and, in the words of Colonel Wylly's history, it had now become necessary 'to punish them'.[4]

The 'Hindustani fanatics' were Pathans who thirty years earlier had been the followers of Saiyid Ahmad Shah, a famous mullah from Bareilly. The Saiyid, who had been associated in 1817 with Amir Khan and the Pindaris, was 'a man of peculiar sanctity' who believed himself to have been 'divinely commissioned to wage a war of extermination, with the aid of all true believers, against the infidel'. Having studied Arabic in Delhi and sailed to Mecca from Calcutta, the saiyid had had considerable influence among the Muslims of Bengal. Transferring his base to the neighbourhood of Peshawar in 1823, he had preached a jihad against the Sikh ruler, Ranjit Singh. Defeated in 1827 by Ranjit's general, Hari Singh, the saiyid had retreated via Swat to Buner.

With support from local Pathans, he set out again to recover his position at Peshawar, but this time the Sikh armies were more forthright. They organised expeditions against the Hindustanis, which, wrote E. E. Oliver, 'were exterminative rather than punitive'.[5] British colonial historians always liked to recall events in which their predecessors were as brutal as themselves.

> The villagers turned out and hunted back the fugitives into the mountains, destroying them like wild beasts. The history of the time is a record of the bitterest hatred. The traditions tell of massacre without mercy ... Something like the Sicilian Vespers was repeated, the fiery cross was passed round the hills as the signal for the massacre of his agents, and in one hour – the hour of evening prayer – they were murdered by the tribesmen almost to a man.[6]

Finally, in 1829, Saiyid Ahmad Shah was killed by the soldiers of Ranjit Singh. Of the 1,600 Hindustanis with him, 300 escaped to Sitana, a territory controlled by Saiyid Akbar Shah, formerly his counsellor and treasurer. Sitana soon became a refuge for outlaws and all kinds of offenders from Yusufzai and Hazara. The surviving Hindustanis established a colony there and built a fort at Mandi.

Called out to help the Hassanzai against the British in 1852, the Hindustanis established themselves at Kotla, but when Colonel Mackeson's force arrived on the banks of the Indus opposite the Kotla fort in January 1853, they withdrew into the hills beyond.

'There was no more trouble in the Peshawar district' until 1857, the year of the Mutiny, wrote Colonel Wylly. The Hindustanis, 'supported by contributions of men and money from traitorous princes and private individuals in India', remained an important focus of resistance on the Yusafzai frontier.[7] Maulvi Inayat Ali Khan 'raised the standard of religious war', and an expedition was sent against him; but the Maulvi himself escaped. The Hindustanis were attacked again by the Ambela Expedition in 1863.

CHAPTER 60

The Burmese Empire Resists Further Invasion

On 12 April 1852, Burmese soldiers in Rangoon put up a stout defence against a fresh British invasion, in which the great Schwe Dagon pagoda came under attack. Fierce resistance kept this symbolically significant structure out of British hands for two days, while elsewhere in the city soldiers were deployed in defending a colossal statue of Buddha. Its established position within the 'White House' stockade was 'burned by the Engineers and the Sappers', and 'the entire roof of the house was destroyed'. One eyewitness recalled the extraordinary effect of 'the huge figure seen from a distance, overtopping the shell of the ruined mansion'.

Burma had been invaded by the British nearly thirty years earlier, in 1824, and the unequal treaty of Yandabo, imposed at war's end in February 1826, had met with lasting resistance. Burmese hostility to this enforced British connection obliged the 'British Resident' imposed by the treaty to withdraw in the 1830s, first from the capital at Ava and then from the port at Rangoon. Succeeding to the Burmese throne in 1846, King Pagan Min had stepped up his country's anti-British campaign, clamping down on the trading privileges that the British had claimed for themselves at Rangoon. Traders were threatened, and the British organised an economic blockade. The king was accused of oppressing the traders and of human rights abuses against his own people; it was said that 6,000 executions had taken place in the first two years of his reign.[1]

Britain soon claimed that its patience was 'exhausted', and in March 1852 King Pagan received an ultimatum from Lord Dalhousie, Viceroy of India: 'hostile operations' would begin on 1 April if Britain's demands for economic redress were not met. Ignoring the threat, the king commanded his soldiers at Rangoon to resist an impending invasion. The viceroy, for his part, ordered some 8,000 sepoys to assemble at Calcutta, Madras and Penang; they sailed to Rangoon under the command of General Henry Godwin, an ageing veteran of the Peninsular War and a participant in the first Burmese invasion, in 1824.

The Burmese monarch was well prepared; he had several Europeans working for his army, including a Portuguese engineer and a British officer from the Madras Artillery. The situation was by no means desperate, but when the British attacked Rangoon the Burmese were unable to prevent the capture of the town, the pagoda, and the Buddha; their soldiers were withdrawn northwards up the Irrawaddy.

The British invading force followed them, capturing the town of Pegu in June 1852. The Burmese commander was General Bandula, the son of Maha Bandula, who had been killed in 1824. This was also the first campaign of Garnet Wolseley, a prominent colonial general, who appears in innumerable later imperial battles – from Canada to South Africa – until the end of the century. Like many of his kind at the time, he was a devout Christian. 'All through my life, sinner though I have been', he noted late in life, 'I trusted implicitly in God's providence, I believed He watched specially over me and intended me for some important work.'[2]

The rainy season brought a halt to the fighting, but when it resumed the Burmese failed to prevent General Godwin's advance on Prome, which was captured in October. King Pagan was informed by Dalhousie that the province of Pegu would now be annexed to the British Empire, linking Arakan and Tenasserim to form British Burma, a new province of British India. The King was left with the provinces of Upper Burma, but he was warned that any further resistance would lead to the destruction of his entire kingdom. He ignored these threats, which the British were in no condition to carry out, and the formal war came to a unilateral end with no formal treaty.

Other Burmese figures questioned the judgment of King Pagan; they resolved to embark on a campaign of guerrilla resistance to the British invasion. Ever since the first British assault on the Burmese Empire, in 1824, large areas of the country remained beyond the control either of the old (Burmese) empire or of the new (British) empire. Local chiefs, variably described as dacoits, robbers, or brigands, operated up and down the rivers, controlling the banks and imposing their own kind of rough justice. Myat Toon was one such chief, much feared by the British, who headed an army of some 7,000 men. He was allied with other chiefs, including Shwe Ban, who possessed a smaller force of around 2,000. Between them, they controlled the river banks of the Irrawaddy between Rangoon and Donabew, and raided the British supply ships that plied between Rangoon and the advanced base at Prome.

Myat Toon fought off successive British efforts to winkle him out of his river fastness at Donahew, notably in early February 1853. He attacked a small British force of 200 soldiers that had arrived close to his base after moving up a small creek off the main river. The banks were low and covered with jungle, and Myat Toon's men had felled trees and driven stakes into the river to prevent the British boats from passing. Muskets were fired from each bank and the British were obliged to retreat, with the loss of twelve killed or wounded, including Captain Loch, the commanding officer.

Later in the month, Myat Toon was faced with a punitive expedition, led by Colonel John Cheape, sent down from Prome to avenge the death of Captain

Loch. Among those with him was Ensign Garnet Wolseley. Cheape's force was more than 1,000 strong, made up of 500 Europeans and 500 Indian sepoys, mostly Sikhs and Bengalis. On arriving close to Donabew, he realised he would need reinforcements, and more soldiers were sent up from Rangoon.

Myat Toon's base at Kyault Azein was defended with stockades, stakes and fences, and Cheape's forces had some trouble finding their way. They had left the Irrawaddy in March, plunging inland; for several days they moved backwards and forwards, uncertain where they were or where the enemy was. The guides were unreliable. With food running short, the soldiers were put on half-rations, and over one hundred men were lost to cholera in the first few days. 'As they drew nearer to Myat Toon's stronghold, it was found that his dispositions for defence exhibited considerable skill, and were admirably adapted to the nature of his position', wrote one historian.[3]

Myat Toon's soldiers, unseen in the jungle, opened fire on the unsuspecting British force. Myat Toon then withdrew to another defended position that was attacked by Cheape's surviving force, aided by the reinforcements from Rangoon, on 19 March. His new position was captured with the assistance of a twenty-four-pound howitzer. The British had prevailed, but the cost, with 140 dead and wounded, was high. Ensign Wolseley was wounded and invalided back to Britain. Myat Toon escaped into the jungle, like so many Burmese guerrillas before and since, to fight another day.

King Pagan, however, was threatened by internal enemies. The defeat by the British led to his overthrow by his half-brother King Mindon, a Buddhist monk. The new regime remained hostile to the British, but only on the surface. Mindon refused to recognise the British seizure of the southern half of the kingdom, yet he quietly made deals quietly with the new rulers and eventually received a British representative at court.[4] He accepted the new imperial order and ruled over his (northern) portion of Burma for a quarter of a century, until his death in 1878. The resistance struggle against the British was later revived in 1885 by Thibaw, his son and successor.

Part X

THE GATHERING STORM, 1854–58

In March 1854 a war broke out between the world's great empires. The British Empire joined forces with the French Empire to declare war on the Russian Empire, which was confronting the Turkish Empire. In September Britain and France landed troops on Russia's Crimean peninsula, on the northern shores of the Black Sea, with the immediate aim of capturing the Russian naval base of Sebastopol. Major battles were fought at the Alma river, at Balaklava and at Inkerman.

In the affairs of the British Empire, the Crimean War marked a watershed. The war brought an end to the world system established after Waterloo in 1815, and to the era of overt military control of the Empire directed by the now-dwindling band of soldiers who had fought in the Peninsular Wars – in Wellington's armies in Spain from 1808 to 1814. The duke himself, prominent in the battle against Tipu Sultan at Seringapatam in 1799, died in 1852, just two years before the Crimean War; he had remained as Britain's commander-in-chief throughout the decade before his death.

Most of Wellington's contemporaries, actively engaged in imperial duties on distant frontiers for nearly fifty years, were at the end of their careers. His alter ego, Lord Fitzroy Somerset, was one of the few still in command (as Lord Raglan). He had been on Wellington's staff during the Peninsular War, his military secretary at the Horse Guards from 1827 to 1852, and his successor as commander-in-chief. He was effectively killed off by the Crimean War, dying of dysentery in 1855. Not having fought a battle for forty years, he continued to refer to the Russian enemy as 'the French'. Raglan himself had had no colonial experience, but his successor as commander-in-chief, General James Simpson, had taken part in fighting the Baluchi amirs in Sind during Napier's campaigns in the 1840s. Admiral Sir James Stirling, the killer of Aborigines in western Australia in 1834, was now commander of naval forces on the China station.

British forces were spread very wide in 1854, with 30,000 troops in India and 40,000 in the other colonies. Some 65,000 remained to guard the turbulent home front. To fight the Crimean War, the British were obliged to withdraw several regiments from their colonial territories. Canada, in particular, was almost denuded of troops, with less than 2,000 regular soldiers remaining to garrison the entire country.

In the early part of the war, opponents of empire everywhere took heart from British misfortune and Russian success. Educated Indians followed the war with close interest, and those hostile to empire 'discussed with malicious glee the ill-success of British arms'.[1] Henry Lawrence, the Resident at Lahore, reported that 'many sensible natives of India think that every Russian is eight feet high, and that Bombay and Calcutta are threatened by a Russian fleet, while an army is coming down the Khyber'.

In Cape Colony, the embattled Xhosa also believed that the Russians would soon come to their rescue. They had heard of the death of Sir George Cathcart, the British commander-in-chief in South Africa, killed at Inkerman in November 1854. Sarili, paramount chief of the Xhosa, told a British priest in 1855 that he expected the Russians to win. So widespread was the belief in an imminent Russian arrival that the Xhosa started looking out to sea for signs of Russian ships. In March 1856, Nongqawuse, the teenage niece of Sarili's adviser, saw visions of strange people who told her that the Russians were coming to expel the British.

Sebastopol remained under siege for more than a year, and the Russians finally withdrew in September 1855, after blowing up its fortifications; in distant Delhi the viceroy, Lord Dalhousie, issued a proclamation welcoming 'the great and glorious victory' of the allies. Nearly a quarter of a million people were dead on both sides, though many through disease rather than in battle. A peace conference took place in March 1856, leading to yet another Treaty of Paris, which guaranteed the status quo ante in the Balkans, whose alteration had been the original cause of the war.

The end of the war brought new immigrants to Cape Colony. More than 2,000 German and Swiss mercenaries, recruited by the British to fight at Sebastopol, were sent for resettlement to British Kaffraria, eventually establishing prosperous settlements along the Tyumi River. These new settlers were mobilised as a militia to defend the frontier in 1857, permitting regular Cape regiments to be sent to India to help in the suppression of the great Indian rebellion of 1857–58.

The Empire was shaken to its roots by this epochal revolt, occurring just one hundred years after the Indian defeat at the battle of Plassey – an anniversary of which the Indians were rather more conscious than the British. The revolt was preceded by several indications of unrest. The uprising of the Santals in West Bengal in 1855 was the first serious peasant rebellion in British India, and the resistance of the Muslim Moplahs in Malabar in the same year was a symptom of trouble beneath the surface calm. The Moplahs sought an end to oppression by Hindu landlords, but the Santals hoped for independence from the Raj.

Other non-colonial wars were fought by the British in the year before the Indian revolt, one with China and one with Persia. War was declared on Persia in November 1856, and the Shah Nasir-u-Din ordered his priests to declare a jihad against the British, hoping (in vain) that the Muslims in India would listen to the appeal.[2] The war's principal cause was the British concern about the Persian occupation of Herat, a city considered to be part of Afghanistan. The five-month war ended with a British victory just as the Indian revolt was beginning. Several officers – notably Henry Havelock and James Outram – hurried back to India to participate in its repression.

Like the war with Persia, the British attack on China – sometimes called the Arrow War or the Second Opium War – took place late in 1856, on the eve of the Indian revolt. Canton, now Guangzhou, came under heavy bombardment between October 1856 and January 1857, in which houses and warehouses were destroyed and hundreds of civilians killed.[3] The city was then occupied for several years. China in the 1850s was itself undergoing a huge upheaval, the Taiping Rebellion,[4] whose ramifications were felt throughout the Chinese communities in Asia, notably in Singapore and Hong Kong. Riots and sabotage directly affected the interests of the British Empire. These were troubled times, and even the most distant colonies took note.

CHAPTER 61

The Taiping Rebellion Spreads Unrest among Chinese Communities Elsewhere

In May 1854, a war broke out between Chinese clans living in and around the British naval base of Singapore; thousands fought in the streets of the city over twelve days. The scale of the fighting took the European authorities by surprise, and they suddenly understood that cheap convict labourers recruited into the settlement, without women, brought frustration and violence with them from China, as well as historic animosities.[1] Some 400 people were killed and 300 homes destroyed. Merchants feared for the safety of their goods and their godowns. Although the immediate cause of the riots was an increase in the price of rice, and the consequent discontent of the labour force, the underlying trouble lay in the inherited feuds between existing secret societies and more recent immigrants from China. China itself was being shaken by the campaigns of the Taiping Rebellion.

The riots were not directed against the European community, but the battles were so extensive that the Europeans organised a self-defence militia, the Singapore Volunteer Rifle Corps – the first white settler militia set up in Asia. William Butterworth, governor of the colony, was appointed its colonel, but his militia did not have the strength to suppress the Chinese quarrels. He asked for assistance from the naval commander of the East India and China station, and the Chinese rebels soon faced Indian sepoys and British marines. 'These people must fully understand that this is not their country', Butterworth declared in a proclamation to the Chinese community on 11 May, 'and they must learn to attend to their own business, instead of molesting each other by going about the country to destroy the houses and properties of their neighbours.' If they continued in these outrages, he went on, 'they must expect to be treated like madmen'.[2]

The fighting spread to the country areas where the Chinese communities were established, and reports told of whole villages being wiped out.[3] Hundreds of Chinese were alleged to be preparing an attack on the city, and troops were deployed to guard the roads into town. Yet after days of sporadic fighting, life returned to normal. According to one report, the warring parties were appeased with the help of influential Chinese merchants. Some 500 Chinese were detained, and half were put on trial; six were sentenced to death, and two were executed. Yet the Europeans remained nervous, and the underlying threat of violence persisted. Similar disturbances were to take place in 1867 and 1872.

On the morning of 15 January 1857, the European community in Hong Kong woke up to discover that their bread had been poisoned. Several hundred people collapsed with arsenic poisoning, among them the wife of the governor, Sir John Bowring. They had all eaten bread supplied by the E-sing Bakery.

The bread poisoning was immediately assumed to be a form of Chinese sabotage against the imperial authorities. The Chinese population was in close touch with the Chinese at the great port of Canton, across the water on the mainland, and a few months earlier, during the so-called Arrow War between Britain and China in October 1856, Canton had come under British bombardment. Fearing that the hostility aroused by this small war might spill over into Hong Kong, the British anchored a gunboat off the Central Market in December – a visible warning to the Chinese population to remain quiet.

The bread-poisoning episode caused considerable alarm among the Europeans. Suspicion fell first on Cheong Ah-lum, the owner of the E-sing bakery, who had left Hong Kong that morning for Portuguese Macao. Yet Cheong Ah-lum was a major player in the bakery business, supplying bread and other provisions to the Europeans during the weeks they had been fighting on the mainland, and he was not the most likely candidate to have organised a poisoning campaign. When he was arrested in Macao, it emerged that he too had eaten the poisoned bread and been extremely ill.

The British authorities then imagined that one of Cheong Ah-lum's bakery workmen might have been guilty of making the poisoned bread, and fifty-one bakers were arrested. They were detained for two weeks in an underground police cell, measuring fifteen feet square, and the Chinese called it the 'Black Hole of Hong Kong', for the colony had recently marked the centenary of Calcutta's 'Black Hole', of 1756.

When the bakers appeared in court, the British prosecutor argued that the poisoning had been ordered from Canton; but since no evidence was forthcoming, the jury called for their acquittal.[4] The authorities ordered their immediate re-arrest. Governor Bowring was concerned by the adverse publicity arising from their gaol conditions, and recommended their deportation. The fifty-one bakers were eventually released and ordered to leave the colony. Several members of the European community thought the island of Formosa would be a suitable destination. Cheong Ah-lum sought refuge in Saigon.

The Chinese in the colony, undaunted by the exile of the bakers, continued in their criticism of the British attacks on Canton. In February, they again took action against the European food supply. The bakery of George Duddwell, which had taken over the task of supplying bread to the European community, was burned down, and again the authorities arrested many people. Some 200 'suspicious-looking characters' were arrested in Bonham Strand, 500 others detained, and 167 deported to Hainan.

By such methods, Chinese passions were slowly brought under control, and by 1858 the atmosphere in the colony was less volatile. The administration was able to recruit a corps of 2,000 Hong Kong 'coolies' to act as porters for an Anglo-French military expedition launched against Peking in 1858.

CHAPTER 62

White Settler Rebellion in Australia and Further Aborigine Resistance

A revolt by gold-diggers in November 1854 became the first significant white settler rebellion in Australia since the events of 'Vinegar Hill' half a century earlier, in 1804, and the 'Rum Rebellion' *coup d'état* of 1808. It was to become one of the founding myths of the white Australian nation. Gold had been discovered near Bathurst in New South Wales in 1851, and a few months later at Ballarat in Victoria. Thousands of prospectors swiftly arrived from distant parts of the world. Most were British and Irish, but Americans came too, as well as adventurers from Europe. Many Chinese joined the gold rush, arousing considerable racist animosity within the mining communities. Nearly 400,000 immigrants arrived in the country in 1852; indeed, it was claimed that more settlers came in that year alone than the total number of convicts brought in during the previous seventy.

The authorities imposed a tax on the diggers, who were required to pay for a licence of thirty shillings a month. Payment was enforced by an embryonic police force, but increasing resentment of the tax came to a head in the Ballarat goldfields towards the end of 1854. The murder of a miner there, and the burning down of the Eureka hostel in revenge, led to a meeting on 11 November of 10,000 enraged prospectors, and the subsequent formation of a Ballarat Reform League. Several leaders of this League had experience of the Chartist movement in England in the 1830s, and of other revolutionary upheavals in Europe in 1848. Their immediate interest was an end to the licence system, but, echoing the Chartists' demands, they also called for 'no taxation without representation' and for manhood suffrage (although not, of course, for Aborigines).

The response of the governor in Melbourne was to send out reinforcements to crush this revolt. An initial armed clash, followed by the ostentatious burning of the licences, led to the creation of a more militant group of miners, led by Peter Lalor, a twenty-seven-year-old Irishman. He quickly organised armed resistance to the force sent from Melbourne. Lalor had once been involved with the Young Ireland movement, and had emigrated to Australia two years earlier. Tall and good-looking, he was a natural leader, though hardly a democrat. He devised the oath that the rebels swore under their new flag: 'We swear by the Southern Cross to stand truly by each other and fight to defend our rights and liberties.' He also organised the construction of a 'stockade' of farm carts within which the rebels assembled. Most were Irish and, echoing past struggles, they used the words 'Vinegar Hill' as their password.

A brief battle took place on 3 December at what became known as the 'Eureka stockade', and more than twenty miners were killed by the military. Lalor himself was wounded, and lost an arm. Martial law was declared and a hundred miners were taken prisoner. Thirteen were taken to Melbourne for trial. The unequal struggle at Eureka Stockade was widely perceived as a massacre, and all were acquitted.

A subsequent Royal Commission recommended the abolition of the license system and the expansion of political representation to the goldfields. Lalor was among a new generation of elected politicians. Visiting the goldfields years later, in 1895, Mark Twain described the episode at the Eureka Stockade as

> the finest thing in Australasian history. It was a revolution – small in size; but great politically; it was a strike for liberty, a struggle for principle, a stand against injustice and oppression . . . It is another instance of a victory won by a lost battle. It adds an honorable page to history; the people know it and are proud of it.[1]

Legends were created around the revolt, and movies were later made to help keep them alive. Chips Rafferty played the part of Peter Lalor in an Ealing Studios film of 1949.[2]

In the year after the miners' revolt at Eureka Stockade, it was the turn of the Aborigines to renew their resistance struggle. In 1855 a series of Aborigine attacks took place on the new settlements on the expanding northern frontier of Queensland, as the native peoples sought to fight against the expropriation of their tribal land. On the night of 23 September 1855, a small group crept into the camp of the Native Police Force at Rannes, and removed the carbines and pistols of seven troopers while they slept. A larger group moved in later that night from the scrub, and speared the troopers before they had time to move. Three were killed and four were wounded; the Aborigines withdrew into the bush, taking guns and clothes with them.[3]

This was an unusually well-planned attack; the Aborigines came not just from the surrounding districts but from as far away as the Fitzroy and MacKenzie rivers, from tribes already active in their opposition to the seizure of their lands by white settlers. Further attacks followed, as part of a concerted plan to destroy the new settlements. Police patrols sent to hunt them down returned without success.

In December, three months after their first attack, the same group returned. Their target this time was a station at Mt Larcom, seventy miles east of Rannes and fourteen miles north of Gladstone. The owner, William Young, was well known for his harsh dealings with Aborigines, and the group had been fired on in earlier weeks by police troopers. On the morning after the attack the bodies of three white men, a white woman, and an Aboriginal boy were found by Lieutenant Murray Young. He guessed that about fifty Aborigines had taken part; the bodies were mutilated, 'being covered with spear and nulla-nulla wounds'. He thought that it had been a surprise attack, for 'the white men killed had been well provided with fire-arms'. Double-barrelled guns and two carbines were found close to their bodies. Sheep had been driven off, the store had been broken open, and quantities of cloth, flour and sugar were missing.

The Aborigines were pursued by Young's troopers, and two further clashes took place over a three-week period in which eleven Aborigines were killed. Yet it was easy for the native fighters to disappear in the difficult terrain – salt-water creeks where no horseman could follow – and Young was obliged to withdraw.

A fresh attack was made a month later, in January 1856, when a hundred Aborigines came to a station some miles north of Grasmere, run by the brothers Elliott. One sheep shearer was killed, and William Elliott was severely wounded. This was a close-run affair, for the Aborigines were faced by twenty well-armed whites with 'a bold and systematic plan'. The Elliott brothers was still awake when they attacked, and the element of surprise was lost.

Another Aborigine group gathered on the northern side of the Fitzroy River the following month. Charles Archer, the owner of the station at Grasmere, claimed that they planned to attack any white man who looked as though he might settle in their direction. Lieutenant Young was again summoned out on patrol, but with only four troopers at his command, he returned empty-handed. The Aborigines continued to resist the Queensland settlers for several more years.

In October the following year, a hundred Aborigines launched a savage attack on the Hornet Bank homestead near Taroom in central Queensland, close to the Dawson River. The Hornet Bank sheep run of some 200 square miles occupied the hunting grounds of the Jiman Aborigines – just one among many such sheep stations operating in Aborigine territory. It had been seized a few years earlier, in 1853, by Andrew Scott, who had subsequently leased it to the Fraser family. Armed with spears and nulla-nullas, the Aborigine band attacked just before dawn, and killed eight members of the Fraser family. Three of them were women, aged between eleven and forty-three, and they were 'violated in their persons and frightfully mangled'. Sylvester Fraser, aged fourteen, was the only one left alive to tell the tale.

All the evidence suggests that the Aborigine fury was aroused for a very simple reason. John and David Fraser, the eldest sons of the family, had raped local Aborigine women and were the authors of their family's misfortune.

Although Martha Fraser, their mother and a widow, had repeatedly asked Native Police officers to reprove her sons 'for forcibly taking the young maidens . . . they were in the habit of doing so, notwithstanding her entreaties to the contrary'. She fully 'expected harm would come' as a result. Several neighbours pointed out that the Fraser boys were 'famous for the young gins', and all agreed that their acts 'were the cause of the atrocity'.[4]

The killings that October morning took place against the background of continuing resistance to white settlement in central Queensland, and the reaction of the settler community to the attack was swift and harsh. The settler newspaper, the *Moreton Bay Courier*, described the attack as 'a fearful outrage committed by blacks under circumstances of peculiar atrocity'. Small gangs of settlers, assisted by detachments from the Native Police Force, now began a six-month campaign against the Aborigines in the district. Rosa Campbell-Praed, a child on a neighbouring settlement who later wrote a book describing the events of her childhood, labelled it 'a little war', but it could 'more accurately' be described as 'a vendetta, a rout, or "an orgy of slaughter".'[5]

There are particular moments in Australian history, writes one of the modern historians of racial conflict there, when the barely suppressed fears and exasperations of the white settlers 'were channelled into an outburst of embittered and uncompromising fury'. Such a flash-point

> was not usually ignited simply by Aborigines killing a disparate number of white individuals, such as shepherds. Rather, it was induced after they had struck down members of that social unit which was virtually identified with the coming of civilisation into the wilds: the European family unit. The themes invoked here of ravished femininity and outraged innocence acted upon other settlers as a goad for revenge which would be pursued with a passion that even transcended their passion for land.[6]

So it was with the killing of the Fraser family at Hornet Bank. It was followed by a full-scale settler pogrom. 'Several hundred Aborigines in broken batches were rounded up over a wide area, and standing mutely, or roped and handcuffed together, or ordered to run, were shot down, while the press called for extermination of "the black fiends by whom we are surrounded" and "full and just revenge" upon the "butchering Aborigines".'

One young man who visited the area early in 1858 was appalled by the revenge attacks of the settlers. George Lang wrote an account of what he had discovered, and forwarded it to his uncle in the city:

> I learned from various sources that a party of twelve – squatters and their confidential overseers – went out, mounted and armed to the teeth, and scoured the country

> for blacks, away from the scrubs of the murder of the Frasers altogether, and shot upwards of eighty men, women and children. Not content with scouring the scrubs and forest country, they were bold enough to ride up to the Head Stations and shoot down the tame blacks whom they found camping there. Ten men were shot in this way at Ross' head station on the Upper Burnet. Several at Prior's station, and at Hays and Lambs several more.[7]

Lang noted that the official custodians of law and order were also active, the Native Police Force claiming to have shot more than seventy blacks. 'One of their acts deserves especial notice. They arrived at Humphrey's station, went to the blacks encamped near the house, bound two of the men, and led them into the scrub and deliberately shot them. The cries of the two poor wretches were heard by the superintendent's family at his house.'

Lang's letter was dated 31 March 1858 – some five months after the killings at Hornet Bank. He had found the repression to be still in full swing:

> On the evening of Friday or Saturday last, the white police, accompanied by some white volunteers, proceeded to the Blacks Camp near Mr Cleary's homestead, between the old and new townships of Maryborough, and drove every man, woman, and child out of it, then set it on fire, destroying all the clothing, bark, tomahawks and weapons of the blacks, and burning wilfully all the blankets which, at no inconsiderable expense, are served out to the blacks yearly by the Government . . . Yesterday, the Native Police force, under the orders of their white officers, performed the same meritorious action for the blacks in Maryborough, setting fire to their camp, destroying their clothing and blankets, and driving numbers of them into the river – in sight of the whole town population.

The Hornet Bank 'massacre' became a famous event in the history of white Australia because an entire settler family was wiped out, yet the provocation was intense and unceasing. The subsequent revenge killings of Aborigines occupy a less significant role in the official memory of Australia's past.

The slaughter of Aborigines by settlers and squatters continued without respite in many parts of Australia in the 1850s, but the indigenous peoples in New South Wales began to organise themselves for fresh resistance. They seemed to have 'some settled plan to murder as many [shepherds] as they can' was the message received by the state's attorney-general in April 1858, sent by W. H. Wiseman, the commissioner of Crown Lands.[8] Wiseman had visited a sheep station at Camboon to investigate the death there of 'two Coolies and two Englishmen', killed by Aborigines. He was alarmed to find that the Aborigines had seized no sheep but had taken the available weapons – 'a carbine, powder and balls, and some axes'. Now well-armed, they had moved on to an isolated sheep station at Banana, where only three shepherds were employed. The shepherds, according to Wiseman's account, were seriously alarmed and offered 'the Aborigines everything they possessed'. The Aborigines told them that 'they would have only their lives; and "that they would take the lives of all the b—y white men in the country"'.

The Aborigines then attacked and wounded the shepherds with spears. The shepherds fought off their attackers and killed one of them. Wiseman noted with some concern that some of the Aborigines 'had long been living with the whites'. Now they had turned to rebellion.

Several shepherds had already been killed in the region, and it had proved difficult, in unfriendly terrain, to find enough police to protect them. Wiseman reported that

> even fifty men is but little to look after the now numerous inimical Blacks which line the Dawson and Fitzroy, on a frontier of more than three hundred miles. The scrubs and broken impracticable country occupy, perhaps, one-third of this district so continuously that the Aborigines can travel, perhaps, from one end to the other under shelter.

Wiseman had no immediate solution, for the existing police force was ill-paid and not up to the task. He recognised that 'the remedy of high wages, securing the services of men for shepherds whose courage will intimidate the Blacks', would be 'ruinous to the capitalist, and would ultimately cause the desertion of the district'. This, he wrote to the attorney general, would 'never be permitted by His Excellency's Government'.

Wiseman turned again to a South African example, perhaps recalling the experience after Myall Creek in 1838. He suggested that 'the substitution of Hottentots as troopers might succeed'. He had stayed some years earlier with Dr Stephen Simpson, the commissioner of Crown Lands of the Moreton Bay district of Woogaroo, who had had two 'Hottentot' troopers in his Border Police Force. 'These troopers were ex-soldiers who, *after conviction in South Africa for military offences*, were transported to the colony of New South Wales. As convicts they were assigned to the Border Police which had been established to serve in the districts *beyond the boundaries of the settlement in the colony*.' This might be a solution for the upcountry regions of New South Wales, Wiseman suggested, though nothing further was done. The frontier resistance struggle continued unabated long into the second half of the century.

CHAPTER 63

The Santals in Bengal and the Moplahs in Malabar

In the remote hills of West Bengal, the first great peasant insurrection in the history of British India broke out in June 1855. Assembling from more than 400 villages in the area of Damun-i-koh, 10,000 Santals gathered at Bhagnadihi, in the hills close to Barhait.[1] Their leaders voiced their opposition to the continuing oppression of tax-collectors and money-lenders, but the peasants themselves had wider ambitions. Their initial plan was to march on Calcutta, 'to take possession of the country and set up a government of their own'. One cause of the rebellion, a British official explained years later, was the yearning of the Santals 'for independence, a dream of the ancient days when they had no overlords'.[2]

The Santals were one of India's many indigenous peoples, a group that had moved into this part of Bengal in the 1830s, clearing the forest and bringing large tracts of land into cultivation. Their principal quarrel was with the tax-collectors, but they also opposed the arrival of fresh settlers and traders, forever pushing into the woods of their pillared territory from the plains. British settlers had established indigo plantations in the area.

Real trouble started in 1854, after European officials arrived to construct a railway. The new line skirted the Santal country for 200 miles, and the construction of embankments, cuttings and bridges created a demand for workmen. It 'completely altered' the relation of capital to labour in Bengal, wrote Sir William Hunter, an official who worked there later.[3] Something else was 'altered' too. One of the witnesses to a commission appointed to examine the causes of the rebellion blamed 'the unwarrantable conduct of some of the railway employees, who insulted their women and refused to pay the Sonthals when [they were] employed on the railway works'.[4]

The rebellion's first leader was a peasant named Kanhu, who was supported by his brothers Sidhu, Chand and Bhairab. Kanhu rapidly acquired a god-like status, and the brothers explained that they had been led to rebel through divine intervention. They had received a visit from Thakur, a Hindu god who was 'like a white man, though dressed in the native style', according to a contemporary account in the *Calcutta Review*. 'On each hand he had ten fingers. He held a white book and wrote therein.' Thakur gave the brothers the book, and then 'ascended upwards and disappeared'. He told them that the time was ripe for rebellion.

Thakur's visitations continued in varying forms. 'There was not merely one apparition of the sublime Thakoor; each day in the week, for some short period, did he make known his presence to his favoured apostles. At one time it was in a flame or fire, with a book, some white paper, and a knife; at another in the figure of . . . a solid cart-wheel.'

Kanhu and Sidhu built a statue of Thakur in their garden, and soon began spreading the news of his revelation. They carried branches of the Sal tree into local marketplaces – a traditional method of communication among the Santals. Asked why he had participated in the revolt, a captured Santal quoted Kanhu saying that 'it was our "Raj" now. We obeyed his words, for he was a Thakur.'[5]

The first Santal action was an attack on a local market. Half a dozen Hindu *mahajuns* – men who worked both as traders and as moneylenders – were killed, and a week after the initial gathering at Bhagnadihi, the rebels killed Mahesh Lal Datta, a *daroga*, or police inspector, who had arrived at the nearby town of Barhait with a small force. A week later, they attacked people working on the railway line, saying that 'the Company's rule is at an end'.

The authorities were initially bewildered. The Santals had never given trouble before. 'Their industry, their perseverance, their love of order, their inquisitiveness, their joviality', said the Reverend Ernest Droese, a missionary, 'are conspicuous to the most casual visitor.' Yet the attack on the police and on the railway line showed that something unusual was underway.

The Santal rebels were soon confronted by a British force, led by Major F. W. Burroughs, sent out from Bhagalpur to crush them. Yet when a battle took place at Pirpainti on 16 July, the Santals were victorious, much to the major's surprise. Six officers and twenty-five soldiers were left for dead. 'The rebels stood their ground firmly', Major Burroughs reported later, 'and shot not only with hand-bows but with bows which they used with their feet, sitting on the ground to pull them, and fought also with a kind of battle-axe.'

The authorities were now thoroughly alarmed. The insurrection has 'assumed all the characteristics of a rebellion', wrote C. F. Brown, the commissioner at Bhagalpur, on 19 July. He issued a proclamation sanctioning 'the destruction of the rebels found in arms'. Large rewards were offered for any leaders captured, and the soldiers were told 'to take all the measures considered necessary for the extirpation of the rebels'. They were asked to ensure that their families were spared, since 'the British government does not make war against women and children'. Commissioner Brown had 'deemed it necessary' to declare martial law, but he does not seem to have done so with adequate formality, and the Calcutta government told him later that his 'proclamations' were illegal.

Concerned by the defeat at Pirpainti, the commissioner told Major-General Lloyd at Dinapur that more troops would be needed if the rebellion was to be suppressed: 'Not a day passes without fresh atrocities being perpetrated, villages plundered and burnt, and the unfortunate inhabitants massacred without respect to age or sex.'

Rebuked by Calcutta for his premature proclamations, Commissioner Brown wrote on 29 July to Frederick Halliday, the governor of Bengal, to restate his case:

> It appears that the Santhals are led on and incited to acts of oppression by the *gowallahs* (milkmen), *telis* (oilmen), and other castes, who supply them with intelligence, beat their drums, direct their proceedings, and act as their spies.
>
> These people, as well as the *lohars* (blacksmiths) who make their arrows and axes, ought to meet with condign punishment, and be speedily included in any proclamation which government may see fit to issue against the rebels.

Government forces were now mobilised to crush the rebels. A. C. Bidwell was appointed by the Bengal governor as the 'Special Commissioner for the Suppression of the Santal Insurrection'. He was ordered to take measures necessary 'for the entire suppression of the insurrection . . . and for restoring tranquillity to the disturbed districts'. At this stage, Halliday believed that Commissioner Brown had overreacted, and Bidwell was urged to err on the side of leniency. He was told to declare that the government would 'freely pardon all who may tender a speedy submission, except those who shall be proved to have been the principal leaders and instigators of the insurrection'. Halliday added further warnings against the burning of Santal villages in reprisal raids. 'It can never conduce to the early settlement of the present unhappy disturbances', he remarked, 'to make large bodies of armed men, our subjects, homeless and desperate.'

In spite of the repression, some 30,000 Santals had been actively mobilised by the middle of August. 'They have as yet shown no signs of submission to the government', Commissioner Brown noted on 11 August, 'but are on the contrary openly at war with our troops.' The Santal rebel army had now divided into two large groups, and further attacks occurred in September. One magistrate noted that 'their numbers average, as nearly as we can ascertain, from 12,000 to 14,000, and are receiving augmentation from all quarters'.

Governor Halliday was lobbied in Calcutta by a deputation from Nelson and Co., the contractors building the railway line. Worried about their investment, they requested firmer action, and told him that 'great consternation prevailed in that neighbourhood among the Europeans as well as the Indians'. It would be difficult to start work again 'unless very active measures be taken to preserve the peace'. Under pressure, Halliday agreed to allow the firm to recruit a paramilitary force with fifty muskets 'for the defence of his people and works, and the neighbouring villages'.

'It is only through striking terror into these bloodthirsty savages . . . that we can hope to quell this insurrection', wrote the editor of the *Friend of India*, published in Calcutta:

> It is necessary to avenge the outrages committed . . . India has not arrived at the point where armed rebellion can be treated with the contemptuous forbearance with which the English ministry can pardon a knot of Chartists or banish a gang of Irish patriots. Let the Santhals' punishment be entrusted to a special Commision as was done in Canada in 1838.

In November the Calcutta authorities reappraised the situation. Martial law was formally declared, and 14,000 soldiers were deployed against the Santals. In the ensuring campaign, innumerable Santal villages were destroyed; the villagers, according to the account of L. S. S. Malley, showed 'the most reckless courage, never knowing when they were beaten, and refusing to surrender'. Armed with axes and bows and arrows, they were mown down by British guns. They refused to surrender:

> On one occasion, forty-five Santhals took refuge in a mud hut which they held against the sepoys. Volley after volley was fired into it, and, before each volley, quarter was offered. Each time, the Santhals replied with a discharge of arrows. At last, when their fire ceased, the sepoys entered the hut and found only one old man was left alive. A sepoy called on him to surrender, whereupon the man rushed upon him and cut him down with his battle axe.

'It was not war', wrote Major Vincent Jervis,

> it was execution. We had orders to go out wherever we saw the smoke of a village rising above the jungle . . . As long as their national drums beat, the whole party would stand, and allow themselves to be shot down. Their arrows often killed our men, and so we had to fire on them as long as they stood . . . There was not a Sepoy in the war who did not feel ashamed of himself. The prisoners were for the most part wounded men. They upbraided us with fighting against them . . . They were the most truthful set of men I ever met; brave to infatuation. A lieutenant of mine had once to shoot down seventy-five men before their drums ceased, and the party fell back.

Months of bloody fighting took place before the rebellion began to falter early in 1856. 'The details of border warfare', wrote Sir William Hunter in 1868, 'in which disciplined troops mow down half-armed peasants, are unpleasant in themselves, and afford neither glory to the conquerors nor lessons in the military art.'

Thousands of Santals were killed. Kanhu and other leaders were captured in February, and hanged at Barhait after a summary trial. Some 200 of those captured were given prison sentences of between seven and fourteen years.

With the rebellion crushed, the railway construction work began afresh, creating a huge new demand for workers, recruited from among the Santals. Some years later, Hunter recorded,

> twenty thousand were required in Beerbhoom alone; and the number along the sections running through, or bordering on, the Santal territories amounted to one hundred thousand men . . . The contractors sent their recruiters to every fair, and in a few months the Santals who had taken service came back with their girdles full of coin, and their women covered with silver jewellery . . .

One lasting outcome of the insurrection, recorded by the historian Kalikinkar Datta in 1940, 'was the direction of missionary activities to the aboriginal races'. Soon the Santal hills were 'studded with missions'. As a result, 'rude tribes have been taught the value of British contact and civilisation, and together with the policy of favourable and special treatment of aborigines and converted Christian aborigines, this made aboriginal discontent a very remote possibility'. The god Thakur conjured up by Kanhu was forced to retreat after a bombardment from Christian missionaries.

While the rebellion of the Santals was well underway, a party of enraged Muslim peasants at the opposite end of India descended in September 1855 on the bungalow of Henry Valentine Conolly, the magistrate and tax collector of Malabar. The peasants, called Moplahs, killed the magistrate as he sat on his verandah reading to his wife. His immediate crime was to have sent the Moplah leader into exile, but the Moplahs had other grievances: he had confiscated their knives and sent many of them to prison.

The Moplahs had rebelled frequently in earlier years, usually against their Hindu landlords. From 1800 to 1802, they had waged a guerrilla war after the overthrow of Tipu Sultan;[6] their most recent actions had been in 1849 and 1850, and in 1851 the British authorities had sent army units to crush them. A report on this perennial Muslim insurgency, prepared in 1852 by Thomas Strange, a government official, had recommended that harsh measures be taken against the peasants. Legislation was drafted to give increased powers to the police. One particular measure that annoyed the Moplahs was the withdrawal of their right to carry knives. Conolly's task had been to disarm them, and he seized more than 7,000 knives. Many peasants were arrested and given long prison terms.

Conolly's decision to send the Moplah leader into exile was the event that sparked his death. His house had been inadequately guarded. After his death, the peasant group was surrounded by military and police guards. The Moplahs refused to surrender and the police took seven days to subdue them. All were killed.

The Moplahs continued to rebel at intervals over the next sixty years, culminating in the great revolt of 1921. British officials remained uncomprehending of their purpose. One described the violence as 'not mere riots or affrays, but murderous outrages, such as have no parallel in any other part of Her Majesty's dominions'.[7]

CHAPTER 64

James Sayers Orr and the 'Angel Gabriel' Riots in Guyana

After the abolition of slavery throughout the Empire in 1834, a number of Portuguese Catholics arrived from Madeira to work as labourers in the South American colony of Guyana. This was one of several publicly funded experiments to bring labour to the sugar plantations after the liberated black slaves proved reluctant to turn themselves into wage slaves. Immigrants came from India and China as well as from Madeira, and none of them had any more taste or aptitude for the plantations than the former slaves. A substantial number of the Portuguese soon established themselves in the urban retail trade, where they became the focus of resentment.

One evening in February 1856 a riot exploded in the centre of Georgetown, as many enraged and impoverished citizens broke into the small shops of the traders, to ransack and to plunder. Rioting spread to settlements along the coast and up the Demerara river, clashes occurring as far away as Essequibo and Berbice. 'The town may be said to have been in open insurrection', wrote the Governor, Sir Philip Wodehouse, 'and the true character of the disturbances was at once revealed.' Wodehouse was an energetic and vindictive colonial official, ordered home from Colombo by the House of Commons after the rebellion in Ceylon in 1848, but given a new posting to Guyana.

The riots were sparked off by the detention of John Sayers Orr, a black evangelical preacher who had recently returned to his native Georgetown after a long sojourn abroad.[1] He had been touring Britain, 'the Protestant parts of Ireland', Canada, and the United States. Nicknamed 'the Angel Gabriel' because of his habit of summoning his flock with the blast of a trumpet, 'he purveyed an inflammable mixture of Protestant zeal, populist radicalism, racism, and appeals to patriotism'.[2] One of the posters printed on his American tour provides a flavour of his eclectic political stand:

> Scorn be on those who rob us of our rights,
> Purgatory for Popery and the Pope,
> Freedom to man be he black or white,
> Rule Britannia!

Orr's powerful oratory, aimed against Catholics and the Portuguese, served to translate into religious and racial terms the black population's sense of oppression. Orr's preaching, wrote the governor, had attracted huge crowds of town and country blacks, 'blending together skilfully and amazingly . . . political and religious subjects in a manner calculated to arouse the passions of the Black and Coloured Population against the Portuguese immigrants'.

Wodehouse had greeted Orr as a distinguished preacher, but he had second thoughts (as he wrote to London) when Orr began 'walking about the Town and its vicinity, carrying a flag, wearing a badge, and blowing a horn occasionally at the corners of the Streets, followed by small groups of the rabble of the place'. Wodehouse believed that a black mutual aid society was behind the rioting, and indeed a group existed that had tried, unsuccessfully, to establish creole shops that might have competed with the Portuguese. No proven link was ever found, although the subject was one of general discussion.

With tension rising in the town, the governor banned all public gatherings. Orr sought to avert the ban by holding a meeting outside his mother's house, but he was arrested and charged with unlawful assembly. News of the arrest sparked off the riots, and the black population began attacking the Portuguese traders – the immediate cause of their resentment against the colonial system. Wodehouse's report noted that 'men, women and children all joined in, and in some parts of the country every creole of the lower orders seems to have been one of the mob'. A Wesleyan missionary introduced an unusual element, describing how a 'large number of Vile and Abandoned Women' had taken part in the riots, as well as 'wild, rude and half-savage children'.

Wodehouse also noted the participation of women:

> Nothing remained in the minds of the actors but the long subsisting hatred and jealousy of the Portuguese Immigrants from Madeira and the love of plunder, aggravated by the gross and brutal character of the female population, who have throughout the Colony taken a most active part in the Riots, and who are of course the most difficult to punish.

He did not understand that many women were simply searching for food.

Wodehouse crushed the rebellion with black troops from the Second West India Regiment. Reinforcements were summoned from Barbados, and offers of assistance from warships stationed in the Dutch and French colonies were gratefully accepted.[3] Hundred of whites and 'respectable' coloureds were sworn in as special constables. So many people were arrested that a special penal camp had to be set up. More than a hundred 'ringleaders' were fined and flogged, and then given three years' hard labour in the cane fields. This was the fate of Orr the preacher. A further 600 prisoners were discharged on condition that they worked on specific estates, signing a contract to provide six months' work for each month of their notional sentence.

A more lasting punishment for the community was the imposition of a registration tax designed to reimburse the Portuguese traders for their losses. Claims for damages of nearly £60,000, more than the colony's annual budget, were accepted by the governor, and compensation was secured through a poll tax that bore heaviest on the poorer sections of society.

The population was resentful and expressed its anger towards Governor Wodehouse at every opportunity. When he left Georgetown on holiday in August 1857, he was pelted at the dockside with stones, cane stalks and offal. Sailing away for the last time, in May 1861, for a fresh imperial posting in Cape Colony, he left at night without ceremony, 'to avoid a salute of dead cats and dogs'.

CHAPTER 65

Nongqawuse and the Self-Destruction of the Xhosa in Cape Colony

On the frontiers of Cape Colony, in March 1856, a teenage girl named Nongqawuse told her uncle Mhalakaza of visions she had seen – of herds of cattle and of strange people who had talked to her.[1] Nongquawuse lived by the Gxara River, to the east of the Kei River, and Mhalakaza was a senior councillor of Sarili, son of Hintsa, the paramount chief of the Xhosa peoples who had been driven into this area as a result of earlier British wars.

The burden of the message received by Nongqawuse was that the Russians, perceived as the victors in the Crimean War, would soon come to South Africa to throw out the British. Her strange and powerful vision sparked off an extraordinary, and suicidal, resistance movement by the Xhosa people, who hoped by following her visionary prophecies to expel the white settlers and recover their land. The eventual outcome was an unqualified disaster.

A man of some education and experience, Mhalakaza had worked for a time with the Reverend Nathaniel Merriman, a Church of England missionary living in Cape Colony since 1849, with a position as the archdeacon of Grahamstown.[2] Mhalakaza soon became the guardian and interpreter of Nongqawuse's vision, and made his own investigations on the spot. He came away with a yet more dramatic story – and a call to action.

Mhalakaza had seen a number of people among whom he recognised his brother, some years dead. These people told him that they had come from across the water; they were the people – the Russians – who had been fighting against the English, with whom they would wage perpetual warfare. They had now come to assist 'the Kaffirs', they said, but first the Xhosa would have to abandon witchcraft. As they would have abundant cattle at the coming resurrection, those now in their possession would have to be destroyed.

The Xhosa had already received optimistic news of the Crimean War in the year before Nongqawuse's vision, learning that things had not gone well for the English. They had heard that their most recent oppressor, George Cathcart, military commander at the Cape since 1852, had been killed at the battle of Inkerman in November 1854.

Sarili, the paramount chief, had been visited by Archdeacon Merriman in 1855, and he had questioned the archdeacon closely about events in the Crimea. Delighted by the various British defeats, Sarili told Merriman that he expected

Nongqawuse (right), Xhosa prophetess who foresaw a great wind sweeping the whites into the sea in 1985 and advocated the killing of all Xhosa cattle to bring this about. Photographed years later with Nonkosi, another prophetess.

the Russians to win, and to follow up their victory by expelling the British from South Africa. This belief spread rapidly among the Xhosa, and they began searching the ocean from the hilltops for signs of the Russian ships that might come to deliver them.

Nongqawuse herself, and others who confirmed the message she had received, claimed that ancient Xhosa heroes would rise again from the dead; those now living would be restored to youth; the choicest English cattle would fill the byres; the grain pits would overflow; wagons, clothes, guns and ammunition would appear in abundance; and a great wind would sweep the whites into the sea. It was an appealing and compelling vision, but there was a price to be paid. For all this to happen, the cattle of the Xhosa would have to be killed, all grain bins would have to be emptied, and no sowing of grain would be permitted. Only after this great sacrifice would the brave new world be ushered in.

The idea of killing cattle as a form of sacrificial cleansing, to celebrate the start of a millennial era, was not new to the Xhosa. Two of their prophets, Makana in 1819 and Mlanjeni in 1850, had called for cattle to be sacrificed, as had several lesser prophets in British Kaffraria in the 1850s. But the impact of Nongqawuse's vision was qualitatively different. Whether she was manipulated by Mhalakaza, or whether she saw her own visions, in the manner of St Joan, is impossible to know. Noël Mostert notes that 'Xhosa who saw her at Gxara at the time of the prophecies said she had a silly look, appeared as if she was not in her right mind, and did not take any pains with her appearance'. Yet colonial officials who questioned her said she was intelligent.[3]

By May that year the story of her vision had spread throughout the country, and Sarili himself came in July to visit the now-sacred site by the Gxara river. Mhalakaza, in his role as a prophet, was able to conjure up visions for him of his recently dead son and his favourite long-dead horse, and Sarili was soon convinced of the importance of obeying the prophetic instructions. On his return home, he gave orders for his large herds of cattle to be destroyed.

Later that month, the seers at the Gxara river announced the imminent arrival of the 'new people', and when nothing happened, a fresh date was scheduled in August. People assembled in their white blankets, wearing new brass wire rings. Mostert describes the visions conjured up for the faithful:

> On the great day itself, two suns would rise over the Amatolas, above which they would collide. The English then would all walk into the sea, which would divide and reveal a road along which they would march back to the place of creation, *uhlanga*, where Satan would dispose of them . . . A day of darkness would follow and then would come the new world. A grand resurrection of the ancestors would be accompanied by herds of new cattle emerging from below the earth . . . New corn would stand in the fields to replace that which had been emptied from the corn bins.

In October the decrees from the Gxara river reached the Xhosa in British Kaffraria, to the west of the Kei River. Their leaders were also persuaded that their cattle should be killed within eight days, and they prophesied that the dead would rise on the eighth day. More than a 150,000 cattle were slaughtered. Soon the voice of other prophets could be heard, and early in 1857 a new prophetess, Nonkosi, appeared on the Mpongo river and claimed to have seen dead heroes from the past: Hintsa and Ndlambe, Ngqika and Nqeno. The old chief Maqoma, son of Ngqika, became an enthusiastic slaughterer of cattle; so too did his half-brother Sandile.

The Xhosa had been deceived by their prophets. By February 1857, the population of the frontier lands was starving. Some 20,000 people died, and 30,000 were forced to move into Cape Colony, desperately seeking food and work. After killing his cattle and destroying his corn, Mhalakaza himself died of starvation.

The tragedy of the Xhosa was an opportunity for the British. The frontier land of British Kaffraria was once again opened up to white settlement. Maqoma was arrested and given a twenty-one-year sentence, and imprisoned on Robben

Island. He died there in September 1873. A military force was sent across the Kei River in February 1858 to occupy the lands of Sarili; he died in 1893, aged eighty-three. Sandile was killed in 1878.

Nongqawuse, the unwitting destroyer of the Xhosa people who had struggled so valiantly against the white settlers for half a century, lived on into the twentieth century, dying in 1905. Further skirmishes with the British continued, but her visions and prophecies, like those of Mlanjeni earlier in the decade, brought the long resistance struggle of the Xhosa to an end.

CHAPTER 66

The Great Rebellion in India

The great Indian rebellion of 1857–58 was the climactic moment of the first century of empire, an anti-British explosion that threatened the entire enterprise. Starting as an outbreak of sepoy insubordination and mutiny, the rebellion concluded two years later after rearguard guerrilla actions had taken place over much of the country. Crushed by the British with almost genocidal violence – the outcome of an unexpected eruption of white racist hatred common in other parts of the Empire but hitherto unusual in India – the rebellion more closely resembled a millenarian revolution than a simple revolt.

What began in April 1857 as a mutiny within the Bengal Army at Meerut – a garrison town north of Delhi in the plain between the Jumna and the Ganges – developed swiftly into a hugely popular Islamic rebellion, particularly along the Ganges in the province of Oudh (now Uttar Pradesh). The initial unrest may have been sparked off among the sepoys by the insensitive introduction of a new cartridge smeared with tallow,[1] but the rebellion was immediately and joyfully welcomed by the Muslim lower classes in the urban areas. An Islamic regime was swiftly established in Delhi and in Lucknow, and the green flag of Islam was unfurled in other cities in the Ganges plain.

The fierce and manifest hatred of Christians, and an intense rejection of the British attempt to introduce Christianity into India – ever more apparent during the preceding two decades – became defining marks of the rebellion. 'Deen ka Jai', or 'Victory to Religion', was the popular cry raised by many insurgents, and Islamic preachers or *maulvis* were prominent among the rebel leaders. Hindu as well as Christian temples were targeted. Paradoxically, most of the sepoys in the Bengal Army were Hindus, yet in practice they had little difficulty in working with Muslims or in giving their allegiance to the nominal focus of the rebellion, the eighty-two-year-old Mughal emperor, Bahadur Shah II, sometimes called the King of Delhi.

The early weeks of the rebellion, in May, were characterised by an unusual degree of ferocity, notably from the enraged *badmashes* – the urban mob living beyond the cantonments of the sepoys. These made short work of Europeans found out in the open (and prisoners were also killed when occasion arose). Yet the most notable incidents of Indian revenge against their conquerors came after a British troop, commanded by Colonel James Neill and advancing inland from Calcutta in June, began systematically disarming and then slaughtering the sepoys at Benares and Allahabad. Colonel Neill's sadistic actions immediately provoked further sepoy mutinies at Faizabad, Fatehpur and Jaunpur, leading inexorably to the much-publicised deaths of European civilians at Cawnpore in July.

The rebellion was an inchoate affair, ill-organised and geographically dispersed. Traditional histories have concentrated on the rebellious outbreaks in cities, crushed within a matter of months; yet the rural areas remained under rebel control throughout much of the following year. Several local chieftains rose up in obscure parts of the country, and only oral accounts survive of their exploits. Some princes remained loyal to the British, and a handful joined the rebellion only after coming under pressure from their own soldiers. Many rebel groups had little in common with their fellows, and few outstanding leaders emerged. Of the dozen or so most prominent, three were Islamic preachers with a huge jihadi following, five were nabobs or princes, and three were ordinary soldiers. Some of the rebel commanders acquired a measure of posthumous celebrity – notably Nana Sahib, Tantya Topi, and the Rani Lakshmi Bai; but there was no Napoleon or Lenin among them. No figure emerged comparable to Haidar Ali or Tipu Sultan, or the other formidable leaders of the anti-British resistance in the eighteenth century.

Many British observers convinced themselves that the rebels were more competent than they actually were. The rebel leaders were widely assumed to have a strategic plan and to be highly organised, their hostility sparked off by the British annexation of Oudh the previous year. Wajid Ali Shah, the Nawab of Oudh, had lost his kingdom in 1856 and been exiled from Lucknow to Calcutta; his army had been disbanded, and the powerful landowners of his territory had been expropriated. Most of the sepoys in the Bengal army came from Oudh, and they did not like what had happened to their homeland. 'This mutiny has been planned since the taking of Oudh', wrote Maria Vansittart, the wife of an official at Agra. 'It was settled about 20 May [1857] that every cantonment all down the country was to rise and murder all the Europeans, seize forts, magazines, treasures.' The court martial of recalcitrant sepoys at Meerut that month had, in her view, 'caused the plot to explode ten days too soon'.[2]

The revolts in May did certainly follow a remarkably similar pattern in different cities. The mutinous sepoys would occupy the parade ground, shoot their European officers, seize the armoury and the treasury, and release all prisoners from the local gaol. They would then set off on the long march to Delhi, to give their support to the Mughal emperor. Yet in spite of these copycat events, none of today's nationalist historians of India, who have searched for evidence of a generalised plot, have ever found the necessary evidence. The rebellion was a spontaneous and largely unheralded explosion that followed an uncharted course.

The rebels caught the British off-guard. There were perhaps 37,000 British soldiers in the country at the time, facing more than 230,000 Indian troops. At many towns between the cantonments of the Punjab in the west and the Calcutta military base at Barrackpore in the east, virtually no British troops were present at all – neither at Bareilly nor Shajahanpur, nor at Cawnpore or Allahabad or Benares. Lord Canning, the relatively new and inexperienced governor-general at Calcutta (he had only arrived in 1856), had to summon troops from near and far to crush the rebellion – from the battle fronts in China and Persia; from Burma, Ceylon and South Africa; and from Britain itself. The capacity of the British to find additional troops available elsewhere in the Empire was their eventual trump card, for which the rebels were unprepared.

Signs of sepoy disaffection first appeared in March, at the major British base at Barrackpore, fifteen miles north of Calcutta. Mangal Pandy, a Hindu sepoy from a Native Infantry regiment, came onto the parade ground on 29 March to urge his fellow sepoys to join him in a rebellion against British rule. A devout Hindu, Pandy had been provoked by the proselytising Christian zeal of the commanding officer, Colonel Steven Wheler. He shot and wounded two British sergeants, but his appeal received no immediate response from other sepoys, and he was detained after a failed attempt at suicide.

Since Barrackpore had been the scene of an earlier rebellion, in 1824, and had already experienced recent outbreaks of insubordination, the authorities had been fearing trouble. A regiment of British soldiers had been ordered to return to Calcutta from Burma. This was quickly sent up to the potentially mutinous base, where it disarmed the Native Regiments. Mangal Pandy was brought before a court martial and executed on 8 April. This was the spark that lit the fuse.

Two weeks later, on 24 April, a mutinous refusal of orders by sepoys took place at the great military encampment at Meerut, forty miles north-east of Delhi. Ninety sepoys were ordered to handle the new greased cartridges being issued to the troops, and eighty-five of them refused to do so. Brought before a court martial, they were sentenced to ten years' hard labour. On 9 May the entire garrison was ordered onto the parade ground to witness the sepoys judged guilty being shackled and stripped of their uniforms. A fresh mood of unrest was created in the camp by this ritual humiliation, and angry sepoys made plans to stage a rebellion the following day.

On 10 May the Native Infantry regiments seized and torched their barracks, and shot their officers. They moved on to the prison to free the court-martialled prisoners, soon sparking a wider rebellion in the town beyond the base. While civilians 'from the bazaar' attacked the bungalows of the Europeans, burning, plundering and slaughtering their inhabitants, the bulk of the rebel sepoys took the road to Delhi – to offer their support to the Mughal emperor.

* * *

In Delhi the next morning, 11 May, an advance force of 300 rebels from Meerut arrived outside the palace of the Mughal emperor – the first wave of thousands that would follow. 'Help, O King', they called out from below his window. 'We pray for assistance in our fight for the faith.'

The white-bearded Bahadur Shah was in two minds. Poet and painter, and in receipt of a large British pension, the emperor had had a hitherto agreeable and uncomplicated life. But he had had his differences with his British overlords: he was but a titular emperor, and his status had been much diminished; his head had been removed from the coins, and the British had refused to recognise his heir. Seeing himself as the legitimate leader of millions of Muslims and Hindus, he felt it to be his duty to support the rebellion, believing he had been born 'to restore the realm of the Great Timur'.[3]

As more of the Meerut rebels arrived, they were joined by sepoys from the Native Infantry regiments based at the Delhi garrison. These had been on parade earlier that morning at the military camp known as the Ridge, two miles north of the city. There, with unfortunate timing from the British point of view, they had been given an official account of the execution of Mangal Pandy at Barrackpore. As his death sentence was made officially known, a murmur of disapproval spread across the parade ground. The assembled sepoys began hissing and shuffling their feet, and soon they too had mutinied.[4] They shot their officers and sought to seize the magazine – the building housing the garrison's arms and ammunition – demanding in the name of 'the King of Delhi' that it should be surrendered.

Their request was rejected by the British commanding officer, who quickly blew up the building, killing and injuring many sepoys as a result. A rumour now spread that the explosion had been engineered specifically to kill them, and the Delhi sepoys joined forces with the Meerut rebels in ever larger numbers. They embarked on the slaughter of the men, women and children living in the European quarter – Europeans, Eurasians and Indian Christians alike. Some fifty prisoners were taken, but they too were subsequently killed. By nightfall, the city had been captured by the rebels.

Unlike their depressed and reluctant father, the sons of Bahadur Shah supported the rebellion with enthusiasm. The twenty-nine-year-old Mirza Mughal, the most prominent of several brothers, was appointed as the commander-in-chief of the rebel forces. A protégé of his powerful stepmother, Zinat Mahal, and for some years the palace chamberlain with responsibility for its finances, Mirza Mughal was a qualified and competent leader.[5]

With the great city of Delhi captured by the sepoy rebels, and the British holding on in the outskirts but powerless in the short term to retrieve the situation, the rebellion proceeded apace. The cities in the valley of the Ganges were soon in rebel hands, and the rebellion spread beyond, to Bundelkhand and

Rajputana. Only at either end of the country, in Bengal and the Punjab – regions with a preponderance of European troops – were British generals able to make desperate plans to contain and roll back the rebellion.

News of the Meerut rebellion reached the town of Bareilly in Rohilkhand, east of Delhi, on 14 May. Its Nawab, Khan Bahadur Khan, was the grandson of Hafiz Rahmat Khan, who had fought against the British in 1774. His sepoys now rose in revolt and occupied the treasury, in what was now a familiar pattern, and burnt the land-registry records. Bakht Khan was their leader – an experienced soldier born in 1797 who had spent forty years in the Bengal Horse Artillery, and had fought for the British in the Afghan War in the 1840s. More significantly, he was closely associated with a group of Islamic fundamentalists led by the *maulvi* Sarfaraz Khan, a prominent local intellectual who had been educated in the *madrasas* of Delhi. 'Our religion is in danger', the *maulvi* declared before the revolt, and as soon as the sepoys rebelled, he called for an anti-British jihad. The Islamic pattern of the rebellion was established at an early stage.

Together with 4,000 Muslim jihadis, Bakht Khan and the *maulvi* set off to join the emperor and the rebels in Delhi. They took with them the funds collected from the treasury, leaving Bareilly in the hands of Khan Bahadur Khan. The Nawab was to control the region for many months, holding out in the city until the following year.

The revolt now spread to Lucknow, east of Cawnpore, the capital city of what until the previous year had been the independent state of Oudh. Minor sepoy uprisings had occurred in the state throughout the month, and the mutinous mood enveloped Lucknow on 30 May. Three British officers were killed that day, and bungalows in the European cantonments were set on fire. The unrest spread to the city, and the green flag of Islam was again on display. Yet this was the limit of the rebellion. The initial mutiny in Lucknow failed to secure wider support, and was crushed by soldiers loyal to the British. Thirty mutinous sepoys were court-martialled and swiftly hanged in batches of eight. The surviving mutineers escaped and set off for Delhi.

The dislike of the British in this region arose from the overthrow the previous year of its Nawab Ali Shah.[6] He had been exiled to Calcutta, but his advisers had remained behind to foment rebellion. The focus of the revolt centred on the Nawab's principal wife, the Begum Hazrat Mahral, and on Birjis Kadr, her ten-year-old son.

Sir Henry Lawrence, the British Resident in Lucknow who had transferred from the Punjab two months earlier, was well aware that the situation might deteriorate. He assembled the 600 Europeans who lived in the city into the thirty-seven-acre compound of his residency. An additional 3,000 Europeans took refuge there, escaping from rebel-held towns in the surrounding areas, as the rebellion continued throughout the state in June. A month later, a fresh rebel army was to seize the city.

West of Lucknow, at the garrison at Cawnpore, a large commercial city on the Ganges, sepoy regiments organised another successful mutiny on 4 June. They seized the magazine with its guns and ammunition, emptied the gaol, and set off for Delhi, leaving their European officers untouched. Passing on their way through Bithur, the home of Nana Sahib, a local Hindu prince, they sought to enlist his support.

Nana, aged thirty-seven, sometimes called Dhondu Pant, was the adopted son, and the appointed heir, of the last of the Peshwas, Baji Rao II – a member of the famous Maratha Confederacy that had fought its final battle against the British in 1817. Captured and pensioned off by the British, Baji Rao had died at Bithur in 1851. Nana, like the Mughal emperor in Delhi, had had serious differences with the British, for after Baji Rao's death, the governor-general had refused to continue the large pension his father had once received. The sum had amounted to £2,500,000 over thirty years, and the British argued that this should not be seen as an hereditary pension; Nana Sahib was perceived as a man possessed of adequate means.[7]

Petitioned by the rebellious Cawnpore sepoys to join their cause, Nana Sahib agreed quickly. Together with his advisers – Rao Sahib, his nephew, and Tantya Topi, his principal commander (sometimes known as Ram Chandra Pandurang) – he persuaded the rebels to abandon their march towards Delhi and to return to Cawnpore to establish a second powerful base for the rebellion. Sepoys from other towns, including Azamgarh and Nowgong, soon came to join them, and Nana Sahib declared himself the new Peshwa in early July, resurrecting the historic title of Baji Rao.

Tantya Topi was appointed as commander, although he had no military training. A fifty-three-year-old Maratha Brahmin, formerly in Baji Rao's service, he had long been a close friend of Nana, and he proved to be a most capable military leader.

Although Cawnpore itself was in rebel hands, Nana Sahib had to reckon, as in Lucknow, with a significant British garrison that remained in the outskirts. Its commander, General Sir Hugh Wheeler, gathered nearly a thousand Europeans into the garrison's two large barrack buildings, initially protecting them with his artillery. Tantya Topi's sepoys shelled this European encampment throughout June, successfully putting the British guns out of action and leaving the Europeans short of water.

* * *

Nana Sahib, Hindu prince and heir to the Peshwa Bai Rao, established his base at Cawnpore in June 1857.

A rebellion had also erupted far away on the North-West Frontier. Sepoys from the 55th Native Infantry regiment mutinied on 22 May at Nowshera, twenty miles from Peshawar, but their rebellion was short-lived. The British at Peshawar had acted quickly on hearing the news from Meerut, and most of the 8,000 sepoys of the Bengal Army stationed around the town were quickly disarmed. The mutiny at Nowshera was bloodily suppressed by General John Nicholson, deputy commissioner at Peshawar; more than 120 sepoys were killed.

The survivors escaped across the hills to Swat, but 150 captured prisoners were brought back to Peshawar. At a special punishment parade witnessed by the entire garrison, forty of them were blown from guns.[8] 'It was a horrible sight', wrote a British captain stationed in the town, 'but a very satisfactory one.' He explained in a letter to his father that 'the pieces were blown about in all directions . . . Since then we have hung a good many more – a dozen or half a dozen at a time and blown away a few more.'[9] A wider revolt in the Punjab was prevented by Nicholson's bloody action, and in September he was to take part in the recapture of Delhi.

* * *

This picture appeared in *Harper's Weekly*, 15 February 1862. The magazine claimed that it was reprinted from an illustration in the *London Illustrated Times* in 1857, depicting an execution in Peshawar on 12 June 1857 where forty sepoy prisoners were blown from guns.

In early June, back on the Ganges, after a month in which much of north India had fallen to the rebels, the insurgents encountered the first British troops sent out from Calcutta to crush them. What were perceived as 'white' soldiers had been brought by sea to Calcutta from Madras in May. India was about to undergo an unparalleled period of violent repression at the hands of two British commanders. One was Colonel James Neill, aged forty-seven, the commander of the 1st Madras Fusiliers; the other was Colonel Henry Havelock, the commander of a Highland regiment hastily summoned from the Persian battlefront.

The Native Regiments at Benares had been about to join the rebellion when Neill arrived there on 3 June after a 500-mile march. He was followed three weeks later by Havelock. Neil quickly sought to dissuade potential rebels from taking any mutinous action, but when the sepoys in the cantonments understood that they were about to be disarmed, and feared that they would then be shot, they did indeed rebel, firing on their British officers. They were then subjected to a broadside from Neill's artillery, and hundreds were killed immediately. The survivors escaped into the city beyond.

This attack on the sepoys at Benares was followed up by other measures of British retribution. 'Rows of gallowses' were to be seen, according to a contemporary account, 'on which the energetic Colonel was hanging mutineer after mutineer as they were brought in.' Martial law was belatedly proclaimed on 9 June, and volunteer hanging parties were sent out into the countryside to round up the rebels. These, when caught, were executed immediately, without benefit of legal process. 'One gentleman boasted of the number he had finished off, quite "in an artistic manner", with mango trees for gibbets and elephants for drops, the victims of this wild justice being strung up, as though for pastime, in "the form of a figure of eight".'[10] This unwonted British violence was counterproductive, for the news of Colonel Neill's actions spread rapidly up the valley of the Ganges, provoking fresh mutinies at Jaunpur, Allahabad and Faizabad.[11]

West of Benares, at Allahabad – a vital communications centre at the junction of the Ganges and the Jumna – sepoys of the 6th Native Infantry rose in revolt towards the evening of 6 June. Six European officers were killed, as well as eight teenage cadets who had just arrived from England. Earlier in the day the officers had offered to march to Delhi to help suppress the rebellion there, but news of Colonel Neill's revenge attacks at Benares had changed their minds.[12]

As in other towns, the rebel sepoys at Allahabad were joined by a city mob of Muslims; they helped in releasing prisoners from gaol and burning European bungalows; they tore down telegraph wires and destroyed railway lines.[13] Soon they had killed every European, Eurasian and Christian they could lay their hands on, and the green flag of Islam was raised at the police station. Here another *maulvi* emerged as their leader: Liaquat Ali, a Muslim schoolteacher, took charge of the city in the name of the emperor at Delhi.[14] The mob opened the town's treasury, and an initial decision to take it to Delhi was dropped in favour of an immediate division of the spoils. In the excitement, the chance to capture the city's great fort was lost, and it remained in the hands of a hundred Europeans.

The rebels at Allahabad soon faced the avenging columns of Colonel Neill; they arrived from Benares a few days later, on 11 June, and the rebels swiftly melted away. Neill ordered the bombardment of the suburb of Daryaganj, rescued the Europeans in the fort, and seized the now deserted city on 18 June. Soon he was engaged in fresh slaughter outside the city: the old and the young, women and children, none were neglected. 'Every day we led expeditions to burn and destroy disaffected villages', wrote the chief of a commission appointed to try offenders, 'and we had taken our revenge . . . Day by day, we have strung up eight or ten men. We have the power of life in our hands; and I assure you we spare not. A very summary trial is all that takes place.'[15]

The vengeance exacted by Neill was yet more severe and indiscriminate at Allahabad than at Benares. British soldiers and civilians turned on the Indian population, killing them regardless of sex or age. They boasted that they had 'spared no one', pointing out that 'peppering away at niggers' was a very pleasant pastime 'enjoyed amazingly'.[16] One British officer described how 'the gallows and trees adjoining it had each day the fresh fruits of rebellion displayed upon them'. A legal officer, he added that 'hundreds of natives in this manner perished, and some on slight proofs of criminality'.[17]

The *maulvi* Liaquat Ali escaped from the city to Cawnpore, 130 miles away, bringing fresh reports of Neill's terror tactics.[18] Cawnpore was still controlled by Nana Sahib's rebel sepoys, who continuously bombarded the surviving Europeans marooned in General Wheeler's barrack encampment.

North of Allahabad, at Fatehpur, further up the Ganges, the standard of revolt was raised on 10 June by Hikmathullah Khan, the deputy collector. With 'an influential band' of Muslims, he proclaimed the independence of the city, and the sepoys opened the gaol and raided the treasury. Hikmathullah secured some military support from Nana Sahib at Cawnpore, who sent soldiers to help defend the city. Individual resistance to the sepoy rebellion came from Robert Tucker, a Christian missionary and a magistrate, who declared his intention of going out with a bible in one hand and a pistol in the other. He did just that, killing a dozen rebels before himself being captured and shot.[19]

Fatehpur remained independent for three weeks, until, in early July, the sepoys faced a force of 700 Europeans and 300 Sikhs, under Major Sydenham Renaud, sent forward from Allahabad by Colonel Neill. Renaud was told to hang the sepoys of mutinous regiments that could not give a good account of themselves, and to destroy all subversive villages and kill their male inhabitants. The instructions were carried out to the letter.[20] Renaud was joined by Colonel Havelock's forces on 7 July, and the town was torched by Havelock's men. Hikmathullah was captured and beheaded, and his head remained on display outside the police station for a week.

Far to the south of the Jumna, in Bundelkhand, sepoys had mutinied at the fort at Jhansi on 5 June. Giving voice to the now popular battle cry of 'Deen ka Jai', Victory to Religion, they killed the garrison commander, Captain Dunlop, and two other officers. They seized the treasury and the magazine, and released prisoners from the gaol. Land tenure records were seized and piled on a bonfire, and European property was plundered. Laying siege to the fort itself, in which fifty Europeans and Eurasians had taken refuge, the sepoys brought up large guns on 8 June and forced the British political officer to negotiate terms for an evacuation. The refugees were marched down to a garden below the fort and killed.

As at Delhi, Bareilly and Cawnpore, the sepoys at Jhansi called on the local ruler to support them. Like other local figureheads, the Rani Lakshmi Bai, aged twenty-three, had had recent problems with the British. Married at the age of eight to the Rajah Gangadhar Rao of Jhansi (as his second wife), she had adopted a son after his death and appointed him as her successor. Yet under rules introduced by Lord Dalhousie (the so-called Doctrine of Lapse), Jhansi was annexed to the Raj and the Rani's son was not permitted to be the new rajah. In such circumstances, the Rani agreed to support the rebel sepoys, providing them with guns, ammunition and money. Lal Bahadur, her most senior infantry officer, took command.

Further mutinies took place in Bundelkhand, at Nowgong and Kurrera, and on 14 June at Hamirpur and Banda.[21] Ali Bahadur, the Nawab of Banda, supported his soldiers, but they left him in no doubt as to who was the master, announcing in a proclamation that 'the world is God's, the country is the emperor's, and the rule is of the soldiers'.

At Gwalior, on the same day, the personal force of the Maharajah Scindia mutinied, and marched off to join up with the forces of Nana Sahib at Cawnpore. Scindia Bahadur was the heir to the noble line of Maratha rulers that had fought against the British half a century earlier, although this latest Scindia remained loyal to the British throughout 1857. His 'Gwalior Contingent' was considered to be one of the best Native Regiments in the country.

In early June the rebels holding Delhi faced their first setback. The city had been seized on 11 May in the name of the emperor, but the rebels now confronted a small British column, the Delhi Field Force, led by General Henry Barnard, the commander-in-chief, advancing from Ambala to the north. A large rebel army moved out of the city on 8 June to confront the British at Badli-Ki-Serai, and Mirza Mughal sent an encouraging message to the emperor: 'Rest assured our enemies will come no closer – I have brought all the troops to the front line to slay the infidels.'[22]

The rebels had the advantage of numbers, but they failed to halt the British column. Their most prominent commander, Khizr Sultan, another son of the emperor, fled early from the battle. The British advanced to a position between the city and the cantonments, known as 'the Ridge', and Delhi itself now came under regular bombardment. Yet the British position was by no means secure, and it too was shelled almost daily by rebel guns from within the city.

Yet rebel morale was affected by their defeat, and Mirza Mughal issued a word of criticism on 23 June:

> Despite the fact that this war started over faith and religion, many of you have not gone to battle, and instead while your time away in gardens and shops. Others are hiding inside their quarters, protecting their lives. His Highness the Emperor has made you all swear on his salt that all the platoons would go on the attack and annihilate the Kafirs, but you no longer show the will to do so. How sad that when this confrontation is about religion and faith, and when His Highness gave you his protection, you still refrain from going for battle.[23]

The fervour of victory in May had been replaced by the hard slog of resistance in June.

In Cawnpore, meanwhile, the rebels had been regularly shelling the barracks buildings filled with European refugees, and on 23 June Nana Sahib ordered a frontal attack on this stronghold to celebrate the hundredth anniversary of the Muslim resistance at the battle of Plassey, in 1757. The refugees lodged there were living in increasingly dismal conditions, and Nana was well aware that Colonel Neill's forces were advancing from Allahabad. He needed to solve the refugee problem before British reinforcements arrived. His anniversary attack on the barracks was ineffective, but two days later he offered the refugees safe passage downriver to Allahabad if they would agree to surrender.

General Wheeler, the Resident, felt obliged to agree, and on 27 June several hundred refugees were escorted down to the riverbank at the Satichaura Ghat. They waded out to boats offshore, and were then fired on from the bank. Many were killed, including Wheeler himself. Nana Sahib eventually ordered a halt to the firing, and those who survived – approximately 125 women and children – were taken back to the city to be lodged in two small houses known as the Bibigarh.

East of Cawnpore, a large rebel army marched on Lucknow at the end of June, led by Barkat Ahmad. An initial rebellion had been crushed in Lucknow at the end of May, but the mood remained markedly hostile to the British presence. 'Seditious placards were found stuck up in the principal streets', noted one British observer, 'calling upon all good Mussulmen and Hindoos to rise and kill the Christians.'[24] Sir Henry Lawrence's large Residency compound, established as a place of refuge for Europeans in the city, was now filled with additional Europeans who had fled from the nearby towns of Oudh.

On 30 June the forces of Barkat Ahmad, one of the more successful military commanders to emerge during the rebellion, confronted troops under Lawrence's command at Chinhat, outside Lucknow. The battle at Chinhat was a major victory for the rebels, enabling them to seize the city. Many of Lawrence's sepoys deserted to join the rebellion. The European survivors retreated behind the barricades of the Residency compound, while Lawrence himself, wounded by a shell, died a few days later.

A rebel government was set up in Lucknow, run by the thirty-seven-year-old Begum Hazrat Mahal, mother of the ten-year-old Birjis Kadr, soon to be crowned as the new King of Oudh. A powerful leader of the rebellion there was the *maulvi* Ahmed Ahmadullah Shah, an itinerant preacher familiar throughout the region from Agra to Faizabad. Often known as 'the *maulvi* of Faizabad', where he had been arrested earlier in the year after preaching in favour of a holy war against the English,[25] he was one of the important Islamic leaders of the rebellion. Considered too dangerous to be kept in an ordinary civil gaol, he had been detained in the military cantonments at Faizabad and released by mutineers in early June. Making his way from Faizabad to Lucknow, he again called for a jihad against the infidels, and circulated leaflets calling on the faithful, Hindus as well as Muslims, 'to arise, or be forever fallen'.

The Begum Hazrat Mahal secured the support of the emperor at Delhi for the independence of Oudh, and Hindus were asked to join her largely Muslim government. She confiscated the lands of a number of pro-British landlords, using their funds to pay her troops, soon to be commanded by Rajah Jai Lal Singh, over the rather stronger claims of Barkat Ahmad. Her troops kept the Lucknow Residency and the area around it under siege for several months.

One of the problems facing the rebel commanders throughout the rebellion was the need to keep Muslims and Hindus working together. In Delhi, an orthodox mullah, the *maulvi* Muhammad Sayyid, had set up a jihadi standard in May outside the Jama Masjid, the city's principal mosque, and called for a Muslim holy war. The emperor told him to desist, arguing that the *purbiya* soldiers (those from the east of Delhi from Allahabad, Oudh and Bihar) were all Hindu. The *maulvi* replied that the Hindus were mostly supporters of the English, but the emperor eventually ordered him to take down the flag, since 'such a display of fanaticism would only tend to exasperate the Hindus'.

Elsewhere, the Nawab of Bareilly had also recognised the need for unity among Hindus and Muslims, and appealed to them to engage in a common struggle:

> All you Hindoos are hereby solemnly adjured, by your faith in the Ganges, Tulsi and Saligram; and all you Mussalmans, by your belief in God and the Koran, as these English are the common enemy of both, that you unite in considering their slaughter extremely expedient, for by this alone will the lives and faith of both be saved.

The Nawab later took advantage of the popular hostility to the spread of Christianity, and proclaimed in March 1858 that 'the English are people who overthrow all religions'. He accused the British occupiers of 'causing books to be written and circulated throughout the country by the hands of their clergymen, and [of bringing] out numbers of preachers to spread their own tenets'. They had done this, he said, 'with the object of destroying the religions of Hindoostan'.

The battle of Chinhat in June 1857 and the occupation of Lucknow were the high point of the rebellion. British commanders were falling like ninepins: Lawrence at Lucknow was dead; Wheeler at Cawnpore was dead; so too was the British commander-in-chief, General George Anson, who died of cholera on 27 May when advancing on Delhi from Simla; his successor, General Henry Barnard, also died of cholera, on the outskirts of Delhi, on 5 July; within two months, Colonel Neill was killed, as was his superior officer Colonel Havelock.

At the start of July, the Begum Hazrat Mahal was in charge in Lucknow, Nana Sahib was in command at Cawnpore, and the emperor held court in Delhi. Elsewhere the rebels were in complete control, without much fear or likelihood of disruption. Yet large numbers of European hostages were held in each of these three cities, and this made an eventual British rescue mission inevitable.

Fresh rebel reinforcements arrived in Delhi on 1 July. Bakht Khan, the leader who had led the mutiny in Bareilly in May, arrived with an immense troop of Rohilla sepoys and 4,000 Muslim jihadis loyal to the *maulvi* Sarfaraz Ali. Respecting his experience, the emperor made Bakht Khan the new commander, giving him the title of Sahib-I-Alam Bahadur ('Lord of the World'). As a member of the war council, he was effectively in charge of both civil and military affairs, and put new energy into the sepoy armies. He organised regular attacks throughout July on the British forces encamped on the Ridge, beyond the city.

Yet at the moment of maximum rebel expansion, the tide began to turn in all three cities. Nana Sahib's forces marched out of Cawnpore on 12 July, to confront a British column commanded by Colonel Havelock advancing from Allahabad. Another obsessive Christian, Havelock was an experienced veteran of earlier imperial wars in Afghanistan and Burma. He had marched from Calcutta with a thousand European soldiers, and had followed in the footsteps of Colonel Neil. He arrived in the area earlier in the month, and he came with orders to drive the rebels from Cawnpore.

He had united his troops with those of Major Renaud outside Fatehpur, and this combined force clashed with Nana Sahib's sepoys on 12 July. The sepoys wilted before the British guns, and were defeated again a few days later at Aong, and in a final battle in the outskirts of Cawnpore. Nana Sahib was obliged to withdraw north to his old base at Bithur, before crossing the Ganges into Oudh. The fates had turned against him.

* * *

In Nana Sahib's absence, the gates of Cawnpore were opened to Havelock's forces on 17 July, but he arrived too late to save the European hostages held in the Bibigarh. On the night of 15/16 July, its European occupants – by now some 200, mostly women and children – had all been killed, an event usually regarded as the worst Indian atrocity of the Mutiny. Their bodies were thrown into a well. While there is no evidence that Nana Sahib himself gave orders for this massacre, a member of his bodyguard may have been involved.

Colonel Havelock left Cawnpore a week later, on 25 July, in a desperate attempt to advance towards Lucknow. Colonel Neill, the butcher of Benares and Allahabad, was left behind to exact revenge on the captured sepoys of Cawnpore, famously ordering them to lick up the blood from the floor of the Bibigarh before their execution.

Far to the north, a European atrocity took place at much the same time, in the district of Amritsar in the Punjab. The author of the crime was an educated Englishman, Frederic Cooper, the deputy commissioner. A large number of sepoys from the 26th Bengal Native Indian regiment, disarmed at Lahore in May, had escaped in July, killing a British officer and a sergeant-major. Detained by villagers in the region of Amritsar, some 150 of them were killed by the police, while the survivors sought shelter on an island in the river Ravi.

They surrendered when Cooper and the cavalry arrived, and 282 of them were taken off to the police station at Ajnala. The sepoys were kept for the night in an ill-ventilated mud-walled bastion of an old fort,[26] and Cooper himself records that they 'were possessed of a sudden and insane idea that they were going to be tried by court-martial'.[27] Not so. They were taken out the next day and shot, in batches of ten.

After 237 of the prisoners had been executed in this manner, Cooper was told that the others refused to come out. He went to look, and, as he recorded, 'behold, they were nearly all dead! Unconsciously the tragedy of Holwell's Black Hole had been re-enacted . . . 45 bodies dead from fright, exhaustion, fatigue, heat and partial suffocation, were dragged into light, and consigned, in common with all the other bodies, into one common pit, by the hands of the village sweepers.'[28]

Cooper's victims had never taken part in a mutiny – indeed, they had been disarmed before they could do so. Only a few of them could have been responsible for killing the British officer and sergeant-major. Most were guilty of no offence except desertion, and for this they were shot without trial.[29]

In spite of setbacks, the rebellion rolled on. At Dinapur – to the west of Patna, far to the east – three Native Infantry regiments joined the revolt on 25 July, provoking a further insurrection in Bihar.[30] British communications between

Calcutta and Benares were now seriously threatened. Marching south to the nearby British garrison at Arrah, the rebels seized the treasury and emptied the prison, but they could not overcome the garrison's defenders, and kept it under siege for several weeks. Here the rebels were joined by Kunwar Singh, a distinguished Hindu Rajput in his seventies who was to become a formidable guerrilla leader.[31] They fought off a British relief force that came up the river by steamer, killing two hundred; but when a second relief force arrived, advancing from Buxar to the west, Kunwar Singh's men were less successful. They abandoned their siege of the Arrah garrison and withdrew. The British commander, Major Vincent Eyre, declared martial law and hanged thirty wounded prisoners.[32]

Kunwar Singh's rebel force travelled west to Banda, and then to Kalpi, on the Jumna. Nana Sahib invited them to join him at Lucknow. The rebel sepoys there were threatened in July by Havelock's small column that had moved east from Cawnpore across the Ganges. Kunwar Singh's actions threatened the entire British supply operation, and several battles took place in the outskirts of Bashiratganj. The sepoys forced Havelock to retreat to Cawnpore, and in August the forces of Tantya Topi, advancing on Cawnpore from Bithur, obliged him to remain there to protect his northern flank. Kunwar Singh's forces were eventually sent back to the east to besiege the British garrison at Azamgarh, where they held out for eight months.

In Delhi, the emperor's advisers received news in August of the advance of fresh British forces from the Punjab. General John Nicholson, butcher of the Punjab, had left Amritsar on 25 July, and, with nearly 10,000 men, he reached the outskirts of Delhi on 14 August. Bakht Khan, the commander, emerged from the city a week later to attack the British siege train travelling in Nicholson's wake, bearing guns and ammunition. He was obliged to retreat after a fierce battle at Najafgarh, some twenty miles west of Delhi.

His defeat created a pessimistic mood in the city, and on 6 September Mirza Mughal issued a message, proclaimed by drum-beat throughout the city: 'This is a religious war. It is being prosecuted on account of the faith, and it behoves all Hindu and Musulman residents of the Imperial City, or of the villages out in the country to . . . continue true to their faiths and creeds, and to slay the English and their servants.'[33]

On 14 September the Delhi rebels were attacked by British troops (although more than half were Indian sepoys). They fought a rearguard action, street by street, and by the evening the British had suffered more than a thousand casualties. General Nicholson was mortally wounded, and two regiments refused orders to advance. But the rebels lost the day. The emperor and his family retreated from the Red Fort to take refuge outside the city, at Humayun's tomb.

Bakht Khan escaped with a large group of sepopys to Lucknow, still in rebel hands, and joined forces with Ahmadullah Shah, the *maulvi* of Faizabad.

Once in control of Delhi, the British began mass killings of the urban population. One observer described how

> all the city people found within the walls when our troops entered were bayoneted on the spot; and the number was considerable, as you may suppose, when I tell you that in some houses forty or fifty persons were hiding. These were not mutineers but residents of the city, who trusted to our well-known mild rule for pardon. I am glad to say they were disappointed.[34]

The day after the city's capture, one officer present commented that the streets were 'deserted and silent, they resembled a city of the dead, on which some awful catastrophe had fallen. It was difficult to realise that we were passing through what had been, only a few days before, the abode of thousands of people.'[35] Several months elapsed before civilian authorities took over from the military.

On 16 September the emperor surrendered to Captain William Hodson, the commander of a group of irregular cavalry. He was taken with his wife, the Begum Zinat Mahal, and held under house arrest in Delhi. Later they were transported to Rangoon, where the emperor died in 1862. A more severe fate awaited his children. Captain Hodson went again to Humayun's tomb and seized the three princes who had been the principal political organisers of the rebellion in Delhi – Mirza Mughal, Khizr Sultan and Abu Bakr. They were taken off in a cart to a spot some miles away, and then ordered to get out, and to strip naked. They were shot dead by Hodson with a Colt revolver, one after another. Their bodies were left out in the open for three days, to be gazed upon by the British troops. 'I cannot help being pleased with the warm congratulations I received on all sides for my success in destroying the enemies of our race', Hodson wrote to his sister the next day. 'The whole nation will rejoice.'[36] Twenty-one lesser princes were hanged a few days later. Hodson himself was killed in an attack on Lucknow the following March.

With the loss of their principal headquarters in Delhi, the rebel sepoys elsewhere found themselves increasingly vulnerable; yet their resistance continued well into 1858. On 21 September the rebel sepoys confronted a British force at Mangalwar on the Ganges, on the road from Cawnpore to Lucknow. A new British commander, General James Outram, had arrived at Cawnpore in early September, and, with Havelock, he made plans to advance to the relief of Lucknow. Clashing with Outram and Havelock at Mangalwar, the sepoys were obliged to retreat, but they made a stand a few days later at the southern entrance to Lucknow. A bloody battle took place, but the forces of the Begum Hazrat Mahal could not prevent the final advance of this large British contingent. They prepared for house-by-house resistance in the city, building blockades across the streets and placing sharpshooters in upper windows. Among the British officers caught in this way was the great murderer, Colonel James Neill, killed on 26 September.

The rebels could do nothing to stop the British force from entering the Residency and rescuing the Europeans that remained within, but they retained control of the city beyond. With reinforcements coming in from the disaster at Delhi, the rebels at Lucknow soon numbered more than 100,000, and they were strong enough to prevent the forces of Havelock and Outram from returning, as planned, to Cawnpore. The struggle was by no means over. In their frustration, the British turned on the sepoys they had captured and slaughtered them.

In November, the Begum's forces were faced by a fresh British column led by General Colin Campbell, with troops that had sailed from South Africa to Calcutta. The rebels were stationed at the Alam Bagh, a shaded enclosure outside the city guarding access to the Residency, where European refugees had taken refuge since June, and where the relieving force of Havelock and Outram had been obliged to remain since September. On 16 November the 2,000 rebel defenders were unable to resist the British onslaught, and all but a handful were slaughtered. The Residency was captured by the British on 22 November, and General Havelock died of dysentery on 29 November.

In spite of this setback, the rebels held on to control of the city itself, for General Campbell was obliged to hurry back to Cawnpore, now surrounded by the superior forces of Tantya Topi and under constant attack. Campbell left a large force, commanded by General Outram, to hold the Alam Bagh, and the rebel sepoys were initially reluctant to move against it.

The Begum made a heartfelt appeal to the troops, pointing out that her entire army was in Lucknow, but complaining that it lacked courage: 'Why does it not attack the Alam Bagh? Is it waiting for the English to be reinforced and Lucknow to be surrounded? How much longer am I to pay the sepoys for doing nothing? Answer now, and if fight you won't, I shall negotiate with the English to spare my life.'[37] The task of attacking Outram's redoubt in the Residency and defending the city against further British attack was now put in the hands of the *maulvi* of Faizabad.

After Delhi and Cawnpore had been re-occupied by the British in September, the rebel leaders were obliged to regroup. They established their new headquarters at Kalpi, a town on the Jumna to the west of Cawnpore. Tantya Topi and Nana Sahib arrived there in October, and more than 12,000 rebel sepoys had joined them by the end of the year. Tantya Topi sought to mobilise local chieftains, and letters and proclamations were sent out to inform them of the progress of the rebellion and of the dangers ahead. His message declared that religion was in danger, and that an outright war should now be launched against the British.

His first task was to attempt the recapture of Cawnpore, and in November his forces advanced from Kalpi to surround the city. His army, which included the followers of Nana Sahib, numbered some 25,000 men, with fifty heavy guns. On 26 November they came under fire from the British troops in the city, commanded by General Charles Windham, the MP for East Norfolk; but they were not deflected, and moved on to attack the city itself. Cawnpore was enveloped in flames, but Tantya Topi was soon faced by Colin Campbell's army, returning hotfoot from Lucknow and crossing the bridge over the Ganges. British siege batteries silenced his artillery.

Early the next month, on 6 December, his rebel force was defeated outside the city by Campbell's army – strengthened by 5,000 infantry, 600 cavalry and thirty-five guns, recently arrived from England.[38] Cawnpore was now lost to the rebels, and Tantya Topi retreated northwards to Fatehgarh, held by the rebels since June. He was pursued there by Campbell, and Fatehgarh was also lost, in January 1858. The surrounding countryside was laid waste by the British, and thousands of sepoys and innocent peasants were slaughtered.

In the course of 1858, when the prospects of ultimate success had virtually disappeared, the rebels showed a surprising determination to defy the British and a remarkable capacity to maintain themselves in the field.[39] But General Campbell's advance was inexorable, and by the end of February his army had grown to become the largest British army ever seen in India, reinforced by a force of Gurkhas sent by the king of Nepal.

The rebels at Fatehgarh had been the first to bear the brunt of his attacks in the new year, but in February it was the turn of Lucknow. The *maulvi* of Faizabad and the other generals of the Begum Hazrat Mahal had assembled a huge army to defend the city, and they had launched a series of attacks on the residual British garrison at the Alambagh. Yet they could not resist Campbell's reinforced army. On 16 March they were obliged to evacuate the city for the last time, resisting to the end. Captain Hodson, the murderer of the royal princes at Delhi, was one of their victims, shot while looting. The Begum and her army left the city, to continue a rearguard action throughout the year.

The next rebel commander in Campbell's sights was Khan Bahadur Khan, the Nawab of Bareilly, the rebel 'viceroy' established in Rohilkhand ever since the initial mutiny, in May 1857. For a while, the Nawab had welcomed the surviving troops of Nana Sahib, but Nana's Hindu nationalism was unpopular in this largely Muslim city. Nana Sahib's soldiers made short work of a handful of Highlander troops that attacked a fort at Ruiya, but they were defeated outside Bareilly on 5 May by Campbell's army, and the Nawab and Nana Sahib were obliged to retreat south, where they joined the surviving rebel commanders at Kalpi.

Meanwhile, to the south, at Jhansi, the fort of the Rani Lakshmi had come under sustained artillery attack on 21 March from fresh British forces led by General Hugh Rose. The barrage lasted for ten days. The Rani Lakshmi's personal efforts had enabled the area to remain under rebel control for almost a year, but the arrival of General Rose at Indore in December soon changed the balance of power. Rose commanded the Central India Field Force, a British-officered and largely Indian army put together with troops assembled from the British bases at Bombay and Madras.

The Rani's sepoys now lined the walls of the Jhansi fort, and the women carrying ammunition to the batteries were subjected to 'a remorseless fire' from Rose's infantry.[40] The walls were finally breached on 29 March, the day on which reinforcements from Kalpi led by Tantya Topi came to her assistance. This fresh army, with Afghan soldiers and sepoys from the Gwalior Contingent, was substantial, but it was no match for Rose's soldiers. At a battle outside Jhansi, the rebel leader lost more than a thousand men, and was forced to return to Kalpi.

The Jhansi fort was captured by the British on 3 April, after ten months in rebel hands, and the British indulged in their customary practice of looting and summary execution. Some 5,000 people were killed.[41] 'The whole city looked like a fiendish burial ground', wrote one inhabitant. 'Innumerable men were slaughtered.'[42] The Rani herself escaped from the walls and withdrew to Kalpi, to join up with Tantya Topi and eventually with Nana Sahib. She was pursued there by Rose's avenging army.

Early in May, Tantya Topi advanced with 20,000 soldiers to Kunch, some forty-two miles south of Kalpi, to confront Rose's troops. After a bloody struggle, the rebels withdrew to the outskirts of Kalpi and took up a defensive position, but they were again defeated by Rose's soldiers and withdrew to the city. Faced with such a powerful enemy, the rebel forces retreated, and moved west towards Gwalior. When Rose entered Kalpi on 24 May, the city was empty.

Gwalior had once been the fort of Scindia Bahadur, but his soldiers – the Gwalior Contingent – had mutinied in June the previous year, and were now loyal to Nana Sahib and Tantya Topi. The rebel leadership had a new stronghold and, to replace Scindia, Nana Sahib was named as the new Peshwa of a revived Maratha government. But the rejoicings were short-lived.

Lakshmi Bai, Rani of Jhansi, circa 1890.

On 17 June 1858, at Kotah-ke-Serai, five miles outside Gwalior, the rebel army met with disaster, in a confrontation sometimes known as 'the battle of Gwalior'. This was the swan-song of the great rebellion. Confronting General Rose's troops and additional British reinforcements brought up from Agra, the Rani herself was killed. Rose chivalrously described her as 'the bravest and best military leader of the rebels'. She was, he wrote later to the Duke of Cambridge, 'the Indian Joan of Arc'.[43]

Defeated at Gwalior, Tantya Topi embarked on a guerrilla resistance campaign that lasted for more than a year. Operating at first in the regions of Sagar and Narbada, he moved later to Khandesh and Rajasthan. Betrayed in March 1859 by Man Singh, chief of Narwar, his close associate, he was captured by the British while asleep in his camp. Taken to Sipri, he was tried by a military court and hanged on 19 April 1859. His close friend Nana Sahib had already disappeared, possibly into Nepal.

In April 1858, Kunwar Singh, the Hindu rajput based at Azamgarh, had been driven from the city by British forces led by Lord Mark Kerr. He retreated across the Ganges to his home at Jagdishpur, in Bihar, and he too engaged in guerrilla

Execution of native mutineers after the Indian Mutiny,
Lucknow, January 1858. Photograph by Felice Beato.

warfare, supported by thousands of peasants recruited by his brother, Ammar Singh. A large British force was despatched against him from Allahabad, and on 23 April he was able to claim a victory against it. Yet he died a few days later, from a wound that had led to the amputation of his right hand. Ammar Singh maintained the guerrilla resistance until late in the year, when he too was killed.

Driven out of Bareilly in May 1858, the Nawab Khan Bahadur Khan also became a skilled guerrilla fighter,[44] although he eventually abandoned guerrilla operations to seek refuge in the forests of Nepal. Captured there in December 1859 by the troops of Jung Bahadur, the maharajah of Nepal and a British ally, he was handed over to the British. He was brought back to Bareilly and hanged outside the police station in February 1860.

The Begum Hazrat Mahal, the heroic leader at Lucknow, was more fortunate. She also took refuge with Jung Bahadur in Nepal, remaining there until her death in 1879 – the last surviving leader of the rebellion. Bakht Khan from Bareilly, who had defended Delhi and fought in Lucknow, and later in Shahjahanpur, also retreated to the forests of Terai, in Nepal, where he died in 1859.

The Muslim leaders fared little better. The *maulvi* Ahmed Ahmadullah Shah, known as 'the *maulvi* of Faizabad', waged a guerrilla war in Oudh after the fall of Lucknow, and eventually withdrew into Rohilkhand. He sought assistance from the rajah of Pawayan, who was sympathetic to the British, and in June 1858 he was shot by the rajah's brothers when attacking their fort on an elephant. His severed head was taken to Shahjahanpur, where the rajah claimed the reward that the British had offered.

One of the other Islamic leaders of the rebellon, Liaquat Ali, the *maulvi* of Allahabad, survived for some fourteen years after the rebellion was crushed, but was eventually captured and tried by the British at Allahabad. He pleaded guilty to leading the mutineers, but asked the court to consider that he had saved the lives of several Europeans, both at Allahabad and at Cawnpore. Sentenced to life imprisonment, he died at the prison colony of Port Blair in the Andaman Islands.

Nana Sahib, the Hindu resistance leader at Cawnpore, was last heard of in April 1859, when he sent a petition to the British authorities asking for clemency. He most probably died in the same year. Although a junior officer suggested that, since an amnesty had been declared, he might come in without fear, Lord Canning, under pressure from public opinion in Calcutta, thought otherwise. 'Whether he surrenders or be taken', wrote Canning, 'he will be tried for the crimes of which he stands charged.'[45] Nana Sahib, the emblematic leader of the rebellion who was most feared and hated by the British, disappeared without trace.

Epilogue

An array of rebels and resistance fighters crowd the pages of this book over the century from 1755 to 1857 – from the Black Hole of Calcutta to the Indian Mutiny, in the traditional formulation of imperial history. A handful are familiar figures; some are only famous in the countries where they fought and died. The great majority have little name-recognition in the twenty-first century; they have disappeared into history's immense oubliette, unremembered and unsung. This book has sought to recover some of their names and their activities, to give them an appropriate place in the imperial record. They were not always forgotten. Nana Sahib, the maligned rebel from Bithur in 1857 and heir to the throne of the Marathas, invoked the memory of Siraj-ud-Daula, the Muslim Nawab of Bengal, who had destroyed the British military base at Calcutta in 1755. Nana planned to avenge the Nawab's defeat at Plassey in 1757 by attacking the British-occupied town of Cawnpore.

A remembered thread of resistance runs through the episodes of this book as rebels recall what once had been, before British soldiers came to seize their countries and settlers came to occupy their land. The early struggles of the mid 1750s in India and North America were but a foretaste of the rebellions that occurred in later years as Britain's imperial tentacles spread into fresh areas of the globe.

In most cases the resistance fighters were unsuccessful, but on occasion their fightback proved effective. The slaves of Haiti defeated a British army of occupation and forced it to withdraw; rebellious slaves elsewhere in the Caribbean helped to accelerate an end to slavery; the map of Indonesia was not painted red for long, although that had once been the ambition of Stamford Raffles; the incorporation of Latin America into the Empire was a pipe dream that did not survive a military victory by the indigenous militias of the River Plate.

White settler rebels were usually more successful than indigenous peoples, although they too did not always prevail. The North American settlers won a permanent victory in 1783, but the Australian settlers failed in 1808, as did the South Africans in 1815. The Canadian rebels of the 1830s were defeated, but their actions brought self-government closer for the settlers. The Dutch farmers in Cape Colony eventually won a victory of sorts, also in the 1830s, by simply walking out of the Empire and then nourishing a tradition of resistance to the British that culminated in the Boer War.

Prominent at the start were the Native American leaders of the 1750s and

1760s, who aimed to drive the British into the sea. Their great rebellion is usually overshadowed by the eventually more successful revolt of the settlers. Yet the story of the resistance of Shingas, Custaloga and Seroweh, and of Neolin and Pontiac, is an important page in the history of Empire, in which the suppression of indigenous peoples is often neglected or underplayed. Elsewhere, the Maori rebels in New Zealand in the 1840s have left a handful of prominent names – Te Here Rangihaeata, Hone Heke, Kawiti, and Topine Te Mamaku. The biographical details of the Aborigine rebels of Australia are more difficult to uncover – Pemulwy, Merridio and Neugavil, and Timninparewa, are among the few whose names have survived.

The leaders of slave revolts in the Caribbean and adjacent territories are also hard to pin down. We know too little about Tacky and Blackwall in Jamaica, or Will and Sharper in Guyana, but some rebellious slave leaders, often Maroons, come into closer focus – Chatoyer, Pharcelle and Polinaire, Quashee and King Samson, Bussa and Nancy Grigg, Quamina Gladstone and Sam Sharpe.

The Indian princes, drawn from high rank, fare better. Indians still honour Mir Kassim and Nana Farnavis, Haidar Ali and Tipu Sultan, as well as Daulat Rao Sindhia and Jeswant Rao Holkar. The rebels of Kandy – Wickrama Sinha, Kapitipola, and Wikrama Sardawa Siddhapa – are also well remembered today. The half-dozen Xhosa chiefs who fought a rearguard action in Cape Colony for half a century have an established place in the contemporary revision of South Africa's troubled history: Ndlambe and Makana, Matiwane and Maqoma, Hintsa and Sandile. The names of the leaders of the Burmese resistance struggle, Maha Bandula, Myat-Toon and Pagan Min, have also survived into the twenty-first century. So too have the fighting amirs of Sind in the 1840s – Mir Shahdad Khan and Sher Mohammed Khan – as well as the Sikh resistance fighters – Sher Singh Attariwala and Sham Singh Attariwala.

Less fortunate are the unremembered pirates of the eastern seas, swept away in particularly vicious campaigns, or the only marginally less forgotten tribal leaders of Assam. Ireland too, for obvious reasons, hides most of its rebellious leaders behind a range of pseudonyms – Queen Sive, Captain Rock, the Whiteboys, the Defenders.

A century is a brief spell in the life-span of an empire, and although the Indian Mutiny marked the end of an era, it did not bring the Empire to a close – or even to its knees. That would take another ninety years. One change in 1858 was the formal winding-up of the East India Company and the transfer of its possessions to the British Crown. Queen Victoria was given the title of empress and her governor-general became the viceroy. The Empire emerged strengthened from this testing time, and the protests of a small band of Radical MPs who had sustained a steady anti-imperial critique at Westminster were marginalised and rendered increasingly irrelevant. The British public were encouraged to support the Empire, and they were taught to remember and highlight the atrocities of the rebel forces during the Indian rebellion – at Cawnpore and elsewhere. The 'frightfulness' unleashed by the British – the hanging and 'cannonading' – was passed over largely in silence.

Imperial arrogance became the hallmark of the subsequent hundred-year period after the Indian rebellion, as the Empire entered a hyperactive period in which military repression of recalcitrant opponents went hand-in-hand with continuing settler land grabs and the concomitant slaughter of indigenous peoples. The settler wars in Australia and New Zealand continued for several more decades, with the Maoris fighting back methodically and the Aborigines lashing out whenever opportunity arose.

Elsewhere, the famous Jamaican uprising at Morant Bay in 1865 was crushed with great brutality, arousing deep disagreements within the British political elite and marking an important and degrading milestone in imperial history. Later that decade came a further rebellion in Ireland, this time by the 'Fenians', as well as a revolt by the Métis in Canada led by Louis Riel. The invasion of Ethiopia in 1868 and the defeat and suicide of the Emperor Tewodros marked the start of a new kind of 'gunboat diplomacy' that has lasted from that day to this. The British learned to use their military power to remove an unfavoured leader without moving on to occupy his country on a permanent basis.

The final decades of the nineteenth century began with important resistance in Ireland and Egypt and ended with the rebellion of the Boers in South Africa. In the years between, the high noon of empire (sometimes called 'the scramble for Africa'), the British faced the freshly awakened resistance forces of Islam in many places in Asia and Africa: in the Sudan, in Uganda, in Malaya and Borneo, in India, in Kenya and Zanzibar, in Somalia, and in Nigeria and Sierra Leone. Some of the most zealous opponents of empire had long been those perceived as 'Mohammedans', and their forces, more often than not, were wrapped in the green flag of Islam. Traditional histories of empire have been reluctant to discuss the British conflict with Islam, yet in much of the Empire, for much of the time, an undeclared struggle with Muslims formed part of the imperial backcloth. Much of this Islamic resistance was caused by the Empire's militant Christianity, in open conflict with Muslim culture and traditions. In the twenty-first century, as this topic has moved again to the top of the international agenda, the British should be able to reflect on the fact that they have been here before, even if this permanent thread has never been adequately absorbed into official memory. Indeed it sometimes seems as if the current enthusiasm for the ideology of 'human rights' is little more than a twenty-first century form of the secular Christianity that played such a central imperial role in the nineteenth century.

Islamic opposition sprang up in the Middle East and the Arab world after

Gladstone's invasion of Egypt in 1882. Nationalist hostility to the invasion, evoked by the Egyptian leader, Colonel Ahmed Arabi, was to nurture an anti-British tradition in the country that would survive through the years of British occupation and beyond. Arabi had given due warning to the British prime minister when the invasion was imminent, invoking the possibility of an Islamic war throughout the Empire:

> Egypt is held by Mohammedans as the key of Mecca and Medina, and all are bound by their religious law to defend these holy places and the ways leading to them. Sermons on this subject have already been preached in the Mosque of Damascus, and an agreement has been come to with the religious leaders of every land throughout the Mohammedan world.
>
> I repeat it again and again, that the first blow struck at Egypt by England or her allies will cause blood to flow through the breadth of Asia and Africa, the responsibility of which will be on the head of England.[1]

The British attack on Alexandria did not go uncontested, but the successful Islamic uprising against the Empire that Arabi had predicted failed to materialise in the short run. Yet over the longer term the invasion of Egypt proved to be one of the turning points of empire. Egypt itself – and its ancillary territory, the Sudan – were to prove difficult and expensive to control and govern. Arabi's appeal for a jihad was ignored in Egypt itself, but was to be taken up repeatedly in the Muslim territories of the Empire in the decades before the outbreak of the First World War in 1914. In the 1890s, on India's north-west frontier bordering Afghanistan, the British faced the most violent and extensive rebellion by Muslim tribesmen since their annexation of the Punjab in the 1840s. Punitive expeditions were sent out against the Mohmands, the Orakzai, and the Afridis – as they would be just over a century later, organised this time by the United States and Pakistan.

In the Sudan in the same period, the victories of Mohammad Ibn Abdullah, the famous 'Mahdi', kept the British at bay for many years; Sudanese resistance was only finally subdued by the intemperate machine-gun massacre perpetrated by British troops at Omdurman in 1898. In Uganda, the British faced prolonged resistance from Islamic factions in Buganda and Banyoro, and in Nigeria in 1903, Sultan Attahiru Ahmadu, a great Muslim warrior, led the resistance to the British invasion and occupation of Sokoto. Machine guns were again used to mow down Muslim resistance, and, as Captain F. P. Crozier noted, officers went over the battlefield to deal with the wounded survivors: 'Soon all was calm. Faithful slaves died by the score round the mystic green flag of the Emir . . . Officers ran out to capture this flag and "finish off" the wounded with sporting rifles.'[2]

Elsewhere, in Somaliland, Haji Mohammad bin Abdullah Hassan, called 'the Mad Mullah' by the British, kept imperial forces at bay for twenty years, defeated eventually in 1920 by aerial bombing – the terror weapon that would be so widely used in the final decades of empire.

Gradually it became clear in the early twentieth century that the Empire had overreached itself. Swallowing up Egypt in 1882, followed by Nigeria and Central Africa in the early twentieth century, was already a step too far. Soon the First World War, involving every country in the Empire, would provide an occasion for endless incidents of rebellion, mutiny and insubordination that would continue well into the 1920s, long after the recalcitrant colonial troops had returned home. The wartime occupation of Iraq, and its inclusion within the Empire behind the fig leaf of a League of Nations 'mandate', was the final straw. Iraq was the last in (in 1920) and the first out (in 1932) – although the Royal Air Force and its ancillary bases remained in place for more than twenty years. The Second World War merely served to accelerate the process of imperial collapse, leaving the Empire prostrate and bankrupt. What had taken two centuries to construct was destroyed, after the end of hostilities in 1945, in just two decades.

Yet this has been not so much a history of the Empire as a history of those who did not wish to participate in the imperial project. Over the years the imperial rebels devised many stratagems to resist, and when possible to defeat, their oppressors – struggles that became more sophisticated as time passed. In the period covered by this book, rebels fought back with the mostly inadequate means they had at their disposal. In the final century of empire their rebellions saw the developing use both of political assassination and of non-violent resistance, techniques not much in evidence in earlier years. (Suicide bombings lay further in the future.) At the same time, the imperial authorities moved from extreme post-rebellion punishment – beatings and hangings – to the use of terror weapons in battle: first the machine gun and then the aerial bomb.

The Empire as it once had been came to a formal conclusion in the 1960s, yet its unhappy legacy is ever-present in today's world, where many conflicts take place in the former colonial territories. This is one of the reasons why the Empire still provokes such harsh debate. If Britain made such a success of its colonies, why are so many of them still major sources of violence and unrest? The British have continued to fight wars in the lands of their former Empire in the twenty-first century, and much of the British population has reverted without question to its old position of accepting unthinkingly what is being done in its name in distant parts of the globe. Yet some British citizens today have other historical memories, from the other side of the battle lines. Tipu's tiger pouncing on a British soldier, portrayed on the jacket of this book, is an appropriate emblem for this alternative view.

Acknowledgements

My debt to many writers, alive and dead, will become apparent to any reader of this book, but I am especially grateful to the late Sir John Fortescue, author of an encyclopaedic thirteen-volume *History of the British Army* that finds space to do justice to the rebel opponents that the army faced; to Noel Mostert, author of *Frontiers*, a path-breaking study of the Xhosa of South Africa and their epic, half-century struggle to hold back the tides of white settlement; and to the late Sir Penderel Moon, whose immense volume on *The British Conquest and Dominion of India* is a magnificent distillation of the British imperial experience as well as a sympathetic account of the Indian predicament, typical of a former member of the Indian Civil Service. In his well-remembered role as my Uncle Pendie, I owe Sir Penderel additional thanks for a timely legacy, shared among his six nephews, that has enabled me (briefly) to work, in that felicitous phrase devised by Hugh Thomas, as 'a historian in private practice'. My boyhood self would also acknowledge a special debt to John Fortescue for his *Story of a Red Deer*, a moving account originally published in 1897 of those free spirits on Exmoor that were hunted down much as the indigenous peoples of Empire.

This book has been researched and written over many years, and several of those who helped and encouraged me are no longer with us. I remember with particular pleasure the enthusiasm with which Raphael Samuel greeted this project in its early days; my old friend John Rettie required endless updates on progress and plied me with books on Native American resistance; John Roberts introduced me to several obscure imperial episodes, both in India and Australia; while Tom Lubbock supplied me with cartoons and enjoyed discussions on the imagery of Empire. These friends are gone, and it is sad that they are no longer around to see the completed volume.

Fortunately, many others who have accompanied me on this long journey are still alive, to be thanked in person. Josh Gilbert read an early version of the manuscript and, urging me to curb my interest in military detail, made excellent and detailed suggestions for improvement; Michael Simmons read a later version and has saved me from many errors; Mary Turner, in at the beginning, argued wisely in favour of starting the book half a century earlier than I had originally planned; while Deborah Rogers was most helpful in the reconstruction of the book's basic framework, obliging me most sensibly to abandon the straitjacket of strict chronology that I had forced myself to adopt.

Verso continues to be a friendly and agreeable publisher and I owe especial thanks to Tariq Ali, who dreamt up the image of Tipu's tiger for the jacket, and to Robin Blackburn, benign expert on slavery. Tom Penn in London and Mark Martin in New York have been wonderful editors, cajoling and threatening in turn, while Charles Peyton has been a fine copy editor. Andrea d'Cruz has done sterling work securing permissions for the illustrations. My thanks to them all.

Vivien Ashley, my wife, has accompanied me on many trips to Latin America, and now she has willingly joined me on virtual expeditions to other continents in earlier centuries. Her father and my grandfather were in the Indian Army long ago, and it has been a strange experience for both of us to re-imagine in the twenty-first century the family haunts of yesteryear. She has come along for the ride with her customary enthusiasm and gaiety, enjoying the good moments and keeping me going when the going has been rough.

Richard Gott
London, 2011

Notes

Introduction

1 Henrietta Elizabeth Marshall, *Our Empire Story: Stories of India and the Greater Colonies Told to Children*, London, 1908.

2 Sven Lindqvist, *Exterminate all the Brutes*, London, 2004.

1 Native American Resistance during the French and Indian War

1 An Iroquois letter written in 1754, quoted in Allan McMillan, *Native Peoples and Cultures of Canada*, Toronto, 1995.

2 Paul E. Copperman, *Braddock at the Monongahela*, Pittsburgh, 1977.

3 Gregory Evans Dowd, *A Spirited Resistance: The North American Indian Struggle for Unity, 1745–1815*, Baltimore, 1992.

4 Francis Jennings, *Empire of Fortune: Crowns, Colonies and Tribes in the Seven Years War in America*, New York, 1988.

5 Ibid.

6 Ibid.

7 Randolph Downes, *Council Fires on the Upper Ohio: A Narrative of Indian Affairs on the Upper Ohio Valley until 1795*, Pittsburgh, 1940.

8 These were contingents from the Shawnees, Ottawas, Chippewas, Hurons, Mingos, and Potawatomis, as well as the Delaware.

9 Fred Anderson, *Crucible of War: The Seven Years War and the Fate of the Empire in British North America, 1754–1766*, London, 2000.

10 Virginia DeJohn Anderson, 'New England in the Seventeenth Century', in Nicholas Canny, ed., *The Oxford History of the British Empire, Volume I: The Origins of the British Empire*, Oxford, 1998, p. 214.

11 Peter C. Mancall, 'Native Americans and Europeans in British America, 1500–1700', *Oxford History of the British Empire, Volume I*, p. 344.

12 James Horn, 'Tobacco Colonies: The Shaping of British Society in the Seventeenth Century Chesapeake', *Oxford History of the British Empire, Volume I*, p. 175.

13 Mancall, 'Native Americans and Europeans in British America', p. 338.

14 Anderson, 'New England in the Seventeenth Century', p. 201.

15 David Corkran, *The Creek Frontier, 1540–1783*, Oklahoma, 1967.

16 The report from the French captain at Fort Duquesne in 1756.

17 Wilbur Jacobs, *Diplomacy and Indian Gifts: Anglo-French Rivalry along the Ohio and North-West Frontiers, 1748–1763*, Stanford, 1950.

18 Anderson, *Crucible of War*.

19 See below, Chapter 3.

20 The Micmacs were members of the Wakanabi Confederacy, a grouping formed earlier in the century by the Passamaquoddies, the Penobscots and the Maliseets. They were much influenced by French priests and usually took the side of the French in the long years of rivalry and hostility between the two European powers.

21 John Mack Faragher, *A Great and Noble Scheme: The Tragic Story of the Expulsion of the French Acadians from Their American Homeland*, New York, 2005

22 Several French Acadian families settled at St Malo, from where they set out ten years later, in 1764, to found a new French colony in the south Atlantic at les îles Malouines, later to be occupied by the British. As Las Malvinas, or the Falkland Islands, they provided the backdrop to the last years of the Empire story some two centuries later.

23 Olive Dickason, *Canada's First Nations: A History of Founding Peoples from Earliest Times*, Oklahoma, 1992.

24 The event was later described in *The Last of the Mohicans*, a novel by James Fenimore Cooper published in 1826.

25 Odanak, known to the French as St François-du-Lac, stood on the banks of the St François river, close to the St Lawrence.

26 Timothy Todish, *The Annotated and Illustrated Journals of Major Robert Rogers*, New York, 2002.

27 McMillan, *Native Peoples and Cultures of Canada.*

2 The Last Great Native American Rebellions

1 David Corkran, *The Cherokee Frontier: Conflict and Survival, 1740–1762*, Oklahoma, 1962.

2 Corkran, *Cherokee Frontier: Conflict and Survival.*

3 Ibid.

4 Gregory Evans Dowd, *A Spirited Resistance: The North American Indian Struggle for Unity, 1745–1815*, Baltimore, 1992.

5 Dowd, *A Spirited Resistance.*

6 Neolin himself was soon lost to history, although his name and teaching were invoked in the early nineteenth century by the Native American leader Tecumseh. John Sugden, *Tecumseh: A Life of America's Greatest Indian Leader*, London, 1999.

7 Quoted in Colin Callaway, *The American Revolution in Indian Country: Crisis and Diversity in Native American Communities*, Cambridge, 1995.

8 Alexander Henry, *Travels and Adventures in Canada and the Indian Territories Between the Years 1760 and 1776*, Toronto, 1901.

9 This, the famous battle of Bushy Run, was a close contest, as Colonel Fortescue's history records:

> The Indians attacked with great gallantry, charging again and again with wild yells up to the line, only to be driven back by steady and telling volleys. But the counter-attack of the bayonet was of little avail against so active an enemy in the forest; and the savages, skipping nimbly from tree to tree, kept themselves under cover, constantly changing the point of assault and pouring in always a destructive fire. For seven long hours the fight raged fiercely . . .

Colonel J. W. Fortescue, *A History of the British Army, Vol. III, 1763–1793*, London, 1902.

10 John Penn, an eyewitness, described how the Indians 'divided into their little families, the children clinging to their parents; they fell on their knees, protested their innocence, declared their love to the British, and that, in their whole lives, they had never done them injury; and in this posture they all received the hatchet! Men, women, and little children were every one inhumanely murdered in cold blood!'

Michael N. McConnell, *A Country Between: The Upper Ohio Valley and Its Peoples, 1724-1774*, Lincoln, 1992.

11 William Trent, 'William Trent's Journal at Fort Pitt, 1763,' ed. A. T. Volwiler, *Mississippi Valley Historical Review*, 11 (Dec. 1924).

12 Colonel Bouquet had some additional ideas about the extermination of the Native Americans, echoing the experience of the Empire of Spain. 'I wish we could make use of the Spanish method', he wrote, 'to hunt them with British dogs, supported by Rangers and some light

horse, who would, I think, effectually extirpate or remove that vermin.' Quoted in Ray Billington, *Westward Expansion: A History of the American Frontier*, University of New Mexico Press; 6th edition, 2001. The settlers in America were already familiar with the Spanish practice in their Cuban colony of using hunting dogs to curb slave rebellions. General Amherst was enchanted with the colonel's additional suggestions, though unsure of their practicality: 'You will do well to try to inoculate the Indians by means of blankets, as well as to try every other method that can serve to extirpate this execrable race. I should be very glad your scheme for hunting down by dogs could take effect, but England is at too great a distance to think of that at present.' Elizabeth A. Fenn, 'Biological Warfare in Eighteenth-Century North America: Beyond Jeffery Amherst', *The Journal of American History*, March 2000, and Jennings, *Empire of Fortune*. Years later, in 1795, the British were to introduce hunting dogs from Cuba to help crush a revolt by the Maroons in Jamaica.

13 This territory stretched to the south and east of a line running south from Fort Stanwix to the Delaware river, west and south to the Allegheny river, and downstream as far as the junction of the Ohio and the Tennessee.

3 Slave Rebellions in the Caribbean

1 Edward Long, *History of Jamaica*, London, 1774.

2 Edward Long's opinionated and tendentious version of events, written from the slave-owners' point of view, is the principal source for the story of the rebellion.

3 Long, *History of Jamaica*. The name 'Maroon' was derived from the Spanish *cimarrón*, describing an escaped slave living on the *cima*, or summit, of the mountains. Happily existing in their free territory in the hills, the Maroons were often intermarried with the Carib natives, and were sometimes referred to as Black Caribs. On some islands, the indigenous Caribs lived a similar existence to that of the Maroons – notably in St Vincent, Dominica and Cuba, which the British seized from Spain in 1762.

4 Ibid.

5 The British had occupied these islands in 1642, and would eventually surrender them to Honduras in 1859. Rebel slaves, Maroons and Black Caribs were often deported there from elsewhere in the Caribbean.

6 J. Philmore, *Two Dialogues on the Man-Trade*, London, 1760. Quoted in Peter Linebaugh and Marcus Rediker, *The Many-Headed Hydra: The Hidden History of the Revolutionary Atlantic*, Verso, London, 2000.

7 As in 1760, Long is the principal source for the rebellion of 1765 (Long, *History of Jamaica*).

8 Linebaugh and Rediker argue that Tacky's revolt sparked a new era of resistance in the Caribbean, with further rebellions taking place in Bermuda and Nevis in 1761; in Suriname in 1762, 1763 and 1768–72; in Jamaica in 1765, 1766 and 1776; in British Honduras in 1765, 1768 and 1773; in Grenada in 1765; in Monserrat in 1768; in St Vincent in 1769–73; in Tobago in 1770, 1771 and 1774; in St Croix and St Thomas in 1770; and in St Kitts in 1778.

9 The British liked to claim that the Caribs were merely the descendants of slaves from the Guinea coast, whose slaving ship had been wrecked off the island in 1675. The slaves had intermarried with a surviving handful of the island's native 'Yellow Caribs'. By making this claim, the British could argue that the Black Caribs were newcomers just like themselves, and had no right to prior ownership. This was one of the perennial claims of settlers throughout the Empire: the belief that apparently indigenous inhabitants had only just arrived.

10 Sir William Young, *An Account of the Black Charaibs in the Island of St Vincent's, with the Charaib Treaty of 1773, and Other Original Documents*, London, 1795.

11 The Black Caribs were not immune to the spirit of unrest creeping over the American mainland in those years, and were well informed about foreign events. The commissioner was surprised to learn that they knew that Britain, France and Spain had been on the brink of war in 1771, as a result of a crisis over the Falkland Islands in the south Atlantic. A Spanish fleet had

forced the British to withdraw their vestigial presence from the islands in June 1770, but the British had returned in September 1771 'after threat of war' with Spain. The British withdrew again in May 1774.

12 Adam Smith, *Lectures on Jurisprudence*, Oxford, 1978.

4 Treaties and Proclamation Mark the End of the French and Indian War

1 Fortescue, *History of the British Army, Vol. III.*

2 Callaway, *The American Revolution in Indian Country.*

5 Muslim Resistance in Bengal and Mysore

1 The Company reciprocated his dislike. One British observer perceived him as an 'excessively blustering and impertinent young man', recalling how Company officials would refuse to allow him into their factory at Kassimbazar or into their country houses. On occasion, they claimed, he 'would break the furniture or, if it pleased him, take it away'. The denigration of local rulers would become an established imperial practice.

2 John Holwell, *Black Hole*, London, 1758.

3 Brijen Gupta, *Siraj-ud-Daullah and the East India Company, 1756–57*, Leiden, 1966.

4 K. K. Datta, *Alivardi Khan and His Times*, Calcutta, 1939.

5 Admiral Watson, who had brought Clive from Madras to Calcutta, was presented with a rose and plume composed of diamonds, rubies, sapphires and emeralds. His descendants sold them at auction in 1982, and they were purchased by London's Victoria and Albert Museum.

6 Penderel Moon, *The British Conquest and Dominion of India*, London, 1989.

7 Among the troops at the disposal of the Nawab of Oudh were some 5,000 'fanatics' from the Afghan border, armed only with swords. When the attack against Patna was launched, according to Colonel Fortescue's account,

> the poor creatures, naked and smeared with ashes, their long hair streaming wildly behind them, rushed forward sword in hand with yells and screams. The British held their fire until they came within close range, and then gave them a volley and a shower of grapeshot, which brought hundreds to the ground and sent the rest shrieking away.

Fortescue, *History of the British Army, Vol. III.*

8 Wayne Broehl, *Crisis of the Raj: The Revolt of 1857 through British Lieutenants' Eyes*, University Press of New England, 1986.

9 Broehl, *Crisis of the Raj.*

10 William Butler, *The Land of the Veda, being personal reminiscences of India . . . together with incidents of the great sepoy rebellion and its results to Christianity and civilisation*, New York, 1875.

11 Colonel Fortescue's history records that something unusual occurred:

> The first four of the culprits were actually about to meet their fate, when four grenadiers of the battalion stepped forward and asked that, as grenadiers and therefore entitled to the post of honour in the field, they might take their place. The request was granted, and they were tied up and blown away.
>
> The whole parade shuddered at the sight; the Europeans were all of them actually in tears; and the officers of the sepoy battalions hurried forward to warn Munro that their men would not allow the execution to proceed. Munro . . . ordered the Europeans

> to load with ball and grape, and drew up the infantry on two lines on either side of the mutineers. Then, ordering the officers back to their posts with the sepoy battalions, he gave those battalions the order, "Ground Arms". Every sepoy instinctively obeyed. "Quick March". The sepoys marched forward, and the Europeans filed down in their rear, so as to cut them off from their grounded arms. The sepoys were then halted and reformed, and the provost-marshal was directed to proceed with his duty. Sixteen more of the doomed men were then blown from the guns, four being reserved for the same fate in another place . . . Then the army was ready again for its work.

Fortescue, *History of the British Army, Vol. III.*

12 Rajat Kant Ray, 'Indian Society and British Supremacy', in P. J. Marshall, ed., *The Oxford History of the British Empire, Volume II: The Eighteenth Century*, Oxford, 1998.

13 Percival Robert Innes, *The history of the Bengal European Regiment, now the Royal Munster Fusiliers, and how it helped to win India*, Simpkin, Marshall & Co, 1885.

14 W. W. Hunter, *The Annals of Rural Bengal, Vol. I: The Ethnical Frontier of Lower Bengal, with the Ancient Principalities of Beerbhoom and Bishenpore*, second edn, New York, 1868.

6 Peasant Resistance in Ireland

1 John Wesley, *The Journal of the Rev. John Wesley*, 4 vols, London, 1827.

2 J. S. Donnelly, 'The Whiteboy Movement, 1761–5,' *Irish Historical Studies* XXI: 81 (March 1978).

3 Wesley, *Journal of the Rev. John Wesley.*

4 Ibid.

5 Ibid.

6 W. E. H. Lecky, *A History of Ireland in the Eighteenth Century, Vol.* 2, London, 1892.

7 Jim Smyth, *The Men of No Property: Irish Radicals and Popular Politics in the Late Eighteenth Century*, London: Macmillan, 1992.

8 Lecky described the impact of this belief on the rival religious establishments:

> Catholic chapels for many months were almost deserted, while the quiet Protestant churches were thronged by wild and tattered congregations come to qualify themselves for midnight outrages, and hands were thrust into the baptismal font for holy water, and beads were counted, and Ave Marias repeated around the communion rails.

9 Smyth, *Men of No Property.*

10 Francis Joseph Bigger, *The Ulster Land War of 1770 (The Hearts of Steel)*, Dublin, 1910.

11 Wesley, *The Journal of the Rev. John Wesley.*

Part II: Introduction

1 Colin Collaway, *The American Revolution in Indian Country: Crisis and Diversity in Native American Communities*, Cambridge, 1995.

7 Episodes of Resistance during the American War of Independence

1 John Spencer Bassett, 'The Regulators of North Carolina, 1765–1771', in the *Annual Report of the American Historical Association*, 1894–95, Washington, 1895.

2 Ibid.

3 Ibid.

4 The Tea Act allowed the East India Company to send tea directly to North America, thereby reducing costs. The settlers were not impressed. They also objected to the fact that the Company now had the right to deal solely with their own chosen merchants.

5 The surveyed land was to be given to officers promised land grants long ago, for their military service during the French and Indian wars of the 1750s. In subsequent years, many officers had sold their entitlements to land speculators, and Major George Washington had a personal interest in these surveys, since he had bought up many of these military land claims.

6 Grace Haber, *With Pipe and Tomahawk: The Story of Logan, the Mingo Chief*, New York, 1959.

7 Douglas Hurt, *The Ohio Frontier: Crucible of the Old Northwest, 1720-1830,* Bloomington, Indiana, 1996.

8 Emily Foster, ed., *The Ohio Frontier: An Anthology of Early Writings*, Lexington, Kentucky, 1996.

9 Eugene Bliss, ed., *The Diary of David Zeisberger, a Moravian Missionary among the Indians of Ohio*, Michigan, 1972.

10 Calloway, *The American Revolution in Indian Country.*

8 Native American Resistance to Fur Traders in Western Canada

1 Arthur Morton, *A History of the Canadian West to 1870–71, being a history of Rupert's Land and of the North-West Territory*, Toronto, 1972.

2 Daniel Williams Harmon, *Sixteen Years in the Indian Country, 1800–1816*, ed. W. Kaye Lamb, Toronto, 1957.

9 The Resistance in Southern India

1 James Mill, *History of British India*, London, 1826

2 'The blunders had been great and flagrant', wrote Colonel Fortescue harshly in his *History*. 'From a military point of view, Munro must be held responsible for one of the greatest calamities that has ever befallen British arms.' Colonel J. W. Fortescue, *A History of the British Army, Vol. III, 1763–1793*, London, 1902.

3 Penderel Moon, *The British Conquest and Dominion of India*, London, 1989.

4 Fortescue, *History of the British Army, Vol. III.*

Part III: Introduction

1 More than sixty years later, in the aftermath of the Indian Mutiny, a penal colony was re-established on the Andaman islands in 1868. As late as 1901 some 12,000 Indian prisoners were held there, guarded by 140 British troops, 300 sepoys and 600 paramilitary policemen.

10 The British Search for Distant Gulags

1 R. Bonney, *Kedah, 1771–1821: The Search for Security and Independence*, Kuala Lumpur, 1971.

2 J. C. Beaglehole, *The Voyage of the Endeavour, 1768–1771*, Cambridge, 1955.

3 Hugh Cobbe, ed., *Cook's Voyages and Peoples of the Pacific*, London, 1979.

4 'The natives of this country are of a middle stature, straight bodied and slender-limbed, their skins the colour of wood, soot, or of a dark chocolate, their hair mostly black, some lank and others curled, they all wear it crop'd short, their beards which are generally black they likewise

crop short or singe off. Their features are far from being disagreable, and their voices are soft and tunable. They go quite naked, both men and women without any manner of cloathing whatever, even the women do not so much as cover their privities.'

5 Quoted in J. C. Beaglehole, *The Life of Captain James Cook*, London, 1974.

6 William Eden, writing on the subject of banishment, was keen to note that Australia was at least preferable to Russia: 'the country of New Wales does not receive them in a bleak hideous solitude, destitute of shelter from the fury of an inclement sky, like the frozen deserts of Siberia'. Yet Siberia it was, a gulag in the southern hemisphere. See William Eden, Lord Auckland, 'An Introductory Discourse on Banishment', in *The History of New Holland, from Its First Discovery in 1616 to the Present Time; with a Particular Account of Its Produce and Inhabitants and a Description of Botany Bay*, London, 1787.

7 Richard Broome, *Aboriginal Australians: Black Response to White Dominance, 1788–1980*, London, 1982.

8 James Bonwick, *The First Twenty Years of Australia: A History Founded on Official Documents*, London, 1882.

9 A surgeon describing the prisoners who arrived in Sydney in three ships in 1792 noted that 'a great number of them were lying nearly quite naked, without either bed or bedding, unable to turn or help themselves . . . The smell was so offensive that I could hardly bear it. Some of these unhappy people died after the ships came into harbour, before they could be taken on shore. Part of these had been thrown into the harbour, and their dead bodies cast upon the shore, and were seen lying naked upon the rocks. The misery I saw amongst them is inexpressible.'

The History of the British Convict Ship "Success" and Its Most Notorious Prisoners: Compiled From Governmental Records and Documents, no author, no publisher, 1912 (reprint Cornell University Library).

10 When the ships arrived in port, the story was much the same, as a Lieutenant Bond recounted:

> The commissioned officers then come on board and, as they stand on the deck, select such females as are most agreable in their persons . . . The non-commissioned officers are then permitted to select for themselves; the privates next; and lastly those convicts who, having been in the country a considerable time, and having realised some property, are enabled to procure the Governor's permission to take to themselves a female convict.

11 David Collins, *An Account of the English Colony in New South Wales*, London, 1798.

12 Colonel Collins, the Marine commander, had already noted in December 1788 that the governor planned to capture one or two people 'whose language it was becoming absolutely necessary to acquire, that they might learn to distinguish friends from enemies'. Collins, *Account of the English Colony*.

13 Bonwick, *The First Twenty Years of Australia*.

14 Ibid.

15 Pemulwy's supernatural powers soon became a matter of concern to the British. 'A strange idea was found to prevail among the natives respecting the savage Pemulwy', noted Colonel Collins. 'Both he and they entertained an opinion that, from his having been frequently wounded, he could not be killed by our fire-arms. Through this fancied security, he was said to be at the head of every party that attacked the maize grounds.' Pemulwy was dead, but his rebellious spirit lived on among the Aborigines for many decades. Collins, *Account of the English Colony*.

16 Quoted in J. L. Kohen, 'Pemulwey' – entry in the *Australian Dictionary of Biography*, Melbourne, 2005.

17 In January 2010, Prince William, the heir to the British throne, was asked for help by a group of Aborigine activists in finding Pemulwy's skull. Research revealed that the skull had been given to the Royal College of Surgeons at some moment in the nineteenth century, but the College

was bombed in 1941 and over half its collection of skulls was destroyed. Those that survived were transferred to the National History Museum in 1948.

11 The Black Settlers of Sierra Leone

1 Perceiving a business opportunity, Smeathman changed his advice, claiming that the area of the Sierra Leone river was 'but thinly populated'. His support for the scheme was welcomed by the British government, though Smeathman died before his claims could be verified, and Sharp's project went ahead without him.

2 Bryan Edwards, a plantation owner in Jamaica in the 1790s, had a Mandingo slave from the region who could write the Arabic alphabet 'with great beauty and exactness' and copy passages from the Koran. Bryan Edwards, *The History of the British Colonies in the West Indies*, London, 1801.

3 Adam Hochschild, *Bury the Chains: The British Struggle to Abolish Slavery*, London, 2005.

4 Nova Scotia was conveniently and suspiciously empty. Taking over the territory from the French nearly forty years earlier, during the French and Indian War, the English had driven out 6,000 of the island's population of French settlers and Native Americans in 1755, scattering them through the various English colonies of America. Now the 'Empire Loyalists' were given plots on this usefully empty land.

5 'King' Jimmy remained suspicious, but eventually understood that the settlers were there to stay. When he died in 1796, his heirs invited the British authorities to his funeral 'to help the people to cry for King Jimmy'. Yet many of the Temne retained doubts about British intentions. Naimbanna's son died on board ship on his way home from his English school, and the Temne believed that he had been murdered. They came to regret the deal that had been struck.

6 James W. St G. Walker, *The Black Loyalists: The Search for a Promised Land in Nova Scotia and Sierra Leone, 1783–1870*, Dalhousie, Halifax, 1976.

7 Thomas Winterbottom, *An Account of the Native Africans in the Neighbourhood of Sierra Leone*, London, 1803; and Christophe Fyfe, ed., *'Our Children Free and Happy': Letters from Black Settlers in Africa in the 1790s*, Edinburgh, 1991.

8 Walker, *Black Loyalists*.

9 Robert Charles Dallas, *The History of the Maroons, from Their Origin to the Establishment of Their Chief Tribe at Sierra Leone*, London, 1803.

Part IV: Introduction

1 The Spanish island of Hispaniola was divided between Spain and France in 1697 under the terms of the Treaty of Ryswick. France received the western third of the island, which was renamed Haiti in 1804.

2 The British army in India at this time had some 70,000 men, of whom 5,000 were 'King's troops' from Britain, 5,000 were European mercenaries recruited by the East India Company, and 60,000 were Indian sepoys.

3 An area of several thousand square miles, with a population one-third Muslim Moplahs (or Mappilas) and two-thirds Hindu, Malabar was to be the site of endless small rebellions throughout the nineteenth century, finally exploding more than a century later, in 1921.

4 Cornwallis returned to India in 1805 to clear up the problems created by his successors – and to die. He gave the ring to his daughter, who married Baron Braybrooke. It was stolen from the house of their descendants at Audley End in 1951.

5 Saint-Domingue, Tobago, Martinique, Guadeloupe, St Lucia and Mariegalante.

6 Henry Dundas, the British trade minister, sent instructions to the governor of Jamaica that spelled out Britain's intentions. In the event of war with France, he wrote, Britain would seek 'to extend the protection of His Majesty's arms to the French West Indies, and secure to them the advantage of being subjects to the Crown of Britain'.

12 Resistance to Empire in the Caribbean in the Wake of the French Revolution

1 Dominica was 'discovered' by Christopher Columbus in the fifteenth century, and remained under Spanish control from 1493 to 1625. The French acquired it that year, and surrendered it to the British under the terms of the earlier Treaty of Paris, in 1763. France regained it during the American War of Independence, and returned it to the British under the terms of the Treaty of Paris in 1783.

2 George Hamilton, the new governor, offered a bargain: Pharcelle and his two wives, Martian and Angélique, plus twelve of his followers, would be freed and given Crown land on which to settle. In exchange, he would be expected to search for runaway slaves.

3 David Geggus, *Slavery, War, and Revolution: the British Occupation of Saint Domingue, 1793–1798*, Oxford, 1982.

4 'I have consecrated my life to the defence of the Blacks', Rigaud recalled in 1799:

> From the beginning of the Revolution, I have braved all for the cause of liberty. I have not betrayed my principles, and I shall never do so. I am too much of a believer in the Rights of Man to think that there is one colour in nature superior to another. I know a man only as a man.

5 Soldiers under the command of General Grey were shipped across in February 1794 to attack Martinique. Yet even with 7,000 soldiers carried in nineteen ships, it took seven weeks to capture the island. Prince Edward, the Duke of Kent (and the future father of Queen Victoria), eventually hoisted the British colours on the French fortress of Morne Fortuné, but only after some 350 British troops had been killed or wounded.

Grey's troops were more swiftly successful at St Lucia in early April, securing a French defeat within a couple of days, and soon the general was arranging for prize-money to be secured from the sale of goods in the island's captured warehouses. A prolonged campaign began the same month in Guadeloupe.

6 Michael Duffy, *Soldiers, Sugar and Seapower: The British Expeditions to the West Indies and the War against Revolutionary France*, Oxford, 1987.

7 Not until the end of the next century did anyone identify the cause of the great imperial nightmare of yellow fever: a mosquito that lived in stagnant pools in tropical ports, and made its home in wooden boats.

8 R. G. Buckley, *Slaves in Red Coats: the British West India Regiments, 1795–1815*, London, 1979.

9 Stephen Alexis, *Black Liberator: The Life of Toussaint Louverture*, London, 1949. Toussaint went on to defeat the forces of André Rigaud in the south in 1799, and to capture the Spanish end of the island in 1801. He fought against Napoleon's troops in 1802, but was detained after signing a peace treaty and exiled to France, where he died in 1803.

13 Slaves and 'Free Coloureds' in the French Islands of the Caribbean Resist Absorption in the Empire

1 There was a precedent for this in Guadeloupe, since Jean-Baptiste Labat had armed the slaves on Basseterre to fight the English in 1703.

2 Colonel Fortescue's history recorded the melancholy event: 'Thereupon 125 ghastly figures staggered out of the lines, "fitter for hospital than to be under arms" – all that remained of what had once been three battalions and twenty-three companies of infantry and two companies of artillery.'

3 The general put in charge of St Lucia, captured in April, was court-martialled on charges of stealing; the general at Martinique had to be transferred; and, at the end of July, General Grey

himself was accused by the London government of rapacity, extortion and oppression in the matter of prize-money. Years later he won his case, and in 1806 some £378,000 was awarded to the captors of the islands – a sum insufficient to provide pensions for those made widows in the campaign. J. W. Fortescue, *A History of the British Army, Vol. IV, Part I, 1789–1801*, London, 1913.

4 'If the losses of the Army, Navy and transports be added together', wrote Colonel Fortescue, 'it is probably beneath the mark to say that 12,000 Englishmen were buried in the West Indies in 1794.'

5 Fortescue noted that 'ever since Cromwell sent his expedition to Hispaniola in 1654, the rule had held good that to assemble any great number of white men together in the West Indies was the certain way to bring about an epidemic of yellow fever, which would not only annihilate them but destroy multitudes of the white settlers also'.

6 Napoleon's government had a change of heart in 1802, re-establishing slavery throughout the French Empire. The French could no longer claim the moral high ground, and paid the price. French forces under General Antoine Richepanse sought to recover Guadeloupe from its radical black government in 1802. Richepanse died of yellow fever, and his slave army rebelled at their camp at Matouba and refused to submit. Rather than accept a return to slavery, the black soldiers blew themselves up.

7 Edward Cox, 'Fédon's Rebellion, 1795–96: Causes and Consequences', *Journal of Negro History* LXVII: l (Spring 1982).

8 In 1805 he became governor of Trinidad, and participated in the extermination of the Pindaris in India in 1817.

9 Richard and Elizabeth Howard, eds, *Alexander Anderson's Geography and History of St Vincent, West Indies*, London, 1983.

10 Bryan Edwards, *The History of the British Colonies in the West Indies*, London, 1801.

11 Earl Kirby and C. I. Martin, *The Rise and Fall of the Black Caribs of St Vincent*, St Vincent, 1972.

12 Howard and Howard, *Alexander Anderson's Geography and History of St Vincent.*

13 One contemporary chronicler, Robert Dallas, reveals the extent of the Maroons' dismay:

> No sooner was it reported to the Maroons that the party who had submitted had been tied [up], and sent [as] prisoners to Montego Bay, than each man, of his own accord, determined to set fire to his house, declaring that he would die rather than surrender and be shipped off the country with his arms in his hand.

Robert Charles Dallas, *The History of the Maroons, From Their Origin to the Establishment of Their Chief Tribe at Sierra Leone*, London, 1803.

14 Dallas, *History of the Maroons.*

15 Edwards, *History of the West Indies, Volume IV*, London, 1819.

16 The chasseurs gave Colonel Walpole a demonstration of what the dogs could do:

> Some of the dogs, maddened by the shout of attack while held back by the ropes, seized on the stocks of the guns in the hands of the keepers, and tore pieces out of them . . . If the greatest exertions had not been made to stop them, they would certainly have seized upon his horses.

17 On arrival at Halifax, Prince Edward, the British commander-in-chief, came on board, and was impressed by what he saw: 'The Maroon men in a uniform dress in lines on each side the whole length of the ship, and the women and children forward, dressed clean and neat.'

18 On one occasion, a member of the Canadian assembly was out riding near their settlement with Colonel Quarrell:

> He saw a large company of them at a little distance, and heard them singing, on which he commented on their happiness in their new situation. 'The singing you hear,' said the commissary, 'is no proof, I doubt, of their happiness.' While the member was

proving singing to be an indication of felicity, they approached the company of Maroons, and found them employed in the interment of one of their friends.

19 Henry Breen, *St Lucia: Historical, Statistical, and Descriptive*, London, 1844.

20 At the end of 1796, hearing of an armistice negotiated on St Vincent by Marin Padre, the rebel chief who was also a landowner in St Lucia, Brigadier Moore suggested that he should be brought over to try out his negotiating talents on his native island. Marin Padre came over in December and exchanged ideas with Captain Lacroix. Their negotiations proving inconclusive, the fighting resumed.

21 Brigadier Moore was offered the governorship of Grenada, but, suffering from fever, he was repatriated to England. He died years later, famously, at La Coruña, during the Peninsula Wars. General Abercromby returned to Britain and was appointed commander-in-chief in Ireland, on the eve of its great eighteenth-century rebellion in 1798.

14 Europe's Revolutionary Conflict Spreads to South Africa

1 A fierce repression of Jacobins was undertaken in 1797 by George Macartney, the civilian governor of Cape Town. As a former governor in the Caribbean, in Madras, and in Ireland, he had experience of such things. Prominent Republicans were exiled, while others had dragoons billeted in their homes. One man, who addressed his guests on the invitation cards to his daughter's wedding as 'Citizen', was given the dragoon treatment and fined a thousand pounds.

2 The security of the new British colony was constantly at risk, not least from its nominal defenders. In October 1797, a mutiny occurred on British ships anchored off Cape Town, echoing the mutinies that had occurred earlier that year in the fleet at Spithead and the Nore. The sailors had complaints about their conditions. The admiral was well disposed towards his men and began negotiations, but Lord Macartney threatened a tougher line and trained the shore guns on the mutinous ships. The mutinous crews surrendered, and their leaders were hanged at the yard arm.

3 Noël Mostert, *Frontiers: The Epic of South Africa's Creation and the Tragedy of the Xhosa People*, London, 1992.

4 Robert Percival, *An Account of the Cape of Good Hope*, London, 1804.

5 John Shipp, *The Extraordinary Military Career of John Shipp*, London, 1829.

6 J. S. Marais, *Maynier and the First Boer Republic*, Cape Town, 1944.

15 The British and the Dutch Empire in Ceylon

1 Captain Robert Percival, *An Account of the Island of Ceylon*, London, 1804.

2 Colvin De Silva, *Ceylon under the British Occupation, 1795–1833*, Colombo, 1953.

3 The governor, Frederick North, was a convert to the Greek Orthodox church and the younger son of the Lord North who had presided over Britain's defeat by the settlers in America in the 1780s.

4 Geoffrey Powell, *The Kandyan Wars: The British Army in Ceylon, 1803–1818*, London, 1973.

5 Colonel Fortescue's history describes how 'the villagers were incensed to madness by the devastation of their fields and the shooting down of their fathers and brothers'. Frederick, Duke of York, the commander-in-chief in London, asked the Colonial Office if the stories of the destruction of paddy fields and the shooting of villagers were true, since, if so, they were 'very disgraceful to the British arms'. After this royal rebuke, the border war was halted. J. W. Fortescue, *A History of the British Army, Vol. V, 1803–1807*, London, 1910.

6 The 'caffres', as they were called, arrived with their families, and cost £45 a head. A further batch of 180 came in October 1804, and by February 1805 there were a total of 700, and the price had gone down to £37. All had to be given military training and taught to speak English.

7 Richard Hall, *Empires of the Monsoon: A History of the Indian Ocean and Its Invaders*, London, 1996.

8 Governor North also recruited Malay soldiers from the former Dutch territories of

Malacca, Penang, Java and St Helena, but it was claimed throughout the nineteenth century that the children of black slaves made the best soldiers.

16 The Great Irish Rebellion of 1798

1 Liz Curtis, *The Cause of Ireland: From the United Irishmen to Partition*, Belfast, 1994.

2 W. E. H. Lecky, *A History of Ireland in the Eighteenth Century*, London, 1892.

3 Roy Foster, *Modern Ireland, 1600–1972*, London, 1988.

4 T. Bartlett, 'Defenders and Defenderism in 1795', *Irish Historical Studies* XXIV: 95 (May 1985).

5 Lecky, *History of Ireland*.

6 Richard Musgrave, *Memoirs of the Different Rebellions in Ireland*, Dublin, 1802

7 David Miller, 'The Armagh Troubles, 1784–95', in S. Clark and J. Donnelly, eds, *Irish Peasants: Violence and Political Unrest, 1780–1914*, Manchester, 1983.

8 Even at the distance of more than a century, Lecky was unusually outraged. 'The measure was as completely illegal as the proceedings of the Defenders themselves', and it should not be confounded with an ordinary press gang. These were not 'professional sailors, but for the most part agricultural labourers, many of whom had never even seen the sea, who were suddenly torn from their families and their homes, and sent to the war-ships, to pestilential climates, and to a great naval war. To such men the fate was more terrible than death.' Lecky, *History of Ireland*.

9 Thomas Pakenham, *The Year of Liberty: The History of the Great Irish Rebellion of 1798*, London, 1969.

10 Particularly notorious were the activities of a Welsh cavalry regiment stationed at Newry, known as the Ancient Britons. John Giffard, an officer in the Dublin militia, observed how these Ancient Britons vied with the Orange yeomanry to see who could wreak the most damage. After going on an arms search in the hills, he noted how simple it was to rejoin the Welsh regiment:

> I was directed by the smoke and flames of burning houses, and by the dead bodies of boys and old men slain by the Britons or the Yeomanry, though no opposition whatever had been given by them, and, as I shall answer to Almighty God, I believe a single gun was not fired, but by the Britons or the Yeomanry. I declare there was nothing to fire at, old men, women, and children excepted. From ten to twenty were killed outright; many wounded, and eight houses burned.

11 Hastings was an Irish peer, Lord Moira, and later, as the Indian governor-general, he was himself to be no stranger to repression when crushing the Gurkhas of Nepal in 1814 and the Pindaris in 1817.

12 Cornwallis was later despatched to perform a similar role in India in 1805, to clear up after a comparably disastrous showing there by General Lake.

13 William Lecky claims there were two rebellions in Ireland in 1798: 'One was purely political . . . The other was a popular movement . . . directed against the owners of property.' Ibid.

14 Lecky, *History of Ireland*.

15 The Byrnes were one of the most prominent rebel families, and Miles Byrne (in Lecky's account) recalled in his memoirs what had most rankled:

> He mentioned that his own father had told him that he would sooner see his son dead than wearing the red uniform of the King, and had more than once shown him the country around his farm, bidding him remember that all this had belonged to his ancestors, and that all this had been plundered from them by the English invaders.

These folk memories, coupled with tales of atrocities against Catholics in the towns and country round about, led many people to believe that a policy of extermination had been decided on by the military, causing waverers to join the rebel ranks. Lecky, *History of Ireland*.

16 According to Lecky's account, 'great numbers of Protestants were brought to the rebel camp, confined in the old windmill, or in a barn that lay at the foot of the hill, and then deliberately butchered'. A further rebel atrocity occurred at the end of the month, at a nearby country house called Scullabogue. No exact record exists of the number of (mostly) Protestant prisoners held there who were killed, but a figure of one hundred seems likely, many of them burned in a barn.

17 This was more of a massacre than a battle, according to Thomas Pakenham's account:

> When the pursuit was called off, after perhaps five hundred fugitives had been cut down, Lake's army celebrated their victory in the usual style of the period. Some found bodies to make targets for sword play; others stripped the dead of clothes and valuables. The worst atrocities were committed in Enniscorthy itself. The rebels had turned one of the town houses into a makeshift hospital, and there they had made their wounded as comfortable as they could. Lake's troops captured the hospital and then set fire to it – patients and all. Next morning the bodies were still hissing in the embers.

Pakenham, *Year of Liberty*.

18 One other rebellion occurred in June that year, organised by the Presbyterian supporters of the United Irishmen in the north, and crushed at the battle of Ballynahinch, south of Belfast.

19 In his memoirs, Holt recalled the assistance of Susy Toole, the daughter of a blacksmith, who became his eyes and ears in enemy territory, acquiring large quantities of ammunition: 'Carrying a basket of gingerbread and fruit, she ranged over many miles of country, collecting the most minute and accurate knowledge about the position, movements, and intentions of every body of troops in the neighbourhood.' T. C. Croker, ed., *Memoirs of Joseph Holt, General of the Irish Rebels*, London, 1838.

20 Ibid.

21 Marianne Elliott, *Robert Emmet: The Making of a Legend*, London, 2003.

17 Tipu Sultan and the Final Resistance of Indian Forces in Mysore

1 Colonel Fortescue's history recalled the scene:

> Scarcely a house was left unpillaged, and bars of gold, jewels, and trinkets of great value were brought into camp for sale by private soldiers and sepoys. The treasure at the palace was saved, except one casket of jewels, said to have been worth £300,000, whereof it appears that at least one officer took his share with the men.

Fortescue, *History of the British Army, Vol. IV, Part 2, 1789–1801*, London, 1906.

2 The St James Chronicle, April 1800, quoted in Susan Stronge, *Tipu's Tigers*, V & A Publishing, London, 2009.

3 Quoted in Anne Buddle, *The Tiger and the Thistle, Tipu Sultan and the Scots in India, 1760-1800*, National Gallery of Scotland, Edinburgh, 1999.

4 Stronge, *Tipu's Tigers*.

5 Colonel John Biddulph, *The Nineteenth and Their Times*, London, 1899.

6 G. S. Sardesai, *New History of the Marathas*, Bombay, 1968.

Part V: Introduction

1 John D. Grainger, *The Amiens Truce: Britain and Bonaparte, 1801–1803*, London, 2004.

2 The British navy was given the task of patrolling the Atlantic, to police the continuing international trade from Africa to Brazil, Cuba and the United States. The West Africa Squadron began surveying the coast of Africa, and securing the naval bases that would facilitate the task of imperial expansion later in the century, when East Africa was brought into the frame. Parliamentary radicals, however, were always opposed to the policy, arguing cogently in the 1840s

that 'our unavailing attempts to suppress the traffic worsened the lot of the slaves by making the misery of the Middle Passage worse than ever'. Their opposition was ineffective. The naval squadron was not phased out until the 1870s, when Britain's taste for empire was well established.

3 The British parliament had originally voted in favour of a motion declaring that 'the slave trade ought to be gradually abolished' in April 1792. The weasel word 'gradually' was introduced by Henry Dundas, the influential imperial politician from Scotland, whose intervention postponed the trade's end for fifteen years. This long postponement allowed the evil practices of the Atlantic passage to continue, as well as permitting the British to purchase blacks in the slave market to serve in their imperial wars. Blacks were imported from Goa and Mozambique to fight the war of conquest in Ceylon in 1803, while 13,000 slaves bought in the Caribbean to help in the suppression of slave rebellions in 1795 were obliged to fight against each other. Black soldiers in the Ranger battalions formed in several islands after 1795 were promised freedom when hostilities ended, but the promise was often forgotten. Rebellions were followed by mutinies, both leading to a litany of floggings and executions.

18 Rebellions, Revolts and Mutinies in the Caribbean

1 Unlike neighbouring Trinidad, Tobago had never been occupied by the Spaniards. Others had claimed it over several centuries – the British, the Dutch and the French. Their successive settlements had proved a mixed blessing, and the island had provoked a measure of resistance by the native inhabitants in 1640, and by slaves in 1771 and 1774. Tobago had fallen to the British in 1762 and to France in 1783. A decade later, in April 1793, it was seized again by the British, and in 1801 it seemed likely to return to France. Gertrude Carmichael, *The History of the West Indian Islands of Trinidad and Tobago, 1498–1900*, London, 1961.

2 Bryan Edwards, *The History, Civil and Commercial, of the British West Indies, Vol. I*, London, 1819.

3 Ibid.

4 A subsequent investigation into Colonel Cochrane's tenure of the island found that his rule had been marked by tyranny and extortion. Accused of keeping a harem on his estate, he was made to resign his commission. He returned to his former position as a member of parliament at Westminster. Years later, he was found guilty of conspiracy at the Stock Exchange and expelled from parliament.

5 Lennox Honychurch, *The Dominica Story*, Kingston, 1995.

6 Ibid.

7 Colonel Ainslie faced a bleak future too. He was recalled to London in June 1814, just as the long rebellion was ending. His repressive measures in Dominica had not gone unnoticed at home, and he was not without critics in London. In retirement he devoted himself to his coin collection.

8 The rebels divided themselves into *convois*, or regiments, each with a name: the Dreadnought Band, the Danish Regiment, and the Monkey Corps. Each regiment had its own king and queen and royal family, with flags and elaborate uniforms that made fun of the military dress of the Europeans. Everyone was given a title, and the kings exchanged messages and visited one another, and were approached with considerable ceremony. Ceremonial feasts were held, as well as mock communion services with secret songs and slogans. Some of the *convois* were Creole and some were African, and some had come from other islands – from Martinique, Guadeloupe and Grenada.

9 Britain had seized Trinidad with hardly a shot being fired, for the Spaniards had capitulated when they saw the size of General Abercromby's armada. Its acquisition was ratified by the Treaty of Amiens of 1802. Although originally a Spanish colony, Trinidad had become largely French-speaking as a result of a decree of 1776 that had encouraged immigration. Many settlers from the French islands had arrived with their slaves after the French Revolution and the revolution in Saint-Domingue.

10 Carmichael, *History of the West Indian Islands of Trinidad and Tobago.*

11 Brigadier Hislop reported to London on 19 December that 'three of them (two styling themselves kings and one a general in chief) were condemned to be hanged this day at twelve o'clock; their heads to be exposed after death on poles erected for the purpose, and their bodies to be hanged in chains on the sea side near the district where they resided'. A month later he recorded the fate of the other six: 'The most culpable are sentenced to lose their ears, to be flogged under the gallows and then banished from the colony for ever. Some less culpable have been sentenced to corporal punishment and to work in chains for a specific period. Those least culpable are to suffer a modest chastisement.'

12 The settlers' militia kept up their harassment of the Maroons. In April 1819 the militia, commanded by Captain Taylor, shot three Maroons and captured twenty-five; in May they captured twenty-seven. In April 1826 they raided a Maroon village at Terre Bouillant, killing two and detaining fifteen, before burning down the village.

13 Thomas Talboys, *An Account of Certain Circumstances between General Hislop, Governor of Trinidad, and Thomas Talboys, Methodist Missionary, in the Year 1811*, Georgetown, 1817.

14 W. J. Gardner, *A History of Jamaica*, London, 1873

15 Bryan Edwards, *A History of the West Indies, Vol. V*, London, 1819.

16 Ibid.

17 Ibid.

18 The Reverend W. J. Gardner noted in his *History of Jamaica* in 1873 that 'the city must have been sadly deficient in all proper police supervision when twenty or thirty so-called negro dukes, generals, etc., could meet in the suburbs to discuss their plans, and practice pistol-shooting at trees every Sunday afternoon'.

19 Edwards, *History of the West Indies, Vol. V.*

19 The Resistance of the Marathas to the British Invasion of Central India

1 Shah Alam had been blinded by an Afghan, Ghulam Qadir Rohila, who had briefly seized Delhi in 1788. He was the grandfather of Bahadur Shah II, who became the focus of the Great Rebellion of 1857.

2 The most recent episode in their history of internecine fighting had occurred in 1802, when Sindhia joined forces with Baji Rao to help defend the Peshwa's city of Poona against an attack from Holkar. After Holkar's capture of Poona, Baji Rao escaped to British territory on the coast and signed a treaty that would provide him with British support against his Maratha opponents. With Baji Rao now operating as a British ally, Sindhia perceived that, if he was to combat the British threat successfully, he would have to join forces with Holkar.

3 General Lake, commander of British forces in India since October 1800, was no stranger to repression, having earlier been a notorious figure during the bloody struggle in Ireland in 1797 and 1798. Lake's army, 10,000 strong, had the advantage over Sindhia. He had some 200 European artillerymen, three regiments of European cavalry, and five of native cavalry. He also had eleven infantry regiments of sepoys and one of Europeans, and was equipped with powerful cannon. Yet Sindhia's army was no pushover, and Lake wrote later of the favourable impression that it made on him.

> Their army is better appointed than ours, no expense is spared whatsoever. They have three times the number of men to a gun we have. Their bullocks, of which they have many more than we have, are of a very superior sort. All their men's knapsacks and baggage are carried upon camels, by which means they can double the distance . . .

See William Thorn, *Memoir of the War in India Conducted by Lord Lake*, London, 1818, and H. W. Pearse, *Memoir of the Life and Military Service of Viscount Lake, 1744–1808*, London, 1908.

4 Wellington lost nearly 1,600 men, killed and wounded – a quarter of his entire force. The Marathas' losses were also heavy – 1,200 dead and perhaps three times as many wounded.

5 General Lake, who later described himself as 'Viscount Lake of Delhi and Laswari', recorded his favourable impressions of the army pitted against him.

> These battalions are most uncommonly well-appointed, have a most numerous artillery, as well served as they possibly can be, the gunners standing to their guns until killed by the bayonet. All the sepoys of the enemy behaved exceeding well, and if they had been commanded by French officers, the event would have been, I fear, extremely doubtful. I never was in so severe a business in my life, or anything like it, and pray to God I may never be in such a situation again.

Thorn, *Memoir of the War in India Conducted by Lord Lake.*

6 Holkar first tried a diplomatic offensive, sending messengers in February 1804 to General Lake's headquarters at Biana. He said he was ready to sign a treaty similar to the one that Sindhia had signed, although his conditions were more stringent: the British should pay him tribute and return the Maratha territory they had occupied in the Bundelkhand and the Doab, the land between the Jumna and the Ganges. 'Friendship' requires that you accept, was his message. 'If not', he concluded with a rhetorical flourish, 'my country and property are upon the saddle of my horse; and, please God, to whatever side the reins of the horses of my brave warriors may be turned, the whole of the country in that direction shall come into my possession.' Holkar sent a further message to Wellesley, warning of the consequences of a refusal: 'Countries of many *coss* [two hundred miles] shall be overrun and plundered. General Lake shall not have leisure to breathe for a moment; and calamities will fall on *lakhs* of human beings, in continual war, by the attacks of my army, which overwhelms like the waves of the sea.'

7 Thorn, *Memoir of the War in India Conducted by Lord Lake.*

8 A version of this epic event occurs in the Holkar Chronicle:

> Monson, being routed by this huge body, beat a precipitate retreat back to the Makundra pass. His Kotah contingent was entirely annihilated near Peeplah, and Lieutenant Lucas was killed on his elephant. The Rajah of Kotah then assisted Monson to cross over the Chambal safely with all his men, but Holkar pursued them, and came upon them in fury, having been assisted by the Bhils of these hilly regions. The small British force was plundered and stripped of their belongings while they were flying away for safety. Another severe attack took place on the river Banas on 24 August, in which Monson lost a great number either killed or drowned in the river, in the close pursuit which he had to suffer at Holkar's hands.

A British version records a similar tale: 'Worn out with fatigue and hunger, and almost at the end of their tether, the broken army streamed into Agra at the end of August in utter demoralisation and disorder, fifty days after the retreat had commenced.' Stewart Gordon, *The Marathas, 1600–1818 (The New Cambridge History of India, Vol II, Part 4)*, Cambridge, 1995.

9 Pearse, *Memoir of the Life and Military Service of Viscount Lake.*

10 General Lake took a leaf from the book of his Irish experiences in 1798, burning towns and slaughtering prisoners. When he captured the fortress of Dig, he found five companies of sepoys who had deserted from Colonel Monson's ill-fated army in July. They had sought Holkar's protection within the fortress, and their fate was recalled in the memoirs of Lieutenant John Shipp: the mutinous sepoys 'stood outside the principal gate of the fort, with their arms ordered, without apparently making any resistance, and frequently crying out, "Englishmen, Englishmen, pray do not kill us; for God's sake do not kill us".'

They received little sympathy from Shipp: 'As these supplications proceeded rather from fear than from penitence for the crime they had been guilty of – that of deserting to an enemy – these men could expect no mercy. We had positive orders to give them no quarter, and most of them were shot.'

11 'From the accursed day that Lord Wellesley set foot in India till the day of his departure', noted one speaker in the House of Commons, 'he has exhibited a constant scene of rapacity, oppression, cruelty and fraud, which goaded the whole country into a state of revolt.'

12 'They are ready to join in my plans of resisting the British', Sindhia told a cousin in a letter describing a meeting with the Sikh princes of Patiala. He even claimed to have received 'friendly approaches' from Ranjit Singh in Lahore and from the Shah of Afghanistan.

13 Thorn, *Memoir of the War in India Conducted by Lord Lake.*

14 Holkar went mad in 1808, and was kept roped up for three years and fed only with milk. His kingdom was taken over by his mistress, Tulsi Bai, who became regent for her son. Yet even in his absence, Holkar's hostility to the Empire remained vibrant within his court. When Tulsi Bai sought to make peace with the British in 1817, she was seized by her counsellors and beheaded.

20 Mutiny and Revolt by Muslim Sepoys and European Officers

1 Quoted in Penderel Moon, *The British Conquest and Dominion of India*, London, 1989.

2 Gillespie had made his name during the occupation of Haiti, where he was fired at when swimming ashore with a flag of truce to demand the surrender of Port-au-Prince. He had only recently been transferred from Jamaica to Arcot, and had arrived a few days earlier. A sergeant named Brady, who had been with his regiment in Jamaica some four years earlier, was amazed to see the colonel. 'If Colonel Gillespie be alive', he said, 'God Almighty has sent him from the West Indies to save our lives in the East.'

3 Eventually, in 1811, Cradock was sent out to be governor of Cape Colony, where he authorised one of the first extermination campaigns against the Xhosa, while Bentinck returned to India in 1828 as governor of Bengal. Colonel Gillespie went on to participate in the capture of Java in 1811, and was shot dead by the Gurkhas when he tried to capture Nepal in 1814.

4 Quoted in Moon, *British Conquest and Dominion of India.*

5 Colonel W. J. Wilson, *History of the Madras Army*, Madras, 1882.

6 H. H. Wilson, *The History of British India from 1805 to 1835, Vol. VII*, London, 1858.

21 Rebellion in Australia and the Slaughter of Aborigines

1 More than a thousand Irish convicts had disembarked in Australia in 1800, and hundreds more sailed in during 1801. More than 600 had been members of the United Irishmen organisation, promoters of the rebellion.

2 Margaret Hazzard, *Punishment Short of Death: A History of the Penal Settlement at Norfolk Island*, Melbourne, 1984.

3 Holt had arrived in Australia in January 1800 on board the *Minerva*, a ship bringing 121 male convicts and twenty-six women convicts to the gulag. Many of the Irish prisoners, it was noted at the time, 'were bred up in genteel habits, and others to light professions, and of course unaccustomed to hard labour'. Always a reluctant revolutionary, Holt was frequently asked by the Irish convicts to support their plans for revolt, and he always refused their requests. Joseph Holt, *Memoirs of Joseph Holt, General of the Irish Rebels*, ed. T. C. Croker, London, 1838.

4 R. W. Connell, 'The Convict Rebellion of 1804', *Melbourne Historical Journal* 5 (1965).

5 With martial law in force, vengeance was swift, as Holt's account makes clear:

> The unfortunate wretches who escaped by flight were arrested by a party of forty soldiers, the constables, and some loyal settlers. Being brought before a Court Martial, it was arranged that lots should be drawn from a hat, and that every third man whose name was drawn should be hanged. Many fine young men were strung up like dogs, but the arrival of the Governor put an end to this extraordinary proceeding.

Holt, *Memoirs of Joseph Holt.*

6 The surviving prisoners, according to D. D. Mann's near-contemporary account, were dealt with equally harshly:

> Ten of the leaders of this insurrection, who had been observed as particularly conspicuous, and zealous in their endeavours to seduce the rest, were tried on March 8, and capitally convicted. Three were executed on the same evening at Parramatta, since it was justly concluded that measures of prompt severity would have a greater effect upon the minds of those who had forsaken their allegiance. On the following day, two others rebels were executed at Sydney, and three at Castle Hill.

A further nine men were sentenced to the lash, receiving between 200 and 500 strokes each. Cunningham had been one of the first to fall, but his body was subsequently hanged on the staircase of the public store in Hawkesbury 'as an example'. D. D. Mann, *The Present Picture of New South Wales*, London, 1811.

7 These included 'twelve male settlers, of whom six had wives, and one a sister; one widow, eight boys and two girls; Mr Coke, a missionary to the Aborigines, with his wife and son; fifteen wives of prisoners, with four boys and two girls; and prisoners and marines.'

8 James Fenton, *A History of Tasmania*, London, 1884.

9 Ibid.

10 W. C. Wentworth, *Statistical, Historical and Political Description of the Colony of New South Wales, and Its Dependent Settlements in Van Diemen's Land*, London, 1819.

11 William Bligh was born in 1754, and commanded a ship on Captain Cook's final voyage to the Pacific in 1776. As captain of the Bounty in 1789, he was placed with eighteen others on an open boat when the crew mutinied, and they sailed on to Timor. He was appointed governor of New South Wales on the recommendation of Joseph Banks, and died in 1817.

12 H. V. Evatt, *Rum Rebellion: A Study of the Overthrow of Governor Bligh by John Macarthur and the New South Wales Corps*, Sydney, 1938.

22 Resistance in South Africa, South America and Egypt

1 Colonel Beresford and Admiral Popham were initially overjoyed and shared quantities of booty between them, reserving the largest share for Colonel Baird, conqueror of Cape Town, who had remained behind in South Africa. Six wagon-loads of looted treasure were loaded on British ships and brought ashore at Portsmouth in September. Popham wrote to City merchants in London pointing out that an extensive new market had been captured and would shortly be opening up for business. Beresford was more realistic, realising the precarious nature of their military position. He sent urgent messages to London and Cape Town requesting reinforcements, though in the event fresh troops were to arrive too late.

2 According to the estimates of an English lieutenant, Alexander Gillespie.

3 One group led by Martín de Pueyrredón was made up of *gauchos* from the interior and of 'pacified' Indians; another was led by Martín de Alzaga, a Spanish merchant who had taken against the free trade programme the British were proposing; and a third was commanded by Captain Jacques (Santiago) de Liniers, an officer of French origin in the Spanish navy.

4 *An Authentic Narrative of the Proceedings of the Expedition under Brigadier-General Craufurd (by an officer of the expedition)*, London, 1808.

5 Other British dreams of imperial expansion in 1806 included a possible attack on Spanish Mexico, with a pincer movement from both east and west. Troops from the black West Indian regiments of the Caribbean would descend on Vera Cruz, on Mexico's Atlantic coast, while sepoys from India would attack Acapulco on the Pacific side, having first captured Manila in the Spanish Philippines. Later in the year, when news arrived in London of the Spanish settler fight-back in Buenos Aires, these imperial pipe dreams had to be abandoned.

6 The government in London was enraged to find that the welcome and unexpected victory

at Buenos Aires in June had been so swiftly followed by such a humiliating defeat in August. The three men deemed responsible – Baird in Cape Town, the governor of St Helena, and Admiral Popham – were recalled to London in disgrace, and Popham was brought before a court martial, though later acquitted.

7 Whitelocke's earlier entry in the imperial story occurred in September 1793, when he was first ashore at the capture of Jérémie, in Haiti.

8 José Luis Molinari, 'Los índios y los negros durante las invasiones inglesas al Río de la Plata, en 1806 y 1807,' *Boletín de la Academia Nacional de Historia* XXXIV, Buenos Aires (1963).

9 Tulio Halperin Donghi, *Politics, Economics, and Society in Argentina in the Revolutionary Period*, Cambridge, 1971. See also, Isabel Hernández, *Los índios de Argentina*, Madrid, 1992.

10 One of those participating in the British attack was Lieutenant Harry Smith, aged twenty – an officer who would later play a prominent role in imperial campaigns in South Africa and India. He left an account of the British advance into the city: 'The tops of the houses were occupied by troops, and such a tremendous fire was produced of grape, canister, and musquetry, that in a short time nearly two columns were annihilated without effecting any impression.' Smith's column suffered severe losses and took refuge in a church, surrendering to the enemy at dusk. See *The Autobiography of Lieutenant-General Harry Smith*, London, 1903.

11 For the English, the military defeat was bad enough, noted Colonel Fortescue in his *History of the British Army*, but the financial implications were worse:

> The pecuniary loss which accompanied it was unendurable. There had been frantic speculation in the new market which Popham, in his vanity, had proclaimed to be open in South America. Not prosperous merchants only, but large numbers of the needy, the rapacious, and the impecunious had staked their all, or their neighbours' all, in the great venture; and, as is usual in such cases, tons of worthless artefacts, which could find no sale in any other quarter, had been shipped over to Buenos Aires. Now it was seen that the long and perilous voyage had been undertaken in vain, and that the whole of the goods exported, whether valuable or worthless, would be returned upon their owners' hands.

Fortescue, *History of the British Army, Vol. V, 1803–1807*, London, 1910.

12 Colonel Craufurd lived on to fight in the Peninsular War with Wellington, and was killed at Ciudad Rodrigo in 1812. General Auchmuty rose to greater prominence as commander-in-chief in Madras in 1810, conqueror of Java in 1811, and commander in Ireland in 1821.

13 J. A. Burdon, *Archives of British Honduras,* 3 vols, London, 1931-34; see also George Henderson, *An Account of the British Settlement at Honduras*, London, 1809.

14 Henderson, *An Account of the British Settlement.*

15 A. A. Paton, *History of the Egyptian Revolution*, 2 vols, London, 1870.

16 According to the account in the *Encyclopaedia Britannica, eleventh edition, 1911.*

17 Mungo Park, *The Journal of a Mission to the Interior of Africa in the Year 1805*, London, 1815, quoted in Maya Jasanoff, *Edge of Empire, Conquest and Collecting in the East, 1750–1850*, London, 2005.

23 Slave Rebellion, Xhosa Resistance, and White Settler Revolt in Cape Colony

1 George McCall Theal, *Records of the Cape Colony, Vol. VI, 1806-1809*, Cape Town, 1900.

2 Quoted in Noël Mostert, *Frontiers: The Epic of South Africa's Creation and the Tragedy of the Xhosa People*, London, 1992.

3 A journal of the campaign, kept by Lieutenant Robert Hart, gives evidence of the impact of Graham's troops. Hart's diary itself has been lost, but it was quoted in the memoirs of a later settler:

> 'From this journal, it appears that the Caffers were shot indiscriminately, women as well as men, wherever found, and even though they offered no resistance. It is true that Mr Hart says the females were killed unintentionally, because the Boers could not distinguish them from the men among the bushes, and so, to make sure work, they shot all they could reach!'

Quoted in Mostert, *Frontiers.*

4 Mostert, *Frontiers.*

5 C. W. Hutton, ed., *The Autobiography of the Late Sir Andries Stockenstrom*, Cape Town, 1887.

6 An Afrikaner historian, J. C. Voight, evoked the scene in a history written in 1899:

> Sobbing and with tearful eyes, the friends of the condemned men see the executioner arrange the cords round the necks of the victims . . . The doomed men submit to their fate. The executioner is now completing his task, and their bodies hang suspended in mid-air. Only for a moment. In the next, the scaffold, clumsily arranged, and not strong enough to bear the weight, gives way, and tumbles to the ground. 'Heaven intervenes for them! Let them live! Give them back to us!' cry the bystanders, as they rush towards the foot of the gallows, where the senseless bodies of the unhappy victims are lying on the ground. The soldiers who are ranged in line on the place of execution are unable, or have not the heart, to keep back the crowd of sympathisers. Men and women, on their knees before Colonel Cuyler, beg for mercy for their brothers, for their husbands, for their sons. Slowly consciousness returns to the five unhappy men. 'Mercy?' Ask it not of a British officer. He must obey his instructions. Again the scaffold is erected, and again the executioners do their work – this time more thoroughly.

J. C. Voigt, *Fifty Years of the History of the Republic in South Africa, 1795–1845*, London, 1899.

24 British Penetration into the Persian Gulf

1 Sultan Mohammed Al-Qasimi, *The Myth of Arab Piracy in the Gulf*, London, 1986.

2 This was a treaty arrangement that would echo down the centuries, for with Oman came Africa. Bolstered by British support, a later Omani sultan, Said ibn Sultan, was to recover Zanzibar, and from there to restore the Kenyan coast of East Africa to the Omani Empire. His British allies were never far behind.

3 See p. 83.

4 Hubert Moyse Bartlett, *The Pirates of Trucial Oman*, London, 1966.

5 'So far from a ready cooperation, there was great trouble in obtaining from His Highness even the assistance of the country boats; the fast of Ramazan was also in celebration, during which the Mohammedans cannot be prevailed upon to work.'

6 Ibid.

7 Ibid.

8 Hassan sent a defiant challenge to the British commander:

> You have been the witness of our endurance and tenacity, in circumstances under which our forces, our valour and number are falling short, since we are only the remaining quarter of the garrison of Ras al Khaima, which counted six thousand combatants. We are enduring all this, taking our stand on nothing but our religion, and preferring the death of the faithful to the life of the reverse; and this, while we are well aware of your condition and forces; but we hold firmly to our purpose, knowing that God is mightier than you, and whenever we deem you strong, we say God is still stronger.

Ibid.

9 See L. G. Johnson, *General T. Perronet Thompson*, London, 1957.

10 Ibid.

25 The British Seizure of Mauritius, the Seychelles and Indonesia

1 The town of St Paul's had been captured in September 1809, and the batteries, the magazines and the public warehouses were all destroyed. Not a gun or cartridge survived, yet with insufficient men available to maintain a garrison, the British were obliged to withdraw.

2 The Battle of Grand Port was the sole French naval victory of the Napoleonic era to be inscribed on the Arc de Triomphe in Paris.

3 The 'Code Noir' was often quoted by the settlers to explain why they could not be expected to do any labouring work themselves: 'As the heat of these climates, and the temperature of ours, prevent Frenchmen from undertaking so painful a labour as the clearing of uncultivated lands in these burning countries, it was necessary to supply this want by means of men accustomed to the heat of the sun and the greatest degree of fatigue.'

4 Moses Nwulia, *The History of Slavery in Mauritius and the Seychelles, 1810–1875*, Toronto, 1981. See also Richard B. Allen, 'Licentious and Unbridled Proceedings: The Illegal Slave Trade to Mauritius and the Seychelles during the Early Nineteenth Century', *Journal of African History* 42, Cambridge (2001).

5 An increase of 20,000 from the 60,000 estimated in 1810. Allen, 'Licentious and Unbridled Proceedings'. See also Richard Allen, *Slaves, Freedmen, and Indentured Labourers in Colonial Mauritius*, Cambridge University Press, 1999.

6 Robert Farquhar, the governor, wished to end the trade, and had sought an alternative source of labour. He had worked previously in Penang, which had secured prisoners for use as forced labour from India, and he planned to use this model for Mauritius. Some 700 Bengali convicts were brought from Calcutta in 1815 and set to work building roads. Many were political prisoners. Twenty years later, the island had a prison population of 8,000 Indian convicts.

7 The Seychelles – named after Moreau de Séchelles, the financial controller of the French King Louis XIV – had been twice occupied by the British during the French war, in 1794 and 1806. Having no spare troops to garrison the island in 1794, the British had left the French military governor, Jean-Baptiste Queau de Quincy, in charge, and he remained there, under successive English and French regimes, until his death in 1827.

8 Seventy political prisoners from France were landed at Mahe in July 1801. Some had been involved in the 'September Massacres' of 1792, others had been accused of trying to assassinate Napoleon. The French settlers objected to their presence, and thirty-six prisoners were diverted to Anjouan, one of the Comoro Islands.

9 Among them were Abdullah Khan, the sultan of Perak, in 1875; Prempeh, king of Ashanti, in 1900; Mwanga of Buganda and Kabarega of Banyoro, kings of Uganda, in 1899; and Sultan Ali of Somaliland, in 1919.

10 Sheila Ward, *Prisoners in Paradise*, Mauritius, 1986.

11 Winston Churchill, when Britain's colonial secretary in the 1920s, earmarked the islands for Irish political prisoners. He cabled the Seychelles' governor in September 1922, noting that the Irish Free State required 'accommodation for large number of political prisoners whose retention in Ireland is embarrassing'. Churchill said that he was considering 'the possibility of giving them temporary control of a suitable portion of some easily-isolated colony'. Could an 'outlying island be made generally suitable for immediate accommodation in huts or tents for 500 prisoners with the necessary guards with the possibility of expansion of up to say 5000?'.

The governor told him that the Côte d'Or estate on Praslin island would be suitable, although the climate 'might be trying to Europeans of the type of Irish political prisoners'. A month later the proposal was abandoned.

12 C. E. Wurtzburg, *Raffles of the Eastern Isles*, Oxford, 1986.

13 Major William Thorn, *Memoir of the Conquest of Java, with the Subsequent Operations of the British Forces in the Oriental Archipelago*, London, 1815.

14 More than a century later, the British were to perform a similar operation – invading independent Indonesia in 1945 in order to return it to Holland after a period of wartime rule by the Japanese.

15 An army of 9,000 sepoys were embarked in a hundred ships. Five thousand were Rajputs from the Bengal army, other units came from the recently mutinous army of Madras. All had been enticed with promises of plunder. Minto was in overall command, but General Sir Samuel Auchmuty, latterly in charge of the River Plate armada in 1807 and now the commander in Madras, had military control of the invasion force, seconded by General Robert Rollo Gillespie, last heard of in 1806 defending the garrison at Vellore. Sailing south via Malacca, the British fleet arrived off the Java coast and captured Jakarta on 8 August, meeting little resistance. The French army defending the island was concentrated at Mester Cornelis, and here, on 26 August, fierce fighting occurred. 'The storm of the lines of Cornelis', noted the military historian Colonel Fortescue, has been 'utterly forgotten by the army and the nation', yet it was 'one of the great exploits of the Napoleonic War'. J. W. Fortescue, *A History of the British Army, Vol. VII, 1809–1810*, London, 1912.

16 Lord Minto sent a triumphant message to London from Jakarta, boasting that

> an Empire, which for two centuries has contributed greatly to the power, prosperity, and grandeur of one of the principal and most respected states of Europe, has been thus wrested from the short usurpation of the French government, and added to the Dominion of the British Crown; and converted from a seat of hostile machination and commercial competition into an augmentation of British power and prosperity.

Ibid.

17 A detachment of Bengali sepoys, stiffened with soldiers from a British regiment, advanced into the rice fields to find 'upwards of two thousand musqueteers regularly drawn up behind a bank'. After a brief skirmish, the Muslim rebels were dispersed by a bayonet charge and 'a considerable number were killed and wounded'.

18 The British demanded a high price for their support, and the new sultan was required to surrender the neighbouring island of Banca, known for its lucrative tin mines. Raffles hoped to establish a permanent military base on Banca and to exploit its tin, fearing that one day he might have to hand back the principal Dutch islands to Holland. Landing there in May, Gillespie renamed it Duke of York Island.

19 Eric Wakeham, *The Bravest Soldier: Sir Rollo Gillespie, 1766–1814, A Historical Military Sketch*, London, 1937.

20 This was a guerrilla tactic employed against Europeans on other occasions, notably during the prolonged 'Java War' against the Dutch between 1825 and 1830.

21 One of the princes, Pangeran Arya Mohamed Abubakar, had been planning to make a pilgrimage to Mecca that year, and he wanted to declare a 'holy war' on the infidel invader. Fond of wearing the long white religious clothes worn by Muslim clerics and by those who had participated in the Hajj, he soon found his dress was too conspicuous, making him an easy target for the British gunners. Given the added danger of wearing white, he decided that a 'holy war' would not be appropriate, and asked for a change of clothes. Peter Carey, ed., *The British in Java 1811–1816: A Javanese Account (a verse-form diary kept by Pangeran Arya Panular)*, Oxford, 1992.

22 The Prangwedana, the Surakarta chief cooperating with the British, pressed forward

> to enter the front courtyard with the firm intention of getting to grips with Sumadiningrat, for the latter is generally known as the champion of the Yogyanese and has made Prangwedana the particular object of his scorn. The Surakarta prince thus feels very bitter towards him. At the doorway (leading into the front courtyard), Prangwedana stamps with his feet on the ground commanding his troops to fire

> volleys, but, when the soldiers penetrate into the courtyard itself, Sumadiningrat is not to be found

Carey, *The British in Java.*

23 One British officer was killed while about to rape the sultan's daughter. Lieutenant Hector Maclean had broken into his private apartments, guarded by a corps of 300 women, equipped with spears, *krises*, and daggers. 'Breaking his way through a wooden door which barred his progress, he came suddenly upon an unexpected object in the person of a dark Javanese girl, who, from some cause unknown, had been left behind when the Sultan and his court made their hasty exit'. Maclean, 'without pausing to consider the imprudence of the act, rashly seized the girl by the waist, and attempted to carry her away by force', but his intended victim had other ideas. 'The princess, as she turned out to be, irritated at the capture of her father's *Kraton*, and the insults now offered to herself, stabbed the young officer in the neck with a *kriss* that she wore concealed in the folds of her sarong, inflicting a wound from the effects of which he died shortly thereafter.' Maclean was buried with many others in the cemetery at Jogjakarta, and the British erected a monument, still visible fifty years later, to 'a brave and gallant youth'. The historian Peter Carey notes decorously that 'although it seems that none of the court ladies were actually physically violated, many were roughly treated by the invading sepoy troops, who stormed into the *Kraton* in search of loot'.
Ibid.

24 Trained in Scotland as a doctor, Crawfurd had gone to India and transferred to Penang. A proficient linguist, he was taken, aged twenty-seven, on the expedition to Java, and he later served in Singapore, Burma and Thailand.

25 C E Wurtzburg, *Raffles of the Eastern Isles*, Oxford, 1986

26 Ibid.

27 Nicholas Tarling, *Piracy and Politics in the Malay World: A Study of British Imperialism in Nineteenth-Century South-East Asia*, Melbourne, 1963.

26 Bulbhadar Singh and the Gurkha Resistance in Nepal

1 Quoted in Moon, *British Conquest and Dominion of India.*

2 Ibid.

27 The British Conquest of Kandy

1 John Davy, *An Account of the Interior of Ceylon and of its Inhabitants*, London, 1821.

2 Wickrama died of dropsy in Vellore in 1832. The other exiles from Kandy were all given liberal allowances by the British, and some of their descendants were found to be living in southern India in 1893, still in receipt of a pension from the government of India. Periodic rebellions in Kandy, the last occurring in 1848, sought unsuccessfully to restore Wickrama's descendants to the throne.

3 The Dissawa was a provincial representative of the ruler of Kandy, while the adigars were members of his ruling council.

4 Geoffrey Powell, *The Kandyan Wars: The British Army in Ceylon, 1803–1818*, London, 1973.

5 The odds were seriously stacked against the British, as Colonel Fortescue's history makes clear:

> More trying work has seldom been assigned to British soldiers. They could only move on steep, narrow mountain paths encompassed by dense jungle; and though their enemy was as a fighting man contemptible, he made up in cunning what he lacked in valour. No isolated soldier, indeed no small party of soldiers, was safe against attack at any time in any place. Every man's hand was against them, and,

> though that hand might be weak, it was invisible and could therefore be deadly. To the commanders, this state of things was more trying even than to the men, for they could obtain no information, and were, therefore, obliged to impose upon their troops endless, long and exhausting marches to no purpose.

J. W. Fortescue, *A History of the British Army, Vol. XI, 1815–1838*, London, 1923.

6 After a ritual Buddhist ceremony, Kapitipola recited some Pali verses, and 'while he was so employed, the executioner struck him on the back of the neck with a sharp sword. A second stroke deprived him of life . . . His head being separated from his body, it was, according to Kandyan custom, placed on his breast.'

7 Ehelapola, Kapitipola's uncle and one-time friend of the British, was also sent to Mauritius, where he died of dysentery in 1829. He had been arrested in March 1818 on suspicion of involvement in the rebellion. A memorial to him still stands on the island, at Morcellement San André, Pamplemousses.

8 Fortescue, *History of the British Army, Vol. XI*.

28 Slave Rebellions in the Caribbean

1 Robert Schomburgk, *The History of Barbados*, London, 1848; see also *Report from a Select Committee of the House of Assembly, Appointed to Inquire into the Origin, Causes, and Progress, of the Late Insurrection*, Barbados, 1818.

2 The British sought to regulate the treatment of slaves in Barbados, promulgating a 'slave code' for the island in 1661, an 'Act for the better ordering and governing of Negroes'. The slaves were defined as 'heathenish', 'brutish', and 'a dangerous kind of people', and the code became the model for use on Britain's other slave islands.

3 Planned over several years, the revolt of 1675 was brutally suppressed. More than one hundred slaves were arrested and brought before a court martial. In the initial proceedings, seventeen slaves were found guilty and executed, of whom six were burned alive and eleven beheaded. Five committed suicide before the trial, and a further thirty-five were executed subsequently. Their owners were reimbursed from the island's treasury for the loss of their capital. A further revolt in 1692 was suppressed after its leaders were captured. Many were tortured, and more than ninety were executed. See *Great Newes from the Barbados, or a True and Faithful Account of the Grand Conspiracy of the Negroes against the English*, London, 1676.

4 Hilary Beckles, *A History of Barbados: From Amerindian Settlement to Nation State*, Cambridge University Press, 1990.

5 Many officers involved in the fighting and the subsequent repression were interviewed by a board of enquiry. Colonel Conrade Adams Howell of the St Michael's Regiment of Militia was one of them. He had been the president of one of the courts martial, and was asked by the enquiry team how long he had held that position:

> A. I was employed in that capacity upwards of seven weeks.
> Q. How many of the insurgents were tried during the period of your being President?
> A. One hundred and fifty – four of which were free people of colour.
> Q. Of this number, how many were capitally convicted, or otherwise?
> A. Three of the free people, and one hundred and eleven slaves, were capitally convicted; ten sentenced to transportation, eleven to corporal punishment, and eighteen acquitted.

Report . . . into the Origin, Causes, and Progress, of the Late Insurrection.

6 Even when slavery was formally ended eighteen years later, on 1 August 1834, the governor of Barbados took no chances, sending military units to Bridgetown on emancipation day. Under the terms of that year's Emancipation Act, slaves over the age of six were freed, although

they were obliged to serve their masters as apprentices for a further twelve years, a figure subsequently reduced to six. More than 80,000 slaves were freed in Barbados on that day – a number vastly in excess of the labour needs of Barbados. Formal slavery was over, but for many decades the former slaves in Barbados and elsewhere in the West Indies became the victims of a free market in cheap labour.

7 A. G. L. Shaw, *Sir George Arthur*, Melbourne University Press, 1980.

8 Nigel Bolland, *The Formation of a Colonial Society: Belize from Conquest to Crown Colony*, Baltimore, 1977.

9 Martin Khan, *Djuka: The Bush Negroes of Dutch Guiana*, New York, 1931.

10 S. G. Checkland, *The Gladstones: A Family Biography, 1764–1851*, Cambridge, 1971.

11 Viotti da Costa, *Crowns of Glory, Tears of Blood: The Demerara Slave Rebellion of 1823*, Oxford, 1994.

12 Robin Blackburn, *The Overthrow of Colonial Slavery*, London, 1988.

13 Mary Turner, *Slaves and Missionaries: The Disintegration of Jamaican Slave Society, 1787–1834*, Illinois, 1982.

14 Ibid.

29 The Battle of Seven Oaks, Canada

1 John Morgan Gray, *Lord Selkirk of Red River*, Michigan, 1964.

2 Lord Selkirk, 'Proposal Tending to the Permanent Security of Ireland', London, 1802.

3 Daniel Williams Harmon, *Sixteen Years in the Indian Country, 1800–1816*, Toronto, 1957.

4 Arthur J. Ray, *Indians in the Fur Trade, 1660–1870*, Toronto, 1974.

5 Prince Maximilian zu Wied, *Travels Through North America in the Years 1832–34*, Taschen, 2001.

30 Revolts and Resistance in Central India

1 See S. B. Chaudhuri, *Civil Disturbances during British Rule in India*, Calcutta, 1955; Stephen Fuchs, *Rebellious Prophets: A Study in Messianic Movements in Indian Religions*, London, 1965; R. C. Majumdar, *History of the Freedom Movement in India, Vol. I*, Calcutta, 1963.

2 Baji Rao II was the grandson of Baji Rao I, a yet more famous Maratha leader of the eighteenth century, who extended the Maratha dominions.

3 Mulhar had replaced Jeswant Rao Holkar, who had died in 1811. Jeswant Rao Holkar was replaced as regent by Tulsi Bai, a woman known to be favourable to a settlement with the British. The Peshwa arranged with the other chiefs that she should be detained and executed, and the youthful Mulhar Rao Holkar was installed as the new ruler.

4 V. Blacker, *Memoirs of the British Army in India during the Mahratta War of 1817, 1818, and 1819*, London, 1821.

5 The inadequacy of General Hislop's preparations was described in Colonel Fortescue's history:

> As the majority of the wounds were inflicted by grape or round shot, they were very severe if not mortal; and, in fact, over 200 out of 600 wounded died, not a little through want of proper surgical treatment. In the field-hospitals, there was scarcely a scrap of dressing-plaster for the officers, and none for the men. Further, there were no surgical instruments except those belonging, as private property, to individual surgeons, some of whom could produce none.
>
> Hence, of the patients who underwent amputation, all suffered unnecessary torture owing to the bluntness of the knives, and two out of three died from lack of proper dressings. It appears to have been the practice in the Madras army to allow the

> medical officers to make their own contracts for medical stores; and to this vicious system hundreds of brave men were sacrificed.

J. W. Fortescue, *A History of the British Army, Vol. XI, 1815–1838*, London, 1923.

6 General Hislop was the governor who had crushed the slave revolt in Trinidad in 1805, and his slaughter of the garrison at Talner caused questions to be asked about his conduct in the British parliament. His murderous behaviour was not the only thing to be held against him, for an argument broke out between him and the governor of Bengal as to who was to receive the prize money from the Maratha campaign. Their legal battle eventually went to the Privy Council in London, which decided that the monies should be divided between them.

7 Two explanations are given by imperial historians for the word 'Pindari'. One suggests it was a Maratha word meaning 'a member of a body of plunderers'; the other argues its derivation from 'the dissolute habits of people visiting wine shops and taking an intoxicating drink called "Pinda".' Neither word is very complimentary. While most of the Pindaris were Muslims, some were Hindus; indeed, they seem to have embraced different religions without qualm. Pindari women were allowed considerable freedom. 'Usually mounted on small horses or camels', they 'were more dreaded by the villagers than the men, whom they exceeded in cruelty and rapacity.'

8 M. N. Roy, *Origin, Growth, and Suppression of the Pindaris*, New Delhi, 1973.

9 Chitu's full title was Nawab Mohammed Kamal Khan Mustakeen Jung Bahadur. A bald man with an oval face, a moustache, a wheatish complexion and several broken teeth, he was of middling height with a fine physique; his personal flag was decorated with a small white snake. Wherever he travelled, he was given a five-gun salute with a roll of drums. Two European gunsmiths worked for him, manufacturing weapons.

10 Roy, *Origin, Growth, and Suppression of the Pindaris.*

11 See Blacker, *Memoir of the Operations of the British Army in India*; and Reginald Burton, *The Maharatta and Pindari War*, Delhi, 1975.

12 Lt Col George Fitzclarence, *Journal of a Route Across India*, London, 1819.

13 Roy, *Origin, Growth, and Suppression of the Pindaris.*

14 As the military frontier extended into civil society, army commanders were wont to suspend civil justice and enforce the rule of martial law instead – executing offenders on the most summary of charges. This gained part-institutionalisation in the cases of travelling people and 'tribal' groups, who often became collectively proscribed and stripped of the individual rights and protections enjoyed by 'civilised' members of society. It was developed further by the claim of the state to prerogatives enabling it to exile 'undesirable' or 'dangerous' people at will and in a manner scarcely different from that of the Russian Tsar. See D. A. Washbrook, 'India, 1816–1860: The Two Faces of Colonialism', in *The Oxford History of the British Empire, Vol. III*, Oxford, 1999.

15 Typical of British arrogance was an episode in central India in 1828 when a mutiny of sepoys occurred in an Indian cavalry unit known as Nizam's Horse, a native troop for the use of the British army by the Nizam of Hyderabad. The regimental commander, Major 'Tiger' Davies, an officer fond of shooting tigers, had gone off to pursue his favourite pastime, leaving Lieutenant Stirling, described as 'a most foolish and injudicious young officer', in temporary command. Stirling took it into his head to order his sepoys to shave off their beards. They agreed to cut them short, but refused to removed them entirely. This was not sufficient for the lieutenant, who ordered two soldiers to be held down and shaved on parade. Major Davies returned the following day to be told that the sepoys had mutinied, and he galloped off to confront them. Arriving with a single servant, he ordered the mutineers to lay down their arms. All would be pardoned, he said, except for the *havildar*, or sergeant, who was perceived as the ringleader. This man approached the major as if begging for mercy, drew his pistol, and shot him. The major managed to gallop home with a score of sabre cuts, but just as he came to the place where his wife was preparing breakfast, he fell dead from his horse. With the death of the commander, the mutineers fled from their barracks out into countryside, pursued by Lieutenant Stirling.

When the mutineers saw him, they took refuge in a mosque. Stirling forced the door and killed the *havildar*; the other mutineers were hanged. Stirling was shot later, in a similar skirmish. See Helen Mackenzie, ed., *Storms and Sunshine of a Soldier's Life: Lt Gen Colin Mackenzie, CB, 1825–1881*, Edinburgh, 1884.

31 Revolt, Fresh Settlement and Extermination in Cape Colony

1 Quoted in Edward Roux, *Time Longer than Rope: A History of the Black Man's Struggle for Freedom in South Africa*, Madison, 1964.

2 Stockenstrom had been told this by Ngqika's interpreter. C. W. Hutton, ed., *The Autobiography of the late Sir Andries Stockenstrom*, Cape Town, 1887.

3 Noël Mostert, *Frontiers: The Epic of South Africa's Creation and the Tragedy of the Xhosa People*, London, 1992.

4 Hutton, *Autobiography of the Late Sir Andries Stockenstrom.*

5 John Philip, *Researches in South Africa, Illustrating the Civil, Moral, and Religious Condition of the Native Tribes*, London, 1828.

6 George Thompson, *Travels and Adventures in Southern Africa*, London, 1827.

7 Philip, *Researches in South Africa.*

8 Hutton, ed., *Autobiography of the Late Sir Andries Stockenstrom.*

9 Stephen Kay, *Travels and Researches in Caffraria*, London, 1833.

32 The British Base and Prison on the Island of Singapore

1 'Although the area had been inhabited since the dawn of time', explains Carl Trocki, 'in 1800 it remained one of the most sparsely populated places on earth. In the main, there was the jungle and the sea. Given traditional technology, human life could sustain itself only in small niches scattered through this desert of forest and water. These habitats were the islands, the beaches, and the riverbanks.' Carl Trocki, *Prince of Pirates: the Temenggongs and the Development of Johor and Singapore, 1784–1885*, Singapore, 1979.

2 Quoted in ibid.

3 Quoted in ibid.

4 Colonel Nahuijs described how

> the Temenggong lives with his dependents a short distance away from the European town, on a site allotted to him by the British Government of Singapore, on account of the frequent quarrels and murders for which his dependents have been responsible. Over all these people, as well as over the Bouginese settled in Singapore, the British Resident has not the least authority, even when they attack Europeans.

Quoted in Trocki, *Prince of Pirates.*

5 Faced with the continuing irritation of piracy, Crawfurd suggested several ways of dealing with it:

> Industrial habits should be encouraged among the natives; a ready and free market should be found for their productions; discovered piracy should be condignly punished; native princes, when found to be implicated, should be heavily fined; the headquarters and haunts of pirates should be destroyed; armed steamboats should be more frequently employed in hunting for and attacking the pirate fleets.

The steamship *Diana*, first used in the Burma war of 1824, arrived in Singapore in 1837, with the specific aim of 'frightening the pirates'. Nicholas Tarling, *Piracy and Politics in the Malay World: A Study of British Imperialism in the Nineteenth Century*, Melbourne, 1963.

6 A British trader, G. F. Davidson, reported after first arriving on the island in 1826 that 'a great deal has been done for Singapore by gangs of convicts from Bengal, Madras and Bombay, who, under an experienced and able superintendent, have cut and made excellent roads, that now extend, east, west, north, and south, for several miles'. G. F. Davidson, *Trade and Travel in the Far East; Or, Recollections of Twenty-One Years Passed in Java, Singapore, Australia, and China*, London, 1846.

7 Twenty years after 1819, Singapore's twenty plantations growing gambier had increased to 350, employing 3,000 labourers. Increasing numbers of Chinese settlers arrived to grow and harvest the tree, in tandem with pepper, first for the Chinese market and then, after 1830, for the expanding tanning industries of Britain. 'The Chinese immigrants wanted crops which produced a quick return', according to the historian Constance Turnbull, 'and called for no special skill or experience.' Gambier and pepper blended well together.

> Gambier waste provided an excellent fertiliser to counteract pepper which exhausted the soil, and usually one acre of pepper was planted to ten acres of gambier. Gambier leaves had to be boiled soon after picking, so that it was necessary to have large areas of forest to supply wood for the burners. The unoccupied jungles of Singapore were ideal for this purpose.

Constance Turnbull, *A History of Singapore, 1819–1988*, Oxford, 1989.
Yet there was a high ecological price to pay:

> Gambier and pepper planting . . . provided a peasant with comparative wealth and for some years gave several thousands a livelihood. But it exhausted the soil, destroyed the forest, and left the ground open to the encroachment of coarse lalang grass, which was more difficult and more expensive to clear than virgin jungle.
>
> By the end of the 1860s, much of the interior of Singapore had been laid waste and stood abandoned. Gambier plantations created a suitable habitat for tigers, hitherto almost unknown. As more gambier was planted, the tiger menace grew. The *Singapore Free Press* carried accounts in 1840 of men being killed by tigers every month; five were killed in July barely two miles outside the town.

Charles Burton Buckley, *An Anecdotal History of Old Times in Singapore, 1819–1867*, Oxford, 1984.

33 Years of Unrest Culminate in a Fresh Revolt in Ireland

1 Better known in his role as foreign secretary, Robert Stewart, Viscount Castlereagh, had acquired the title of Londonderry the previous year, on the death his father; he was barely six months away from his own death by suicide. Stanley Palmer, *Police and Protest in England and Ireland, 1780–1850*, Cambridge, 1988.

2 Thomas Wright, *The History of Ireland, from the Earliest Period of the Irish Annals to the Rebellion of 1848*, 3 vols, London, 1854.

3 Thomas Moore, *Memoirs of Captain Rock, the Celebrated Irish Chieftain, with some Account of his Ancestors*, London, 1824.

4 Signor Pastorini's *General History of the Christian Church*, published under a pseudonym half a century earlier, in 1771, was actually the work of Charles Walmesley, an English Catholic bishop.

5 James Donnelly, 'Pastorini and Captain Rock: Millenarianism and Sectarianism in the Rockite Movement of 1821–24', in Samuel Clark and James Donnelly, eds, *Irish Peasants: Violence and Political Unrest, 1780–1914*, Manchester, 1983.

6 Charles Grant, a former chief secretary (and later to play a significant imperial role in the 1830s as Lord Glenelg), strongly criticised the new force in June 1822. It would, he said, 'place the

whole of Ireland under an armed police' and 'subject it to a species of gendarmerie', making 'the whole of the magistracy of the country liable to the control of the lord-lieutenant'.

7 Charles Jeffries, *The Colonial Police*, London, 1972. See also R. Curtis, *The History of the Royal Irish Constabulary*, London, 1869, and Broeker Galen, *Rural Disorder and Police Reform in Ireland, 1812–1836*, London, 1970.

34 Aborigine Resistance in Australia and White Retaliation

1 General Brisbane was another veteran of the Peninsular Wars who was no stranger to the crushing of rebellions, having seen service with General Abercromby in Haiti and the Caribbean in the 1790s.

2 Niel Gunson, ed., *Australian Reminiscences and Papers of L. E. Threlkeld, Missionary to the Aborigines, 1824–1859*, Australian Institute of Aborigine Studies, Canberra, 1974.

3 Ibid.

4 Ibid.

5 General Darling was also a veteran of the Peninsular Wars, and another expert at destroying rebellions. Like Brisbane, he had campaigned with General Abercromby in the West Indies in the 1790s. Living for many years in Grenada, he had taken part in the suppression of the revolt of Julien Fédon in 1793. See Brian Fletcher, *Ralph Darling: A Governor Maligned*, Oxford, 1984.

6 Gunson, ed., *Australian Reminiscences . . . of L. E. Threlkeld.*

7 Saxe Bannister, *British Colonisation and Coloured Tribes*, London, 1838.

8 *The Times*, London, 2 January 1828.

9 A contemporary journal recorded an ironic commentary after a visit to the spot:

> The whole tribe was seated round their fires, partaking of their hard-earned fare, when down rushed the band of fierce barbarians thirsting for the blood of these unprotected and unoffending people. They fled, leaving their provision. Some rushed into the sea, others scrambled round the cliff, and what remained the monsters put to death. Those poor creatures who had sought shelter in the cleft of the rock they forced to the brink of an awful precipice . . . and threw the bodies down.

35 The Ashanti Defeat the British at Esamankow

1 Colonel McCarthy came from an Irish family that had settled in France. Having joined the British army after the French Revolution, he saw service in the West Indies in 1795 and 1796, and later in Canada. A lieutenant-colonel in the Royal African Corps in 1811, he had been appointed the governor of Sierra Leone in 1812.

2 Keeping order on shore had always been a hit-and-miss affair. In memory of an Englishman called Meredith, killed at Cape Coast in 1812, it became the practice for British ships passing the spot 'to pour in a broadside', as a hint that Europeans could not lightly be murdered.

3 W. W. Claridge, *A History of the Gold Coast and Ashanti*, London, 1915. See also J. F. A. Ajaji and Michael Crowder, eds, *History of West Africa, Vol. II*, London, 1974.

4 H. I. Ricketts, *A Narrative of the Ashantee War*, London, 1831.

36 The Burmese Empire Fights Back

1 Henry Gouger, a British trader visiting Ava, found King Bagyidaw to be accessible and unpretentious. At the end of a great hall, he found

> a young man, about thirty years old, with a pleasant, good-humoured countenance, seated cross-legged on a gilded arm-chair of European make, manifesting no sign or symbol of state other than the chair he sat in, which sat on a stage very slightly raised from the floor . . . His costume did not vary from that of his courtiers, except that the silk cloth worn round the loins was a bright scarlet check, a colour confined to the use of the Royal family.

Henry Gouger, *Personal Narrative of Two Years' Imprisonment in Burmah*, London, 1860.

2 One of the officers, Captain Michael Symes, had written a book about his trip. Michael Symes, 'An Account of an Embassy to the Kingdom of Ava', *SOAS Bulletin of Burma Research*, London, 2006.

3 A Lieutenant Rodgers, known as Yadza, had attached himself to the Burmese court in 1782, and two American Baptist missionaries had settled there and given the court a view of a wider world. Henry Gouger, a British merchant and arms trader, had established himself up in Rangoon in 1822, to try his hand at the silk trade. Travelling up the Irrawaddy to Ava, he had had no trouble in meeting King Bagyidaw in his Audience Hall, noting that he found 'far less difficulty in gaining an audience of His Majesty than I should have had in getting an interview with our Secretary of State in Downing Street'.

4 Prince Tharrawaddy, King Bagyidaw's younger brother, reminded Henry Gouger of the courage and cleverness of his countrymen:

> You know nothing of the bravery of our people in war. We have never yet found any nation to withstand us. They say your soldiers, when they fight, march up exposing their whole bodies. They use music, to let us know when they are coming. They do not know our skill and cunning. They will all be killed if they attack us in this way.

Gouger, *Personal Narrative*.

5 'In courage and readiness of resource', wrote a contemporary chronicler, H. H. Wilson, in his history of the war, 'he displayed great abilities to maintain the contest. He was a low and illiterate man who had risen to power by his bravery and audacity.' H. H. Wilson, *Narrative of the Burmese War in 1824–26, as Originally Compiled from Official Documents*, London, 1852.

6 Bandula was ready, wrote H. H. Wilson 'to lead a Burman army to the capital of British India, and wrest from its government the lower districts of Bengal'.

7 Henry Gouger, visiting Ava in January 1824, had been privileged to attend the New Year military pageant, and to witness the country's military preparations:

> The Burmese general, Mengee Maha Bundoola, the Wellington of the army . . . had levied a picked force of 6,000 men, who had been assembled at the capital and were now to cross the river . . . in the presence of the king and court. My house commanded the river view, which gave me an opportunity of witnessing this brilliant spectacle to great advantage.
>
> A fleet of magnificent war-boats, many of them richly gilded, were in readiness to receive the troops at midday, who embarked in perfect order; each man was attired in a comfortable campaigning jacket of black cloth, thickly wadded and quilted with cotton, and was armed with a musket and spear, as suited the corps to which he belonged.
>
> A profusion of flags, with gay devices, were unfurled to the breeze, martial music resounded, the chiefs took their seats at the prows of their boats . . . and in the middle of each boat, a soldier, selected for his skill, danced a kind of hornpipe. When all was ready, the whole fleet, lining the bank for a considerable distance, dashed all at once across the river, nearly a mile wide; the loud song bursting from six thousand lusty throats, while the stroke from thousands of oars and paddles kept time to their music.

8 Quoted in Courtney Anderson, *To the Golden Shore, the life of Adoniram Judson*, Michigan, 1972,

9 'The happy news quickly spread to their comrades', Fortescue's *History of the British Army* recalls, 'and by nightfall the British soldiers, almost to a man, were either prostrate and insensible or rambling, blissfully intoxicated, with lighted torches from house to house, in search of plunder.' Half the town went up in flames, and the rest was only saved 'by the exertions of sailors landed from the fleet'. Fortescue, *History of the British Army, Vol. XI*.

10 General Campbell's officers had a good eye for a bargain. Captain F. B. Doveton had noted the large number of gilded statues of the Buddha to be found in the Rangoon temples: 'Some of these alabaster images were of a very large size, and many that were rescued from the general wreck that followed our occupation of Rangoon were despatched to India and to England . . . One or two of these occupy a conspicuous and honourable position in the entrance-room of the British Museum.' F. B. Doveton, *Reminiscences of the Burmese War*, London, 1852.

11 One British officer who later became famous, Lieutenant Henry Havelock, was more sober. A devout Baptist, he held services for his men in the cloisters of the Schwe-Dagon pagoda, where his soldiers placed their regimental colours in the hands of a Buddhist statue. Campbell referred to them as 'Havelock's saints'.

12 Later that month, the Burmese produced some of their special weapons, floating down 'a huge fire-raft, consisting of thirty or forty canoes linked together and piled up with faggots, which had been soaked in crude petroleum, for the destruction of British shipping'. The British chronicler noted with relief that 'this formidable engine of destruction drifted ashore and burned itself out long before it reached Rangoon'.

13 Elements in the Burmese expedition, wrote Colonel Fortescue, 'provoke comparison with the worst epidemic of yellow fever in the West Indies'. Fortescue, *History of the British Army, Vol. XI*.

14 Ibid.

15 Ibid.

16 Ibid.

17 Combermere was reputed to have been Wellington's best cavalry officer in the Peninsular campaign. He had commanded the advance guard sent from Cape Town to Saldanha Bay, which witnessed the surrender of the Dutch ships in 1795, and had gone on, with his regiment, to India and participated in the downfall of Tipu Sultan at Seringapatam, in 1799. From 1817 to 1820 he had been governor of Barbados, arriving just after the slave rebellion of 1816.

18 Durjan Singh had a secret weapon. A British artilleryman, Sergeant Herbert, had deserted from the British force and come over to assist the Jats. On arriving outside the fortress, the British were surprised by the accuracy of the firing in the area around General Combermere's headquarters. One of his servants was hit while moving a chair from the table. Colonel Fortescue explains in his history that Sergeant Herbert was now seen to be 'directing the Jat gunners, heedless of the projectiles that hummed around him, with the greatest coolness and self-possession'. Fortescue, *History of the British Army, Vol. XI*.

19 Metcalfe wrote of this 'glorious' affair:

> Our first mines were bungling, but the latter ones were very grand. That to the right did a great deal of mischief to ourselves, for the people assembled in the trenches were too near, and the explosion of the mine took effect afterwards. It was a grand sight, and was immediately followed by that of the advance of the storming columns up the two grand breaches.

J. W. Kaye, *Life and Correspondence of Charles Lord Metcalfe*, London, 1854.

20 Metcalfe, euphoric at the outcome, wrote to his sister to outline the darker side to the operation:

> Then came the miseries even of victory. The numerous dead of the enemy – the wounded imploring succour – on one side, hundreds of the enemy crushed and

> jammed together in a chasm into which they had rushed in their confused flight – on the other, a number of our own noble fellows blown up by one of the enemy's mines, some dead, some living and calling to be dug out.

Ibid.

21 Colonel Cotton was another Peninsular veteran, and became commander in Jamaica from 1829 to 1834, where he presided over a period of martial law in 1831 and crushed a slave rebellion.

22 Bandula's servant told Major John Snodgrass, a participant-observer in the British campaign, what had occurred:

> Yesterday morning, between the hours of nine and ten, while the chief's dinner was preparing, he went out to take his usual morning walk round the works, and arrived at his observatory . . . where, as there was no firing, he sat down upon a couch that was kept there for his use. While he was giving orders to some of his chiefs, the English began throwing bombs, and one of them, falling close to the Wongee, burst, and killed him on the spot; his body was immediately carried away and burnt to ashes; his death was soon known to every body in the stockade, and the soldiers refused to stay and fight under any other commander.

J. J. Snodgrass, *Narrative of the Burmese War*, London, 1827.

23 Maha Nemiao's army included 8,000 Shans from Burma's territory on the Chinese border, and among them were three handsome young women, 'prophetesses endowed by magic with invulnerability, who had risen up among them with predictions of a speedy victory'. These Amazons, 'dressed in warlike costume', rode among the troops to give them courage. According to the account of Major Snodgrass, they were said 'to be endowed not only with the gift of prophecy and foreknowledge, but to possess the miraculous power of turning aside the balls of the English, rendering them wholly innocent and harmless.' Snodgrass, *Narrative of the Burmese War*.

24 King Bagyidaw put a brave face on these developments, issuing his own version of what had occurred, later translated for John Crawfurd by Adoniram Judson, an American Baptist missionary:

> White strangers of the west fastened a quarrel upon the Lord of the Golden Palace. They landed at Rangoon, took that place and Prome, and were permitted to advance as far as Yandabo . . . The strangers had spent vast sums in their enterprise, so that by the time they reached Yandabo their resources were exhausted. They then petitioned the King, who in his clemency and generosity sent them large sums of money to pay their expenses back, and ordered them out of the country.

See Anderson, *To the Golden Shore, the life of Adoniram Judson.*; and see also John Crawford, *Journal of an Embassy from the Governor-General of India to the Court of Ava in the Year 1827*, 2 vols, London, 1834.

25 Ibid.

26 Penderal Moon, the historian of British India, spelled out the cost:

> Of the five British regiments that originally landed at Rangoon, only 471 out of 3,586 of the men survived, the vast majority succumbing to disease rather than to the enemy; and the losses among the 150 officers, though much less severe, were heavy, 45 dying of disease and 16 falling to the enemy. The Indian regiments also suffered terrible losses, but the sepoys stood up to the climate and poor food rather better than the British.

Penderel Moon, *The British Conquest and Dominion of India*, London, 1989.

37 Tea and Strategy: The Rajahs and Hill Peoples of Assam Rebel

1 Ibid.

2 As a result of the reform to its charter, the Company lost its lucrative trade in China tea, and the search began for a replacement. Although left in charge of India's administrative affairs, the Company was deprived of its monopoly over trade with China.

3 H. K. Barpujari, *Assam in the Days of the Company*, Gauhati, 1980.

4 Another frontier expert, Alexander Mackenzie, repeated this pessimistic forecast half a century later:

> Tribes, over whom we can exercise no control, come surging up against our outposts from the unknown mountains of Burma and from valleys yet unsurveyed. Of the causes that press them forward, we know nothing. New names crop up. A raid by savages of a strange fashion of hair tells us a tribal change has taken place across our frontier, and we have nothing for it but to strengthen our outposts, increase our patrols, and watch to see what follows.

Alexander Mackenzie, *History of the Relations of the Government with the Hill Tribes of the North-East Frontier of Bengal*, Calcutta, 1884.

5 Heneswar Dihingia, *Assam's Struggles Against British Rule, 1826–1863*, Delhi, 1980.

6 The Khasi historian, Hamlet Bareh, explains that

> according to local tradition, the soldiers took away the articles and foodstuffs from the poor sellers in the market without paying for them. Wood cutters and peasants were oppressed. They ill-treated the Khasi labourers employed in the service of the Company. Such attitudes came from the lower ranks of the soldiers. The country became infuriated with the arrogant and disgraceful behaviour of the soldiers.

Hamlet Bareh, *The History and Culture of the Khasi People*, Calcutta, 1967.

7 Dihingia, *Assam's Struggles Against British Rule.*

8 Major Adam White, *Memoir of the Late David Scott*, Calcutta, 1832.

9 Dihingia, *Assam's Struggles Against British Rule.*

10 Quoted in Jagdish Chandra Jha, *The Kol Insurrection of Chota-Nagpur*, Calcutta, 1964. In a vivid report to the authorities in Calcutta, John Master, the Commissioner of the Patna Division, described what he imagined was going on:

> Restless, wild and ferocious, they rushed into an insurrection scarcely paralleled for ferocity and eager for plunder, universally prone to inebriation and infuriated by real or imaginary wrongs, the whole population yielded to the unobstructed tide of rebellion – fire, rapine and murder marked their paths, nor was their vindictive spirit confined to those to whom their injuries were ascribed, but madly extended to unoffending females and helpless infants with the subtle determination of exterminating the whole race.

11 Ibid.

Part VII: Introduction

1 'Report of the Parliamentary Select Committee on Aboriginal Tribes (British Settlements)', London, 1837.

2 Quoted in Noël Mostert, *Frontiers: The Epic of South Africa's Creation and the Tragedy of the Xhosa People*, London, 1992.

3 'Report of the Parliamentary Select Committee on Aboriginal Tribes'.

4 Angus Macintyre, *The Liberator: Daniel O'Connor and the Irish Party, 1830–1847*, London, 1965.

38 Slave Rebellions in the Caribbean Hasten the End of Slavery

1 Mary Turner, *Slaves and Missionaries: The Disintegration of Jamaican Slave Society, 1787–1834*, Illinois, 1982. See also Michael Craton, *Testing the Chains: Resistance to Slavery in the British West Indies*, London, 1982.

2 Henry Bleby, *Death Struggles of Slavery*, London, 1853.

3 Britain was not the first European country to abolish slavery. The French revolutionaries had decreed it in 1794 (though it did not finally end in the French Empire until 1848); the Mexicans had done so in 1829; and even the Bolivians, early in 1831, had pre-empted the British.

4 A rebellion exploded in 1831 on the French island of Martinique, sparked off by the arrival of a shipload of failed revolutionaries from the July Revolution of 1830 in Paris. Making common cause with the exiled revolutionaries, the slaves burned down eleven sugar plantations near the capital, St Pierre, in February 1831. The authorities declared martial law, and 500 people were arrested. Chéry, the slave leader, and twenty-two others were hanged on a single day. Many who survived the repression fled to other islands.

5 Turner, *Slaves and Missionaries.*

6 Ibid.

7 Ibid.

8 Last heard of advancing up the Irrawaddy river in Burma in 1824, General Cotton was later to fight in the Afghan War of 1838–39, and to end his career as the commander-in-chief at Bombay from 1847 to 1850.

9 An eyewitness recorded events at Montego Bay:

> The gibbet erected in the public square in the centre of the town was seldom without occupants, during the day, for many weeks. Generally four, seldom less than three, were hung at once. The bodies remained, stiffening in the breeze, till the court martial had provided another batch of victims . . . [The executioner] would ascend a ladder and with his knife sever the ropes by which the poor creatures were suspended and let them fall to the ground. Other victims would then be suspended in their places and cut down in their turn, the whole heap of bodies remaining just as they fell until the workhouse negroes came in the evening with carts and took them away, to cast them into a pit dug for the purpose, a little distance out of town.

Bleby, *Death Struggles of Slavery*, quoted in Turner, *Slaves and Missionaries.*

10 Ibid.

11 I. Duffield, 'From Slave Colonies to Penal Colonies: The West Indian Convict Transportees to Australia', *Slavery and Abolition* 17: 1 (May 1986).

12 A. B. Ellis, *The History of the First West India Regiment*, London, 1885.

13 Edward Joseph, *A History of Trinidad*, Trinidad, 1839.

14 This was a commonly held view at the time. A year later, in Guyana, twenty Bengalis escaped from a group of 400 labourers brought from India to work on John Gladstone's estate; they 'cut through the bush due east in the hope of reaching Bengal'.

15 The story is also told by Charles Kingsley in *At Last: A Christmas in the West Indies*, London, 1871.

39 White Settlers Devise New Ways to Hunt the Australian Aborigines

1 A. G. L. Shaw, *Sir George Arthur*, Melbourne, 1980. See also Clive Turnbull, *Black War: The Extermination of the Tasmanian Aborigines*, Melbourne, 1948; Robert Travers, *The Tasmanians: The Story of a Doomed Race*, Melbourne, 1968; Mark Cocker, *Rivers of Blood, Rivers of Gold: Europe's Conflict with Tribal Peoples*, London, 1998.

2 Jan Kociumbas, *The Oxford History of Australia, Vol. II*, Oxford, 1992.

3 *Historical Records of Australia, Series 1, Governor's Despatches to and from England, Volume XIX, July 1837–January 1839*, Sydney, 1923. See also Henry Reynolds, *The Other Side of the Frontier: Aboriginal Resistance to the European Invasion of Australia*, Melbourne, 1982, and Jean Woolmington, ed., *Aborigines in Colonial Society, 1788–1850: From 'Noble Savage' to 'Rural Pest'*, Sydney, 1973.

4 *Historical Records of Australia,* and see also R. H. W. Reece, *Aborigines and Colonists: Aborigines and Colonial Society in New South Wales in the 1830s and 1840s*, Sydney, 1977.

5 Kociumbas, *Oxford History of Australia, Vol. II*, Oxford, 1992.

40 The Whitefeet in Ireland Oppose the Payment of Tithes and Rent

1 G. Poulett Scrope, *How Is Ireland to be Governed?*, London, 1834.

2 Angus Macintyre, *The Liberator: Daniel O'Connor and the Irish Party, 1830–1847*, London, 1965.

3 Henry Paget was the brother of General Edward Paget, the officer who shot the sepoys at Barrackpur in 1824.

4 Macintyre, *The Liberator.*

5 See the earlier, eighteenth-century version of the Whiteboys oath in Chapter 6 (page 50). The Whitefoot oath of allegiance, recorded in 1832, was as follows:

> 1st. I solmly sware to be loyall and true to the New Ribbon Act.
>
> 2nd. I sware, I will to the best of my power, Cut Down Kings, Queens and Princes, Duks, Earls, Lords, and all such with Land Jobin and herrisy.
>
> 3rd. I sware that I will never Pity the moans or groans of the Dying, from the Cradell to the Crutch, and that I will wade knee Deep in Orange Blood.
>
> 4th. I sware I am to Bear My right arm to be Cut of and trow over the left shoulder and nailed to the traples Door of Armagh before I will way lay or betray or go in to any Court to Prosecute a Brother, known him to be such.
>
> 5th. I sware I will go 10 miles on foot and 15 Miles on horse Back in five minutes warning.
>
> 6th. I sware I will give Money to Purchase and repair fire arms amunition and the Like, and every other weapon that may Be wanting.
>
> 7th. I sware I never will tell the man's name nor the man's name that stood By making me a Ribbonman or whitefoot to any one under the Cannopy of heaven, not even to Priest, Bishop, or any in the Church.
>
> 8th. I sware I will not stand to hear hell or confusion Drank to a whitefoot or Ribbonman without resisting the same or quitting the Company.
>
> 9th. I sware I never will Keep a robber's company Nor harbour him, except for fire Arms
>
> 10th. I sware I will not make foul freedom with a Brother's wife or Sister Known them to be as Such.
>
> 11th. I sware I will not Keep the second Coat or the Second Shilling and a Brother to Be in want or relief, Known him to be as Such.

> 12th. I sware I will not Be present at the Making of a ribbonman or White foot without Praper orders from our Captain.
> In pursuance of this spirituall Oblagation So Healp mee God.

This version of the Whitefoot oath was given by an informer to Hugh Boyd Wray, Queen's County Police, in January 1832. 'Evidence of Hugh Boyd Wray, Esq., to the Select Committee on the State of Ireland', *Parliamentary Papers*, 1831–32 xvi (677).

6 'Report from the Select Committee appointed to examine the State of the Disturbed Counties in Ireland, into the immediate causes which have produced the same, and into the efficiency of the laws for the suppression of Outrage against the Public Peace', *Parliamentary Papers*, 1831–32 xvi (677).

7 Scrope, *How Is Ireland to be Governed?*

8 Details of this and other incidents in County Wexford, Kilkenny, and County Cork come from Richard Barry O'Brien, *Fifty Years of Concessions to Ireland, 1831–1881*, 2 vols, London, 1883.

9 Ibid.

10 Violent resistance was often deemed necessary, but a strategy of passive resistance was also effective. 'The complicated machinery for bringing a tithe defaulter to book', writes the historian R. B. McDowell,

> was quite inadequate for coping with a widespread, collective refusal to pay. A process had to be secured, served, and moved, a decree obtained and executed, and the whole procedure bristled with hampering technicalities. Cattle could only be seized between sunrise and sunset. If under lock and key, they could not be touched, for the law did not empower the driver to force a door or a bolt, or even to raise a latch.

R. B. McDowell, *Public Opinion and Government Policy, 1801–1846*, London, 1952.

11 O'Brien, *Fifty Years of Concessions to Ireland*. Giving evidence to the House of Commons committee in 1832, General Sir Richard Hussey Vivian had described 'a new proceeding' of the Whitefeet, which partly explained how they were able to mobilise so many people so rapidly:

> It appears that strangers entered some of the towns [Wicklow, Wexford, Carlow, Waterford, Cork and Kildare] . . . in the middle of the night, either with pieces of lighted turf, parcels of powder, lighted sticks, or pieces of brown paper; those they gave to the Catholics, and told them they were charms against the cholera, or that some of the neighbouring towns had been destroyed by fire from heaven, and that they would be burned if they did not give the charm, in some instances, to four other Catholics, and those to whom it was given were to do the same to others, until the whole Catholic population had received the blessed turf; this set the whole population in motion; they were running in all directions without waiting to dress, and they appeared to be inspired with indescribable zeal in serving the stipulated number; some had many miles to travel . . . My belief is that the object was to ascertain in how short a time the Catholic population could receive a summons, for the purpose of intimidation regarding tithes . . . an experiment in order to see how soon they could convey a communication, and how rapidly they could get large bodies together.

12 Scrope, *How Is Ireland to be Governed?*

13 Quoted in Macintyre, *The Liberator*.

14 O'Brien, *Fifty Years of Concessions to Ireland*. See also Michael Beames, *Peasants and Power: The Whiteboy Movements and their Control in Pre-Famine Ireland*, Brighton, 1983; Galen Broeker, *Rural Disorder and Police Reform in Rural Ireland, 1812–1836*, London, 1970; and Samuel

Clark and J. S. Donnelly, eds, *Irish Peasants: Violence and Political Unrest, 1790–1914*, Manchester, 1983.

15 The situation was similar in Leinster, General Wellesley reported: 'Lawless combinations, secret councils, and nightly outrages are exhibited in full force. A complete system of legislation, with the most prompt, vigorous, and severe executive power, sworn, equipped, and armed for all excesses of savage punishment, is established in almost every district.'

41 White Settler Rebellions and Buddhist Resistance in the East

1 The Commissioners, John Bigge and Major William Colebrooke, were in South Africa from 1823 to 1826, and came to Mauritius in 1827. The task was so large that a third Commissioner, William Blair, was appointed in 1825. An enquiry into Ceylon was subsequently added, first to look into its finances, and subsequently into 'the whole state' of the colony, with Charles Cameron as an additional Commissioner. See V. K. Samaraweera, *The Commission of Eastern Enquiry in Ceylon, 1822–1837: A Study of a Royal Commission of Colonial Inquiry*, (unpublished) Oxford University D.Phil thesis, 1969.

2 Henry Taylor, head of the West Indian section, October 1832, quoted in Peter Burroughs, 'The Mauritius Rebellion of 1832 and the Abolition of British Colonial Slavery', *Journal of Imperial and Commonwealth History* IV (May 1976).

3 Quoted in Burroughs, 'The Mauritius Rebellion of 1832'.

4 Thomas Skinner, *Fifty Years in Ceylon: An Autobiography*, London, 1891.

42 Resistance in the Strait of Malacca

1 Captain Peter Begbie, *The Malayan Peninsula*, Madras, 1834.

2 C. M. Turnbull, *The Straits Settlements, 1826–67, Indian Presidency to Crown Colony*, London, 1972.

3 Admiral Henry Keppel, *A Sailor's Life under Four Sovereigns*, 3 vols, London, 1899.

4 Charles Burton Buckley, *An Anecdotal History of Old Times in Singapore, 1819-1867*, Oxford, 1984.

5 The three boats had 130 men on board, with a twelve-pound gun, a six-pound gun, a dozen small guns and much ammunition. They had just been refitted on the south side of the islands, and been re-launched 'with their gongs beating' and with much singing by the crew. Two members of the crew of the *Andromache*, Midshipman Montagu Burrows and Lieutenant Colin Mackenzie, had joined the ship at Singapore earlier in the month, and both wrote letters and diaries describing what they saw. Burrows was a midshipman, later to be professor of history at Oxford. Mackenzie was a lieutenant who went on to have a distinguished military career in India. See Montagu Burrows, *Memoir of Admiral Sir Henry Ducie Chads GCB, by an Old Follower*, Portsea, 1869; Stephen Burrows, ed., *Autobiography of Montagu Burrows, Captain RN*, London, 1908; Helen Mackenzie, ed, *Storms and Sunshine of a Soldier's Life, Lt General Colin Mackenzie CB, 1825–1881*, Edinburgh, 1884.

6 Mackenzie, *Storms and Sunshine of a Soldier's Life.*

7 Lieutenant Mackenzie discovered an example of these licences in a captured boat: 'among the papers found in the *prahus* were actual commissions from the Rajahs of Rhio, Johore, and Selangor to the Pangleemahs [boat captains], authorising them to commit piracy, and furnishing them with means to do so'.

8 Begbie, *Malayan Peninsula.*

9 George Windsor Earl, *The Eastern Seas, Or Voyages and Adventures in the Indian Archipelago, in 1832, 33, 34*, London, 1837.

10 E. G. Festing, ed., *Life of Commander Henry James RN*, London, 1899.

11 Ibid.

12 Taking advantage of Chads's 'good humour', Mackenzie showed him the severed head of

the chief. The good Christian captain was 'amazed and horrified', but he 'gave me a small cask and sufficient arrack to preserve it'. The ship's doctor prepared the specimen, and asked to be given one of the chief's teeth. These had 'had the enamel filed away so as to make them concave outside, with the addition of a black dye, and finally a St Andrew's cross let into each in gold, another mark of the rank of the deceased'.

13 Montagu Burrows himself retained his neck, eventually retiring to a fellowship at All Souls College, Oxford, where he was Chichele professor of Modern History from 1862 to 1905.

14 Carl Trocki, *Prince of Pirates: The Temenggongs and the Development of Johor and Singapore, 1784–1885*, Singapore, 1979.

43 Resistance on the Gambia River in West Africa

1 Taxes on gum arabic, exported through the French port of St Louis on the Senegal River, had become the cause of hostility towards the French by local traders, leading to a war between France and the Emir of Trarza in southern Mauritania in 1825.

2 William Fox, *A Brief History of the Wesleyan Missions on the Western Coast of Africa*, London, 1851.

3 Reverend William Moister, *Memorials of Missionary Labour in West Africa and the West Indies, and at the Cape of Good Hope*, London, 1866.

4 Ibid.

5 Ellis, *History of the First West India Regiment.*

6 Sir Henry Huntley, *Seven Years Service on the Slave Coast of West Africa*, 2 vols, London, 1850.

7 J. M. Gray, *A History of the Gambia*, Cambridge, 1940.

44 The End of Slavery in Cape Colony, the Rebellion of Maqoma, and the Flight of the Boer Farmers

1 John Philip, *Researches in South Africa, Illustrating the Civil, Moral, and Religious Condition of the Native Tribes*, London, 1828.

2 Ngqika had long been ill and withdrawn from tribal government, and his power had already devolved to his son. He died in December 1829. Maqoma was described by Colonel Richard Collins, who had met him in 1809 at the age of eleven, as 'a noble specimen of a savage prince, capable of being moulded into a Christian hero'. Another officer called him 'the most daring Caffre of the whole, a gallant bold fellow, and as a friend, a most excellent one; but as an enemy a most dangerous one'.

3 Mostert, *Frontiers.*

4 C. W. Hutton, ed., *The Autobiography of the Late Sir Andries Stockenstrom*, Cape Town, 1887.

5 Ibid.

6 In 1834, and again in 1846, the Xhosa took their revenge on the Khoi-Khoi and destroyed their farms. Later still, in 1850, the two African nations buried the hatchet, rising up in a joint rebellion against the white settler regime.

7 Philip, *Researches in South Africa.*

8 Mostert, *Frontiers.*

9 J. C. Voigt, *Fifty Years of the History of the Republic of South Africa, 1795–1845*, London, 1899.

10 C. J. F. Bunbury, *Journal of a Residence at the Cape of Good Hope*, London, 1848, quoted in Frank Welsh, *A History of South Africa*, London, 1998.

11 Quoted in Mostert, *Frontiers.*

12 Quoted in Mostert, *Frontiers.*

13 W. F. A. Gilfillan, *The story of One Branch of the Gilfillan Family*, Johannesburg, 1970, quoted in Mostert, *Frontiers*.

14 Mostert, *Frontiers*.

15 Quoted in Mostert, *Frontiers*. See also *The Autobiography of Harry Smith*, London, 1903.

16 The family names of those who accompanied Trichard were to resonate down the years as famous figures in the Boer community: Botha, Pretorius, Strydom and Van Rensburg.

17 Robert Godlonton, *A Narrative of the Irruption of the Kafir Hordes, 1834–35*, Cape Town, 1965.

18 Frank Welsh has written that Dingaan 'shared many of Shaka's psychological abnormalities – he was sterile and probably impotent – but being grossly fat and slothful was less inclined to warlike activity, delegating much responsibility to his ministers'. Welsh, *A History of South Africa*.

19 J. A. Wahlberg, *Travel Journals*, Cape Town, 1992.

20 Stephen Taylor, *Shaka's Children: A History of the Zulu People*, London, 1994.

21 *Encyclopaedia Britannica, Eleventh Edition*, 1911.

22 See Percival Kirby, *Andrew Smith and Natal*, Cape Town, 1955.

45 White Settler Rebellions in Canada

1 A third Canada also existed, of Indian nations beset by fur-trappers and settlers, but their resistance struggles only came to the fore later in the nineteenth century.

2 John Mercier McMullen, *The History of Canada*, London, 1893.

3 Ibid.

4 The government in London proved reluctant to put the middle-class leaders of this first Quebec rebellion on trial, still less to execute them. A new governor of Lower Canada, John Lambton, Lord Durham, arrived in May 1838, and among his first tasks was to decide what should be done with the prisoners held in the Montreal gaol. Unwilling to send them before a court martial, and aware that no local jury would convict them, Lord Durham devised a scheme hitherto unknown to English law. Wolfred Nelson and the seven other principal rebels were to plead guilty to high treason, to place themselves, without trial, at his disposal, and then to be banished to Bermuda. The prospect of a possible death sentence would continue to hang over them, to prevent their return.

Nelson and the others were sent to Bermuda in July 1838, and the remaining prisoners were released. In October Durham's ingenious scheme for dealing with them unravelled, since his proposal was rejected by the parliament in London. He felt obliged to resign. Bermuda then refused to accept the Canadian prisoners, and they were sent to England and eventually pardoned. General Colborne was left in charge in Canada as the acting governor.

5 A nineteenth-century historian records how

> people met after nightfall in the corners of quiet fields, in the shadow of the woods, and in other sequestered places, and there received such instruction in military drill and movement as was possible under the circumstances. Old muskets, pistols and cutlasses were furbished up after long disuse, and pressed into service once more. Small quantities of rifles and ammunition were surreptitiously obtained from the United States. Disaffected blacksmiths in the rural districts devoted themselves to the manufacture of rude pike heads, which, after being fitted to hickory handels of five or six feet in length, formed no contemptible weapons for either attack or defence.

The blacksmith's shop of Samuel Lount at Holland Landing was for some weeks largely given up to this work. 'As there was no interference with these proceedings, the disaffected became bolder, and began to assemble at regular periods to engage in rifle practice, pigeon-matches, and the slaughter of turkeys.' J. C. Dent, *The Story of the Upper Canada Rebellion*, Toronto, 1885.

6 He remained there for more than a decade, finally returning to Canada after an amnesty, and once more joining the national assembly.

7 Among the clauses of Robert Nelson's independence declaration were the following:

> 1. from this day forward, the People of Lower Canada are absolved of all allegiance to Great Britain, and that the political connection between that power and Lower Canada is now dissolved.
> 2. the Republican form of Government is best suited to Lower Canada, which is this day declared to be a Republic.
> 3. the Indian shall no longer be under any civil disqualification, but shall enjoy the same rights as all other citizens in Lower Canada.
> 4. all union between Church and State is hereby declared to be dissolved . . .
> 5. the feudal or seignorial tenure of land is hereby abolished . . .
> 8. imprisonment for debt shall no longer exist . . .
> 9. sentence of death shall no longer be passed nor executed, except in cases of murder . . .
> 16. every male person of the age of 21 years and upwards shall have the right of voting . . .

8 McMullen, *History of Canada.*

9 Ibid.

10 Ibid.

Part VIII: Introduction

1 The treaty ports were at Shanghai, Canton, Ningpo, Fuchow and Amoy. Under the treaties, the ports were opened up to foreign trade and the establishment of foreign communities. Foreign nationals accused of crimes were tried by their consular officials rather than under Chinese law.

2 Penderel Moon, *The British Conquest and Dominion of India*, London, 1989.

3 In 1841, 24,000 people sailed from Britain for Canada, 14,500 for Australia and New Zealand, and 130 for Cape Colony. Later in the decade, in the five years from 1846 to 1851, 60,000 emigrants left Britain for Australia alone.

4 Hugh Tinker, *A New System of Slavery: The Export of Indian Labour Overseas, 1830–1920*, Oxford, 1974.

5 David Northrup, 'Migration from Africa, Asia, and the South Pacific', in *Oxford History of the British Empire, Vol. III*, Oxford, 1999.

6 Napier had warned in 1839 that

> we have the physical force, not they. They talk of their hundred thousands of men. Who is to move them when I am dancing round them with cavalry and pelting them with cannonshot? What would their 100,000 men do with my 100 rockets wriggling their fiery tails among them, roaring, scorching, tearing, smashing all they came near? And when in desperation and despair they broke to fly, how would they bear five regiments of cavalry careering through them? Poor men! How little they know of physical force!'

Gabrielle Lambricke, *Sir Charles Napier and Sind*, Oxford, 1952.

7 See Captain Henry Keppel, *The Expedition to Borneo of HMS Dido for the Suppression of Piracy*, London, 1846, and Admiral Henry Keppel, *A Sailor's Life under Four Sovereigns*, 3 vols, London, 1899.

8 See S. G. Checkland, *The Gladstones: A Family Biography, 1764–1851*, Cambridge, 1971.

46 The Capture of Useful Imperial Harbours

1 Among those participating in the British assault was Captain Sparkhall Rundle, whose daughter was to marry Sir Reginald Wingate – another great imperial operator in this zone later in the century.

2 Jung-Fang Tsai, *Hong Kong in Chinese History: Community and Social Unrest in the British Colony, 1842–1913*, New York, 1993.

3 'Coolies' were originally from India, but over time the word came to be used for all migrant labourers of Asian origin. Some 30,000 'coolies' left Hong Kong for Canada between 1868 and the end of the nineteenth century, and even larger numbers went to the United States – 300,000 between 1848 and 1882, according to one estimate.

47 Revolts among the Hill Tribes of Assam

1 Alexander Mackenzie, *History of the Relations of the Government with the Hill Tribes of the North-East Frontier of Bengal*, Calcutta, 1884.

2 Hemeswar Dihingia, *Assam's Struggles Against British Rule, 1826–1863*, Delhi, 1980.

3 See Adam White, *Considerations on the State of British India*, Edinburgh, 1822, and *Memoir of the Late David Scott*, Calcutta, 1832.

4 Dihingia, *Assam's struggles Against British Rule.*

5 Ibid.

6 R. G. Woodthorpe, *The Naga Hills Expedition*, London, 1877.

7 Major John Butler, *Travels and Adventures in the Province of Assam during a Residence of Fourteen Years*, London, 1855.

8 Mackenzie, *History of the Relations of the Government with the Hill Tribes of the North-East Frontier of Bengal.*

9 Ibid.

10 Ibid.

11 Ibid.

12 L. W. Shakespear, *History of Upper Assam, Upper Burmah, and the North-Eastern Frontier*, London, 1914.

48 Resistance to the British Invasion of Afghanistan

1 Mohan Lal, *Life of the Amir Dost Mohammed Khan, of Kabul, Including the Victory and Disaster of the British Army in Afghanistan*, London, 1846. See also Henry Durand, *The First Afghan War and its Causes*, London, 1879, J. W. Kaye, *History of the War in Afghanistan*, London, 1878; and J. A. Norris, *The First Afghan War, 1838–1842*, London, 1967.

2 Archibald Forbes, *The Afghan Wars, 1839–42 and 1878–80*, London, 1892.

3 Florentia Sale left a lively account of her travails: Florentia Sale, *Journals*, London, 1843.

4 Charles Low, *The Life and Correspondence of Field Marshal Sir George Pollock, Bart*, London, 1873.

5 Moon, *British Conquest and Dominion of India.*

49 The Resistance of the Amirs of Sind Is Reinforced by Their Baluchi Soldiers

1 George Pottinger, *Sir Henry Pottinger, First Governor of Hong Kong*, New York, 1997.

2 Captain A. B. Rathborne, one of those involved in the British conquest, argued

subsequently that the amirs' 'system would have been just as good as ours . . . and much better for the country . . . than the most perfect system of English law, for under it people have what they could not have under a most perfect system, the speediness of decisions accompanied by a freedom from costs'. See Colonel James Outram, *The Conquest of Scinde: A Commentary*, London, 1846.

3 James Richardson, *Travels in the Great Desert of Sahara in 1845 and 1846*, London, 1848.

4 Henry Pottinger, *Travels in Beloochistan and Sinde*, London, 1810.

5 In September 1844, the surviving amirs in Bengal sought an interview with General Sir Henry Hardinge, the new governor-general. According to their own account, the general 'openly averred that he was aware an injustice had been done to the Amirs, but that he had no power to assist them'. The amirs then wrote to say that 'if it was not in his power to redress their wrongs, they entreated he would, at least, suffer them to send some of their number to the Queen'. Mir Nasir sent three emissaries to London in 1844, and the three men – Akhund Habibullah, Diwan Mittaram and Diwan Dayaram – secured lodgings at No. 19 Harley Street. They sought to lobby Queen Victoria and members of parliament, and they issued statements outlining the grievances of the amirs, but no one took much notice. After Mir Nasir's death in 1845, their funds ran out and they were obliged to return to Bengal.

6 W. Cooke Taylor and P. J. McKenna, *Ancient and Modern India*, London, 1860.

7 Lionel Trotter, *The Bayard of India: A Life of General Sir James Outram*, London, 1925.

8 Cooke Taylor and McKenna, *Ancient and Modern India*.

50 The Long Struggle of the Sikhs in the Punjab

1 Moon, *British Conquest and Dominion of India*.

2 Lady Emma Edwardes, *Memorials of the Life and Letters of Sir Herbert Edwardes*, London, 1886.

3 Lady Lena Login, *Sir John Login and Duleep Singh*, London, 1890.

4 A full account of the battle appears in Colonel Fortescue's *History of the British Army, Vol. XII, 1839–1852*, London, 1927.

5 The Sikhs called Hardinge *tunda lat* – 'the one-armed lord' – for he had lost an arm in battle.

6 'A few shot fell among the transport', wrote Colonel Fortescue in his account of the battle in his *History of the British Army*, and the drivers were thrown into a panic.

> The Sikhs, taking advantage of the confusion, attacked the baggage-train and succeeded in carrying off a great part of it, including the sick and wounded. At one moment Ranjur pressed more closely, but was checked by the fire of Smith's guns, which were massed in rear; and then with great skill he drew out a line of seven battalions, with cannon in the intervals, across the rear of Smith's column, as if to attack in earnest. Smith willingly took up the challenge, and would have assailed this line had not his infantry been utterly exhausted . . . The men were disheartened and dispirited by the result of the day's work.

Fortescue, *History of the British Army, Vol. XII*.

7 Moon, *British Conquest and Dominion of India*.

8 The calculations of Colonel Fortescue in his *History of the British Army, Vol. XII*.

9 Khushwant Singh, *History of the Sikhs*, 2 vols, Princeton, 1963–66.

10 Lawrence James, *Raj: The Making and Unmaking of British India*, London, 1997.

11 Singh, *History of the Sikhs*.

12 Ibid.

13 Ibid.

14 Moon, British *Conquest and Dominion of India*; and see Charles Gough and A. D. Innes, *The Sikhs and the Sikh Wars*, London, 1897.

15 According to Colonel James Hope Grant,

> the diamond Koh-i-noor was passed from hand to hand to be admired. It was set in an armlet, and fastened to the wearer's arm with a thread of red silk. It was upwards of an inch in length, three-quarters of an inch in breadth, and thick in proportion. Two smaller stones, each of immense value, were attached to either side of the jewel.

Incidents in the Sepoy War of 1857–58, Compiled from the Private Journal of General Sir Hope Grant, KCB, London, 1873.

Now, by the terms of the Lahore treaty, the diamond was to be surrendered to the Queen of England. When it was exhibited at the Great Exhibition in London in 1851, the crowds were disappointed by its 'Indian cut'. In 1852 it was re-cut to 'western taste', diminishing its size considerably. Nearly a century later, in 1937, it was incorporated into a royal crown.

16 Singh, *History of the Sikhs*, Princeton, 1963.

51 Aborigine Resistance in Victoria and Queensland

1 M. Doyle, ed., *Extracts from the Letters and Journals of George Fletcher Moore, Esq., Now Filling a Judicial Office at the Swan River Settlement*, London, 1834; George Moore, *Diary of Ten Years Eventful Life of an Early Settler in Western Australia*, London, 1884.

2 M. F. Christie, *Aborigines in Colonial Victoria, 1835–1886*, Sydney, 1979.

3 See J. J. Knight, *In the Early Days: History and Incidents of Pioneer Queensland*, Brisbane, 1895; C. C. Petrie, *Tom Petrie's Reminiscences of Early Queensland*, Sydney, 1932; and Alison Palmer, *Colonial Genocide*, London, 2001.

4 Christie, *Aborigines in Colonial Victoria.*

5 Clive Turnbull, *Black War: The Extermination of the Tasmanian Aborigines*, Melbourne, 1948.

6 Raymond Evans, *A History of Queensland*, Cambridge, 2007.

7 The tale of the strychnine massacre at Kilcoy Creek was told many times, and some fifty years later an old Queenslander called Tom Petrie recalled being told the story by 'several very old blackfellows' present at the Creek:

> These men told him that a great many blacks and gins [women] and pickaninnies were poisoned at Kilcoy Station . . . The white fellows gave them a lot of flour, and it was taken to camp and made into dampers and eaten. Shortly after some of those who had eaten of it took fits, and ran to the water, and died there; others died on the way, and some got very sick, but recovered. The old man showed how each poor poisoned wretch had jumped about before he died.

Palmer, *Colonial Genocide;* see also Petrie, *Tom Petrie's Reminiscences.*

52 Maori Resistance in New Zealand

1 James Belich, *Making Peoples: A History of the New Zealanders, from Polynesian Settlement to the End of the Nineteenth Century*, Auckland, 1996.

2 James Cowan, historian of the New Zealand wars, told the following story:

> The old medicine-man went into the bush and returned with armfuls of branches of the mahoe-tree, and made a fire, which he kept burning until all the wood was reduced to glowing embers. The earth was heaped up around this fire, and the head, neck downwards, was placed over it, and all openings at the sides were closed, so that the fumes from the charcoal oven would pass up into the head. The brains had

> previously been removed and the eyes stuffed up. As the smoking went on, the old man smoothed down the skin of the face with his hands to prevent it wrinkling and wiped off the moisture, until the head was thoroughly smokedried and quite mummified. For several hours the head-smoking went on, and in the morning the trophies of the chase were packed for the final march.

James Cowan, *The Adventures of Kimble Bent*, London, 1911.

3 Ian Wards, *The Shadow of the Land: A Study of British Policy and Racial Conflict in New Zealand, 1832–1852*, Wellington, 1968.

4 James Cowan, *The New Zealand Wars: A History of the Maori Campaigns and the Pioneering Period*, Wellington, 1922; and James Belich, *The New Zealand Wars and the Victorian Interpretation of Racial Conflict*, Auckland, 1986.

5 See R. Burrows, *Extracts from a Diary, Kept During Heke's War in the North in 1845*, Auckland, 1886; Robert Hattaway, *Reminiscences of the Northern War*, Auckland, 1889; and T. L. Buick, *New Zealand's First War or the Rebellion of Hone Heke*, Wellington, 1926.

6 Belich, *New Zealand Wars.*

7 Ibid. 'A not uncommon practice of both sides', Belich adds.

8 Ibid.

9 The battle at Ohaeawai, suggests James Belich, was 'a military debacle comparable in intensity and feats of courage to the attack of the British Light Brigade at Balaclava ten years later'.

10 Belich, *New Zealand Wars.*

11 Cowan, *New Zealand Wars.*

12 Ibid.

13 Ibid.

53 Muslim Resistance in Sarawak

1 'I carry with me presents which are reported to be to his liking; gaudy silks of Surat, scarlet cloth, stamped velvet, gunpowder, etc., besides a large quantity of confectionary and sweets, such as preserved ginger, jams, dates, syrups, and, to wind up all, a huge box of Chinese toys for his children.'

2 'Der Macota, unlike other Malays, neither smokes tobacco nor chews *sirih*. He sought our society, and was the first person who spoke to me on the subject of the trade. His education has been more attended to than that of others of his rank. He both reads and writes his own language, and is well acquainted with the government, laws, and customs of Borneo. From him I derived much information on the subject of the Dayaks and the geography of the interior.'

3 Both Makhota and Muda Hassim were at pains to explain to Brooke that 'were it not for the underhand assistance of the Sultan of Sambas, who had constantly supplied them with food and ammunition, the insurgents would long since have been dispersed'.

4 When HMS *Samarang* had first arrived in the archipelago in June 1844, Belcher had slaughtered a boatload of seafarers off Gillolo – men who were employed by the Dutch authorities to attack 'pirates'. When the Dutch heard of their fate they complained about Belcher's activities to the British, who took no notice. Those on board the *Samarang* received the official bounty for eliminating 'pirates'. Since some 350 were killed, the bounty amounted to nearly £12,000. Captain Edward Belcher, *Narrative of the Voyage of HMS Samarang During the Years 1843–46*, London, 1848.

5 William Laird Clowes, *The Royal Navy: A History, vol. 6*, London, 1901.

6 Midshipman Marryat, who had sailed on HMS *Samarang*, described the scene as the British threatened to blow up the sultan if he did not do what he was told:

> The barge was so placed that the assassination of Mr Brooke and the Europeans would have been revenged on the first discharge of our gun by the slaughter of hundreds;

> and in the main street lay the steamer, with a spring on her cable, her half ports up, and guns loaded to the muzzle . . . The platform admitted one of the steamer's guns to look into the audience chamber, the muzzle was pointed directly at the Sultan, a man held the lighted tow in his hand.

Frank M. Marryat, *Borneo and the Indian Archipelago, with Drawings of Costume and Scenery*, London, 1848.

7 Marryat, *Borneo and the Indian Archipelago.*

8 Clowes, The Royal Navy: A *History, vol.6.*

9 Nicholas Tarling, *Piracy and Politics in the Malay World*, Melbourne, 1963.

10 A more critical account recorded that he had gone 'to sweep together a number of Bisaya girls to fill his harem, when he was fallen upon by the natives at night and killed'.

54 The Penultimate Battles of the Xhosa in Cape Colony

1 The invasion of Xhosa land formed 'one of the most inglorious episodes in the history of the British army in the nineteenth century. Blunder and disaster, timidity, muddle and stupidity, quarrel and disagreement and dismal ineptitude, marked every stage of this dismally ill-considered initiative.' Noël Mostert, *Frontiers: The Epic of South Africa's Creation and the Tragedy of the Xhosa People*, London, 1992.

2 Quoted in ibid.

3 Quoted in B. Le Cordeur and C. Saunders, eds, The *War of the Axe*, Johannesburg, 1981.

4 S. M. Mitra, *The Life and Letters of Sir John Hall*, London, 1911, quoted in Mostert, Frontiers.

5 Quoted in Le Cordeur, *War of the Axe.*

6 Quoted in J. B. Peires, *The Dead Will Arise: Nongqawuse and the Great Xhosa Cattle-Killing Movement of 1856–7*, London, 1989.

Part IX: Introduction

1 James Fenton, *A History of Tasmania*, London, 1884.

55 William Smith O'Brien and the Rising of the Young Irelanders

1 L. Fogarty, ed., *James Fintan Lalor: Patriot and Political Essayist, 1807–1849*, London, 1918.

2 Denis Gwynn, *Young Ireland and 1848*, Cork, 1949.

3 The programme of the Irish Republic, as later remembered by Father Thomas Fitzpatrick:

> 1. Whole and absolute independence of England.
> 2. Declaration of an Irish Republic.
> 3. Political equality of all creeds.
> 4. Confiscation of the property of all found in arms against the Irish Republic.
> 5. Immediate formation of a National Guard, into which the military and police were admissible.
> 6. Strict observance of all private and commercial contracts.
> 7. Contributions in money and kind to be levied on the faith of the Irish Republic.
> 8. Oblivion of all distinctions of race and creed.

4 F. S. L. Lyons, *Ireland Since the Famine*, London, 1971.

5 Sean Cronin, '"The Country Did Not Turn Out": the Young Ireland Rising of 1848', *Eire-Ireland: Journal of Irish Studies* XI: 2 (1976).

6 Virginia Crossman, *Politics, Law and Order in Nineteenth Century Ireland*, Dublin, 1996.

56 Dr Christopher Elliott, Wikrama Sardawa Siddhapa and the Rebellion of the Kandy Pretenders

1 A full account of the rebellion occurs in Lennox Mills, *Ceylon under British Rule, 1795–1932*, London, 1933.

2 Captain John Macdonald Henderson, *The History of the Rebellion in Ceylon during Lord Torrington's Government*, London, 1868.

3 Sir James Tennent later amplified this explanation:

> In all the former rebellions there has been a member of the royal family of Kandy in the island; but in no instance . . . has that person himself taken the field or placed himself at the head of his own forces; not one only, but a number of pretenders, each assuming the name of the king, personate him throughout the various districts, and in the event of success he would come forward and take the place which had been usurped by them.

Tennent further explained that several members of the old royal family were still alive in 1848, and although they had all been transported to India's Coromandel coast in 1815, they were frequent visitors to Ceylon. Whenever an insurrection looms, said Tennent, 'this circumstance gives great facility of obtaining a claimant to the throne to place himself at the head of any discontented party'. 'Third Report from the Select Committee on Ceylon, Session 1850, Volume VIII, Part One (evidence of Sir James Emerson Tennent), HMSO, 1851'. See also James Emerson Tennent, *Ceylon: An Account of the Island, Physical, Historical, and Topographical*, London, 1859.

4 Colonel Jonathan Forbes, *Recent Disturbances and Military Executions in Ceylon*, London, 1850.

5 Sir James Tennent, evidence to the Select Committee on Ceylon, London, March 1850. Tennant explained its fiscal signficance:

> We raise a considerable revenue from the sale of the monopoly of taverns for the disposal of arrack. In order to ensure to the occupants of those taverns the enjoyment of that monopoly, we prevent the inhabitants from drawing the juice from their own cocoa-nut trees, which when fermented they use as a substitute for ardent spirits. The Kandyans complain that the establishment of these taverns throughout their country . . . has led to extensive demoralisation as the consequence of extended intoxification; and they likewise complain of their being prevented from drawing the juice of their own cocoa-nuts . . .

6 P. D. Millie, *Thirty Years Ago, Or, The Reminiscences of the Early Days of Coffee Planting in Ceylon*, Colombo, 1878.

7 Henderson, *History of the Rebellion in Ceylon.*

8 'First, Second and Third Report from the House of Commons Select Committee on Ceylon', HMSO, London, 1850.

9 Millie, *Thirty Years Ago.*

10 'First, Second and Third Report from the House of Commons Select Committee on Ceylon'.

11 K. M. de Silva, *Letters on Ceylon: The Administration of Viscount Torrington and the 'Rebellion' of 1848*, Colombo, 1965.

12 R. W. Kostal, 'A Jurisprudence of Power: Martial Law and the Ceylon Controversy of 1848–51', *Journal of Imperial and Commonwealth Studies* 28 (2000).

13 'Evidence before the House of Commons Select Committee on Ceylon', 20 July 1849.

14 'Third Report from the Select Committee on Ceylon, Session 1850, Volume VIII, Part One (evidence of Sir James Emerson Tennent)'.

15 Forbes, *Recent Disturbances and Military Executions in Ceylon.*

16 Nothing could have been more calculated to inflame the Kandyans, as Tennent explained in his evidence of March 1850:

> I have already alluded to the general impatience which exists in the minds of all Kandyans of the presence of the British government, and the causes which have operated in conjunction with that are, in a great degree, to be traced to the operation of coffee planting, and the introduction not only of Europeans as settlers in the midst of their hills and forests, but likewise to that which has given them much greater offence, viz. the introduction of Malabar coolies, who came there in search of labour; that is what chiefly affected the mass of the people.
>
> The higher classes of the body of the people . . . complain of the sale of their forests for the purpose of converting them into coffee estates . . . The result of that has been likewise very distasteful to the mass of the people, by the opening up of the roads . . . It has poured into the villages the low-country Cingalese, who come there as tradesmen and mechanics, and of whom the Kandyans have a great dislike; and still more, it has let in an influx of Malabar coolies, who are wholly distasteful to the Kandyans, and whom they accuse of robbing their plantains and gardens, and carrying off their poultry . . . They have repeatedly complained of this to the government, but it must be obvious that these are grievances to which we can apply no remedy, because they arise out of legitimate causes which it be injudicious in us to control – I mean to check coffee planting.

'Third Report from the Select Committee on Ceylon, Session 1850, Volume VIII, Part One (evidence of Sir James Emerson Tennent).

57 The Final Rebellion of the Xhosa in Cape Colony

1 The Xhosa resistance lasted for more than twenty-seven months; the Anglo-Boer war, half a century later, lasted for thirty-two months.

2 John Fortescue, *History of the British Army, Vol. XII, 1839–1852*, London, 1913.

3 Ibid.

4 Noël Mostert, *Frontiers: The Epic of South Africa's Creation and the Tragedy of the Xhosa People*, London, 1992.

5 Ibid.

6 This was James Read, son of a British missionary and a Khoi-Khoi woman, who had lived all his life at the Kat River settlement. Quoted in ibid.

7 Ibid.

8 Quoted in J. B. Peires, *The Dead Will Arise: Nongqawuse and the Great Xhosa Cattle Killing Movement of 1856–7*, London, 1989.

9 Quoted in ibid. This was the view of Governor Cathcart.

10 Ibid.

11 Quoted in ibid.

12 From a new High Commissioner in Cape Town, Philip Wodehouse, formerly in Ceylon and Guyana.

58 West African Resistance

1 William Laird Clowes, *The Royal Navy: A History from the Earliest Times to the Death of Queen Victoria, Vol. VII*, London, 1903. Clowes wrote of 'those too soon forgotten police duties which confer so many benefits upon the Empire, and often lack . . . any chronicler other than the officer who reports them dryly to the Admiralty'.

2 See also S. J. S. Cookey, *King Jaja of the Niger Delta, His Life and Times, 1821–1891*, UGR Publishing, Sutton, Surrey, 2005.

3 Christopher Fyfe, *History of Sierra Leone*, Oxford, 1962.

59 The Start of an Endless Saga: The North-West Frontier Territories of India

1 Penderel Moon, *The British Conquest and Dominion of British India*, London, 1989.

2 Colonel H. C. Wylly, *From Black Mountain to Waziristan, Being an Account of the Border Countries and the More Turbulent of the Tribes Controlled by the North-West Frontier Province, and of Our Military Relations with Them in the Past*, London, 1912.

3 Lt-Col W. H. Paget, *A Record of the Expeditions against the North-West Frontier Tribes Since the Annexation of the Punjab*, London, 1884.

4 Wylly, *From Black Mountain to Waziristan.*

5 E. E. Oliver, *Across the Border, Or Pathan and Biloch*, London, 1890.

6 Ibid.

7 Ibid.

60 The Burmese Empire Resists Further Invasion

1 R. S. V. Donnison, *Burma*, London, 1970.

2 Sir Garnet Wolseley, *A Soldier's Life*, London, 1903.

3 Frederick Maurice, *The Life of Lord Wolseley*, London, 1924.

4 Myo Myint, *The Politics of Survival in Burma: Diplomacy and Statecraft in the Reign of King Minden, 1853–1878*, Ann Arbor, 1990.

Part X: Introduction

1 Penderel Moon, *The British Conquest and Dominion of India*, London, 1989.

2 Barbara English, *John Company's Last War*, London, 1971.

3 J. Y. Wong, *Deadly Dreams: Opium, Imperialism and the Arrow War (1856–1860) in China*, Cambridge, 1998.

4 Jonathan Spence, *God's Chinese Son: The Taiping Heavenly Kingdom of Hong Xiuquan*, London, 1996.

61 The Taiping Rebellion Spreads Unrest among Chinese Communities Elsewhere

1 In 1857, the directors of the Chamber of Commerce and Manufacturing in Glasgow claimed that there were 50,000 Chinese males in Singapore, and no females. Wong, *Deadly Dreams.*

2 Charles Burton Buckley, *An Anecdotal History of Old Times in Singapore, 1819–1867*, Oxford, 1984.

3 Lee Poh Ping, *Chinese Society in Nineteeenth Century Singapore*, Kuala Lumpur, 1978.

4 Jun-Fang Tsai, *Hong Kong in Chinese History: Community and Social Unrest in the British Colony, 1842–1913*, Columbia, 1993.

62 White Settler Rebellion in Australia and Further Aborigine Resistance

1 Mark Twain, *Following the Equator: A Journey Around the World*, New York, 1897.

2 *Eureka Stockade*, dir. Harry Watt, 1949.

3 L. E. Skinner, *Police of the Pastoral Frontier: Native Police, 1849–59*, Queensland, 1975.

4 The events at Hornet Bank were retold half a century later by Carrabah George, a survivor of the Dawson River tribe, and he reported the story as he himself had been told it:

> He was a young lad at the time, about nine or ten years of age. An overseer of the [Hornet Bank] station was doing the usual round of the shepherds' huts and discovered, in the camp of one of the Aborigines, some rations which he knew was part of the shepherd's issue. He accused the Aborigine of stealing them but, when the boy tried to explain that the shepherd had given him the tucker in payment for lending his gin for prostitution, the overseer drew his revolver and shot him [the Aborigine] dead. The overseer is said to have later found, at the camp, that the boy's explanation was true. The tribe, in their fury at this wanton act, held a council of war, and decided in revenge to kill all the white occupants of the station.

Quoted in J. W. Bleakley, *The Aborigines of Australia: Their History, Their Habits, Their Assimilation*, Brisbane, 1961.

5 Rosa Campbell-Praed, *My Australian Girlhood*, London, 1902.

6 Henry Reynolds, 'The Other Side of the Frontier: Early Aboriginal Reactions to Pastoral Settlement in Queensland and Northern New South Wales', *Australian Historical Studies* 17 (April 1976).

7 Quoted in Jonathan Richards, *The Secret War: A True History of Queensland's Native Police*, Queensland, 2008.

8 L. E. Skinner, *Police of the Pastoral Frontier*, Queensland, 1975. See also Bleakley, *Aborigines of Australia*; and Henry Reynolds and Noel Loos, 'Aboriginal Resistance in Queensland', *Australian Journal of Politics and History* 22 (April 2008).

63 The Santals in Bengal and the Moplahs in Malabar

1 Their land was called Damun-i-koh, 'the skirt of the hills', though some officials translated it as 'within the pillars'. The government had surveyed and marked off this area in 1832 by constructing a ring fence around it of masonry pillars.

2 H. McPherson, *Final Report on the Survey and Settlement Operations in the District of Santal Parganas, 1898–1907*, Calcutta, 1909.

3 William Wilson Hunter, *Annals of Rural Bengal*, London, 1897.

4 One captured Santal, Dullas Manee, was more specific about the nature of the insults, referring to 'the Sahibs of the Railway who created great oppression at Seetapaharee'. One such Sahib, a Mr Thomas, 'used to go out with a Mussaul [torch-bearer] at night and dishonour the women of the Sonthals, and carry off goats, fowls and kids by force'. Kalikinkar Datta, *The Santal Insurrection of 1855–57*, Calcutta, 1940.

5 See Stephen Fuchs, *Rebellious Prophets: A Study of Messianic Movements in Indian Religions*, London, 1965.

6 See Conrad Wood, 'Historical Background of the Moplah Rebellion: Outbreaks,

1836–1919', *Social Scientist* 3: 1 (August 1974); and Conrad Wood, 'The First Moplah Rebellion against British Rule in Malabar', *Modern Asian Studies* 10: 4 (1976).

7 Minute by J. D. Sim, Madras, 1874, quoted in Wood, 'Historical Background of the Moplah Rebellion'.

64 James Sayers Orr and the 'Angel Gabriel' Riots in Guyana

1 V. O. Chan, 'The Riots of 1856 in British Guiana', *Caribbean Quarterly* 16 (1970).

2 Michael Craton, *Empire, Enslavement, and Freedom in the Caribbean*, Oxford, 1997.

3 Ibid.

65 Nongqawuse and the Self-Destruction of the Xhosa in Cape Colony

1 See J. B. Peires, *The Dead Will Arise, Nongqawuse and the Great Xhosa Cattle Killing Movement of 1856–7*, London, 1989.

2 N. J. Merriman, *The Journals of Archdeacon N. J. Merriman, 1848–1855*, Cape Town, 1957.

3 Noël Mostert, *Frontiers: The Epic of South Africa's Creation and the Tragedy of the Xhosa People*, London, 1992.

66 The Great Rebellion in India

1 The new Enfield rifle used a cartridge greased with tallow, usually defined as rendered beef or mutton fat. Since the cheapest fat available in India was that of cow or pig, both Hindu and Muslim soldiers were affronted. The British became immediately aware of this self-inflicted problem and sought to withdraw the offending cartridges, but the damage had been done.

2 Quoted in Christopher Hibbert, *The Great Mutiny*, London, 1978.

3 Mohan Lal Kashmiri, quoted in William Dalrymple, *The Last Mughal: The Fall of a Dynasty*, London, 2006.

4 Hibbert, *Great Mutiny*.

5 William Dalrymple, after examining the archives, has paid tribute to Mirza Mughal's energy:

> From the first week, Mirza Mughal produced an incessant stream of orders and commands: attempting to get the sepoys out of the city and into a series a coherent military camps; sending policemen or palace guards to rescue any bazaars that were being plundered or noblemen whose houses were being attacked; promising the sepoys pay and raising the money to provide it; finding sufficient food for both the sepoys and the people of Delhi; receiving and attending to the petitions of individual sepoys; providing spades, shovels, axes and sandbags for entrenchments and defence works; imposing a strict code of conduct on the military so that, for example, there could be no house searches without a permit; negotiating to restrain the Gujar tribes outside the walls; establishing a mint to produce coins with Zafar's portrait upon them; and, not least, attempting to rally his increasingly depressed father and control his own brothers.

Dalrymple, *Last Mughal*.

6 The annexation of Oudh forms the background to Satyajit Ray's 1977 film, *The Chess Players*.

7 Nana had sent an emissary, Azimullah Khan, to London to argue his case with the directors of the East India Company. Azimullah failed in his mission, but made a considerable impression on society women in London before returning to India via the Crimea. He formed a low opinion of the military strength of the Empire after witnessing the later stages of the siege of Sebastopol, and communicated this view to Nana Sahib.

8 T. Rice Holmes, *A History of the Indian Mutiny*, London, 1904.

9 Quoted in Hibbert, *Great Mutiny*.

10 Quoted in Moon, *British Conquest and Dominion of India*. See also John Kaye, *The History of the Sepoy War in India, Vol. 2*, London, 1880.

11 The sepoys at Jaunpur, thirty miles north-west of Benares, mutinied on 5 June, and remained in control of their town until the arrival of a force of Gurkhas from Azamgarh in September. The sepoys regained control in November, and not until May 1858 was their rebellion crushed.

12 Moon, *British Conquest and Dominion of India*.

13 Hibbert, *Great Mutiny*.

14 Moon, *British Conquest and Dominion of India*.

15 Quoted in Moon, *British Conquest and Dominion of India*.

16 Penderel Moon, quoting Kaye. 'After Neill's reign of terror', writes Moon, 'the local population were more inclined to run away and hide than to come forward with offers of labour and supplies. Neill's strong measures were in this respect counter-productive.' Moon, *British Conquest and Dominion of India*.

17 Quoted in Hibbert, *Great Mutiny*.

18 Andrew Ward, *Our Bones Are Scattered*, London, 1996.

19 Hibbert, *Great Mutiny*. The enthusiastic Tucker had erected columns at the entrances to the city inscribed with the Ten Commandments in both Hindi and Urdu. Moon, *British Conquest and Dominion of India*.

20 Moon, *British Conquest and Dominion of India*.

21 Tapti Roy, 'Visions of the Rebels: A Study of 1857 in Bundelkhand', *Modern Asian Studies* 27: 1 (1993).

22 Quoted in Dalrymple, *Last Mughal*.

23 Quoted in ibid.

24 Saul David, *The Indian Mutiny: 1887*, London, 2002.

25 'It is more than likely', Moon comments, 'that during his travels he incited the sepoys to mutiny'. Moon, *British Conquest and Dominion of India*.

26 Ibid.

27 Frederic Cooper, *The Crisis in the Punjab from the 10th of May until the Fall of Delhi*, London, 1858.

28 Cooper, *Crisis in the Punjab*.

29 Moon, *British Conquest and Dominion of India*.

30 The 12th Irregular Cavalry at Segowlee on the Nepal border rebelled in June 1857, and joined the rebels at Lucknow after a 300-mile march. The thirty-two Native Infantry in Orissa also rebelled in June 1857 and joined the rebels at Banda in Central India.

31 Moon, *British Conquest and Dominion of India*.

32 Hibbert, *Great Mutiny*.

33 Quoted in Dalrymple, *Last Mughal*.

34 Quoted in Moon, *British Conquest and Dominion of India*.

35 Quoted in ibid.

36 Dalrymple, *Last Mughal*.

37 Quoted in P. J. O. Taylor, *A Feeling of Quiet Power: The Siege of Lucknow, 1857*, London, 1994. See also P. J. O. Taylor, ed., *A Companion to the 'Indian Mutiny' of 1857*, Oxford, 1996.

38 Hibbert, *Great Mutiny*.

39 Moon, *British Conquest and Dominion of India*.

40 Hibbert, *Great Mutiny*.

41 Ibid.
42 Quoted in Julian Spilsbury, *The Indian Mutiny*.
43 The Rani was killed, wrote Rose,

> dressed in a red jacket, red trousers and white puggary; she wore the celebrated necklace of Scindia, which she had taken from his treasury, and heavy gold anklets; as she lay mortally wounded in her tent she ordered these ornaments to be distributed among her troops; it is said that Tantya Topi intercepted the necklace. The whole rebel Army mourned for her; her body was burned with great ceremony under a tamarind tree under the Rock of Gwalior, where I saw her bones and ashes.

Quoted in Spilsbury, *Indian Mutiny*.

44 Khan Bahadur Khan gave useful instructions to his troops about the nature of irregular warfare:

> Do not attempt to meet the regular columns of the infidels because they are superior to you in discipline and organisation, and have big guns. But watch their movements, guard all the *ghauts* on the rivers, intercept their communications; stop their supplies, cut up their *daks* and posts; keep constantly hanging about their camps; give them no rest.

Quoted in Hibbert, *Great Mutiny*.

45 David, *Indian Mutiny*.

Epilogue

1 Quoted in Wilfred Scawen Blunt, *Secret History of the English Occupation of Egypt*, London, 1907.

2 F. P. Crozier, *Five Years Hard, Being an Account of the Fulani Empire, and a Picture of the Daily Life of a Regimental Officer among the Peoples of the Western Sahara*, London, 1932.

Bibliography

North America

American Friends Service Committee, *The Wabanakis of Maine and the Maritimes*, Bath, Maine, 1989.

Anderson, Fred, *Crucible of War: The Seven Years' War and the Fate of the Empire in British North America, 1754–1766*, London, 2000.

Bassett, John Spencer, 'The Regulators of North Carolina, 1765–1771', in the *Annual Report* of the American Historical Association, 1894–95, Washington, 1895.

Bliss, Eugene, ed., *Diary of David Zeisberger: A Moravian Missionary among the Indians of Ohio*, St Clair Shores, Michigan, 1972.

Butterfield, Willshire, *History of the Girtys*, Columbus, Ohio, 1890.

——— *Washington–Irvine Correspondence*, Madison, 1882.

Callaway, Colin, *The American Revolution in Indian Country: Crisis and Diversity in Native American Communities*, Cambridge, 1995.

Corkran, David, *The Cherokee Frontier: Conflict and Survival, 1740–1762*, Norman, Oklahoma, 1962.

——— *The Creek Frontier, 1540–1783*, Norman, Oklahoma, 1967.

Dowd, Gregory Evans, *A Spirited Resistance: The North American Indian Struggle for Unity, 1745–1815*, Baltimore, 1992.

Downes, Randolph, *Council Fires on the Upper Ohio: A Narrative of Indian Affairs on the Upper Ohio Valley until 1795*, Pittsburgh, 1940.

Eccles, W. J., *The Canadian Frontier, 1534–1760*, Albuquerque, 1983.

Flexner, J. T., *Mohawk Baronet: Sir William Johnson of New York*, New York, 1959.

Fortescue, J. W., *A History of the British Army, Vol. III, 1763–1793*, London, 1902.

Gist, Christopher, *The Journal of Christopher Gist, 1750–1751*, Boston, 1825.

Harper's Encyclopaedia of United States History, London, 1902.

Hawkes, Francis, 'Battle of the Alamance, War of Regulation', in William Cooke, ed., *Revolutionary History of North Carolina*, New York, 1853.

Historical Account of the Expedition against the Ohio Indians, Philadelphia, 1766.

Jacobs, Wilbur, *Diplomacy and Indian Gifts: Anglo-French Rivalry along the Ohio and North-West Frontiers, 1748–1763*, Stanford, 1950.

Jennings, Francis, 'The Indians' Revolution', in Alfred Young, ed., *The American Revolution: Explorations in the History of American Radicalism*, Illinois, 1976.

——— *Empire of Fortune: Crowns, Colonies and Tribes in the Seven Years War in America*, New York, 1988.

Kimbrough, Mary, *Louis-Antoine de Bougainville, 1729–1811: A Study in French Naval History and Politics*, Lewiston, New York, 1990.

King, Duane, ed., *The Cherokee Indian Nation: A Troubled History*, Knoxville, Tennessee, 1979.

Kopperman, Paul E., *Braddock at the Monongahela*, Pittsburgh, 1977.

Labaree, Benjamin, *The Boston Tea Party*, New York, 1964.

Louis, Wm Roger, *The Oxford History of the British Empire volume IV*, Oxford, 1998.

McConnell, Michael, *A Country Between: The Upper Ohio Valley and its Peoples, 1724–1774*, Lincoln, Nebraska, 1992.

Metcalf, Samuel, ed., *A Collection of Some of the Most Interesting Narratives of Indian Warfare in the West*, New York, 1821.

Morrison, Kenneth M., *The Embattled Northeast: The Elusive Ideal of Alliance in Abenaki–Euramerican Relations*, Berkeley, 1984.

Parkman, Francis, *The Conspiracy of Pontiac*, 2 vols, Boston, 1851.

Peckham, Howard H., *Pontiac and the Indian Uprising*, Princeton, 1947.

Powell, William, ed., *The Regulators in North Carolina*, Raleigh, 1971.

Quarles, Benjamin, *The Negro in the American Revolution*, Chapel Hill, 1961.

Trigger, Bruce, ed., *Handbook of North American Indians: The Western Tribes, Vol. 15*, Washington, 1978.

Thwaites, Reuben, ed., *The Documentary History of Dunmore's War, 1774*, Madison, 1905.

Upton, Leslie, *Micmacs and Colonists: Indian–White Relations in the Maritimes 1713–1867*, Vancouver, 1979.

Wallace, Anthony F. C., *King of the Delawares, Teedyuscung, 1700–1763*, Syracuse, 1990.

Wheeler, John, *Historical Sketches of North Carolina, from 1584 to 1851*, Philadelphia, 1851.

White, Richard, *The Middle Ground: Indians, Empires, and Republics in the Great Lakes Region, 1650–1815*, Cambridge, 1991.

Canada

Allen, Robert, *His Majesty's Indian Allies: British Indian Policy in the Defence of Canada, 1774–1815*, Toronto, 1992.

Carter, Sarah, *Lost Harvests: Prairie Indian Reserve Farmers and Government Policy*, Montreal, 1990.

Christie, Robert, *A History of the Late Province of Upper Canada*, 6 vols, Montreal, 1848.

De Bougainville, Louis-Antoine, *Ecrits sur le Canada*, Quebec, 1993.

DeCelles, Alfred, *Papineau, Cartier*, London, 1905.

Dent, J. C., *The Story of the Upper Canadian Rebellion*, Toronto, 1885.

Dickason, Olive Patricia, *Canada's First Nations: A History of Founding Peoples from Earliest Times*, Oklahoma, 1992.

Edgar, Matilda, ed., *Ten Years of Upper Canada in Peace and War, 1805–1815*, Toronto, 1819.

Gray, John Morgan, *Lord Selkirk of Red River*, Michigan, 1964.

Guillet, E. C., *The Lives and Times of the Patriots*, Toronto, 1968.

Hamilton, Edward, *Adventures in the Wilderness: The American Journals of Louis-Antoine de Bougainville, 1756–1760*, Oklahoma, 1964.

Harmon, Daniel Williams, *Sixteen Years in the Indian Country, 1800–1816*, ed. W. Kaye Lamb, Toronto, 1957.

Head, Francis Bond, *A Narrative*, Toronto, 1969.

Henry, Alexander, *Travels and Adventures in Canada and the Indian Territories Between the Years 1760 and 1776*, Toronto, 1901.

Jenness, Diamond, *The Indians of Canada*, Ottawa, 1932.

Landon, Fred, *An Exile from Canada to Van Diemen's Land*, Toronto, 1960.

Lindsey, Charles, *The Life and Times of William Lyon Mackenzie*, Toronto, 1862.

Maximilian zu Wied, Prince, *Travels in the Interior of North America during the Years 1832–1834*, London, 1843.

McMillan, Alan, *Native Peoples and Cultures of Canada*, Toronto, 1995.

McMullen, John Mercier, *The History of Canada*, London, 1893.

Morton, Arthur, *A History of the Canadian West to 1870–71, Being a History of Rupert's Land and of the North-West Territory*, Toronto, 1972.

Ray, Arthur J., *Indians in the Fur Trade, 1660–1870*, Toronto, 1974.

Read, Colin, and Ronald Stagg, *The Rebellion of 1837 in Upper Canada: A Collection of Documents*, Toronto, 1985.

Sellar, Robert, *The History of the County of Huntingdon*, Toronto, 1885.

Senior, Elinor Kyte, *Redcoats and Patriotes: The Rebellions in Lower Canada, 1837–38*, Ontario, 1985.
Sosin, Jack, *Whitehall and the Wilderness: The Middle West in British Colonial Policy, 1760–1775*, Lincoln, Nebraska, 1961.
Thwaites, R. G., *Early Western Travels, 1748–1846*, Cleveland, 1906.

The Caribbean, Honduras and Guyana

Adamson, Alan, *Sugar Without Slaves: The Political Economy of British Guiana, 1838–1904*, New Haven, 1972.
Alexis, Stephen, *Black Liberator: The Life of Toussaint L'Ouverture*, London, 1949.
Anderson, Alexander, *Geography and History of St Vincent, West Indies*, ed. Richard and Elizabeth Howard, London, 1983.
Aptheker, Herbert, *American Negro Slave Revolts*, New York, 1968.
Atwood, Thomas, *History of the Island of Dominica*, London, 1791.
Beckles, Hilary, *A History of Barbados: From Amerindian Settlement to Nation State*, Cambridge, 1990.
Blackburn, Robin, *The Overthrow of Colonial Slavery, 1776–1848*, London, 1988.
Bleby, Henry, *Death Struggles of Slavery*, London, 1853.
Bolland, Nigel, *The Formation of a Colonial Society: Belize from Conquest to Crown Colony*, Baltimore, 1977.
Boyer-Peyreleau, Eugène, *Les Antilles françaises*, Paris, 1823.
Breen, Henry, *St Lucia: Historical, Statistical, Descriptive*, London, 1844.
Brereton, Bridget, *A History of Modern Trinidad, 1783–1962*, Kingston, 1981.
Buckley, R. G., *Slaves in Red Coats: The British West India Regiments, 1795–1815*, London, 1979.
Burdon, J. A., *Archives of British Honduras*, 3 vols, London, 1931.
Campbell, Mavis, *The Dynamics of Change in a Slave Society, 1800–1865*, Rutherford, New Jersey, 1976.
Carmichael, Gertrude, *The History of the West Indian Islands of Trinidad and Tobago, 1498–1900*, London, 1961.
Chan, V. O., 'The Riots of 1856 in British Guiana', *Carribean Quarterly* 16: 1 (1970).
Checkland, S. G., *The Gladstones: A Family Biography, 1764–1851*, Cambridge, 1971.
Cornford, Philip, *Missionary Reminiscences; Or, Jamaica Retraced*, Leeds, 1856.
Cox, Edward, 'Fedon's Rebellion 1795–96: Causes and Consequences', *Journal of Negro History* LXVII: I (Spring 1982).
Craton, Michael, *Empire, Enslavement and Freedom in the Caribbean*, London, 1997.
——*Testing the Chains; Resistance to Slavery in the British West Indies*, Ithaca, 1982.
Da Costa, Emilia Viotti, *Crowns of Glory, Tears of Blood: The Demerara Slave Rebellion of 1823*, Oxford, 1994.
Daly, Vere, *A Short History of the Guyanese People*, London, 1975.
Dallas, Robert Charles, *The History of the Maroons, from Their Origin to the Establishment of Their Chief Tribe at Sierra Leone*, London, 1803.
Duffield, I., 'From Slave Colonies to Penal Colonies: The West Indian Convict Transportees to Australia', *Slavery and Abolition* 17: 1 (May 1986).
Duffy, Michael, *Soldiers, Sugar and Seapower: The British Expeditions to the West Indies and the War against Revolutionary France*, Oxford, 1987.
Duncan, Peter, *Narrative of the Wesleyan Mission to Jamaica*, London, 1849.
Edwards, Bryan, *The History, Civil and Commercial, of the British Colonies in the West Indies*, London, 1793.
——*The History of the British Colonies in the West Indies*, London, 1801.

——*A History of the West Indies, Vol. IV*, London, 1819.
Ellis, A. B., *The History of the First West India Regiment*, London, 1885.
Fortescue, J. W., *A History of the British Army, Vol. III, 1763–1793*, London, 1902.
——*A History of the British Army, Vol. IV, Part I, 1789–1801*, London, 1906.
——*A History of the British Army, Vol. V, 1803–1807*, London, 1910.
Fraser, L. M., *History of Trinidad*, Port of Spain, 1891.
Furness, A. E., 'The Maroon War of 1795', *Jamaican Historical Review, vol.* 5 (1965).
Gardner, William, *A History of Jamaica*, London, 1873.
Geggus, David, *Slavery, War, and Revolution: The British Occupation of Saint Domingue, 1793–8*, Oxford, 1982.
Hall, Douglas, *In Miserable Slavery: Thomas Thistlewood in Jamaica, 1750–86*, London, 1989.
Hart, Richard, *Slaves Who Abolished Slavery*, Jamaica, 1980.
Henderson, George, *An Account of the British Settlement at Honduras*, London, 1809.
Heuman, Gad, *Between Black and White: Race, Politics, and the Free Coloureds in Jamaica, 1792–1865*, Westport, 1981.
Honychurch, Lennox, *The Dominica Story*, Kingston, 1995.
Jackson, Thomas, *A Memoir of the Rev. John Jenkins, Late a Wesleyan Missionary in the Island of Jamaica*, London, 1832.
Joseph, E. L., *History of Trinidad*, London, 1839 (1970).
Khan, Martin, *Djuka: The Bush Negroes of Dutch Guiana*, New York, 1931.
Kirby, I. Earl, and C. I. Martin, *The Rise and Fall of the Black Caribs of St Vincent*, Caracas, 1985.
Lacour, M. A., *Histoire de la Guadeloupe, Vol. II, 1789–1798*, Basseterre, 1857.
Lara, Oruño, *La Guadeloupe dans l'histoire*, Paris, 1979.
Laurence, K. O., 'The Tobago Slave Conspiracy of 1801', *Caribbean Quarterly* 28: 3 (September 1982).
Lémery, Henry, *La Révolution française à la Martinique*, Paris, 1936.
Linebaugh, Peter, and Marcus Rediker, *The Many-Headed Hydra: Sailors, Commoners, and the Hidden History of the Revolutionary Atlantic*, London, 2000.
Long, Edward, *History of Jamaica*, London, 1774.
Lyttelton, William Henry, *An Historical Account of the Constitution of Jamaica*, London, 1792.
Marshall, Bernard, 'Slave Resistance and White Reaction in the British Windward Islands, 1763–1833', *Caribbean Quarterly* 28: 3 (September 1982).
Pardon, Jean-Marie, *La Guadeloupe depuis sa découverte jusqu'à nos jours*, Paris, 1881.
Report from a Select Committee of the House of Assembly, Appointed to Inquire into the Origin, Causes, and Progress, of the Late Insurrection, Barbados, 1818.
Robinson, Carey, *The Fighting Maroons of Jamaica*, London, 1969.
Rodway, James, *The History of British Guiana*, 3 vols, Georgetown, 1891.
Schomburgk, Robert, *The History of Barbados*, London, 1848.
Sewell, W. G., *The Ordeal of Free Labour in the British West Indies*, New York, 1862.
Shaw, A. G. L., *Sir George Arthur*, Melbourne, 1980.
Shephard, Charles, *Historical Account of St Vincent*, London, 1831.
Smith, Raymond, *British Guiana*, Oxford, 1964.
Talboys, Thomas, *An Account of Certain Circumstances Between General Hislop, Governor of Trinidad, and Thomas Talboys, Methodist Missionary, in the Year 1811*, Georgetown, 1817.
Turner, Mary, *Slaves and Missionaries: The Disintegration of Jamaican Slave Society, 1787–1834*, Illinois, 1982.
Walker, James W. St G., *The Black Loyalists: The Search for a Promised Land in Nova Scotia and Sierra Leone, 1783–1870*, New York, 1976.
Walvin, James, ed., *Slavery and British Society, 1776–1846*, Louisiana, 1982.
Williams, Eric, *History of the People of Trinidad and Tobago*, London, 1964.
Young, William, *An Account of the Black Charaibs in the Island of St Vincent's, with the Charaib Treaty of 1773, and Other Original Documents*, London, 1795.

India

Ball, Charles, *The History of the Indian Mutiny*, London, 1858–59.

Biddulph, John, *The Nineteenth and Their Times*, London, 1899.

Blacker, Valentine, *Memoir of the Operations of the British Army in India during the Mahratta War of 1817, 1818, and 1819*, London, 1819.

Braddon, Sir Edward, *Thirty Years of Shirkar*, London, 1895.

Bradley-Birt, J. B., *The Story of an Indian Upland*, London, 1905.

British Army in India during the Mahratta War of 1817, 1818, and 1819, London, 1819.

Brittlebank, Kate, *Tipu Sultan's Search for Legitimacy: Islam and Kingship in a Hindu Domain*, Delhi, 1997.

Broehl, Wayne, *Crisis of the Raj: The Revolt of 1857 through British Lieutenants' Eyes*, Hanover, 1986.

Buckland, Charles Edward, *Bengal under the Lieutenant-Governors, 1854–1898*, Calcutta, 1901.

Burton, Reginald, *The Maharatta and Pindari War*, Delhi, 1975.

Butler, John, *A Sketch of the Services of the Madras European Regiment during the Burmese War*, London, 1839.

Butler, William, *The Land of the Veda, Being Personal Reminiscences of India ... Together with Incidents of the Great Sepoy Rebellion and its Results to Christianity and Civilisation*, New York, 1875.

Chaudhuri, S. B., *Civil Disturbances during British Rule in India, 1765–1857*, Calcutta, 1955.

Cooke Taylor, W., and P. J. McKenna, *Ancient and Modern India*, London, 1860.

Cotton, Mary (Lady Combermere), *Memoirs and Correspondence of Field-Marshal Viscount Combermere*, London, 1866.

Creighton, J. N., *Narrative of the Siege and Capture of Bhurtpore*, London, 1830.

Culshaw, W. J., and W. G. Archer, 'The Santal Rebellion', *Man in India* XXV, Ranchi, 1945.

Datta, Kalikinkar, *The Santal Insurrection of 1855–57*, Calcutta, 1940.

Fitzclarence, George, *Journal of a Route Across India*, London, 1819.

Fortescue, J. W., *A History of the British Army, Vol. III, 1763–1793*, London, 1902.

——*A History of the British Army, Vol. IV, Part II*, London, 1913.

——*A History of the British Army, Vol. VII, 1809–1810*, London, 1912.

——*A History of the British Army, Vol. XI, 1815–1838*, London, 1923.

Fuchs, Stephen, *Rebellious Prophets: A Study in Messianic Movements in Indian Religions*, London, 1965.

Gleig, G. R., *The Life of Sir Thomas Munro*, London, 1830.

Goldsmid, Frederick, *James Outram: A Biography*, 2 vols, London, 1881.

Gordon, Stewart, 'The Marathas, 1600–1818', *The New Cambridge History of India, Vol. II, Part 4*, Cambridge, 1995.

Grant Duff, James, *History of the Mahrattas*, London, 1826.

Gupta, Brijen, *Siraj-Ud-Daullah and the East India Company, 1756–57*, Leiden, 1966.

Gupta, P. C., *Baji Rao II and the East India Company, 1796–1818*, New York, 1964.

Holdich, Thomas, *The Gates of India*, London, 1910.

——*The Indian Borderland, 1880–1900*, London, 1901.

Holmes, Thomas Rice, *A History of the Indian Mutiny*, London, 1883.

Holwell, John, *Black Hole*, London, 1758.

Hunter, William Wilson, *The Annals of Rural Bengal, Vol. I. The Ethnical Frontier of Lower Bengal, with the Ancient Principalities of Beerbhoom and Bishenpore*, 2nd edn, New York, 1868.

James, Lawrence, *The Making and Unmaking of British India*, London, 1997.

Jha, Jagdish Chandra, *The Kol Insurrection of Chota-Nagpur*, Calcutta, 1964.

Kaye, John William, *A History of the Sepoy War in India, 1857–58*, 4 vols, London, 1875–80.

Lambrick, Hugh, *John Jacob of Jacobabad*, London, 1960.

Latthe, A. B., *Memoirs of His Highness Shri Shahu Chhatrapati, Maharajah of Kolhapur*, Bombay, 1924.

Mackenzie, Helen, ed., *Storms and Sunshine of a Soldier's Life: Lt General Colin Mackenzie CB, 1825–1881*, Edinburgh, 1884.
McPherson, H., *Final Report on the Survey and Settlement Operations in the District of Santal Parganas, 1898–1907*, Calcutta, 1909.
Majumdar, R. C., *History of the Freedom Movement in India, Vol. I*, Calcutta, 1963.
——*The Sepoy Mutiny and the Revolt of 1857*, Calcutta, 1957.
Malcolm, John, *A Memoir of Central India*, London, 1823.
Malleson, George Bruce, *The Decisive Battles of India, from 1746 to 1849*, London, 1883.
——*Final French Struggles in India*, London, 1878.
Man, E. G., *Sonthalia and the Sonthals*, London, 1867.
Maude, Francis Cornwallis, *Memories of the Mutiny*, London, 1894.
Military Sketches of the Goorka War in India, Woodbridge, 1822.
Mill, James, *A History of British India, Vol. VI*, London, 1840.
Moon, Penderel, *The British Conquest and Dominion of India*, London, 1989.
Namboodripad, E. M. S., *The Peasant Movement in Kerala*, Bombay, 1953.
Natarajan, L., *Peasant Uprisings in India, 1850–1900*, Bombay, 1953.
Nevill, H. L., *Campaigns on the North-West Frontier*, London, 1912.
O'Malley, L. S. S., *History of Bengal, Bihar and Orissa*, Calcutta, 1917.
Orans, Martin, *The Santal: A Tribe in Search of a Great Tradition*, Detroit, 1965.
Paget, Lt Col W. H., *A Record of the Expeditions against the North-West Frontier Tribes since the Annexation of the Punjab*, London, 1884.
Pearse, H. W., *Memoir of the Life and Military Service of Viscount Lake, 1744–1808*, London, 1908.
Prinsep, Henry, *History of the Political and Military Transactions in India during the Administration of the Marquess of Hastings, 1813–1823*, London, 1825.
Ray, Rajat Kant, 'Indian Society and British Supremacy', *The Oxford History of the British Empire, Vol. II*, Oxford, 1998.
Rottger-Hogan, Elizabeth, 'Insurrection … or Ostracism: A Study of the Santal Rebellion of 1855', *Contributions to Indian Sociology*, January 1982.
Roy, M. P., *Origin, Growth, and Suppression of the Pindaris*, New Delhi, 1973.
Sardesai, G. S., *New History of the Marathas*, Bombay, 1968.
Savarkar, V. D., *The Indian War of Independence of 1857*, London, 1909.
Scrafton, Luke, *Reflections on the Government of Indostan, from 1739 to 1756*, Edinburgh, 1761.
Sen, Surendra Nath, *Eighteen Fifty-Seven*, Delhi, 1957.
Shaw, A. G. L., *Sir George Arthur*, Melbourne, 1980.
Sherer, J. W., *Daily Life during the Indian Mutiny*, London, 1910.
Shipp, John, *Memoirs of the Extraordinary Military Career of John Shipp*, London, 1829.
Sinha, Narendra, *Haidar Ali*, Calcutta, 1941.
Sinha, S. P., *Santal Hul: Insurrection of Santal, 1855–56*, Ranchi, 1990.
Stokes, Eric, *The Peasant Armed: The Indian Revolt of 1857*, Oxford, 1986.
Thompson, Edward John, *The Life of Charles Lord Metcalfe*, London, 1937.
——*The Making of the Indian Princes*, London, 1943.
——and G. T. Garratt, *Rise and Fulfilment of British Rule in India*, London, 1934.
Thorn, William, *Memoir of the War in India Conducted by Lord Lake*, London, 1818.
Trotter, Lionel, *The Bayard of India: A Life of General Sir James Outram*, London, 1925.
Wakeham, Eric, *The Bravest Soldier: Sir Rollo Gillespie, 1766–1814, A Historical Military Sketch*, London, 1937.
Wilson, H. H., *The History of British India from 1805 to 1835, Vol. VII*, London, 1858.
Wilson, William, *History of the Madras Army*, 5 vols, Madras, 1832.
Wylly, H. C., *From Black Mountain to Waziristan, Being an Account of the Border Countries and the More Turbulent of the Tribes Controlled by the North-West Frontier Province, and of Our Military Relations with Them in the Past*, London, 1912.

Assam

Allen, William Joseph, *Report on the Administration of the Cossyah and Jynteah Hills Territory*, Shillong, 1900.
Banerjee, A. C., *The Eastern Frontier of British India*, Calcutta, 1943.
Barbujari, H. K., *Assam in the Days of the Company*, Gauhati, 1980.
Bareh, Hamlet, *The History and Culture of the Khasi People*, Calcutta, 1967.
Boulger, D. C., *Lord William Bentinck*, Oxford, 1892.
Dihingia, Hemeswar, *Assam's Struggles against British Rule, 1826–1863*, Delhi, 1980.
Gait, Edward, *A History of Assam*, Calcutta, 1967.
Hooker, Joseph, *Himalayan Journals; Or, Notes of a Naturalist in Bengal, the Sikkim, and Nepal Himalayas, the Khasia Mountains, etc.*, 2 vols, London, 1854.
Huxford, H. J., *History of the 8th Gurkha Rifles, 1824–1949*, Aldershot, 1952.
Mackenzie, Alexander, *History of the Relations of the Government with the Hill Tribes of the North-East Frontier of Bengal*, Calcutta, 1884.
Mills, A. J. M., *Report on the Khasi and Jaintia Hills, 1853*, Shillong, 1901.
Moon, Penderel, *The British Conquest and Dominion of India*, London, 1989.
Pemberton, R. B., *Report on the Eastern Frontier of British India*, Calcutta, 1835.
Shakespear, L. W., *History of Upper Assam, Upper Burmah and North-Eastern Frontier*, London, 1914.
White, Adam, *Considerations on the State of British India*, Edinburgh, 1822.
——*Memoir of the Late David Scott*, Calcutta, 1832.
Woodthorpe, R. G., *The Lushai Expedition, 1871–1972*, London, 1873.
——*The Naga Hills Expedition*, London, 1877.

Afghanistan, Sind and the Punjab

Alexander, Michael and Sushila Anand, *Queen Victoria's Maharajah: Duleep Singh, 1838–93*, London, 1980.
Bell, Thomas Evans, *The Annexation of the Punjab and the Maharaja Duleep Singh*, London, 1882.
Buist, George, *Outline of the Operations of the British Troops in Scinde and Affghanistan*, Bombay, 1843.
Burnes, James, *A Narrative of a Visit to the Court of Sinde*, Edinburgh, 1831.
Cook, H. C. B., *The Sikh Wars: The British Army in the Punjab, 1845–49*, London, 1975.
Cunningham, J. D. A., *A History of the Sikhs, from the Origins of the Nation to the Battles of the Sutlej*, London, 1849.
Durand, Henry, *The First Afghan War and its Causes*, London, 1879.
Eastwick, Edward Backhouse, *Dry Leaves from Young Egypt*, Hertford, 1851.
Edwardes, Emma, *Memorials of the Life and Letters of Sir Herbert Edwardes*, 2 vols, London, 1886.
Edwardes, Herbert, *The Political Diaries of Lieutenant Herbert Edwardes, 1847–1849*, Allahabad, 1911.
———*A Year on the Punjab Frontier in 1848–49*, 2 vols, London, 1851.
Fortescue, J. W., *A History of the British Army, Vol. XII, 1839–1852*, London, 1927.
Gibb, William, *Naval and Military Trophies and Personal Relics of British Heroes: A Series of Water Colour Drawings*, London, 1896.
Gough, Charles and A. D. Innes, *The Sikhs and the Sikh Wars*, London, 1897.
James, Lawrence, *Raj: The Making and Unmaking of British India*, London, 1997.
Kaye, J. W., *History of the War in Afghanistan*, London, 1878.
Khuhro, Hameeda, *The Making of Modern Sind, British Policy and Social Change in the Nineteenth Century*, Karachi, 1978.

Lal, Mohan, *Life of the Amir Dost Mohammed Khan, of Kabul, Including the Victory and Disaster of the British Army in Afghanistan*, London, 1846.
Lambricke, Gabrielle, *Sir Charles Napier and Sind*, Oxford, 1952.
Lee-Warner, Willliam, *The Life of the Marquis of Dalhousie*, 2 vols, London, 1904.
Login, Lena, *Sir John Login and Duleep Singh*, London, 1890.
Low, Charles, *The Life and Correspondence of Field Marshal Sir George Pollock*, London, 1873.
Moon, Penderel, *The British Conquest and Dominion of India*, London, 1989.
Napier, Priscilla, *I Have Sind, Charles Napier in India, 1841–1844*, Salisbury, 1990.
Napier, William, *The Conquest of Scinde*, London, 1845.
Norris, J. A., *The First Afghan War 1838–1842*, London, 1967.
Outram, James, *The Conquest of Scinde: A Commentary*, London, 1846.
Pearse, Hugh, ed., *Soldier and Traveller: The Memoirs of Alexander Gardner, Colonel of Artillery in the Service of Maharaja Ranjit Singh*, London, 1898.
Pottinger, George, *Sir Henry Pottinger, First Governor of Hong Kong*, London, 1997.
Rait, Robert, *The Life and Campaigns of Hugh, First Viscount Gough*, London, 1903.
Richardson, James, *Travels in the Great Desert of Sahara in 1845 and 1846*, London, 1848.
Ryder, M., *Four Years Service in India*, Leicester, 1853.
Sale, Florentia, *Journals*, London, 1843.
Singh, Khushwant, *A History of the Sikhs*, 2 vols, Princeton, 1963–66.
Smith, Harry, *The Autobiography of Lieutenant-General Sir Harry Smith*, London, 1903.

Burma

Anderson, Courtney, *To the Golden Shore: The Life of Adoniram Judson*, Michigan, 1972.
Bell, Henry, *An Account of the Burman Empire*, Calcutta, 1852.
Butler, John, *A Sketch of the Services of the Madras European Regiment during the Burmese War*, London, 1839.
Crawford, John, *Journal of an Embassy from the Governor-General of India to the Court of Ava in the Year 1827*, 2 vols, London, 1834.
Donnison, F. S. V., *Burma*, London, 1970.
Doveton, F. B., *Reminiscences of the Burmese War*, London, 1852.
Fortescue, J. W., *A History of the British Army, Vol. XI, 1815–1838*, London, 1923.
Fytche, Albert, *Burma, Past and Present*, 2 vols, London, 1878.
Gouger, Henry, *Personal Narrative of Two Years' Imprisonment in Burmah*, London, 1860.
Havelock, Henry, *Memoir of the Three Campaigns of Major-General Sir Archibald Campbell's Army in Ava*, Serampore, 1828.
Keeton, Charles, *King Theebaw and the Ecological Rape of Burma, 1878–1886*, Delhi, 1974.
Laurie, W. F. B., *Our Burmese Wars and Relations with Burma*, London, 1885.
——*Pegu, Being a Narrative of Events during the Second Burmese War*, London, 1854.
——*The Second Burmese War: A Narrative of the Operations at Rangoon*, London, 1853.
Lehmann, Joseph, *All Sir Garnet: A Life of Field-Marshal Lord Wolseley*, London, 1964.
Marshman, J. C., *Memoirs of Maj-Gen Sir Henry Havelock*, London, 1876.
Moon, Penderel, *The British Conquest and Dominion of India*, London, 1989.
Myint, Myo, *The Politics of Survival in Burma, Diplomacy and Statecraft in the Reign of King Minden, 1853–1878*, Ann Arbor, 1990.
Phayre, Arthur, *History of Burma*, London, 1883.
Pollak, Oliver, *Empires in Collision: Anglo-Burmese Relations in the Mid-Nineteenth Century*, London, 1979.
Singha, D. P., *British Diplomacy and the Annexation of Upper Burma*, Delhi, 1981.
Snodgrass, J. J., *Narrative of the Burmese War*, London, 1827.
Symes, Michael, *An Account of an Embassy to the Kingdom of Ava in the Year 1795*, London, 1827.

Wilson, H. H., *Narrative of the Burmese War in 1824–26, as Originally Compiled from Official Documents*, London, 1852.
Wolseley, Garnet, *A Soldier's Life*, London, 1903.
Wyllie, Macleod, *The Gospel in Burma*, Calcutta, 1859.

Ceylon

Baker, Samuel, *Eight Years in Ceylon*, London, 1874.
Bennett, John Whitchurch, *Ceylon and its Capabilities*, London, 1843.
Cordiner, James, *A Description of Ceylon*, 2 vols, London, 1807.
Davy, John, *An Account of the Interior of Ceylon and of its Inhabitants*, London, 1821.
De Silva, Colin, *Ceylon under the British Occupation, 1795–1833*, Colombo, 1953.
De Silva, K. M., ed., *History of Ceylon, Volume III: From the Beginning of the Nineteenth Century to 1948*, Colombo, 1973.
De Silva, K. M., *A History of Sri Lanka*, London, 1981.
——'Indian Immigration to Ceylon: The First Phase, c.1840–1855', *Ceylon Journal of Historical and Social Studies* IV (1961), Colombo.
——*Letters on Ceylon: The Administration of Viscount Torrington and the 'Rebellion' of 1848*, Colombo, 1965.
Forbes, Jonathan, *Recent Disturbances and Military Executions in Ceylon*, London, 1850.
Fortescue, J. W., *A History of the British Army, Vol. V, 1803–1807*, London, 1910.
Grey, Henry Earl, *The Colonial Policy of Lord John Russell's Administration*, 2 vols, London, 1853.
Hall, Richard, *Empires of the Monsoon: A History of the Indian Ocean and its Invaders*, London, 1996.
Henderson, John Macdonald, *The History of the Rebellion in Ceylon During Lord Torrington's Government*, London, 1868.
HMSO, 'First, Second and Third Report from the House of Commons Select Committee on Ceylon', London, 1850.
HMSO, 'Third Report from the Select Committee on Ceylon, Session 1850, Volume VIII, Part One (evidence of Sir James Emerson Tennent)', London, 1851.
Hulugalle, A. J., *British Governors of Ceylon*, Colombo, 1963.
Kostal, R. W., 'Martial Law and the Ceylon Controversy of 1848–51', *Journal of Imperial and Commonwealth Studies* 28 (2000).
Lewis, J. P., *Tombstones and Monuments in Ceylon*, Colombo, 1913.
Ludowyk, E. F. C., *The Modern History of Ceylon*, London, 1966.
——*The Story of Ceylon*, London, 1962.
Marshall, Henry, *Ceylon: A General Description of the Island and its Inhabitants; with an Historical Sketch of the Conquest of the Colony by the English*, London, 1846.
Methley, V., 'The Ceylon Expedition of 1803', *Transactions of the Royal Historical Society* IV: i, London, 1918.
Millie, P. D., *Thirty Years Ago; Or, the Reminiscences of the Early Days of Coffee Planting in Ceylon*, Colombo, 1878.
Mills, Lennox, *Ceylon under British Rule, 1795–1932*, London, 1933.
Morrell, W. P., *British Colonial Policy in the Age of Peel and Russell*, Oxford, 1930.
Percival, Robert, *An Account of the Island of Ceylon*, London, 1804.
Pieris, P. E., *Sinhale and the Patriots*, Colombo, 1950.
Pohath-Kehelpannala, T. B., *The Life of Ehelapola, Prime Minister to the Last King of Kandy*, Colombo, 1896.
Powell, Geoffrey, *The Kandyan Wars: The British Army in Ceylon, 1803–1818*, London, 1973.
Skinner, Thomas, *Fifty Years in Ceylon: An Autobiography*, London, 1891.
Tennent, James Emerson, *Ceylon: An Account of the Island – Physical, Historical, and Topographical*, London, 1859.

Tolfrey, William, *A Narrative of Events Which Have Recently Occurred in Ceylon, by a Gentleman on the Spot*, London, 1815.
Turner, L. J. B., *Collected Papers on the History of the Maritime Provinces of Ceylon, 1795–1805*, Colombo, 1923.
Tylden, T., 'The Ceylon Regiments 1796–1874', *Journal of the Society of Army Historical Research* 30 (1952).
Wickremeratne, V. C., *The Conservative Nature of the British Rule in Sri Lanka, with Particular Emphasis on the Period, 1796–1802*, New Delhi, 1996.

Indonesia, Mauritius, the Seychelles and the Gulf

Al-Qasimi, Sultan Mohammed, *The Myth of Arab Piracy in the Gulf*, London, 1986.
Beaton, Patrick, *Creoles and Coolies: Or, Five Years in Mauritius*, London, 1859.
Bradley, J. T., *The History of the Seychelles*, London, 1940.
Carey, Peter, ed., *The British in Java, 1811–1816: A Javanese Account*, Oxford, 1992 – a verse-form diary kept by Pangeran Arya Panular (1772–1826).
Crawfurd, John, *History of the Indian Archipelago*, Edinburgh, 1820.
D'Almeida, William, *Life in Java, with Sketches of the Javanese*, London, 1864.
Fauvel, Albert Auguste, *Unpublished Documents on the History of the Seychelles Islands, Anterior to 1810*, Mahé, 1910.
Fortescue, J. W., *A History of the British Army, Vol. VII, 1809–1810*, London, 1912.
Johnson, L. G., *General T. Perronet Thompson*, London, 1957.
Lees, A. W. H., 'A Forgotten Battle: Belad Beni Bu Ali, 1821', *Journal of the Society for Army Historical Research* 14 (1935).
Keppel, Henry, *The Expedition to Borneo of HMS Dido for the Suppression of Piracy*, London, 1846.
Mackenzie, W. C., *Colonel Colin Mackenzie, First Surveyor-General of India*, Edinburgh, 1952.
Mauritius, Royal Commission (Investigating Coolie Abuse), London, 1871.
Moyse-Bartlett, Hubert, *The Pirates of Trucial Oman*, London, 1966.
Nwulia, Moses, *The History of Slavery in Mauritius and the Seychelles, 1810–1875*, Rutherford, New Jersey, 1981.
Raffles, Lady Sophia, *Memoir of the Life and Public Services of Sir Thomas Stamford Raffles*, London, 1830.
Scarr, Deryck, *Seychelles since 1770: A History of a Slave and Post-Slavery Society*, London, 2000.
Tarling, Nicholas, *Piracy and Politics in the Malay World: A Study of British Imperialism in Nineteenth Century South-East Asia*, Melbourne, 1963.
Temple, R., *Sixteen Views of Places in the Persian Gulf*, London, 1813.
Thorn, William, *Memoir of the Conquest of Java, with the Subsequent Operations of the British Forces in the Oriental Archipelago*, London, 1815.
Wakeham, Eric, *The Bravest Soldier: Sir Rollo Gillespie, 1766–1814, A Historical Military Sketch*, London, 1937.
Ward, Sheila, *Prisoners in Paradise*, Mauritius, 1986.
Waterfield, Gordon, *Sultans of Aden*, London, 1968.
Wurtzburg, C. E., *Raffles of the Eastern Isles*, Oxford, 1986.

Singapore, Malaya and Hong Kong

Begbie, Peter, *The Malayan Peninsula*, Madras, 1834.
Buckley, Charles Burton, *An Anecdotal History of Old Times in Singapore, 1819–1867*, Oxford, 1984.
Burrows, Montagu, *Memoir of Admiral Sir Henry Ducie Chads GCB, by an Old Follower*, Portsea, 1869.

Burrows, Stephen, ed., *Autobiography of Montagu Burrows, Captain RN*, London, 1908.
Davidson, G. F., *Trade and Travel in the Far East; Or, Recollections of Twenty-One Years Passed in Java, Singapore, Australia, and China*, London, 1846.
Earl, George Windsor, *The Eastern Seas; Or, Voyages and Adventures in the Indian Archipelago, in 1832, 33, 34*, London, 1837.
Eitel, E. J., *Europe in China*, London, 1895.
Festing, E. G., ed., *Life of Commander Henry James RN*, London, 1899.
Keppel, Henry, *A Sailor's Life under Four Sovereigns*, 3 vols, London, 1899.
Lee Poh Ping, *Chinese Society in Nineteeenth Century Singapore*, Kuala Lumpur, 1978.
Mackenzie, Helen, ed., *Storms and Sunshine of a Soldier's Life: Lt General Colin Mackenzie CB, 1825–1881*, Edinburgh, 1884.
McNair, J. F. A., *Prisoners Their Own Warders*, London, 1899.
Read, W. H. M., *Play and Politics: Recollections of Malaya by an Old Resident*, London, 1901.
Pottinger, George, *Sir Henry Pottinger, First Governor of Hong Kong*, London, 1997.
Rait, Robert, *The Life and Campaigns of Hugh First Viscount Gough, Field Marshal*, London, 1903.
Tarling, Nicholas, *Piracy and Politics in the Malay World: A Study of British Imperialism in the 19th Century*, Melbourne, 1963.
Thomson, J. T., *Translations from the Hayakit Abdullah*, London, 1874.
Trocki, Carl, *Prince of Pirates: The Temenggongs and the Development of Johor and Singapore, 1784–1885*, Singapore, 1979.
Tsai, Jung-Fang, *Hong Kong in Chinese History, Community and Social Unrest in the British Colony, 1842–1913*, New York, 1993.
Turnbull, C. M., *A History of Singapore, 1819–1988*, Oxford, 1989.
——*The Straits Settlements, 1826-67, Indian Presidency to Crown Colony*, London, 1972.
Wurtzburg, C. E., *Raffles of the Eastern Isles*, Oxford, 1986.

Sarawak

Baring-Gould, S., and C. A. Bampfylde, *A History of Sarawak under its Two White Rajahs, 1839–1908*, London, 1909.
Belcher, Edward, *Narrative of the Voyage of HMS Samarang during the Years 1843–46*, London, 1848.
Buckley, Charles Burton, *An Anecdotal History of Old Times in Singapore, 1819–1867*, Oxford, 1984.
Clowes, William Laird, *The Royal Navy: A History, Vol. VI*, London, 1901.
Earl, George, *The Eastern Seas; Or, Voyages and Adventures in the Indian Archipelago, in 1832, 33, 34*, London, 1837.
Forbes, Frederick Edwyn, *Five Years in China: From 1842 to 1847, with an Account of the Occupation of the Island of Laban and Borneo by Her Majesty's Forces*, London, 1848.
Irwin, Graham, *Nineteenth Century Borneo*, Singapore, 1955.
Jibah, Matassim, 'Pengiram Indera Makhota … and James Brooke in the History of Brunei', *Brunei Museum Journal* 4:3 (1979).
Keppel, Henry, *The Expedition to Borneo of HMS Dido for the Supression of Piracy*, London, 1846.
——*A Sailor's Life under Four Sovereigns*, 3 vols, London, 1899.
Marryat, Frank M., *Borneo and the Indian Archipelago, with Drawings of Costume and Scenery*, London, 1848.
Mundy, Rodney, *Narrative of Events in Borneo and the Celebes*, London, 1848.
Pringle, Robert, *Rajahs and Rebels: The Ibans of Sarawak under Brooke Rule, 1841–1941*, New York, 1970.
Saint John, Spenser, *Life of Sir James Brooke Rajah of Sarawak, from His Personal Papers and Correspondence*, London, 1879.

Saunders, Graham, 'James Brooke's Visit to Brunei in 1844: A Reappraisal', *Sarawak Museum Journal* 17:34–5 (1969).
Tarling, Nicholas, *The Burthen, the Risk, and the Glory: A Biography of Sir James Brooke*, Oxford, 1982.
Templer, John C., *The Private Letters of Sir James Brooke*, London, 1853.
Wright, Leigh, 'The Lanun Pirate States of Borneo', *Sabah Society Journal* 7:4 (1979–80).

Australia

Bannister, Saxe, *British Colonisation and Coloured Tribes*, London, 1838.
Barrington, George, *The History of New South Wales*, London, 1810.
Beaglehole, J. C., *The Life of Captain James Cook*, London, 1974.
——*The Voyage of the Endeavour, 1768–1771*, Cambridge, 1955.
Blainey, Geoffrey, *The Triumph of the Nomads*, South Melbourne, 1975.
Bleakley, J. W., *The Aborigines of Australia: Their History, Their Habits, Their Assimilation*, Brisbane, 1961.
Bonwick, James, *The First Twenty Years of Australia: A History Founded on Official Documents*, London, 1882.
——*The Last of the Tasmanians*, London, 1870.
Broome, Richard, *Aboriginal Australians: Black Response to White Dominance, 1788–1980*, Sydney, 1982.
Campbell-Praed, Rosa, *My Australian Girlhood*, London, 1902.
Christie, M. F., *Aborigines in Colonial Victoria, 1835–1886*, Sydney, 1979.
Clark, Charles Manning, *A History of Australia*, 6 vols, 1962–87.
Cobbe, Hugh, ed., *Cook's Voyages and Peoples of the Pacific*, London, 1979.
Cocker, Mark, *Rivers of Blood, Rivers of Gold: Europe's Conflict with Tribal Peoples*, London, 1998.
Collins, David, *An Account of the English Colony in New South Wales*, London, 1798.
Connell, R. W., 'The Convict Rebellion of 1804', *Melbourne Historical Journal* 5 (1965).
Denholm, David, *The Colonial Australians*, Sydney, 1979.
Ellis, M. H., *John Macarthur*, Sydney, 1955.
Evans, Raymond, and Kay Saunders and Kathryn Cronin, *Race Relations in Colonial Queensland: A History of Exclusion, Exploitation and Extermination*, St Lucia, 1993.
Evatt, H. V., *Rum Rebellion*, Sydney, 1938.
Fenton, James, *A History of Tasmania*, London, 1884.
Fletcher, Brian, *Ralph Darling: A Governor Maligned*, Oxford, 1984.
Gunson, Niel, ed., *Australian Reminiscences and Papers of L. E. Threlkeld, Missionary to the Aborigines, 1824–1859*, Canberra, 1974.
Hazzard, Margaret, *Punishment Short of Death: A History of the Penal Settlement at Norfolk Island*, Melbourne, 1984.
Historical Records of Australia, Series 1, Governor's Despatches to and from England, Vol. XIX, July 1837–January 1839, Sydney, 1923.
Holt, Joseph, *Memoirs of Joseph Holt, General of the Irish Rebels*, ed. T. C. Croker, London, 1838.
Kennedy, Gavin, *Bligh*, London, 1978.
Kiernan, T. J., *The Irish Exiles in Australia*, Dublin, 1954.
Knight, J. J., *In the Early Days: History and Incidents of Pioneer Queensland*, Brisbane, 1895.
Kociumbas, Jan, *Possessions – Oxford History of Australia, Vol. II: 1770–1860*, Oxford, 1992.
Mann, D. D., *The Present Picture of New South Wales*, London, 1811.
Melville, Henry, *The History of the Island of Van Diemen's Land from the Year 1824 to 1835*, London, 1835.
Miller, James, *Koori: A Will to Win: The Heroic Resistance, Survival, and Triumph of Black Australia*, London, 1985.

Palmer, Alison, *Colonial Genocide*, London, 2001.
Petrie, C. C., *Tom Petrie's Reminiscences of Early Queensland*, Sydney, 1932.
Reynolds, Henry, *The Other Side of the Frontier: Aboriginal Resistance to the European Invasion of Australia*, Melbourne, 1982.
——'The Other Side of the Frontier: Early Aboriginal Reactions to Pastoral Settlement in Queensland and Northern New South Wales', *Australian Historical Studies* 17 (April 1976).
——and Noel Loos, 'Aboriginal Resistance in Queensland', *Australian Journal of Politics and History* 22 (April 2008).
Reece, R. H. W., *Aborigines and Colonists*, Sydney, 1974.
Richards, Jonathan, *The Secret War: A True History of Queensland's Native Police*, Brisbane, 2008.
Robson, L., *A History of Tasmania*, Oxford, 1983.
Shaw, A. G. L., *Sir George Arthur*, Melbourne, 1980.
Skinner, L. E., *Police of the Pastoral Frontier, Native Police, 1849–59*, Queensland, 1975.
Tench, Watkin, *Sydney's First Four Years*, Sydney, 1961.
Travers, Robert, *The Tasmanians: The Story of a Doomed Race*, Melbourne, 1968.
Turnbull, Clive, *Black War: The Extermination of the Tasmanian Aborigines*, Melbourne, 1948.
Wentworth, W. C., *Statistical, Historical and Political Description of the Colony of New South Wales, and its Dependent Settlements in Van Diemen's Land*, London, 1819.
Willey, Keith, *When the Sky Fell Down: The Destruction of Tribes of the Sydney Region, 1788–1850s*, Sydney, 1979.
Withey, Lynne, *Voyages of Discovery: Captain Cook and the Exploration of the Pacific*, London, 1987.
Woolmington, Jean, ed., *Aborigines in Colonial Society, 1788–1850: From 'Noble Savage' to 'Rural Pest'*, Sydney, 1973.

New Zealand

Belich, James, *Making Peoples: A History of the New Zealanders, from Polynesian Settlement to the End of the Nineteenth Century*, Auckland, 1996.
——*The New Zealand Wars and the Victorian Interpretation of Racial Conflict*, Auckland, 1986.
Bridge, Cyprian, *Journal of Events on an Expedition to New Zealand*, 1845.
Buick, T. L., *New Zealand's First War; Or, The Rebellion of Hone Heke*, Wellington, 1926.
Burrows, R., *Extracts from a Diary, Kept during Heke's War in the North in 1845*, Auckland, 1886.
Cowan, James, *The New Zealand Wars: A History of the Maori Campaigns and the Pioneering Period*, Wellington, 1922.
Hattaway, Robert, *Reminiscences of the Northern War*, Auckland, 1889.
Manning, Frederick, *Old New Zealand*, London, 1876.
Rose, J. Holland, ed., *The Cambridge History of the British Empire, Vol. VII, Part II: New Zealand*, Cambridge, 1933.
Rutherford, J., *Hone Heke's Rebellion, 1844–46: An Episode in the Establishment of British Rule in New Zealand*, Auckland, 1947.
Wards, Ian, *The Shadow of the Land: A Study of British Policy and Racial Conflict in New Zealand, 1832–1852*, Wellington, 1968.

Ireland

Bartlett, T., 'Defenders and Defenderism in 1795', *Irish Historical Studies* XXIV: 95 (May 1985).
Beames, Michael, *Peasants and Power: The Whiteboy Movements and Their Control in Pre-Famine Ireland*, Brighton, 1983.

Benn, George, *The History of the Town of Belfast*, Belfast, 1823.
Bigger, Francis Joseph, *The Ulster Land War of 1770: The Hearts of Steel*, Dublin, 1910.
Broeker, Galen, *Rural Disorder and Police Reform in Ireland, 1812–36*, London, 1970.
Byrne, Miles, *The Memoirs of Miles Byrne, Chef de Bataillon in the Service of France*, ed. Fanny Byrne, Paris, 1863.
Christianson, Gale, 'Secret Societies and Agrarian Violence in Ireland, 1790–1840', *Agricultural History* XLVI (1972).
Clark, Samuel, *Social Origins of the Irish Land War*, Princeton, 1980.
——and James S. Donnelly, eds, *Irish Peasants: Violence and Political Unrest, 1780–1914*, Manchester, 1983.
Cronin, Sean, '"The Country Did Not Turn Out": The Young Ireland Rising of 1848', *Eire-Ireland, A Journal of Irish Studies* XI: 2 (1970).
Crossmann, Virginia, *Politics, Law and Order in Nineteenth Century Ireland*, Dublin, 1996.
Curtis, Robert, *The History of the Royal Irish Constabulary*, London, 1869.
Curtis, Liz, *The Cause of Ireland: From the United Irishmen to Partition*, Belfast, 1994.
Doheny, Michael, *The Felon's Track*, New York, 1867.
Donnelly, James S., 'Pastorini and Captain Rock: Millenarianism and Sectarianism in the Rockite Movement of 1821–24', in Samuel Clark and James S. Donnelly, eds, *Irish Peasants: Violence and Political Unrest, 1780–1914*, Manchester, 1983.
——'The Whiteboy Movement, 1761–5', *Irish Historical Studies* XXI: 81 (March 1978).
Duffy, Charles Gavan, *Four Years of Irish History, 1845–1849*, London, 1883.
Fogarty, L., ed., *James Fintan Lalor: Patriot and Political Essayist, 1807–1849*, London, 1918.
Foster, R. F., *Modern Ireland, 1600–1972*, London, 1988.
Gahan, Daniel, *Rebellion! Ireland in 1798*, Dublin, 1997.
Galen, Broeker, *Rural Disorder and Police Reform in Ireland, 1812–1836*, London, 1970.
Gordon, James, *History of the Rebellion in the Year 1798*, London, 1801.
Gwynn, Dennis, *Young Ireland and 1848*, Cork, 1949.
Hay, Edward, *History of the Insurrection in the County of Wexford*, Dublin, 1803.
Holt, Joseph, *Memoirs of Joseph Holt, General of the Irish Rebels*, ed. T. C. Croker, London, 1838.
Jefferies, Charles, *The Colonial Police*, London, 1972.
Jordan, Hoover, *Bolt Upright: The Life of Thomas Moore, 1779–1852*, Salzburg, 1975.
Knight, Denis, *Cobbett in Ireland: A Warning to England*, London, 1984.
Leadbeater, Mary, *The Leadbeater Papers: The Annals of Ballitore*, London, 1862.
Lecky, W. E. H., *A History of Ireland in the 18th Century, London, Vol. II*, London, 1892.
Lewis, George Cornwalle, *On Local Disturbances in Ireland, and on the Irish Church Question*, London, 1836.
Lyons, F. S. L., *Ireland Since The Famine*, London, 1971.
McDowell, R. B., *Public Opinion and Government Policy, 1801–1846*, London, 1952.
MacHenry, James, *The Hearts of Steel: An Irish Historical Tale of the Last Century*, London, 1825.
Macintyre, Angus, *The Liberator: Daniel O'Connor and the Irish Party, 1830–1847*, London, 1965.
Mansergh, Nicholas, *The Irish Question, 1840–1921*, London, 1965.
Miller, David, 'The Armagh Troubles, 1784–95', in S. Clark and J. Donnelly, eds, *Irish Peasants: Violence and Political Unrest, 1780–1914*, Manchester, 1983.
Mitchel, J., *Jail Journal*, Dublin, 1913.
Moore, Thomas, *Memoirs of Captain Rock: The Celebrated Irish Chieftain, with Some Account of His Ancestors*, London, 1824.
Musgrave, Richard, *Memoirs of the Different Rebellions in Ireland from the Arrival of the English*, Dublin, 1801.
Nowlan, K. B., *The Politics of Repeal, 1841–1850*, London, 1965.
O'Brien, R. Barry, *Fifty Years of Concessions to Ireland, 1831–1881*, London, 1883.

O Broin, Leon, *Charles Gavan Duffy: Patriot and Statesman*, Dublin, 1967.
Pakenham, Thomas, *The Year of Liberty: The History of the Great Irish Rebellion of 1798*, London, 1969.
Palmer, Stanley, *Police and Protest in England and Ireland, 1780–1850*, Cambridge, 1988.
Reade, George, *Protest and Punishment*, Oxford, 1978.
'Report from the Select Committee appointed to examine the State of the Disturbed Counties in Ireland, into the immediate causes which have produced the same, and into the efficiency of the laws for the suppression of Outrage against the Public Peace', P.P. 1831–2 (677).
Scrope, G. Poulett, *How is Ireland to be Governed?*, London, 1834.
Taylor, George, *An History of the Rise, Progress, and Suppression of the Rebellion in the County of Wexford in the Year 1798*, Dublin, 1800.
de Tocqueville, Alexis, *Journeys to England and Ireland*, 1835.
Townsend, Molly, *Not by Bullets and Bayonets: Cobbett's Writings on the Irish Question, 1795–1835*, London, 1983.
Townshend, Charles, *Political Violence in Ireland: Government and Resistance since 1848*, Oxford, 1983.
Vaughan, W. E., ed., *A New History of Ireland, Vol. V, 1801–70*, Oxford, 1989.
Wesley, John, *The Journal of the Rev. John Wesley, 1735–1790*, London, 1903.
Williams, T. D., ed., *Secret Societies in Ireland*, Dublin, 1973.
Wright, Thomas, *The History of Ireland, from the Earliest Period of the Irish Annals to the Rebellion of 1848*, 3 vols, London, 1854.

South Africa

Adas, Michael, *Prophets of Rebellion*, Cambridge, 1987.
Archives Year Book for South African History, Pretoria, 1949.
Baines, Thomas, *Journal of a Residence in Africa, 1842–53*, 2 vols, Cape Town, 1961.
Barrow, John, *An Account of Travels into the Interior of South Africa*, London, 1801.
Bird, John, *The Annals of Natal*, Pietermaritzburg, 1888.
Booth, A. R., *The US Experience in South Africa, 1784–1870*, Cape Town, 1976.
Boyce, W. B., *Notes on South African Affairs from 1834 to 1838*, Grahamstown, 1838.
Brown, George, *Personal Adventure*, London, 1855.
Brownlee, Charles, *Reminiscences of Kaffir Life and History*, Lovedale, 1896.
Bunbury, C. J. F., *Journal of a Residence at the Cape of Good Hope*, London, 1848.
Campbell, John, *Travels in South Africa*, London, 1815.
Chalmers, J. A., *Tiyo Soga*, Edinburgh, 1877.
Cory, G. E., *The Rise of South Africa, Vol. I*, London, 1913.
Delegorgue, Adolphe, *Travels in Southern Africa*, Natal, 1990.
Du Toit, A. E., *The Cape Frontier, 1847–1866*, Pretoria, 1954.
Ellenberger, D. F., *History of the Basuto*, London, 1912.
Gardiner, A. F., *Narrative of a Journey to the Zoolu Country in South Africa*, London, 1836.
Godlonton, R., *A Narrative of the Irruption of the Kaffir Hordes, 1834–35*, Cape Town, 1965.
Harington, A. L., *Sir Harry Smith: Bungling Hero*, Cape Town, 1980.
Hockly, H. E., *The Story of the British Settlers of 1820 in South Africa*, Cape Town, 1957.
Kay, Stephen, *Travels and Researches in Caffraria*, London, 1833.
Kirby, Percival, *Andrew Smith and Natal*, Cape Town, 1955.
Kotze, D. J., ed., *Letters of the American Missionaries*, Cape Town, 1950.
Le Cordeur, Basil, *The Politics of Eastern Cape Separatism, 1820–1854*, Oxford, 1981.
——and Christopher Saunders, *The War of the Axe, 1847*, Johannesburg, 1981.
Lehman, J., *Remember You Are An Englishman*, London, 1977.
Lucas, T. J., *The Zulus and the British Frontiers*, London, 1879.

Mackay, J., *The Last Kaffir War*, Cape Town, 1978.
Marais, J. S., *Maynier and the First Boer Republic*, Cape Town, 1944.
Merriman, N. J., *The Journals of Archdeacon N. J. Merriman, 1848–1855*, Cape Town, 1957.
Midgley, J. F., 'The Orange River Sovereignty, 1848–1854', in *Archives Year Book for South African History*, Pretoria, 1949.
Mitford-Barberton, I., *Commandant Holden Bowker*, Cape Town, 1970.
Moodie, D. F. C., *The History of the Battles and Adventures of the British, the Boers, and the Zulus in Southern Africa*, 2 vols, Cape Town, 1888.
Morrell, W. P., *British Colonial Policy in the Age of Peel and Russell*, Oxford, 1930.
Mostert, Noel, *Frontiers: The Epic of South Africa's Creation and the Tragedy of the Xhosa People*, London, 1992.
Peires, J. B., *The Dead Will Rise, Nongqawuse and the Great Xhosa Cattle Killing Movement of 1856–7*, London, 1989.
Percival, Robert, *An Account of the Cape of Good Hope*, London, 1804.
Phillip, John, *Researches in South Africa, Illustrating the Civil, Moral, and Religious Condition of the Native Tribes*, London, 1828.
Pringle, Thomas, *Narrative of a Residence in South Africa*, London, 1835 (containing excerpts from Lieutenant Hart's diary, which is otherwise lost).
Read, James, *The Kat River Settlement in 1851*, Cape Town, 1852.
Report of the Select Committee on Aborigines, 1836, vols 1 and 2, London, 1837.
Roux, Edward, *Time Longer than Rope: A History of the Black Man's Struggle for Freedom in South Africa*, Madison, 1966.
Shipp, John, *The Extraordinary Military Career of John Shipp*, London, 1829.
Smith, Harry, *The Autobiography of Harry Smith*, London, 1903.
Sparrman, A., *Travels in the Cape, 1772–1776*, Cape Town, 1976.
Stapleton, T. J., *Maqoma: Xhosa Resistance to Colonial Advance*, Johannesburg, 1994.
Stockenstrom, Andries, *The Autobiography of the Late Sir Andries Stockenstrom*, ed., C. W. Hutton, Cape Town, 1887.
Stuart, James, and D. Malcolm, eds, *The Diary of Henry Francis Fynn*, Pietermaritzburg, 1950.
Taylor, Stephen, *Shaka's Children: A History of the Zulu People*, London, 1994.
Theal, George McCall, *History of South Africa since September 1795, Vol. I*, London, 1908.
——*Records of the Cape Colony, Vol. VI: 1806–1809*, Cape Town, 1900.
Thompson, George, *Travels and Adventures in Southern Africa*, London, 1827.
Tylden, G., *The Rise of the Basuto*, Cape Town, 1950.
Voigt, J. C., *Fifty Years of the History of the Republic of South Africa, 1795–1845*, London, 1899.
Wahlberg, J. A., *Travel Journals*, Cape Town, 1992.
Welsh, Frank, *A History of South Africa*, London, 1998.

West Africa

Ajayi, J. F. A., 'The British Occupation of Lagos, 1851–1861', *Nigeria Magazine* 69 (August 1961).
Ajaji, J. F. A., and Michael Crowder, eds, *History of West Africa, Vol. II*, London, 1974.
Beecham, John, *Ashantee and the Gold Coast*, London, 1841.
Claridge, W. W., *A History of the Gold Coast and Ashanti*, London, 1915.
Clowes, William Laird, *The Royal Navy: A History from the Earliest Times to the Death of Queen Victoria, Vol. VII*, London, 1903.
Dallas, Robert Charles, *The History of the Maroons, from Their Origin to the Establishment of Their Chief Tribe at Sierra Leone*, London, 1803.
Ellis, A. B., *The History of the First West India Regiment*, London, 1885.
Fox, William, *A Brief History of the Wesleyan Missions on the Western Coast of Africa*, London, 1851.

Fyfe, Christopher, *A History of Sierra Leone*, Oxford, 1962.
Gray, J. M., *A History of the Gambia*, Cambridge, 1940.
Huntley, Henry, *Seven Years Service on the Slave Coast of West Africa*, London, 1850.
Moister, William, *Memorials of Missionary Labour in West Africa and the West Indies*, London, 1866.
Ricketts, H. I., *A Narrative of the Ashantee War*, London, 1831.
Walker, James W. St G., *The Black Loyalists: The Search for a Promised Land in Nova Scotia and Sierra Leone, 1783–1870*, New York, 1976.
Winterbottom, Thomas, *An Account of the Native Africans in the Neighbourhood of Sierra Leone*, London, 1803.

Argentina

An Authentic Narrative of the Proceedings of the Expedition under Brigadier-General Craufurd, London, 1808.
Besio Moreno, Nicolás, *Buenos Aires, Puerto del Rio de la Plata, Estudio Crítico de su Población*, Buenos Aires, 1939.
Fortescue, J. W., *A History of the British Army, Vol. V, 1803–1807*, London, 1910.
Graham-Yooll, Andrew, *The Forgotten Colony: A History of the English-Speaking Communities in Argentina*, London, 1981.
Halperin Donghi, Tulio, *Politics, Economics, and Society in Argentina in the Revolutionary Period*, Cambridge, 1971.
Hernández, Isabel, *Los indios de Argentina*, Madrid, 1992.
Molinari, José Luis, 'Los indios y los negros durante las invasiones inglesas al Río de la Plata, en 1806 y 1807', *Boletín de la Academia Nacional de Historia* XXXIV, Buenos Aires, 1963.
Smith, Harry, *The Autobiography of Lieutenant-General Harry Smith*, London, 1903.

Illustration Credits

Every effort has been made to secure permission from the copyright holders before reproducing the illustrations appearing in this volume. The publisher apologizes for any omission or inaccuracy in the credits that follow, and, on being alerted to such an error, will make appropriate emendations in all future editions.

The portrait of Chief Pontiac, by John Mix Stanley. © The Granger Collection.

Blowing from Guns in British India, by Vasily Verestchagin. © The Bettmann Collection.

Haidar Ali in his younger years. From C. Hayavadana Rao, *History of Mysore*, Bangalore, 1943

Pimbloy (or Pemulwy), a native of New Holland, by Samuel John Neele. From James Grant, *The Narrative of a Voyage of Discovery performed in H. M. Vessel Lady Nelson . . . in the years 1800, 1801, and 1802*, London, 1803. © State Library of New South Wales.

Tipu Sultan's sons being handed over as hostages to General Lord Cornwallis at Seringapatam, by Robert Home. © The Council of the National Army Museum, London.

Chatoyer, the Chief of the Black Charaibes in St Vincent with his five wives, by Augustin Brunyas. From Bryan Edwards, *The History, Civil and Commercial, of the British West Indies*, London, 1819, and currently held at the John Carter Brown Library at Brown University.

'Rebels Destroying a House and Furniture during the Irish Rebellion of 1798', by George Cruikshank. Commissioned to appear in William Maxwell's *History of the Irish Rebellion in 1798*, published in 1845. © CartoonStock.com.

Four head-and-shoulder vignettes engraved by Samuel Daniell, 1804. From Samuel Daniell, *African Scenery and Animals at the Cape of Good Hope*, London, 1804. © The Bridgeman Art Library.

Ra's al-Khaymah, fortress of the Qawasim, under attack by British forces, 13 November 1809, by I. Clark after an aquatint by R. Temple. © The Bridgeman Art Library.

Governor Davey's Proclamation to the Aborigines 1816. © National Gallery of Australia, Canberra.

Proclamation to the Aborigines of Van Diemen's Land; *The Conciliation*, by Benjamin Duterrau. © State Library of New South Wales.

Dr Wolfred Nelson. © Library and Archives Canada.

Rebel French settlers in Canada; French settler forces flee the burning town of St Eustache, west of Montreal. © Library and Archives Canada, Ottawa.

Dost Mohammed, king of Cabaul, and his youngest son, by Lieutenant James Rattray. From James Rattray, *Scenery, Inhabitants and Costumes of Afghanistaun, from drawings made on the spot*, London, 1848. © The Bridgeman Art Library.

Te Rangihaeata, chief of Ngati Toa, by Captain Richard Oliver. From R. A. Oliver, *A Series of Lithographic Drawings, from Sketches in New Zealand*, London, 1852.

The settlement at Kororareka in the Bay of Islands; sketch drawn on stone by William Nicholas and lithographed by E. D. Barlow, Sydney. © National Library of Australia.

Topine Te Mamaku, photographed by Alfred Burton. © Te Papa Museum of New Zealand, Wellington.

William Smith O'Brien, by Henry O'Neil. © Archives Office of Tasmania.

Thomas Francis Meagher. © Montana State University Libraries.

Nana Sahib. From James Grant, ed, Cassell's *Illustrated History of India*, vol.ii, London, 1880. © The Bridgeman Art Library.

'British Civilisation'. © *Harper's Weekly*.

Lakshmi Bai, Rani of Jhansi. © Heritage-Images.

Execution of native mutineers after the Indian Mutiny, photographed by Felice Beato. © Getty Images.

Index